# Forensic Psychology

## An Applied Approach
### Second Edition

**Christopher Cronin**
*St. Leo University*

**Kendall Hunt**
publishing company

i

Book Team

Chairman and Chief Executive Officer **Mark C. Falb**
President and Chief Operating Office **Chad M. Chandlee**
Vice President, Higher Education **David L. Tart**
Director of National Book Program **Paul B. Carty**
Editorial Manager **Georgia Botsford**
Editor **Melissa M. Tittle**
Assistant Vice President, Production Services **Christine E. O'Brien**
Senior Production Editor **Carrie Maro**
Permissions Editor **Elizabeth Roberts**
Cover Designer **Suzanne Millius**
Photo Research **Jodi Klostermann**

Copyright © 2009 by Kendall Hunt Publishing Company

ISBN 978-0-7575-6174-0

Printed in the United States of America
10 9 8 7 6 5 4 3 2 1

# Brief Contents

# Contents

# Preface

Forensic psychology has witnessed a surge in interest among students and professionals over the past two decades. As an educator and practicing forensic psychologist of 15 years, I have watched as courses on forensic psychology swell with interested undergraduate and graduate students. I have also observed the proliferation of continuing education seminars packed with professionals desiring to enter the field. Much of this new interest has been accompanied by misunderstanding and misconceptions regarding the practice of forensic psychology. This misunderstanding is fueled to some extent by inaccurate portrayals of forensic psychologists in the popular media. Students and professionals demonstrate confusion regarding the activities and realm of practice of forensic psychologists. Recent movies and numerous television series feature characters portraying forensic psychologists. These savvy fictional characters profile serial killers and death row inmates feigning mental illness. Students fantasize about working as in-demand criminal profilers, assisting detectives at crime scenes by offering elaborate personality and behavioral descriptions of the elusive perpetrator. Unfortunately, even some professional seminars fall prey to the media hype. I actually attended a seminar at which the presenter recommended psychologists learn to evaluate blood splatter patterns. Psychologists should develop expertise in psychological techniques and not attempt to conduct crime scene investigations as part of their psychological duties. Finally, even the professional scholarly literature adds to the confusion with authors adopting their own idiosyncratic definitions of forensic psychology, suggesting that the field encompasses nearly anything that touches on the legal system and psychology. Such a broad conceptualization of the field can include well-known areas of legal psychology, such as expert testimony by cognitive psychologists on the fallibility of eyewitness testimony, but can also include more esoteric areas, such as offering psychological expert opinion on trademark infringement or services provided as a trial consultant. Indeed, there is some debate in the literature as to whether most trial consultants are trained as psychologists or, rather, possess advanced degrees in communications. The fact that many trial consultants are not psychologists makes it difficult to suggest that this endeavor is part of forensic psychology. Because some psychologists are involved in trial consultation, it is included in this text as part of legal psychology. However, these broad, all-encompassing definitions of forensic psychology confuse students and professionals alike. Although it may, at first glance, seem glamorous to visit a crime scene to analyze blood splatter patterns, or testify that a famous celebrity fits a particular criminal profile; these examples are not what forensic psychology is all about.

The goal of this book is to present the *practice* of forensic psychology. Forensic psychology is an exciting field comprised of a variety of interesting opportunities for students and professionals. The impetus to write this textbook was triggered by a general dissatisfaction with current textbook offerings and a desire to disavow students of the misconceptions surrounding forensic psychology. Forensic psychology, as defined by the American Psychological Association, is the application of clinical specialties to the legal arena. This definition emphasizes the application of clinical services in forensic settings. Perhaps the most frequent duty of forensic psychologists is the psychological assessment of individuals who are involved, in one way or another, with the legal system.

One of the most common types of forensic psychological assessment is a competency to stand trial evaluation and will serve as an illustrative example of the work of forensic psychologists. In conducting a competency to stand trial evaluation, a forensic psychologist is asked to use his or her clinical skill in addressing a specific psycholegal question: is the defendant competent, as defined by a legal standard, to proceed to trial. The forensic psychologist evaluates the individual and reports back to the court his or her expert opinion on the defendant's competency. The majority of forensic evaluations follow this format. The forensic psychologist must address a specific psycholegal question and provide an expert opinion back to the court based on the psychologist's evaluation and clinical experience. A competency to stand trial evaluation is just one type of the many forms of forensic assessments a psychologist may be asked to perform. Forensic psychologists can also perform assessments for emotional damages in civil trials. Or a psychologist may assess a defendant's mental state at the time of an offense to offer an expert opinion on criminal responsibility. Police psychologists may conduct fitness-for-duty evaluations of police officers. Correctional psychologists may evaluate incarcerated sexual predators to offer an opinion as to whether the inmate continues to pose a threat or should be released.

These assessments are just a few examples of forensic work discussed in the text. It should be obvious that many of these assessments are complicated and require expert clinical skills and a thorough understanding of the legal issues involved in the referral. Additionally, the forensic psychologist's opinion can have a significant impact on people's lives. For example, in civil cases involving a tort action for psychological damage, the forensic psychologist's opinion can play a major role in the jury's decision to award monetary damages to the plaintiff. Similarly, the Supreme Court has ruled that sexual predators can be civilly committed for an indefinite period if a forensic psychologist determines that the inmate continues to pose a threat to society. Finally, a forensic psychologist's testimony on aggravating and mitigating circumstances during the sentencing phase in a capital trial can mean the difference between life and death for the defendant. Certainly, due to the potential significant consequences of their work, forensic psychologists are expected to perform to high standards of ethics and competence.

As previously stated, this is a textbook about the *practice* of forensic psychology. As an academic and practitioner, I hope to convey the spirit of the scientist-practitioner model. Readers of the text will appreciate the fact that psychologists can be practitioners of the craft as well as scholars of the literature that drives the field. The focus of the text is on the applied, clinical aspect of the field, though several chapters do address popular areas in legal psychology. Legal psychology refers to the nonapplied areas of psychology that interface with the legal system. The text is not a "how-to" guide on the practice of forensic psychology, but rather offers students and professionals interested in the field a broad overview of the many opportunities available to forensic psychologists. Each chapter focuses on specific areas of forensic practice. Chapters are structured similarly, first offering an overview of the particular area of practice and then providing details on the specific practices within that area of forensic psychology. Key concepts are presented at the beginning and the reader is encouraged to review these terms before reading the chapter. This review will alert the reader to important concepts encountered in the chapter and may indicate a good time to break out the highlighter. Case examples are provided when appropriate, including examples from my own clinical work. Definitions of new terms are provided in the margins on the page where the concept first appears. Chapters also include career information for each area of practice. The information provided includes types of training opportunities and necessary skills to perform the work in the particular area. Results from job satisfaction surveys along with salary information from professionals working in the area are also provided when available. Each chapter ends with a brief summary reviewing the major themes of the chapter.

In this second edition, each chapter has been updated and new material added, when appropriate. Instructors familiar with the first edition will note the continuity of topics, although new research is presented throughout. Despite the addition of current research and new material, perhaps the most exciting additions are pedagogical tools to help students understand the concepts. For example, each chapter now has "essential questions" that will help guide the reader to identify key concepts presented in the chapter. These essential questions can also be used as review questions for tests as the majority of test items in the test bank directly relate to these essential questions. All the chapters also have a "Test Your Knowledge" section that provides practice with the multiple-choice questions similar to those in the text bank. Many of the chapters also have "active learning" exercises that challenge students to solve ethical dilemmas or offer forensic psychological recommendations based on case vignettes. These exercises can be worked on in small groups in the classroom or completed at home to be discussed during class. Finally, based on students' recommendations, a glossary has been added as well as a list of landmark court cases discussed in the text along with the implications these cases have for the practice of forensic psychology.

After several introductory chapters, the book focuses on specific practice opportunities in forensic psychology. The first three introductory chapters should be read sequentially and lay the basic foundation for the rest of the text. Chapter 1 provides an introduction to the field of forensic psychology and an overview of the text. Chapter 2 addresses the complex ethical and legal issues involved in the practice of forensic psychology. An entire chapter is devoted to the ethical and legal issues involved in forensic psychology due to the complexity and heightened significance of providing ethical services. Chapter 3 provides an introduction to psychological assessment and an overview of instruments frequently used in forensic practice. Each of the remaining chapters provides a detailed overview of specific practice areas in forensic psychology. The reader may choose to read these chapters in any particular order, as they stand alone. Each chapter presents the work of forensic psychologists in the specific area. These remaining chapters cover criminal responsibility and competency to stand trial evaluations, police psychology, correctional psychology, child custody evaluations, and personal injury evaluations. Three chapters are devoted to areas akin to forensic psychology and include chapters on criminal investigative psychology, trial consultation, and the collection and use of eyewitness testimony. Finally, the last chapter identifies some emerging trends in the field that are of particular relevance to individuals entering the practice of forensic psychology. An emphasis is placed on the future training models for forensic psychologists and professional implications due to the increased collaboration between the legal and psychological professions.

It is my hope that this text instills in the reader an excitement and enthusiasm for the practice of forensic psychology. It is also hoped that the text helps to clarify what opportunities exist in the profession and encourages readers to enter the practice of forensic psychology.

# Acknowledgments

The revision of a textbook poses unique challenges. Questions linger regarding what to leave in and what to leave out, as well as the temptation to polish the final product indefinitely. The revision of a textbook actually starts the day after you send the final manuscript of the previous edition to the publisher. It is always easy to find new and exciting information to add to a text. One of the challenges is to keep the text manageable.

My thanks for this revision go to the many students that I have taught over the years. Their comments and suggestions have been incorporated into this revision and perhaps best reflect the new additions in the text. I also want to express my gratitude to the numerous professors who have reviewed the text. Their comments have also helped to shape this second edition.

A special word of thank goes to the team at Kendall Hunt, my editor Melissa Tittle, the Editorial Manager, Georgia Botsford, and the Senior Production Editor, Carrie Maro. Melissa demonstrated the patience of Job as she reluctantly watched unmet deadlines slide by. She managed to keep me on the task despite the numerous professional distractions. Georgia showed an uncanny ability to track me down to keep me on task, and Carrie helped to bring the final book together. I am very sure they had colleagues who also assisted, to whom I am grateful for their professionalism.

Finally, as before, I wish to thank my wife, Michelle. As many people know, once you have a partner in life, no task is too large to accomplish, or too small to do well.

# About the Author

Christopher Cronin received his BS in psychology at the University of Wisconsin, Madison, and his MA and PhD in clinical psychology at the University of Delaware. He completed his internship at the University of California, Davis in the Department of Psychiatry at the University Medical Center in Sacramento. He has also completed a Post-doctoral Certificate in Clinical Psychopharmacology at Fairleigh Dickinson University. Dr. Cronin is a licensed clinical psychologist who has held academic positions in Europe (University of Maryland, Munich Campus), Australia (Flinders University of South Australia), and the United States (Transylvania University and Saint Leo University). He has practiced forensic psychology since 1991, conducting competency to stand trial and criminal responsibility evaluations for the Commonwealth of Kentucky. He is Professor of Psychology at Saint Leo University in Florida and has conducted over 4,000 court-ordered forensic evaluations in the Tampa Bay area. In addition to various journal articles, Dr. Cronin is the editor of *Military Psychology: An Introduction*, which was translated into Chinese, and author of *Forensic Psychology*, both now in their second editions. He regularly consults as a subject matter expert for the development of online and ground-based undergraduate and graduate courses in forensic psychology. Additionally, he presents continuing education workshops to mental health professionals on topics related to forensic psychology.

# Chapter One

# Introduction to the Field of Forensic Psychology

## Learning Objectives

- Distinguish between forensic and legal psychology and give examples of each.
- Define stare decisis.
- What area in psychology is forensic psychology a subspecialty?
- What are the four applied areas of psychology?
- What is the difference between clinical and counseling psychology?
- Be able to give examples of forensic evaluations and distinguish between criminal and civil evaluations.
- What is the most common forensic criminal evaluation?
- Define board certification and describe what a vanity board is and the notion of a grandparenting clause for membership.
- Distinguish between a master's degree and a doctorate degree in psychology regarding both professional practice and oversight by the APA.
- Describe the training required for a doctorate degree and licensure as a forensic psychologist.
- Define cognitive psychology, developmental psychology, and social psychology and the roles these professions play in legal psychology.
- What is a change of venue request and why would such a request be made?
- Define empiricism.
- Where do most psychologists receive their training in forensic psychology?

*Many of the key concepts presented in this chapter are elaborated on throughout the rest of the text. However, it is beneficial to start now to become familiar with the terminology used in forensic psychology.

## Key Terms*

- A *priori* method
- American Board of Forensic Psychology
- American Board of Professional Psychology
- American Psychological Association
- Applied fields in psychology
- Board certification
- Case law
- Child custody evaluations
- Civil law
- Clinical psychology
- Cognitive psychology
- Competency
- Correctional psychology
- Counseling psychology
- Criminal law
- Criminal profiling
- Criminal responsibility
- Developmental psychology
- Didactic training
- Diplomate
- Empiricism
- Epidemiology
- Ethics
- Expert witness
- False memory syndrome
- Forensic psychologists
- Forensic psychology
- Grandparenting clause

*(continued)*

## Key Terms *(continued)*

- Industrial/organizational psychology
- Investigative hypnosis
- Legal psychologists
- Legal psychology
- Licensure
- Malingering
- Personal injury evaluations
- PhD
- Police psychology
- Postdoctoral training
- Professional psychology

- Psychological autopsy
- Psychology
- PsyD
- Recovered memory
- School psychology
- Social psychology
- Student affiliate
- Terminal degree
- Trial consultants
- Vanity boards

■ **Criminal profiling**

Any process used to infer distinctive personality traits, behavioral tendencies, physical and demographic characteristics, or even geographic locations of individuals responsible for committing criminal acts from physical and/or behavioral evidence

Forensic psychology is a specialty area of psychology that has seen a great increase in attention over the past decade. This increase has involved the public as well as mental health professionals. Part of this new attention is due to the appearance of forensic psychology in the popular culture. Forensic psychology is portrayed in the media through films such as *Silence of the Lambs*, *Primal Fear*, and a steady stream of television shows featuring psychologists conducting **criminal profiling**. This media exposure has led to a whole new generation of psychology and criminal justice majors wanting to become criminal profilers. Mental health professionals have also turned their attention to forensic work as an avenue of potential revenue free of the bureaucracy of managed care. Partly due to the mass media's portrayal of forensic psychologists and partly due to a lack of knowledge, there are numerous misconceptions among both the public and professionals as to what exactly forensic psychologists do.

This book will introduce the reader to the field of forensic psychology, with an emphasis on the *applied* aspects of the profession. The forensic psychologist may be involved in a variety of activities, including, but not limited to, insanity pleas, competency to stand trial hearings, child custody evaluations, assessment of dangerousness, trial consultation, and personal injury evaluations for emotional distress. The majority of the work involves the direct delivery of services to a client and typically requires the psychologist to be licensed in the state in which he or she practices.

# Definition of Forensic Psychology

Before we can define forensic psychology, it would be useful to have a good working definition of psychology. Despite the fact that modern psychology has been around for over 120 years, there still is a lack of consensus regarding the domain of the science of psychology. Psychology is a broad field that it touches on many disciplines. Ludy Benjamin, a well-known historian of psychology, summed up the diversity of the discipline recently:

> No doubt many psychologists were drawn to their field because of its diversity of subject matter. Biologists and chemists can find a home in psychology. Physicists can find much interest in contemporary work in perception. Anthropologists, sociologists, economists, and political scientists could be happy in social psychology, cognition, develop-

ment, and other subfields. Business people, educators, and healers all can find a home. The quantitatively inclined are welcomed, as are the computer scientists. Sports fans too can pursue their love in psychology. Even historians can find work in this field. (2001, p. 740)

Indeed, psychology is a diverse field where one can earn a doctorate (**PhD**) in a variety of subfields including clinical psychology, counseling psychology, developmental psychology, experimental psychology, **industrial/organizational psychology**, personality psychology, physiological psychology, social psychology, and sport psychology, to name just a few of the subfields. Frequently, there is a great deal of overlap among the subfields. Psychologists from different subfields may be investigating a common topic, like violence or maximizing performance, but approaching the problem from different perspectives. Additionally, psychologists use common methods of inquiry grounded in science. Although all of these areas have some things in common, there are also important differences and areas of expertise. For example, a psychologist with a background in physiological psychology may attempt to understand what role neurotransmitters in the brain play in triggering violence, whereas a social psychologist may want to understand how group norms facilitate or inhibit violent behavior. A clinical psychologist might attempt to understand violent behavior as a form of psychopathology in the individual. A developmental psychologist may attempt to understand violent behavior as a result of inadequate psychological development. A cognitive psychologist might want to understand the brain's mechanisms and lack of behavioral or impulse control.

Regardless of their specialty area, psychologists are also involved in a wide variety of professional activities including teaching, working with the public as therapists and consultants, conducting research, and administrative work. Because of the diversity of professional opportunities, psychologists are also employed in a range of settings, such as independent or group practice, hospitals and clinics, research groups, universities and colleges, industry, correctional facilities, police departments, medical and law schools, government, the FBI and CIA, and even with the Olympic team and professional sports teams, to name a few. It is partly due to this diversity of opportunities that psychology is a popular major on college campuses (American Psychological Association, 2000). Again, there are important differences among the subfields. Just as the public views all forensic psychologists as criminal profilers, many people believe that all psychologists listen to people's problems while the patient reclines on the ever-present couch. Actually, the reality is far different. Not all psychologists are qualified to provide counseling or therapy. Typically, only counseling and clinical psychologists provide clinical services and account for approximately 50% of all doctoral-level (possessing the PhD) psychologists. The American Psychological Association has recognized four *applied* or *professional* areas in psychology:

1. clinical psychology
2. counseling psychology
3. school psychology
4. industrial/organizational psychology

Clinical and counseling psychologists represent the common perception of a psychologist in that these specialties are involved in providing counseling or therapy. Clinical and counseling psychologists account for approximately 50% of all psychologists. School

**Figure 1.1**

A social psychologist may want to understand how group norms facilitate or inhibit violent behavior.
© 2009 Lars Christensen. Used under license from Shutterstock, Inc.

■ **Industrial/organizational psychology**
Specialty in psychology that works with industry on assessment and classification of workers, organizational morale and culture, and workers' performance.

psychologists conduct intellectual assessments on schoolchildren and consult with teachers on implementing programs to enhance student performance. Industrial/organizational (I/O) psychologists examine factors in the workplace that affect job performance such as organizational climate. I/O psychologists are also involved in testing and assessment of employees. Psychologists in these four subfields provide direct services to the public (clients, the schools, and industry) and are regulated by state licensing boards, although specific licensing requirements vary by state. Psychologists in the other subfields are frequently involved in teaching and research at the college level. They cannot "hang a shingle" and become involved in the *professional practice* of psychology, which is the state-regulated delivery of services to the public.

For the purpose of this text, and while recognizing the diversity of the field, we will adopt a simple, introductory textbook definition of **psychology** and define it as the "science that seeks to understand behavior and mental processes" (Bernstein & Nash, 2005, p. 3). It is important to emphasize the word *science* in the definition of psychology. Psychology was founded on the philosophy of **empiricism**, the view that knowledge comes from experience and observation. This philosophical heritage emphasizes the role of the scientific method and recognizes the falsifiability of knowledge. As we will see later, one important distinction between law and psychology is the different approaches to knowledge. Whereas psychology uses the method of science to obtain knowledge, law uses both the method of authority (courts) and the *a priori* **method**, based on precedent and logical, deductive reasoning. We will return to this and other differences between psychology and law later in the book.

In light of the discussion above, it should not be surprising that forensic psychology appears to have a variety of definitions (i.e., Bartol & Bartol, 1999; Goldstein, 2003; Wrightsman, 2001). The major distinction among the various definitions appears to be how broadly the field is defined. Some authors have suggested a broad definition for the field, suggesting that forensic psychology "is reflected by any application of psychological knowledge or methods to a task faced by the legal system" (Wrightsman, 2001, p. 2). Similarly, Bartol and Bartol suggest that

> It is both (a) the research endeavor that examines aspects of human behavior directly related to the legal process (e.g., eyewitness memory and testimony, jury decision making, or criminal behavior), and (b) the professional practice of psychology within or in consultation with a legal system that encompasses both **criminal** and **civil law** and the numerous areas they interact. Therefore, forensic psychology refers broadly to the *production* and *application* of psychological knowledge to the civil and criminal justice systems. (1999, p. 3, original emphasis)

Hess and Weiner (1999) have suggested that forensic psychology consists of three main areas: "the application of basic psychological processes to legal questions; research on legal issues, such as the definition of privacy or how juries make decisions; and knowledge of legal issues" (p. 24).

Other authors have defined forensic psychology using a more applied context. In the "Petition for the Recognition of a Specialty in Professional Psychology," forensic psychology is defined as the "professional practice by psychologists within the areas of **clinical psychology**, counseling psychology, neuropsychology, and **school psychology**, when they are engaged regularly as experts and represent themselves as such, in an activity primarily intended to provide professional psychological expertise to the judicial system" (Heilbrun, 2000, p. 6). The **American Board of Professional Psychology** (ABPP), which recognizes forensic psychology as a specialty, defines the field as the "practice of psychology as related to the law and legal system." The reader should note that the two major distinctions in the various definitions of forensic psychology are in the breadth of the field and as to whether the

■ **Psychology**
The study of behavior and mental processes.

■ **Criminal law**
The area of law that deals with offenses committed against the safety of society or acts against the state.

■ **Civil law**
The area of law that deals with the infringement upon the civil rights of an individual or organization; noncriminal law.

focus is on the professional practice of psychology or both the professional practice of psychology along with the application of psychological research to legal issues.

Recently, there has been a trend toward separating the applied aspect of forensic psychology from the experimental portion of the specialty. The term **forensic psychology** is used to identify the **application** of clinical specialties to the law, and the term **legal psychology** is used to refer to the other, more experimental areas of psychology as applied to legal questions (Bersoff et al., 1997; Packer & Borum, 2003).

Most individuals who define themselves as forensic psychologists are actually clinical psychologists who specialize in forensic work (Bartol & Bartol, 2004). Since the trend is to define forensic psychology as the portion involving clinical work, and the majority of forensic psychologists are clinicians, the emphasis of this text will be on the applied aspect of forensic psychology. This is not a "how-to" book, but rather a description of the possible professional activities of a forensic psychologist. One goal of the text is to inform students of the numerous options available in the specialty of forensic psychology. Chapters in the text cover the more applied areas of forensic psychology, although the contributions that psychological research has to offer the legal system are not ignored. Naturally, psychologists with training in subfields other than clinical or counseling psychology also work in the legal arena. For example, social psychologists may work as trial consultants and cognitive psychologists may appear as expert witnesses regarding the accuracy of eyewitness testimony. This application of psychology to the law has recently been termed *Legal Psychology* (Bersoff et al., 1997; Packer & Borum, 2003) to distinguish it from the clinical aspect of forensic psychology. In this text, we define *forensic psychology* as the application of clinical specialties to legal institutions and people who come into contact with the law. The emphasis of the text is on the *practice* of forensic psychology. The practice of forensic psychology includes conducting forensic assessments, testifying in court, and providing treatment to specific populations.

It is reassuring to note that there has been a recent trend among textbook authors to follow the American Psychological Association's definition of forensic psychology as an applied specialty. Both new books as well as revisions have shifted toward the narrow definition of forensic psychology (Bartol & Bartol, 2008; Huss, 2009), although some books continue to offer the broader perspective combining legal psychology and forensic psychology as one specialty (Fulero & Wrightsman, 2009). In a similar vein, many of the scholarly works for professionals focus on the practice of forensic psychology as narrowly defined here (e.g., Goldstein, 2007; Melton, Petrila, Poythress, & Slobogin, 2007).

First, we briefly identify some of the areas of legal psychology. We then review a more detailed description of the field of forensic psychology and the necessary

■ **Forensic psychology**
The application of clinical specialties to legal institutions and people who come into contact with the law.

■ **Legal psychology**
The scientific study of the effect of the law on people, and the effect people have on the law. Areas of legal psychology discussed in the text include eyewitness identification and investigative psychology.

## Distinction between Forensic Psychology and Legal Psychology        Table 1.1

■ **Forensic psychology** The *application* of clinical specialties to legal institutions and people who come into contact with the law.
■ **Legal psychology** *Experimental* or research-oriented areas of psychology as applied to legal questions; the scientific study of the effect of law on people, and the effect people have on the law.

training to practice as a forensic psychologist. Rather than adopting the broad definition of legal psychology proposed by Ogloff (2000) to include the area of forensic psychology, we define legal psychology as its own domain, distinguished from forensic psychology. Legal psychology is defined as the "scientific study of the effect of law on people; and the effect people have on the law" (Ogloff, 2000, p. 467). This distinction between the applied practice of forensic psychology and the research-oriented area of legal psychology will help avoid the confusion that frequently occurs among the public between researchers and practitioners. The public has a difficult time distinguishing between licensed psychologists (generally clinical and counseling psychologists) and psychologists in the more research-oriented fields, such as social psychologists or cognitive psychologists. Using the same term (e.g., **legal psychologists**) to identify these diverse fields in the legal system would only contribute to the confusion. Therefore, practitioners who apply their skills to legal issues are referred to as forensic psychologists and researchers in the area of legal psychology are referred to as legal psychologists (Ogloff, 2000).

# Areas in Legal Psychology

The areas of legal psychology are briefly reviewed here as well as discussed in more detail in several chapters later in the book. It should be noted that professionals involved in legal psychology may or may not possess the doctoral degree in their subfield of psychology. Since they are not, nor can be, licensed as practicing psychologists, the doctoral degree would not be a prerequisite for employment, as is the case with a clinical or counseling degree. The advantage is that students can enter the field of legal psychology with a master's degree. On the other hand, the additional training of the doctoral degree would certainly enhance an individual's skills and their perceived credibility when appearing as an expert witness. Training in legal psychology occurs at the graduate level working with a faculty member whose interest is in an area of legal psychology. Some departments have developed minors in psychology and the law and eight doctoral programs offer specialty training in legal psychology (Packer & Borum, 2003). See Table 1.2 for a list of doctoral programs offering training in legal psychology. In addition to the required coursework in psychology, students interested in legal psychology are encouraged to gain an understanding of legal issues through law-related courses. Students focusing on legal psychology can obtain a degree in any specialty in psychology. The more common areas are **social psychology**, **cognitive psychology**, and **developmental psychology**. Table 1.3 highlights a few of the subfields of psychology that relate to the area of legal psychology.

■ **Social psychology**
The study of how people influence others' behavior and attitudes; the study of the individual within a group.

■ **Cognitive psychology**
A subfield of psychology concerned with the study of cognition and mental processes including memory and eyewitness testimony.

■ **Developmental psychology**
A subfield of psychology that focuses on the study of the changes in behavior and mental processes over time due to aging and maturation.

## Table 1.2 Graduate Programs in Legal Psychology

- Florida International University, North Miami
- Simon Fraser University, Burnaby, British Columbia, Canada
- University of Illinois, Chicago
- University of Kansas, Lawrence
- University of Nevada-Reno
- University of Texas, El Paso
- University of Virginia, Charlottesville

## Social Psychology

Social psychologists study how people influence others' behavior and attitudes. If psychology were to be roughly defined as the study of the individual, social psychology would be the study of the individual in groups. Psychologists with training in social psychology may work as trial consultants in the legal arena. However, the majority of individuals who identify themselves as trial consultants are not trained in psychology and most trial consultants indicate that they do not have a doctoral degree (Wrightsman, 2001). Social psychologists who work in legal psychology may focus on identifying and understanding how group processes affect jury deliberations and decision making. This information is then used to assist attorneys in jury selection. Social psychologists may also conduct research on the effects of pretrial publicity. This data can then be used to support an attorney's arguments for a change of venue. Social psychologists working as trial consultants sometimes hold mock jury trials to determine the most persuasive arguments for a courtroom case. Additionally, they may help attorneys prepare witnesses for testifying in a case and assist the witness to develop the most compelling testimony. The role of trial consultant is discussed in Chapter 9, "Trial Consultation," along with the ethical issues involved.

Most social psychologists are employed in academic settings, teaching and conducting research at colleges and universities. Social psychologists working in legal psychology conduct research applying the principles of psychology to legal questions. The most popular research areas involve juror selection, pretrial publicity, and jury decision making. However, there is a wealth of other areas that can be pursued. Students wishing to pursue this area may work with a mentor in graduate school conducting research in legal psychology. Social psychologists who consult as trial consultants generally do it on a part-time basis.

## Cognitive Psychology

Cognitive psychology is the study of cognition and mental processes. The focus of research is on the mental processes underlying judgment, decision making, memory, perception, and problem solving. An area that has received a lot of attention from cognitive psychologists in legal psychology is the accuracy of eyewitness testimony (e.g., Wells & Loftus, 2003). Eyewitness testimony can be one of the most convincing pieces of evidence used by a jury to convict a defendant. A growing body of evidence suggests that there is a high rate of false identifications of suspects by bystanders and victims. In fact, false identifications by mistaken witnesses account for more convictions of innocent persons than all other causes combined (Scheck, Neufeld, & Dwyer, 2000). Cognitive psychologists have developed a variety of techniques to improve the accuracy of eyewitness testimony (Wells et al., 1998).

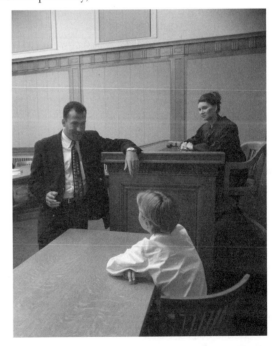

Figure 1.2

A developmental psychologist may have determined that this boy is mature enough to be a credible witness.
Brand X.

Cognitive psychologists also serve as expert witnesses refuting inaccurate or dubious eyewitness testimony. Related to this area is the study of memory and "recovered memories." Recovered memories usually involve memories of childhood sexual abuse that are repressed for many years until adulthood when the memories are recalled through therapy. These recollections of alleged sexual abuse have resulted in criminal trials regarding behaviors that are alleged to have occurred 20–30 years prior and have pitted daughters against their fathers. There is an academic as well as public debate regarding the accuracy of recovered memories. Skeptics of the accuracy of recovered memories have termed this phenomenon "false memory syndrome." Cognitive psychologists attempt to understand memory processes and how false memories can occur as well as how actual memories can be repressed. These areas of legal psychology are discussed in Chapter 11, "Eyewitness Memory and Recovered Memory."

## Developmental Psychology

Developmental psychologists study the changes in behavior and mental processes over time due to aging and maturation. One legal area of particular relevance for developmental psychologists is how the courts treat children. In civil cases, this can involve child custody disputes and the impact of custody arrangements on the emotional health of the child. In the criminal justice system, issues of development and maturity affect the child's credibility as a witness as well as his or her competency to proceed to trial. Developmental psychologists may research the accuracy and suggestibility of children's testimony, particularly in cases of alleged physical or sexual abuse. Researchers also study the ability of children and adolescents to make legally relevant decisions such as waving *Miranda* rights or offering a confession. A recent Supreme Court case cited psychological data regarding the developmental stages of the adolescent brain to rule that it is unconstitutional to execute a minor.

### Table 1.3    Areas of Psychology Related to Legal Psychology

- **Social psychology** Subfield of psychology that studies the effect of the social world on the mental processes and behavior of individuals and groups; examples in legal psychology include the effects of attitudes on jury decisions, pretrial publicity on verdicts, and scientific jury selection.
- **Cognitive psychology** Subfield of psychology that studies mental processes underlying cognition including such areas as decision making, judgment, memory, perception, and problem solving; examples in legal psychology include accuracy of eyewitness identifications and recovered memories.
- **Developmental psychology** Subfield of psychology that studies social, moral, intellectual, and emotional development over the course of the life span; examples in legal psychology include maturity of the adolescent brain and competency to waive legal rights and competency to be executed.

## Training in Forensic Psychology

In 2001, the American Psychological Association formally recognized forensic psychology as a specialty within psychology. The specialty designation indicates that the field has developed a substantial body of professional literature and specialized knowledge that distinguishes forensic psychology from other specialties (Packer & Borum, 2003). This also suggests that individuals practicing within the specialty require specific educational programs that prepare them to practice the specialty. The Commission for the Recognition of Specialties and Proficiencies in Professional Psychology defines the specialized knowledge in forensic psychology as follows:

> Specialized knowledge in forensic psychology is important in three areas. These are as follows: (1) clinical (e.g., diagnosis, treatment, psychological testing, prediction and intervention measurement, **epidemiology** of mental disorders, **ethics**), (2) forensic (e.g., response style, forensic ethics, tools and techniques for assessing symptoms and capacities relevant to legal questions) and (3) legal (e.g., knowledge of law and the legal system, knowledge of where and how to obtain relevant legal information). (http://www.apa.org/crsppp/archivforensic.html, 2004)

This set of skills is consistent with the narrow definition of forensic psychology and places the emphasis on the development of solid clinical skills. Although it is necessary to have specialized training in areas of law and forensic psychology, these competencies come after the development of clinical expertise. Therefore, anyone wishing to pursue a career in forensic psychology should first develop clinical skills in assessment, interviewing, understanding psychopathology, report writing, diagnostic interviewing, and case presentation. Just as not all clinicians typically treat all possible problems and populations, most forensic psychologists may not necessarily have the competence and expertise to work with all populations in all areas of forensic psychology (Packer & Borum, 2003).

# Doctoral Degrees

Most psychologists are practitioners who apply psychology to human problems as opposed to researchers and academics. To practice psychology in the United States or Canada, an individual needs to be licensed by their state or provincial board. The American Psychological Association (APA), the largest professional association of psychologists, recommends that individuals be eligible to sit for **licensure** upon completion of the following education and training (Williams, 2002):

1. A doctoral degree in psychology from an APA-accredited or Canadian Psychological Association (CPA)–accredited university.
2. The equivalent of 2 years of organized, sequential, supervised professional experience, 1 year of which is an APA- or CPA-accredited predoctoral internship. It is recommended that professional training, whether at the predoctoral-level practicum, internship, or postdoctoral level, is organized, sequential, and well supervised with ongoing evaluation of competence in a breadth of professional areas.

Thus, in order to practice **professional psychology**, the student needs to obtain a PhD or **PsyD** (Doctor of Psychology) degree. Though the above recommendations are not binding in all states, many states have adopted the APA recommendations and thus require licensure candidates to have their degrees granted from an APA-accredited program. The APA does not accredit all institutions of higher education that offer the doctoral degree in clinical or counseling psychology. Accreditation by the APA is different from accreditation by the regional education-accrediting agency. Although an institution is accredited to award the doctoral degree by the institution's regional accrediting agency, such as the Southern Association of Colleges and Schools, the APA may not accredit the institution. Students graduating with a doctoral degree not accredited by the APA may not be able to obtain licensure as a psychologist in a number of states. The APA does not accredit programs offering only the master's degree. Individuals can identify APA-accredited institutions from a list published on the APA web site (www.apa.org).

A doctoral degree can require 5–8 years of formal education after the bachelor's degree. The median number of years of full-time study from the bachelor's degree to the doctoral degree is nearly 7 years (Nixon, 1990). In order to obtain the doctorate in clinical or counseling psychology the student must complete a 1-year internship. Once the degree is awarded, most states require a second, postdoctoral year of supervised experience before the candidate can apply for licensure. Finally, candidates are required to obtain a passing score on the *Examination for Professional Practice in Psychology* (EPPP), would also need to pass any state exam, and may need to sit for an oral exam, depending on the state. The Association of State and Provincial Psychology Boards (ASPPB) publishes information on each state's licensing requirements.

The difference between degrees in clinical psychology versus counseling psychology was traditionally one of focus. Clinical psychologists were trained to work with the more severe mental disorders whereas counseling psychologists were trained to work with individuals experiencing adjustment problems. This distinction between clinical and counseling psychology has gradually become blurred over the past two decades. In order to practice independently, both specialties require the PhD—an academic degree requiring intensive study of research methods, personality theories, developmental psychology, psychopathology, assessment, and psychotherapy and counseling skills. Clinical psychologists are trained to diagnose and treat individuals with serious mental illness such as major depression and anxiety disorders. Clinical psychologists frequently do their 12-month internship in a psychiatric hospital setting or the psychiatric unit of a general hospital. Counseling psychologists receive much of the same training as clinical psychologists, though they may be enrolled in the Department of Education as opposed to the Department of Psychology at a university. In this case, the degree awarded may be a Doctor of Education (EdD). Counseling psychologists are generally trained to work with individuals who are struggling with adjustment issues in life, such as moving away from home, transitioning through a divorce, or adjusting to a new location. Frequently, a counseling psychologist may do their 12-month internship at a university counseling center. However, as noted, the distinction is not as great as it was in the past and there is now a great deal of overlap in populations served by the two specialties. Table 1.4 compares sample curriculums between a counseling doctoral program and a clinical doctoral program.

Another type of doctoral degree in clinical psychology is the PsyD, indicating the Doctor of Psychology degree. The original intent of the PsyD degree was to distinguish between the scientist role (PhD) and the practitioner role (PsyD). The focus of training for a PsyD is on clinical service as opposed to research and teaching (Stricker & Cummings, 1992). However, there are many practitioners with PhDs and academics and scientists with the PsyD degree. The major differences between the two degrees are training opportunities and training focus. Students are encouraged to discuss with their advisors the benefits and tradeoffs associated with both degree types before making decisions that will have consequences that carry well into one's career (Norcross, Castle, Sayette, & Mayne, 2004).

A number of graduate programs have developed coursework and supervision opportunities for individuals wishing to pursue specialized work in forensic psychology. Clinical psychologists are the most active in the legal setting and constitute the largest percentage of individuals who identify themselves as forensic psychologists (Bartol & Bartol, 2004). Indeed, approximately 85% of the membership of the American Psychology-Law Society identifies themselves as clinicians (Grisso, 1991). Relatively few graduate programs offer formal training in exclusively forensic psy-

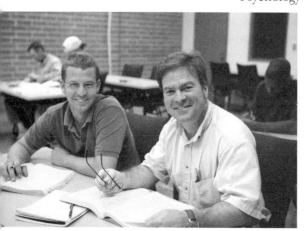

**Figure 1.3**

It appears that the majority of psychologists entering the specialty of forensic psychology obtain most of their training through continuing education.
© 2009 Lisa F. Young. Used under license from Shutterstock, Inc.

## Comparison of Typical Graduate Programs in Clinical and Counseling Psychology — Table 1.4

### Counseling Psychology
- Introduction to Professional Counseling
- Legal and Ethical Issues in Counseling
- Multicultural Counseling
- The Mental Health Counselor as Professional, Practitioner, and Consultant
- Masters Research
- Addictive and Compulsive Disorders
- Psychopathology
- Advanced Human Growth and Development
- Individual Assessment
- Group Counseling
- Marriage and Family Counseling
- Psychodiagnostics and Treatment Planning
- Crisis Intervention Counseling
- Research Methods
- Advanced Clinical Methods
- Counseling Internship–2,000 hours
- Dissertation Research

### Clinical Psychology
- Research Methods I
- Graduate Statistics I and II
- Advanced Social Psychology
- Advanced Developmental Psychology
- Physiological Psychology
- Human Cognition and Behavior
- Masters Research
- Fundamentals of Clinical Psychology I–Interviewing and Diagnosis
- Theory of Assessment
- Advanced Psychopathology
- Methods of Assessment
- Assessment Practicum
- Systems of Psychotherapy
- Fundamentals of Clinical Psychology II–Ethics
- Practicum in Clinical Psychology
- Advanced Seminar in Clinical Psychology
- Advanced Clinical Techniques–Practica
- Internship in Clinical Psychology–2,000 hours
- Dissertation Research

chology (Bartol & Bartol, 2004). However, some practitioners have questioned the long-term viability and advisability of such specialized degrees (Otto, 2005; Packer & Borum, 2003). It appears that a specialized degree in forensic psychology may limit an individual's professional options more so than a general degree in clinical or counseling psychology. Rather, in order to work as a clinical forensic psychologist, it is advisable to obtain a doctoral degree in clinical or counseling psychology with specialized coursework, supervised clinical experiences, and continuing education in forensic psychology. Table 1.5 lists graduate programs in psychology that indicate they offer specialized training in forensic psychology.

Individuals can also pursue **postdoctoral training** in forensic psychology. This typically requires a year of specialized training with intensive supervision and additional formal coursework in forensic psychology. Currently, there are only 11 identified postdoctoral programs in forensic psychology and these programs accept only one or two applicants a year (Packer & Borum, 2003). With so few postdoctoral training opportunities, it seems unlikely that this will become the requisite for practice in the specialty. Table 1.6 lists the postdoctoral training programs in forensic psychology (Packer & Borum, 2003).

Due to the relatively recent development of **didactic training** and supervision opportunities in forensic psychology at the graduate level, many current practitioners

## Table 1.5 — Clinical PhD/PsyD Programs Offering Specialized Training in Forensic Psychology

- *University of Alabama* (clinical PhD with a psychology-law concentration)
- *University of Arizona* (PhD and/or JD)
- *Alliant International University* (PhD in Forensic Psychology or PsyD in Forensic Psychology)
- *Carlos Albizo University in Miami* (PsyD in Clinical Psychology with a concentration in Forensic Psychology)
- *Drexel University* (JD/PhD)
- *Drexel University* (PhD with a concentration in Forensic Psychology)
- *University of Florida* (Counseling PhD with psychology-law concentration or JD)
- *Fordham University* (Clinical PhD with a concentration in Forensic Psychology)
- *John Jay College of Criminal Justice-CUNY* (MA or PhD)
- *University of Nebraska* (joint JD and PhD or joint JD and MA in Psychology)
- *Nova Southeastern University* (PsyD with a concentration in Clinical Forensic Psychology)
- *Sam Houston State University* (PhD in Clinical Psychology with an emphasis in forensics)
- *Simon Fraser University* (PhD in Clinical Forensic Psychology).
- *West Virginia University* (Ph D in Clinical Psychology with an emphasis in forensics)
- *Widener University* (JD/PsyD joint degree)

## Table 1.6 — List of Postdoctoral Training Programs in Forensic Psychology

- Center for Forensic Psychiatry, Ypsilanti, Michigan
- Federal Bureau of Prisons, Springfield, Missouri
- Federal Medical Center, Rochester, Minnesota
- Florida State Hospital, Chattahoochee, Florida
- Kirby Forensic Psychiatric Center, New York, New York
- Massachusetts General Hospital, Juvenile Track, Boston, Massachusetts
- Patton State Hospital, Highland, California
- St. Louis Hospital, St. Louis, Missouri
- University of Massachusetts Medical School, Worcester, Massachusetts
- University of Southern California, Los Angeles, California
- Western State Hospital, Tacoma, Washington

did not have access to this training during their graduate school years. The majority of psychologists entering the specialty of forensic psychology appear to gain the greater part of their forensic training through continuing education workshops. Licensed psychologists must complete continuing education (CE) as part of their license renewal process. The number of CE hours per licensure period varies by state. Professionals in the specialty have noted an increase in attendance at CE workshops in forensic psychology. Some have suggested that the increase may be prompted in part by the desire for psychologists to avoid the billing and oversight complexities associated with managed care (Otto, 1998).

One of the foremost providers of continuing education in forensic psychology is the American Board of Forensic Psychology (*www.abfp.org*). A typical 3-day workshop series offered by the Academy might include the following topics: Ethical Issues in Forensic Practice, Forensic Applications of the MMPI-2, Violence Risk Assessment, Comprehensive Child Custody Evaluations, Sex Offender Commitment: Risk Assessment and Treatment, Assessing Malingering and Defensiveness, Effective and Ethical Testimony, and Psycholegal Issues in Criminal Cases. As one can see from the workshop topics, the focus of the training is on the applied aspects of the specialty. There are other providers of continuing education in forensic psychology including workshops at state psychological association meetings and the annual meeting of the APA.

Some individuals may elect to become *board certified* in forensic psychology. Concurrent with the increased interest in forensic psychology, there has been a growth in the number of private agencies offering **board certification**. It should be noted that the APA does not award board certification, or diplomats, as they are sometimes called, in any specialty nor does it endorse any of the credentialing agencies. In 1978, the **American Board of Forensic Psychology** (ABFP) was formed to credential psychologists who were practicing at an advanced level in forensic psychology. In 1985, the ABFP joined the American Board of Professional Psychology (ABPP; *www.abpp.org*). The ABPP was incorporated in 1947 with the support of the APA. It is one of the oldest and most respected of the credentialing organizations in psychology. Board certification (awarding of a Diploma in a specialty) is accomplished through examination by specialty boards affiliated with the ABPP. In forensic psychology, the ABFP has the authority to certify psychologists as Diplomats in Forensic Psychology. The letters ABPP after the individual's degree, typically a PhD, denote this certification (e.g., name, PhD, ABPP).

Just as college degrees from different universities (e.g., Harvard compared to Chris's School of Professional Psychology and Television Repair) are not viewed as equal in regards to quality, there is a wide range of standards regarding board certification among the various private organizations, many of which are relatively new. Whereas some boards, such as the ABFP, require individuals to possess a license and experience in the specialty before they may even apply for examination, other certifying organizations appear to be "little more than **vanity boards** that offer checkbook credentials" (Otto & Heilbrun, 2002, p. 13). The emergence of these new boards offering "expertise" in the name of "board certification," "**diplomate**" status, or "fellow" status has prompted criticism of the boards that appear to provide a credential based on minimal criteria. Golding (1999) suggested ways to evaluate credentialing agencies. Specifically, he recommends the prospective candidate determine whether the status is based on a work-sample review, oral examination, and specific requirements for training and supervision and warns against organizations with "**grandparenting**" clauses. Often, these liberal grandfather clauses allow individuals to apply for certification prior to the implementation of more rigorous standards. The practice of extending the grandfathering privileges suggests that the clause may only truly serve as a marketing ploy and detract from the credibility of the credential

■ **Vanity boards**
Certification boards that have minimal or nonexistent requirements for board certification.

■ **Diplomate**
Recognition by a professional association that a member has advanced training, skills, and competence; commonly referred to as board certified.

(Otto & Heilbrun, 2002). It is necessary to note that board certification is a voluntary process and some psychologists question the value of obtaining certification. Although the vanity boards are a relatively painless process, at times requiring no more than a current vita and a signed check, others can require a rigorous 2-year process of application and examination. There is no evidence to indicate that board-certified psychologists are more or less competent than their non-board-certified colleagues (Otto & Heilbrun, 2002).

# Practicing Forensic Psychology at the Master's Level

A master's degree in psychology typically requires 1–2 years of formal school after the bachelor's degree. Although an individual with a master's degree usually cannot present him- or herself as a psychologist, they may be able to practice in various states under the title of licensed professional counselor, licensed mental health counselor, or other such titles. Thus, a degree in counseling or clinical psychology may allow one to practice independently, depending on the jurisdiction. The master's degree could then open the door to working in the specialty of forensic psychology.

Working as a master's-level counselor in forensic psychology usually entails providing basic mental health services within correctional or police settings (Kuther & Morgan, 2004). Master's-level counselors may lead psychoeducational groups in correctional facilities or for individuals serving probation in the community. The focus of treatment can involve anger management, domestic violence, parenting skills, substance abuse and relapse prevention, or the development of problem-solving skills, to name just a few. Depending on the jurisdiction, individuals with a master's degree may conduct court-ordered psychological and mental health assessments. When deciding to pursue a master's degree in psychology, it is important to understand the laws of the state in which you plan to practice. It is just as important to keep in mind that state laws can evolve rapidly and it is best to stay abreast of any changing in licensing requirements.

In addition to the necessary educational and internship requirements to practice as a forensic psychologist, other skills can be of particular benefit. Most forensic psychologists are involved in some form of psychological assessment. These assessments may address a wide range of issues before the court such as competency evaluations, **criminal responsibility** evaluations (insanity plea), child custody evaluations, psychological trauma evaluations, sex offender risk, dangerousness, sexual abuse, accuracy of children's testimony, disability evaluations, civil commitment, psychological autopsy, and so on. Therefore, it is important for the forensic psychologist to have excellent assessment skills. These skills include strong statistical skills to understand the psychometric properties of the instruments being used, training and supervision in using psychological tests, and strong writing skills to produce understandable psychological reports for the court. Additionally, psychologists who testify in court should develop their oral presentation skills along with having a well-groomed social presence.

Students interested in careers in forensic work can consult the American Psychology-Law Society web site for information on careers, graduate programs, and job listings (http://www.ap-ls.org/students/careersIndex.html). The American Psychology-Law Society is Division 41 of the **American Psychological Association**. Students interested in pursuing a career in law and psychology are encouraged to become **student affiliates** of the APA and to join Division 41. The Careers and

■ **Criminal responsibility**
Culpability for a crime; accountability for criminal behavior; often discussed with the insanity defense.

■ **American Psychological Association**
Based in Washington, D.C., the American Psychological Association (APA) is a scientific and professional body that represents psychology in the United States (www.apa.org).

Training Committee of the American Psychology-Law Society also publishes a booklet titled *Careers in Psychology and the Law: A Guide for Prospective Students* (Careers and Training Committee, 2004). *Your Career in Psychology: Psychology and the Law* (Kuther, 2004) also provides career information for students interested in psychology and law. The Appendix of this textbook provides a list of web sites along with a brief description of numerous professional associations associated with forensic psychology. These sites should help with both your scholarly research and career decision.

# Full-Time versus Part-Time Forensic Work

The majority of psychologists who do forensic work generally do so on a part-time basis and are engaged in other activities such as general counseling or clinical work, teaching, research, and administrative work. Although some psychologists work solely in forensic practices or full time in a correctional or police setting, many individuals supplement their clinical practice with forensic work. In addition, most forensic psychologists specialize in one or two areas of forensic psychology, such as conducting child custody evaluations and evaluations for the termination of parental rights, as opposed to providing the full range of forensic services.

# Overview of This Book

The following chapters present in detail the practice of forensic psychology. **Chapter 2** discusses ethical and legal issues related to the practice of forensic psychology. A forensic evaluation is quite different from most other psychological evaluations. Perhaps the most striking difference is the lack of confidentiality. Forensic evaluations are used to answer a psycholegal question, such as **competency to stand trial** or criminal responsibility. By their very nature, the results of a forensic evaluation need to be made public so that the courts can make a legal ruling. Another important distinction is *whom* the evaluation helps. There are times when the results of the evaluation may actually not be in the best interest of the examinee. For example, a forensic psychologist may decide that a client is feigning emotional distress in an attempt to win a lawsuit. Also covered will be the potential conflicts between law and psychology regarding both ethical issues and decision-making procedures. Professionals in law and psychology adhere to their own professional code of conduct. In addition to maintaining professional ethical standards, psychologists and attorneys must practice within the boundaries of the law. At times, these two professionals' codes of ethics and the law can be in conflict. Lawyers are required to zealously represent the best interest of their client. A psychologist functioning as an **expert witness** is required to remain objective and impartial, despite the retaining attorney's commitment to his or her client. Chapter 2 also presents **case law** regarding expert witness testimony. Testimony by expert witnesses differs from testimony by fact witnesses. One important difference is that experts are asked to form an opinion. In most cases, experts are also allowed to testify regarding the ultimate issue of the case. The ultimate issue is the question that must be decided by the trier of fact, either the judge or the jury. Most forensic psychologists are subpoenaed to testify in court at one time or another. Chapter 2 discusses the potential pitfalls of expert testimony and offers some suggestions for trial preparation.

■ **Competency**
The ability or capacity to perform a specific task or function with rationality. The Dusky standard is used to determine competency to stand trial.

■ **Expert witness**
Any individual who has been qualified as an "expert" by the trial judge due to specialized knowledge or skill. A fact witness is generally not allowed to offer an opinion, whereas an expert witness may.

**Figure 1.4**

One of the responsibilities of a police psychologist is to aid in selecting police officers.
© 2009 JupiterImages Corporation.

■ **Malingering**

An individual attempts to feign symptoms or exaggerate symptoms during assessment, usually for secondary gain. For example, a defendant may fake a mental illness with the intention of being found incompetent to stand trial.

**Chapter 3** introduces the reader to psychological assessment. Psychological assessment is one area that distinguishes psychology from the other mental health care professions. Psychologists receive rigorous training in assessment skills in graduate school. The strong foundation in assessment skills is what enables most psychologists to readily enter into the specialty of forensic psychology, with its heavy reliance on assessment. Chapter 3 builds upon the discussion of ethical issues from Chapter 2 and presents the ethical and legal complexities of forensic assessment. General principles of assessment are presented including the four psychometric properties of psychological tests: reliability, validity, standard error of measurement, and normative groups. The differences between forensic assessment and clinical assessment in a therapeutic setting are vast and these differences present liability pitfalls for the unwary practitioner. These differences are reviewed and recommendations provided on how to navigate through the complexities of forensic work. Chapter 3 provides an overview of common clinical and forensic instruments used in practice. The instruments reviewed are the standards in the field and do not represent a comprehensive list of all possible psychological tests. New instruments are routinely introduced. A student of forensic psychology should understand the basic psychometric issues and have familiarity with the commonly used assessment instruments.

**Chapter 4** presents the two assessment areas most frequently associated with forensic psychology, competency to stand trial and criminal responsibility. Competency to stand trial (CST) is the most common forensic assessment performed by psychologists with estimates as high as 60,000 CST evaluations per year. Criminal responsibility is referred to informally as the insanity plea. Some of the myths of the insanity plea are reviewed and debunked. Most people greatly overestimate the frequency of use and the success of the insanity plea, tending to believe that guilty defendants use the plea as a way to "get off." **Malingering**, or the attempt to feign mental illness, is a unique aspect of forensic work covered in some detail in this chapter. Certainly, defendants and plaintiffs involved in civil lawsuits may be motivated to fake or exaggerate their symptoms of mental illness. The public and court officials frequently confuse these two evaluations with one another. Criminal responsibility evaluations address the mental state of the defendant at the time of the crime, which could be as much as a year or so prior to the date of the evaluation. Competency to stand trial evaluations assess the defendant's mental state at the time of the assessment as well as ability to progress through a trial. The chapter presents the ethical issues and case law regarding criminal responsibility and competency evaluations. Instruments used in the evaluations are reviewed and several case examples taken from forensic practice are provided. This chapter is particularly interesting since it is a common avenue for psychologists to use as they start working in forensic psychology.

**Chapter 5** examines the subspecialty of **police psychology**. Police psychologists work with law enforcement personnel, providing psychological services to police agencies. Police psychologists do not work with criminal defendants; rather, they conduct evaluations on police officers and officer candidates, provide counseling to law enforcement personnel and their families, and consult to police agencies. The two most common activities of police psychology work are counseling and selection of police officers. In addition to preemployment assessment, police psychologists assess officers for special assignments, such as SWAT duties, and conduct fitness-for-duty evaluations. Policing is an extremely stressful occupation. The stress of police work affects the officer as well as his or her family. Psychologists provide counseling to officers and their families. The issues of confidentiality and the importance of understanding the police officer's job are presented as important considerations for the psychologist provide psychological services to law enforcement personnel. Police psychologists also provide training to sworn and unsworn personnel. Training topics include stress management and inoculation, dealing with the mentally ill suspect, hostage negotiation, communication skills, sensitivity training, diversity training, and peer counseling skills, to name a few. In addition to training, police psychologists consult with law enforcement personnel on investigative techniques such as criminal profiling, **investigative hypnosis**, and psychological autopsies. Along with consulting on investigative techniques, police psychologists can consult on organizational issues such as department morale, departmental communication, and management decision-making policies. Again, the student will note the emphasis on the applied aspects of the profession, particularly in regards to psychological assessment.

**Chapter 6** turns to another subspecialty of forensic psychology and examines the role psychologists play in correctional facilities. Correctional psychologists work with the prison inmate population. Correctional psychologists provide psychological services to incarcerated individuals and work to rehabilitate inmates for their successful return to society. Although many of the clinical skills for working with the general population are also necessary for working with inmates, **correctional psychology** is not simply the psychological treatment of people who happen to be in prison. A variety of unique obstacles and issues confront the correctional psychologist. The number one problem facing prisons today is overcrowding. The overcrowding of prisons exacerbates the difficult conditions already in place, making the need for psychological services all the more important. To compound the problem, nearly one-half million men and women with mental illness are incarcerated. This chapter reviews the current condition of prisons in the United States with an emphasis on the psychological needs of incarcerated individuals. Theories of punishment from the criminal justice literature are discussed, including retribution, deterrence, incapacitation, rehabilitation, and restorative justice. One current issue regarding the goal of incapacitation is the use of selective incapacitation. Selective incapacitation refers to the civil commitment of individuals to prevent him or her from committing crimes in the future. The legal, ethical, and constitutional questions related to selective incapacitation are presented. Correctional psychologists spend the majority of their time doing administrative work. They also conduct assessments on inmates and provide counseling, including crisis intervention. Suicide is an ever-present problem among the inmate population and psychologist can play a major role in screening and training correctional officers in detecting and preventing suicidal behaviors. The types of assessments that correctional psychologists conduct are presented from the initial classification assessment when an inmate first enters a facility to the risk assessment often required prior to parole. The chapter reviews treatment programs from various state and federal facilities and discusses the unique challenges facing the correctional psychologist. Correctional psychology is a growth area. In the 1940s, there were fewer

■ **Police psychology**
Area of forensic psychology that focuses on law enforcement personnel; includes the assessment and treatment of law enforcement personnel.

■ **Investigative hypnosis**
A tool used to help enhance a victim's recollection of a crime.

than 100 correctional psychologists. Today, there are over 2,500 correctional psychologists and the future looks bright for the profession.

**Chapters 7 and 8** present the practice of forensic psychology under civil law. Chapter 7 reviews tort law and personal injury evaluations. Citizens who feel that they have been wronged can have the dispute settled in civil court. Civil courts can impose sanctions in the form of monetary payments but cannot impose prison time. Many people are familiar with the work of trial attorneys and personal injury lawsuits. Individuals claiming to have been harmed can sue for compensation for their injuries. Personal injury lawsuits involve emotional damages as well as physical injuries. Plaintiffs can sue for emotional damages when the damages were caused either intentionally or through negligence. For example, a mother who suffers emotional distress after witnessing the injury of her child at

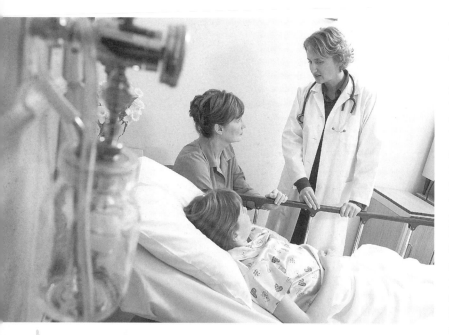

**Figure 1.5**

A forensic psychologist may evaluate this child and mother to determine the extent of psychological impairments suffered because of the child's injuries.
© 2005 JupiterImages Corporation.

an amusement park may be entitled to compensatory and punitive damages if the injury was due to the park operator's negligence. An individual who was sexually molested as a child may file a civil lawsuit against the perpetrator as well as his or her employer if the abuse occurred in the work environment, as seen in the media with priests or teachers. The role of the forensic psychologist in **personal injury evaluations** is to assess the nature and extent of psychological impairments suffered by the plaintiff. The psychologist must also determine the likely cause of each impairment or injury and the nature of any treatment that may return the plaintiff to the level of functioning he or she experienced before the injury. This type of assessment is complicated, as the psychologists must distinguish between any psychological impairment that was pre-existing from impairments caused by the alleged injury. In addition, even clients who suffered emotional damages may be tempted to malinger or exaggerate their impairments due to fears of being denied compensation. The most common diagnosis in personal injury cases is posttraumatic stress disorder (PTSD). PTSD is a severe anxiety disorder that can occur after someone experiences a traumatic event. It is characterized by flashbacks, sleep disturbances, nightmares, irritability, depression, and hypervigilance.

**Chapter 8** presents juvenile law with particular attention to **child custody evaluations**. Child custody evaluations can be the most complex, difficult, and challenging of all forensic evaluations. Rather than evaluating one individual, the forensic psychologist involved in a child custody case will need to possibly evaluate several children, two parents, and possibly stepparents, stepsiblings, and grandparents. The adversarial nature of child custody disputes complicates the issue of determining the best placement for the child. Frequently parents engaged in a child custody dispute may use the child as weapons in the battle. The psychologists must determine what the best placement situation is for the interests of the child and parents. Many factors need to be considered in formulating a recommendation for the court. A disgruntled parent who disagrees with the psychologist's recommendation can present a liability risk for the psychologist. Case law regarding custody decision making along with guidelines for performing custody evaluations are reviewed.

**Chapters 9, 10, and 11** present select topics from the field of legal psychology. Legal psychology is the research-oriented application of psychological principles and methods to legal questions. These three chapters look at how psychological methods have been used to assist lawyers in the courtroom, assist law enforcement personnel in the field, and assist the trier of fact in the jury deliberation chambers. Each chapter presents an area in which psychologists can play a "behind-the-scenes" role in the legal process. Chapter 9 presents the relatively new practice of trial consultation. **Trial consultants** assist attorneys with jury selection, witness preparation, change of venue requests due to pretrial publicity, and even the evaluation of trial strategy. Psychologists are uniquely skilled to work as trial consultants due to their extensive background in social science research and understanding of human behavior. This chapter first presents the new field of trial consultation. The process of traditional jury selection versus scientific jury selection is reviewed. Attorneys really do not select jurors but they can dismiss potential jurors with or without cause. The process of jury selection is governed by rules exclusive to each jurisdiction. Psychologists may survey potential jurors in the community to identify attitudes, traits, and/or demographic characteristics that would either favor or prejudice a defendant or a defense strategy. Attorneys can use this information to help shape the jury. Psychologists can also assist attorneys by determining the effects of pretrial publicity on potential jurors. When a community survey indicates that many of the potential jurors have already made a decision of guilt or innocence based on pretrial publicity, an attorney may decide to seek a change of venue, citing the survey data as support for the change. Testifying on the witness stand can be a harrowing experience for even the most seasoned attorney. An adversarial cross-examination can confuse and intimidate a witness. Trial consultants work with attorneys to prepare witnesses for courtroom testimony. The consultant can assist the witness to provide a credible and consistent testimony. The consultant should not, however, alter or enhance the witness's statements. The ethics of trial consultation are also discussed in this chapter.

Legal psychology can assist law enforcement procedures in the criminal investigative process. Investigative psychology is the application of psychological principles and methods to investigating criminal behavior. The chapter on investigative psychology presents several examples from the field including criminal profiling, methods used to detect deception, investigative hypnosis, and psychological autopsies. Criminal profiling is the use of psychological methods to help identify potential suspects. Criminal profiling involves a variety of approaches such as looking for similar criminal personality characteristics for specific crimes (i.e., the "typical" rapist) to a detailed crime scene analysis, searching for the perpetrator's "signature" and *modus operandi*. Although criminal profiling has been glamorized in the media, it is infrequently used and continues to be more art than science. Students wishing to become criminal profilers need to reexamine their career plans due to the scarcity of profiling training and jobs.

Psychologists have long been interested in detecting deception. The current standard in lie detection is the use of the polygraph, an instrument that measures physiological changes thought to be related to the arousal that accompanies deception. As with any sophisticated technique, there are a variety of approaches to using the polygraph. These approaches as well as the scientific validity and admissibility of polygraph evidence are discussed. New methods of detecting deception include recording brain wave patterns with positron emission tomography (PET) and magnetic resonance imaging (MRI) scanners, facial thermography (skin temperature),

Figure 1.6

A legal psychologist may do a detailed crime scene analysis in an effort to identify the perpetrator's "signature" or *modus operandi*.
© 2009 Simone van den Berg. Used under license from Shutterstock, Inc.

demeanor, and even word usage. Although the research is still in the early stages, some of these methods should help to provide a theoretical basis to the detection of deception as well as practical tools for evaluating victims' and suspects' self-reports. One promising area is the use of specific electroencephalogram (EEG) patterns, called event-related potentials, to indicate that an individual has specific knowledge. This area is called brain fingerprinting and provides an example of the thin line between scientific validity and junk science. Investigators have also used investigative hypnosis as attempts to increase the amount and accuracy of a victim's or witness's recall. The validity and admissibility of hypnotically refreshed memories is reviewed. Psychological autopsies are used when the manner of death is uncertain. Manner of death is classified as natural, accidental, suicide, or homicide (NASH). When there is a question about the manner of death, usually when it was a suicide or an accident, forensic psychologists can provide a **psychological autopsy**, attempting to understand the deceased's state of mind at the time of death.

**■ Psychological autopsy**

A retrospective examination of social and psychological events prior to an individual's death.

Chapter 11 covers the large area of literature examining the accuracy of eyewitness testimony and the role psychologists play as expert witnesses to the courts in presenting this data. Inaccurate eyewitness testimony is perhaps the most frequent cause of convicting an innocent person. Numerous innocent bystanders have gone to prison primarily based on a witness's erroneous testimony that he or she saw the person commit the crime. Memories do not work like videotapes, but rather, we appear to reconstruct our memory of events based on expectations and mental schemas. Cognitive psychologists attempt to educate juries about the low accuracy rates of eyewitness testimony and help defense lawyers scrutinize the accuracy of such testimony. Cognitive psychologists also work with law enforcement on methods to increase the accuracy of eyewitness identification, as in the case of a police lineup. Recommendations from psychologists as well as organizations such as the Innocence Project and law enforcement agencies are provided for reforming the eyewitness identification procedure. This chapter also addresses the phenomenon of recovered memories and the issue of **false memory syndrome**. Several high-profile court proceedings have highlighted the complex phenomenon of recovered memories of childhood sexual abuse. Victims confront their abusers years after the incident allegedly took place. The only evidence is the word of the accuser against the word of the accused. The question of the accuracy of these recovered memories has been intensely debated. Recent cases have used physical evidence to prove that the **recovered memory** was false. Patients who have "recovered" false memories of sexual abuse as part of therapy have successfully sued their therapists.

**■ False memory syndrome**

False memories that have been implanted inadvertently through suggestive therapy techniques but the individual believes the memories to be real.

Finally, **Chapter 12** explores four emerging trends in the field of forensic psychology. Specifically, the chapter examines the growth of forensic psychology and the impact this increased interest has had on the development of the specialty. The increase in the number of students and professionals entering the field of forensic psychology has led to a greater sophistication in methods used as well as more scrutiny of the quality of services provided by **forensic psychologists**. As psychologists become better acquainted with the legal profession, they can work to influence public policy. Psychologists engage in political activism to promote the profession's agenda. These activities can include lobbying, political contributions, class action lawsuits, and even running for state and federal office. One mechanism that the profession has used frequently is the amicus brief. An amicus brief is used to inform the court on issues related to a case and is submitted by an impartial party who is not directly involved in the case but may have a stake in the court's ruling. The American Psychological Association has submitted over 100 such briefs on a wide range from psychologists' right to make psychiatric diagnosis to the constitutionality of executing juvenile offenders. Experts in the field of forensic psychology recently held the

Villanova Conference to discuss future training models in forensic and legal psychology. It offered several recommendations for training in the specialty. Current training models are presented along with recommendations from the Villanova Conference. As the fourth emerging trend in forensic psychology, Chapter 12 introduces the relatively new area of therapeutic jurisprudence (TJ). TJ attempts to use the law in a therapeutic way, helping both offenders and victims. Psychologists involved in TJ can use methods developed in clinical and **counseling psychology** and apply them to the legal system. For example, methods used to enhance treatment compliance in a clinical setting can also be used to enhance compliance to the terms of probation in the criminal justice system. Procedures such as publicly communicating a commitment to adhere to the rules and using family and friends to support the probationer can increase compliance. TJ has already made a mark in specialty courts, such as drug courts and family courts. Forensic psychologists can collaborate with lawyers and legislators to help shape the law into a therapeutic intervention.

Forensic psychology is a broad applied field that offers numerous opportunities to the practitioner. Forensic psychologists may conduct assessments, provide clinical services, and work in administration. The practice of forensic psychology is expanding with new roles for the forensic psychologist. Legal psychology also offers a variety of opportunities for research into psycholegal questions. Psychologists have examined the effects of pretrial publicity, attitudes, and conviction rates, and even ways to enhance compliance with jury duty. Tables 1.7 and 1.8 provide examples of the type of work psychologists can do in forensic psychology and in legal psychology.

## Activities in Forensic Psychology  Table 1.7

- Competency to stand trial
- Competency to waive *Miranda* rights
- Competency to confess
- Civil commitment
- Criminal responsibility (insanity plea)
- Child custody
- Psychological damages
- Disability determinations
- Risk assessment–violence
- Sexual predator evaluations
- Evaluation of child sexual abuse
- Evaluation of mitigating and aggravating factors in capital sentencing
- Court-ordered psychological evaluations
- Anger-management evaluations
- Fitness-for-duty evaluations
- Psychological preemployment evaluations of police officer candidates

| Table 1.8 | Activities in Legal Psychology |
|---|---|

- Trial consultation
- Jury selection
- Witness preparation
- Mock trials to evaluate courtroom strategy
- Evaluating effects of pretrial publicity
- Expert witness on a variety of psychological and social science research issues such as trademark infringement, effects of adult entertainment, sexual harassment, discrimination, etc.
- Expert witness testimony on accuracy of eyewitness
- Research on a variety of factors affecting the courts such as jury size and qualified jurors

# TEST YOUR KNOWLEDGE

1. Although the textbook discusses a broad definition of forensic psychology, others define it more narrowly, considering it a specialization of
   a. social psychology
   b. clinical psychology
   c. experimental psychology
   d. developmental psychology

2. Current training practices in forensic psychology suggest that the majority of psychologists get their forensic specialty training
   a. at the predoctoral level on internship
   b. at the postdoctoral level in the form of continuing education hours
   c. during their graduate school years
   d. typically self-taught through scholarly endeavors

3. Psychology was founded on the philosophy of empiricism. This view suggests that knowledge
   a. comes from authority
   b. comes from precedent and deductive reasoning
   c. comes from experience and observation
   d. is elusive and never accurately assessed

4. Dr. Debra Long has a degree in developmental psychology. She was asked to testify as an expert witness. She would most likely testify on
   a. a defendant's competency to stand trial
   b. effects of pretrial publicity on potential jurors
   c. an adolescent's ability to understand her waiver of the *Miranda* rights
   d. a defendant's mental state at the time of the offense

5. Dr. William Moore has his doctoral degree in cognitive psychology. He would most likely be interested in
    a. how individuals can persuade a group of jurors
    b. how memory affects eyewitness testimony
    c. why people break the law
    d. how to treat antisocial personalities

Answer Key: (1) b, (2) b, (3) c, (4) c, (5) b

# Chapter Two

# Ethical Issues Related to the Practice of Forensic Psychology

## Learning Objectives

- Describe the three roles a forensic psychologist can play as an expert witness (i.e. philosopher/advocate, hired gun, conduit-educator) and describe advantages or disadvantages to each.
- Distinguish between a fact witness and an expert witness.
- Who may serve as an expert witness?
- Distinguish between qualifying as an expert witness and admissibility of expert witness testimony.
- Name and define the standards used to determine admissibility of expert testimony.
- What are the penultimate issue and the ultimate issue? What is the APA's position on psychologists testifying as to the ultimate issue? What are arguments for and against testifying on the ultimate issue?
- What are the three critical elements necessary for expert witness testimony?
- What is reliability and what are the four standards of reliability defined by the Supreme Court?
- Describe good-faith immunity laws and the function of these laws. Which states have adopted good-faith laws?
- Be able to describe the following court decisions:
  *Kumbo Tire Co. v. Carmichael* (1999)
  *Daubert v. Merrell Dow Pharmaceuticals* (1993)
  *General Electric Co. v. Joiner* (1997)
  *Frye v. United States* (1923)
- What is the Dusky standard?
- Describe the Federal Rules of Evidence.
- What are dual relationships and the ethical concerns regarding dual relationships?
- What are some of the ethical differences between psychology and law?

## Key Terms

- Adversarial
- Advocate
- Amicus curiae brief
- Case law
- Character
- Coaching
- Common law
- Conduit-educator
- Core competencies
- *Daubert v. Merrell Dow Pharmaceuticals* (1993)
- Ethical absolutism
- Ethical relativism
- Ethical standards
- Ethics
- Expert witness
- Fact witness
- Federal Rules of Evidence
- Fitness
- Foundational competencies
- *Frye v. United States* (1923)
- General Acceptance Rule
- *General Electric Company v. Joiner* (1997)
- Hired gun
- Immunity laws
- Impartiality as the best advocacy
- *Jenkins v. United States* (1962)
- Jurisdiction
- *Kumbo Tire Company v. Carmichael* (1999)
- Learned treatise method
- Legal sufficiency
- Legislative law
- Malingering
- Multiple relationships

*(continued)*

# Key Terms *(continued)*

■ **Standard of care**

The appropriate practice for the delivery of mental health or medical services; a standard of care should be based on scientific evidence and is the expected minimum care within the profession.

■ **Advocate**

One who pleads on behalf of another individual; an advocate will promote the interests of their client. An attorney typically serves as a legal advocate for their client.

- ■ Peer review
- ■ Penultimate issue
- ■ Philosopher-advocate
- ■ Practice guidelines
- ■ Relevancy
- ■ Reliability
- ■ Specialty competencies
- ■ Specialty Guidelines
  for Forensic Psychologists (SGFP)

- ■ Standard of care
- ■ Stare decisis
- ■ Statutory law
- ■ Trier of fact
- ■ Ultimate issue
- ■ Validity
- ■ Witness immunity

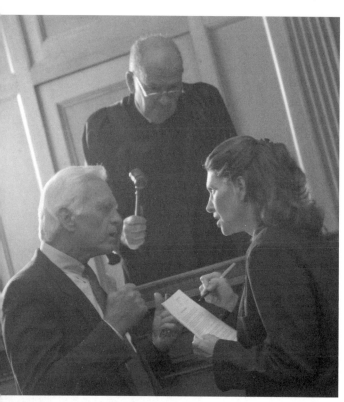

Figure 2.1

Lawyers argue their case before the judge, citing previously decided cases to confirm precedence.
© 2009 BXP

This chapter addresses the ethical issues involved in the practice of forensic psychology. Most professional organizations have ethical codes and standards of conduct to which the members are expected to adhere. There are also a variety of **practice guidelines** recommending "best practices" or **standards of care** for particular services a forensic psychologist may provide. Finally, there are also legal standards including both statutory and case law that psychologists must follow. Whereas ethical standards and guidelines are recommended, they are not necessarily legally binding. Unfortunately, there are numerous circumstances in which one can act unethically though still be within the law. This raises an interesting point that is discussed later in the chapter, what to do when the ethical code and the law conflict. Many of the ethical codes state the types of behaviors that are prohibited and are therefore proscriptive in nature. The ethical codes do not address all possible ethical dilemmas nor do they indicate the most ethical action for particular situations. Rather, the code indicates what a professional should *not* do, not what the professional should do. As a result, the decision to practice as an ethical professional requires more than an understanding of ethical codes, practice guidelines, and the rules and laws of the jurisdiction in which one practices. It requires the development of an identity as an ethical psychologist (Handelsman, Gottlieb, & Knapp, 2005).

To complicate matters, the ethical rules that govern the practice of law to which attorneys must adhere are not the same as the ethical rules that govern the practice of psychology. This clash in ethical obligations between psychologists and attorneys is nowhere more apparent than when a forensic psychologist performs the role of the expert witness at a trial. In the courtroom, lawyers must be their client's **advocate** and are expected to zealously represent their clients. The expert witness does not assume the role of advocate. Rather, the expert functions as the impartial, uninterested third party that has been asked to render an expert opinion to the court. Because of the ethical conflicts surrounding expert testimony, this chapter addresses the permissibility and role of expert testimony in the courtroom. Included in this discussion are the standards used to determine who can be certified as an expert and what type of expert testimony is permissible in court.

The chapter will end with a discussion on some of the cultural differences between psychology and law. For example, the legal system uses laws, a man-made concept, to reach consensus. Laws are enacted by the legislature and are a reflection of society's values (Woody, 1988). Courts use **case law** to help guide new decisions. Many readers have seen popular television shows where the lawyers present their legal arguments before a judge, each lawyer citing decisions from cases previously decided. Court decisions are based on precedent; the decision handed down in a prior case stands. The science of psychology, and science in general, reaches decisions using empirical evidence. Empirical evidence is evidence that can be observed, replicated, and verified by others. Therefore, in addition to differences in ethical codes and the professional culture, another source of conflict between the disciplines of law and psychology deals with how decisions are made. Law uses precedence to help guide new decisions whereas psychology relies on the scientific method and empiricism.

# Ethics, Morality, Competence, Professionalism, Character, and Law

The word **ethics** is derived from the Greek work *ethos* meaning "character" (Swenson, 1997, p. 57). Ethics is a specialty within philosophy that examines the conduct of humans and moral decision making. Ethics and morality involve judgments about good and bad or right and wrong. It is important to note that these judgments are based on the context of the culture or society. Moral beliefs are influenced by a multiple of factors, including upbringing, values, religious beliefs, and culture (Remley & Herlihy, 2005). Ethical relativists believe that judgments regarding right and wrong are culturally determined. If members of a group or culture believe that an action is morally right, then it is morally right to perform that behavior within the context of that culture. The opposing argument to **ethical relativism** is **ethical absolutism**. Ethical absolutism is the philosophical belief that there are some absolute universal standards of right and wrong that apply to all cultures, regardless of the cultural beliefs (Freeman, 2000).

Mental health professionals have formal written statements that define ethical behavior. Each profession has their own ethical principles and code of conduct that begin to define competence within that profession. The American Psychological Association has recently published the revised Ethical Principles of Psychologists and Code of Conduct (American Psychological Association, 2002). There is an important distinction between the Ethical Principles and Code of Conduct, also referred to as the **Ethical Standards**. The *Principles* are aspirational in nature, reflect the highest ethical ideals of the profession, and are not mandatory. The Ethical Standards are obligations and failure to follow the standards can result in sanctions. The American Counseling Association has published the ACA Code of Ethics and Standards of Practice (American Counseling Association, 1995). Similarly, the National Association of Social Workers publishes the Code of Ethics. Lawyers, psychiatrists, and other mental health professionals all can point to a formalized code of ethics established by their profession. In addition to a code of ethics, many professional associations have developed guidelines for members of the profession to follow. For example, the American Psychological Association has developed the *General Guidelines for Providers of Psychological Services* (1987) as well as the *Specialty Guidelines for Forensic Psychologists* (Committee on Ethical Guidelines for Forensic Psychologists, 1991). The APA has developed other guidelines, some of which are discussed later in the text, such as the *Guidelines for Psychological*

| **Table 2.1** | General Principles of the APA Ethics Code |
| --- | --- |

**Principle A: Beneficence and Nonmaleficence**

Psychologists strive to benefit those with whom they work and take care to do no harm.

**Principle B: Fidelity and Responsibility**

Psychologists establish relationships of trust with those with whom they work. They are aware of their professional and scientific responsibilities to society and to the specific communities in which they work.

**Principle C: Integrity**

Psychologists seek to promote accuracy, honesty, and truthfulness in the science, teaching, and practice of psychology.

**Principle D: Justice**

Psychologists recognize that fairness and justice entitle all persons to access to and benefit from the contributions of psychology and to equal quality in the processes, procedures, and services being conducted by psychologists.

**Principle E: Respect for People's Rights and Dignity**

Psychologists respect the dignity and worth of all people, and the rights of individuals to privacy, confidentiality, and self-determination.

| **Table 2.2** | American Psychological Association Ethical Standards |
| --- | --- |

1. Resolving Ethical Issues
   1.01 Misuse of Psychologists' Work
   1.02 Conflicts Between Ethics and Law, Regulations, or Other Governing Legal Authority
   1.03 Conflicts Between Ethics and Organizational Demands
   1.04 Informal Resolution of Ethical Violations
   1.05 Reporting Ethical Violations
   1.06 Cooperating With Ethics Committees
   1.07 Improper Complaints
   1.08 Unfair Discrimination Against Complainants and Respondents
2. Competence
   2.01 Boundaries of Competence
   2.02 Providing Services in Emergencies
   2.03 Maintaining Competence
   2.04 Bases for Scientific and Professional Judgments
   2.05 Delegation of Work to Others
   2.06 Personal Problems and Conflicts
3. Human Relations
   3.01 Unfair Discrimination
   3.02 Sexual Harassment
   3.03 Other Harassment
   3.04 Avoiding Harm

*Evaluations in Child Custody Matters* (APA Committee on Professional Practice and Standards, 1998) and other guidelines, which will not be covered in any depth, such as the *Guidelines for Psychological Practice with Older Adults* (2004).

These codified ethical standards among the professions as well as the guidelines allow a profession to define a standard of care. A standard of care reflects what professionals regard as the appropriate practice for the delivery of services. Membership in a professional organization requires adherence to the ethical standards of the organization. Standards are mandatory and failure to adhere to the standards can result in disciplinary action by the professional organization. Some state licensing laws require adherence to the professional's ethical standards and a violation may result in a complaint to the licensing board. However, it is important to realize that the ethical principles are not the law and may, at times, be in conflict with the law. Guidelines are not mandatory, but rather suggest or recommend professional behavior. In this regard, they are aspirational in nature (American Psychological Association, 2004). However, the courts have tended to use guidelines to define standard of care when questions of malpractice have been raised (Bednar, Bednar, Lambert, & Waite, 1991). With regard to the courts, any professional must follow their profession's code of ethics and standards even if they are not a dues-paying member of the professional organization. Furthermore, if the professional has an identity with more than one professional organization, such as forensic psychology and sex therapy, then the professional is expected to adhere to the code of ethics of the professional organizations representing each specialty area (Woody, 1988).

Swenson (1997) cites two purposes for the development of ethical rules by professional organizations. The primary purpose is to protect the public, the consumers of psychological services, and clients of the professionals. The secondary propose is to protect the profession from the possibility of questionable behavior by members of the profession and consequently, attacks from members of the public. A good example of a public attack on forensic psychology is the book titled *Whores of the Court: The Fraud of Psychiatric Testimony and the Rape of American Justice* (Hagen, 1997). Margaret Hagen, a psychologist with a degree in child development and a professor at Boston University, is critical of psychologists, psychiatrists, and social workers testifying as expert witnesses who "mislead" judges and juries. Hagen contends that the "witch doctors" and "psychoexperts" are motivated by financial gain or blind advocacy for a particular cause. Although she does address ethical concerns relevant to the practice of forensic psychology, the book tends to rely on provocation and generalizations. Public attacks of this kind can tarnish the reputation of the profession and invite regulation by outside agencies. Swenson (1997) suggests that the publication and enforcement of ethical guidelines within a profession helps to limit the amount of regulation by the government. If a profession can police itself, there is less need for an outside agency to do so.

The establishment of ethical codes and guidelines also serves to enhance the professional services provided to the public. For example, the *Specialty Guidelines for Forensic Psychologists* (SGFP; Committee on Ethical Guidelines for Forensic Psychologists, 1991) developed by Division 41 of the American Psychological Association and the American Psychology-Law Society and endorsed by the American Academy of Forensic Psychology, are intended to be used by psychologists who function in the legal arena. "The primary goal of the SGFP is to improve the quality of forensic psychological services by providing guidance to psychologists delivering services to courts, members of the bar, litigants, and persons housed in forensic, delinquency, or correctional facilities" (Otto & Heilbrun, 2002, p. 7). Although general in nature, the guidelines help professionals identify competent forensic practice. Similarly, the *Guidelines for Child Custody Evaluations in Divorce Proceedings* established by the American Psychological Association have as their goal to "promote proficiency in using psychological expertise in child custody evaluations" (1994, p. 677). A final example is the *Guidelines for Psychological Evaluations in Child Custody Matters* (Committee on Professional Practice and Standards, 1998). The stated goal of these guidelines is to "facilitate the continued systematic development of the professional and help to assure a high level of practice by psychologists" (p. 2).

It has recently been argued that a *competent* professional engaged in the applied practice of psychology possesses **foundational competencies, core competencies, and specialty competencies** (Kaslow, 2004). Specialty competencies are the skills distinctive to a particular specialty. Core competencies include engaging in a scientifically minded practice, competence in psychological assessment, intervention, consultation and interprofessional collaboration, supervision, and professional development. Foundational competencies consist of diversity and ethical practice. Nadine Kaslow (2004), when accepting the Award for Distinguished Contributions to Education and Training in Psychology, described ethical competency as follows:

> Competence in ethics involves the following overlapping components: knowledge of ethical/professional codes, standards and guidelines, statutes, rules, regulations, and case law; ability to recognize ethical and legal issues across the range of psychological activities; ability to recognize and reconcile conflicts among relevant codes and laws and to deal with convergence, divergence, and ambiguity; capacity to apply the aforementioned knowledge and skills in situations related to professional activities; skill in seeking out information and ability to know when to consult as well as how to offer consultation; skills in assertively and appropriately raising ethical and legal issues; ability to adopt or adapt one's own ethical decision-making model and apply it with personal integrity and contextual sensitivity; ability to build and participate in a collaborative, supportive peer network; and capacity to self-assess; and knowledge and awareness of self. (pp. 777–778)

This description of ethical competence clearly involves more than an understanding of the ethical standards and practice guidelines. Guidelines and ethical standards do not address all the ethical quandaries a professional may encounter (Swenson, 1997). Professionals need to develop an identity as an ethical psychologist. This assumes that psychology, as a profession, "represents a discrete culture with its own traditions, values, and methods of implementing its ethical principles" (Handelsman et al., 2005, p. 59). This ethical culture may in fact differ significantly from the value traditions of students entering the field, or professionals in other professions. These authors have proposed an acculturation model of ethical training, suggesting that students will develop the identity of an ethical psychologist through a process of adaptation just as an immigrant to a new country might adapt to the new culture.

Nevertheless, the question remains as to whether an individual can be taught to make moral and ethical decisions. Knowing the ethical culture does not ensure that an individual will make the ethical or morally correct choice. For example, the American Psychological Association (2002) ethics code and many state laws prohibit sexual relationships between therapist and client or teacher and student. However, in one survey, 28% of the psychologists who reported engaging in an unethical sexual relationship stated that they continued the relationship despite knowing that it violated ethical standards (Lamb & Catanzaro, 1998). Knowledge of the ethical guidelines is not sufficient to ensure that all professionals behave in an ethical manner. However,

■ **Core competencies**
Skills and knowledge that enable a professional to engage in a scientifically minded practice. Suggested core competencies in the practice of psychology include competence in psychological assessment, interventions, consultation and interprofessional collaboration, supervision, and professional development.

■ **Specialty competencies**
Skills distinctive to a particular specialty; for example, legal knowledge is a specialty competency for forensic psychologists. See Core competencies.

research does suggest that ethical codes are a deterrent to engaging in unethical behavior for the majority of professionals (Lamb, Catanzaro, & Moorman, 2004).

If ethical codes are insufficient to prevent all transgressions, other alternatives to increasing ethical conduct among professionals may be possible. One possibility is to use ethical behavior as a criterion for selection into doctoral training programs. Some professionals have recommended **character** and **fitness** criteria as necessary but not sufficient for competence in professional psychology (Johnson & Campbell, 2002). Johnson (2003) has suggested that *character* serves as a foundation for ethical decision making and can help guide professional activities. Moral character is demonstrated by moral excellence or uprightness in the way one lives. "Character represents the honesty and integrity with which a person deals with others" (Johnson & Campbell, 2004, p. 406). Fitness, in this use, is an indication of an individual's emotional stability. Essential *fitness* requirements are

1. healthy personality adjustment,
2. absence of a serious psychological illness, and
3. appropriate use of psychoactive substances, when the use of such substances is warranted.

Essential *character* requirements include

1. integrity,
2. prudence, and
3. caring (Johnson & Campbell, 2002).

Lack of sound psychological fitness or character, such as the presence of a severe mental disorder, threatens a psychologist's ability to function competently.

The law profession has required bar examiners to screen applicants on the basis on character and fitness (National Conference of Bar Examiners, 2000). State Bar examining boards usually have a committee to examine issues of character and fitness. Issues addressed by these committees can include mental illness, history of a mental illness, criminal conduct, drug or alcohol misuse, neglect of professional obligations, lack of civility, lack of respect for authority, failing to accept responsibility for conduct, plagiarism, and cheating in school (National Conference of Bar Examiners, 2000). Law school faculty are obligated to report character and fitness concerns to the appropriate Bar examining board (Oswald & Johnson, 1994). Character is defined as moral character comprised of honesty, discretion, a sense of honor, and fiduciary responsibility. An examining board can deny admission to the Bar for behavior that "would cause a reasonable man to have substantial doubts about an individual's honesty, fairness and respect for the rights of others . . ." (Jackson, 2003, p. 10). Although it has been recommended, there is currently no such screening process in the profession of psychology. This difference in the cultural ethic between the professions of law and psychology is discussed later in the text.

Finally, there is the matter of law. Forensic psychologists must be aware of the laws within the jurisdiction in which they function. **Jurisdiction** refers to the authority of a court to decide a particular legal question. The jurisdiction must be over both the subject matter, or type of case, and the person (Woody, 1988). The forensic psychologist is obligated to be aware of the ethical, legal, and professional jurisdictional obligations for any work he or she accepts (Weissman & DeBow, 2003). Failure to understand the complexities of interjurisdictional practice can result in disciplinary actions ranging from board sanctions to incarceration (Tucillo et al., 2002). This responsibility is particularly important for forensic psychologists who provide their expertise in states other than where they are licensed (Shuman,

**■ Jurisdiction**

Synonymous with the word "power" and is the authority to preside over a given case.

Cunningham, Connell, & Reid, 2003). There are two sources of law: statutory or **legislative law** and case law, also called **common law** or judge-made law. The legislature of a state is the source of **statutory law** and includes acts, statutes, and ordinances. Case law is derived from rulings made by trial judges and sets a precedent for future decisions. Statutory law prevails over case law (Woody, 1988).

## Relevant Legal Terms  Table 2.3

- **Jurisdiction:** the authority of a court to decide a particular legal question. The jurisdiction must be over both the subject matter, or type of case, and the person.
- **Statutory law:** written by the state legislature and includes acts, Statutes, and ordinances.
- **Case law:** derived from rulings made by judges in particular cases.

There are times when the ethical standards may conflict with the law. For example, the APA Ethics Code addresses the issue of multiple relationships. A **multiple relationship** occurs when a psychologist who is in a professional role or relationship with a client or student finds him- or herself in a second role or relationship with that individual (Lamb et al., 2004). Multiple relationships can occur when a psychologist has a professional role with a client and then enters into a second relationship in one or more of the following three forms:

1. sexual relationship,
2. nonsexual social or professional relationship, or
3. financial–business relationship.

For example, a psychologist should avoid employing a client who is a contractor to do work on her home. Similarly, a psychologist should avoid an invitation to a client's family reunion. Nonsexual social or professional relations with a client can be detrimental to the counseling relationship (Moleski & Kiselica, 2005).

It should be obvious that a sexual relationship between a therapist and a client would be harmful to the therapeutic process for a number of reasons (see Pope, 1990). The APA Ethics Code forbids sexual relationships between a psychologist and a client. However, with regard to sexual intimacies with former therapy clients the Ethics Code states, "Psychologists do not engage in sexual intimacies with former clients/patients for at least two years after cessation or termination of therapy" (2002, p. 15). The Ethics Code does state that such a relationship with a former client should only occur in the "most unusual circumstances" and the burden is on the psychologist to demonstrate that no exploitation occurred. State laws may prohibit any sexual contact with former clients regardless of the elapsed time since cessation of therapy. For example, sexual contact between a psychologist and client or ex-client is a second- to third-degree felony in the state of Florida (Pettrila & Otto, 1996). The relationship between the psychologist and the client is considered to

| Table 2.4 | Definition of a Multiple Relationship |
|-----------|----------------------------------------|

A multiple relationship occurs when a psychologist is in a professional role with a person and

1. at the same time is in another role with the same person,
2. at the same time is in a relationship with a person closely associated with or related to the person with whom the psychologist has the professional relationship, or
3. promises to enter into another relationship in the future with the person or a person closely associated with or related to the person. (American Psychological Association, 2002, p. 6)

continue in perpetuity with regard to sexual involvement. In this situation, the state law is more restrictive than the Ethics Code. The APA Ethics Committee Task Force felt that an in-perpetuity rule might not survive a challenge in state courts (Knapp & VandeCreek, 2003). On the other hand, the APA Ethics Code prohibits sexual relations between psychologists and their students. State law does not address this issue. The Ethics Code does state that when a conflict between the Code and law occurs, the psychologist may adhere to the requirements of the law. That would be true in the first example regarding state law and sexual relationships with former clients. When the Ethics Code establishes a higher standard than the standard of conduct required by law, psychologists are required to meet the higher ethical standard (American Psychological Association, 2002).

It is important to realize that the Ethics Code is not part of either criminal or civil law. The law prescribes the minimum standards of acceptable behavior; ethics represent the ideal standards expected by the profession (Remley & Herlihy, 2005). Adherence to the Ethics Code does not protect a psychologist from criminal prosecution or civil liability. Likewise, a violation of the Ethics Code does not automatically determine whether legal consequences occur. However, two states have recently introduced "good faith" **immunity laws** regarding civil liability when performing child custody evaluations during divorce proceedings. Child custody evaluations during divorce proceedings tend to be one of the more complicated forensic assessments a psychologist can be asked to do and account for numerous civil lawsuits and complaints to licensing boards against psychologists. In contested custody cases, there is frequently a great deal of hostility between the parents. The parent who is dissatisfied with the psychologist's custody evaluation may decide to seek satisfaction through the courts or a complaint to the licensing board. In fact, research indicates that only 1% of complaints to the licensing board regarding child custody evaluations resulted in disciplinary action against the clinician (Kirkland & Kirkland, 2001). Licensing boards are not lax in their duty to protect the public (Van Horne, 2004). Rather, the low percentage of complaints *resulting* in disciplinary action indicates the frivolous nature of these complaints. Because of the high number of complaints and lawsuits brought in child custody cases, Florida and West Virginia have enacted *"good faith" immunity laws*. The law states that a complaint to the licensing board charging bias, incompetence, or a similar allegation by a court-appointed psychologist can no longer be made anonymously. If a civil action is filed, the complainant must pay all legal fees for both parties if the judge rules the lawsuit is frivolous (Greer, 2004). These laws state that if a psychologist has followed the APA's *Guidelines for Child Custody Evaluations in Divorce Proceedings* then the psychologist or psychiatrist has performed the evaluation in "good faith." Prior to the enactment of the Florida law, nearly 80% of all complaints to the licensing board involved child custody evaluations (Greer, 2004). Although it was not the original intent of ethical codes or practice guidelines, in some situations, they may serve to legally protect clinicians. Furthermore, in a criminal or civil trial, a psychologist who can show that they were functioning within the bounds of the ethical code and guidelines for their profession will have an easier time demonstrating that they met the required standard of care.

# A Clash of Cultures: Ethics, Psychology, and the Legal Profession

Psychology, as both a profession and a scientific discipline, has been described as a discrete culture consisting of its own traditions, values, methods of knowing, and ethical principles (Handelsman et al., 2005). It takes years of training, mentoring, and supervision for a new psychologist to become acculturated to the ethical culture and develop a professional ethical identity. In the same manner, the profession of law is a discrete culture with traditions, values, methods of knowing, and ethical principles. This professional identity also takes years of training, mentoring, and acculturation. When psychologists function within the legal arena, there is likely to be a clash of cultures (Rowley & MacDonald, 2001). This conflict can occur in a variety of areas, such as ethical issues, values, or even how decisions are formed.

Attorneys have an ethical obligation to serve as an advocate for their client. The attorney's duty is to protect the best interests of their client. The attorney works as an advocate for their client in an **adversarial** system. Stakes can be high for both the attorney and the client. The attorney faces risk for professional liability and reputation, finances, and substantial fiduciary responsibility. The client may face significant financial risks, the possible loss of liberty and life, and loss of various rights, such as visitation or guardianship. Attorneys carry a significant burden as an advocate for their client and their actions need to be evaluated within their professional culture (Weissman & DeBow, 2003). Rules of professional conduct published by state Bar associations are modeled on the American Bar Association's Model Rules of Professional Conduct (2003) and typically state that the lawyer shall represent a client *zealously and diligently* within the bounds of the law. The role of an advocate requires the lawyer to seek advantages for their client. This model can differ sharply with the role of the unbiased, neutral expert witness.

An example of the clash between the two professional cultures relevant to forensic psychologists is the use of assessment instruments. Forensic psychologists will frequently use psychological assessment instruments to evaluate clients that engage in legal disputes, such as personal injury cases for emotional damages or head injury, child custody disputes, insanity plea, or competency to stand trial evaluations (Ackerman, 1999). Assessment and testing in forensic settings is often prone to distortion and/or malingering by the examinee (Rogers, 1988). There is strong incentive to distort test results, particularly when the outcomes of cases rely on psychological assessment results, as is the case with neuropsychological testing (Sherrod, Anderson, & Tyron, 1991).

With high stakes and the lawyer's duty to perform as an advocate for their client, it is understandable that a lawyer may seek to prepare their clients for psychological assessments. One survey found that 48% of attorneys believed that they should inform their clients about the nature of psychological tests that will be administered in an assessment and should inform the client about any scales used to detect **malingering** (Wetterm & Corrigan, 1995). Another survey found that 75% of lawyers report preparing their clients for assessment including suggesting how clients should respond to the tests (Victor & Abeles, 2004). To be sure, there is a wealth of information readily available both in libraries and on the Internet on psychological assessment and malingering (Pope, n.d.; Ruis, Drake, Glass, Marcotte, & van Gorp, 2002). Some of this information can be used by individuals hoping to distort test results on a psychological evaluation and possibly to avoid the detection of malingering.

Lawyers may also *coach* their clients on how to take psychological tests and on how to present themselves to examiners and in court (Gershman, 2002; Lees-Haley, 1997). **Coaching** is defined as "any attempt to alter the results of psychological or neuropsychological tests in such a way that distorts the true representation of the examinee's cognitive, emotional, or behavioral status or hinders an accurate assessment of such attributes" (Victor & Abeles, 2004). Numerous published materials and continuing education workshops exist for lawyers to gain the skills necessary to coach their clients successfully. Attorneys hiring a forensic psychologist as an expert may attempt to enlist the psychologist's assistance in preparing a client for assessment. Based on the above-mentioned surveys and practices, it appears that many attorneys feel that it is ethical to coach their clients. Attorneys may even feel that it is their ethical obligation to assist their clients in this way and failure to do so could be construed as malpractice (Youngjohn, 1995). Attorneys also suggest that their coaching of a client may be legally lied about in court and is protected under attorney–client privilege (Lees-Harley, 1997). Coaching does appear to make clients seem more impaired, though researchers suggest psychologists would be able to detect coached examinees (Victor & Abeles, 2004). Although some authors argue that the American Bar Association considers influencing a witness's testimony as unethical practice (Huss, 2009), an attorney may not feel that preparing a witness for a psychological examination is the same as influencing testimony. However, it is clearly unethical for a psychologist to coach a client on how to respond to items on a psychological test. This difference in approaches to coaching clients for psychological assessments provides a clear example of the intense clash between the ethical cultures of the two professions.

Ethical violations in forensic practice can happen for a variety of reasons, only one of which is the fact that psychologists are functioning in a profession with a different cultural ethic. Weissman and DeBow (2003) provide a comprehensive list of other impediments to the ethical practice of forensic psychology. Their list includes the following obstacles:

1. ignorance of specialized psycholegal knowledge;
2. advocacy for a client or advocacy for a particular agenda or position as opposed to remaining neutral and objective;
3. lack of specialized forensic training;
4. assuming that the attorney will provide the expert the necessary legal, ethical, and professional information;
5. assuming that different jurisdictions are similar in laws and how the laws are implemented;
6. not appreciating the different levels for the burden of proof between the disciplines and within the legal system;
7. economic concerns—psychologists are prohibited from working on a contingency-fee basis and may feel that their services will not be used if they do not perform as the hiring attorney requests;

8. entering into multiple relationships such as expert witness and consultant or expert witness and therapist;
9. failure to understand the unique issues associated with confidentiality and privilege communications in forensic work;
10. failure to appreciate the unique role assessment plays in forensic settings and using inappropriate tests;
11. inadequate documentation and failing to recognize the need for meticulous notes; and
12. failure to use all the appropriate sources of information expected in a forensic evaluation such as interviews with third parties (Weissman & DeBow, 2003).

Forensic psychologists working with lawyers as experts need to address in the form of a written contract potential conflicts of interest and ethical conflicts at the beginning of the business relationship. This approach will help to identify and avoid potential ethical problems before they arise. Psychologists should address

1. ethical and standard of care concerns;
2. role definitions, role boundaries, and scope of the assignment; and
3. professional fees (Weissman & DeBow, 2003).

**Figure 2.2**

A "Fact Witness" may testify about things they know or have perceived, or about opinions that do not need special expertise.
© 2009 Stephen Coburn.
Used under license from Shutterstock, Inc.

Communication between the two parties is critical to avoid misunderstandings. Ethical problems can be avoided through continuing education and obtaining consultation and supervision from colleagues who are experienced and perceived as possessing an ethical professional identity. When confronted with an ethical dilemma, psychologists are encouraged to consult with professionals within the professional organization and can call the APA Office of Ethics for guidance.

A recent contribution to the field of forensic psychology is a book that guides professionals through a decision-making process when confronted with ethical dilemmas (Bush, Connell, & Denny, 2006). These authors provide a decision-making model including systematic steps a forensic psychologist should use when resolving ethical dilemmas. The standard decision-making model includes the following steps:

- Identify the problem.
- Develop possible solutions to the problem.
- Consider the potential consequences of various solutions.
- Choose and implement a course of action.
- Assess the outcome and implement changes as needed.

To this standard decision-making model, the authors add an additional three steps for forensic psychologists. These three steps are to

1. consider the significance of the context and the setting,
2. identify and use ethical and legal resources,
3. consider personal belief and values.

These three additional steps are considered a major contribution to the current literature regarding ethical decision making in forensic work (Holcomb, 2006). Throughout the book, several chapters present scenarios with ethical dilemmas faced by forensic psychologists. Students are encouraged to use this decision-making model to answer these ethical problems.

# Expert Witness Testimony

Rules of evidence governed what is admissible as evidence in a trial. These rules of evidence pertain also to testimony from witnesses. Most courts only allow a witness to testify to what they know as facts, limiting testimony to things of which they have firsthand knowledge through their own perceptions. A **fact witness** is called to testify about things they know or have perceived (i.e., heard, saw, felt, etc.). They may not form opinions about events that would require special expertise in order to form the opinion. For example, fact witnesses cannot be asked to determine if an individual was intoxicated or suffering from an emotional disorder at the time. That is forming an opinion requiring expertise. A fact witness can testify to opinions that do not require special expertise (Greenberg, 1999). They can be asked if the person slurred their words, stumbled when walking, or smelled of alcohol. On the other hand, witnesses recognized by the court as "experts" due to their training, skills, or experience may testify about both facts and opinions that they formed. They may also offer conclusions based on their expertise (Ewing, 2003).

Both forensic psychologists and psychologists involved in the area of legal psychology testify in court as expert witnesses. An **expert witness** is any individual who has been qualified as an "expert" by the trial judge. The role of the expert witness is to assist the **trier of fact** (the judge or the jury) to understand a complicated subject and/or to provide an expert opinion. Ideally, an expert summarizes their work or research findings in a clear and impartial manner. Psychologists have testified as expert witnesses on a wide range of issues such as criminal responsibility, competency to stand trial, reliability of eyewitness testimony, and even the influence of psychological expert testimony on jury decisions. Frequently, a forensic psychologist will be asked to testify regarding their opinions and conclusions based on a psycho-

■ **Fact witness**
A person who testifies about things they know or have personally perceived.

■ **Expert witness**
Any individual who has been qualified as an "expert" by the trial judge due to specialized knowledge or skill. A fact witness is generally not allowed to offer an opinion, whereas an expert witness may.

---

**Table 2.5** Examples of Issues on which Psychologists Testify as Expert Witnesses

- Insanity defense
- Mitigating or aggravating circumstances in death penalty sentencing
- Competence to stand trial
- Competence to confess
- Competence to waive *Miranda* rights
- Competence to be executed
- Civil commitment
- Civil competence–guardianship and conservatorship
- Child custody
- Termination of parental rights
- Psychological damages in civil suits (mental and neuropsychological)
- Trademark litigation
- Eyewitness testimony
- Impact of pretrial publicity
- Assessing the risk to the community of releasing convicted sex offenders
- Social issues (i.e., pornography, same-sex parental adoption, etc.)

logical assessment they performed on a defendant or plaintiff. For example, a psychologist may be asked to assess the mental state of an individual at the time of the offense to determine if they meet the criteria for legally insane at the time of the crime. The psychologist may testify during the trial about what opinion they formed as to the defendant's mental state at the time of the offense. A psychologist involved in legal psychology may be asked to summarize to the court research results related to a psycholegal question such as the reliability of eyewitness testimony. In both instances, an expert witness can testify to not only facts and their own perceptions, but also may provide opinions and conclusions as part of their testimony (Ewing, 2003).

# Who Can Be Qualified as an Expert Witness?

As noted above, there are well-defined rules determining what is admissible as evidence in a trial. Many jurisdictions have established their own evidence rules, frequently modeled after the federal code called the *Federal Rules of Evidence*. The Advisory Committee to the U.S Congress enacted Federal Rule of Evidence 702 that governs who may be qualified as an expert witness. The committee set a low standard in stating who can be an expert allowing the decision to be left to the trial judge. The committee reports:

> The rule is broadly phrased. The fields of knowledge which may be drawn upon are not limited merely to the "scientific" or "technical" but extend to all "specialized" knowledge. Similarly, the expert is viewed, not in the narrow sense, but as a person qualified by "knowledge, skill, experience, training or education." Thus, within the scope of the rule are not only experts in the strictest sense of the word, e.g., physicians, physicists, and architects, but also the large group sometimes called "skilled" witnesses, such as bankers or landowners testifying to land values. (*Federal Rules of Evidence Handbook*, 2000–2001 Ed., 2000, p. 104)

Therefore, in the broad terms that the Rule was conceived, an expert could be qualified by education and training, but also by experience. The courts have been lenient in qualifying witnesses as experts in their field.

The initial purpose for allowing experts to come into the courtroom and offer "expert opinion" was to assist the trier of fact, the jury, to understand the issues of the case. The concern was that the evidence presented in court would be too complicated for a jury of ordinary laypersons to understand sufficiently to reach an informed verdict. Indeed, research suggests that more than 20% of cases heard in federal courts have a strong scientific or technological aspect (Slind-Flor, 1994). The original common law standard to allow expert testimony was whether the issues presented were something the average juror would not understand. This approach has given way in many jurisdictions to the "helpfulness" standard (Ewing, 2003). The "helpfulness" standard addresses whether the ordinary person would have sufficient understanding of the issues such that they would not need the assistance of an expert to reach a verdict. If the material is complex and the jury would benefit from being educated by an expert, the judge can grant permission for the expert to testify. If the expert's testimony is deemed to be common knowledge, than the judge can exclude the testimony as a "superfluous and a waste of time" (*Federal Rules of Evidence Handbook*, 2000–2001 Ed., 2000, p. 104).

# Admissibility of Expert Testimony

The courts have been generally lenient as to who is qualified as an expert witness. However, meeting the qualifications as an expert witness does not necessarily mean the expert's testimony will be admitted into evidence. Although a low standard has been established to be qualified as an expert, the admissibility of expert testimony must also meet certain standards. It is possible to be qualified by the court as an expert only to have the court prevent the expert's testimony from being admitted as evidence during the trial. Judges have a great deal of discretion and flexibility in deciding whether to admit expert testimony. In fact, it is very difficult to overturn on appeal a trial judge's decision to either admit or reject an expert's testimony unless it can be shown that the judge's ruling constituted a flagrant abuse of discretion (Ewing, 2003).

Due to the broad discretion judges exercise in deciding to admit or reject expert testimony, there tends to be inconsistencies regarding the admission of psychological evidence (Penrod, Fulero, & Cutler, 1995). For example, some trial judges have allowed testimony regarding the inaccuracy of eyewitness identification whereas other judges have rejected such testimony. Judges may exercise their discretion in their courts and may reject testimony on several grounds. Judges may decide the data presented does not meet the scientific standards required of expert testimony. Alternatively, the judge may be skeptical of psychological evidence in general (Kovera & McAuliff, 2000). Finally, the judge may reject the testimony if he or she decides that the testimony would confuse the jurors, initiate or contribute to a "battle of the experts," or that the testimony would have too great an impact on jurors' decisions. Judges can use case law for guidance in deciding to admit or reject expert testimony. Below is a discussion of case law regarding the admissibility of expert testimony.

## Case Law Regarding Admissibility of Expert Testimony

An important court ruling regarding expert testimony decided in 1962 paved the way for the development of the field of forensic psychology. At issue in the case was whether psychologists could offer expert testimony on the diagnosis of a mental illness. Clinical psychology was a very young profession in the late 1950s. Psychologists, trained with academic degrees, were primarily involved in research and assessment. It was the end of World War II and the immense need for clinical services that helped move clinical psychology into providing diagnostic and treatment services. Over half of the nearly 75,000 hospitalized veterans at the end of the war were hospitalized for psychiatric reasons. In 1946, the Veterans Administration hospitals set up training programs at major universities to turn out clinical psychologists whose duties would include therapy as well as diagnosis (Leahey, 1997).

In *Jenkins v. United States* (1962), three psychologists testified regarding the criminal responsibility of a defendant, stating that he had a mental illness at the time of the crime. The trial court told the jury to disregard the psychologists' testimony since they were not physicians. At the defendant's appeal of his conviction, the defense argued that the testimony of the psychologists should have been admitted as evidence. Both the American Psychiatric Association (against admitting the testimony) and the American Psychological Association (for admitting the testimony) submitted **amicus curiae brief**s to the court. An amicus brief is a letter to the court from a "friend of the court." Frequently, professional associations will submit a brief to the court on behalf of its membership. In an advocacy brief, the organization attempts to present information to the court to sway the court's opinion. In the Jenkins' case, the defense prevailed and the court ruled that the

■ *Amicus curiae* **brief**

Letter to the court from a "friend of the court," typically a person or organization that provides information to the court relevant to a case before the court.

training required for a PhD in clinical psychology did qualify an individual to testify regarding criminal responsibility and mental illness. This ruling had significant implications for the field of forensic psychology and undoubtedly opened the doors for psychologists to provide expert testimony on a wide range of issues (Ewing, 2003).

## *Frye v. United States* (1923)

The Frye test was originality decided in 1923 on a case involving the use of an early model of the polygraph test (*Frye v. United States*, 1923). With this ruling, the court established the **general acceptance rule** regarding the admissibility of scientific testimony. The court ruled that for scientific expert testimony to be admissible, it must be based on generally accepted scientific methods. This ruling established a general acceptance test for the admissibility of scientific testimony, known as the general acceptance rule. Broadly interpreted, the general acceptance rule states that an expert's testimony must be based on scientific techniques that have reached a general acceptance in the scientific field.

■ **General acceptance rule**
For scientific expert testimony to be admissible, it must be based on *generally accepted* scientific methods.

The Frye test governed the admissibility of evidence in federal courts for nearly 70 years, from 1923 to 1993. Some social scientists felt that the general acceptance rule was too restrictive. It is difficult to determine how many scientists must agree with data before it is deemed to meet the criteria of general acceptance. For example, does 51% of those polled indicate general acceptance, or would a consensus of 80% indicate general acceptance? In addition, social science is very tolerant of dissenting viewpoints, allowing researchers to "battle it out" in the pages of scholarly journals. However, these dissenting voices can give the impression of a lack of "general acceptance" on a scholarly issue (Kassin, Ellsworth, & Smith, 1989). Another concern with the general acceptance rule is whether general acceptance indicates scientific validity. Two examples serve to illustrate this concern. For decades, it was generally accepted that young children should always be placed with the mother in child custody decisions. This model is known as the *tender-years doctrine*. However, this assumption has been challenged and is no longer used to determine child custody decisions. The second example involves the "science" of phrenology. Phrenology was an accepted science in the late 1800s. Phrenology was the study of brain function by measuring bumps on a person's skull. There were professional associations, conferences, and even the *American Phrenological Journal* was first published in 1838. Even if a notion is generally accepted in the scientific community, it still may not be a valid science.

## Federal Rules of Evidence

Additional guidelines for the admissibility of scientific evidence were established in 1975 with the adoption of the *Federal Rules of Evidence* (see Table 2.6). However, the Frye test continued to be used in most jurisdictions until the Supreme Court rendered its decision in the *Daubert v. Merrell Dow Pharmaceuticals* (1993) case. The U.S. Supreme Court ruled that the Federal Rule of Evidence 702 superseded the Frye test when the Rule was adopted in 1975 (Ewing, 2003). In the Supreme Court's ruling, the justices clarified the requirements of the Federal Rules of Evidence. The Court ruled that the Federal Rules of Evidence requires the judge, when ruling on the admissibility of scientific testimony, to determine if the scientific evidence is relevant to the case at issue, reliable (scientifically valid), and likely to assist the trier of fact in coming to a decision. Federal Rule of Evidence 702 considers the importance of the *general acceptance rule* (the Frye test) but extends the guidelines by emphasizing relevance.

■ **Relevancy**
Expert testimony must be directly related to the issues of the case; one criterion used to determine admissibility of expert testimony.

■ **Legal sufficiency**
A criterion used in determining the admissibility of expert testimony. Legal sufficiency relates to whether the testimony is likely to assist the jury. Expert testimony on the fallibility of eyewitness identification has sometimes been refused on the premise that it is unlikely to assist the jury.

**Relevancy** refers to the requirement that the expert testimony is directly related to the issues of the case. If counsel who has called the expert witness fails to show the relationship between the expert testimony and the facts of the case, the expert evidence can be rejected by the judge. The judge can decide if the testimony is relevant to the facts at hand. **Legal sufficiency** is the term used to describe if the information is likely to assist the trier of fact, the jury (Bartol & Bartol, 2004). The judge must consider if the testimony will assist the jury to understand the information or whether it will it confuse or prejudice the jury. As stated by Ladd (1952) and frequently cited:

> There is no more certain test for determining when experts may be used than the common sense inquiry whether the untrained layman would be qualified to determine intelligently and to the best possible degree the particular issue without enlightenment from those having a specialized understanding of the subject involved in the dispute. (p. 418)

By specifying that the evidence must be reliable, the Rule states that the evidence must be based on scientific methods and procedures. Specifically, Federal Rule 702 states that the testimony must be based upon sufficient facts or data, the testimony is the product of reliable principles and methods, and the witness has applied the principles and methods reliably to the facts of the case (*Federal Rules of Evidence Handbook*, 2000).

---

**Table 2.6**    **Federal Rules of Evidence, Article VII Opinions and Expert testimony**

### Rule 701

Opinion Testimony by Lay Witnesses

If the witness is not testifying as an expert, the witness' testimony in the form of opinions or inferences is limited to those opinions or inferences which are (a) rationally based on the perception of the witness and (b) helpful to a clear understanding of the witness' testimony or the determination of a fact in issue, and (c) not based on scientific, technical, or other specialized knowledge within the scope of Rule 702.

As amended effective December 1, 2000.

### Rule 702

Testimony by Experts

If scientific, technical, or other specialized knowledge will assist the trier of fact to understand the evidence or to determine a fact in issue, a witness qualified as an expert by knowledge, skill, experience, training, or education, may testify thereto in the form of an opinion or otherwise, if (1) the testimony is based upon sufficient facts or data, (2) the testimony is the product of reliable principles and methods, and (3) the witness has applied the principles and methods reliably to the facts of the case.

As amended effective December 1, 2000.

### Rule 703

Bases of Opinion Testimony by Experts

The facts or data in the particular case upon which an expert bases an opinion or inference may be those perceived by or made known to the expert at or before the hearing. If of a type reasonably relied upon by experts in the particular field in forming opinions or inferences upon the subject, the facts or data need not be admissible in evidence. Facts or data that are otherwise inadmissible shall not be disclosed to the jury by the proponent of the opinion or inference unless the court determines that their probative value in assisting the jury to evaluate the expert's opinion substantially outweighs their prejudicial effect.

As amended effective December 1, 2000.

### Rule 704

Opinion on Ultimate Issue

(a) Except as provided in subdivision (b), testimony in the form of an opinion or inference otherwise admissible is not objectionable because it embraces an ultimate issue to be decided by the trier of fact.

(b) No expert witness testifying with respect to the mental state or condition of a defendant in a criminal case may state an opinion or inference as to whether the defendant did or did not have the mental state or condition constituting an element of the crime charged or of a defense thereto. Such ultimate issues are matters for the trier of fact alone. (As amended October 12, 1984.)

### Rule 705

Disclosure of Facts or Data Underlying Expert Opinion

The expert may testify in terms of opinion or inference and give reasons therefor without first testifying to the underlying facts or data, unless the court requires otherwise. The expert may in any event be required to disclose the underlying facts or data on cross-examination.

# *Daubert v. Merrell Dow Pharmaceuticals* (1993)

The Supreme Court used the *Daubert v. Merrell Dow Pharmaceuticals* (1993) decision to clarify the admissibility of scientific testimony under the Federal Rules of Evidence. Joyce Daubert had a son born with a physical deformity. During her pregnancy, Ms. Daubert used Bendectin, a drug marketed by Merrell Dow Pharmaceuticals to treat morning sickness. Although the drug had been approved by the Food and Drug Administration (FDA) for this use, the pharmaceutical company eventually removed the drug from the market in 1983 due to the cost of continued litigation and insurance arising from claims regarding the alleged teratogenic effects of the medication.

Clearly, the issues involved in determining if a drug causes birth defects is a complicated matter that may not be easily understood by the ordinary person. The drug was approved by the FDA and the manufacturer pointed to numerous epidemiological studies indicating no association between the drug and birth defects. Still, the plaintiffs had more than a handful of expert witnesses who cited other studies indicating that the drug was a teratogen, a drug that can cause birth defects. At issue was the scientific validity of the studies cited by the plaintiff's experts.

This case reflects some of the concerns courts have expressed regarding expert scientific testimony in civil liability trials (Wrightsman, 2001). The concerns focus on "junk science" in the courtroom that simply prolongs litigation, forcing companies to settle to avoid costly legal battles. The *Daubert* case gradually weaved its way through the judicial system and court of appeals to the U.S. Supreme Court. The argument centered on which standard to use in allowing expert testimony. The plaintiff had argued for a liberal standard, stating that the Frye test should be used and questioned the lower court's interpretation of the general acceptance rule. The U.S. Supreme Court handled down the "*Daubert* decision" in 1993 in a 7–2 vote (Wrightsman, 2001).

As mentioned earlier, the Supreme Court ruled that Federal Rule of Evidence 702 superseded the Frye test and was the standard to be used for determining admissibility of scientific evidence. The Court then offered criteria to use in determining if the evidence met the "reliability" requirement of the Federal Rule of Evidence 702. Recall that **reliability** refers to scientific validity. The Court stated that trial judges may, but are not required to, consider the following factors in deciding whether to admit expert testimony with a purported scientific basis

1. Whether the principles and methodology underlying the testimony have been or can be tested.
2. Whether they have been subjected to peer review and publication.
3. Whether the known or potential error rate is acceptable.
4. Whether the underlying principles have gained general acceptance in the scientific community.

None of the four conditions is either a necessary or a sufficient basis for allowing expert testimony. The judges stated that the trial judge had a great deal of flexibility in deciding whether to admit expert testimony (Ewing, 2003).

With the *Daubert* decision, trial judges are asked to perform a "gatekeeping" role with regard to admissibility of expert testimony. The dissenting judges in the *Daubert* Court decision expressed doubts that trial judges had the inclination or the expertise to make these sorts of scientific judgments. Judges would be required to evaluate the methods used in scientific research to reach scientific and technical decisions well beyond their realm of expertise. Indeed, research suggests that judges are poorly equipped to perform this "gatekeeping" role. In a national survey of 400 state court judges, results indicated a lack of scientific sophistication among the judges. Although 71% of the judges understood the scientific peer review process and 82% understood the concept of general acceptance, fewer than 5% understood the concept of known or potential error rate and only 6% understood the meaning of testability (Gatowski et al., 2001). Judges also appear to have a bias against psychological evidence. One study found that only 17% of judges out of 144 would admit psychological evidence in a sexual harassment case, suggesting a general bias against psychological research (Kovera & McAuliff, 2000).

In the aftermath of the *Daubert* ruling, there are now efforts to educate judges about scientific methodology so that they can perform the gatekeeping duty responsibly (Costanzo, 2004). The Federal Judicial Center, serving as the research arm of the federal courts, has established training programs for judges. Universities such as the Adjudication Center at Duke University and the National Judicial Center offer workshops for judges to learn how to evaluate scientific expert testimony. However, this program was subsequently cancelled, leaving an unfilled need for the judicial bench. There has also been the publication of a reference text for judges to use to help evaluate scientific testimony (Faigman, Kaye, Saks, & Sanders, 1997).

The U.S. Supreme Court has issued two additional rulings after the *Daubert* case addressing the limits of admissibility of expert testimony. Both cases are relevant for the expert testimony of psychologists. In the first case, Robert Joiner was suing General Electric and others for damages. Joiner claimed that his work of 18 years as an electrician exposed him to chemicals that contributed to his development of lung cancer. The trial judge ruled that the experts for the plaintiff failed to demonstrate the scientific link between his lung cancer and the chemicals to which he was exposed. Joiner appealed, and the trial judge's decision was overturned in appellate court. The case eventually made its way to the U.S. Supreme Court. The Supreme Court sided with the trial judge and ruled that the district court could exclude the plaintiff's experts (Bartol & Bartol, 2004). The *Joiner* decision established that a trial judge's decision to allow or reject expert testimony under Rule 702 may not be overturned on appeal unless the judge's ruling constituted a clear abuse of discretion—a very difficult standard to meet (Ewing, 2003).

The second Supreme Court decision extended the *Daubert* ruling to nonscientific expert witnesses who claimed a specialized knowledge (*Kumbo Tire Co. v. Carmichael*, 1999). This court ruling focused on an engineer's testimony regarding the role a defective tire played in an automobile accident. The engineer presented himself as a "tire-failure expert" and his testimony had been classified as technical. The questioned addressed by the court was whether the engineer's "technical," as opposed to "scientific," testimony met the Daubert test. The Supreme Court stated "*Daubert*'s general holding—setting forth the trial judge's general "gatekeeping" obligation—applies not only to testimony based on "scientific" knowledge, but also to testimony based on "technical" and "other specialized knowledge" (p. 142). Forensic psychologists frequently based their testimony on a combination of science and professional experience (Ewing, 2003). The Court indicated that the same level of rigor applies to all expert testimony, whether it is based on the scientific literature or professional experience. Federal judges should apply the same standards (methods have been tested, subject to peer review, analysis of error rates, general acceptance) to both technical and clinical experts. The application of scientific rigor to clinical experts is particularly relevant for forensic psychologists, who base much of their opinion on clinical experience. Research shows that judges and attorneys (Redding, Floyd, & Hawk, 2001) as well as the public (Boccaccini & Brodsky, 2002) find practitioners who see patients as more believable as expert witnesses than those who engage solely in academic activities, such as research and scholarly writing.

# Ultimate Issue and Penultimate Issue

Courts have traditionally allowed expert witnesses to testify regarding the **ultimate issue**. The ultimate issue is the final question that must be decided by the court (e.g., insane at the time of the crime, incompetent to stand trial). The ultimate issue is considered the duty of the trier of fact. Experts testifying on the ultimate issue were thought to be assuming the duty of the trier of fact. However, that reasoning no longer continues and most jurisdictions allow the expert to address the ultimate issue. However, Federal Rule of Evidence 704 explicitly prohibits experts from addressing the ultimate issue in insanity cases. This amendment to the Federal Rules of Evidence was adopted by Congress with the Insanity Defense Reform Act of 1984 following the assassination attempt of President Ronald Reagan and subsequent acquittal "by reason of insanity" of John Hinckley, Jr. This prohibition of addressing

■ **Ultimate issue**
The final question that must be decided by the court; usually left to the trier of fact to decide (i.e., guilt or innocence).

the ultimate issue in a criminal responsibility trial only applies in federal courts. Many state and local courts allow and even request that the mental health professional give an opinion on the ultimate issue.

Whether forensic psychologists should testify on the ultimate issue is not without debate in the profession. Some writers caution against giving testimony on the ultimate issue (Melton, Petrila, Poythress, & Slobogin, 1997; Sales & Shuman, 1993), and some authors have even suggested that it is unethical to do so (Koocher & Keith-Spiegel, 1998). Arguments include the contention that preventing expert witnesses from addressing the ultimate issue will not help avoid the "battle of the experts" since the battle can rage over penultimate opinions. Another argument suggests that preventing ultimate issue testimony deprives the judge and jury of valuable information (Lipsitt, 2007). The APA does not take a position one way or another on whether psychologists should provide ultimate issue testimony. Rather, it recommends that psychologists who testify should be aware of both sides of the debate regarding ultimate issue testimony and are able to separate opinion from fact in their testimony.

Arguments have been made for and against psychologists expressing an opinion on the ultimate issue. Smith (1991) has argued against ultimate issue testimony, suggesting that it is common for experts to make errors in ultimate issue testimony. Smith's arguments address the topic of this chapter and are not errors as much as ethical violations. First, he argues that psychologists may not understand the legal issues involved in a case, such as the criteria for criminal responsibility or competency. However, the Ethics Code and the *Specialty Guidelines for Forensic Psychologists* state that psychologists are responsible "for a fundamental and reasonable level of knowledge and understanding of the legal and professional standards that govern their participation as experts in legal proceedings" (1991, p. 658). The Guidelines further require that "Forensic psychologists provide services only in areas of psychology in which they have specialized knowledge, skill, experience, and education" (1991, p. 658).

Smith (1991) also raises the possibility that forensic psychologists may apply their own value judgments to their decision-making process as opposed to maintaining objectivity based on the scientific literature. Personal values can interfere with a competent, objective opinion from a forensic psychologist. For example, a forensic psychologist who is adamantly against the death penalty may have a difficult time providing an objective testimony regarding aggravating and mitigating circumstances during the sentencing phase of a capital trial. Again, the *Specialty Guidelines* are clear on the ethical course of action. "Forensic psychologists recognize that their own personal values, moral beliefs, or personal and professional relationships with parties to a legal proceeding may interfere with their ability to practice competently. Under such circumstances, forensic psychologists are obligated to decline participation or to limit their assistance in a manner consistent with professional obligations" (1991, p. 658).

Smith's third objection is that forensic psychologists may simply function as a "**hired gun**," espousing the viewpoint of the side that is paying for their services. This is clearly not a source of error but rather an ethical violation. Again, the *Specialty Guidelines* are clear:

> When testifying, forensic psychologists have an obligation to all parties to a legal proceeding to present their findings, conclusions, evidence, or other professional products in a fair manner. This principle does not preclude forceful representation of the data and reasoning upon which a conclusion of professional product is based. It does, however, preclude an attempt, whether active or passive, to engage in

partisan distortion or misrepresentation. Forensic psychologists do not, by either commission or omission, participate in a misrepresentation of their evidence, nor do they participate in partisan attempts to avoid, deny, or subvert the presentation of evidence contrary to their own position. (1991, p. 664)

Smith's (1991) arguments against ultimate issue are sound if we assume forensic psychologists will behave unethically. However, these sources of error in ultimate testimony are not errors, but rather ethical breaches. Although ethical violations occur, practice guidelines should not be based on the assumption that they will occur.

Saks (1990) has argued against ultimate issue testimony, stating that the expert's opinion unduly influences the jury. However, research suggests that juries are not overwhelmed by an expert's opinion (Nietzel, McCarthy, & Kern, 1999). The one situation where the expert's opinion on the ultimate issue tends to carry significant weight in the trier of fact's decision is at a pretrial hearing to determine competency to stand trial (Melton et al., 1997). Judges frequently, though not always, will abide by the expert's opinion regarding whether a defendant is competent to stand trial. This makes sense since the forensic psychologist has spent a significant amount of time with the defendant and conducted a thorough competency to stand trial evaluation. The judge has neither the time nor the expertise to duplicate the forensic psychologist's work and relies on the expert for an opinion on the ultimate issue. An argument for ultimate issue testimony is that judges and prosecutors frequently request the opinion of the expert as to the ultimate issue (Redding et al., 2001). An opposing attorney should be able to mitigate any undue influence an expert's testimony may have on the jury with a thorough cross-examination (Rogers & Ewing, 1989).

## Pros and Cons Regarding Expert Testimony on the Ultimate Issue — Table 2.7

- Arguments against ultimate issue testimony
  1. Concerns about the accuracy of the opinion based on three common sources of errors (Smith, 1991):
     (a) expert may not understand legal criteria for decision
     (b) may apply value judgments
     (c) may simply want a particular end result for their client
  2. Expert's opinion on ultimate issue may have too much influence on the trier of fact (Saks, 1990).
- Arguments for ultimate issue testimony
  1. Judges and prosecutors depend on it and frequently request the expert to voice an opinion on the ultimate issue (Redding et al., 2001).
  2. The possible undue influence of expert testimony on the ultimate issue can be mitigated through cross-examination (Rogers & Ewing, 1989).

■ **Penultimate issue**
Elements that define the
ultimate issue and do not
appear to unduly influence
the jury.

Others have suggested that the forensic psychologist could testify on the penultimate issues (Fulero & Finkel, 1991). The **penultimate issues** are the elements that define the ultimate issue and do not appear to unduly influence the jury. For example, rather than testifying that the defendant was criminally insane at the time of the crime, the forensic psychologist could state that the defendant was delusional at the time of the crime and believed that the victim was an alien trying to kill him. The psychologist could further elaborate that the defendant, in his delusional state, most likely did not appreciate that shooting the victim was wrong. The expert could also state that due to the defendant's hallucinations, he probably did not have complete control over his behavior and most likely would have committed the act had a police officer been standing next to him. This testimony would address the penultimate issues regarding criminal responsibility. The psychologist could refrain from testifying if the defendant was insane at the time of the offense, stating that the ultimate decision is the duty of the jury. However, many attorneys and judges may not be satisfied with such a response. Furthermore, the jury may interpret the expert's failure to offer an opinion as uncertainty, thus undermining the expert's testimony.

# The Three Possible Roles for an Expert Witness

Saks (1990) has suggested that there are three roles the psychologist can assume as an expert witness in relating their expertise to the case at hand. These three roles represent a continuum ranging from testifying as an objective, neutral expert to presenting a partisan, biased case.

The role of **conduit-educator** presents an objective, neutral view of the current state of psychological knowledge. An accurate representation of the field of psychology is the first priority for the conduit-educator. Saks (1991) suggests that this position places the expert witness in a dilemma when the testimony may go against the expert's own values: "The central difficulty of this role is whether it is all right for me to contribute hard-won knowledge to causes I would just as soon see lose."

The second role is that of **philosopher-advocate**. In this assumed role, the expert witness recognizes the adversarial nature of the courtroom and decides to "play by those rules." The witness advocates for a position or outcome regardless of the data at hand. The philosopher-advocate allows their own values to shape their testimony, believing there is a greater good at stake. They feel justified in shaping their testimony to reflect the "greater good." This shaping of the testimony may involve a "careful editing, selecting, shading, exaggerating, or glossing over" of contrary evidence during testimony (Saks, 1990, p. 296).

The third role, which has been written about elsewhere in the literature (e.g., Cooper & Neuhaus, 2000; Jensen, 1993) is that of the *hired gun*. The hired gun essentially advances their employer's agenda, regardless of the data at hand. Though similar to the philosopher-advocate concerning biasing their testimony, the hired gun is not pursuing what they believe to be a greater good, but rather what they believe their employer (the contracting attorney) wants them to say.

It should be obvious to the reader that these three roles fall on a continuum of ethical behavior for forensic psychologists. The APA Ethics Code as well as the *Specialty Guidelines for Forensic Psychologists* seek to ensure impartial testimony in the courtroom. The ethical obligations of lawyers demand a diligent advocacy for their clients. Lawyers retaining forensic psychologists as expert witnesses may expect a partisan loyalty from their expert. Experts often feel trapped, forced to choose between ethical, impartial testimony and partisan advocacy. Experts who do not con-

## Roles the Forensic Psychologist May Assume as an Expert Witness    Table 2.8

1. Conduit-educator: the impartial representation of the field of psychology is the first priority.
2. Philosopher-advocate: adopts a legal-adversary approach, volunteering only research that supports their side and omitting flaws, etc.
3. Hired gun: motivation is to help the lawyer who hired them; serves their employer's values.

form to the adversarial needs of the retaining lawyer fear the loss of future income and risk gaining a reputation in the legal community of being uncooperative (Shuman & Greenberg, 2003). However, experts who misrepresent the facts, for whatever reason, may face ethical and legal sanctions.

**Impartiality as the best advocacy** has been proposed as a way to strike a balance between the adversarial needs of the trial and the ethical obligations of the forensic psychologist (Shuman & Greenberg, 2003). These authors recommend the application of five principles: competence, relevance, perspective, balance, and candor. "Experts should first identify each legal question on which their opinion is being sought and then determine if and how their competence permits them to offer an expert opinion to assist in the resolution of these legal questions" (Shuman & Greenberg, 2003, p. 221). By relevance, the authors suggest that the expert can work with the retaining attorney to disclose only information that is relevant to the expert's proffered opinion, and selectively shield information that is not relevant to the issues questioned. "To integrate neutrality and advocacy effectively, experts have an obligation to test their opinions on the issues they have been asked to address from the perspective of the parties' competing versions of the case, without insulation from opposing views" (p. 222). Experts must then weigh each perspective fairly. Acting in a balanced manner toward each perspective enhances credibility with the fact finder. Finally, " . . . having identified the issues they have been asked to address and having considered them fairly from the perspective of all parties, experts have an obligation to present all perspectives considered candidly and explain the weights assigned to each in presenting their findings" (p. 223).

The argument presented above for impartiality as the best advocacy assumes that an expert's credibility is crucial if the expert is to serve as an advocate, and that credibility derives from the expert's impartiality (Shuman & Greenberg, 2003). The believability of the expert witness depends largely on how they are perceived by the members of the jury. Experts typically assume that the content and delivery of their testimony determines their credibility (Brodsky, 1999). However, a number of other factors can also affect how members of the jury perceive the expert. For example, highly paid experts are often perceived as being "bought" and are associated with the role of the hired gun discussed above (Cooper & Neuhaus, 2000). It is common practice to attempt to discredit an expert witness by questioning their fee during cross-examination (Ewing, 2003). Courts have allowed opposing counsel to question the expert regarding their fee during cross-examination. In survey research, respondents indicated that they would most likely believe an expert who received no fee for their testimony (Boccaccini & Brodsky, 2002). Other results from the survey indicated that jurors find local experts more believable than experts from out of state. In addition, experts who had never testified before or testified for both the prosecution and the defense in the past are viewed as more credible than a "professional" expert witness or one who routinely testifies for just one side. Respondents also indicated a preference for experts who see patients as opposed to experts who are engaged in academic activities. It seems that many of the characteristics of the less credible expert are associated with the professional expert witness or hired gun. These characteristics conjure up the image of the out-of-state, highly paid academic who has written extensively on a topic and is brought in to pontificate to the jury. Attorneys would do better to hire local practitioners who do not make it a habit of testifying as an expert witness.

The Ethics Code and *Specialty Guidelines* conform closest to Sak's (1990) conduit-educator role. Psychologists' primary loyalty must be to their discipline (Costanzo, 2004). Certainly, there have been times when unscrupulous experts have assumed the role of the hired gun in court. In the past, experts enjoyed **witness immunity**, and could not be held criminally or civilly liable for their actions or testimony. It is rare for an expert to be prosecuted for misconduct. Since an expert is offering an opinion, it is virtually impossible to charge an expert witness with perjury, even when the testimony is clearly a biased opinion. However, several recent cases have started to place limits on the doctrine of absolute immunity for expert witnesses (Ewing, 2003). Psychologists have been subjected to disciplinary action from their licensing boards due to misconduct while functioning as an expert witness. Courts have refused to allow witness immunity to protect the psychologists from a state licensing board's disciplinary action. Other courts have allowed plaintiffs to file civil lawsuits against their own experts when the plaintiffs felt that the expert's performance was negligent. Alternatively, other courts have dismissed such suits, stressing that witness immunity helps to ensure the expert's objectivity and willingness to assist the court.

**■ Witness immunity**
When an expert witness is exempt from criminal or civil liability for actions or testimony as an expert witness.

# Possible Pitfalls for the Expert Witness

Wrightsman (2001) has presented five possible temptations for the psychologist as expert witness:

1. promising too much,
2. substituting advocacy for scientific objectivity,
3. letting values overcome empirically based findings,
4. doing a cursory job, and
5. maintaining dual relationships and competing roles.

These pitfalls are discussed here since each is actually addressed by the ethical guidelines.

Psychologists, who rely on earning a living, may be tempted to make claims of their success that is inconsistent with reality. Likewise, developers of psychological assessment instruments may promote their instruments as more reliable and valid than the data shows. The temptation to surrender objectivity to the adversarial nature of the trial has been discussed above. Psychologists need to remain objective and adopt the model of impartiality as the best advocacy. Many questions that the forensic psychologist is asked to address are, by their nature, value-laden issues. Most people will have an opinion on the topics, based to some extent, on their own value system. Examples of these emotionally charged topics include the death penalty, childrearing practices, sexual orientation of parents, child sexual abuse, and sexual assault. Psychologists need to remain objective and resist the temptation to allow their own value systems to influence their testimony. A thorough forensic evaluation requires a great deal of time and work. One study found that the average child custody evaluation took over 26 hours (Ackerman & Ackerman, 1997). However, with busy schedules and tight deadlines, there is always the temptation to perform a cursory job, particularly if the fee is less than adequate. Some states reimburse psychologists at relatively low rates for their forensic work. For example, a county in Florida pays $300 for a *termination of parental rights evaluation*. At such a low rate, psychologists may be tempted to do a cursory job, justifying the work based on the fee. It is better to turn down such work and only ethical to be thorough and professional in one's work. The last temptation is maintaining dual or multiple relationships. Dual relationships account for one of the top two reasons for disciplinary action against psychologists (Schoenfeld, Hatch, & Gonzalez, 2001). A common example is the treating therapist who is asked to perform forensic work, as with a child therapist who becomes involved in a child custody battle (Greenberg & Gould, 2001). However, frequently the multiple-role demands extend beyond the conflict of providing therapeutic and forensic services (Shuman & Greenberg, 2003).

In all of the discussed temptations, psychologists need to evaluate carefully all forensic referrals. Hess (1998) provides a list of 15 questions the forensic psychologist can answer prior to accepting a case as a strategy for avoiding the ethical temptations discussed above as well as other ethical and professional complications. Downing Hansen and Goldberg (1999) have proposed a seven-category matrix to use when evaluating ethical and legal dilemmas. Their matrix includes examining the following considerations:

1. moral principles and personal values,
2. clinical and cultural considerations,
3. professional ethics code(s),
4. agency or employer policies,
5. statutes,
6. professional rules and regulations governing the practice of psychology, and
7. case law.

Through careful consideration and consultation, ethical breaches are avoidable. However, as professionals, when a colleague does appear to behave unethically,

## Possible Ethical Pitfalls for the Expert Witness    Table 2.9

1. Promising too much
2. Substituting advocacy for scientific objectivity
3. Letting values overcome empirically based findings
4. Doing a cursory job
5. Maintaining dual relationships and competing roles

whether through lack of knowledge, poor performance of professional duties, or ethical violations, it is incumbent upon psychologists to confront their colleague prior to making a professional complaint. Brodsky and McKinsey (2002) provide sample letters to assist in the ethical confrontation of an unethical forensic colleague.

# Surviving the Witness Stand

Much has been written about the stress of cross-examination on the witness stand (Shapiro, 1984). Although a hostile cross-examination can be stressful, there are strategies the forensic psychologist can use to prepare for the worst. Understanding the procedure and knowing what to expect helps the expert witness to prepare and deliver their testimony in a credible and professional manner.

An expert witness will want to present their qualifications to the court at the beginning of their testimony. As was noted above, the judge has the authority to qualify experts based on their education, training, experience, or skill. Courts have generally used wide discretion when qualifying an individual as an expert witness. Frequently the judge and the opposing counsel accept the witness's qualifications, precluding the legal need to qualify the witness on the stand. Even though the legal need may not be present, it is still recommended that the expert witness publicly recite their qualifications. The jury will be judging both the expert's testimony along with the expert's credibility. This is done in a forthright and confident manner without appearing to boast. The forensic psychologist can provide the retaining attorney questions to ask the psychologist on the witness stand to allow the jury to hear the expert's qualifications. Experts should neither be modest nor exaggerate their credentials. Though some of the questions are routinely used, others might be formulated to address issues of the case at hand. See Table 2.10 for a series of sample questions used to qualify an expert witness (Ewing, 2003; Greenberg, 1999).

All jurisdictions follow the *order of examination* (Ewing, 2003). The attorney who calls them to testify first questions the witnesses. They are then subject to cross-examination by the opposing counsel. Cross-examination is limited to issues raised on direct examination and matters affecting the credibility of the witness. Judges can use their discretion to allow a broad range of issues to be addressed on cross-examination. After cross-examination, there may be questions again by the retaining attorney, called redirect examination. Questions during the redirect examination are again limited to the scope of questions raised during the cross-examination. This process can continue until each side has completed their questioning. The expert witness may or may not be present when other experts testify. An attorney will ask a judge for a "rule on witnesses," meaning that others testifying on the same matter must be excluded from the courtroom when testimony is given. Attorneys who want the other expert witness out of the courtroom suggest that allowing an expert to hear the testimony of the other experts gives an unfair advantage. The expert who heard the prior testimony may use his or her own testimony as a chance to subtly rebut the previous opinion (Shapiro, 1984).

It is important for the expert witness to remember that the trial is an adversarial process and the opposing counsel will attempt to discredit the expert witness. Some lawyers feel that they must attack the expert witness to discredit his or her testimony. Some cases are decided by the expert's opinion and the only chance an attorney has is to discredit that opinion. For example, an affirmative defense such as the insanity plea rests on whether the jury finds the defendant insane at the time of the crime. This decision is based almost entirely on the expert's opinion. An expert witness must remember not to take the attacks personally and to remained poised during testimony. An attorney will attempt to discredit both the testimony and the expert's credibility.

## Sample Qualifying Questions for a Forensic Psychologist

Table 2.10

Please state your full name for the record.
What is your profession?
What positions have you previously held?
When were you first licensed? Where are you licensed?
Do you specialize in any area in psychology?
Please describe what forensic psychology is.
What is your educational background?
Do you have any advanced training in forensic psychology?
Are you a member or fellow of any professional organizations?
Are you board certified?
Please describe the board certification process.
Have you published any books or journal articles?
Do you present at professional meetings?
Have you received any awards or honors for your professional work in psychology?
Approximately how much time do you spend in seeing patients, conducting research, and teaching?
Have you qualified as an expert witness before? In what courts? On what subject matter?
Approximately how many forensic evaluations have you conducted?
Approximately how many times have you testified as an expert witness in the past?
Do you testify more for the defense or the plaintiff/prosecution?
What did you understand your task to be in this matter before the court?

There are several strategies an attorney can use to discredit the witness during cross-examination. The attorney may decide to attack the expert's opinion. However, if they are too harsh on the opinion they may undercut their own expert's opinion. For example, in a criminal responsibility trial, if the attorney dismisses the scientific value of forensic assessment, then his or her own expert will have a difficult case if his or her opinion is based on forensic assessment. If the opinion is solid and cannot be attacked, then the attorney will attempt to discredit the expert's credibility. The attorney may attack the expert based on their credentials, or lack of credentials. This can be a particular problem for experts who exaggerate their accomplishments or who apply for board certification through so-called "vanity boards" (Ewing, 2003). The attorney may also attempt to discredit the expert by asking the expert to inform the jury of the fee they are receiving for their opinion. Jurors tend to view experts who receive high fees as less credible than experts who are providing services pro bono, meaning for no fee. Exorbitant fees may give the impression that the expert's opinion was "bought." However, most jurors realize that experts also need to earn a living and reasonable compensation for one's time is to be expected. The attorney may try to impeach the expert during cross-examination. This is accomplished by using inconsistent statements the expert may have made in a previous case. Since prior testimony is public record, a diligent opposing counsel may uncover contradictory statements from previous testimony provided by the expert in a different case. Another form of impeachment is the **learned treatise method** (Ewing, 2003). An attorney may confront the expert with other authoritative works that contradict or challenge the expert's opinion. Ziskin (1995) has prepared a series of texts to assist lawyers in challenging psychological testimony.

Finally, if all else fails, the attorney may try to attack the expert personally. This is an attempt to rattle the expert and place him or her on the defensive (Shapiro, 1984). I recall testifying in a criminal responsibility case. I had been retained by the county to conduct a criminal responsibility evaluation. This is an enviable position since I am working for neither the prosecution nor the defense. The results indicated that the defendant met the criteria for sanity at the time of the offense. The opposing counsel enlisted a psychiatrist who stated that the defendant was insane at the time of the crime. Near the end of the cross-examination, the attorney asked in a rather pejorative manner, "You are not a real doctor, are you?" I simply asked him to supply a definition of a real doctor and then I could tell him if I met that definition since I was not sure what a "real doctor" was. Shapiro (1984) suggests that once the attacks are personal, the expert should feel confident in that their testimony and credibility were solid enough to force the attorney to resort to personal abuse. Several excellent texts are available for the mental health professional to use as preparation for direct testimony and cross-examination (e.g., Bernstein & Hartsell, 2005; Melton et al., 2007).

# A Clash of Cultures: Knowledge, Psychology, and the Legal Profession

In addition to stark ethical differences between the two professions, there is also a difference in how decisions are formed. Psychology is the scientific study of human behavior rooted in empiricism. Empiricism is the belief that knowledge comes from observation and experience. Psychologists believe that there is an absolute truth that can be discovered through the application of the scientific method. Psychologists attempt to advance their understanding of human behavior through the systematic testing of hypotheses and accumulation of empirical data. It is common for a lively debate to exist in journal articles related to scholarly topics on which professionals disagree. Although at times, even these debates may go well beyond scholarly objectivity (e.g., Karon & Widener, 1998; Pendergrass, 1999).

Whereas psychology is based on empiricism, law is based on authority (Goldberg, 1994). Unlike psychology, law advances through the accumulation of decisions made by judges in the courts. Laws are either handed down by the legislature (statutes) or decided by trial judges (case law). Part of the method of law is deference for past rulings (Costanzo, 2004). The legal system relies heavily on precedent. Legal arguments are typically based on past rulings. Judges follow the doctrine of *stare decisis*, meaning *let the decision stand*.

■ *Stare decisis*

Latin meaning *let the decision stand*; used in case law as the standard that states that legal rules decided in cases govern subsequent cases; contributes to the consistency of laws.

These two different approaches to solving disputes can lead to different outcomes. For example, competency to stand trial is a legal term based on the *Dusky* standard (*Dusky v. United States*, 1960). In a more recent ruling, the U. S. Supreme Court applied the *Dusky* standard to all forms of competency, such as competency to plead guilty or competency to confess (*Godinez v. Moran*, 1993). Psychologists argue that different legal issues require differing levels of competence (Powers-Stafford, 2003). Psychologists would argue that competence to stand trial involves different abilities than competence to plead guilty. The psychologists will point to a variety of research studies demonstrating the relevance of different cognitive skills for the two types of competence. However, the law rests its opinion on precedent.

This leads to another important difference between the two professions. Psychology, as a science, seeks the objective truth. Law does not seek the truth as much as the resolution to a conflict. Law strives to achieve justice (Costanzo, 2004). As an example, nearly 90% of all criminal cases result in plea bargains. The role of plea-bargaining in the criminal justice system is crucial to allowing the system to run smoothly. Plea bargains do not seek the truth; rather, they seek to resolve a conflict. Even if a case goes to trial, there are numerous rules regarding what evidence can be admitted. Evidence that clearly indicates guilt may be deemed inadmissible by a trial judge if obtained improperly. On the other hand, one cannot imagine that a scientist would ignore data because it was "obtained" improperly. "Justice for all parties replaces truth as the predominant goal" (Wrightsman, Greene, Nietzel, & Fortune, 2002, p. 21).

# TEST YOUR KNOWLEDGE

1. "Well-recognized standards regarding the principles or evidence for a particular field should determine the admissibility of expert testimony" describe which of the following?
   a. The Warren Standard
   b. The Federal Rules of Evidence
   c. The Frye Test
   d. The Daubert Rule
   e. The Kumbo Tire Ruling

2. The Court ruled that expert testimony should have three critical elements. They are
   a. reliability, validity, and norms
   b. relevancy, legal sufficiency, and reliability
   c. clear and convincing, preponderance, and beyond a reasonable doubt
   d. falsifiability, *a priori*, and tenacity

3. The "general acceptance" rule regarding admissibility of evidence is also called
   a. the Dusky Standard
   b. the Federal Rules of Evidence
   c. The Frye Test
   d. the Daubert Decision

4. The Federal Rules of Evidence determines who can be an expert witness. This standard is
   a. fairly stringent, allowing very few "experts" to testify
   b. fairly lenient, allowing the decision up to the discretion of the trial judge
   c. absent of regulations regarding who can serve as an expert witness
   d. requires a *general acceptance* rule for an expert witness

5. Which Supreme Court decision was related to admissibility of evidence of an early version of the polygraph?
   a. *Kumbo Tire Co. v. Carmichael* (1999)
   b. *Daubert v. Merrell Dow Pharmaceuticals* (1993)
   c. *General Electric Co. v. Joiner* (1997)
   d. *Frye v. United States* (1923)

Answer Key: (1) d, (2) b, (3) c, (4) b, (5) d

# Chapter Three

# Psychological Assessment

## Learning Objectives

- What is the distinction between psychological assessment and psychological testing?
- Be able to list and define differences between clinical assessment and forensic assessment.
- What are the four components of a clinical interview?
- What is rapport?
- What was the Supreme Court ruling in the *Kansas v. Hendricks* (1997) case?
- Describe the different types of reliability and different types of validity used in psychological testing.
- How do reliability and validity relate to one another?
- What is a correlation and how are the strength and direction of a correlation expressed?
- What is the standard error of measurement?
- What does *mens rea* mean and why is this concept important?
- What is the Dusky standard?
- What are the differences between competency to stand trial and competency to confess?
- What is an affirmative defense? Cite a few examples.
- What are aggravating and mitigating circumstances in capital case sentencing procedures?
- What is the method–function match in psychological assessment?
- Describe some of the differences between civil law and criminal law.
- List a few examples of assessment in civil law and assessment in criminal law.
- What are the three categories of assessment instruments with regard to forensic work presented in the text? Give an example of a test from each of the three categories.
- What is the distinction between projective and objective techniques? Give an example of each.
- List and describe the seven criteria presented in the text as a way to evaluate the appropriateness of a psychological test for use in forensic settings.
- Be able to list commonly used instruments for assessment of intellectual ability and personality measures.
- What is the average IQ score?
- What can we infer about scores that are normally distributed? What percentage of scores falls within one standard deviation? What percentage of scores falls within two standard deviations?
- What is a test battery?

## Key Terms

- Affirmative plea
- Assessment interview
- Civil law
- Competency
- Concurrent validity
- Content validity
- Correlation coefficient
- Criminal law
- Criterion keying
- Criterion-related validity
- DSM-IV
- Dusky standard
- Equivalence
- Face validity
- Forensic assessment instruments
- Forensically relevant instruments
- Internal consistency
- Interrater reliability
- Involuntary commitment
- Likert scale
- Malingering
- *Mens rea*
- Mental status
- Method–function match
- Method–mode match
- Millon Clinical Multiaxial Inventory (MCMI)
- Minnesota Multiphasic Personality Inventory–2 (MMPI-2)
- Negative correlation
- Normal distribution
- Normative group
- Objective personality measures

*(continued)*

## Key Terms *(continued)*

- Parallel forms reliability
- Positive correlation
- Predictive validity
- Privilege communication
- Projective hypothesis
- Projective personality measures
- Psychological assessment
- Psychometrics
- Rapport
- Reliability
- Rorschach Inkblot Test
- Slosson Intelligence Test

- Standard deviation
- Standard error
  of measurement
- Structured interview
- Test battery
- Test–retest reliability
- Therapeutic interview
- Unstructured interview
- Validity coefficient
- Wechsler scales
- Wide Range Intelligence Test
- Wonderlic Personnel Test

One of the most prominent roles the forensic psychologist plays in the legal arena is that of conducting a psychological assessment and providing a report of the assessment to the court. Though the process of conducting an assessment and reporting on the results appears fairly straightforward, there are a number of important conceptual, ethical, and legal considerations of which the forensic psychologist must be aware. This chapter provides an overview of psychological assessment and presents the legal considerations involving expert witness testimony. Several assessment instruments will be briefly introduced. However, due to the pervasive role assessment plays in forensic psychology, subsequent chapters will go into more detail regarding specific assessment activities.

# Types of Assessment Activities

Psychologists are involved in a wide range of assessment activities in the legal setting. Forensic psychological assessment is an attempt to identify important variables regarding human behavior so that past and present behavior can be appraised within a set of specific legal guidelines and/or some aspects of future behavior can be predicted. Forensic assessment occurs in both criminal and civil cases and also outside of courtroom proceedings, as in the use of assessment for screening, selection, and training of law enforcement personnel.

## Table 3.1    Types of Forensic Assessments

- Assessment in Criminal Proceedings (e.g., criminal responsibility, competency, risk assessment for dangerousness, mitigating and aggravating circumstances for capital sentencing)
- Assessment in Civil Proceedings (e.g., child custody evaluations, personal injury cases, sexual harassment cases)
- Assessment in Selection and Screening (e.g., selection of law enforcement personnel, fitness for duty evaluations)

# Forensic Assessment in Criminal Proceedings

In criminal proceedings, assessment can be informative to the courts in at least *five* stages of the legal process discussed by Bartol and Bartol (2004) and a *sixth* stage presented here. *First*, assessment can play a role at the time of arrest and the pretrial process. Psychologists can be asked by the courts to assess a defendant's competencies, such as **competency** to waive legal rights, to plead guilty, or competency to stand trial. For example, consider the hypothetical case of a 12-year-old accused of murder. Is the child competent to waive his *Miranda* rights and discuss the incident with the police without the presence of an adult who has the child's best interest in mind, such as a court-appointed lawyer or legal guardian? Important issues to be assessed would include the child's understanding of the gravity of the situation, possible penalties they may incur if found guilty, and other options available to him or her. For statements of confessions to be admissible in court, the defendant must have waived his or her *Miranda* rights *knowingly, intelligently, and voluntarily* (Ackerman, 1999). Courts have recognized the potential intellectual or emotional limitations of juveniles that may invalidate the waiver of *Miranda* rights.

At this first stage of the criminal proceedings, a frequent question for the forensic psychologist is a defendant's competency to stand trial. One study reports that 25,000 defendants were evaluated for competency to stand trial in the United States in one year alone and of those evaluated, 6,500 were hospitalized as incompetent to stand trial (Steadman, Monahan, Harstone, Davis, & Robbins, 1982). This problem has been exacerbated by the "deinstitutionalization" of the mentally ill. With the development of psychotropic medications that help to control psychotic symptoms, many patients have been released from public psychiatric hospitals and, partially due to their circumstances, have found themselves caught up in the legal system. The role of the forensic psychologist is to determine if the individual is competent to stand trial. Competency to stand trial is defined as having "sufficient present ability to consult with his lawyer with a reasonable degree of rational understanding—and whether he has a rational as well as factual understanding of the proceedings against him" (*Dusky v. United States*, 1960, p. 789).

At the *second* stage of assessment, a forensic psychologist may be asked to conduct an evaluation when the defendant raises an **affirmative plea**, such as extreme emotional disturbance, duress, self-defense, or insanity at the time of the offense. An *affirmative defense* indicates that the defendant admits committing the offense, but can offer an "excuse" that the defendant did not posses *mens rea* at the time of the offense. Thus, even though they broke the law, they can offer a reason that would exonerate him or her. A broad definition of *mens rea*, or a "guilty mind," refers to the defendant's state of mind at the time of the offense. If the defendant lacked the capacity for rational thought at the time of the offense or was compelled to act, then they did not possess *mens rea* at the time of the crime. Though the definition of *mens rea* varies by jurisdiction, it basically refers to whether the individual possessed free will with the intention of doing harm. A lack of *mens rea* suggests that although an individual committed the offense, they are not morally responsible for the act. As U.S. Supreme Court Justice Oliver Wendell Holmes stated, even a dog knows the difference between being stumbled over and being kicked, though the injury may be the same (Goldstein, Morse, & Shapiro, 2003).

An example of an affirmative defense evaluation is the assessment of criminal responsibility at the time of the offense, typically referred to as the insanity plea.

■ **Competency**
The ability or capacity to perform a specific task or function with rationality. The Dusky standard is used to determine competency to stand trial.

■ *Mens rea*
A "guilty mind" or free will with the intention of doing harm; required for conviction in criminal court.

Figure 3.1

The role of a forensic psychologist is to determine if the individual is competent to stand trial.
© 2009 Gina Sanders. Used under license from Shutterstock, Inc.

## Table 3.2    Six Stages of Forensic Assessment in Criminal Proceedings

- Time of arrest and pretrial hearing on competency
- At the time the defendant enters a plea, especially an affirmative plea
- At the time the defendant is placed into custody; assessment of dangerousness to self or others
- Assessment of victims of a crime, such as allegations of sexual abuse made by children or rape trauma
- Assessment during sentencing phase regarding potential benefits of mandated treatment; mitigating/aggravating circumstances in capital cases
- Assessment at the time of release from prison to predict dangerousness or likelihood of reoffending and potential benefits of mandated treatment

Consider the case of a person with paranoid schizophrenia whose mental condition is deteriorating due to discontinuance of medications. The defendant had a verbal confrontation with another customer in the drive-through lane of a fast-food establishment late at night. The police were called and the defendant felt that he was physically abused and subsequently filed a police brutality charge against the officers involved. His condition continued to deteriorate over the course of several weeks as evidenced by bizarre telephone calls to the CIA, FBI, DEA, and his family. Approximately 1 month after the incident at the drive-through, a concerned relative living approximately 100 miles away in a nearby city called the police and asked them to check up on his relative. When the police knocked on his apartment door and identified themselves, he was convinced, because of his delusional state, that they had come to harm him. Rather than answering the door, he used a pistol to fire a "warning shot" into his ceiling. The police retreated, called for backup, and set up a watch in the apartment across the hall. A SWAT team arrived on the scene and took position in the parking lot of the apartment building. This show-of-force reinforced the defendant's paranoid delusion that the police were out for revenge due to his earlier filing of police brutality charges. The police charged the door of his apartment and he leaped out the second-floor window amidst a flurry of shots fired by both the defendant and the police. No officers were hit but the defendant suffered a bullet wound to the groin area. It was obvious to the arresting officers that the defendant was behaving in a bizarre manner and appeared delusional. A subsequent forensic assessment found the defendant to meet the legal criteria for being insane at the time of the offense.

The *third* stage that may involve the use of forensic assessment is after the defendant is placed into custody. A psychologist may be asked to help the courts in making decisions regarding bail. Individuals who pose a risk to themselves or others may not be appropriate for release. Consider the hypothetical case of an elderly couple in which one individual is suffering from a terminal illness. This couple may decide that it is in their best interests to die together and avoid a lengthy, painful illness in which the surviving spouse will then be alone to deal with the grief and isolation that frequently characterizes old age. The couple may form a murder-suicide pact in which the stronger of the two kills the consenting spouse and then commits suicide. However, if the suicide is unsuccessful and the stronger spouse is rescued, he or she may face murder charges. Before bail can be set, it would be prudent to assess the risk of suicide and to deny bail if the individual poses a serious risk to harm one's self. Similarly, a battering husband who is charged with domestic violence may pose a substantial risk to his spouse were he to be released on bail while pending trial. A forensic psychologist may be asked to assess the likelihood of this individual harming another before bail would be considered.

A *fourth* stage of assessment in criminal cases involves the assessment of victims of a crime. This could include the assessment of allegations of sexual abuse by children and allegations of rape. In the first instance, children are susceptible to suggestions by interviewers and may have difficulty in determining whether they obtained information from their own experiences or from other sources (Poole & Lindsay, 1995). The child victim is typically the only witness to the crime, psychological symptoms can result from a variety of causes, medical symptoms are not always present, and confessions by the accused perpetrator are rare (Myers, 1998). As such, a forensic psychologist may be asked to evaluate the accuracy of sexual abuse allegations made by children.

Forensic psychologists have also introduced testimony regarding the presence of battered woman syndrome (Follingstad, 2003). Frequently, domestic violence cases escalate to murder. More often than not, the person killed is the wife. However, at times the battered spouse kills the abusive male. These cases typically result in murder charges against the wife who must prove that she killed her husband in self-defense, an example of an affirmative defense discussed above. The defense of the battered woman syndrome rests on the evidence that battering is a causative factor in the behavior of the abused spouse (Gillespie, 1989). A forensic psychologist will be asked to determine if the defendant suffers from battered woman syndrome and perhaps to determine what role that played in the alleged offense.

A *fifth* area of assessment occurs at the sentencing phase. This is particularly relevant in death penalty cases. A forensic psychologist may be asked to conduct and assessment and provide testimony regarding mitigating and aggravating factors regarding the defendant's background as well as circumstances of the crime that may influence the sentence the defendant is to receive (Cunningham & Goldstein, 2003). Mitigating factors in capital cases may involve a wide range of factors. Examples include a history of mental illness, a history of child physical or sexual abuse, substance abuse prior to or at the time of the crime, lack of a prior criminal record, subintellectual functioning, or lack of adequate psychiatric care preceding the offense. The prosecution may also introduce aggravating factors and, in federal cases, each juror must find, beyond a reasonable doubt, that one or more aggravating factors exist. Aggravating factors typically involve specifics related to the offense, such as the age of the victim and the premeditation of the crime, but may also include the assessment of risk that the defendant poses to the community. Twenty-one states allow for future dangerousness to be considered as a statutory aggravating factor in death penalty cases (Cunningham & Goldstein, 2003).

In addition to their role in capital sentencing, forensic psychologists may be asked to address the likelihood of rehabilitation at the time of sentencing. A judge may be interested to know if a defendant would benefit from treatment. For example, should an individual found guilty of domestic violence be recommended for outpatient treatment while on probation? In a sex offense case, the court may want to know if the perpetrator is a good candidate for treatment on an inpatient or outpatient basis. Numerous jurisdictions have developed outpatient treatment programs for first-time offenders to address anger management, domestic violence, substance abuse, and sex offenses.

Finally, a *sixth* stage in the criminal justice system in which forensic psychologists are asked to provide assessment and testimony is upon the release and parole of incarcerated individuals. Increasingly, the correctional system is turning to forensic psychologists to provide expert opinion when individuals are to be released from prison. In

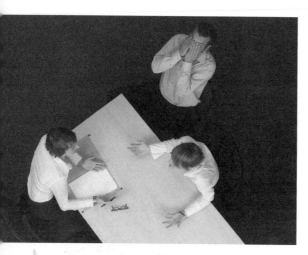

some jurisdictions, it has become routine practice for parole boards to require parolees to obtain a psychological evaluation and follow any recommendations for treatment while on parole. Individuals on parole may be required to participate in anger management classes or substance abuse treatment as a condition of their parole.

More recently, the courts have turned to forensic psychologists to evaluate sex offenders. These evaluations focus on identifying treatment needs, understanding psychopathology, and predicting the likelihood of reoffending (Conroy, 2003). With the recent development of sexual predator laws, forensic psychologists are being asked to provide predictions regarding the future dangerousness of sex offenders. In the recent U.S. Supreme Court landmark case of *Kansas v. Hendricks* (1997), the court allowed for the postincarceration civil commitment of "any person who has been convicted of or charged with a sexually violent offense and who suffers from a mental abnormality or personality disorder which makes the person likely to engage in the predatory acts of sexual violence" (p. 2077). Forensic psychologists are asked to predict the dangerousness of individuals and these individuals may be civilly committed for crimes they *may* commit in the future.

The need to predict future dangerousness has prompted the development of forensic instruments used to assess risk for violence among sex offenders (i.e., Viljoen et al., 2008). Others have attempted to combine a variety of risk factors with various weightings to develop actuarial risk assessments (Grann & Langstrom, 2007; Harris & Rice, 2007; Langton et al., 2007). Finally, some researchers have suggested looking at dynamic risk factors that are changeable, such as criminal behavior and behavior while incarcerated (Listwan, van Voorhis, & Ritchey, 2007; Reitzel, 2006). Instruments have been developed for use with adults as well as juveniles (Meyers & Schmidt, 2008). It is very likely that this area of assessment will continue to become more sophisticated, pushed by the need for accurate predictive assessments. A comprehensive review of risk assessment for violent and sexual offenders examining both static and dynamic variables is provided by Kroner and his colleagues (2007). They discuss the current state of risk assessment strategies, how risk assessment is communicated to decision makers, and methodological considerations in risk assessment research.

# Forensic Assessment in Civil Proceedings

In addition to criminal proceedings, the role of forensic psychologists has expanded in the area of civil court proceedings. **Civil law** deals with noncriminal matters pertaining to the rights and duties of citizens. For example, the following areas are within the scope of forensic assessment in the civil legal arena: child custody evaluations, termination of parental rights, personal injury examinations regarding emotional damages, employment discrimination and harassment, disability claims, workman's compensation, civil commitment proceedings, and the evaluation of individuals in high-risk occupations such as law enforcement. These roles are briefly described below.

Frequently, in contested divorce proceedings, psychologists will be asked to recommend to the court custody rights of parents involved in a divorce. These evaluations are often the most complex that forensic psychologists must face involving evaluation of numerous parties with respect to multiple issues and capacities (Otto, Buffington-Vollum, & Edens, 2003). One survey found that the mean length of time to conduct a child custody evaluation was 26.4 hours (Ackerman & Ackerman, 1997).

The American Psychological Association published guidelines for child custody evaluations in divorce proceedings in 1994. It should be noted that child custody evaluations pose one of the highest liability risks for forensic psychologists and account for the majority of licensing board complaints.

A related issue is the termination of parental rights. Parental rights may be terminated voluntarily by the parents or they may be terminated involuntarily by the state. The latter is initiated by the courts if it can be shown that a parent has either abandoned their child or that the parent's abuse and neglect present a serious and ongoing threat to the life or well-being of the child.

A general misconception regarding personal injury cases is that they only involve individuals who suffer some form of physical injury usually resulting from an accident, such as a motor vehicle accident. The reality is that personal injury cases can include any situation where an individual is injured physically or psychologically in which damages occur. Public policy allows for individuals to collect compensation when they have been harmed, even if no crime has occurred. Examples of personal injury claims for psychological damages can include medical malpractice cases resulting in psychological injury; accidents resulting in psychological damages; claims of sexual abuse, harassment, and discrimination; and misconduct cases resulting in psychological injury. Psychologists are typically asked to assess the amount of psychological damages resulting from the claim and are employed by the lawyer for the plaintiff, the individual claiming damages. However, psychologists may be asked to testify for the defendant in cases alleging liability issues when the professional conduct of mental health professionals is called into question.

**Figure 3.3**

Sexual harassment that causes psychological injury may result in a personal injury lawsuit.
© 2009 Phase4Photography. Used under license from Shutterstock, Inc.

The Civil Rights Act of 1964 identified race, sex, religion, and national origin as discrimination criteria in the workplace. More recent laws have also added protection against discrimination based on age and disability status. The Civil Rights Act of 1991 provides for injunctive relief from discrimination (i.e., correction of the problem) and, in some instances, monetary damages. Monetary damages to those harmed by the discrimination can be for compensation of loss wages and benefits as well as for emotional pain and suffering. Psychologists may testify in court regarding what the psychological research indicates regarding workplace discrimination and harassment such as the effects of stereotyping and prejudice or they may be asked to provide a psychological assessment of an individual who is filing a claim (Vasquez, Baker, & Shullman, 2003). This type of assessment would be similar to personal injury evaluations, discussed previously.

Both disability claims and workman's compensation require the forensic psychologist to make a determination of a psychological disorder that prevents the individual from working. The major distinction between the types of claims is that workman's compensation claims allege that the psychological injury is a result of the workplace. There has been a large increase in the number of claims filed for disability based on mental disorders over the past few years. Individuals can collect disability payments for psychological disorders such as depression and bipolar disorder.

Civil commitment proceedings typically involve the **involuntary commitment** of individuals deemed to pose a danger to self or society. Though the law varies according to jurisdiction, most require the individual to be diagnosed with some type of mental disorder and some type of dangerousness (i.e., to self or others) for the involuntary commitment statue to apply (Kane, 1999a). Typically, involuntary commitment is for individuals with

1. severe mental illnesses who, because of their mental illnesses,
2. pose a danger to self or others, or are gravely disabled, and for whom
3. inpatient hospitalization is the least restrictive alternative (Parry, 1994).

The role of the forensic psychologist is to determine if there is the presence of a severe mental illness and if, as a result of the illness, the individual poses a danger or is gravely disabled. The criteria of dangerousness refers to danger to others (i.e., a person with paranoid schizophrenia who threatens to harm others) or self (i.e., a suicidal patient or someone who self-mutilates). Gravely disabled includes persons who are unable to independently conduct the activities of daily living necessary for survival (Kane, 1999a).

Recent years have seen a substantial increase in the role of psychological assessment in law enforcement agencies (Delprino & Bahn, 1988). Forensic psychologists can assist in the screening and selection of recruits and individuals eligible for promotion. Additionally, psychologists may be asked to conduct a "fitness for duty" evaluation. This assessment occurs after the individual has been engaged in an incident that raises concern about the psychological suitability of the individual to perform his or her job duties or concerns that the individual may pose a risk to self or others (Borum, Super, & Rand, 2003). The selection of law enforcement personnel poses unique challenges for the forensic psychologist. Certainly the screening process should rule out individuals with severe psychological pathology, but research on what makes for a "good cop" is less clear (Ainsworth, 1995). Psychologists may also provide training and program evaluation to law enforcement personnel. Though the bulk of this work involves working with law enforcement agencies, it can also be applied to other high-risk occupations such as correctional officers, firefighters, airline pilots, air traffic controllers, and nuclear power plant operators (Rigaud & Flynn, 1995.)

The above discussion is not meant to provide an exhaustive list of the assessment activities of forensic psychologists. Rather, it is an attempt to present an overview of some of the more common assessments forensic psychologists perform. Psychologists face a wide range of challenges when conducting assessments. As the field continues to expand and assessment procedures become more sophisticated, it is likely that opportunities for forensic psychologists will also increase. Indeed, a particular strength in the training of psychologists is a background in **psychometrics**. Psychologists enter the legal arena with a stronger background in statistics and assessment than other mental health professionals. We now turn to an overview of assessment procedures and basic psychometric concepts of psychological tests.

# Psychological Assessment and Psychological Testing

■ **Psychological assessment**
The entire evaluative process used to measure a person's psychological status.

**Psychological assessment** refers to the entire evaluative process used to measure a person's psychological status. This can refer to any time period including the past, present, and future. The assessment process employs a variety of techniques including interviews with the individual, interviews with others such as witnesses, arresting officers, relatives, and other informants, a review of records and case files, behavioral observations, psychological testing, situational tests, and neuropsychological tests.

Forensic psychological assessments are conducted in order to answer a specific question and do not provide global descriptions of personality or behavior. For example, the courts may wish to know the likelihood that an incarcerated sex offender will benefit from treatment. Courts frequently refer first-time offenders for an evaluation to see if they would benefit from various forms of group treatment, such as anger management classes or substance abuse treatment. Another example of a forensic referral question is whether a defendant is competent to stand trial, and if not, can the defendant achieve competence through treatment in a reasonable amount of time. Each assessment will involve techniques unique to the referral question. Thus, the assessment techniques selected should reflect the referral question and the decision-making purpose for which the assessment will be used and the nature of the disorder being assessed (Hemphill & Hart, 2003). This matching of assessment tools to the decision-making process and to the disorder being assessed has been referred to as **method–function match** and **method–mode match**, respectively (Haynes, Richard, & Kubany, 1995).

There are a number of similarities between forensic assessments and clinical assessments that occur in a therapeutic setting. For example, the psychologist may use many of the same assessment tools in a clinical setting as they would use in a forensic setting, such as an interview, intellectual assessment, projective and objective measures of personality, collateral informants, and behavioral observation. However, there has been a recent flurry in the number of assessment tools specific to forensic assessments (Otto & Heilbrun, 2002).

With these similarities in mind, it is important to note the differences between clinical assessments and forensic assessments. The differences between clinical interviews and forensic interviews are particularly important to note due to the potential outcomes of the interview and how it will affect the individual. The purpose of forensic assessments is usually litigation, not treatment. The report is entered into the legal system, which is adversarial by nature. In a **therapeutic interview**, the client anticipates benevolence and assistance from the clinician. In a forensic setting, the individual being evaluated cannot assume that the evaluation will result in what the client considers to be his or her best interest.

Differences between a clinical evaluation and a forensic evaluation include purpose of the evaluation, examiner–examinee relationship along with the therapist–patient privilege, who is the client, motivation of the examinee, written report, the psychologist's cognitive set, professional accountability, and temporal focus of the assessment (Goldstein, 2003; Greenberg & Shuman, 1997; Heilbrun, Warren, & Picarello, 2003).

## Differences between a Forensic Assessment and a Clinical Assessment

**Table 3.3**

|  | Forensic | Clinical |
| --- | --- | --- |
| Purpose of the evaluation | Psycholegal question | Treatment |
| Examiner–examinee relationship | Neutral, objective | Therapeutic |
| Therapist–patient privilege | No privilege exists | Patient possesses privilege |
| Who is the client | Attorney/courts | Patient |
| Motivation of the examinee | Secondary gain | Truthful, candid |
|  | Possibility of malingering |  |
| Written report | Extensive report to courts | Private notes for therapist |
| Psychologist's cognitive set | Neutral, objective | Supportive, trusting |
| Professional accountability | To the courts, attorneys | To the client |
| Temporal focus | Past, future | Present |

# Purpose of the Evaluation

The purpose of a *clinical evaluation* is for diagnosis and treatment with the goal of helping the client. The information obtained is used to help the client resolve psychological difficulties and achieve personal growth. The psychologist and client collaborate to identify goals for therapy and work together to help the client achieve these goals. However, in forensic psychology the goal of the assessment is quite different. The forensic psychologist is conducting the assessment to shed light on a psycholegal issue and to assist the court in its decision-making process. The court's decision may in fact be detrimental to the client. For example, the court may find the defendant criminally responsible in an insanity plea case or may rule against a parent in a child custody case based on the information provided by the psychologist. The client or someone who has the client's best interest in mind, such as a parent or spouse, typically initiates a clinical assessment. An attorney, or the court, not the individual being examined, initiates the forensic assessment.

# Examiner–Examinee Relationship

In a clinical assessment, the clinician assumes a helper role toward the client. Therapist–client privilege exists in that information obtained in the therapeutic relationship may not be disclosed to third parties without the client's informed consent except in a very limited number of exceptions to the law. The APA ethical principle of benevolence applies to the therapeutic relationship. The therapist strives to do no harm to the client. There is no guarantee that the outcome of a forensic assessment will be beneficial to the client. For example, a psychologist who testifies as an expert witness in the sentencing stage of a capital case may sway the court's decision toward imposing the death penalty. The forensic psychologist assumes an objective role toward the examinee. Their role is to inform the court, the trier of fact, to come to a just conclusion regarding the examinee (Greenberg, 1999). Therefore, the role of the forensic psychologist is not to help the examinee, but rather, to help the court. It is important and ethical in all forensic assessments that the examinee understands this distinction. It is necessary for forensic psychologists to document the examinee's understanding of this unique aspect of the forensic assessment through signed informed consent. For example, at times an examinee may wish to share information "off the record." It may be tempting for a forensic psychologist to agree to this condition. The psychologist may feel that doing so would be "therapeutic" for the examinee or that information that would otherwise not be disclosed by the examinee may be revealed. However, to agree to "off the record" material would be unethical. The forensic psychologist should take the opportunity to remind the examinee that any information disclosed may be included in the report that goes to the attorneys and the court.

# Who is the Client?

In a clinical assessment, the client is usually the individual being examined by the psychologist. The client approaches the psychologist for assistance with a personal problem and expects the psychologist to work with the client on resolving these issues. Even when the client is a minor and the parents brought the child in for treatment, the clinician still has ethical responsibilities to the child. However, in a forensic assessment, the client may be the court, the attorney, or the individual being examined. For example, a court-appointed psychologist might be asked to conduct a competency to stand trial evaluation and to report back to the court. An attorney may request a psychologist to evaluate their client for psychological damages pending a personal injury case. Finally, a parent may ask for a custody evaluation prior to initiating court proceedings regarding divorce and child custody. Others have broadened the definition of the client to include not only the attorney and the courts (the judge and the jury) but also those potentially affected by the expert's opinion including society as a whole (Goldstein, 2003; Monahan, 1980).

# Motivation of the Examinee

In a clinical assessment, it is assumed that the information provided to the psychologist by the client is accurate and truthful to the best of the client's ability. Rarely would a psychologist doubt the integrity of the information provided by a client in an assessment. Any inaccuracies in self-report data would be attributed to faulty memory, lack of insight, or other nondeliberate motives. However, in forensic evaluations there is frequently a strong motivation in the form of secondary gain for an examinee to misrepresent their symptoms. For example, it is obvious that a defendant may wish to be found incompetent to stand trial and/or not guilty by reason of insanity at the time of the offense. Similarly, an individual suing for psychological damages may not want to put their best mental health foot forward, so to say. Rather, an examinee may attempt to feign mental illness or even exaggerate genuine emotional distress. Consequently, forensic psychologists must always be skeptical of an examinee's self-report, whether in an interview situation or on psychological test instruments. Forensic psychologists can use collaborating information to substantiate an examinee's report, such as third-party information. Third-party information may include a review of case documents and/or interviews with collateral informants (Heilbrun et al., 2003).

# Written Report

In clinical assessments, a formal report may or may not be written. Frequently, the treating clinician will keep records of what was done, though these records are usually brief, omitting many of the details of the assessment and treatment (Welch, 1998b). Most importantly, these notes are written for the benefit of the therapist with the expectation that only the therapist will have access to the notes. However, the majority of forensic evaluations require a formal, detailed report to be submitted to the attorneys involved and to the court. Thus, a lengthy, detailed report documenting exactly what was done and what the results mean is the final end product of the forensic evaluation. Since the report will be scrutinized by opposing counsel, the judge, and the jury in many circumstances, the forensic psychologist must take a conservative approach to the use of data and opinions expressed based on the data. For example, any notes the examiner make that are related to the final expert opinion or help to form the basis of the opinion are discoverable, meaning that they may be obtained by the attorneys and the court for scrutiny and review (Ackerman, 1999). A forensic psychologist should include in the report all the information including information that may conflict with the final conclusion of the report. It is the responsibility of the trier of fact to weigh all the information and to make the final decision.

# The Psychologist's Cognitive Set

In a clinical setting, psychologists approach their clients with a benevolent, empathic orientation. Their role is to be supportive and trusting of the client. As is obvious from the above discussion, the forensic psychologist approaches the **assessment**

**interview** with a detached, neutral, and objective cognitive mindset (Greenberg & Shuman, 1997). The forensic psychologist typically provides more structure to the assessment interview than would be the case in a therapeutic setting. The psychologist must control the interview so as to facilitate the collection of information. Often in a therapeutic setting, the clinician allows the client to control the topics discussed and the flow of information. Most importantly, the forensic psychologist must remain neutral and objective and cannot present information to the courts in a partisan or advocacy manner. This is in opposition to a therapeutic relationship in which a client may have legitimate expectations of support from their therapist.

# Professional Accountability

The American Psychological Association published the *Ethical Principles and Code of Conduct* with a recent revision in 2002. The *Ethical Principles and Code of Conduct* apply to all areas of psychology. Additionally, the *Specialty Guidelines for Forensic Psychologists* addresses the specific practice of forensic psychology (Committee on Ethical Guidelines for Forensic Psychologists, 1991). Psychologists are thus held accountable to the APA for the ethical practice of forensic psychology. Psychologists must also answer to state licensing boards as well. However, the psychologist in a forensic setting is obligated to provide objective, accurate, and complete information to all parties involved in any legal proceeding. As stated above, the psychologist must maintain a neutral and objective approach to the examinee. The forensic psychologist frequently provides the same information to the attorneys who initially retained their services as well as the attorneys for the opposing side. The judge and the jury will also use the expert's opinion to reach a decision and as such the psychologist is accountable to these participants in the legal arena. Finally, the psychologist is obligated to the examinee to provide as accurate information as possible. There are usually not so many parties involved in a clinical assessment setting.

# Temporal Focus of the Assessment

Most clinical assessments are concerned with the client's current level of functioning. The referral question wants to know the client's intellectual or psychological functioning at the time of the assessment. Though there may be some attention given to future functioning, particularly in regards to any outcomes expected with treatment, the request for the assessment is to understand the client's current condition. In contrast, forensic assessments often focus on the examinee's emotional state at the time of the offense or attempt to predict future behavior. For example, a forensic assessment of criminal responsibility will address the examinee's mental state at the time of the offense, which can be several months to several years prior to the assessment. Or, an examiner may be asked to predict the likelihood of a sex offender reoffending should they be released into the community.

# Assessment Instruments

It is apparent from the above discussion that there are similarities and differences between clinical assessments and forensic assessments. It is reasonable to assume that a competent forensic psychologist must possess strong clinical skills. However, they must also have a set of skills specific to the forensic issue at hand. The forensic skills necessary to conduct a competency to stand trial evaluation and a criminal responsibility evaluation differ from the skills necessary to conduct a child custody evaluation. Just as the assessment skills of the clinician vary for clinical and forensic evaluations, so too do the assessment tools available to psychologists. We now turn to a brief overview of assessment tools used by forensic psychologists.

## Assessment Tools: The Interview

Perhaps the most widely used assessment tool is the clinical interview. Clinical interviews can be broadly categorized as either a *therapeutic interview* or an *assessment (diagnostic) interview*. Sarason and Sarason (2005) suggest that all clinical interviews have the following four components: rapport, technique, mental status, and diagnosis. **Rapport** characterizes how the psychologist and the client relate to each other during the interview. The psychologist attempts to establish good rapport by putting the client at ease and demonstrating interest in the client's self-report. Technique can vary during the interview and refers to skills the psychologist may use, such as open-ended questions, active listening skills, and confrontation. **Mental status** is an assessment of the client's short- and long-term memory, understanding of the interview process, and their current situation. Clinicians will frequently state that the individual was "oriented times 3," meaning that the client knew the date (time), where they were (place), and who they were (person). The most basic assessment of mental status is to determine if the client is in touch with reality. More detailed approaches assess cognitions, memory, and any sign of deterioration over time. Most interviews have a goal of determining a diagnosis, if any, for both clinical categories and personality disorders.

## Four Components of a Clinical Interview
Table 3.4

- Rapport–how the client and therapist relate to each other during the interview
- Technique–clinical skills used by the therapist such as open-ended questions, active listening skills, and confrontation
- Mental status–assessment of client's cognitive functioning
- Diagnosis–diagnosis of clinical (Axis I) and personality (Axis II) disorders using the *Diagnostic and Statistical Manual of Mental Disorders* (American Psychiatric Association, 2002)

Interviews may be either *structured* or *unstructured*. By far, the vast majority of interviews conducted by clinicians would fall into the unstructured format. The psychologist asks the questions he or she feels are most relevant to the client at hand. The types of questions (i.e., open-ended or closed) and the topics vary based on the clinician's understanding of the case. A wide variety of factors can influence the information obtained in an **unstructured interview**. Interviewers may not note or correctly interpret what is taking place during the assessment. Characteristics unique to the examiner as well as the examinee may influence the course of the interview and its content.

This is in contrast to a **structured interview**. In a structured interview, questions are predetermined and answers from the client determine the follow-up questions. Most structured interviews allow for the clinician to digress from the standardized format under specific circumstances. The interviewer is also provided with rating scales to assess the presence and severity of symptoms. Numerous structured interviews are now commercially available to assess a variety of presenting problems. The majority of the available structured interviews are for use in clinical settings. Examples include the Diagnostic Interview Schedule (DIS; Robins, Tipp, & Przybeck, 1991) and the Structured Clinical Interview for DSM (SCID; Spitzer et al., 1992). Structured interviews for specific disorders related to forensic issues, such as the assessment of personality disorders, also exist. Two structured interviews that might be used to assess antisocial personality disorder are the Structured Clinical Interview for DSM-IV, Axis II (SCID-II; First et al., 1995) and the International Personality Disorder Examination (IPDE; Loranger et al., 1994).

However, structured interviews have also been specifically developed for forensic assessments. An example of a commercially available forensic structured interview is the Miller Forensic Assessment of Symptoms Test (M-FAST; H. A. Miller, 2001). The M-FAST is a structured interview designed to assess the malingering of psychiatric disorders.

## Assessment Tools: Psychological Tests

Testing instruments and techniques can be divided up into three categories based on the relevance the instruments have to forensic issues (Heilbrun, Rogers, & Otto, 2000; Otto & Heilbrun, 2002). The first category, *clinical measures and assessment techniques*, refers to instruments that were not developed specifically to address an issue related to forensic psychology. Rather, the instruments were developed for the assessment, diagnosis, or treatment planning of a clinical population (Bartol & Bartol, 2004). These instruments assess a wide variety of issues and comprise the assessment armamentarium of general practitioners. This category includes measures of intellectual functioning, personality measures, tests of aptitude as well as achievement, neuropsychological test batteries, and assessment for learning disabilities. Tests from this category may be an important part of a forensic assessment, such as administering a test of intellectual functioning as part of a competency to stand trial assessment. However, it is also important for the examiner to understand the limitations of applying the results of instruments in this category to legal issues. Since the tests were not specifically developed to address legal questions, the results and interpretation may not be applicable to all forensic assessments.

**Table 3.5** Forensic Classification of Assessment Instruments

- Clinical measures and assessment techniques–instruments developed for work with a clinical population
- Forensically relevant instruments–instruments developed outside of the forensic area but have direct applicability to forensic questions
- Forensic assessment instruments–instruments that are directly relevant to a psycholegal issue and developed to answer a specific legal question

The second category consists of what has been termed **forensically relevant instruments** (FRIs). Otto and Heilbrun (2002) classified instruments in this category as those that have been developed outside of the forensic arena but have direct applicability to addressing forensic questions. Examples of instruments from this category include tests developed to assess psychopathology, malingering, violence risk assessment, and measures of personality traits such as anger and impulse control, and instruments used to assess substance abuse. An example would include the use of the Thematic Apperception Test (TAT), a projective measure of personality frequently used in child custody evaluations (Ackerman & Ackerman, 1997).

Finally, the third category, **forensic assessment instruments**, is defined as "measures that are directly relevant to a specific legal standard and reflect and focus on specific capabilities, abilities, or knowledge that are embodied by the law" (Otto & Heilbrun, 2002, p. 9). These are tests that have been developed to answer a specific legal question, such as competence to stand trial, criminal responsibility, prediction of a sex offender reoffending, and so on. These instruments frequently address the psychological as well as legal issues involved in the assessment. The most common psychological assessment in the criminal courts involves the assessment of competency to stand trial (Otto et al., 1998; Steadman & Hartshorne, 1983). Tests used to assess competency to stand trial were the first instruments developed for use in forensic settings (Otto & Heilbrun, 2002). Competency to stand trial refers to the defendant's ability to understand the legal proceedings and to assist the attorneys in preparing and conducting the defense. This definition of competency has not changed since the U.S. Supreme Court clarified it in 1960 in *Dusky v. United States*. This definition has become known as the **Dusky standard**. Instruments used to assess competence to stand trial thus include assessing aspects of the legal definition of competence as established by the courts and provide an example of forensic assessment instruments. Instruments in this third category assess psychological functioning (i.e., cognitive abilities) within specific legal guidelines.

It should be apparent to the astute reader that not all psychological tests are suited for forensic assessments. However, even some *forensic-relevant instruments* and *forensic instruments* may not be suited for use in a forensic assessment with the subsequent introduction into the courtroom. Many tests lack criteria considered necessary for use in forensic settings. When forensic assessments are introduced into the court proceeding, they are subjected to scrutiny by opposing counsel. A prudent opposing counsel is likely to hire their own forensic psychologist to point out to the jury any shortcomings in the selection or application of the psychological assessment techniques. A well-known series of texts in the field coaches attorneys on how to attack the credibility of expert psychological and psychiatric testimony (e.g., Ziskin, 1995).

As stated earlier in the text, forensic psychology has been a growth field in the past few decades. This growth is also reflected in the number of recently developed forensic assessment instruments. Prior to 1990, a total of 10 forensically relevant instruments and forensic assessment instruments existed; during the 1990s, 33 new assessment instruments were developed for forensic settings (Heilbrun et al., 2000). Frequently, psychological tests can suffer from fundamental shortcomings. These shortcomings include a lack of

1. commercial publication, making it difficult for others to obtain the instrument;
2. inadequate data regarding the instrument's psychometrics including the test's reliability and validity;
3. a comprehensive test manual detailing the development of the instrument; and
4. data on the standardization of the instrument and the appropriate norms (Bartol & Bartol, 2004; Heilbrun et al., 2000; Poythress et al., 1999).

Heilbrun (1992) has suggested seven criteria to be used to evaluate the use of psychological test instruments in forensic settings.

1. The test is commercially available and documented in at least two sources. A manual describing the test's development, psychometric properties, and administration accompanies the test.
2. The test has demonstrated adequate reliability among forensic samples. Reliability coefficients for forensic samples should be .80 or higher.
3. The test should assess constructs that are relevant to the legal question. The choice of the test should be justified in the report submitted to the court.
4. The examiner should follow the standardized administration procedures presented in the test manual.
5. The instrument should assess response style (how the examinee approached answering the test questions, such as feigning mental illness). Interpretation of test data should be within the context of the examinee's response style.
6. Objective test data should be combined with base rates and accuracy rates for the test. Any limitations should be explicitly stated in the report.
7. The legal question and population the examinee is from should drive the selection of the instrument. The more the population used in the validation research matches the individual being assessed, the more confidence can be expressed in the results.

In a perfect world all of the above criteria suggested by Heilbrun would be followed. However, it is not a perfect world and there are times that not all the above criteria are met by an assessment instrument. This does not mean that the test cannot be used in a forensic assessment. However, it is necessary, more so than usual, for the psychologist to justify in the report and to be prepared to justify on the witness stand how the test addresses the relevant psychological and legal issues (Ackerman & Kane, 1998).

Psychological assessment is one of the strengths of the forensic psychologist's "professional black bag." The use of psychological tests in the assessment process is a valuable addition to the forensic psychologist's skills. As such, as a forensic psychologist, it is necessary to understand concepts related to test development and test psychometrics. Tests vary in complexity with regard to administration, scoring, and interpretation. Some tests require a trained clinician to administer the test under a controlled situation whereas untrained individuals may administer other tests.

Psychological tests allow for obtaining detailed information about the examinee in a structured, standardized format. It usually reduces the amount of time needed to obtain the information and allows for comparison of results to other individuals that have completed the test, called the **normative group**.

Figure 3.4

The TAT, a projective measure of personality frequently used in child custody evaluations, is similar to the Rorschach ink-blot test. Subjects are shown pictures and asked to tell a story based on what they see.
© 2009 Dvirus. Used under license from Shutterstock, Inc.

# Psychometric Properties of Assessment Instruments

There are four important psychometric concepts that are important to understand concerning assessment instruments: *reliability, validity, normative group,* and *standard error of measurement* (Bartol & Bartol, 2004). These are the criteria by which psychologists—and, in the forensic setting, attorneys, judges, and juries—evaluate assessment instruments. This is particularly relevant to the legal arena as there are specific criteria required by the courts before expert testimony, including the results of tests, may be admissible.

# Reliability

**Reliability** refers to the consistency of the test. There are several types of reliability, including *internal consistency, test–retest reliability*, and *interrater reliability*. A test must be reliable before it can be valid. Therefore, reliability is one of the most basic psychometric properties of an instrument. A highly reliable test may adequately meet all three reliability measures. Reliability is usually expressed as a **correlation coefficient**.

A correlation coefficient is a mathematical expression of how two or more variables vary together. For example, generally speaking, the taller a person is, the more they weigh. Thus, height and weight vary together in a **positive correlation**. A positive correlation means that the variables vary together in the same direction. Therefore, as one variable increases (height) the other variable (weight) also increases, or as one variable decreases, the other variable decreases. On the other hand, a **negative correlation** means that the two variables move in opposite directions, so as one increases the other variable decreases. An example of a negative correlation is time spent watching television and grades in school. Generally speaking, the more a student watches television, the less time they have to study and grades can suffer. However, it is not a perfect relationship as some students need to study more than others to achieve the same grades.

In addition to the direction of the relationship, correlation coefficients also describe the *strength* of the relationship. In the above example, height and weight are not perfectly correlated. There are tall individuals who weigh less than shorter individuals. The correlation coefficient ranges from 0.0 (no correlation) to 1.0 (a perfect correlation). A correlation of .7 is stronger than a correlation of .3. The direction of the correlation *does not* affect the strength of the relationship; a correlation of −.7 is stronger than a correlation of .3. You may recall that one of the seven criteria for selecting a test was that the correlation coefficient for reliability was at least .80 or above.

It is also important to note that a correlation does not indicate a cause-and-effect relationship. For example, you will find that the number of annual pregnancies and houses of worship in a town are positively correlated. The more houses of worship a town has, the higher the birth rate. Houses of worship do not cause pregnancy. A third variable, population density, can help explain the correlation. The higher the population density, the more houses of worship in a town. Also, the higher the population density, the higher the birth rate. Correlations simply indicate how two or more variables vary together. Correlations do not indicate a cause-and-effect relationship between the correlated variables.

There are four common types of reliability: *test–retest reliability, parallel forms, interrater agreement*, and *internal consistency*.

## Four Common Types of Test Reliability    Table 3.6

- Test–retest–consistent over time
- Parallel forms–two forms of the same test produce comparable scores
- Interrater reliability–two raters using the same assessment instrument obtain comparable results
- Internal consistency–items on the instrument correlate with the instrument's total score

**Test–retest reliability**, also referred to as stability, indicates how consistent, or stable, the test scores are over time. To establish test–retest validity, a test or measure is administered to a group. Some time later the same test is readministered to the same group. One usually expects the scores to be highly correlated. For example, we could administer a measure of *psychopathy*, such as the Psychopathy Checklist—Revised (PCL-R; Hare, 2003). Psychopathy is considered a stable personality trait and therefore any assessment instrument assessing psychopathy should have consistent or stable scores over time. We would then readminister the test to the same group of individuals 6 months after the first administration. We could then establish the 6-month test–retest reliability of the PCL-R.

**Parallel forms reliability**, also called **equivalence**, requires different forms of the same tests. Different forms of the same test (i.e., Form A and Form B) are administered to the same group and the scores are correlated. The correlation coefficient between the two scores indicates if the two forms of the same test are equivalent. Aptitude tests, such as the SAT and GRE, frequently have alternate forms of the same test.

**Interrater reliability** indicates the amount of agreement between two or more raters who are using the same rating form. The question addressed is if two or more raters using the same rating form are consistent in their ratings. For example, two parents may be asked to rate their child on the Bricklin Perceptual Scales (BPS; Bricklin, 1984). The amount of agreement between the two parents rating the child would comprise the interrater reliability coefficient.

**Internal consistency** is perhaps the most common form of reliability reported in the literature. Internal consistency refers to how closely each item of the test correlates with the total score on the test. The question addressed here is how well does each item measure the content or construct under consideration. For example, test items on an exam in a forensic psychology course should all relate to the topic of forensic psychology. An item on the test measuring algebra skills would presumably have a low correlation with the total test score and would therefore lower the internal consistency of the test. This is the most common form of reliability reported and typically is stated as the coefficient alpha. The coefficient alpha, as stated above, should be at least .80.

## Validity

All psychological assessment instruments must demonstrate that they are *valid* measures of the psychological or legal construct that they claim to measure. The question of validity addresses whether an instrument is an accurate measure of what it claims to measure. An example often seen in the news media is the issue of intelligence tests. Critics of intelligence tests frequently question the validity of these tests, claiming that they do not measure intellectual aptitude but rather scores are more related to economic and educational background. Just as there are a variety of reliability coefficients, so are there various forms of validity. The main types of validity that will be discussed here are *content validity* and *criterion-related validity* including *predictive validity* and *concurrent validity*.

Essential properties of any measure are that the test is both reliable and valid. An instrument can be reliable, but not valid. Validity is really a matter of degree and not "all or nothing." The process of validation is a combination of logical argument and empirical validation. Strictly speaking, one validates the use to which a measure is used rather than the instrument itself. Each unique use must be specifically validated. Tests or measures valid for one use aren't necessarily valid for another. This is particularly relevant for forensic assessments when we recall the distinct differences between a clinical assessment and a forensic assessment. For example, a measure of parenting skills validated on a clinical sample of parents seeking treatment for their

## Five Common Types of Validity
**Table 3.7**

- Content validity–items on the test cover a representative sample of the domain of the behavior or construct to be measured
- Criterion-related validity–how well scores on the test correlate with performance on another measure of the same construct
  - Predictive validity–using performance on the measure to predict future performance related to what is being measured
  - Concurrent validity–comparing performance on the test to performance on another measure, known to be reliable and valid
- Face validity–not a measurement concept; degree to which an instrument appears to measure what it purports to measure

child may not be appropriate for use in a child custody evaluation. Ideally, forensic assessment instruments should be validated on a forensic population for a forensic use.

**Content validity** refers to whether or not the items on the test cover a representative sample of the domain of the behavior or construct to be measured (Anastasi, 1998). Content validity is based on a combination of logical argument and subject matter expertise. For example, an exam in a forensic psychology course should only have questions related to forensic psychology, the content of the course. A question on chemistry would be inappropriate and indicate poor content validity. Likewise, the questions on the exam should cover the range of material that was presented. A content-valid test should have at least moderate levels of internal consistency. This suggests that the items measure a common domain. For example, an assessment instrument used to determine competency to stand trial should have only items related to the criteria used to determine competency as established by the courts.

Courts frequently confused "**face validity**" with content validity. Face validity is not a measurement concept. It is the degree to which an instrument *appears* to measure what it says it does. A test has "face validity" if it looks like it measures what it is supposed to measure, even if there is no empirical support that the test actually measures what it purports to measure. There are well-respected psychological tests, such as the **Minnesota Multiphasic Personality Inventory** (MMPI/MMPI-2), that do not have face validity. However, face validity can have some value for both the individual being assessed and for the courts. The MMPI-2 is a personality inventory with over 500 true–false questions. Many questions on the MMPI-2 lack face validity for individuals taking the test. This lack of face validity can interfere with a respondent's willingness to answer all the questions. Otto et al. (1998) have suggested that face validity is particularly important in the legal arena as the test should look relevant to the legal question being addressed.

**Criterion-related validity** refers to how well scores on the test correlate with performance on another measure known to be both reliable and valid (i.e., a criterion).

Performance on the first measure should be highly correlated with performance on the second (i.e., known to be valid and reliable) measure. Criterion-related validity is

**■ Face validity**
Refers to whether a test *appears* to measure what it purports to measure.

■ **Concurrent validity**

Two measures of a construct are assessed at the same time and should correlate with one another; one measure is compared with an already established measure.

■ **Predictive validity**

How well test scores predict future behavior.

established empirically by a correlation coefficient, called a **validity coefficient**. There are two types of criterion-related validity, predictive validity and concurrent validity.

**Concurrent validity** is established by comparing performance on one measure against performance on another measure, known to be valid, reliable, and considered a "standard." An example is comparing a short aptitude test to a much longer version. If scores on the short version correlate highly (>. 80) with scores on the longer version, then the shorter version demonstrates concurrent validity. Most test developers demonstrate concurrent validity by administering the two tests at the same time (i.e., concurrently). The scores on the new instrument are compared to the scores on the established instrument. However, scores on the new instrument could also be compared to other criteria, such as performance on a task. For example, we may want to compare scores on a test measuring parent–child relationship with the rating of a 5-minute interaction between the parent and the child.

**Predictive validity** refers to how well scores on the test predict future behavior related to what the test is supposed to measure. A common example is the use of SAT scores for admission to college. SAT scores are thought to predict success in college. A current area of research is the development of assessment instruments that can be used to predict future dangerousness. Forensic psychologists are asked to predict if individuals who have committed a sex offense will reoffend after being released from prison.

Establishing the validity of a test involves numerous research studies. One study demonstrating concurrent or predictive validity is not sufficient to state that a test is valid. The validation process requires a number of studies all showing that the test is reliable and valid. Test developers need to demonstrate content validity as well as criterion-related validity. This is an expensive and time-consuming process. Take the example of developing a test to predict if a sex offender will reoffend. To establish predictive validity, we would want to demonstrate that scores on the test predict the occurrence of a future sex offense. The test could be administered to a random sample of 100 sex offenders who are about to be released. We would then want to know which offenders reoffend during a certain time period after their release. Some of the limitations of such a proposed study should be obvious. First, we would need to ensure that the individuals taking the test answer in a candid manner. Second, we would need to know which individuals reoffend. Relating the scores to rearrest rates may not be sufficient since many other factors can account for rearrest, such as postrelease supervision. Knowing the actual number of reoffenses may be impossible due to the nature of the act, it is secretive and illegal.

In another example, we may want to see how well a test predicts job performance as a correctional officer. We could give the test to 100 random candidates for correctional officer positions. We would then need to hire all 100 candidates regardless of scores on our test. We could then compare scores to supervisor ratings and other job-performance measures. Again, this would be a costly and time-consuming process as we may wish to wait 1–2 years before identifying someone as successful at their job.

As a result, most tests need to have their reliability and validity demonstrated for each particular sample and use. It is important to note that a test itself is neither reliable nor valid. Rather, it is reliable for a particular sample and valid for a specific use. Reliability and validity need to be repeatedly demonstrated for each new sample and new use of the instrument. It is important to note that reliability is not part of the test, but rather specific to the test along with the population completing the test (APA Task Force, 1999).

## Normative Group

A psychological test is initially developed for work with a specific population. For example, a test may be developed to assess competency among juveniles to waive

*Miranda* rights. This test would then need to be *normed* for this population. Interpretation of results on any test is based on the normative distribution. For example, a student frequently wants to know how the class performed on a test or quiz so that they have a general idea of where they stand in relation to the group. Similarly, it is important to establish a normative distribution for the given instrument so examiners know where the respondent stands in relation to the group. The development of a normative distribution can be a complicated process. For example, the Wechsler Adult Intelligence Scale—Third Edition (WAIS-III) is based on a national standardization sample representative of the U.S. population taking into consideration age, sex, race/ethnicity, educational level, and geographic region (The Psychological Corporation, 1997).

## Standard Error of Measurement

When we hear a report of a poll on television about how people feel about some issue, the results are reported with a margin of error, typically plus or minus a few percentage points. The margin of error suggests that the actual way respondents feel may be plus or minus a few percentage points of the reported results. Similarly, when an individual takes a test, whether it is a measure of personality or an achievement test, the scores may vary from one testing to the next. There are a number of factors that could affect the scores. These factors could include distractions in the testing environment, fatigue, carelessness, failure to understand the directions, or even preoccupation with other life concerns. The **standard error of measurement** (SEM) indicates how much variation we can expect in a test score each time a person takes a test (Bartol & Bartol, 2004). This is the difference between the *actual score* (the individual's "true" score) and the *observed score*. The SEM is an indication of how much error there is in the test score. This is of particular interest to courts when basing decisions on psychological test scores. Obviously, the lower the SEM the more confidence one can have in that the observed score is an accurate indication of the actual score.

■ **Standard error of measurement**
The amount of variation in a score each time it is assessed, which is considered the result of measurement error.

# Assessment Instruments

Psychological assessment usually involves a variety of instruments and assessment techniques selected by the examiner for the specific purpose. This is a **test battery** and can include measures of intellectual functioning (IQ tests), measures of personality, an interview, and other tests appropriate to the referral question. The following section briefly presents some of the more frequently used assessment instruments.

■ **Test battery**
A group of assessment instruments and techniques selected to answer a specific referral question.

## Measures of Intellectual Ability

Perhaps the most frequently used IQ tests are the **Wechsler scales** (Camara, Nathan, & Puente, 2000). Gregory (1999) has suggested that the Wechsler Adult Intelligence Scale "is *the* cornerstone of adult intellectual assessment" (p. xiii). A majority of experts in the field support the use of the Wechsler scales for intellectual assessment (Lally, 2003). David Wechsler started work on measures of intelligence in 1939. These instruments have been revised and updated periodically, with the most recent revisions appearing in 2004. The Wechsler scales consist of three measures of intellectual ability designed for three different age groups. The Wechsler Preschool and Primary Scale of Intelligence (WPPSI) is designed for children ages 2½ to 7 years, 3 months. The Wechsler Intelligence Scale for Children (WISC) is designed for children ages 6–17, and the Wechsler Adult Intelligence Scale (WAIS) is designed for individuals ages 16–89. The three scales are similar in construction and the following comments apply to all three scales.

The Wechsler scales provide a Verbal IQ and a Performance IQ score as well as a total or Full Scale IQ score. The tests are made up of a variety of subtests assessing the multidimensional aspects of intelligence. Wechsler originally defined intelligence as the "capacity of the individual to act purposefully, to think rationally, and to deal effectively with his environment" (Wechsler, 1944, p. 3). Each subtest taps into an area assumed to comprise intelligence, with the subtests broadly classified into verbal tests and performance tests. Examples of the verbal tests include tests of Vocabulary and Similarities. Examples of the performance tests include Picture Completion (identifying the missing feature in a drawing) and Block Design (arranging color blocks to match illustrated designs).

## Table 3.8    Measures of Intellectual Functioning

**Individual Measures**

- The Wechsler Preschool and Primary Scale of Intelligence
- The Wechsler Intelligence Scale for Children
- The Wechsler Adult Intelligence Scale
- The Standford-Binet Intelligence Scale

**Group Measures**

- The Wide Range Intelligence Test
- The Slosson Intelligence Tests
- The Wonderlic Personnel Test

Another popular intelligence test is the Stanford–Binet Intelligence Scale, now in its fifth revision (SB5). This test consists of 15 subtests measuring cognitive domains assumed to be related to intelligence. The manual provides norms for individuals ages 2–85+. The test is popular among school psychologists due to its appeal to children and is used frequently in the school setting. However, the Wechsler scales appear to be the more common individual measure of intellectual functioning in forensic settings (Ackerman & Ackerman, 1997; Boccaccini & Brodsky, 1999; Lees-Haley, Smith, Williams, & Dunn, 1996).

The Wechsler scales and the Stanford–Binet are all individual measures of intelligence. These instruments are administered by trained examiners and usually require between 60 and 90 minutes to complete. The examiner must be trained in the administration of the test as well as scoring responses. Training usually requires graduate-level coursework in assessment with specific training and supervision on the instrument. Scoring the test and report writing can take an additional 1–2 hours.

Group measures of intellectual functioning are also available. These include paper-and-pencil tests that may be administered to groups of individuals, saving time and expense. Most of the group intelligence tests do not require extensive training to administer. The **Wide Range Intelligence Test** (WRIT) is an example of a test that can be administered to a group of individuals. The test can be used on individuals ages 4–85 and takes approximately 30 minutes to complete. The **Slosson Intelligence Test** can be administered to a similar age range of individuals and takes approximately 15 minutes to complete. Finally, the **Wonderlic Personnel Test** is a 12-minute group intelligence test.

There are obvious advantages to group measures of intellectual functioning. The use of a group test saves time and reduces cost. Additionally, most group tests do not require extensive training in administration and can be administered by an assistant. These tests are frequently used in human resource departments for employment decisions as well as in schools and other mass-testing situations. However, it is best to caution against their use in forensic assessments. In addition to an IQ score, individual measures of cognitive ability provide important information relevant to the legal question and an examiner would lose the richness of this data by relying on a group measure of IQ (Ackerman, 1999).

Most IQ tests produce an IQ score with an average of 100 and a standard deviation of 15 points. A **standard deviation** is a statistic that indicates the amount of variability around the mean. Most psychological constructs, including intelligence, are assumed to follow a normal distribution or bell curve. It is assumed that the majority of people taking the test will fall around the mean and only a few individuals will achieve extreme scores on each end of the distribution. A **normal distribution** indicates that approximately 68% of the population will fall within one standard deviation of the mean (scores between 85 and 115 on an IQ test). Approximately 95% of the population will score within two standard deviations of the mean (scores between 70 and 130). Scores below 70 on an IQ test are one of the criteria for a diagnosis of mental retardation. Approximately 2% of the population will score below 70. The Supreme Court recently ruled that individuals with mental retardation may not be sentenced to death (*Atkins v. Virginia*, 2002).

Measures of intelligence used in a variety of forensic assessments include issues related to competency, child custody, termination of parental rights, personal injury cases, and child protection cases, to name a few. The majority of forensic examiners prefer to use individual measures of intelligence, with most turning to the Wechsler scales (Lally, 2003).

■ **Standard deviation**
The amount of variability among scores on a test around the mean score.

■ **Normal distribution**
The scores of a sample of a population that, when graphed, fall on or close to a normal curve, where the highest frequency is in the middle, and this frequency diminishes the farther you get away from the center on either end.

# Measures of Personality—General

The majority of assessment batteries will also include measures of personality. Personality inventories can take many forms depending on how one defines personality. Since personality is a theoretical construct, it should come as no surprise that there is not a general consensus regarding the definition of personality. This is particularly relevant for the forensic examiner who may be called upon the witness stand to justify the selection of a specific instrument. Rather than struggle to defend a definition of personality in court, the most prudent approach is to use personality assessment instruments that have been demonstrated to meet most of the criteria for selecting forensic assessment instruments. Personality measures are most useful in forensic settings when they assess specific traits or characteristics that are thought to be relevant to the legal question at hand. For example, tests that assess conscientiousness may be assumed to be relevant when a psychologist is asked to assess the suitability of a candidate for police work. Another example would be the assessment of antisocial

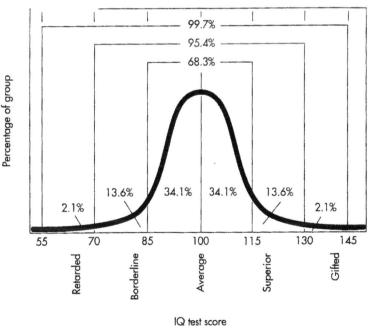

Figure 3.5

The normal curve.

personality features, or psychopathy, when asked to predict the future dangerousness of an individual about to be paroled from prison.

It is worthwhile to reiterate that individual tests are never to be used as the sole basis of any forensic decision. Rather, tests should always be considered as one of many sources of hypothesis for decision making. In fact, tests can be wrong. I had the opportunity to take the Minnesota Multiphasic Personality Inventory (MMPI) while a graduate student in clinical psychology. Much to my dismay and amusement, the resultant MMPI profile was suggestive of schizophrenia. I am happy to report 20 years later that I am still fine with no obvious symptoms of psychosis. The point is that tests are used to generate hypothesis that the forensic clinician can then explore further in an interview and with other collateral sources of information. A test result should not be assumed to be always accurate.

Personality measures may be broadly classified into *objective* and *projective* techniques. The distinction between the two is based on the theoretical development of the instrument as well as the stimuli used to elicit the respondent's answers. Projective techniques rely on the **projective hypothesis**, which assumes that people project their unconscious into their responses to ambiguous stimuli (Rabin, 1981). Examples of ambiguous stimuli include the famous ink blots of the **Rorschach Inkblot Test** as well as incomplete sentence stems (e.g., "My childhood was . . .") or illustrations of people involved in daily activities for which the respondent is asked to create a story. The main principle behind the use of ambiguous stimuli is that there is no right or wrong answer; rather the respondent projects their unconscious into their responses. Projective techniques are usually associated with *psychodynamic* viewpoints of personality, which assume that a great deal of the causes of behavior derives from unconscious motives.

Some authors have suggested that projective techniques are neither reliable nor valid (Grove & Barden, 1999) whereas others have suggested projective techniques have no standard scoring key and thus lack interrater agreement regarding test results. Actually, some projective techniques do lack psychometric reliability, although they may be quite useful clinically, a point to which we'll return shortly. Additionally, some projective techniques have standardized scoring systems increasing interrater agreement. An example would be the Comprehensive System for the Rorschach Inkblot Test (Exner, 1991). It is best to use the Rorschach cautiously, if at all, in forensic settings due to a number of problems with the normative sample (Garb, Wood, Lilienfeld, & Nezworski, 2002). Some projective techniques have no standardized scoring keys, leaving the interpretation of the results up to the individual clinician. Obviously, the lack of a standardized scoring key may allow the biases of the examiner to interfere with an objective interpretation of the respondent's answers.

Objective techniques, on the other hand, use questions that are not ambiguous and for which there is a correct answer for the respondent. Most of these measures are pencil-and-paper "self-report" instruments, the type of which many students are already familiar with. The respondent is asked to answer true or false to statements that describe their attitudes or behavior. Some of these inventories many use a **Likert scale** in which the respondent answers on a scale from, say, 1 to 5, with the range being "strongly disagree" to "strongly agree." In addition to unambiguous questions, the scoring of **objective personality measures** is standardized, usually through the use of a scoring key. Michel and Michel (1977) suggest that an objective personality measure avoids any examiner bias in the administration, scoring, and interpretation of the test. Once norms are established for the test, a forensic psychologist can state that individuals with similar scores have been known to behave in particular ways based on these norms.

■ **Projective hypothesis**
Assumes that people project their unconscious into their responses to ambiguous stimuli and is associated with the use of projective assessment techniques.

## Projective Techniques

Perhaps the most popular example of a projective test is the Rorschach Inkblot Test. This test consists of 10 bilaterally symmetrical inkblots on 5″× 8″ cards, originally developed in 1939 by Herman Rorschach. It is interesting to note that Dr. Rorschach originally had 15 inkblots but could only find a publisher who agreed to print the manuscript if the number of cards was reduced to 10. Respondents are asked to describe what they "see" in the inkblots. This is an excellent example of asking individuals to make sense of an ambiguous stimulus (the inkblot) with the expectation that their response reflects their unconscious. There are a number of scoring systems for the Rorschach Inkblot Test (e.g., Beck, Beck, Levitt, & Molish, 1961; Exner, 1991). Contrary to popular opinion, the interpretation of the test is not based on the image the individual reports. Rather, there are complex scoring guidelines based on characteristics of the examinee's responses, such as whether they report movement in the image or describe an animate versus an inanimate object. Norms have been established for the response characteristics and the clinician can then report that the examinee's responses are similar to the responses of other individuals who have a particular diagnosis or personality trait.

### Common Projective Measures of Personality                    Table 3.9

- Rorschach Inkblot Test
- Thematic Apperception Test
- Children's Apperception Test
- Rotter's Incomplete Sentences Blank

Another popular projective technique is the Thematic Apperception Test (TAT). This test consists of 29 cards (8″× 11″) with illustrations of people engaged in various activities, such as an individual staring out a window or a man and a woman having a discussion. Individuals are usually told that this is a measure of creativity and are asked to make up a story for each of the cards. The examiner may choose to use only some of the cards or may administer, one at a time, all 29 of the cards plus an additional blank card. The respondent is asked to describe what is going on in the scene, what actions preceded the scene, how the scene evolves, and the emotional state of the individuals depicted in the illustration. The clinician then looks for themes throughout the stories presented. It is assumed that any underlying themes reflect unconscious concerns of the respondent. There are variations on the TAT including two versions of a Children's Apperception Test (CAT). One version utilizes color illustrations of children and adults involved in various activities. A second version is for younger children and depicts animals involved in human activities, such as a family of bears dressed in clothes and preparing dinner. The administration and interpretation of these tests are similar to the original TAT.

Another form of a projective technique is Rotter's Incomplete Sentences Blank (Rotter, Lah, & Rafferty, 1992). Respondents are asked to complete 40 incomplete sentence stems. Items attempt to elicit information of clinically relevant issues. An example of an incomplete sentence stem would be: "I am best when . . ." In the Objective Scoring System, responses are coded as Conflict Responses, Positive Responses, or Neutral Responses. Based on the level of conflict expressed or the strength of the positive response, numerical weights ranging from 0 (strong positive) to 6 (severe conflict) are assigned, resulting in an Overall Adjustment Score. The authors argued that the Objective Scoring System is both reliable and valid.

Projective techniques have a number of critics who question the psychometric properties of the tests. Anastasi (1988) has suggested that the interpretation of projective tests may tell us more about the unconscious biases of the examiner rather than the examinee. It is true that many of the projective techniques have failed to meet the minimum standards of reliability and validity expected of psychological instruments (Lilienfeld, Wood, & Garb, 2001). However, it can be argued that these tests do have clinical utility. Additionally, as presented above, no one test should be used for decision making in isolation of other sources of information. It is best to use the results of a test to generate hypotheses that need to be evaluated against other sources of information. If a test is used in this context, the psychometric limitations of the test need

## Projective Techniques and Children

For example, this author had the opportunity to evaluate a 7-year-old boy who was referred to the clinic by the school psychologist. The child, "Jeffrey," had done well in the first grade but was experiencing both academic and behavioral difficulties in the second grade. His grades had deteriorated and he was fighting routinely with other children. The second grade teacher had requested an evaluation by the school psychologist, suspecting that the schoolwork in the second grade was either too easy for Jeffrey and he was bored, or too difficult and he was frustrated. An intellectual evaluation by the school psychologist suggested that Jeffrey was on par with his peers and that his change in behavior was not due to the challenges of the schoolwork. The school psychologist recommended that Jeffrey see a clinical psychologist.

Children at this age have neither the vocabulary nor emotional insight to be able to describe their inner feelings and psychological state. This appeared to be an excellent opportunity to administer a projective technique. Jeffery was asked to make up stories to 10 of the TAT cards selected on the basis of their potential relevance to a 7-year-old boy. As stated above, the clinician looks for similar themes throughout the stories. In Jeffrey's stories, there was a recurring theme of family conflict. Interestingly, in his stories with a young boy as the protagonist, the character was worried about both his parents and younger siblings. It was obvious from Jeffrey's stories that his parents were going through a dif-

ficult time and that their marital discord was affecting his performance in school. However, neither Jeffrey nor his parents indicated any problems at home when asked and certainly did not make the connection between the marital problems and school performance. Armed with Jeffrey's stories, it was easier to consult with the parents regarding the home situation. In true Columbo-like fashion, the stories were presented to the parents with a puzzled expression about what underlying theme may be present and what could it tell us about Jeffrey's emotional state. The parents quickly recognized the effect their arguments were having on Jeffery and the other children and immediately entered into marital therapy.

The above vignette is presented as an example of the clinical utility of a projective technique. Clearly, the information may have been obtained through other means with a similar outcome. However, this is a good example of using the results or interpretation of a test to develop hypotheses about the referral question. Other collateral information is then used to evaluate each hypothesis. When used in this manner, projective techniques can offer valuable information not readily available from other sources. Projective techniques appear to frequently be used with children in child custody evaluations (Ackerman & Ackerman, 1997), though many in the field find the use of projective techniques in forensic evaluations unacceptable (Lally, 2003).

not preclude its use. The use of projective techniques for assessment in forensic settings should be cautiously approached (Garb et al., 2002). Projective techniques should not be discarded and may be useful in therapeutic settings as an aid for exploration.

## Objective Techniques

The most widely used objective personality measure is the Minnesota Multiphasic Personality Inventory (MMPI). The MMPI was first published in 1942 and has been used extensively ever since. It is an excellent example of a paper-and-pencil self-report inventory. Respondents are asked to respond to 566 true or false questions. The questions sampled a wide range of activities, including many questions that lacked face validity for most respondents. Face validity is not a true form of validity but rather indicates the degree to which an instrument *appears* to measure what it says it does. For example, whereas some questions ask about sleep patterns and symptoms associated with depression, other questions covered preference for reading magazines on popular mechanics or preference for reading romance novels or repairing a door latch. Individuals in clinical settings or forensic settings frequently have a difficult time understanding how their enjoyment in repairing a door latch relates to their legal situation. Despite this lack of face validity, the MMPI is the most widely researched personality inventory and has a wealth of normative data associated with its scores.

## Common Objective Personality Measures | Table 3.10

- Minnesota Multiphasic Personality Inventory–2
- Millon Clinical Multiaxial Inventory–III
- Personality Assessment Inventory
- Personality Assessment Screener
- Sixteen Personality Factor Questionnaire

Due to outdated questions and concerns regarding the original normative sample, the MMPI was revised in 1989 (MMPI-2). Questions were updated to replace outmoded expressions that were seen as offensive, such as sexist language. However, researchers were reluctant to drastically change the MMPI since there was such a large body of data associated with the original version. As such, many of the changes in the MMPI-2 appear more cosmetic than substantive and researchers and clinicians readily apply the normative data collected on the original MMPI to individual scores on the MMPI-2.

The original MMPI was designed to identify psychopathology and resulted in three validity scales and 10 clinical scales. The validity scales attempted to assess the response set of the individual taking the test. For example, did the respondent randomly respond to the questions, or attempt to make a particularly favorable impression? The 10 clinical scales assess typical forms of psychopathology, such as depression, schizophrenia, paranoia, and anxiety. These scales were all originally developed using a technique termed **criterion keying**. The original authors of the MMPI, Drs. Hathaway and McKinley, identified a criterion group of patients for the clinical scales as well as a control group. For example, to develop the depression scale, the entire pool

■ **Criterion keying**

Identifying a criterion group and a control group, and using their responses to identify which questions reliably distinguish between the two groups; the method used to develop the MMPI scales.

of 566 true–false questions is administered to 100 patients who are known to have a diagnosis of clinical depression. The same pool of questions is administered to a control group, say 100 individuals who are known *not* to have a diagnosis of depression. The researcher would then identify which questions reliably distinguish between the two groups. For example, the majority of depressed patients may respond true to a particular item whereas the majority of "normals" may respond false to the same item. This item could then be one of the items used to comprise the Depression scale.

| Table 3.11 | MMPI 10 Clinical and Validity Scales |
|---|---|

| Validity Scales | | Clinical Scales | |
|---|---|---|---|
| ? - | Cannot Say Scale | 1 - | Hypochondriasis (Hs) |
| L - | Lie Scale | 2 - | Depression (D) |
| F - | Faking Bad | 3 - | Hysteria (Hy) |
| K - | Faking Good | 4 - | Psychopathic Deviant (Pd) |
| | | 5 - | Masculinity–Femininity (Mf) |
| | | 6 - | Paranoia (Pa) |
| | | 7 - | Psychasthenia (Pt) |
| | | 8 - | Schizophrenia (Sc) |
| | | 9 - | Hypomania (Ma) |
| | | 0 - | Social Introversion (Si) |

There are several interesting features to using this approach. First, it is atheoretical; that is, there is no particular theory offered as to why any one particular item differentiates between groups. Second, the opportunities for scale development are limitless. Researchers could develop scales for a wide range of constructs. Researchers could ask respondents to take the test while attempting to appear "insane," as if they were trying to plea insanity in a criminal case. These responses could then be compared to responses from individuals who did successfully plead insanity. Researchers would then need to identify items that differentiate between the individuals who were told to fake insanity from individuals who were actually judged to be insane at the time of the crime. The result would be a scale that identifies individuals who are attempting to fake insanity. Numerous secondary scales have been developed in just this manner for the MMPI and the MMPI-2 for almost everything, including potential for happiness in marriage (Fowler, 1976). Greene et al. (2002) list over 150 secondary scales for the MMPI-2. However, it is important to note that the majority of these secondary scales have not been well validated (Meyer, 1983). There is also an adolescent version of the MMPI, the MMPI-A, published in 1992.

The MMPI is widely used in forensic settings (Lally, 2003). Studies have found that the MMPI/MMPI-2 is used by forensic psychologists as much as 94% of the time in competency to stand trial evaluations (Borum & Grisso, 1995) and emotional injury evaluations (Boccaccini & Brodsky, 1999) and 92% of the time in child custody evaluations (Ackerman & Ackerman, 1997). Much of its popularity is based on ease of administration and scoring as well as the large normative database that has been developed over the years. The MMPI-2 is simply handed to examinees and they complete the 566 items, typically "bubbling" in their answers to a machine-readable answer sheet. A computer can score the questionnaire and even produce a narrative report. Despite the popularity of it use in forensic settings, there are also several drawbacks. First, the MMPI requires at least a sixth-grade reading level. Second, the length of the questionnaire can be a hindrance for examinees who may tire of the tedium of answering over 500 true–false questions and start to respond to the items haphazardly. This is compounded by the lack of face validity for the items, which only increases the frustration of all but the most determined test-takers.

Another popular objective personality measure is the Millon Clinical Multiaxial Inventory, now in its third version (MCMI-III; Millon & Davis, 1994). However, clinicians recommend the use of the older, 175-item MCMI-II for use in forensic assessments (Ackerman, 1999; McCann & Dyer, 1996). This instrument is based on Millon's personality theory and assesses 13 personality styles that closely match the *personality disorders* of the fourth edition of the *Diagnostic and Statistical Manual of Mental Disorders* (**DSM-IV**; American Psychiatric Association, 2000a) as well as nine clinical syndromes seen in a variety of treatment settings, including forensic. Like the MMPI, the **MCMI** also has several validity scales to assess response styles that may call into question the validity of the results. An advantage of the MCMI is that it is shorter than the MMPI, requiring about 20–25 minutes to administer. The MCMI is reported to be used in slightly over 30% of forensic evaluations (Ackerman & Ackerman, 1977; Boccaccini & Brodsky, 1999; Borum & Grisso, 1995). The MCMI appears to be particularly useful in forensic settings for identifying characterological or personality disorders (McCann, 1990) as well as substance abuse disorders (National

## Clinical Scales for the MCMI-II                                      Table 3.12

### Clinical Personality Patterns

1   Schizoid
2   Avoidant
3   Dependent
4   Histrionic
5   Narcissistic
6A  Antisocial
6B  Aggressive-sadistic
7   Compulsive
8A  Passive-aggressive
8B  Self-defeating

### Severe Personality Pathology

S   Schizotypal
C   Borderline
P   Paranoid

### Clinical Syndromes

A   Anxiety
H   Somatoform
N   Bipolar: Manic
D   Dysthymia
B   Alcohol dependence
T   Drug dependence

### Severe Syndromes

SS  Thought disorder
CC  Major depression
PP  Delusional disorder

Institute on Alcohol Abuse and Alcoholism, 1995). Additionally, there are specific resources available for the application of the MCMI-II to forensic assessment (McCann & Dyer, 1996).

A much briefer objective personality measure is the Personality Assessment Screener (PAS; Morey, 1991). This brief screening instrument is a 22-item self-report inventory that includes a validity scale along with scores on 10 scales measuring "potential problem areas in mental health." These scales include forensically relevant constructs such as Anger Control, Hostile Control, Acting Out, and Alcohol Problem. The PAS is a shorter version of the 344-item Personality Assessment Inventory (PAI; Morey, 1991). This scale has been shown to be useful in predicting the potential for alcohol abuse, aggression, and suicide. Both the PAS and PAI can be machine-scored along with a computer-generated narrative report. The ease of administration of the PAS makes this a particularly useful instrument for generating hypotheses in a forensic evaluation.

Another commonly used objective personality measure is the Sixteen Personality Factor Questionnaire (16 PF; IPAT Staff, 1972). The 16 PF, developed primarily by Raymond Cattell and Herbert Eber, is commonly used to assess personality patterns. There are several different forms of the test, though Form A is the most commonly used version. It has 187 items and allows three response choices including *undecided*. The questionnaire takes approximately 50 minutes to complete and can be either machine- or hand-scored. Along with the 16 personality trait subscales, the 16 PF can be scored for faking good or faking bad (Myers, 1983). This allows for the opportunity to detect the possibility of malingering, an important consideration in forensic settings.

## Table 3.13    Sixteen Personality Factor Trait Subscales

| | |
|---|---|
| A | Sizothymia (reserved) v. Affectothymia (outgoing) |
| B | Lower scholastic mental capacity (Less intelligent) v. Higher scholastic mental capacity (More intelligent) |
| C | Lower ego strength (Affected by feelings) v. Higher ego strength (Emotionally stable) |
| E | Submissiveness (Humble) v. Dominance (Assertive) |
| F | Desurgency (Sober) v. Surgency (Happy-go-lucky) |
| G | Weaker superego strength (Expedient) v. Stronger superego strength (Conscientiousness) |
| H | Threctia (Shy) v. Parmia (Venturesome) |
| I | Harria (Trusting) v. Premsia (Tender-minded) |
| L | Alaxia (Trusting) v. Protension (Suspicious) |
| M | Praxemia (Practical) v. Autia (Imaginative) |
| N | Artlessness (Forthright) v. Shrewdness (Astute) |
| O | Untroubled adequacy (Self-assured) v. Guilt proneness (Apprehensive) |
| Q1 | Conservatism of temperament (Conservative) v. Radicalism (Experimenting) |
| Q2 | Group adherence (Group-dependent) v. Self-sufficiency (Self-sufficient) |
| Q3 | Low integration (Undisciplined self-conflict) v. High strength of self-sentiment (Controlled) |
| Q4 | Low ergic tension (Relaxed) v. High ergic tension (Tense) |

In summary, there are a number of commercially available personality inventories available for the forensic clinician to include in the assessment armamentarium. The choice of using a general personality measure in a forensic assessment depends on the issues that need to be addressed and the clinician's familiarity with the instrument as well as the criteria discussed above. It should be noted that while tests are commercially available, they are sold only to professionals appropriately trained to administer, score, and interpret psychological tests. Psychological tests are rated according to the qualification level needed by the individual using the test. Qualification level A requires no specialized training. Qualification level B requires a 4-year college degree in psychology or a closely related field as well as coursework in psychological testing or a closely related area. Qualification level C requires all qualifications for level B plus an advanced professional degree with appropriate training in administration and interpretation of psychological tests. Tests like the Rorschach, TAT, MMPI, and PAI all require qualification level C. Companies typically require documentation of one's qualifications before they will sell any restricted tests. The purpose of restricting the sale of tests to only qualified individuals is obvious. This prevents tests from being misused while also protecting the integrity of the test materials.

# Measures of Personality—Forensically Relevant Instruments

Now we can turn to our next category of assessment measures, forensically relevant instruments. Otto and Heilbrun (2002) describe forensically relevant instruments as tests that focus on clinical issues that are relevant to forensic evaluations. Unlike forensic assessment instruments, which are developed to address specific legal questions (i.e. competency to stand trial), a forensically relevant instrument may also be used outside of the forensic setting. For example, a test of malingering is categorized as a forensically relevant instrument (Bartol & Bartol, 2004).

Malingering has been defined by the American Psychiatric Association in the DSM-IV as the "intentional production of false or grossly exaggerated physical or psychological symptoms" (1994, p. 683). It is obvious that a criminal defendant may be motivated to produce false psychological symptoms in the hopes of avoiding prosecution. It is just as likely that a plaintiff filing a personal injury lawsuit may be motivated to feign physical and emotional trauma in the hopes of winning a large financial settlement. Forensic psychologists need to always be alert to the possibility of malingering. The development of tests to detect malingering is particularly useful in this regard.

Once again it is best to understand the real value of tests as generators of hypothesis that need to be tested against other sources of information. Although some authors have suggested that no *single* instrument has been particularly successful in the detection of malingering (Bartol & Bartol, 2004), some currently available instruments are useful in alerting the clinician to the possibility. The forensic psychologist should not base any decisions on only one source of information. It is best to use a variety of methods to obtain information. If several different instruments along with reports from collaterals as well as past history all suggest the presence of malingering, the examiner will have a stronger presentation on the witness stand than relying on any one source of information.

Additionally, the detection of malingering in an evaluation does not necessarily suggest that the examinee has no psychological symptoms. An individual may attempt to exaggerate symptoms in order to make a stronger or more compelling case for their claim. For example, consider the hypothetical case of a married man and father of four who is wrongly accused of child sexual abuse. He may lose custody of his children and certainly experience a great deal of strain in his marriage. Depending on his job, he may be terminated or required to take an unpaid leave of absence. Friends and neighbors will most certainly judge him differently, regardless of the trial's outcome. If he is wrongly accused and the prosecution withheld evidence that would exonerate him, he may have grounds for a lawsuit. In his lawsuit, he may seek compensation for psychological damages suffered as a result of the ordeal. He may indeed have experienced psychological trauma resulting in depression and anxiety. However, he may feel that it is necessary during the examination with the forensic psychologist hired by the defendant to exaggerate his symptoms. If the psychologist is successful in detecting the malingering, it would be necessary to report back to the court the severity of the psychological damages and the presence of malingering. Thus, the forensic psychologist would be faced with the difficult task of teasing apart the actual symptoms from the feigned, or malingered, symptoms.

Several instruments have been developed to assess malingering of psychiatric symptoms and cognitive impairments. Although these instruments lend themselves to use in forensic evaluations, individuals may also feign symptoms in other than legal settings. For example, as an intake worker at a crisis center, it was necessary to identify homeless individuals who were searching for a comfortable place to stay for the night from individuals who were experiencing true psychiatric problems. Several instruments used to assess the presence of malingering are reviewed below.

The Miller Forensic Assessment of Symptoms Test (M-FAST; H. A. Miller, 2001) is a brief 25-item screening interview to detect feigned psychiatric illness. The M-FAST is a brief interview that can be used to quickly screen individuals for the possibility of malingering and indicates if there is the need for the use of a more extensive evaluation for malingering. The M-FAST identifies response styles that are characteristic of individuals who feign psychiatric illness. The test has seven subscales that are reported to successfully identify individuals attempting to feign psychiatric symptoms:

1. Reported vs. Observed Symptoms,
2. Extreme Symptomatology (ES),
3. Rare Combinations (RC),
4. Unusual Hallucinations (UH),
5. Unusual Symptom Course (USC),
6. Negative Image (NI), and
7. Suggestibility (S).

Another brief screening instrument for the detection of malingering is the Rey Visual Memory Test (Lezak, 1983; Rey, 1964). This is simply 15 items presented on a sheet of paper in 3 columns by five rows. The 15 items are extremely common (i.e., 1, 2, 3; A, B, C; a, b, c; a circle, square, and triangle; and I, II, III) and typically would be recalled by most individuals. The examinee is told that it is a test of memory and is asked to look at the items for a specified period, anywhere from 10 to 60 seconds. This period can be timed with a stopwatch to increase the "perceived" validity of the task. The examinee is then asked to write down all the items they observed. In reality, the task is quite simple. Very few individuals will miss more than six of the items regardless of psychiatric symptoms (Goldberg & Miller, 1986). Individuals who are unable to recall more than eight items are most certainly feigning or suffering from a severe neurological disorder or mental retardation that would be obvious without any need for testing. A cutoff from seven to nine has been suggested to distinguish likely malingerers from individuals suffering from brain injury (Lee, Loring, & Martin, 1992).

Both of these screening instruments, as well as many others that focus on detecting malingering, work on the substantiated premise that the majority of individuals

## Detection of Malingering

For example, this writer had the opportunity to conduct a criminal responsibility evaluation on a gentleman who had shot and killed a man. His lawyer had requested a competency to stand trial evaluation and a criminal responsibility evaluation. The man was brought to the evaluation by his wife. He was using what can loosely be called the "I don't remember defense." He simply stated that he did not recall the event in question. However, he went on to state that he did not recall who he was or what he did for a living. He could not even recall how he arrived at the interview!

He was under the naive impression that if he did not recall anything about the incident he would not be charged. He was administered the Rey Visual Memory Test. Not only could he only recall 2 of the 15 items after viewing the sheet for 60 seconds but he also reported that he remembered other items that were not on the test. No individual, regardless of psychopathology or cognitive impairment, would perform so poorly. As is frequently the case, individuals attempting to feign a psychological disorder exaggerate their symptoms to an almost ludicrous degree.

feigning psychological symptoms exaggerate their symptoms. The majority of individuals suspect that people with a mental illness or cognitive impairment are "obviously" disturbed. Therefore, individuals attempting to feign mental illness typically behave in an extreme manner.

A more thorough measure of malingering is the Structured Interview of Reported Symptoms (SIRS; Rogers, Gillis, Dickens, & Bagby, 1991). This is a 172-item structured interview that can be administered in less than 60 minutes. Of the 172 items, 32 are repeated to detect inconsistency in responses. The interview is appropriate for individuals 18 years old or older and focuses on detection of individuals feigning psychological disorders and the way this feigning is likely to occur. For example, the subscales may suggest an exaggeration of symptom severity as opposed to the reporting of improbable and/or absurd symptoms (Rogers, 1988). Thus, if a malingering screening instrument such as the Rey Visual Memory Test suggested the possibility of malingering, the examiner may wish to then administer a more thorough instrument such as the SIRS.

In addition to instruments that assess malingering, we can also add several personality measures to the category of forensically relevant instruments. Examples include the Substance Abuse Subtle Screening Inventory (SASSI) and the Hare Psychopathology Checklist—Revised (PCL-R; Hare, 2003). These two instruments are frequently used in forensic evaluations for the assessment of substance abuse disorders and antisocial personality features, respectively.

The SASSI is a brief screening instrument administered in self-report format. It identifies individuals who have a high probability of having a substance abuse disorder and also provides information to select appropriate treatment. The SASSI is available in English and Spanish and requires a fifth-grade reading level and can be used with individuals 18 years old or older. There is also an adolescent version (SASSI-A2) that can be used with individuals from 12 to 18 years old. Both tests can be administered in individual or group format and takes less than 15 minutes to administer and only about 5 minutes to score.

The PCL-R is a semi-structured interview used to assess psychopathic or antisocial personality traits in adults 18 years old or older. The scale is specifically designed to identify criminal psychopaths in forensic populations and is used in 60,000–80,000 evaluations annually (Otto & Heilbrun, 2002). The PCL-R is a 20-item symptom construct rating scale based on information obtained through a semi-structured interview and review of collateral information. The interview consists of 125 questions and can take approximately 90–120 minutes to complete. A collateral review is mandatory to score the PCL-R and usually takes about 60 minutes to complete, depending on the amount of information available. The type of collateral information varies depending on the setting. For example, in a correctional facility, information such as prison files, police reports, criminal records, presentence reports, court transcripts, institutional logs, intake reports, and parole or probation records would be available. In forensic psychiatric and pretrial settings, police reports as well as interviews with family, friends, arresting officers, and results of any psychological or medical testing may be available. The PCL-R is based on two major facets of psychopathology: the callous, selfish, remorseless use of others and a chronically unstable and antisocial lifestyle. The scoring is based on a dimensional measure of psychopathology as opposed to a categorical measure. Thus, individuals are not classified as either psychopath or nonpsychopath but rather are placed on a continuum based on the amount of psychopathic features the individual displays. There is also a briefer form called the Psychopathology Checklist: Screening Version (PCL:SV). The PCL:SV consists of a semi-structured interview of approximately 85 questions and takes approximately 60–90 minutes to administer. The PCL:SV does not use collateral information and thus can be used in settings in which no criminal background information is available, as in personnel selection for law enforcement, correctional work, or military recruiting (Hart, Cox, & Hare, 1995). There is also a youth version of the PCL-R (PCL-R:YV) for adolescents age 13 years and older. The research group is also working on a French-Canadian version as well as a self-report version (Hart et al., 1995).

# Forensic Assessment Instruments

Forensic assessment instruments, first defined by Grisso (1986), are those instruments "that are directly relevant to a specific legal standard and reflect and focus on specific capacities, abilities, or knowledge that are embodied by the law" (Otto & Heilbrun, 2002, p. 9). These tests address specific legal questions such as competency to stand trial, competency to waive *Miranda* rights, civil competency, and allegations of child abuse, child custody issues, and criminal responsibility. These instruments constitute the backbone of most forensic assessments and are usually restricted to use by clinicians involved in forensic work. These measures are only briefly introduced here, as they are covered in more depth in the following chapters related to each specific form of assessment.

There has been a proliferation of forensic assessment instruments in the past decade. Heilbrun et al. (2000) identified a minimum of 33 assessment instruments developed for forensic work during the 1990s and contrasts that with only 10 forensic instruments developed prior to 1990. Some of this rapid development of instruments may be due to increased awareness of the need for forensic assessment instruments and some of the increase may be prompted by economic considerations. Regardless of the reasons, the rapid proliferation of forensic assessment instruments has not been without problems. Previously, research on forensic assessment instruments was published in journal articles and clinicians wishing to use the instrument would need to obtain a copy from the author. Through this process some instruments developed a following of researchers who would publish data on the instrument. Other tests that were not adopted were simply forgotten (Otto & Heilbrun, 2002). More recently, there are numerous commercially available instruments. Publishers of psychological tests have tapped into the forensic market. Many of these instruments have not been rigorously developed and lack the necessary research to support their use (Heilbrun et al., 2000). The *Standards for Educational and Psychological Testing* (American Educational Research Association, American Psychological Association, & National Council on Measurement in Education, 1999) requires that test instruments have comprehensive test manuals describing the psychometric properties of the tests, normative data, and administration and scoring standards. However, many tests lack the comprehensive manuals, adequate normative sample sizes, proper validation studies, and psychometric properties discussed earlier in this chapter (Heilbrun et al., 2000).

Forensic assessment instruments addressed specific legal questions. Perhaps the most common forensic assessment is the competency to stand trial evaluation. It is estimated that over 25,000 requests for a competency to stand trial evaluation are made annually (Steadman & Hartstone, 1983). The determination of whether an individual is competent to stand trial is a legal question based on case law known as the Dusky standard. This two-prong standard asks "whether the defendant has sufficient present ability to consult with his attorney with a reasonable degree of rational understanding; and a rational as well as factual understanding of proceedings against him" (*Dusky v. United States*, 1960, p. 402). Other forms of competency include competency to waive *Miranda* rights, competency to plead guilty, competency to be sentenced, competency to be executed and civil competence. The assessment of competency to stand trial is covered in detail in Chapter 4.

Another area that has spawned forensic assessment instruments is the evaluation of criminal responsibility, commonly referred to as the insanity plea. Again, case law has established several standards that are used to determine criminal responsibility. Perhaps the most frequently cited assessment instrument for criminal responsibility is the Rogers Criminal Responsibility Scales (R-CRAS; Rogers, 1984). These scales are used by the clinician to rate the defendant regarding possible malingering, the presence of organic impairment, mental retardation, symptoms of mental illness, cognitive impairment, and loss of behavioral control at the time of the offense. These are all factors that relate to the various standards determined by the courts to consider a defendant insane at the time of the offense. The assessment of criminal responsibility is covered in depth in Chapter 4.

Yet another area that has prompted the development of forensic assessment instruments is child custody evaluations in divorce proceedings. Child custody evaluations can be quite litigious by their very nature. During an acrimonious divorce, parents can use custody proceedings as a tool to harm the "other side." This acrimony can make the custody evaluation a particularly high-risk endeavor for the psychologist. The parent who feels they did not receive a fair decision can bring malpractice charges against the psychologist. In fact, the APA (1994) has published guidelines to be used in child custody evaluations. Prompted in part by the number of frivolous lawsuits brought against psychologists by disgruntled parents, Florida and West Virginia have past immunity laws protecting psychologists who followed the APA guidelines in child custody evaluations. The laws stipulate that any civil action filed against a psychologist must cite a specific breach of APA's guidelines. Failure to cite the breach is cause for dismissal (Greer, 2004).

Forensic psychologists spend an average of 30 hours on each custody evaluation and charged approximately $2,600 for the evaluation in the late 1990s (Ackerman & Ackerman, 1997). The burden of using instruments that will withstand the scrutiny of the court system is immense. In a survey of doctoral-level psychologists who conduct child custody evaluations, Ackerman and Ackerman (1997) found that the most frequently used custody tests were the Bricklin Perceptual Scales (Bricklin, 1984) for children and the Ackerman–Schoendorf Scales for Parent Evaluation of Custody (ASPECT; Ackerman & Schoendorf, 1992) for adults. However, these scales have not been without their critics (Melton et al., 1997; Otto & Helibrun, 2002). Child custody evaluations will be discussed in detail in Chapter 6. Melton et al. (2007) as well as Goldstein (2007) provide two excellent compendiums on forensic assessment with numerous case examples and sample reports.

Recently, several authors have proposed a principles-based approach to forensic mental health assessment (Heilbrun, Marczk, DeMatteo, & Mack-Allen, 2007). It is suggested that a principles-based approach will improve the quality of forensic practice. The authors suggest that this approach will

1. improve training of mental health professionals conducting forensic evaluations,
2. have a positive impact on research and theory development in forensic assessment, and
3. could assist in shaping policy, both within the legal arena and the practice of forensic assessment.

The authors proposed 29 principles covering four areas of forensic mental health assessment: Preparation, Data Collection, Data Interpretation, and Communication. Some of the principles put forth are considered *established* within the profession whereas others are viewed as *emerging* principles. These authors note that the work on the principles is continuing as the field of forensic mental health assessment evolves. Students interested in pursuing a career in forensic assessment will undoubtedly become acquainted with these developing principles.

## Table 3.14    Principles of Forensic Mental Health Assessment

### Preparation
1. Identify relevant forensic issues
2. Accept referrals only within area of expertise
3. Decline the referral when evaluator impartiality is unlikely
4. Clarify the evaluator's role with the attorney
5. Clarify financial arrangements
6. Obtain appropriate authorization
7. Avoid playing the dual role of therapist and forensic evaluator
8. Determine the particular role to be played within the forensic assessment if the referral is accepted
9. Select the most appropriate model to guide date gathering, interpretation, and communication

### Data Collection
10. Use multiple sources of information for each area being assessed
11. Use relevance and reliability (validity) as guides for seeking information and selecting data sources
12. Obtain relevant historical information
13. Assess clinical characteristics in relevant, reliable, and valid ways
14. Assess legally relevant behavior
15. Ensure that conditions for the evaluation are quiet, private, and distraction-free
16. Provide appropriate notification of purpose and/or obtain appropriate authorization before beginning
17. Determine whether the individual understands the purpose of the evaluation and the associated limits on confidentiality

## Data Interpretation

18. Use third-party information in assessing response style
19. Use testing when indicated in assessing response style
20. Use case-specific (idiographic) evidence in assessing clinical condition, functional abilities, and causal connection
21. Use nomothetic evidence in assessing causal connection between clinical condition and functional abilities
22. Use scientific reasoning in assessing causal connection between clinical condition and functional abilities
23. Do not answer the ultimate legal question
24. Describe findings and limits so that they change little under cross-examination

## Communication

25. Attribute information to sources
26. Use plain language; avoid technical jargon
27. Write report in section, according to model and procedures
28. Base testimony on the results of the properly formed forensic mental health assessment
29. Testify effectively

Source: A principles-based approach to forensic mental health assessment by Heilbrun et al. (2007) p. 50. In A. M. Goldstein (Ed.), *Forensic psychology: Emerging topics and expanding roles.* New York: Wiley.

# Summary

This chapter has covered basic issues related to forensic assessment. Assessment in criminal and civil cases was discussed. Important differences between clinical assessment and forensic assessment were presented. Clinical assessment differs from forensic assessment along the following dimensions: purpose of the evaluation, examiner–examinee relationship, who is the client, motivation of the examinee, the written report, the psychologist's cognitive mindset, professional accountability, and temporal focus of the assessment. Basic psychometric properties related to testing were reviewed and included reliability, validity, normative group, and standard error of measure. These were discussed in detail and the concept of a correlation coefficient was covered. Three classifications for tests as they relate to forensic work were presented. These classifications are clinical measures and assessment techniques, forensically relevant instruments, and forensic assessment instruments. Measures of intellectual functioning were reviewed along with projective and objective measures of personality. Examples of commonly used tests were presented for each category.

# TEST YOUR KNOWLEDGE

1. A test can be
   a. reliable but not valid
   b. valid but not reliable
   c. if it is not valid, it cannot be reliable
   d. if it is reliable, then it must be valid

2. The standard error of measurement indicates
    a. the validity of a test
    b. an indication of the amount of error in a test or measure
    c. how well the examinee did on the test.
    d. all of the above

3. Which of the following is *not* a standard of proof?
    a. Clear and convincing evidence
    b. Beyond a reasonable doubt
    c. Relevance-of-truth standard
    d. Preponderance of the evidence
    e. All of the above are used in civil or criminal trials

4. *Dusky v. United States* (1960) established the standard for
    a. criminal responsibility
    b. sexual predators
    c. incarceration of the mentally ill
    d. competency to stand trial

5. Instruments that have been developed outside of the forensic arena but have direct applicability to addressing forensic questions are classified as
    a. clinical measures and assessment instruments
    b. forensically relevant instruments
    c. forensic assessment instruments
    d. none of the above

Answer Key: (1) a, (2) b, (3) c, (4) d, (5) b

# Chapter Four

# Insanity Pleas and Competency Evaluations

## Key Terms

- Adjudicative competency
- Affirmative defense
- American Law Institute
- ALI Standard
- Antisocial personality disorder
- Beyond a reasonable doubt
- Brawner rule
- Burden of proof
- Clear and convincing proof
- Cognitive prong
- Competency evaluation
- Competency restoration
- Competency Screening Test
- Competency to stand trial
- Competency to Stand Trial Assessment Instrument (CAI)
- Decisional competence
- Delusions
- Duress
- Durham rule
- Dusky standard
- *Dusky v. United States* (1960)
- *Farretta v. California* (1975)
- Foundational competence
- Georgia Court Competency Test
- Guilty But Mentally Ill (GBMI)
- *Godinez v. Moran* (1993)

*(continued)*

## Learning Objectives

- Define *mens rea*.
- What burden of proof is used in the competency to stand trial hearing?
- Who can raise the issue of competency to stand trial?
- What burden of proof is used in the criminal responsibility hearing?
- Who can raise the issue of criminal responsibility?
- How often is the insanity defense used? How often is the insanity defense successful?
- What types of defendants are most successful with the insanity plea?
- Be able to describe the various standards for criminal responsibility including the McNaughten Rule, Durham Standard, the Brawner Rule, the "policeman at the elbow test," and the ALI Standard.
- Be able to explain the decisions related to the following court rulings: *Jackson v. Indiana* (1972), *Dusky v. United States* (1960), *Godinez v. Moran* (1993).
- What are some of the ethical considerations for a forensic psychologist conducting a competency to stand trial or criminal responsibility evaluation?
- What happens to individuals found incompetent to stand trial?
- What happens to defendants found not guilty by reason of insanity?
- What is the difference between GBMI and NGRI?
- What crime prompted Congress to pass the Insanity Defense Reform Act and what are the major outcomes of this law?
- Who decides if a defendant is competent to stand trial? Who decides if a defendant is criminally responsible?
- How are defendants found incompetent to stand trial brought to competency?
- What is the distinction between the ultimate and penultimate issue? Can psychologists testify on the ultimate issue? What does the APA suggest regarding testimony on the ultimate issue?
- What is an MSO evaluation?

## Key Terms *(continued)*

- Hallucinations
- Incompetent to stand trial (IST)
- Informed consent
- Insanity
- Insanity Defense Reform Act
- Irresistible impulse test
- *Jackson v. Indiana* (1972)
- MacArthur Competence Assessment Tool—Criminal Adjudication (MacCAT-CR)
- McNaughten Rule
- *Mens rea*
- Mental state at time of the offense (MSO)
- Model Penal Code
- Not guilty by reason of insanity (NGRI)
- *Pate v. Robinson* (1966)
- Policeman at the elbow test
- Preponderance of the evidence
- Product rule
- Provocation
- Restoration to competency
- Rogers Criminal Responsibility Assessment Scales
- Trier of fact
- Ultimate issue
- Volitional prong
- *Westbrook v. Arizona* (1966)
- Wild beast knowledge test

Forensic psychologists and psychiatrists are routinely asked by the courts to conduct criminal responsibility evaluations and **competency to stand trial** evaluations. Though these two evaluations are frequently combined, they should be viewed and conducted as two separate evaluations. This chapter reviews the case law and issues involved in conducting criminal responsibility evaluations, commonly referred to as the insanity plea. The chapter also addresses the issue of **competency evaluations**. Perhaps the most common competency evaluation conducted by a forensic psychologist is competency to stand trial. Previously it was estimated that over 25,000 requests for a competency to stand trial evaluation were made annually (Steadman & Hartstone, 1983). Estimates that are more recent suggest that 60,000 criminal defendants are annually evaluated with respect to competence (Bonnie & Grisso, 2000). This number takes on perspective in light of the estimate that of the 30,000 psychiatrists in the United States, fewer than 1,000 practice forensic psychiatry (Caplan, 1984).

# Criminal Responsibility

Criminal responsibility evaluations are commonly known as the insanity plea by the public. An insanity plea is termed an **affirmative defense.** An affirmative defense means that the commission of the crime is not disputed. Rather, the defendant claims that committing the offense is attributed to special circumstances, such as insanity, duress, necessity, provocation, or extreme emotional disturbance (Ewing, 2000). With a defense of **duress**, the defendant claims that there was a threat of death or harm, the defendant reasonably believed that the threat was real, that the only way to avert death or injury was to commit the act, and that the defendant was not at fault for placing themselves in the situation. A defense of *necessity* is based on the belief by the defendant that he or she faced imminent harm, the defendant was not at fault for creating the situation, and the harm imposed by the criminal act must be less than the harm avoided. A defendant may also claim an affirmative defense based on **provocation**. The defendant claims that he or she was provoked to commit the act and that any reasonable person would have behaved the same way. For example, a defendant may admit to shooting his wife's paramour when he caught them in bed together. Although he would not be found innocent of the crime, a defense of provocation may

■ **Affirmative defense**

Defendant admits guilt, but claims he did not possess "mens rea" at the time of the offense. Examples include self-defense, insanity, and committing a crime under duress.

■ **Duress**

Unlawful threat or coercion used to cause another to act in a manner that they otherwise would not.

reduce a murder charge to a manslaughter charge. The "mere words rule" states that words alone are not sufficient to support a provocation defense. An *extreme emotional disturbance* defense was developed to remedy flaws in the provocation doctrine. This defense states that there is a reasonable explanation for the defendant's extreme emotional state and can be used to reduce a murder charge to manslaughter. For example, a father referred for a criminal responsibility evaluation was charged with murder. The father had arrived home to find his 12-year-old daughter being sexually molested by his 40-year-old neighbor. As the neighbor ran from the house, the father shot him in the back. The father claimed that he did not know if he hit the neighbor. The neighbor was found dead several days later not far from where he had been shot. The father did not meet the legal criteria for insane at the time of the offense. However, his lawyer did decide to plea extreme emotional disturbance, arguing that there was a reasonable explanation for his behavior at the time of the offense.

## Affirmative Defenses    Table 4.1

- *Duress*, the defendant claims that
  - (1) there was a threat of death or harm
  - (2) the defendant reasonably believed that the threat was real
  - (3) that the only way to avert death or injury was to commit the act
  - (4) the defendant was not at fault for placing themselves in the situation.
- *Necessity*, the defendant claims
  - (1) the belief by the defendant that he or she faced imminent harm,
  - (2) the defendant was not at fault for creating the situation
  - (3) the harm imposed by the criminal act must be less than the harm avoided.
- *Provocation/passion doctrine*
  - an intentional murder is reduced to voluntary manslaughter if the defendant can demonstrate that they were in the "heat of passion" due to a provocation that would have caused a reasonable person to be in that state.
- *Extreme mental or emotional disturbance*, defendant claims
  - there is a reasonable explanation for the defendant's extreme emotional state
    - can be used to reduce a murder charge to manslaughter
    - developed to remedy flaws in the provocation/passion doctrine.

When a person meets the legal criteria for being insane at the time of the offense, they are not considered criminally responsible. The astute reader will note three important issues related to the insanity defense. First, the definition of insanity is a legal term, not a mental health term, and the defendant must meet the legal definition of being insane. The exact definition of insanity varies by jurisdiction. Each state has its own statutes regarding criminal responsibility, though several standards do exist, which are discussed later in this chapter. Not everyone who suffers from a mental illness is judged by the courts to be insane. Indeed, many individuals who suffer from a psychosis and

■ **Delusions**

Irrational beliefs, such as believing that one is being controlled by powerful transmissions from another planet; often associated with severe mental illness.

■ **Hallucinations**

Hearing, seeing, or feeling things that are not actually present, typically associated with severe mental illness.

■ **Burden of proof**

The necessity of proving facts in dispute, the burden of proof typically rests with the prosecution in criminal trials *(beyond a reasonable doubt)* and the plaintiff in civil trials *(preponderance of the evidence)*.

■ **Beyond a reasonable doubt**

A standard of proof of such convincing nature that one would be willing to rely upon it in his or her own personal affairs; typically defined as a belief to a moral certainty.

■ **Clear and convincing proof**

A level of proof or persuasion that produces a firm belief as to the facts; greater than *a preponderance of the evidence* but not as strict as *beyond a reasonable doubt*.

■ **Preponderance of the evidence**

The evidence for one side is more convincing than the evidence for the other side; the lowest burden of proof. Used in competency evaluations as well as civil court.

commit a crime do not meet the legal criteria for insanity. Second, the insanity plea is based on the defendant's state of mind at the time of the offense. The forensic psychologist is faced with the challenge of determining the defendant's mental state at the time of the offense (MSO). The difficulty that this poses is that the criminal responsibility evaluation may take place months or even years after the criminal act occurred. Therefore, although an assessment of the individual's present state is necessary, it is also important to obtain collateral information regarding the defendant's behavior at the time of the offense. It is not uncommon to assess individuals who are legally sane at the time of the assessment, but were psychotic with **delusions** and **hallucinations** at the time of the offense. Delusions are irrational beliefs, such as believing that one is being controlled by powerful transmissions from another planet. Hallucinations are hearing (auditory), seeing (visual), or feeling (tactile) things that are not actually present. The most common form of hallucinations is hearing voices. Sometimes the voices tell the person to do certain acts and are termed command hallucinations. Frequently after an individual is arrested, they receive treatment in jail while awaiting the legal proceedings. At the time of the assessment by a forensic psychologist, the defendant may have recovered from the psychotic episode and may even express dismay and surprise at his or her current predicament. Finally, insanity pleas only occur in criminal court; it is not an issue that is raised in civil proceedings.

# *Mens Rea*

There are two elements to all crimes: *actus reas* and *mens rea*. *Actus reas* is the criminal act. This can also include omissions of behavior that result in a criminal act. For example, Good Samaritan laws require the first individual who comes upon the scene of an accident to render assistance; failure to render assistance is a criminal offense. *Mens rea* is the mental element of a crime and refers to the criminal state of mind. In the legal system, an individual must possess *mens rea*, or a "guilty mind," to be found guilty of a crime. A broad definition of *mens rea* refers to the defendant's state of mind at the time of the offense. There are a few exceptions to the *mens rea* element, such as bigamy or statutory rape. Guilt for a crime requires both the commission of the act along with understanding the implications of the behavior. Thus, very young children are typically not held accountable for their behavior, as most people would suggest that a 5-year-old child does not understand right from wrong. Similarly, we do not hold friends accountable for an act if we recognize it was an unintended accident. Thus, if I hit my friend's thumb with a hammer while they are helping me hang a picture, my friend may not blame me for the offense, although they may not help me hang pictures in the future. Better yet, they may elect to be the one with the hammer in hand. However, sometimes we are not sure of our friend's intention and may be uncertain of how to proceed. Or, we may feel that they were partly responsible even though they did not intend for us to get hurt. The point is that there are many shades of gray when attempting to determine "intent." The same issues arise when attempting to determine *mens rea*. In determining guilt, there has to be both free will and intent to do harm (*Durham v. United States*, 1954).

It is worthwhile to note that not all forensic evaluations come down with an unequivocal yes or no answer. Rather, the decision is typically based on the amount of evidence for one decision versus the other. In legal terms, this is called the **burden of proof**. There are three levels of burden of proof used in the courts. The highest level, **beyond a reasonable doubt**, is used in criminal court. This is the level of proof that falls just short of certainty. The intermediate standard, required in some civil proceedings, is **clear and convincing proof**. The lowest level of proof is the **preponderance of the evidence**. This is when one side has more evidence in its favor than the other side. The Supreme Court ruled that states could require defendants to prove their *incompetence to stand trial* by a preponderance of the evidence but no more than that. However, it is a different standard for *criminal responsibility*. The federal government and most state courts previously required defendants to prove their **insanity** by a preponderance of the evidence, the lowest standard. After the unpopular acquittal of John Hinckley, Jr. for the attempted assassination of President Ronald Reagan and others (*United States v. Hinckley*, 1982), the U.S. Congress passed the federal **Insanity Defense Reform Act** (1984). Among other changes, the Act placed the burden of persuasion on the defendant to prove *insanity* by clear and convincing evidence (Goldstein et al., 2003).

■ **Insanity**

A legal term addressing a defendant's culpability for a crime. Different standards are used in different jurisdictions, such as the McNaughten standard and the Durham standard.

## Burden of Proof: Three Levels                                    Table 4.2

**Beyond a Reasonable Doubt**

"In evidence means fully satisfied, entirely convinced, satisfied to a moral certainty."

**Clear and Convincing Proof**

"Clear and convincing proof will be shown where the truth of the facts asserted is highly probable."

**Preponderance of the Evidence**

"Evidence which is of greater weight or more convincing than the evidence which is offered in opposition to it; that is, evidence which as a whole shows that the fact sought to be proved is more probable than not."
(Black, 1990)

# Myths Regarding the Insanity Defense

Research suggests that the public has several misconceptions regarding the insanity defense (Melton et al., 1997). There is a general misconception among the public that the insanity plea is frequently used in the courts to allow defendants to go free. When asked, most students will estimate that the insanity plea is used anywhere from 25 to 50% of the time in criminal cases. Additionally, the public also feels that it is generally successful as a way to avoid incarceration. One study found that the public thought the insanity plea was used as a ploy in nearly 50% of all criminal cases and that it was successful approximately 20% of the time (Pasewark & Pantle, 1981). Actually, the plea of **not guilty by reason of insanity** is used in approximately less than 1% (Silver, Cirincione, & Steadman, 1994) to 3% of all criminal cases (Golding, Skeem, Roesch, & Zapf, 1999). The insanity defense is used much less frequently than generally thought. It also has a much lower success rate than most people believe. Several studies have found that the plea is successful (termed *not guilty by reason of insanity*, or NGRI) approximately 25% of the time (Cirincione, Steadman, & McGreevy, 1995; Golding et al., 1999). Approximately 70% of the insanity acquittals are the result of a plea bargain or similar arrangements rather than through a jury trial (Melton et al., 1997). This is not too surprising in light of the fact that juries tend to hold negative attitudes toward the insanity defense (Ballis, Darley, Waxman, & Robinson, 1995). Furthermore, research demonstrates that defendants found NGRI tend to spend more time incarcerated in a psychiatric facility than they would have spent in a correctional facility had they been found guilty of the crime (Golding et al., 1999; Silver, 1995).

| Table 4.3 | Myths Regarding the Insanity Plea |
|---|---|

- ■ *Myth*: The insanity plea is used excessively by criminal defendants.
- ■ *Reality*: The insanity plea is used in approximately 1–3% of criminal cases.

- ■ *Myth*: The insanity defense is almost always successful.
- ■ *Reality*: The insanity defense is successful in approximately 25% of times it is used. Since the insanity defense is used so infrequently, its actual success rate is less than one-half of 1% of criminal cases.

- ■ *Myth*: Individuals acquitted by reason of insanity go free or spend very little time in jail.
- ■ *Reality*: Individuals acquitted of insanity spend more time incarcerated in psychiatric facilities than do individuals found guilty of the same crime.

# Historical Perspectives of the Insanity Defense

The notion that the mentally ill are not to be held responsible for criminal behavior has existed for centuries. However, the evolution of this standard has changed over time with an increase understanding of mental illness as well as a change in how society judges individual responsibility. One of the earliest legal notions of insanity is termed "Lord Hale's dictum" (Maudsley, 1898). This was essentially the notion that individuals who are *partially insane* (lunacy) are held accountable for their actions whereas individuals who are *perfectly insane* (idiots) are not held accountable. Thus, if a person could handle their affairs, then they could not claim insanity. In a trial in 1723, this doctrine was enunciated as follows: "It is not every kind of frantic humour, or something unaccountable in a man's actions, that points him out to be such a madman as is exempted from punishment: it must be a man that is totally deprived of his understanding and memory, and doth not know what he is doing, no more than an infant, than a brute or a wild beast; such a one is never the object of punishment" (Maudsley, 1898, p. 96).

This doctrine may be considered the "**wild beast knowledge test**"—did the accused have any more understanding of their behavior, all of their behavior all the time, than a wild beast. If they did have more understanding than a wild beast, then they would be deemed criminally responsible and found guilty. However, this standard gradually changed to a requirement to understand the difference between right and wrong. In a trial in 1812, Bellingham was found guilty of murder and executed. However, during the trial, Chief Justice Mansfield stated, "It must be proved beyond all doubt that at the time he committed the atrocious act, he did not consider that murder was a crime against the laws of God and nature." The wild beast knowledge test was subtlety changed in the early 1800s to a test of knowing the difference between right and wrong at the time of the offense.

This approach continued to be used until a sensational trial in 1843. Daniel McNaughten suffered from delusions believing that members of the governing Tory Party were following him, blasting his character, and plotting to murder him (Maudsley, 1898; Moran, 1981). (In the literature, there are several different spellings, including M'Naghten and McNaughton.) McNaughten traveled to London with the intention of killing the Tory Prime Minister, Sir Robert Peele. Instead, he mistakenly killed Peele's secretary, Edward Drummond. McNaughten pled insanity and was subsequently acquitted of the murder, being found not guilty by reason of insanity. McNaughten had conducted business a short time before the murder and had demonstrated no apparent signs of insanity throughout his daily activities. McNaughten was committed to the Broadmoor asylum for the insane and remained there for the rest of his life.

McNaughten's acquittal led to a public outcry, led by Queen Victoria herself. There had been a series of assignation attempts on the Queen's ministers, members of the English royal house, and on the Queen herself. The possibility that criminals making assassination attempts against public figures could escape punishment on the grounds of insanity outraged the Queen. Public indignation was so high that the House of Lords called the Judges of England to the House to explain their decision (Finkel, 1980). This debate led to the so-called **McNaughten rule.** The McNaughten rule states that:

> To establish a defense on the ground of insanity, it must be clearly proved that, at the time of the committing of the act, the party accused was laboring under such a defect of reason, from disease of the mind, as not to know the nature and quality of the act he was doing: or, if he did know it, he did not know he was doing what was wrong. (Maudsley, 1898)

This McNaughten standard was widely adopted in the United States after its adoption in English law. This standard has two issues the courts must consider in finding someone legally insane. There must be a defect of reason caused by a mental disease that prevents the defendant from knowing either the nature and quality of their actions or its wrongfulness. Thus a defendant can be excused of criminal behavior if, as a result of a "disease of the mind,"

1. the defendant did not know what he was doing (e.g., believed he was slaughtering a pig as he killed a human) or
2. did not know what he was doing was wrong (e.g., believed it was "right" to kill prostitutes).

Knowing the nature or quality of an act requires interpretation by the courts. Extreme examples are helpful to illustrate the concept, but frequently cases are not so clear-cut. For example, a defendant who runs a wooden stake through his son's heart believing that by doing so he will free his son from possession of a vampire clearly does not know the nature and quality of the act. Similarly, a manic individual who is delusional and believes that he is making a police training film when he involves the police in a high-speed chase does not understand the nature and quality of his actions. Both these examples are fairly straightforward based on the first prong of the McNaughten standard.

As another example, suppose a defendant delusionally believes that their neighbor is controlled by alien beings who are plotting the destruction of the planet. The defendant believes the only way to save the planet is to kill his neighbor. The defendant understands that it is wrong to kill his innocent neighbor; after all, it is not his neighbor's fault that the aliens have taken over his mind. On the other hand, by killing his neighbor, he can save the entire planet from alien domination. In one sense, the defendant understands the quality and nature of his actions. On the other hand, the rationale is bizarre and out of touch with reality. A court would need to decide between a narrow interpretation of the McNaughten standard versus a broader interpretation. The interpretation of understanding the nature and quality of an act depends on social, moral, and legal issues (Goldstein et al., 2003).

The second prong of the McNaughten rule addresses the issue of knowing right from wrong. There is debate as to whether this addresses the issue morally wrong or legally wrong. The more common interpretation by the courts is moral wrongfulness (Goldstein et al., 2003). The individual did not know what they were doing was wrong if they did not understand that the act would offend the mores of society. For example, some individuals may claim that it is morally acceptable to kill physicians who perform abortion. However, they may also recognize that their view is not accepted by society and would be judged to understand the wrongfulness of their behavior.

The McNaughten rule is the standard for defining insanity in approximately one-third of the states. However, it is primarily a cognitive test and does not consider the ability to control behavior. As a result, several states adopted an **irresistible impulse test** for cases in which an individual may understand the difference between right and wrong but lacked the capacity to control their behavior. An irresistible impulse test, or control test, addresses criminal behavior that may be the result of disorders of impulse control, such as intermittent explosive disorder. However, the difficulty is determining how strong an impulse must be before it can be resisted. Indeed, what is the difference between an irresistible impulse and an impulse that one decides not to resist? If you need to study this evening, but decide to go out with friends at the last minute, was that an irresistible impulse? Some states adopted the informal "**policeman at the elbow test**" to evaluate the irresistible impulse. Essentially, the criterion is whether the defendant would have committed the act had a police officer been standing at their side. However, most legal experts and forensic clinicians were dissatisfied with this test, primarily based on the difficulty with assessing it, and it is now rarely used.

The abandonment of the irresistible impulse test left many states with a strictly cognitive standard for determining legal insanity. Some critics of this approach felt that many individuals with mental illness would be convicted of crimes that are the result of delusional beliefs. If an individual knew right from wrong but felt compelled to obey command auditory hallucinations, he may be found legally sane under a purely narrow interpretation of a cognitive standard. However, a broad interpretation of the McNaughten rule would find him insane, in that obeying command auditory hallucinations is out of touch with reality. It was inevitable that modifications to the law would occur.

Both the legal profession and the psychiatric community were dissatisfied with the McNaughten rule. The case of Monte Durham gave Judge Bazelon of the U.S. Court of Appeals, District of Columbia Circuit an opportunity to reform the McNaughten rule. Durham, who had a long history of criminal behavior and psychiatric problems, was convicted of robbing a house in 1951. His lawyer appealed the decision, stating that the McNaughten rule was obsolete. By this time, the influence of psychiatry was spreading and psychoanalysis was becoming a household word. The U.S. Court of Appeals overturned the conviction and stated that a new standard would be used for the determination of insanity. Judge Bazelon stated that the widest authority should be provided to expert evaluation and expert testimony by the psychiatric community. The **Durham rule**, also known as the **product rule**, stated "that an accused is not criminally responsible if his unlawful act was the product of a mental disease or mental defect."

The Durham rule, enunciated in 1954, was initially applauded as progress in dealing with the criminally insane. It also led to an influx of mental health professionals into the courtroom as expert witnesses (Wrightsman et al., 2002) and is perhaps partially responsible for the growth of forensic psychology. Several years later, the American Psychological Association successfully argued against the American Psychiatric Association's attempt to prevent psychologists from qualifying as mental health experts in U.S. courts. The American Psychological Association submitted a brief as a friend of the court (*amicus curiae brief*) arguing clinical psychologists were qualified to reach "informed decisions as to the nature and existence of mental disease or defect in a given subject and as to the causal relationship or lack thereof between such mental disease or defect and the subject's overt behavior" (*Jenkins v. United States*, 1962). A ruling in favor of the psychiatrist's position would have been a serious setback for the emerging field of forensic psychology. Although this ruling pertained only to the role of psychologists as expert witnesses in criminal responsibility cases, it clearly paved the way for psychologists to testify as expert witnesses to a wide variety of issues within their scientific expertise (Ewing, 2003).

However, the Durham rule was not without its detractors. It was difficult for experts to agree if a particular act was the product of a mental disease. Additionally, experts were not able to agree on what constituted a mental disease or defect. For example, alcoholics or drug addicts could claim that their behavior was the result of a mental disease and thus should be acquitted of criminal conduct related to their illness. Courts were also weary of the role that mental health professionals were playing in the decision-making process of the court. Insanity defenses inevitably led to a battle of the experts, pitting one expert witness against another. In 1962 the courts attempted to reign in the experts by restricting the definition of mental disease or defect to "any abnormal condition of the mind which substantially impairs mental or emotional processes and substantially impairs behavioral controls" (*McDonald v. United States*, 1962).

Further restrictions were placed on the role of mental health experts in the courts by the United States District Court in the case of *Washington v. United States* (1967). The influence of mental health professionals in the court room was increasing and many judges felt that these experts were hijacking the role of the **trier of fact** (the judge or jury). In court proceedings, the *trier of fact* is tasked with making decisions regarding the **ultimate issue.** In this example, mental health experts were no longer able to address the ultimate issue, that is, did the mental illness "cause" the criminal behavior in question. Rather, mental health experts could testify about whether the defendant had a mental illness and address questions in general about mental illness, but could not address the issue that is traditionally left to the judge or jury to decide.

■ **Ultimate issue**
The final question that must be decided by the court; usually left to the trier of fact to decide (i.e., guilt or innocence).

Frustration continued with the Durham standard and it was eventually overruled by the Federal Court of Appeals in the District of Columbia in 1972 (*United States v. Brawner*, 1972). Judge Bazelon, writing for the U.S. Court of Appeals, ended what he had started 18 years earlier in 1954 with the Durham rule (Bartol & Bartol, 2004). In 1962 a group of legal scholars, sponsored by the **American Law Institute (ALI)**, developed the **Model Penal Code**. In 1972 the Bazelon court unanimously repealed the Durham rule and adopted a slightly modified version of the Model Penal Code Rule, also known as the **Brawner rule**. This rule states that:

1. A person is not responsible for criminal conduct if at the time of such conduct as result of mental disease or defect he lacks substantial capacity either to appreciate the criminality (wrongfulness) of his conduct or to conform his conduct to the requirements of the law.
2. . . . the terms "mental disease or defect" do not include an abnormality manifested only by repeated criminal or otherwise antisocial conduct.

There are two important changes to note with the Brawner rule, also known as the ALI standard. The ALI standard contains both a cognitive and a control component. Thus, like all other insanity defense tests, it required the presence of a mental illness (mental disease or defect). However, the ALI standard included a cognitive

| **Table 4.4** | Chronological Order of Rulings Regarding Criminal Responsibility |
| --- | --- |

- *Wild beast knowledge test* (1723) – did the accused have any more understanding of their behavior, all of their behavior all the time, than a wild beast.
- *Justice Mansfield ruling* (1812) – did the defendant know right from wrong.
- *The McNaughten rule* (1843) – "To establish a defense on the ground of insanity, it must be clearly proved that, at the time of the committing of the act, the party accused was laboring under such a defect of reason, from disease of the mind, as not to know the nature and quality of the act he was doing: or, if he did know it, he did not know he was doing what was wrong."
- *Durham rule* (1954), also known as the *product rule*, stated "that an accused is not criminally responsible if his unlawful act was the product of a mental disease or mental defect."
- *Brawner rule* (1972), also known as the ALI standard. This rule states that:
  - A person is not responsible for criminal conduct if at the time of such conduct as result of mental disease or defect he lacks substantial capacity either to appreciate the criminality (wrongfulness) of his conduct or to conform his conduct to the requirements of the law.
  - . . . the terms "mental disease or defect" do not include an abnormality manifested only by repeated criminal or otherwise antisocial conduct.

■ **Antisocial personality disorder (APD):**

A personality disorder listed in the *Diagnostic and Statistical Manual of Mental Disorders* characterized by infringing on the rights of others; includes behaviors such as aggressiveness, deceitfulness, impulsivity, recklessness, lack of remorse, and failure to conform to social norms.

test—"lacks substantial capacity to appreciate the criminality (wrongfulness) of his conduct"—and the control test—"or conform his conduct to the requirements of the law." The ALI standard also recognized differences in jurisdictions regarding the cognitive test and offered the option of "criminality" versus "wrongfulness."

Another important change with the ALI standard was the introduction of the phrase "lacks substantial capacity." No longer were the consequences of mental illness an all-or-none decision. Rather, the ALI standard recognizes that mental illness can be a matter of degree. This change enabled expert witnesses to testify about the degree that a mental illness can influence behavior. The introduction of the word "appreciate" indicated that insanity is more than simple knowledge regarding wrongfulness or criminality, but requires an understanding of the consequences. For example, a 5-year-old may know that it is against the law to kill another. They may also know that shooting another person with a gun can kill the individual. However, if a 5-year-old child was playing "cops and robbers" and shot their sibling using their parent's gun, the courts would not try the 5-year-old child. The term "appreciate" recognizes that the defendant needs to understand the significance and consequences of his or her actions to be found not criminality responsible (Goldstein et al., 2003).

Finally, the ALI standard states that the terms mental disease or defect do *not* include "abnormality manifested only by repeated criminal or otherwise antisocial conduct." This caveat was included to specifically not allow individuals identified as psychopaths and sociopaths to claim insanity. Psychopathy is characterized by a disregard for others' rights and lack of remorse for doing harm to others. Though the DSM-IV does not offer a diagnosis of psychopathy, it does include the diagnosis of **antisocial personality disorder** (APD). APD is characterized by, among other things, repeated infringements on the rights of others including illegal behavior. This section of the ALI standard is usually applied to individuals diagnosed with APD.

The ALI standard appeared to be a popular solution to a long-standing problem. It addressed many issues that were seen as flaws in the other tests for legal insanity and was adopted by numerous states and all but one U.S. Courts of Appeals. However, it was bound to be changed. If you recall, it was the failed assassination attempt by McNaughten on the Tory Prime Minister that led to the establishment of the McNaughten rule. (McNaughten mistakenly killed the Prime Minister's secretary.) The case of John Hinckley, Jr. led to the eventual modifications of the ALI standard.

John Hinckley, Jr. attempted to assassinate President Ronald Reagan and others as a way to impress Jodie Foster, an actor. Hinckley's assassination attempt and belief that he would gain Jodie Foster's attention and love were apparently loosely based on his delusional beliefs related to her portrayal of a prostitute in the film *Taxi Driver*. In the film, a psychotic New York taxi driver, played by Robert De Niro, tries to save the child prostitute, played by Jodie Foster. De Niro's character also becomes infatuated with a political campaigner. When his plans do not work out, he goes on a violent rampage. Apparently, Hinckley's delusions led him to believe that he could gain the affections of Jodie Foster by imitating the violent behavior from the film. He was acquitted of the attempted murder of President Reagan, being found not guilty by reason of insanity. Low, Jeffries, and Bonnie (1986) provide a synopsis and analysis of the Hinckley case.

After Hinckley's acquittal, there was a public outcry due to the fact that Hinckley was not punished for his actions. The ensuing debate in Congress eventually led to the Insanity Defense Reform Act passed by Congress in 1984. Professional organizations offered their opinions. The American Medical Association proposed doing away with the insanity plea altogether while both the American Psychiatric Association and

Figure 4.1

A child who shoots another child playing "cops and robbers" with a real gun would not be prosecuted.
© 2009 Mityukhin Oleg Petrovich. Used under license from Shutterstock, Inc.

## Tests of Legal Insanity | Table 4.5

- *McNaughten standard*
  Did the defendant know what he or she was doing? If so, did they know that what they were doing was wrong in the moral sense?
- *Durham standard (product rule)*
  Was the defendant's action the result (product) of a mental disease?
- *Brawner-ALI standard*
  As a result of mental disease or defect, did the defendant lack substantial capacity to appreciate the criminality of the conduct or to conform their conduct to the requirements of the law?
- *Insanity Defense Reform Act*
  An affirmative defense to a prosecution under any Federal statute that, at the time of the commission of the acts constituting the offense, the defendant, as a result of severe mental disease or defect, was unable to appreciate the nature and quality or the wrongfulness of his acts. Mental disease or defect does not otherwise constitute a defense.

American Bar Association proposed reforming the standard by abolishing the control test. The American Psychological Association did not offer a specific position, but cited the need for more empirical data (Goldstein et al., 2003).

The **Insanity Defense Reform Act** kept the insanity defense in federal courts, but modified the defense, making it more difficult for persons pleading insanity in federal courts to be acquitted. The Act had several major changes to the insanity plea. Among the changes were:

1. it shifted the burden of persuasion onto the defendant to prove legal insanity by clear and convincing evidence;
2. it eliminated the control or volitional component of the insanity standard;
3. it placed a limitation on the role of the expert witness;
4. it established parity between psychologists and psychiatrists in conducting mental state examinations;
5. it excludes any partial affirmative defense based on mental illness.

Each of these reforms are discussed briefly.

Perhaps one of the most influential reforms regarding the insanity defense was shifting the burden of proof onto the defendant. Prior to the Insanity Defense Reform Act, the burden was on the prosecution to prove beyond a reasonable doubt that the defendant was sane. The Act requires the defendant to prove legal insanity by clear and convincing evidence. This standard of proof required of the defendant is less rigorous than proof beyond a reasonable doubt but more rigorous than the standard used in civil law. Civil law merely requires a preponderance of the evidence. It is probable that Hinckley was acquitted due to the state's inability to prove beyond a reasonable doubt that he was legally sane at the time of the offense. The jury heard numerous expert witnesses offer testimony regarding Hinckley's mental state that was consistent with mental illness. This alone would have made it difficult for the jury to rule that he was sane "beyond a reasonable doubt" (Goldstein et al., 2003). The reform of shifting the burden of persuasion to the defendant from the state appears to have reduced the success rate of insanity defenses (Steadman et al., 1993). Since the Insanity Defense Reform Act of 1984, virtually every state, and the federal government, places the burden of proof on the defendant.

Congress eliminated the volitional or control standard of the insanity test. The Act is strictly cognitive; no longer can a defendant claim an inability to conform his or her conduct to the requirements of the law. However, in making this change, Congress broadened the scope of the cognitive test over other standards such as the McNaughten standard. First, the Act states that an individual must have a *severe mental disease or defect*, the change being that the mental illness must be severe. This change probably has had little impact on jury decisions since most defendants who are successful with an insanity defense have a prior history of psychiatric hospitalizations and have been diagnosed with severe forms of mental illness, usually psychoses (Nicholson, Norwood, & Enyart, 1991). Cochrane, Grisso, and Frederick (2001) found that defendants with a diagnosis of psychosis had the highest rates of insanity, followed by affective disorders and mental retardation. The Act kept the term used in the ALI standard: "*appreciate* the nature and quality or the wrongfulness of his acts." As noted above, this allows for a broader interpretation than the term to *know* the nature and quality or the wrongfulness of the act.

The Insanity Defense Reform Act prohibits expert witnesses from giving their opinion on the *ultimate issue*. The ultimate issue is the final question that must be decided by the courts. This decision is up to the trier of fact, either the judge or a jury. The Act states, "No expert witness testifying with respect to the mental state or condition of a defendant in a criminal case may state an opinion or inference as to whether the defendant did or did not have the mental state or condition constituting an element of the crime charged or of a defense thereto. Such ultimate issues are matters for the trier of fact alone." The ultimate issue in an insanity defense case is whether or not the defendant was insane at the time of the crime. The expert witness can describe the defendant's behavior and whether or not this behavior would constitute a diagnosis of mental illness, but they cannot give an opinion on whether or not the defendant met the legal criteria for being insane at the time of the offense. It is important to note that the Insanity Defense Reform Act applies only to federal court, though other jurisdictions have adopted parts of the Act. The question of whether or not an expert witness can testify as to the ultimate issue has been debated for some time and this debate does not look like it will be resolved any time soon (Bonnie & Slobogin, 1980; Morse, 1978; Rogers & Ewing, 1989; Shapiro, 1999). In fact, the APA has not taken a stand one way or the other on the issue, but rather suggests that the forensic psychologist is aware of both sides of the issue and is prepared to justify their own viewpoint.

Courts frequently expect the expert witness to offer an opinion on the ultimate issue, particularly in insanity defense cases, as well as in competency hearings (Melton et al., 1997; Redding et al., 2001). Despite the concerns of some psychologists that expert witnesses will usurp the role of the trier of fact by offering opinion on the ultimate issue (Saks, 1990; Slobogin, 1989), research suggests that this is not the case in insanity defense trials. Fulero and Finkel (1991) examined the effects of the prohibition of ultimate opinion testimony on the outcomes of trials. They looked at trials that had diagnosis-only testimony, trials with penultimate testimony, and trials with ultimate issue testimony and found practically no difference in the outcome. It appears that juries can weigh the opinions of the experts and arrive at their own decisions (Nietzel et al., 1999). Indeed, there is no evidence to suggest that this reform has had an impact on either the use of or success of the insanity defense (Borum & Fulero, 1999). Refer back to Chapter 2 for a detailed discussion regarding the role of expert witness testimony and the issue of ultimate and penultimate decisions.

# Evaluation of Insanity

An evaluation of a defendant's mental state at the time of the offense (MSO) requires multiple sources of data. Each source of data can be used to generate and test hypotheses regarding the defendant's MSO. Just as no one psychological test can provide conclusive information and should only be used to generate hypotheses, different sources of data should be used in the same way. Data sources can include interview, psychological testing, collateral informants, and a thorough review of pertinent records. The forensic evaluation should integrate data from the various sources (Goldstein et al., 2003). Novice forensic psychologists may mistakenly rely on traditional methods of clinical evaluation when conducting a forensic exam. It is not sufficient to conduct an interview with the defendant and administer psychological tests for a criminal responsibility determination. A MSO evaluation requires forming an opinion about the defendant's mental state at the time of the defense, which could be several months or more prior to the evaluation. The forensic expert's final opinion is based on all the available date regarding the defendant's behavior at the time of the offense.

The use of multiple sources of data will invariably produce inconsistencies among data sources. The inconsistencies need to be presented to the trier of fact. Any inconsistencies among data sources should be noted in the report and discussed in terms of conclusions and opinions formed. The forensic psychologist should note any inconsistent or missing information and qualify any conclusions related to missing or inconsistent data. The open presentation of inconsistencies and missing data enhance the credibility of the expert's opinion. The expert is not an advocate for the client, but rather an impartial evaluator. Recall from Chapter 2 the suggestion that impartiality is the best form of advocacy. The expert can increase credibility and waylay a hostile cross-examination by noting and addressing in the report any inconsistencies or shortcomings

**Figure 4.2**

While testifying, a forensic psychologist should note any inconsistent or missing information, and qualify any conclusions related to missing or inconsistent data. This enhances credibility.
Brand X.

in the data used to generate the expert opinion. Potential inconsistencies can arise from a variety of sources for a multitude of reasons. Examples of inconsistencies in data sources include conflicting witness interviews, psychological test data that conflicts with clinical impressions, or conflicts between police reports and the defendant's version of the incident. All inconsistencies need to be noted in the report. Not only does noting all aspects of the data enhance credibility of the expert witness but it is also a requirement of the APA Ethics Code.

A MSO evaluation is an intellectual puzzle. The evaluator needs to obtain and review multiple sources of data in an attempt to reconstruct what an individual's state of mind was months prior to the evaluation. Fortunately, the MSO evaluation only needs to address the psycholegal question of insanity in the particular jurisdiction in which the case is being tried. Numerous obstacles can occur while trying to solve the puzzle. Obstacles include inconsistent or contradictory data sources; missing data; malingering by the defendant; uncooperative or hostile examinees, lawyers, and/or witnesses; defendants with severe mental disorders that prohibit testing; unrealistic deadlines; incarcerated defendants in facilities with poor testing and interview rooms; falsification of information prompted by secondary gain by both defendants and witnesses; and unavailability or unreliability of collateral informants. The use of multiple sources of information helps to mitigate potential shortcomings in reaching an opinion.

A MSO evaluation should include the following data sources: conversations with the retaining and (possibly) opposing attorney; assessment interview with the defendant; psychological testing of the defendant; review of all available records to include police reports and witness statements; medical and psychological history; school records, if relevant; jail records and any examinations conducted during the incarceration or by other mental health professionals; interviews with immediate family members; interviews with friends and coworkers, if warranted, and the arresting officers.

Initially, a conversation with the retaining attorney should be conducted prior to any other data collection. If the forensic psychologist is retained by the court, ideally a conversation with both the defense and prosecuting attorneys regarding the case is conducted. This initial conversation will establish communications with the lawyers involved in the case and give them the opportunity to express any thoughts they may have regarding an insanity plea and why it was requested. In addition, the psychologist can request the lawyers to furnish all relevant records including arrest report, prior medical records, and so on. It is also an opportunity for the forensic psychologist to explain his or her role in the case and to inform/reassure both sides of the forensic psychologist's impartiality in the case.

Before contacting any other principals involved in the case, the forensic psychologists should request and review as many relevant records as possible. Most readily obtainable records typically include the police report with witness' statements, all jail records, and prior criminal records. Some records cannot be obtained until the defendant signs a released form. In the initial conversation with the attorney, the psychologist should attempt to identify any potential relevant records and request the attorney to obtain the necessary signatures. Release forms should be mailed to the attorney immediately after the initial contact.

Prior to meeting with the defendant, the psychologist will want to interview third-party informants. Conducting these interviews prior to meeting with the defendant is for both logistical and assessment purposes. Frequently, defendants are incarcerated in a correctional facility and as a result, access to the defendant is limited. Interviews with third parties can help generate hypotheses regarding the defendant's MSO and guide both questioning of the defendant and choice of assessment instruments. Interviews with third-party informants should include the arresting officers, witnesses identified from the police report, immediate family members, and any health care professionals who were involved with the defendant's treatment. Many of these interviews can be conducted over the telephone and do not need to be recorded. However, the clinician should take copious notes and use verbatim quotes from witnesses in the report when indicated. Verbatim quotes help to convey both the content and the essence of the respondents' answers. Interviews with other third-party informants may be indicated depending on the case. Examples include school officials, jail personnel, coworkers, and acquaintances such as church members or club members.

Prior to conducting any interviews, the psychologist should attempt to review as many records as possible. It typically is the case that during the course of an interview with either the defendant or a third party, the issue of other records may arise that will also need to be reviewed after the interview is completed. However, reviewing records prior to the interview helps to generate hypotheses that can be pursued during the interview. Records can typically be obtained through the lawyers, courts, and law enforcement. Records to be reviewed include police reports, witness statements, jail records, and hospital records. Other records that may be appropriate can include prior treatment records, any recent psychological or psychiatric records, school records, military records, work records, and any records from other organizations with which the defendant may have had contact. For example, in one case, a defendant had telephone contact with the FBI, CIA, and Secret Service reporting his delusional beliefs regarding drug smugglers. These organizations were able to provide transcripts of these telephone contacts indicating dates that supported the opinion that the defendant suffered a gradual deterioration of his mental state prior to the offense. Some records may be available without a release, such as police records. Other records can only be obtained with a signed release from the defendant. Typically, the attorney can obtain the necessary signature on forms sent to him or her by the psychologist.

**Figure 4.3**

It is important for the psychologist to review as many records as possible before meeting with the defendant.
© 2009 Steven Coburn. Used under license from Shutterstock, Inc.

| Suggested Psychological Test Battery for Mental State at the Time of the Offense Evaluation | Table 4.6 |
|---|---|

- Wechsler Adult Intelligence Scale–III
- Minnesota Multiphasic Personality Inventory–2
- Rogers Criminal Responsibility Assessment Scales
- Millon Clinical Multiaxial Inventory–III
- Personality Assessment Inventory
- Rey Fifteen Item Visual Memory Test
- Structured Interview of Reported Symptoms

In preparing for the evaluation with the defendant, it is important to select a variety of assessment instruments to comprise the psychological test battery. The test battery should consist of tests appropriate to the psycholegal referral question. The referral question as well as hypothesis generated by third-party information guides the selection of the assessment instruments. Most forensic psychologists recommend at minimum the use of a measure of intellectual functioning and an objective personality test. The most frequently used test for intellectual functioning is the current version of the Wechsler Adult Intelligence Scale (WAIS). The Minnesota Multiphasic Personality Inventory–2 (MMPI–2) is the most frequently used personality measure. However, these two tests would be insufficient as a test battery. The forensic examiner should not rely on only one instrument in forming an opinion. Other personality measures can include the Personality Assessment Inventory or Personality Assessment Screener and the Millon Clinical Multiaxial Inventory (MCMI-III) as a measure of personality disorders and characterological traits. Some forensic psychologists find neuropsychological assessments acceptable. It is recommended to screen for neuropsychological impairment and if warranted, to refer for a full neuropsychological test battery. An examiner may want to include a measure of malingering such as the Rey Fifteen Item Memory Test or the Structured Interview for Reported Symptoms. If either of these instruments suggests malingering, a more thorough evaluation should be conducted, as multiple measures should be used to detect malingering (Heilbrun, Marczyk, & DeMatteo, 2002).

One instrument that is recommended for MSO evaluations is the **Rogers Criminal Responsibility Assessment Scales** (R-CRAS; Rogers, 1984). The R-CRAS is a forensic assessment instrument developed to "provide a systematic and empirically based approach to evaluations of criminal responsibility" (Rogers, 1984, p. 1). The R-CRAS is actually a rating scale in which the examiner uses multiple sources of information in a systematic way to evaluate the psycholegal question of criminal responsibility. The R-CRAS has 25 variables, which the examiner uses to rate the defendant on issues related to criminal responsibility. See Table 4.7 for a list of the 25 variables from the R-CRAS. The forensic examiner uses all the sources of information gathered, including one or more clinical interviews with the defendant, to answer each of the variables. Note that none of the variables by themselves is exculpatory, that is, proving the defendant is free of guilt. The R-CRAS is completed by the forensic examiner immediately after the last interview with the defendant after all the records have been reviewed and collateral interviews completed. The R-CRAS provides a decision tree that the examiner can use, if he or she wished, to determine whether the legal standard for insanity is met. The R-CRAS also provides a decision tree to determine if the defendant meets the ALI standard of insanity or if they meet the **Guilty But Mentally Ill** (GBMI) standard. The R-CRAS has attained adequate construct validity in several studies (Rogers & Sewell, 1999; Rogers, Wasyliw, & Cavanaugh, 1984).

It is important to note that many of the psychological tests presented above require quite a bit of time to complete. For example, the WAIS can require anywhere from 45 to 75 minutes to administer. The defendant might require an additional 45 minutes to complete the MMPI-2 and approximately 35 minutes to complete the MCMI-III. A neuropsychological test battery can require between 6 and 8 hours to administer, although this is often not warranted. When selecting psychological assessment instruments, the forensic psychologist needs to consider the defendant's education level, reported mental state, general health, and the testing facility. For example, physically frail defendants, due to either age or health, may not be able to tolerate long assessment sessions without a rest. Defendants with poor reading skills or visual impairments will have difficulty completing the paper-and-pencil tests such as the MMPI-2 and MCMI-III. The forensic psychologist may need to conduct the assessment at the facility where the defendant is incarcerated. Some jails and prisons have very poor testing rooms lacking privacy, quiet, and even an adequate desk for completing tests, which can all interfere with optimal test performance. The other alternative is to have law enforcement escort the defendant, usually in handcuffs and shackles along with the orange prison jumpsuit, to the psychologist's office. Though possible, this can prove disruptive to other professionals and clients using the same office suite.

## Variables Rated on the Rogers Criminal Responsibility Assessment Scales (Rogers, 1984, pp. 25–32)

Table 4.7

- Reliability of the patient's self-report, which is under his voluntary control.
- Involuntary interference with the patient's self-report.
- Level of intoxication at the time of the alleged crime.
- Evidence of brain damage or disease.
- The relationship of brain damage to the commission of the alleged crime.
- Mental retardation.
- The relationship of mental retardation to the commission of the alleged crime.
- Observably bizarre at the time of the alleged crime.
- General level of anxiety at the time of the alleged crime.
- Amnesia for the alleged crime.
- Delusions at the time of the alleged crime.
- Hallucinations at the time of the alleged crime.
- Depressed mood at the time of the alleged crime.
- Elevated or expansive mood at the time of the alleged crime.
- Patient's level of verbal coherence at the time of the alleged crime.
- Intensity and appropriateness of affect during the commission of the alleged crime.
- Evidence of formal thought disorder at the time of the alleged crime.
- Planning and preparation for the alleged crime.
- Awareness of the criminality of his/her behavior during the commission of the alleged crime.
- Focus of the alleged crime.
- Level of activity in the commission of the alleged crime.
- Responsible social behavior during the week prior to the commission of the alleged crime.
- Patient's reported self-control over alleged criminal behavior.
- Examiner's assessment of the patient's self-control over alleged criminal behavior.
- Was the loss of control over the criminal behavior a result of a psychosis? Additional Assessment Criteria for GMBI and M'Naghten Standards
  - Impaired judgment on the basis of a mental disorder during the period of the alleged crime.
  - Psychopathologically-based impairment of behavior at the time of the alleged crime.
  - Impaired reality testing at the time of the alleged crime.
  - Capacity for self-care of personal and home-environmental needs at the time of the alleged crime.
  - Awareness of the wrongfulness of the alleged criminal behavior.

Prior to the start of the interview, the forensic psychologist must obtain signed **informed consent.** Informed consent differs from simple consent in that the examinee is informed of all uses of the information to be provided. Informed consent is crucial in all aspects of providing psychological services, as indicated in the APA Ethics Code (2002). For example, practitioners have provided written consent forms for clients to complete prior to entering outpatient therapy (Pomerantz & Handelsman, 2004). However, as discussed in Chapters 2 and 3 of this text, the forensic assessment differs in a number of ways from the provision of therapeutic services. Forensic psychologists must take extra precautions to ensure that the individual being examined has a complete and accurate understanding of how the information will be used.

In a criminal responsibility evaluation, the information the defendant provides, or does not provide, can make a difference between liberty and incarceration and even life or death. A good practice is to obtain signed inform consent on a sheet indicating the limits of confidentiality. The form should be clearly written in easy-to-understand language. Bullet points indicating the limits of confidentiality, to whom the information may be disclosed, under what circumstances the information may be disclosed, and the fact that disclosure of information may be used against the defendant are all important facts to convey to the defendant. The examiner can ask the defendant to read aloud each bullet point. This provides the examiner with a rough estimate of the defendant's reading ability. The examiner should then ask the defendant to paraphrase each bullet point in his or her own words. This ensures comprehension of the informed consent form and provides a rough estimate of the defendant's reading comprehension. The clinical impressions of reading ability and comprehension only serve to indicate if further evaluation of these skills is required.

Once informed consent is obtained, the interview and psychological testing can proceed. The examiner can use a structured interview to obtain a psychosocial and medical history. Starting with this line of questioning, which is less threatening than discussing the alleged criminal offense, helps to establish rapport. The psychosocial history should cover the defendant's early childhood; relationships to parents, siblings, and significant others; school performance; dating and sexual development; peer interactions and friendships; and employment history. Examiners should specifically ask about any history of physical or sexual abuse, alcohol or drug use, fights or violent behavior, psychological treatment, difficulties in school or work performance, and interactions with the legal system. History of any psychiatric or psychological treatment should be explored in detail as well as any family history of a mental illness. It is important to note that mental illness often goes undetected and untreated; therefore, merely asking about treatment is insufficient. It is more informative to ask about symptoms associated with significant mental illnesses such as depression, mania, and psychosis.

The examiner may decide to intersperse the interview with psychological testing. For example, the examiner may conduct a 1-hour interview, followed by a brief break and then the intellectual assessment. This can be followed by more time devoted to the interview and then another break. It is important to have all testing scored before the end of the interview, or to provide for testing to be completed prior to the interview. Either way, psychological tests provide their optimal value when the examiner can use the results to generate hypotheseses that he or she can then evaluate with the examinee. Testing provides information about the defendant's intellectual and psychological functioning at the time of testing, not a portrayal of the defendant's functioning at the time of the offense. However, it can provide valuable insight into enduring behavior patterns that may be relevant to the defendant's MSO. For example, intellectual functioning and personality disorders are conceptualized as enduring characteristics that do not fluctuate over time. In addition, attempts at malingering and current psychopathology add data to the evaluation that needs to be considered in formulating the final opinion.

A unique part of the forensic MSO interview is the defendant's version of the offense. Once rapport has been established, the examiner should ask open-ended questions to obtain an uninterrupted account of the offense. The examiner can then clarify any details regarding the defendant's version of the events. After a full, detailed description of the alleged offense is provided, the examiner can explore any discrepancies between third-party reports and the defendant's version. In the final report, the examiner must address any inconsistencies or contradictions among the various sources of data. It is helpful to have a detailed description of the defendant's behavior prior to and after the offense. In addition, a full explanation as to why the defendant committed the offense is crucial to determining the defendant's MSO (Goldstein et al., 2003).

All of the various sources of data are integrated into a comprehensive report. The report should present the referral question, collateral sources of information including third-party interviews, records and any video or audio tapes reviewed, tests administered and their results, the defendant's demographic and psychosocial history, the defendant's narrative of the offense, and the expert's opinion and a rationale as to how the opinion was derived. As discussed previously, the report may or may not address the ultimate issue. Additionally, forensic examiners may or may not render a DSM diagnosis. Some authors have suggested that a diagnosis not be included as individuals who are not mental health professionals may misunderstand the diagnosis (Golding & Roesch, 1987; Grisso, 1986). See Tables 4.8 and 4.9 for sample criminal responsibility reports. These actual reports have been altered to maintain the confidentiality of individuals involved.

## Sample Criminal Responsibility Evaluation    Table 4.8

DATE

The Honorable Judge
Southern County Circuit Court
Main Street

RE: Defendant
DOB: mm/dd/yyyy

Judge:

Defendant is a 40-year-old single, black female charged with Assault–First Degree. Specifically, she is alleged to have splashed Liquid Fire, a liquid drain cleaner, onto another woman's face, incidentally splashing five other bystanders. Ms. Defendant is referred per your order for evaluation of her criminal responsibility at the time of the alleged crime. A previous evaluation has found her competent to stand trial. At the time of the evaluation, Ms. Defendant was in the Southern County Detention Center. I met with Ms. Defendant on Date. Defendant is informed that the results of the evaluation will be released to the court and that the results may be used against her in court. Ms. Defendant gave her written consent to be evaluated

PSYCHOLOGICAL EVALUATION

Instruments Administered:

Wechsler Adult Intelligence Scale
Minnesota Multiphasic Personality Inventory–2
Millon Clinical Multiaxial Inventory–II
Whitaker Index of Schizophrenic Thinking

*(continued)*

Sample Criminal Responsibility Evaluation (*continued*)

Bender Visual Motor Gestalt Test
Trail Making Test
Carlson Personality Survey (CPS)
Rogers Criminal Responsibility Assessment Scale

Interviews Conducted:

Defendant
- Defense Attorney
- Prosecuting Attorney
- Arresting Officer
- Arresting Officer
- Ms. Defendant's church minister
- Witness, acquaintance
- Witness 1
- Witness 2
- Witness 3
- Witness 4
- Psychiatrist for the defense

Records Reviewed:

Police Case Summary – Arresting Officer
Mental Status Evaluation – Southern Care Center (Date)
Competency to Stand Trial Evaluation – Correctional Psychiatric Facility (Date)
Initial Assessment, Physical, Discharge Summary – Correctional Psychiatric Facility (Date, Date)
Psychosocial Evaluation – Correctional Psychiatric Facility (Date)
Psychological Evaluation – Correctional Psychiatric Facility (Date)
Psychiatric Evaluation – (Date)
Notes from conversation between Ms. R, Ms. Defendant's sister, and E. (Date)

Psychosocial History:

Only limited information is available regarding Ms. Defendant's background. She is a lifetime resident of the state. Her mother died of cancer at the age of 79 on Date. Her father, L. Defendant, is 84 years old and is a retired farmer. Ms. Defendant has five living sisters, four brothers, and two deceased siblings. Three of her sisters have received inpatient psychiatric treatment. One sister lives in Close Town, one in Europe with her husband who is in the military, and one sister died in a drowning accident. One brother committed suicide by hanging himself. There is no history of psychiatric problems among the other brothers.

Ms. Defendant completed tenth grade. She is literate. Ms. Defendant worked on an assembly line for 5 years until 1988 when the factory closed. She then worked at an office-cleaning job. Her reasons for leaving this position are vague. She was unemployed for several years and supported by her family. She lives in rent-free government housing. Her church pastor, Reverend, arranged for her to get employment at Helpful Industries through the vocational office at State Psychiatric Hospital. She was employed at Helpful Industries for approximately 2 months prior to the incident.

Ms. Defendant has never married. She has a 13-year-old son who lives with his father.

Psychiatric History:

Ms. Defendant denies any previous psychiatric treatment. Family members and individuals who know Ms. Defendant state that she has a long history of psychiatric symptoms such as loose associations and persecutory delusions. Ms. Defendant's sister, Ms. Sister, reports that Ms. Defendant has been violent in the past, threatening her niece with a knife. Her emotional difficulties were also apparently common knowledge among her congregation. As stated above, Ms. Defendant has a positive family history for psychiatric illness. Ms. Defendant is currently on haloperidol, an antipsychotic medication.

Ms. Defendant denies any alcohol or substance abuse. She states that she has one previous arrest for prostitution in 1975. She spent 6 months in jail for this offense.

Report of the Crime:

When asked to report what happened, Ms. Defendant states, "It happened so fast, I just remember I threw it on her. I didn't mean to." She continues, "I threw Liquid Fire on her. She was always causing me trouble. (Q) She was picking with me all the time. (Q) Sometimes she would step on my feet." "I didn't mean to do it, it happened so quick I didn't understand myself." "That morning when I went to church, I was standing by a table and she came over, starting trouble with me." (Q) Came over and said, "My Name."

Ms. Defendant was guarded in her responses and at one point asked what the court would do with her if she said she "just didn't know why I did it." Her report conflicts with several eyewitness reports. All the eyewitnesses interviewed claimed that Ms. Defendant yelled at Ms. Victim. Mr. Witness 1 states that Ms. Defendant approached Ms. Victim and said, "I'm getting sick and tired of you picking on me everyday at church." He states that she then started splashing Ms. Victim with the drain cleaner. Ms. Witness 2's account is similar. She states that "as soon as First Name (Ms. Victim) entered, Defendant's First Name grabbed her purse and started throwing the solution on her saying, "I told you I was gonna get you. I'm tired of you getting me in trouble."

Ms. Witness 3's report of the incident is also similar. Additionally, Ms. Witness 3 states that Ms. Defendant would frequently deny making threats when confronted with an issue, claiming that she did not make such a threat or did not remember making it. Ms. Witness 3 also states that Ms. Defendant reported experiencing auditory hallucinations telling her to get people. Ms. Defendant has consistently denied hallucinations.

Test Results:

Ms. Defendant was administered a battery of psychological tests on 3 days (Dates) at Correctional Psychiatry Facility. Those test results are briefly summarized here. Her results on the WAIS-R are considered a valid assessment of her current intellectual functioning. Ms. Defendant scored a Verbal IQ of 75, a Performance IQ of 79 and a Full Scale IQ of 76. This places her overall intellectual functioning in the Borderline to Low Average range.

Although a full neuropsychological assessment was not performed at Correctional Psychiatric Facility, results on the WAIS-R, Bender Visual Motor Gestalt Test, and Trail Making Test are not suggestive of organic dysfunction.

*(continued)*

Sample Criminal Responsibility Evaluation (*continued*)

Her responses on the MMPI-2, while guarded, were reported to be characteristic of Schizophrenia, Paranoid Type or Paranoid Disorder. Her responses on the MCMI-II are reported to be suggestive of a Dependent Personality Disorder. In addition, her results on the Whitaker Index of Schizophrenic Thinking (Form A) were suggestive of moderate disorganized thinking on logical tasks.

Her results on the CPS were valid and not indicative of substance abuse or a thought disturbance.

Criminal Responsibility:

The Rogers allows for a determination of whether the defendant met the statutory criteria for "insanity" at the time of the crime. State law states that, "A person is not responsible for criminal conduct if at the time of such conduct, as a result of mental disease or defect, she lacks substantial capacity either to appreciate the criminality of her conduct or to conform her conduct to the requirements of law." The determination is made based on a sequential consideration of several factors.

The first area of inquiry is whether the defendant is exaggerating or feigning a report of symptoms at the time of the crime. Ms. Defendant does not report any psychiatric symptoms at the time of the incident. She states that "everything happened so fast" and that "she didn't mean to do it." She denies hallucinations and delusions. Her report of the incident was guarded. She expressed concern on several occasions that she may be incriminating herself. Thus, her self-report may not be inclusive and/or reliable.

The second focus of study has to do with the presence of involuntary intoxication, mental retardation, or brain damage at the time of the crime. Ms. Defendant denies alcohol or drug use. There is no evidence to suggest involuntary intoxication. Ms. Defendant functions at the Borderline to Low Average range of intellectual functioning and is not mentally retarded. There is nothing in the history or psychological testing to suggest the presence of brain damage.

The Rogers asks if the defendant suffered from a major psychiatric disorder based on the presence or absence of specific symptoms. Both Ms. Defendant's self-report and third-party reports suggest a long history of psychiatric symptoms including persecutory delusions and possibly auditory and visual hallucinations. However, Ms. Defendant denies any hallucinatory experiences. The delusional content appears to involve suspicions that people are out to harm her reputation socially. She blames others for her misfortunes and becomes defensive and accusatory when criticized. For example, several choir members remarked that Ms. Defendant blamed the victim, Ms. Victim, when she was singled out by the pastor for needing help with her singing 2 weeks prior to the incident. Witnesses state that Ms. Defendant believed Ms. Victim picked on her. Ms. Defendant also states that she believes someone is responsible for her current predicament.

The admission note (Date) at Correctional Psychiatric Facility states that her mood was appropriate and thought processes were intact. The note further states that there were no delusions or hallucinations at the time. However, the psychological evaluation from Correctional Psychiatric Facility did note evidence persecutory delusions. There is also evidence of loose associations in her speech that is suggestive of a thought disorder. There is no indication of bizarre behavior on the morning of the alleged crime. Several eyewitness reports state that she was "more quiet" than usual. However, both her own report and witness reports suggest that her mood was calm on the morning of the incident. When asked about her mood, Ms. Defendant replied, "I'm a calm person, I wasn't even angry that morning." There is no report of verbal incoherence, mania, or clinical depression at the time of the incident.

There is evidence to suggest that Ms. Defendant had planned the assault. Witnesses state that Ms. Defendant had threatened the victim 2 weeks prior to the assault. Ms. Witness 2 also states that 1 week prior to the assault, Ms. Defendant purchased a large purse. Ms. Witness 2, who is aware of Ms. Defendant's finances, stated that Ms. Defendant would not have budgeted money for a purse. Ms. Witness 2 states Ms. Defendant was very protective of the purse and would not allow others near it. When I questioned Ms. Defendant as to why she had Liquid Fire in her purse, she stated that she had it for "a while." She also stated that she did not always carry the Liquid Fire in her purse. She further stated that the Liquid Fire had been in her purse for "a while and I forgot it was in my pocketbook. I don't know why I looked in my purse." However, Dr. Psychiatrist's report states that she had "procured the acid the night before the incident as a protective measure." When asked about this apparent contradiction, she stated, "I didn't put it in that morning, no way." Dr. Psychiatrist also states that Ms. Defendant claimed she felt physically threatened by Ms. Victim. However, both her responses and remarks by Ms. Witness 2 and the Reverend contradict Ms. Defendant's earlier statements. There is no way to determine if Ms. Defendant is fabricating her responses. There is no reason to suspect fabrication from the two witnesses.

Further behavior suggests intent occurred on the morning of the incident. Ms. Defendant did not join the choir in prayer and did not join the choir in the processional to enter the church at the start of services. Rather, she waited by a file cabinet with her purse. The victim was on a church bus that was late. Once the victim entered the vestibule, Ms. Defendant approached her and splashed the Liquid Fire onto her face. Witnesses also state that Ms. Defendant yelled at the victim, indicating that she had told her she would get her. Ms. Defendant then quickly ran out of the church. Ms. Defendant admits that she would not have splashed the Liquid Fire on anyone else. She states that if the victim had not arrived at church on that Sunday, the incident would not have happened. She also states that if someone had asked her that morning if it was wrong she probably would not have done it, suggesting control over her behavior.

Additionally, she states that she was not aware that the Liquid Fire splashed onto five other people. She states, "I wasn't aware it splashed on five other people when I splashed it on her, not until I got my indictment letter. I'm not guilty of five counts. I wasn't thinking about five people when I did it. They were sitting in the hallway." Her behavior does not appear to have been an impulsive act.

Ms. Defendant states that she does not know why she committed the behavior. She does admit to having previous difficulties with the victim. However, when asked if she feared the victim, Ms. Defendant states, "I wasn't thinking that nobody was out to hurt me. No, she just always picked at me. She would walk on my feet. Once she pushed me when we were out of town with the church in Close Town. I was standing at the end of line; she walked up to me and pushed me. I don't know why, I never said anything to her. But that ain't why I did it." She further states, "I never wanted to do nothing like that to nobody, not even her." Both the Reverend and Ms. Witness 2 report that Ms. Defendant never mentioned that she was afraid of the victim or felt

*(continued)*

Sample Criminal Responsibility Evaluation (*continued*)

threatened by the victim or anyone else. Based on her own account, it does not appear that Ms. Defendant acted in response to a perceived physical threat.

Ms. Defendant states that she is aware that splashing Liquid Fire onto someone else is wrong and against the law. Her behavior at the time of the incident suggests that she realized splashing the Liquid Fire was illegal since she attempted to flee the church. In addition, when the Reverend tried to speak with Ms. Defendant after the incident she fled from him twice. She went to Defendant's friend's home to tell him "somebody started trouble with me." She believes that Mr. Friend is a detective. He states that she appeared at the door with the police. The police rang the bell and asked him if he knew her. She was saying that she "didn't mean to do it" and pleading with him to not allow her to be arrested. She states that she was not thinking about being arrested when she did it. Her self-report and behavior suggest that Ms. Defendant appreciated the criminality of her conduct.

In conclusion, Ms. Defendant appears to suffer from Schizophrenia, Paranoid Type. Ms. Victim became the focus of Ms. Defendant's persecutory delusions. However, Ms. Defendant states that she did not feel threatened by Ms. Victim. Additionally, Ms. Defendant admits to appreciating the criminality of her conduct at the time of the incident. Also, her self-report and behavior indicate control over her behavior at the time of the incident.

Conclusions:

Defendant is a 40-year-old single, black female charged with Assault–First Degree. Specifically, she is alleged to have splashed Liquid Fire, a liquid drain cleaner, onto another woman's face, incidentally splashing five other bystanders.

Ms. Defendant functions in the Borderline to Low Average range of intellectual functioning. She completed school to the tenth grade.

She has worked primarily in unskilled, manual labor positions. She lives in rent-free government housing. She has a 13-year-old son who lives with his father.

Ms. Defendant has a long history of psychiatric symptoms such as loose associations and paranoid delusions. She has never received treatment for these symptoms. She also has a positive family history for mental illness.

A previous evaluation conducted at Correctional Psychiatric Facility found Ms. Defendant competent to stand trial. Additionally, Ms. Defendant is currently on haloperidol, an antipsychotic medication.

Ms. Defendant has the mental capacity to appreciate the nature of the charges against her. She has the capacity to rationally participate in her own defense.

Ms. Defendant did not, as the result of a mental disease or defect at the time of the alleged crime, lack substantial capacity to appreciate the criminality of her conduct. Ms. Defendant did not, as the result of a mental disease or defect at the time of the crime, lack substantial capacity to conform her conduct to the requirements of the law.

Diagnosis DSM-III-R:

Currently:

Axis I – Schizophrenia, Paranoid Type

Axis II – Deferred

Axis III – None

Axis IV – Psychosocial Stressors: unemployed, poverty,
incarceration
Severity: 4 – Severe
Axis V – Current Functioning (GAF): 50 Serious
Symptoms

Best Functioning Past Year (GAF): 40 Serious
Symptoms

At Time of Crime:

Axis I – Schizophrenia, Paranoid Type

Axis II – Deferred

Axis III – None

Axis IV – Psychosocial Stressors: unemployed, poverty
Severity: 4 – Severe

Axis V – Current Functioning (GAF): 40 Serious
Symptoms

Best Functioning Past Year (GAF): 40 Serious
Symptoms

Note: This defendant was found Guilty But Mentally Ill (GBMI) and sentenced to 20 years in a correctional psychiatric facility. If she were to recover from her mental illness while in the correctional psychiatric facility, she would be transferred to a prison to serve out the remainder of her sentence.

## Table 4.9    Sample Criminal Responsibility Evaluation

Date
The Honorable Judge
Southern Circuit Court
Main Street

RE: Defendant<br>DOB: mm/dd/yyyy

Judge:

Defendant is a 30-year-old white, married male charged with Attempted Murder, Assault – 2nd Degree and Wanton Endangerment–First Degree. Mr. Defendant is referred per your order for evaluation of his competency to stand trial and criminal responsibility at the time of the crime. Mr. Defendant is currently in the Southern County Detention Center and was evaluated on February 21 and February 31, 1990. Mr. Defendant was informed that the results of the evaluation will be released to the court and that the evaluation may be used against him in court. Mr. Defendant gave his written permission to be evaluated.

**PSYCHOLOGICAL EVALUATION**

**Instruments Administered:**

> Wechsler Adult Intelligence Scale—Revised
> Bender Visual Motor Gestalt Test
> Minnesota Multiphasic Personality Inventory (MMPI)
> Michigan Alcoholism Screening Test (MAST)
> Beck Depression Inventory
> Millon Clinical Multiaxial Inventory-II (MCMI-II)
> Lipsitt, Lelos and McGarry Competency to Stand Trial
>     Assessment Instrument
> Rogers Criminal Responsibility Assessment Scale

**Interviews Conducted:**

> Defendant
> Defense Attorney
> Prosecutor
> Defendant's Wife, Witness
> Social Worker, Detention Center
> Maintenance man at Mr. Defendant's apartment complex
> Dr. Psychiatrist, attending psychiatrist at Detention Center

### Records Reviewed:

State Hospital - Complete charts from
   5 previous hospitalizations
(5 dates of hospitalizations provided)
County Detention Center – Progress Notes Arrest date – present
Police Investigative Report

Statements from the following individuals:
Officer 1, Officer 2, Officer 3, Officer 4, Officer 5,
Officer 6, Officer 7, Officer 8, Officer 9, Officer 10, Officer 11
Detective 1, Detective 2, Detective 3
Sergeant 1, Sergeant 2, Sergeant 3

Transcribed taped statements of the following individuals:
Sergeant 1 - Lt. Commander of Emergency Response Unit
June and Cleave Defendant - Defendant's mother and stepfather
Sergeant 1, Sergeant 2, Sergeant 3, Sergeant 4, Sergeant 5
Sergeant 6
Detective 1
Mr. K. Defendant (Mr. Defendant's uncle)

Tape of negotiation between Mr. Defendant and Detective 5
Tape of phone calls made by Mr. Defendant to Hometown
Police Department

### Psychosocial History:

Mr. Defendant was born in Town, State m/dd/yy as the only child of his parents who were divorced shortly before he was born. He states that he never knew his biological father. His mother, Mom, has been married to Dad Lastname for approximately 21 years. His mother is employed as a teacher and his stepfather works for a chemical company. His parents live in Town, State.

Mr. Defendant states that he "always experienced some friction" with his stepfather and therefore started living with his grandparents in Another County when he was approximately 14 years old. He states that his stepfather was too strict a disciplinarian as he was growing up. He states that his stepfather is "somewhat hateful." He feels that most of his problems are due to coming from a "dysfunctional family." When asked to elaborate on this he states, "My mom has blinders to my stepfather's real intentions; he hates me and intends me harm." He also states that his stepfather "has not loved me or cared about me; he cheated me out of a mother; felt like I was competing for mom against dad, like we were adversities (sic) instead of friends." Mr. Defendant claims that his family background is the reason he uses marijuana. Mrs. Defendant, Mr. Defendant's spouse, stated that her husband claims his stepfather tried to sexually abuse him when he was young. Mrs. Defendant also states that Mr. Defendant's parents "worship the devil."

Mr. Defendant states that he was "smart" in high school. He also states that he played basketball in grammar school and high school at County, a recognized basketball "powerhouse," and that he was playing to advance his education. He states that his first psychiatric hospitalization at 17 "doused his aspirations to be a pillar of society" as he obtained a reputation as "crazy Name." Mr. Defendant was hospitalized a

*(continued)*

Sample Criminal Responsibility Evaluation (*continued*)

second time while a senior in high school; his second hospitalization was a 60-day court-ordered commitment to State Hospital.

Mr. Defendant finished high school and attempted a semester at State University but dropped out due to emotional difficulties. He states that he also attempted classes at Small College 1 and Small College 2 and claims to have about two semesters of college credit completed.

Mr. Defendant attempted to work at an unskilled manual labor job cleaning office equipment that he states he obtained through "political ties." After working for approximately 6 to 8 months, he states he lost the job due to his emotional difficulties. He states that he has not worked since and is supported by his grandparents and parents.

Mr. Defendant met his wife approximately 8 years ago and was married in month, year. His wife has investment income and SSI; they feel that their income is sufficient so that neither one is employed. Mr. Defendant states that his wife is on SSI for "multiple personality disorder."

Mr. Defendant states that he smokes "quite a bit" of marijuana. He states that he has been smoking for the past 15 years; he denies an alcohol or drug problem. He states that the "region has some of the best marijuana in the world and an abundant supply." He states that he smokes a "connoisseur line, the best grade I could find." He states, "I feel tobacco is an organic plant, government gets taxes; marijuana is illegal, government don't get its cut, therefore illegal."

**Psychiatric History:**

Mr. Defendant was first hospitalized for four days in Month, Year at the Inpatient Unit with a diagnosis of mania. He was placed on lithium carbonate and discharged. However, Mr. Defendant was non-compliant with follow-up appointments and medications and was readmitted following suicidal threats and a combative episode with his grandfather in Month, Year. A review of his charts revealed that he has continually attributed his bizarre behavior to "bad marijuana."

Mr. Defendant has been hospitalized at State Hospital on at least five occasions starting in Month, Year with the last hospitalization in Month, Year. Four hospitalizations all appear to be due to manic behavior with psychotic features, usually prompted by aggressive, threatening behavior. For example, he was arrested in Month, Year while wearing eye mascara and black lace panties. At that time, he was threatening to burn down the jail and kill himself and others. Mr. Defendant was arrested in Month, Year for threatening his mother. At this time, it was necessary for State Hospital staff to place Mr. Defendant in leather restraints for self-protection and protection of others.

A review of Mr. Defendant's psychiatric history suggests that he has poor insight into his problem and is not motivated to obtain treatment. Mr. Defendant appears to respond well to medications while hospitalized, but apparently discontinues his medications after leaving the hospital. It is noted that Mr. Defendant frequently went AWOL or "escaped" from the hospital.

Mr. Defendant states that he is "coming to the realization that I have some type of mental impairment that I may need to take medications for possibly for the rest of my life. I never accepted that . . . felt people and situations just did me in. This incident has brought this home to me."

Mr. Defendant states that his maternal grandmother has a "great deal" of emotional difficulties and has been on antipsychotic medication for the past 25 years. He states that his grandmother's brother is an alcoholic and that his mother may have made a suicide attempt and/or had a nervous breakdown and has been on tranquilizers in the past.

<u>Report of the Crime:</u>

Mr. Defendant states that he was going through a "manic episode with acute paranoia" at the time of the crime. He reports that 2–3 days prior to the incident, he had called the "DEA in Miami, Florida, and the FBI in Virginia regarding the FBI's case involving corrupt cops in Another County." He states he also contacted the Secret Service in Washington, D.C., and in Town. He also had telephone contact with the CIA to report Nazi spies.

He reports that he could not sleep prior to the incident. Mrs. Defendant confirms that Mr. Defendant went for 2 days without sleep immediately preceding the incident. Mr. Defendant also made numerous calls to the Town, State police reporting that his parents were missing and/or dead. His phone calls to the Town police became increasingly aggressive and incoherent over the period leading up to the incident.

Mr. Defendant states that several days prior to the incident he started unplugging the television and VCR since he felt subliminal messages pertaining to Satan and the forces of evil were coming through to him. He reports also calling his mother to tell her that the devil is dead. He denies having audio/visual hallucinations at the time of the crime.

On the night of the incident, Mr. Defendant's uncle called Mr. Defendant at the urging of Defendant's mother to check on how Mr. Defendant was doing. Mr. Defendant states that he went into a "rage of anger" since his uncle neglected to show concern for him 10 years earlier when he needed financial help. Mr. Defendant states that his wife went to the store at this time. Approximately 10 minutes later, there was a knock on the door. When he asked who it was, the police responded by identifying themselves. He asked if they had a warrant and states that they did not reply. He states that he had seen that it was Sgt. X, the same officer who he had filed a police brutality complaint against several months earlier. He states that he was convinced the police had come to "get me, kill me." Mr. Defendant's recall of the following details is sketchy. He states he looked out the bedroom window to see if Sgt. X came in a police car or "on his own." He recalls seeing "two or three (police) cars, walkie-talkies, etc." At this time, he states that he was convinced the police had come to murder him due to his brutality complaint.

He states that his phone rang and the "jerk identified himself as Mr. Park (of Park Place), did not say he was a cop, and said "First name, step outside, we want you to step outside," tauntingly, cold and cruel like we want to blow your fuckin' shit away, like challenging me."

He recalls sitting on the sofa with the gun when "the dam thing accidentally went off." He states that he was holding the gun because he "was scared for his life." He states that he got "disgusted with it, they're here and are just gonna kill me." He

*(continued)*

Sample Criminal Responsibility Evaluation (*continued*)

states that he "walked out, picked up the 9mm, and shot it straight up into the air and emptied it." When questioned why he did this, he states that he was "in panic, schizophrenic, manic episode, insane."

He reports that he then went to his bed, shouted that he was loading his 357 magnum, and was going to walk out the door and leave. He states that when he opened the door, the opposite apartment door slammed open. He then "saw a thing like a fire cracker, heard a shot, and felt it." He returned fire in the direction of the door, threw down his gun, and jumped off the patio. He states that he laid there shot when a member of "SWAT team put a boot on my head and says 'you son-of-a-bitch'; they're animals (referring to the police)."

Mr. Defendant reports experiencing delusions for several days prior to the incident. These reports are substantiated by his wife, witness, and taped conversations of Mr. Defendant with County police. Dr. Psychiatrist reports that Mr. Defendant was quite delusional and manic when initially brought to the jail.

### Test Results:

Mr. Defendant scores a Verbal IQ of 96, a Performance IQ of 91 and a Full Scale IQ of 93, placing his overall intellectual functioning in the Average range. Mr. Defendant approaches the testing with an eagerness to be cooperative and successful. He readily moves on to a new task after failure. Mr. Defendant successfully completed high school and approximately 1 year of college.

Though a full neurological evaluation is not done, neither the WAIS-R nor the Bender suggest organic neurological dysfunctions.

Mr. Defendant's MMPI profile appears to be valid. His responses suggest an attempt to maintain a facade of adequacy and control while admitting no weaknesses. His profile is characteristic of individuals who lack insight into their problems and are defensive about any perceived inadequacies. Individuals with this MMPI profile tend to display insensitivity and disregard for social consequences of their behavior and will act out impulsively. Following periods of acting out these individuals tend to feel guilty, remorseful, and self-deprecating about having exhibited such behaviors. The profile is also characteristic of someone who may be diagnosed schizophrenia. Due to difficulties forming interpersonal relationships, interventions of a purely psychological nature have a poor prognosis; psychopharmacological interventions are often warranted.

Mr. Defendant's responses to the MCMI-II are valid and suggestive of someone who is anxious to conform to the expectations of others, particularly those in authority. Individuals with this profile are described as cooperative and willingly submit to the wishes of others in order to maintain their affections. However, intense anger and oppositional feelings tend to brood behind the passivity and public compliance. This profile is characteristic of someone who is socially skilled and manipulative.

Both the MAST and the MMPI are suggestive of a problem with alcohol. Mr. Defendant reports that his drinking has created problems for him in his relationships and that he drinks before noon. He also admits to an arrest due to drunken behavior and an arrest for drunk driving. There was no evidence of depression on the BDI.

## Competency to Stand Trial:

When asked how he can defend himself against the charges, Mr. Defendant states "I feel that I had a manic episode, which created severe temporary insanity experiencing manic paranoia and schizophrenia; also feel City Police Department bungled handling of answering call to my residence, which in turn led to the turn of events that has created these problems." He states that at the time of the incident he felt that it was a conspiracy by the police department and apartment complex to kill him. He states that his paranoia was "put in progress" by the alcohol intoxication arrest (Date) and his subsequent police brutality complaint.

He knows that he must control himself in the courtroom. He realizes that he could be found in contempt of court if he spoke out or moved around without permission.

Mr. Defendant knows his lawyer well and expresses confidence in him. He feels that his lawyer is doing a good job and agrees with the way he has handled the case thus far. He understands the concept of plea-bargaining.

Mr. Defendant knows the roles of the courtroom principals. He is aware of his right against self-incrimination. He is aware of the adversarial nature of the trial.

Mr. Defendant states that he is charged with attempted murder, second-degree assault, and wanton endangerment. He states that these are major crimes. He is unsure of the possible sentencing for these crimes but states "I think I've heard 10 to 20 or something from inmates here." Mr. Defendant understands the concept of probation.

Mr. Defendant states that he has an 80 to 100% chance of being found innocent. When questioned how strong he thinks the case against him is, he states, "With all factors considered, I think a weak case."

Mr. Defendant is able to discuss his case with his lawyer and is able to testify relevantly in a trial. He knows to tell his lawyer if someone lies about him in court. He states that the police officers may lie about him in court because "they shot first and were in the wrong." He is able to sustain a self-preserving motivation during a trial.

## Criminal Responsibility:

The Rogers allows for a determination of whether the defendant met the statutory criteria for "insanity" at the time of the crime. This determination is made based on a sequential consideration of several factors.

The first area of inquiry is whether the defendant is exaggerating or feigning a report of symptoms at the time of the crime. Mr. Defendant states that he was in a manic episode with a "period of acute paranoia" during the time of the crime. Mr. Defendant appears to have been manic with delusions of persecution and grandiosity at the time of the crime. Witness reports along with taped conversations substantiate this claim. Furthermore, Mr. Defendant's psychiatric history is consistent with his apparent symptomatology at the time of the crime. Thus, Mr. Defendant's report of his mental state during the incident appears reliable.

The second focus of study has to do with the presence of involuntary intoxication, mental retardation, or brain damage at the time of the crime. There is nothing to indicate involuntary intoxication. Additionally, Mr. Defendant denies any alcohol or

*(continued)*

Sample Criminal Responsibility Evaluation (*continued*)

drug use at the time of the crime. Mr. Defendant is not mentally retarded in his overall mental functioning. Nothing in the psychological testing indicates brain damage nor is there any medical history suggestive of possible brain damage.

The Rogers asks if the defendant suffered from a major psychiatric disorder based on the presence or absence of specific symptoms. There is clear evidence of bizarre behavior immediately preceding and during the commission of the crime. His delusions of persecution are viewed as the predominant force in the commission of the crime. Additionally, Mr. Defendant was apparently in a manic episode that had a major impact on his behavior at the time of the crime.

There was no planning or preparation for the crime by Mr. Defendant prior to the arrival of the police. Although Mr. Defendant states that he is aware that firing a weapon at the police is a crime, he was convinced that the police were there to kill him and therefore did not feel that this was relevant at the time. Mr. Defendant was in control of his behavior at the time of the crime. However, Mr. Defendant lacked substantial cognitive control to conform his behavior to the requirements of the law as a direct result of a mental disorder during the time of the crime.

### Conclusions:

Mr. Defendant is a 30-year-old white, married male charged with Attempted Murder, Assault-Second Degree, and Wanton Endangerment-First Degree. Mr. Defendant has an extensive psychiatric history starting when he was 17 years old. He has been diagnosed with bipolar disorder and the majority of his hospitalizations appear to have resulted from manic behavior with psychotic features and aggressive behavior. Mr. Defendant responds well to medications. Dr. Psychiatrist reports that Mr. Defendant is doing demonstratively better due to his current medications. However, Mr. Defendant has demonstrated very poor compliance in obtaining follow-up treatment and taking his medications. His noncompliance appears to be related to his lack of insight into his mental disorder and his poor judgment.

Mr. Defendant has the mental capacity to appreciate the nature of the charges against him. He has the capacity to rationally participate with his attorney in his own defense. Mr. Defendant, at the time of the crime, lacked substantial capacity to appreciate the criminality of his conduct and to conform his conduct to the requirements of the law.

### Diagnosis DSM-III-R:

### Currently:

Axis I – Bipolar Disorder, Manic Type with psychotic
features, in partial remission

Axis II – Rule out Personality Disorder, Mixed Type

Axis III – Post gunshot wound to thigh

Axis IV – Psychosocial Stressors: incarceration,
trouble with family
Severity: 3 – Moderate

Axis V – Current Functioning: 40

Best Functioning Past Year: 60

**At Time of Crime:**

Axis I – Bipolar Disorder, Manic Type with psychotic features

Axis II – Rule out Personality Disorder, Mixed Type

Axis III – None

Axis IV – Psychosocial Stressors: trouble with family
Severity: 3 – Moderate

Axis V – Current Functioning: 20

Best Functioning Past Year: 60

**Note: This defendant was found Not Guilty by Reason of Insanity and the charges were dismissed.**

# Competency to Stand Trial

In contrast to a criminal responsibility evaluation that assesses mental state at the time of the offense, a competency to stand trial evaluation (CST) assesses mental functioning at the time of the assessment. This is easily the most common mental health inquiry in the legal system, with nearly 80,000 CST evaluations conducted annually (Bonnie & Grisso, 2000). It is estimated that pretrial determination of competency is sought in 2–8% of all felony cases (Hoge, Bonnie, Poythress, & Monahan, 1992). A request for competency is typically raised by the defense counsel before the trial begins. However, a request for a competency determination can be raised anytime during the trial by the defense, the prosecution, or the court, *sua sponte* (on its own motion) (Westendorf, 1999). In *Pate v. Robinson* (1966), the U.S. Supreme Court ruled that a trial judge *must* raise the issue of competency if any evidence presented creates a "bona fide doubt" about the defendant's competency. Although judges and lawyers estimate that competency is a legitimate issue in approximately 5% of criminal cases (LaFortune & Nicholson, 1995), only approximately two-thirds of these cases are referred for an evaluation. Although a question of the defendant's ability to proceed is the most frequently cited reason for a CST evaluation, the forensic examiner should recognize that there are other possible reasons for the requested evaluation. A request for a CST evaluation may be used by the defense counsel to gain additional time to prepare for the trial or may be motivated by the desire to obtain immediate treatment for the defendant. It has been suggested that the increase in requests for CST evaluations reflects an indirect way of obtaining treatment for individuals with mental illness who would otherwise not receive treatment (Cooper & Grisso, 1997).

There are four rationales for wanting to ensure that a defendant is competent before proceeding with a criminal trial (Wulsch, 1980). First, due process requires that the defendant can assist in their defense and exercise their rights, such as selecting their defense counsel and testifying on their own behalf. Second, the defendant must be competent so that the court can ascertain the facts of the case. Third, prosecuting an incompetent defendant would question the integrity of the entire judicial process. Fourth, meting out punishment to an incompetent defendant who does not comprehend the process or reasons for punishment undermines the goals of punishment.

## Table 4.10    Rationales for Trying Only Competent Defendants

- Due process requires defendants to exercise their rights.
- Defendant must assist the court in obtaining the facts of the case.
- Dignity and integrity of the process depends on the defendant's competency.
- Punishing an incompetent defendant undermines the goals of punishment.

The determination of competency is a legal decision, not a clinical decision (Melton et al., 1997). The most common procedure is for the court to hold a pretrial hearing to determine the competency of a defendant before proceeding with the trial. The decision of competency is made by a judge; juries are not involved in competency proceedings. The court will request that an expert offer an opinion regarding competency of a defendant. Depending on the jurisdiction, the forensic mental health expert (either a psychologist or a psychiatrist) will evaluate the defendant and submit a report to the court within a reasonable amount of time, such as 30 days. A pretrial hearing is held where the expert may be subpoenaed to testify as to his or her finding. As discussed in Chapter 2, some professionals in the field caution against expert testimony on the ultimate issue. However, the attorneys and the judge usually want to know the expert's opinion regarding the ultimate issue, in this case, whether the defendant is competent to stand trial Judges are responsible for making the final ruling regarding competency. Judges usually, but not always, are swayed by the expert's ultimate issue testimony in competency proceedings (Melton et al., 1997).

# Defining Competency

■ **Dusky standard**

The standard used to determine competency to stand trial. A defendant must understand the nature of the proceedings against him or her and must be able to rationally assist his or her attorney.

The question of competency to stand trial is a legal issue. The U.S. Supreme Court established the current minimal constitutional standard for competency in 1960 (*Dusky v. United States*, 1960). The **Dusky standard** articulates two conditions for competency: the defendant has sufficient present ability to consult with his or her attorney with a reasonable degree of rational understanding, and the defendant has a rational as well as factual understanding of the proceedings against him or her. The Dusky standard is used in all federal courts and, with minor variations, in all state courts (Westendorf, 1999).

It is important to note that there are different types of competency. In addition to competency to stand trial, there is also competency to waive rights, competency to plead guilty, competency to be executed, and competency to waive counsel (Stafford, 2003). This is in addition to competency to care for self, as is the case with older adults or those with mental illness (Baker, Lichtenberg, & Moye, 1998). Over the years, courts have ruled on whether the same Dusky standard should apply to these other forms of competency in criminal trials, such as competency to waive counsel. For example, in *Westbrook v. Arizona* (1966) the U.S. Supreme Court ruled that competency to stand trial was not sufficient to determine that the defendant was competent to waive their right to counsel and to conduct their own defense. Interestingly, the court ruled that competency to waive one's right to counsel had no relationship to the defendant's actual ability to represent themselves (*Faretta v. California*, 1975).

The U. S. Supreme Court clarified the issue of competency in the landmark decision *Godinez v. Moran* (1993). The Court ruled that no different or higher standard was required for the waiver of important rights than the Dusky standard. The Court reasoned that the defendant must be competent throughout the course of a trial, from arraignment, to pleading, to trial, conviction, and sentencing. The defendant who is competent to stand trial must make a number of decisions throughout the course of the entire process. This suggests that the Dusky standard should not be viewed narrowly (Stafford, 2003). The *Godinez v. Moran* ruling indicates that competency to stand trial also encompasses competency to waive important rights, such as right to counsel, and pleading guilty. The result could be that judges and evaluators will expect a higher level of competency for CST evaluations (Melton et al., 1997). A defendant must prove his or her incompetence by a preponderance of the evidence, the lowest burden of proof.

After the CST evaluation and at the pretrial hearing, the defendant is found either competent or incompetent. If the defendant is found competent, the criminal process continues. If the defendant is found **incompetent to stand trial** (IST), the criminal proceedings are suspended. Courts struggle with defendants who are found IST. The disposition of incompetent defendants is one of the more problematic areas for judges (Roesch, Zapf, Golding, & Skeem 1999). If the defendant is found incompetent, there are various options. If it is a minor crime, the charges may be dismissed with the condition that the defendant seek and comply with appropriate treatment. If the charges are more serious, the defendant can be involuntarily committed to a mental health facility for treatment *if* the defendant can be brought to competency in a reasonable period of time. Once a defendant is found to be IST, the goal of civil commitment is **restoration to competency**. Not all individuals found incompetent can be expected to be restored to competency with treatment. For example, a developmentally disabled individual with a diagnosis of moderate mental retardation and an IQ score of 50 is unlikely to be deemed competent to stand trial. Treatment will not help this individual achieve competency. In such an example, the state may agreed to dismiss the charges with guarantees of adequate supervision. In a recent case, a defendant with mental retardation who did not pose a danger to himself or society was ordered released since he would never achieve trial competency (*United States v. Duhon*, 2000).

In the *Jackson v. Indiana* (1972) decision, the U.S. Supreme Court ruled that if a defendant is determined incompetent, the state may involuntarily hospitalize and treat the defendant for a "reasonable" period of time to determine the probability that the person can achieve trial competency in the foreseeable future. The term "reasonable" is interpreted differently depending on the jurisdiction but is usually no longer than 365 days. An individual in an active psychotic episode who is delusional or hallucinating may be restored to competency with appropriate psychotropic medications. The majority of defendants found IST suffer from psychotic symptoms and schizophrenia (Morse, 2003; Nicholson & Kugler, 1991). However, one study found that permanently incompetent defendants had been confined for an average of over 4 years even after they were eligible for special conservatorship for the mentally ill who were not deemed violent (Morris & Meloy, 1993). The majority of these individuals were diagnosed with schizophrenia and the majority did not have a history of violent behavior. These results suggest that some jurisdictions ignore the requirements of the *Jackson v. Indiana* decision and civilly commit permanently incompetent defendants.

The majority of individuals found IST are restored to competency with average rates from nearly 75% (Cunero & Brejle, 1984) to 95% of all defendants (Nicholson & McNulty, 1992). **Competency restoration** is generally inpatient treatment and can vary from an average of 2 months to a year. Most hospital-based treatment programs consist of psychoactive medications and knowledge-based programs to help defendants understand the judicial proceedings. Knowledge-based programs teach defendants found IST about the legal system and provide role-playing opportunities (e.g., Anderson & Hewitt, 2002). One program used mock trials for defendants to gain experience (Davis, 1985) and another didactic program offered seven modules including written work, videotaped vignettes, simulated courtroom proceedings, and role-play activities along with presentations by attorneys (Brown, 1992). A variety of studies have found the average period for inpatient treatment for restoration of competence is 4–6 months, although there are many examples of defendants being held much longer (Bennett & Kish, 1990; Miller, 2003).

The U.S. Supreme Court ruled that a defendant found incompetent could be administered medication against their will if the state can show that the medication is essential for the defendant's safety or the safety of others, or that there are no other "less intrusive" means to obtain an adjudication of guilt or innocence (*Riggins v. Nevada*, 1992). One study compared defendants who had been restored to competence with the assistance of forced medication versus defendants who voluntarily complied with medication treatment (Laddis, Convit, Zito, & Vitrai, 1993). The results indicated there was no difference between the two groups in the defendant's ability to obtain a favorable plea bargain or to succeed at trial using an insanity defense.

Competency restoration can also occur on an outpatient basis. In fact, individuals found IST have not been convicted of the crime for which they are charged and are presumed to be innocent. Involuntary treatment is only permissible if there is a likelihood that treatment will restore the defendant to competence and there is no less intrusive means to do so (Stafford, 2003). Professionals in the field have called for greater access to outpatient treatment for defendants rather than involuntary hospitalization (Miller, 2003; Roesch et al., 1999). Defendants who do not pose a risk to self or society should be allowed to receive treatment on an outpatient basis. However, this is typically not the case. Nonforensic civilly committed patients are usually released in several days to a few weeks. Forensically committed patients are typically held for

## Competency to Stand Trial: An Ethical Quagmire

Dr. Steven Roberts has been appointed by the courts to conduct a competency to stand trial (CST) evaluation on a 17-year-old male defendant accused of sexual assault and battery. The defendant is a legal resident residing in the United States and is originally from a coastal village in Chile and speaks his native language, Mapudungun, and appears to understand some Spanish. However, he can also understand and speak rudimentary English. Dr. Roberts works in Appalachia in West Virginia. He is only able to locate someone who can speak Spanish, the national language of Chile. However, this individual is not a professional translator and the county does not have the financial resources to contract with a professional translator.

The CST evaluation was requested by the defendant's public defender due to her concerns that the defendant appears to have a low IQ and also appears to have "paranoid ideas."

Dr. Roberts needs to weigh his options on how to best conduct the CST evaluation. He cannot simply refuse to conduct the evaluation due to the language barrier. The prosecutor has already indicated that the defendant appears to speak and understand English sufficiently to proceed with the trial. The pertinent questions are issues related to the Dusky standard. The defendant's ability to meet this standard would be influenced by a low IQ and/or paranoid delusions. Due to the severity of the charges, a finding of incompetence would result in civil commitment until competency is reached. Because of the nature of the assault, the charge carries a minimum sentence of 10–15 years.

How should Dr. Roberts proceed with the evaluation? What, if any, testing should be conducted? Should he use an individual who speaks Spanish to assist with the evaluation? What are the ethical issues faced by Dr. Roberts? How should he resolve these ethical dilemmas?

months to years (Miller, 2003). The overuse of hospitalization of individuals found IST contributes to the abuse of these defendants' civil rights. Some states even mandate the hospitalization of defendants found IST. Bartol and Bartol (2004) report that 18 states *require* the hospitalization of defendants found IST, whereas 21 states *permit* the involuntary hospitalization of these defendants. In only five states defendants needed to meet civil commitment criteria before they could be involuntarily hospitalized.

# Competency to Stand Trial (CST) Evaluation

There is frequently confusion among attorneys and the public as to the distinction between a criminal responsibility evaluation and a competency to stand trial evaluation. These are two separate evaluations addressing different psycholegal questions. The criminal responsibility evaluation attempts to determine the defendant's state of mind at the time of the offense to determine if the defendant possessed *mens rea*. The competency to stand trial evaluation assesses the defendant's decision-making abilities before, during, and after the trial. Both the temporal focus of the evaluation as well as the cognitive issues involved are distinctly different between the two evaluations. Clinicians can add to the confusion by not treating the evaluations as separate issues. Frequently, a referral for an MSO evaluation will also include a referral for a CST evaluation. The evaluations even include some overlap in assessment instruments, such as a measure of intellectual functioning. When the two are requested together, they can either be completed as two separate reports or clearly distinguished in the report submitted to the court. Although some authors caution against offering a conclusory opinion regarding the ultimate issue (Grisso, 1988), Federal Rule of Evidence 704 allows mental health experts to testify to the ultimate issue of the defendant's pretrial status (competence to stand trial). Some jurisdictions also expect and may even require the mental health expert to offer an opinion on the ultimate issue.

Many of the same caveats that apply to criminal responsibility evaluations extend to competency to stand trial evaluations. In particular, the defendant should have a clear understanding of the implications of the evaluation and must sign an informed consent. The defendant should understand prior to giving consent the purpose of the evaluation; potential uses of disclosed information; conditions under which the defense counsel, prosecutor, and court will have access to the evaluation; and the consequences of refusal to cooperate with the evaluation. Again, it is useful to have the defendant read the informed consent form aloud and to paraphrase the confidentiality limits. Clients are frequently under the assumption that every consultation with a psychologist is privileged communication and therefore confidential. The burden is on the forensic psychologist to dissuade the defendant of this belief. Videotaping or audiotaping of the evaluation, with the written permission of the defendant, provides an evidentiary record that can prove to be useful in disputed testimony.

The Dusky standard requires that a defendant is able to consult with his or her lawyer and has a rational and factual understanding of the proceedings against him or her in order to be found competent. Bonnie (1992) suggested a two-prong model of competence consisting of **foundational competence** and **decisional competence**. Foundational competence refers to the ability to assist the attorney. This includes

■ **Decisional competence**
The ability to make necessary decisions before, during, and after a trial.

1. the ability to understand the charges, the purpose of the criminal trial, and the adversary nature of the trial and the role of the defense counsel and prosecutor;
2. understanding the role of the defendant in a criminal trial; and
3. the ability to communicate pertinent information regarding the case to the defense attorney.

Decisional competence refers to the ability to make necessary decisions before, during, and after a trial. For example, a defendant must decide whether to choose a jury trial, to enter a plea, whether to accept a plea bargain, or to refuse representation.

Competency evaluations typically include an interview, psychological testing, and third-party information, such as legal records, mental health records, and interviews with jail personnel and the attorneys involved in the case. The assessment interview with the defendant can be structured using a variety of commercially available instruments designed to assess knowledge-based competence. Traditional psychological testing can be used to assess intellectual functioning and psychopathology. Traditional assessment instruments include the WAIS-III as a measure of intellectual functioning and the MMPI-2 for psychopathology. Forensic assessment instruments are designed to assess the legal question of competency and include interview-based instruments as well as rating scales and questionnaires.

# Forensic Instruments Used in CST Evaluations

A recent survey of board-certified forensic psychologists (Lally, 2003) found that the most frequently recommended forensic instrument for the assessment of competency was the **MacArthur Competence Assessment Tool—Criminal Adjudication** (MacCAT-CA). The MacCAT-CR is a 22-item instrument consisting of three scales—Understanding (8 items), Reasoning (8 items), and Appreciation (6 items)—and requires approximately 35 to 45 minutes to administer. The instrument requires an eighth-grade reading level and can be read to the defendant as he or she follows along on his or her own form. The Understanding scale assesses the ability to understand information related to law and the legal process. The Reasoning scale assesses the ability to reason about specific choices that face the defendant. The two scales consist of items based on hypothetical legal scenarios. The Appreciation scale assesses the ability to appreciate the implications and consequences of the defendant's own particular case. The MacCAT-CR is based on Bonnie's (1992) reformulation of competence as foundational competence and decisional competence.

Another instrument deemed acceptable for CST by the forensic experts is the **Competency to Stand Trial Assessment Instrument CAI**; (Lipsitt & Lelos, 1970). The CAI is one of the first competency assessment instruments and assesses 13 functions related to the ability to cope with the trial process in a self-protective manner. Each of the 13 functions is defined in statements with two or three sample questions for each function. The functions were developed by a multidisciplinary team and reflect case law, clinical experience, courtroom experience, and the research literature. Although the manual provides clinical examples for rating the degree of incapacity on each function, there is no standardized administration or scoring key. The CAI is an interview-based instrument and takes approximately 1 hour to complete. See Table 4.11 for the 13 functions assessed by the CAI (Lipsitt & Lelos, 1970). As is apparent from the list, the 13 functions possess face validity, rendering it acceptable by judges and attorneys (Melton et al., 1997).

The Interdisciplinary Fitness Interview (IFI) utilizes a joint interview by a psychologist and a lawyer to assess clinical psychopathology and understanding of legal concepts (Golding, Roesch, & Schreiber, 1984). The IFI is a semi-structured interview that assesses legal items and the presence of symptoms of psychopathology. Understanding of legal items is rated on a 0–2 scale and symptoms are rated as present or absent. Both legal items and symptoms are also rated on their significance. Evaluators can derive an overall rating of competent or incompetent and a rating of their confidence in that judgment. One of the instrument's original authors has updated the IFI (Golding, 1993). The Interdisciplinary Fitness Interview—Revised (IFI-R) has two sections: current clinical condition and psycholegal abilities. The IFI-R attempts to incorpo-

## The Thirteen Functions Assessed by the Competency to Stand Trial Assessment Instrument

### Table 4.11

- Appraisal of available legal defenses
- Quality of relating to the attorney
- Planning of legal strategy including guilty pleas to lesser charges where pertinent
- Appraisal of the role of legal actors (e.g., defense counsel, prosecutor, judge, jury, etc.)
- Understanding of court procedure
- Appreciation of charges
- Appreciation of the range and nature of possible penalties
- Appraisal of likely outcome
- Capacity to disclose to attorney available pertinent facts surrounding the offense including the defendant's movements, timing, mental state, and actions at the time of the offense
- Capacity to realistically challenge prosecution witnesses
- Unmanageable behavior in the courtroom
- Capacity to testify relevantly
- Self-defeating versus self-serving motivation

rate both legal and psychological concepts into a comprehensive assessment (Westendorf, 1999). The interview is tailored to the individual's case and the use of the attorney ensures the lawyer's input into the decision process. In the survey of forensic experts, 62% rated the use of the IFI-R as acceptable for a CST evaluation (Lally, 2003).

The **Competency Screening Test** (CST) is a 22-item sentence completion instrument in which the sentence stems suggest various legal scenarios (Lipsitt, Lelos, & McGarry, 1971). The CST is a brief screening measure that can be administered in 25 minutes to identify competent individuals and avoid a lengthy hospitalization and full competency assessment. The defendant is asked to complete a sentence stem such as, "When I go to court the lawyer will. . . ." Scores for completed sentence stems range from 0 for inappropriate responses to 2 for a response that reflects a high level of legal comprehension. The CST assesses three constructs: potential for a working relationship between defendant and counsel, defendant's understanding of the court process, and ability of defendant to emotionally deal with the court process. The CST is easy to administer and reliability data appear to be good (Westendorf, 1999). However, the CST is a screening measure and not suitable by itself for a complete CST evaluation. Seventy-seven percent of the surveyed board-certified forensic psychologists rated the CST as acceptable for a CST evaluation (Lally, 2003).

The **Georgia Court Competency Test** (GCCT) was developed as a screening tool to identify clearly competent individuals and can be administered in 10 minutes. The test uses a drawing of a courtroom to prompt defendants on questions about the roles and functions of court participants. The GCCT consists of 17 items assessing four abilities:

1. ability to communicate with an attorney,
2. understanding of the courtroom procedure,
3. knowledge of the charge against the defendant, and
4. possible penalties the defendant faces.

■ **Competency Screening Test (CST)**

A brief screening instrument consisting of 22 sentence stems related to legal scenarios used to help determine competency to stand trial.

■ **Georgia Court Competency Test (GCCT)**

A screening instrument that uses a drawing of the courtroom to prompt defendants on courtroom protocol and personnel.

The GCCT was revised at a Mississippi state hospital and is referred to as the GCCT-MSH (Nicholson, Robertson, Johnson, & Jensen, 1988). The revision added several questions regarding the defendant's knowledge of courtroom proceedings and slightly changed the scoring procedure. An example of the additional questions is, "What will you do during the trial?" Answers are scored from 0 to 10, with a possible total score of 50. The total is multiplied by 2 for a possible score of 100; scores of 70 or above are indicative of a competent defendant. Sixty-five percent of the forensic experts rated the GCCT as acceptable for a CST evaluation (Lally, 2003).

A written report should be completed if the retaining attorney requests one. It may be best to meet with the attorney to discuss findings before generating a report. Thus, if the results are not advantageous for the defendant, the defense counsel may not wish a report to be produced with the intention of withholding the information from the court. On the other hand, if the courts requested the report, a written report must be prepared for the courts and copies distributed to each party by the court (Westendorf, 1999). Grisso (1988) provides an outline of information that should be provided in the CST report. See Table 4.12 for a list of topics to be covered in the written report. Tables 4.13 and 4.14 provide two competency to stand trial evaluations. Identifying information has been altered to protect the identities of people involved in each case. Melton et al. (2007) also provide several CST and MSO reports along with numerous case studies.

**Table 4.12**  **Information to Include in a Competency to Stand Trial Report**

### Purposes and Methods
- Purpose of the evaluation
- Demographic and other information identifying the defendant
- Nature of the contacts with the defendant
- All third-party information sources
- Psychological assessment instruments

### Defendant's Background
- Psychosocial history
- Mental health history
- Legal history
- Observations relevant to inferences about competency

### Competency Abilities and Deficits
- Examples of competency abilities and deficits
- Current mental condition (can include a DSM diagnosis)

### Causes and Significance of Deficits
- Underlying reasons for deficits

### Summary Conclusions and Recommendations
- Opinion section that may or may not address the ultimate issue
- Recommendations for restoration to competence, as is relevant

| Sample Competency to Stand Trial Evaluation | Table 4.13 |

Date

The Honorable Judge
Southern Town, Southern State

RE: Defendant
DOB: mm/dd/yyyy

Judge:

Defendant is an 18-year-old single, white male charged with Receiving Stolen Property Worth Over 100 Dollars. Specifically, he is charged with possession of a stolen automobile. Mr. Defendant is referred per your order for evaluation of his competency to stand trial. At the time of the evaluation, Mr. Defendant was in the County Detention Center. I met with Mr. Defendant on May 17. Mr. Defendant is informed that the results of the evaluation will be released to the court and that the results may be used against him in court. Mr. Defendant gave his written consent to be evaluated.

### PSYCHOLOGICAL EVALUATION

Instruments Administered:

    Wechsler Adult Intelligence Scale—Revised
    Bender Visual Motor Gestalt Test
    Minnesota Multiphasic Personality Inventory (MMPI)
    Michigan Alcoholism Screening Test (MAST)
    Lipsitt, Lelos and McGarry Competency to Stand Trial
      Assessment Instrument

Interviews Conducted:

    Defendant
    Defense Attorney
    Prosecuting Attorney
    Ms. Center Director

Records Reviewed:
    Video Record
    Detention Center Records
    Adolescent Center Records including psychological test results

Psychosocial History:

Mr. Defendant was born in Town, State, and moved to State when he was approximately 5 years old. His parents separated when he was 18 months old. He lived "off and

*(continued)*

Sample Competency to Stand Trial Evaluation (*continued*)

on" with his mother between placements in foster homes. He has three older sisters in State with whom he maintains contact. His mother has been living in Town, State, since 1988. She also remarried in 1988. Mr. Defendant's father is in a nursing home in Different State after suffering two strokes. Mr. Defendant last saw his father in 1987.

Mr. Defendant completed school through the 11th grade at County High School. He states that he did not sign up for his senior year due to the lack of a birth certificate. Although he did not like school, he states his grades were As and Bs. He was suspended once for fighting. He claims that he had plenty of friends in high school and in his numerous placements.

Mr. Defendant does not have a work history. He was employed in a summer youth program in 1990 and has worked at the various placements where he has lived. He was never married and has no children.

During his spare time, Mr. Defendant states that he is involved in sports such as swimming, biking, and repelling. He also watches movies on television. He has been on medications in the past for acne; however, he is currently on no medications. He denies alcohol and drug use but does admit to smoking approximately one-half pack of cigarettes per day.

Mr. Defendant states that he has been arrested on numerous occasions. All arrests have been for theft either in the form of shoplifting or automobile or horse theft.

Mr. Defendant's future plans are to be employed as a truck driver. However, Mr. Defendant does not have a driver's license. His reason for the lack of an operator's license is because he is "too lazy to try."

Psychiatric History:

Mr. Defendant has been in several treatment centers for adjudicated delinquents. Mr. Defendant's last placement was at Adolescent Center in City. Mr. Defendant was at Adolescent Center from December 30, 1987, to June 15, 1989. He was referred to this program due to behavioral problems at an earlier placement. He had been charged with Burglary-Third Degree. There Mr. Defendant did not complete the program. Rather, he left the program without permission and stole an automobile. He was required to spend several months in a juvenile detention center after the incident. Ms. Center Director states that Mr. Defendant was difficult to work with in that he would continually cause disruptions with his peers. She describes him as needy, likable, and nonviolent.

Mr. Defendant has no history of treatment with psychotropic medications. Records at Adolescent Center indicate he has a diagnosis of conduct disorder; inhalant abuse, in remission; developmental articulation disorder; and developmental expressive language disorder.

Report of the Crime:

Mr. Defendant states that he was walking home in Town at 11:50 p.m. on January 19. He states that it was cold out when he stopped in front of an automobile lot with a car he hoped to purchase. He then decided he would take the car. He had a

BB gun with him and a pair of gloves. He broke the glass window to the office with the BB gun. He cleaned up the glass on the outside of the building before getting the keys to the car he wanted. He removed the sales slip from the car but adds that he forgot the "pink slip."

He was driving around in the car thinking of a place to park the car until he could retrieve it the next day. At this point he decided to drive to Small City. He was in small Town when he passed a gas station where a police car had just arrived. He states that he then panicked and lost control of the car while doing approximately 80 miles per hour. The car hit a curb and spun around in the street until hitting the curb again, dislodging the back wheel.

He was then arrested. Initially he tried to claim ownership of the car, and then he stated that the car belonged to an aunt and finally while in the police car admitted that the vehicle was stolen. He was then taken to the station and processed. He denies alcohol or drug use on the night of the incident.

Test Results:

Mr. Defendant was cooperative and appeared motivated during the testing. His results on the WAIS-R are considered a valid assessment of his current intellectual functioning. Mr. Defendant scored a Verbal IQ of 81, a Performance IQ of 103, and a Full Scale IQ of 89. This places his overall intellectual functioning in the Low Average range between Average and Borderline. Records from Adolescent Center indicate Mr. Defendant was tested in October 1989 and received a Verbal IQ of 76, a Performance IQ of 100, and a Full Scale IQ of 84. Mr. Defendant's relatively low score on the Verbal subtests is suggestive of a Developmental Expressive Language Disorder.

Though a full neuropsychological evaluation was not conducted, results on the Bender Visual Motor Gestalt Test do not suggest an organic neurological dysfunction.

Mr. Defendant did not complete a sufficient number of items on the MMPI to allow for a valid interpretation. His responses to items on the MAST suggest that Mr. Defendant does not have a problem with alcohol.

Competency to Stand Trial:

When asked how he can defend himself against these charges, Mr. Defendant states, "I know I did it. I'll plead I'm guilty."

Mr. Defendant states that he has been to court "tons of times" and understands the courtroom procedure. He realizes that he must control himself in the courtroom. He understands that he could be found in contempt of court if he were to speak out or move around in the courtroom without permission. Mr. Defendant knows the roles of the courtroom principals. He is aware of his right against self-incrimination. He understands the adversarial nature of the trial.

Mr. Defendant knows that his attorney is Defense Attorney and understands how he came to represent him. He expresses confidence in Mr. Attorney. He feels that he is "doing his best" and agrees with the way he has handled the case thus far. Mr. Defendant states, "If I do the crime, I should do the time."

*(continued)*

Sample Competency to Stand Trial Evaluation (*continued*)

Mr. Defendant states that he is charged with auto theft. He states that it is either a class D or class C felony. He states that the burglary charge against him has been dropped. He states that this is a "major" offense. He thinks that he could receive 1 to 5 years in prison or possibly probation. He understands the concept of probation and plea-bargaining. He states that "probation is hard to do. I've broken it plenty of times."

He thinks that the State has a strong case against him but feels that he has a 50% chance of getting off.

Mr. Defendant is able to discuss his case with his lawyer and is able to testify relevantly in a trial. He realizes he would need to tell his lawyer if a witness were to tell a lie against him in court. He is able to sustain a self-preserving motivation during a trial.

Conclusions:

Defendant is an 18-year-old single, white male charged with Receiving Stolen Property Worth Over 100 Dollars. Specifically, he is charged with possession of a stolen automobile. Mr. Defendant has an extensive arrest record with numerous arrests for burglary.

Mr. Defendant functions in the Low Average range of intellectual functioning. Mr. Defendant's verbal skills are limited. His diction is poor, suggestive of Developmental Articulation Disorder. The individual fails to use expected speech sounds, giving the impression of "baby talk." Mr. Defendant tends to think in concrete terms. However, Mr. Defendant has had extensive experience with the judicial system and understands the process adequately.

Mr. Defendant has the mental capacity to appreciate the nature of the charges against him. He has the capacity to rationally participate in his own defense.

Diagnosis DSM-III-R:

Currently:

Axis I – Conduct Disorder, undifferentiated, moderate

Axis II – Developmental Articulation Disorder
Developmental Expressive Language Disorder

Axis III – None

Axis IV – Psychosocial Stressors: unemployment,
incarceration, speech problems
Severity: 4 – Severe (primarily
enduring circumstances)

Axis V – Current Functioning: GAF 50 – Serious Symptoms

Best Functioning Past Year: GAF 50 – Serious
Symptoms

## Sample Competency to Stand Trial Evaluation  Table 4.14

Date

The Honorable Judge
County Circuit Court
Town, State

RE: Defendant
DOB: mm/dd/yyyy

Judge:

Defendant is a 32-year-old divorced, white male charged with Wanton Endangerment–First Degree, Driving Under the Influence–First Offense and Leaving the Scene of an Accident. Mr. Defendant is referred per your order for evaluation of his competency to stand trial. At the time of the evaluation, Mr. Defendant was out on bond. I met with Mr. Defendant on June 5, 1992. Mr. Defendant is informed that the results of the evaluation will be released to the court and that the results may be used against him in court. Mr. Defendant gave his written consent to be evaluated.

### PSYCHOLOGICAL EVALUATION

Instruments Administered:

Wechsler Adult Intelligence Scale—Revised
Bender Visual Motor Gestalt Test with Canter Background
    Interference Procedure
Minnesota Multiphasic Personality Inventory (MMPI)
Millon Clinical Multiaxial Inventory-II (MCMI-II)
Trail Making Test, Parts A and B
Lipsitt, Lelos and McGarry Competency to Stand Trial
    Assessment Instrument

Interviews Conducted:

Defendant
Defense Attorney
Prosecuting Attorney's Detective
Mr. Defendant's father
Mr. Defendant's girlfriend

Records Reviewed:

Uniform Citation: County Sheriff Department (date/92)
Surgery Notes: University Hospital, City (date/83)
Surgery Notes: University Hospital, City (date/83)
Progress Notes: University Hospital, City (date–date/83)

*(continued)*

Sample Competency to Stand Trial Evaluation (*continued*)

Operative Note: Humana Hospital, City (date/88)
Discharge Summary: Humana Hospital, City (date/88)

Psychosocial History:

Mr. Defendant was born in A County and has spent the majority of his life in State. He currently lives with his 72-year-old retired father. Mr. Defendant's parents were divorced in the late 1960s. Mr. Defendant lived with his mother who was on welfare and moved frequently. Mr. Defendant's mother died of a heart attack in the mid-1980s. After his mother's death, Mr. Defendant started living with his father. Neither Mr. Defendant nor his father were sure of the exact dates and were only able to give close approximates. Mr. Defendant has two brothers and two sisters who all live in the same county in State. Mr. Defendant states that he "sometimes" gets along with them. Mr. Defendant also had a brother who committed suicide in 1989.

Mr. Defendant states that he quit school in the seventh grade. When asked why, he states that he "just quit." He adds that he had not done well in school. When asked about his employment history, Mr. Defendant states that he had a job for six months while in a reform school in Town. He states that he was sent to a reform school for 6 months for vandalizing property. He and several friends had broken out the windows of a house under construction. While at the reform school Mr. Defendant states that he was required to do house cleaning. He has no other employment history and currently does not work. His father states that Mr. Defendant would quit farm jobs he was able to secure for Mr. Defendant after working for only a few hours. Mr. Defendant collects $422 per month on SSI.

Mr. Defendant was married when he was 20 years old. The marriage lasted one year, although Mr. Defendant states that he and his wife remained together for only 6 months. He has a daughter named Sue from this marriage. Mr. Defendant has no contact with either his wife or daughter. He states that the marriage ended because his wife "tried to tell him what to do." Mr. Defendant was never in the military, stating that he had tried to enlist but was judged not capable.

Mr. Defendant states that he enjoys sitting around the house and listening to his stereo. Mr. Defendant states that he likes to "crank up the stereo" when his father is not home. Mr. Defendant admits that he is very restless and frequently goes for long walks "all over" town. Mr. Defendant's father added that Mr. Defendant knows everyone in town and will stop and talk with everyone.

Mr. Defendant smokes cigarettes and states that he drinks "every once in a while." He admits that he has been arrested twice for alcohol intoxication, once several years ago and the current incident. He denies getting into fights while drinking. He also denies any other drug use.

Mr. Defendant's father recently had surgery for jaw cancer and is scheduled for surgery again in November. Both Mr. Defendant and his father become visibly upset when discussing the upcoming surgery. Mr. Defendant's father states that he does not know who will take care of Mr. Defendant when he dies. Mr. Defendant states that he would probably "hitchhike to Mexico." It does not appear that Mr. Defendant realizes he would most likely be unable to care for himself.

Mr. Defendant has been dating Ms. Girlfriend for approximately one year. Ms. Girlfriend appears to understand Mr. Defendant's intellectual and social limitations. She describes the relationship as good and states that Mr. Defendant has a great deal of freedom regarding the amount of time they spend together. Mr. Defendant states that he is unable to stay in one place for more than a few hours. During the evaluation, Mr. Defendant frequently got up to walk around in the office. It was also necessary to take two extended breaks during the evaluation.

Psychiatric History:

In 1983 Mr. Defendant was in a motor vehicle accident and suffered an open head injury. Mr. Defendant apparently received damage to the frontal and temporal lobes of the brain. Head injuries sustained in a motor vehicle accident frequently cause damage in other parts of the brain in addition to the area of penetration. Individuals with frontal lobe injury are apt to be impulsive, disinhibited, and out of touch with common social concerns. Mr. Defendant has amnesia for events preceding and following the accident. He was initially in a coma after the accident. Upon awakening, he needed to be fed and taught how to dress. His recuperation lasted approximately 18 months. He is now able to get around in familiar settings by himself. Mr. Defendant has a noticeable indentation in his skull in the right temporal area. Individuals with low premorbid intellectual functioning and a frontal open head injury have a poor prognosis for returning to work.

In 1988 Mr. Defendant was again in a motor vehicle accident suffering primarily facial lacerations and body injuries. Mr. Defendant's brother was also a passenger in the vehicle and was confined to a wheelchair after the accident. One year after the accident, his brother committed suicide using a shotgun. Mr. Defendant's father states that this brother had a drinking problem. Mr. Defendant's father becomes visibly upset when discussing this accident.

Mr. Defendant claims that he has threatened suicide in the past. Once when he was arrested for public intoxication, Mr. Defendant tried to hang himself in jail with his shoelaces. When asked what happened when he tried this, he laughingly states that the jailor took everything from him except his underwear. He does not appear to have the insight to appreciate the seriousness of a suicide attempt. Mr. Defendant states that he also tried to kill himself when his mother died. He apparently went out into a field and fired off a shotgun. When his family asked him later what happened, he simply stated that he had missed.

Report of the Crime:

Mr. Defendant states that a friend of his father's was visiting the defendant's home on the day of the incident. His father had gone to bed and he and the visitor stayed up and were drinking alcohol. His father's friend asked Mr. Defendant to give him a ride into town. He states that they drove to a friend's house. Mr. Defendant was then asked to go to the liquor store. He drove to the liquor store but forgot what he was doing and did not stop at the liquor store. He continued driving. When asked where he was going he states that he was not sure. He admits to being intoxicated at the time.

He states that he then hit the pickup truck. He stopped and asked the driver of the vehicle if he was going to call the police. When the driver indicated that he would call the police, Mr. Defendant states that he "got scared and took off." He denies the reports that he almost hit a pedestrian. He states that he drove approximately one-half

*(continued)*

Sample Competency to Stand Trial Evaluation (*continued*)

mile further before hitting a telephone pole. Mr. Defendant was arrested at the scene and placed in jail.

Mr. Defendant remained in jail for 3 days because he did not know how to get in touch with his father. His father does not have a telephone and Mr. Defendant does not know anyone else's phone number. Mr. Defendant's father discovered Mr. Defendant's whereabouts after being informed by a friend who read about the incident in the newspaper. When asked, Mr. Defendant is unable to accurately recall his home address or his girlfriend's phone number.

Mr. Defendant states that he gave his driver's license to the police because he thought he lost it automatically. Mr. Defendant obtained his driver's license several years ago. He has also sold his car since the accident.

Test Results:

Mr. Defendant was alert and cooperative during the testing. His results on the WAIS-R are considered a valid assessment of his current intellectual functioning. Mr. Defendant scored a Verbal IQ of 62, a Performance IQ of 63, and a Full Scale IQ of 61. This places his overall intellectual functioning in the Mild Mentally Retarded range. However, there is no record of Mr. Defendant's intellectual functioning prior to his automobile accident. Mr. Defendant did quit school during the seventh grade. He also states that while in school his performance was poor. Thus, it is not possible to determine if his current intellectual functioning is a result of the accident or indicative of his premorbid intellectual functioning.

Although a full neuropsychological evaluation was not conducted, results on the Bender Gestalt Test and the WAIS-R are suggestive of an organic impairment. Mr. Defendant performed significantly worse on the Bender Gestalt Test using the Background Interference Procedure (BIP). Individuals with brain damage typically perform poorly when copying the Bender Gestalt figures onto a sheet of paper with irregular wavy lines. Additionally, Mr. Defendant's performance on the Trail Making Test is suggestive of brain damage. This diagnosis would be consistent with Mr. Defendant's history of an open head injury. Mr. Defendant demonstrated poor long-term memory, being unable to recall his age, address, or girlfriend's phone number. His short-term recall was marginal as he had difficulty recalling three words after 15 minutes and was only able to recall 9 of 15 common items immediately after viewing them. Most individuals are usually able to recall an average of 12 items.

Mr. Defendant is illiterate and thus could not complete the MMPI or the MCMI-II by himself. These two tests were administered orally. Mr. Defendant's responses on the MMPI are considered valid, though the unique testing situation must be taken into consideration. His response pattern is characteristic of individuals who are admitting to personal and emotional difficulties. Individuals with similar validity scale configurations are described as having poor impulse control and inappropriate behavior. This response pattern represents a chronic level of marginal adjustment. These individuals tend to withdraw and isolate themselves, experiencing depression and agitation.

Mr. Defendant's responses on the MCMI-II are valid. His responses are characteristic of individuals who are tense, indecisive, and restless. Somatic complaints such as tightness, ill-defined muscular aches, and nausea are common. There was no indication of a thought disorder or major psychiatric syndrome based on his responses.

Competency to Stand Trial:

When asked how he can defend himself against these charges, Mr. Defendant states, "I don't know." He does not appear to have an awareness of his possible legal defenses.

Mr. Defendant realizes that he must control himself in the courtroom. He states that he would "probably get locked up" if he were to speak out or move around in the courtroom without permission. Although Mr. Defendant realizes that he must control his behavior in the courtroom, he may be unable to remain seated for more than an hour. Mr. Defendant frequently got up and walked around the office during the evaluation. Additionally, Mr. Defendant engages in socially inappropriate behaviors, apparently oblivious to social custom. At one point he completely unbuttoned his shirt in order to tuck it into his trousers. Additionally, he attempted to smoke on several occasions, having forgotten the request to refrain from smoking stated only several minutes earlier.

Mr. Defendant knows his lawyer is Mr. Attorney and understands how he came to represent him. He states that he has confidence in his lawyer. When asked if he thinks his lawyer can help him, Mr. Defendant replies, "I don't know. I hope he can." When asked if he thinks his lawyer is doing a good job, he replies, "No. He won't sit still long enough to talk to you. He is never in his office or he is always leaving." Mr. Defendant states that he does not know how is lawyer is planning to handle the case. Mr. Defendant expressed frustration at not having sufficient access to Mr. Attorney in order to review his case with him.

Mr. Defendant does not understand the concept of a plea bargain. Mr. Defendant's father states that Mr. Defendant was offered a plea bargain consisting of a 2-year jail term in exchange for a guilty plea. Additionally, Mr. Defendant did not understand what the word "testify" means. When asked about the role of the courtroom principals, Mr. Defendant stated that the jury's responsibility is to "put you in jail." When questioned about the judge's role, Mr. Defendant states, "Well, he has a hand in it too." He did not appear to understand the impartiality of the judge or jury. Mr. Defendant does not understand the terms "defense counsel" or "prosecutor." However, he does understand the role of his lawyer.

Mr. Defendant is not aware of his right against self-incrimination. He is aware of the adversarial nature of the trial and does understand the nature of probation.

When asked what he is charged with, Mr. Defendant states, "hit and run, leaving the scene of an accident, and wanton endangerment." When questioned further, he is able to recall that he is also charged with driving under the influence. When asked about possible sentencing should he be found guilty, Mr. Defendant states that he was told he would go to jail for 2–5 years. He states that he would most likely have to serve such a sentence at "La Grange." Mr. Defendant expresses concern about his ability to remain incarcerated. He is aware of his restlessness and recognizes that it would be difficult for him to remain in a secured environment.

He states that he does not know what his chances are to be found innocent but adds that he "probably don't have no chance." He appears to feel that the outcome of his trial is completely out of his control.

Mr. Defendant is able to relate the details of the incident to his lawyer. He is able to sustain a self-preserving motivation during a trial. However, Mr. Defendant's

*(continued)*

Sample Competency to Stand Trial Evaluation (*continued*)

low level of intellectual functioning and lack of formal education impair Mr. Defendant's ability to understand, participate, and cooperate with his counsel in planning a defense strategy. In addition, due to Mr. Defendant's low level of intellectual functioning, it is unlikely that he would be able to testify relevantly in a trial.

Conclusions:

Defendant is a 32-year-old divorced white male charged with Wanton Endangerment – First Degree, Driving Under the Influence–First Offense, and Leaving the Scene of an Accident.

Mr. Defendant functions in the Mildly Retarded range of intellectual functioning. He quit school while in the seventh grade and has never held a steady job. In 1983, at the age of 22, Mr. Defendant was in a motor vehicle accident and suffered an open head injury. Although a complete neuropsychological examination was not conducted, current test results are suggestive of brain damage.

Mr. Defendant does not have the mental capacity to appreciate the nature of the charges against him. He does not have the capacity to rationally participate in his own defense. It is unlikely that Mr. Defendant will achieve competency in the foreseeable future.

Diagnosis DSM-III-R:

Currently:

Axis I – Dementia, Moderate (Provisional)

Axis II – Mental Retardation, Mild (Provisional)

Axis III –Post right temporal skull fracture and
partial right temporal lobectomy

Axis IV – Psychosocial Stressors: unemployed, pending
trial
Severity: 4 – Severe

Axis V – Current Functioning (GAF): 40 – Serious
Symptoms

Best Functioning Past Year (GAF): 40 –
Serious Symptoms

**Note: The judge ruled the defendant competent to stand trial at the pretrial hearing.**

# Summary

This chapter reviewed two common evaluations that forensic psychologists perform in the criminal justice system: criminal responsibility and competency to stand trial. The concept of *mens rea*, or a guilty mind, was presented along with various affirmative defenses. The three levels of burden of proof used in court were reviewed. Myths and statistics of the insanity plea (criminal responsibility) were presented. The history of the criminal responsibility standard was discussed and relevant case law was reviewed. Important standards regarding the insanity plea include the McNaughten test, the Irresistible Impulse test, the Durham or Product test, the American Law Institute test, and the Insanity Defense Reform Act. The evaluation of mental state at the time of the offense (MSO) was reviewed and psychological and forensic assessment instruments were presented, with particular attention to the Rogers Criminal Responsibility Scales. The ethical issues related to a MSO evaluation were reviewed with emphasis on the limits of confidentially and the need for the defendant's informed consent. Two sample reports were presented with differing outcomes.

The chapter then discussed competency to stand trial evaluations. Four rationales for trying only competent defendants were discussed. The court's definition of competency was presented as the Dusky standard. Other relevant case law was reviewed, including the *Godinez v. Moran* decision and the *Jackson v. Indiana* decision. The issue of restoration to competency on both an inpatient and outpatient basis was presented as well as the disposition of defendants found incompetent to stand trial (IST). Several assessment instruments used in competency evaluations were reviewed, including the MacCAT-CR, CAI, CST, IFI, and GCCT. Descriptions of the instruments and general scoring procedures were provided. The process of conducting a CST evaluation was elaborated on and report writing was briefly discussed. Sample competency evaluations were provided.

# Role of the Forensic Psychologist in Capital Punishment Sentencing

Mr. Fryer has a long history of psychiatric hospitalizations related to his diagnosis of paranoid schizophrenia. His delusions revolve around the belief that uniform spies have been sent to execute him. He reports auditory and visual hallucinations when not on his medication. He was arrested for trespassing after he was found sleeping in the delivery shed of a warehouse.

During his stay in jail he was put on antipsychotic medications and was released for time-served after spending 54 days in jail. Upon his release he returned to living on the streets and stopped taking his medications. While sleeping on a park bench he was assaulted by several youths who hit and kicked him, leaving him on the ground but with no serious injuries. Mr. Fryer was convinced that the juveniles who assaulted him were spies who would later return to assassinate him.

He found a 17-inch pipe and hid in the shadows the remainder of the evening, fearing for his life. In the early dawn, he saw two uniformed youths approaching him. A 12-year-old boy and his 14-year-old brother were on their way to a Boy Scout meeting. Mr. Fryer ran up behind the boys and started swinging the pipe wildly, screaming that they would never take him alive. He struck the 12-year-old in the head causing severe brain trauma. The 14-year-old was able to flee but only after receiving a blow in the face. Mr. Fryer returned to the 12-year-old and bludgeoned him to death.

He was still hitting the lifeless body when the police arrived. As soon as the police car pulled up he dropped the pipe and sat in silence as he was subdued. He was found incompetent to stand trial and was committed to a state hospital. After 8 months of pharmacological treatment he was found competent, tried, and convicted of capital murder.

In the jurisdiction, mitigating circumstances are that the offender was, at the time of the offense, (1) under extreme emotional or mental distress, and (2) substantially unable to appreciate the wrongfulness of his act or conform his behavior to the requirements of the law.

Aggravating circumstances are that (1) the crime was committed in a wanton, atrocious, and cruel manner, and (2) the offender has the probability of committing criminal acts in the future.

You are hired by the defense to assist in the sentencing phase. Analyze the case study and address the following:

- How should you proceed? Provide reasons to support your answer.
- What role do the mitigating and aggravating circumstances play in capital sentencing?
- What issues as a forensic psychologist will you address? How will you support your opinion to the court? Provide examples and references.

# TEST YOUR KNOWLEDGE

1. The most common type of forensic evaluation conducted by psychologists is the
   a. criminal responsibility evaluation
   b. competency to stand trial evaluation
   c. child custody evaluation
   d. affirmative defense evaluation

2. *Mens rea* refers to
   a. a guilty mind
   b. guilt beyond a reasonable doubt
   c. being guilty but mentally ill
   d. use of an affirmative defense

3. What is the chronological order of the following standards?
   a. The McNaughten Rule, the Durham Standard, the Brawner Rule
   b. The Brawner rule, the McNaughten rule, the Durham standard
   c. The Durham standard, the McNaughten rule, the Brawner rule
   d. The Brawner rule, the Durham rule, the McNaughten rule

4. The ruling that defendants may only be held for a reasonable amount of time if they can be brought to competence was
   a. *Dusky v. United States*, 1960
   b. *Jackson v. Indiana*, 1972
   c. *Godinez v. Moran*, 1993
   d. Insanity Defense Reform Act, 1984

5. The Insanity Defense Reform Act was the result of what historical event?
   a. The assassination of President John F. Kennedy
   b. The assassination attempt of President Bill Clinton
   c. The assassination attempt of President Ronald Reagan
   d. None of the above

Answer Key: (1) b, (2) a, (3) a, (4) b, (5) c

# Chapter Five

# Police Psychology

## Learning Objectives

- Define police psychology and the multiple roles of the police psychologist.
- Be able to discuss the ethical limitations of evaluations conducted by police psychologists, such as officer selection and fitness-for-duty evaluations.
- List the types of evaluations police psychologists conduct.
- What approaches have been used in selecting police officers?
- What personality traits have been linked to potential problems in working as a law enforcement officer?
- According to the guidelines discussed in the text, what should preemployment evaluations include?
- Identify psychological test instruments used in preemployment police officer evaluations.
- What are the types of determinations made after preemployment evaluations and fitness-for-duty evaluations?
- Describe what a fitness-for-duty evaluation is and what circumstances might warrant such an evaluation.
- Describe what constitutes a critical incident and cite several examples.
- Describe the profession's approach to evaluations for special assignments.
- Identify the different types of special assignments to which police officers may be assigned.
- What are some of the advantages of using peer counselors in counseling police officers?
- Be able to list some of the essential skills required of police psychologists and describe the training of most police psychologists.
- What consultative duties might a police psychologist be asked to perform?
- To whom might a police psychologist provide counseling services?
- What is gender role conflict and how might this affect a police officer's performance?
- What is meant by the professionalization of law enforcement?

## Key Terms

- Academy of Police Psychologists (APP)
- Americans with Disabilities Act
- Behavioral Science Unit
- *Bonsignore v. City of New York* (1982)
- California Psychological Inventory
- Commission on Accreditation of Law Enforcement Agencies
- Concurrent validity
- Confidentiality
- *Conte v. Horcher* (1977)
- Correction Validity Scale (K)
- Council of Police Psychological Services (COPPS)
- Criminal profiling
- Critical incident
- Critical incident counseling
- *David v. Christian*, 1987
- Employee Polygraph Protection Act of 1988
- Fitness-for-duty evaluations
- Gender role conflict (GRC)
- Hostage negotiation
- Impact phase
- Infrequency Validity Scale (F)
- Investigative hypnosis
- Investigative psychology

*(continued)*

## Key Terms *(continued)*

- Investigative services
- Inwald Personality Inventory
- Lie Validity Scale (L)
- Mandatory Accreditation Standards
- Minnesota Multiphasic Personality Inventory–2
- NASH
- Organizational services
- Other-than-mandatory standards
- Peer-counselor programs
- Police psychology
- Posttraumatic phase
- Predictive validity
- Preemployment screening
- Privilege communication

- Psychological autopsy
- Psychological profiling
- Psychological suitability
- Psychopathology
- Recoil phase
- Research services
- Special Unit Assignments
- Special-purpose police agencies
- Standards for Law Enforcement Agencies
- Stockholm syndrome
- Stress inoculation
- Suicide by cop
- SWAT team
- Training services

**Police psychology** is the "research and application of psychological principles and clinical skills to law enforcement and public safety" (Bartol & Bartol, 2004, p. 34). Police psychologists are engaged in a broad range of activities, including selection of police officers, counseling, training of police officers, fitness-for-duty evaluations and special unit evaluations, operational support (e.g., field consultation on hostage situations), and organizational development and consultation. The majority of police psychologists are clinical or counseling psychologists who have gained specialized experience in law enforcement–related situations. Police psychologists are normally not sworn officers, although it is important to have an understanding of police work to be an effective police psychologist. There are postdoctoral fellowships and training programs for psychologists to gain a better understanding of policing. A major theme throughout this text on forensic psychology has been the importance of assessment. Police psychologists spend a large percentage of their time in assessment activities. These assessment activities will be covered in detail in this chapter. Police psychologists also provide counseling, training, and conduct research and program evaluation. Before discussing the specific roles of police psychologists, it will be helpful to have a general understanding of police work and police departments.

# Police Department's History with Psychology

In the United States, there are nearly 18,000 law enforcement agencies. This figure includes local police departments, state agencies such as the state police and highway patrol, and federal agencies such as the Federal Bureau of Investigation, the Drug Enforcement Administration, and the Secret Service. There are also **special-purpose police agencies** such as campus police, transit authority, park police, airport police, and school system police. It should not be surprising that there is no single "model" police agency (Territo, Halstead, & Bromley, 2004). Agencies vary widely in number of personnel, responsibilities, and specialization in terms of officer duties. However, most people form their opinion about the police from television shows and the news media. When asked to describe the "typical" police department, people may use schemas adapted from television, such as *NYPD Blue*. Alternatively, they may recall information gleaned from the news media regarding an incident at a large police department, such as the Los Angeles or Chicago police departments. The vast majority of law enforcement agencies are local police departments. There are approximately 13,000 local police departments, and over half of these departments employ fewer than 10 police officers.

It is relatively recently that police departments have started to utilize the services of psychologists. Although many other government agencies employed psychologists, law enforcement was one of the last major bureaucracies to call on psychologists (Blau, 1994). For example, as early as 1918, psychologists were involved in the assessment of military troops during World War I. In World War II, psychologists refined their assessment skills and played a major role in the selection and classification of military recruits (Cronin, 2003). By the end of World War II, over 13 million persons had taken the Army General Classification Test. Psychologists were even involved in the establishment of the United States' first major espionage organization—the Office of Strategic Services (OSS) (Blau, 1994). Henry Murray, a Harvard psychologist, completed a psychological profile of Adolph Hitler in 1943 while working for the OSS. Despite psychologists' success in assessing recruits and developing investigative techniques, law enforcement showed little interest in the profession until only recently. As Blau suggested in 1994, the police psychology movement is only beginning.

Psychologists had worked with law enforcement in a supportive role doing tasks such as crisis intervention as early as the 1950s (Hoover, 1989). Chandler (1990) traces the beginning of modern police psychology to a paper presented in 1968 at a regional psychological association's annual meeting. The paper was presented by a psychologist, Martin Reiser, employed full time by the Los Angeles Police Department, and was aptly titled, "The Police Department Psychologist." The paper was published several years later (Reiser, 1972). Another advance for the emerging role of police psychologists came from the FBI. The **Behavioral Science Unit** (BSU) of the Federal Bureau of Investigation has played a major role in helping to develop the field of police psychology. From its inception, BSU used psychological principles and research to understand criminal behavior. The FBI gave police psychology an important boost when it hosted a conference in 1984 at the Academy on the role of psychologists and the services they can provide to local police departments. The conference was attended by nearly 150 psychologists and law enforcement personnel and generated over 60 papers describing the types of services psychologists were providing to law enforcement agencies (Blau, 1994). The success of this conference led to a second major conference, the International Conference on Police Psychology, hosted again by the FBI Academy. The FBI hosted a third major conference on critical incidents in policing in 1989. The networking that was initiated at these conferences among psychologists and law enforcement personnel led to the development of several professional police psychologists organizations. The **Academy of Police Psychologists** (APP) and the **Council of Police Psychological Services (COPPS)** were a direct outgrowth of these conferences and helped to promote the field of police psychology.

Another major factor in promoting the psychological services to law enforcement was the development of accreditation standards for law enforcement agencies. In 1979, four major law enforcement agencies established the Commission on Accreditation for Law Enforcement Agencies as an independent accrediting authority. The four agencies are

1. International Association of Chiefs of Police (IACP),
2. the National Organization of Black Law Enforcement Executives (NOBLE),
3. the National Sheriff's Association (NSA), and
4. the Police Executive Research Forum (PERF).

Together, they represent approximately 80% of law enforcement personnel in the United States. The establishment of voluntary accrediting standards is part of the trend in policing toward professionalism (Territo et al., 2004). The **Standards for Law Enforcement Agencies** was first published in 1983; the fourth edition was published in January 1999. The last edition contains 446 standards organized into 38 chapters and addressed nine major law enforcement subjects. See Table 5.1 for a list of the nine subject areas addressed by the *Standards for Law Enforcement Agencies*.

| **Table 5.1** | **Nine Subject Areas Addressed by the *Standards for Law Enforcement Agencies*** |
|---|---|

- Role, responsibilities, and relationships with other agencies
- Organization, management, and administration
- Personnel structure
- Personnel process
- Operations
- Operational support
- Traffic operations
- Prisoner and court-related activity
- Auxiliary and technical services

### Figure 5.1

The Accreditation Standards mandate use of psychological screening for selection of police officers to a special operations unit. © 2009 Julien. Used under license from Shutterstock, Inc.

The process of accreditation is voluntary and can take several years to complete. Agencies must comply with all applicable standards. The standards are categorized as **mandatory** or **other-than-mandatory** and are a key element of the accreditation process (Territo et al., 2004). The standards strive to establish the best professional practices among law enforcement agencies and provide a structure for policies and procedures that ensure the highest quality of services. For a law enforcement agency to be accredited, it must comply with all mandatory standards and 80% of the other-than-mandatory standards. Though voluntary, police chiefs and sheriffs view accreditation as a way they can upgrade the quality of services they provide to the community. The standards enable law enforcement agencies to demonstrate publicly that they meet the professional criteria recognized by their profession.

The national standards secured the role of police psychologists in law enforcement agencies. The Accreditation Standards mandate the use of psychologists in police work both directly and indirectly. Indirectly, the standards require psychological screening of all police candidates prior to their probationary appointment to ensure that the candidate can succeed as a police officer. The standards also addressed psychological screening for selection to a special operations unit, such as assignment to a **Special Weapons and Tactical (SWAT)** team. Furthermore, the standards mandate the use of psychological testing, including the use of the **Minnesota Multiphasic Personality Inventory (MMPI)**, for selection to hostage negotiation teams. Finally, the standards directly mandate that a licensed psychologist or psychiatrist conduct psychological screening, including use of a clinical interview. Although the standards do not address the entire range of services provided to law enforcement by police psychologists, it is an important initial step in the development of the profession.

As stated earlier, Chandler (1990) traced the beginning of modern police psychology to the presentation of a scholarly paper by the lone psychologist hired at the Los Angeles Police Department. Today, the LAPD operates the Behavioral Sciences Services (BSS) and employs a staff of over 20 psychologists working in the BSS and out in the field. These police psychologists specialize in law enforcement–related situations and crisis intervention. The BSS provides counseling to departmental personnel and their families, training, organizational consultation, and debriefings. The services provided by the BSS is a prime example of the range of activities that police psychologists can be involved in and helps to define the field of police psychology. The LAPD is a large police department that can offer a wide range of services employing a number of psychologists. The current supervisor of the LAPD Behavioral Science Services is Chief Police Psychologist, Dr. Debra Glaser. See Table 5.2 for a brief description of Dr. Glaser's career. Not all departments can offer such a wide range of psychological services. In the late 1980s Delprino and Bahn (1988) found that over 50% of the police departments they surveyed utilized psychological services. Today, the number of departments using psychologists has increased to slightly over 90% (Bureau of Justice Statistics, 1999). With the number of departments seeking accreditation on the rise, it is likely that the need for psychological services to law enforcement will continue to increase.

## Chief Police Psychologist Dr. Debra Glaser, LAPD — Table 5.2

Dr. Glaser's career path to Chief Police Psychologist of the LAPD is illustrative of how many psychologists become involved in the area of police psychology. She has a master's degree in social psychology and a master's and PhD in clinical psychology. She initially started as a predoctoral student with the LAPD and then stayed on as a postdoctoral fellow. After her fellowship, Dr. Glaser worked with the LAPD as a consultant, eventually joining the agency as a staff psychologist in the Behavioral Science Services. Her specialty is in the area of investigative hypnosis, allowing her the opportunity to consult with detectives on homicide cases as well as other cases on which they are working. Dr. Glaser performs all the roles of a police psychologist including providing counseling services to sworn officers, civilian employees, and their family members, as well as conducting staff training. She has taught classes on stress management, smoking cessation, workplace violence, critical incident stress debriefing, suicide prevention, communication skills, and interpersonal skills. When asked to describe her job, Dr. Glaser states, "It's a fun job, I like it. It is never boring. We do everything from the mundane run-of-the-mill sitting in the office seeing clients to handling emergencies, going out on a SWAT call-out, investigative hypnosis, and consultation with the detectives on cases." She elaborated that the public frequently confuses police psychology with working with the defendants or inmates. She stressed that police psychology is working with law enforcement personnel and differs from conducting court-ordered evaluations on defendants or correctional psychology. It is especially satisfying to highlight Dr. Glaser's accomplishments in this text as she exemplifies the opportunities for women in a field many students perceive to be dominated by men.

| Table 5.3 | Four Roles Filled by the Police Psychologist |
|---|---|

- Provide traditional psychological services to individual and establishment
- Train and educate
- Management consultant on innovation, attitude change, and morale
- Research and program evaluator with appropriate feedback to encourage change

(Blau, 1994)

Blau (1994) states that the police psychologist must fulfill four roles (see Table 5.3): provide traditional psychological services to the individual officers, their families, and the department; train and educate departmental personnel, their families, and the public; serve as a management consultant on organizational behavior such as morale, *esprit de corps*, attitude change, and innovation; and conduct research and program evaluation and provide appropriate feedback to encourage change. See Table 5.4 for a detailed description of services offered by a Behavioral Science Unit in a typical mid-size law enforcement agency (Blau, 1994). Not all agencies can offer such a wide range of services as presented in Table 5.4. Indeed, most psychologists would not be qualified to offer the entire range of services listed. Many police psychologists complain that they are asked to provide services beyond their expertise or to be all things to all people (Super, 1999). Police psychologists spend the majority of their time in screening and selection of law enforcement officers and the provision of psychological counseling (Bartol, 1996).

Although the LAPD employs over 20 psychologists in-house, the majority of police psychologists work as consultants or contract employees to one or more police departments (Blau, 1994). A police psychologist does not have to be a sworn officer to work effectively. Some police officers do obtain an advanced degree in psychology, whereas some psychologists become sworn officers. However, probably fewer than 100 psychologists working with law enforcement agencies are also sworn officers. To be effective, the police psychologist does need to have an understanding of what a police officer does (Bittner, 1990). Despite recent strides in the field, there continues to be some skepticism and suspicion among law enforcement personnel of the role of psychology in police work (Blau, 1994). Some officers will leave therapy because they feel the therapist does not understand police work. One innovative program in San Francisco helps mental health professionals develop expertise in working with law enforcement personnel. Part of the training is learning about the police culture. The training includes ride-alongs with officers, a crisis-response team simulation, a visit to dispatch, a firearms training exercise, and a lesson in incident-report writing. One psychologist who has been through the training states, "I cannot imagine anybody trying to work with officers who haven't had this type of training. You have to walk in their shoes first to have a frame of reference" (Chamberlin, 2000). These types of orientation training programs have proven useful in helping psychologists understand police work (Hatcher, Mohandie, Turner, & Gelles, 1998).

There are both advantages and disadvantages to being both a psychologist and a police officer (Blau, 1994). One obvious advantage is an appreciation of the polic-

## Services Offered by a Behavioral Science Unit in a Mid-Size Law Enforcement Agency

Table 5.4

A.  Organizational Services
    1. Consultation to Management
    2. Officer Personnel Selection
    3. Fitness-for-Duty Evaluations
    4. Special Unit Evaluation (annual evaluations required by Accreditation Standards)
    5. Hostage Negotiation Consultation
    6. Deadly Force Incident Evaluation

B.  Investigative Services
    1. Investigative Hypnosis
    2. Criminal Profiling (serial murderers, serial rapists)
    3. Sex Crimes Analysis
    4. Psychological Autopsy

C.  Training
    1. Stress Reduction Seminars
    2. Domestic Violence Detection, Prevention, and Intervention
    3. Training Seminars (expert witness, road rage, credibility of child witness, etc.)
    4. Peer Group Counselor Training

D.  Personal Services
    1. Individual Counseling
    2. Group Counseling
    3. Family Counseling
    4. Critical Incident Counseling
    5. Stress Reduction Counseling
    6. Health and Wellness Programs (smoking cessation, drug and alcohol use, etc.)

E.  Research Services
    1. Effectiveness of Selection Procedures
    2. Effectiveness of Intervention Programs
    3. Effectiveness of Training Seminars

(Blau, 1994, pp. 315–322)

ing job that comes with the experience of working as a law enforcement officer. In addition to understanding the police experience, the psychologist–police officer also understands "cop language." Blau (1994) provides a five-page glossary of police slang to assist the novice police psychologist. A psychologist–police officer can generally establish empathy and trust with their clients quicker than one who is not "in the job." Police even express a preference for sworn officers, although most police psychologists do not perceive animosity from police officers (Bergen, Aceto, & Chadziewicz, 1992). This preference for working with sworn personnel has led to the development of **peer-counselor programs**. These programs train police officers in skills such as active listening and problem solving so that they can help other officers who are experiencing stress (Chamberlin, 2000). There are also disadvantages to being a psychologist–police officer. There may be resentment since the psychologist is taking up a police slot that could be filled by a police officer doing standard police work. The psychologist–police officer loses some of the mystique associated with the doctor title, and some police clients prefer not to be evaluated by a fellow police officer.

The other alternative is to either work as a civilian psychologist as a consultant or on staff. Again, there are advantages and disadvantages to both arrangements. A consultant can work for multiple agencies, accept the workload he or she is most comfortable with, avoid dual or multiple relationships, and generally earn a higher salary. The ability to maintain autonomy and avoid the office politics characteristic of most bureaucracies allows the consulting police psychologist greater flexibility in terms of services he or she provides. Disadvantages to the consulting role stem primarily from the consultant being viewed as an outsider. The consultant may not have access to all the necessary information, may not get sufficient feedback regarding services, and may experience a certain level of distrust or skepticism regarding recommendations. On the other hand, the in-house or staff police psychologist has ready access to confidential personnel information and can get to know many of the police officers in the department, enhancing credibility and accessibility. However, the increased accessibility can be a double-edged sword as the staff police psychologist may have numerous demands placed on his or her time and expertise. The in-house psychologist sacrifices the flexibility of the consultant for the security of the staff member. The department as well as the official job description dictates the workload and schedule.

For many psychologists their first experience in the field of police psychology is as a consultant (Bartol & Bartol, 2004). Psychologists may initially consult with a variety of local agencies providing counseling to department personnel and their families and provide police candidate screening and selection assessments. The consulting work may evolve into providing other services, such as training and special unit evaluations or fitness-for-duty evaluations. We now turn to a more detailed review of the types of services provided by police psychologists. See Table 5.5 for a summary of services provided by a police psychologist.

## Table 5.5    Services Provided by Police Psychologists

- ■ Psychological Assessment
  - • Preemployment assessment
  - • Fitness-for-duty evaluations
  - • Special unit assessment
- ■ Psychological Counseling
  - • Critical incident counseling
  - • Individual and family counseling
  - • Health and wellness counseling
- ■ Training
- ■ Consultation

## The Thin Blue Line

Dr. Shayleigh Jackson is a newly hired police psychologist for a large city police department. Although Dr. Jackson has had forensic psychology courses in graduate school and completed an internship with a different police agency, she still considers herself a novice to police work. In order to improve her status and gain respect among the police officers, she asks to do several ride-alongs, in which she accompanies officers on patrol. She agrees to accompany two officers on night patrols for a week. On the third night, the officers respond to a noise complaint. Apparently someone living in an apartment building is disturbing the neighbors by playing the stereo too loud. The officers consider the neighborhood to be safe and think of this as a routine call and agree that Dr. Jackson can accompany them to the door, although they caution her to stand behind them and to return to the car if there appears to be any trouble.

The officers knock on the door but there is no response, most likely due to the loud music drowning out their knocks. They again knock forcefully on the door and hear a male shout "Come in." The officers open the door and immediately see four men sitting in the front room dividing up what appears to be a rather large amount of powder cocaine. The officers also see a large sum of cash on the table as well as two weapons, a shotgun and a revolver. The police immediately pull their weapons and order the men onto the floor. Dr. Jackson is through the door and in the room when an officer orders her back to the car. The men are arrested without incident and a second squad car arrives to take Dr. Jackson back to the station.

The following day the station is bustling about the arrest and the "Doc's" involvement in apprehending four wanted drug dealers. Some officers joke with her, asking her to accompany them on patrol since she is obviously good luck. She enjoys the notoriety and feels that she is earning the respect of the officers on the force. However, approximately 1 week after the arrest, she learns that the arresting officers only reported the powder cocaine as evidence and did not report the cash or the weapons. With just a little checking, it becomes apparent that the arresting officers took the cash and the weapons. Dr. Jackson starts to wonder who else knows about the disappearance of the evidence and wonders if the earlier comments about her being good luck referred to this apparent cover-up. She wonders if she should report the incident to her supervisor. She feels that if others know, and she does not report, her integrity will be questioned. However, if she does report the incident, she is concerned that she may cross the "thin blue line" and alienate officers on the force.

How should Dr. Jackson proceed? How do the ethical guidelines for psychologists inform her decision? What are the ethical and professional issues she needs to consider? What will be the consequences of either decision?

# Police Officer Evaluations

There are five general reasons for a psychological assessment of law enforcement personnel (see Table 5.6). The first contact a law enforcement officer may have with a police psychologist is when they apply for a position as a police officer. Police psychologists spend a large amount of their professional time in preemployment screening and selection of recruits. In addition, a seasoned veteran who transfers from one law enforcement agency to another may also be required to undergo a psychological evaluation. For example, if a police officer with 15 years "in the job" in Florida moves with his spouse to Texas and seeks employment with the local police department, part of the application process is a preemployment psychological screening. A promotional assessment may be conducted to differentiate the skills of potential candidates for promotion. Police officers requesting special duty assignments, such as on a SWAT team, undercover work, or the sex crimes unit, are asked to undergo psychological testing. Due to the high levels of stress associated with these special assignments, the Commission on Accreditation for Law Enforcement Agencies recommends testing prior to taking high-risk assignments and then annually thereafter. A fifth reason an officer may be asked to obtain a psychological evaluation is when there is a question about his or her ability to perform his or her duties or a suspicion that the officer poses a risk to self or others. In this circumstance, a fitness-for-duty evaluation is mandated. In addition to psychological testing assessing intelligence and personality characteristics, the above evaluations may include physical agility tests, a background check, and performance ratings (Whisenand, 1989).

**Table 5.6**    Reasons for a Psychological Evaluation of a Police Officer

- Entry level (before or after academy training)
- Lateral move—experienced police personnel enter from outside agency
- Promotional testing
- Special assignments (SWAT, undercover work)
- Fitness-for-duty evaluations

As with other forensic evaluations discussed in this text, there are important distinctions between a psychological evaluation for law enforcement personnel and psychological evaluations conducted in a therapeutic setting. The main distinctions are the issues of **confidentiality** and privileged communication. Confidentiality refers to the psychologist's ethical and legal obligation to keep the client's communications private. Privilege is the law's recognition of the confidentiality of information that would otherwise be subject to disclosure in a legal proceeding (Petrila & Otto, 1996). Generally, when a psychologist evaluates a client all communications are confidential and the client holds privilege to the communications. This means that the client can refuse to disclose and prevent others from disclosing any communications made for the purpose of diagnosis or treatment of a mental disorder. However, when a police psychologist conducts one of the assessments presented above, the examinee or police officer is not the client. The employing agency is the client and the police psychologist cannot promise confidentiality (Borum et al., 2003). In addition, the police psychologist conducting an assessment cannot provide counseling to the examinee. The police psychologist has the ethical duty to notify the examinee prior to starting the evaluation that all communications are not confidential. The psychologist needs to clarify that his or her role is only to gather information about the examinee's **psychological suitability** for the position and not to provide treatment or therapeutic services.

In addition to the lack of confidentiality, another distinction between a therapeutic psychological evaluation and a law enforcement evaluation of the types discussed above is the issue of feedback. The police psychologist must inform the examinee prior to the evaluation that no feedback or interpretation of the results will be given. If the examinee requests feedback, it can only be provided with the consent of the agency as the holder of confidentiality. The right of the examinee to receive feedback on a preemployment psychological assessment has been tested in the courts. The courts have upheld the employing agency's right not to disclose the results of a preemployment evaluation (*Roulette v. Department of Central Management Services*, 1987; Super, 1997). Thus, prior to the start of the assessment, the police psychologist needs to clarify the limits of confidentiality, the psychologist's role as an evaluator and not as a counselor, and the fact that feedback will not be provided unless the agency gives the psychologist permission to do so. All of this information should be documented on an informed consent sheet signed by the examinee.

# Preemployment Evaluations

As early as the 1950s, the LAPD was using psychological screening procedures as part of its selection process for all potential police officers (Blau, 1994). The five-step selection process included a background check, a written civil service examination, an interview, a physical examination, and psychological assessment. The psychological assessment consisted of a brief clinical interview and testing including the MMPI, a group Rorschach Inkblot Test, and a tree drawing. The use of the last two projective techniques would be difficult to defend today.

The *National Advisory Commission on Criminal Justice and Goals: Police* (1967) advocated the use of psychological tests for officer selection. Later, in 1973, the *President's Commission on Law Enforcement and Administration of Justice* (1973) directed that psychological screening be incorporated in a law enforcement agency's selection procedures by the year 1975. Finally, as stated above, the Commission on Accreditation for Law Enforcement Agencies (CALEA) mandates **preemployment psychological screening** for police and sheriff's departments seeking accreditation. The Accreditation Standards from CALEA required that personality testing and a clinical interview be part of the recruit selection process. Guidelines for recruit selection developed and adopted by the Police Psychological Services Section of the International Association of Chiefs of Police (IACP Preemployment Psychological Evaluation Guidelines; IACP, 1998) suggest that preemployment psychological screenings should include psychological testing using objective assessment instruments and a job-related, semi-structured interview. The recently revised guidelines provide 22 recommendations for preemployment psychological screening (Curran, 1998). These IACP guidelines are consistent with best practices in police psychology and the CALEA standards (Borum et al., 2003).

The psychological screening is typically conducted after the police department has made a conditional offer of employment to the candidate (Hibler & Kurke, 1995). This is in accordance with the requirements of the **Americans with Disabilities Act** (ADA; Equal Employment Opportunity Commission, 1992). The ADA guarantees equal opportunity in employment, public services, transportation, public accommodations, and telecommunications for individuals with physical and mental disabilities. With regard to employment opportunities, the ADA prohibits discriminating against persons with physical or mental disabilities who can perform the *essential* functions of the job. The ADA prohibits questioning potential employees about disabilities before a job offer has been made. The job offer can be conditional on passing a medical examination. The Equal Employment Opportunity Commission has divided the inquiry of potential disabilities into two stages: preoffer of employment and postoffer but prehire (Bartol & Bartol, 2004). Prior to offering employment, the employer can only ask general questions about job performance. Once the agency makes a conditional offer, the agency can require candidates to undergo a medical and/or psychological evaluation. The agency can only withdraw the offer if it can show that the candidate is unable to perform the essential functions of the position even with reasonable accommodations (Bartol & Bartol, 2004).

The use of preemployment psychological evaluations has been challenged in the courts. However, the courts have consistently ruled that police agencies have a right to included psychological evaluations in their screening process (*Conte v. Horcher*, 1997; *McCabe v. Hoberman*, 1969). In fact, the courts have indicated that it is not only a right of the police agency to screen applicants but has suggested that it is the police agency's duty and that the police agency can be held liable for the actions of employees who were not properly screened (*Bonsignore v. City of New York*, 1982). Because of these court rulings and federal and professional guidelines, police psychologists play an essential role in the selection process of law enforcement applicants (Moriarty & Field, 1994). National surveys of police departments indicate that more police agencies are using psychological testing in their selection process. For example, one survey in the late 1980s found that approximately 50% of the responding police agencies indicated the use of psychological testing for police applicants (Delprino & Bahn, 1988). Fifteen years later, a national survey of 155 police agencies indicated that over 90% of the police agencies use psychological screening for police recruit selection (Cochrane, Tett, & VandeCreek, 2003). These studies also found a shift away from the use of projective techniques and psychometrically unsound instruments toward objective and standardized psychological instruments. Recall that in the 1950s the LAPD used a group Rorschach Inkblot Test and a tree drawing. The use of projective measures in forensic settings has routinely been criticized as unsound due to the lack of data supporting the validity of these instruments in forensic uses (Garb et al., 2002; Lally, 2003).

# Preemployment Assessment Instruments

Despite the trend toward the use of standardized measures, surveys indicate that departments use a variety of instruments and there is no standard for tests or interviews used (Cochrane et al., 2003; Strawbridge & Strawbridge, 1990). The need for normative and validity data on preemployment assessment instruments is critical due to the widespread use of psychological testing in preemployment selection (Scogin, Schumacher, Gardner, & Chaplin, 1995). The most frequently used tests continue to be group-administered paper-and-pencil tests along with an interview (Cochrane et al., 2003; Lefkowitz, 1977). Time spent in testing ranges from 30 minutes to 4 hours. Police departments use other screening measures in addition to the psychological tests and interview such as background checks, medical exams, polygraph testing, drug tests, and physical fitness tests.

The use of psychological testing for preemployment testing has traditionally used two different approaches: identifying the traits that make for a good cop and screening out pathology or potentially problem cops. The first approach presented is the use of psychological testing to identify the traits that make for a "good cop." If you ask a police officer or a friend what personality traits are necessary for someone to be a good police officer, you are likely to hear a litany of favorable personality traits. Nearly everyone has an opinion about the positive traits required to be a good police officer. A good exercise to do now is to write a list of the personality traits that should be *required*, and those personality traits that are *desirable* for a recruit to have to be hired as a police officer. Undoubtedly, you could generate a number of positive personality descriptors. Researchers have looked at personality traits such as bravery or courage, decisiveness, consistency and reliability, resistance to stress, cooperativeness, traditional values, and respect for authority (Smith & Scotland, 1973). Research has not been promising on identifying characteristics of the ideal police officer, partly because some of the desired traits cannot be reliably measured, such as "street smarts" (Charles, 1986), and also due to lack of agreement as to what the ideal traits are (Ainsworth, 1995). This lack of agreement is due in part to the lack of studies examining the personality traits of "good" and "bad" police officers.

One frequently identified desirable trait is "honesty" or "integrity" (Blau, 1994). Many departments use a polygraph screening to determine if the recruit has been truthful in the vetting process. One common question to ask the recruit during the polygraph exam is, "Is there any other information that you have not disclosed that would jeopardize your candidacy to be a police officer?" If the recruit fails this polygraph exam due to this question, it is likely they are attempting to hide something, such as a previous arrest or other unfavorable information. There has been a recent proliferation of paper-and-pencil integrity tests. This interest in alternative measures of honesty is due to the ban on polygraph testing for employment purposes in the private sector with the passage of the **Employee Polygraph Protection Act of 1988**. Polygraph testing for employment purposes is still permissible by government agencies including police departments. Chapter 10 of this text provides a detailed description of the polygraph technique.

Paper-and-pencil measures of honesty fall into two categories. The first category consists of tests that directly ask the applicant about his or her honesty and attitudes he or she may hold toward employee theft, telling lies, and so on. The second category consists of broad-based measures of personality thought to be related to integrity. The rush to market these tests has prevented the necessary psychometric development and standardization. Few studies on the validity of these tests have been subjected to peer review and the large number of tests is an obstacle to a systematic evaluation of their usefulness (Blau, 1994). Though used in the private sector, these tests do not seem to be part of the preemployment process for police recruits. This may be due to the lack of evidence supporting their usefulness or, more likely, the fact that police departments can continue to use polygraph testing as a measure of honesty.

The second approach to recruit selection is the use of testing to *screen out* psychopathology. Departments wish to avoid hiring police recruits who would later be an embarrassment to the Force or are a liability risk for the department, possibly causing expensive litigation costs (Blau, 1994). Rather than use testing to identify the qualities that make for a "good cop," psychological screening was first adopted as a way to identify individuals who were at risk for developing psychological problems (Reiser, 1982). Similarly, psychological testing was used to identify applicants who may be at an increased risk for job-related behavioral problems or who might pose a substantial risk to public safety due to psychological problems (Janik, 1994). This screening-out approach is somewhat supported by psychologists involved in the testing process. Most of these psychologists are trained as clinical psychologists, an area that traditionally has emphasized the identification of pathology as opposed to personality strengths (Blau, 1994). The search for pathology focused on personality traits that might be considered detrimental to the police profession. These traits include, among others, rigidity, suspiciousness, difficulty dealing with authority figures, and antisocial attitudes (Inwald, 1992; Resiser & Geiger, 1984). Other researchers have looked at what types of skills are necessary for performing the duties of a police officer and screen out individuals who lack these skills. For example, job analysis of a police officer's duties suggests that successful officers need good interpersonal skills (Spielberger, Ward, & Spaulding,1979). It may then be useful to screen out individuals who do not possess good interpersonal skills. The difficulty is operationally defining these skills and developing a valid measure of these kinds of skills.

In addition, other writers in the field report that the personality traits measured at preemployment selection have little predictive value over the police officer's career (Dunnette & Motowidlo, 1976). Personality traits can change with experience. Police recruits are exposed to a variety of strong influences during their police careers that can influence behavioral patterns and personality traits. Researchers have commented on the socialization process of rookie police officers. Studies show that the informal socialization leads to changes in personality traits as well as attitudes toward their job and the public (Niederhoffer, 1967; Skolnick, 1966). Obviously, screening out individuals with severe forms of mental illness or emotional problems is a sensible approach.

The use of psychological testing as a method of screening out candidates who present with psychological problems or undesirable personality traits appears to be the norm in preemployment screening and will continue to be the primary use of testing in the foreseeable future. Although a wide variety of tests is used, recent surveys have identified at least several tests that are used more frequently than others are (Cochrane et al., 2003; Strawbridge & Strawbridge, 1990). Perhaps the most commonly used test in preemployment screening of police officers is the MMPI. Chapter 3 of this text provides a detailed description of the MMPI and its recent revision, the MMPI-2. See Table 5.7 for a list of the validity and clinical scales on the MMPI–2. Another test specifically developed to screen law enforcement candidates is the **Inwald Personality Inventory** (IPI; Inwald, 1992). The IPI and the MMPI-2 are both primarily measures of pathology and are best used to screen candidates out based on evidence of pathology. A third test that is used in preemployment screening of law enforcement is the **California Psychological Inventory** (CPI; Gough, 1987). The CPI was developed to assess normal personality traits, as opposed to the MMPI-2 and the IPI, which are measures of pathology.

The MMPI-2 is perhaps the most widely used objective personality measure. The MMPI-2 is used in preemployment screening by over 70% of police departments responding to a recent survey (Cochrane et al., 2003). The original MMPI was designed to identify psychopathology and resulted in three validity scales and 10 clinical scales. The validity scales attempt to assess the response set of the individual taking the test. For example, did the respondent randomly respond to the questions, or attempt to make a particularly favorable impression? The three validity scales are L (**Lie**), F (**Infrequency**), and K (**Correction**). The 10 clinical scales assess typical forms of psychopathology, such as depression, schizophrenia, paranoia, hypomania, social introversion, somatic concerns, and anxiety.

## Table 5.7  MMPI-2 Validity Scales and Clinical Scales

**Validity Scales**

? - Cannot Say Scale
L - Lie Scale
F - Faking Bad
K - Faking Good

**Clinical Scales**

1 - Hypochondriasis (Hs)
2 - Depression (D)
3 - Hysteria (Hy)
4 - Psychopathic Deviant (Pd)
5 - Masculinity–Femininity (Mf)
6 - Paranoia (Pa)
7 - Psychasthenia (Pt)
8 - Schizophrenia (Sc)
9 - Hypomania (Ma)
0 - Social Introversion (Si)

The original MMPI had been used extensively in police candidate screening (Shaw, 1986). The MMPI-2 is a revised version of the original MMPI and is quite similar to the original, prompting some writers to suggest the revision was guided by financial motives as opposed to developing better psychometric properties (Rodgers, 1992). The switch from using the MMPI to the MMPI-2 was relatively slow (Levitt & Webb, 1922) and there continues to be a need for validation studies and normative data using the MMPI-2 with police recruits (Detrick, Chibnall, & Rosso, 2001). With so few validation studies of the MMPI-2 for police officer preemployment screening, it appears that police psychologists are relying on normative data from the original MMPI when making recruitment decisions using the MMPI-2. Although there does appear to be a high correlation between scores on the MMPI and MMPI-2, validation research is still needed to ensure that the employment decision-making process is fair to examinees (Hargrave, Hiatt, Ogard, & Karr, 1994; Kornfield, 1995). Over 70% of the police agencies responding to the survey reported using the MMPI-2 in their police officer screening process (Cochrane et al., 2003).

The IPI is another paper-and-pencil inventory developed to identify negative behavior patterns and personality traits that might interfere with work as a law enforcement officer. The IPI has 310 true–false questions that yield 26 different scores along with a validity scale. Scales assess potential emotional adjustment problems, coping methods, and potential antisocial characteristics such as alcohol abuse, drug abuse, employment difficulties, interpersonal and family problems, legal difficulties, excessive use of leave time or absence from work, and societal problems. See Table 5.8 for the list of scales on the IPI. The IPI is used to screen out individuals who may not be suitable for police work. The instrument requires less than 45 minutes to administer and was originally normed on over 9,000 law enforcement personnel. Although initially showing some promise as a preemployment screening tool (Blau, 1994), only slightly over 10% of police departments report using the IPI (Cochrane et al., 2003).

## Scales on the Inwald Personality Inventory     Table 5.8

- Guardedness (validity scale)
- Alcohol Use
- Drug Use
- Driving Violations
- Job Difficulties
- Trouble with the Law
- Absence Abuse
- Substance Abuse
- Antisocial Attitudes
- Hyperactivity
- Rigid Type
- Type A
- Illness Concerns
- Treatment Programs

- Anxiety
- Phobic Personality
- Obsessive Personality
- Depression
- Loner
- Unusual Experiences
- Lack of Assertiveness
- Interpersonal Difficulties
- Undue Suspiciousness
- Family Concerns
- Sexual Concerns
- Spouse Conflicts
- Acting-Out Composite

The CPI is a personality inventory with 462 true–false questions that yield 20 scales assessing "normal" personality traits as opposed to identifying pathology. The CPI was originally developed to assess vocational and career goals. The CPI has validity scales as well as scales that measure traits such as empathy, self-confidence, self-control, good impression, socialization, social presence, tolerance, well-being, independence, self-acceptance, communality, and responsibility. Table 5.9 lists the scales on the CPI. The CPI has been normed on law enforcement personnel and is used by approximately 25% of the police departments responding to the survey (Cochrane et al., 2003). The CPI has shown some success in predicting police officer job performance (Hargrave & Hiatt, 1989). One recent meta-analysis compared scores on the MMPI, the IPI, and the CPI for predicting current and future job performance of law enforcement officers (Varela, Boccaccini, Scogin, Stump, & Caputo, 2004). The authors report that prediction was strongest for the CPI than for the other two instruments. However, they note that relationship between personality test scores and job performance, though statistically significant, were modest. Table 5.9 lists the 20 scales and seven special-purpose scales from the third edition of the CPI (Atkinson, 2003).

## Table 5.9    California Personality Inventory Scales

- Dominance
- Capacity for Status
- Sociability
- Social Presence
- Self-Acceptance
- Independence
- Empathy
- Responsibility
- Socialization
- Self-Control
- Good Impression
- Communality
- Well-being
- Tolerance
- Achievement via Conformance

- Achievement via Independence
- Intellectual Efficiency
- Psychological Mindedness
- Flexibility
- Feminity/Masculinity

**Special-Purpose Scales**

- Managerial Potential
- Work Orientation
- Creative Temperament
- Leadership Potential
- Amicability
- Law Enforcement Orientation
- Toughmindedness

■ **Concurrent validity**

Two measures of a construct are assessed at the same time and should correlate with one another; one measure is compared with an already established measure.

Much of the research on the use of these three tests has examined how law enforcement personnel currently employed perform on the MMPI-2, the CPI, or the IPI and how these instruments relate to one another or other standard measures of personality (Bartol & Bartol, 2004). For example, one study found the IPI added incremental predictive power to the MMPI in classifying correctional officers' performance behavior ratings (Shusman & Inwald, 1991). This type of study attempts to establish concurrent validity. **Concurrent validity** is established by comparing performance on one measure against performance on another measure, known to be valid, reliable, and considered a "standard." The standard may be performance ratings by superiors or scores on another assessment instrument. Concurrent validity indicates that the two measures, such as scores on the assessment instrument and supervisor ratings, are assessed concurrently, or at the same time.

Ideally, an assessment instrument for preemployment selection should demonstrate predictive validity. **Predictive validity** refers to how well scores on the test predict future behavior related to what the test is supposed to measure. The process of establishing predictive validity is costly and time consuming. Predictive validity can be established by administering the screening instrument to all applicants at the time of initial employment. All applicants completing the assessment instrument are hired, regardless of scores on the screening instrument. The performance of each applicant is followed over a 1-, 2-, or 3-year period and correlated with scores on the screening instrument. Theoretically, applicants who performed poorly on the screening instrument would also perform poorly on the job.

There are a few logistical hurdles to establishing predictive validity. First, the process is time consuming. A 3-year period may be insufficient to identify job performance failures. In response to the difficulty of following recruits over an extended period, some researchers have used assessment instruments to predict performance at the police academy, a relatively brief period in an officer's professional career. For example, one study found that scores on the Revised NEO Personality Inventory (NEO PI-R; Costa & McCrae, 1992) showed some promise in predicting performance and graduation from the academy (Detrick, Chibnall, & Luebbert, 2004). The NEO PI-R is a personality measure designed to assess the "Big Five" personality traits:

1. openness to experience,
2. conscientiousness,
3. extraversion,
4. agreeableness, and
5. neuroticism (OCEAN).

Another study found that the NEO PI-R, MMPI-2 and IPI, when combined, were useful predictors of academic performance among police recruits (Chibnall & Detrick, 2003). Performance at the police academy is a relatively short period compared to a police officer's career. Although this is a promising start, an instrument used for preemployment screening should demonstrate predictive validity over a longer period. One study found that the IPI was successful in predicting supervisor performance ratings after 1 year of active duty (Detrick & Chibnall, 2002). Another obstacle to establishing predictive validity is the need to hire all recruits, regardless of performance on the measure. If we are attempting to select-in, that is, identify personality traits that will make an individual a particularly good police officer, this procedure might be feasible. However, if we are screening out pathology, it may be difficult to justify hiring candidates who perform poorly on a measure of psychological health to function as police officers.

There is still no consensus regarding the standard for psychological testing in preemployment decisions. Rather, the consensus in the field suggests that there are at least two recommendations of what *not* do to in the preemployment screening process. First, preemployment assessment instruments of personality should be objective personality tests rather than a projective technique. Chapter 3 of this text discusses the distinction between objective and projective techniques. Second, validation research should exist to justify any instrument's use in preemployment screening (Hargrave & Berner, 1984).

The use of psychological tests for the selection of law enforcement personnel is still in its early stages. As Blau points out, despite three-quarters of a century of efforts, the "gap between what psychological research and methodology in the area of testing could do and what it is actually doing for law enforcement is significant" (1994, p. 75). Several factors may be contributing to the lack of progress. First, using instruments that

**■ Predictive validity**
How well test scores predict future behavior.

were designed for one purpose to fulfill another purpose may never prove to be success-ful (Bartol & Bartol, 2004). The MMPI-2 was designed to assess pathology in clinical populations. Using this instrument to predict academic performance at the police acad-emy or police officer performance in the field may also produce unsatisfactory results. Second, with minor exceptions, the use of instruments to predict performance has been lacking any theoretical conceptualization. It appears that the majority of instruments are selected based on their psychometric properties or due to the instrument's general acceptance in the field. Simply because an instrument has sound psychometric prop-erties does not indicate that it can serve all testing purposes. However, the lack of a the-oretically based instrument does not justify the marketing and use of instruments that have not been scientifically validated for employment decisions. The federal and pro-fessional recommendations along with the recent court decisions for psychological test-ing in preemployment selection has created a huge market, with over 18,000 law enforcement agencies. The temptation to market unproven assessment instruments is readily apparent with new instruments appearing on the market. However, police psy-chologists will need to use caution when using instruments that have not been vali-dated. Court rulings allowing psychological screening do not give license for the use of poorly developed instruments. On the other hand, a student entering this area could make a significant contribution to the field with the development of a valid instrument.

# Preemployment Interview

Despite criticism by some writers regarding the utility of face-to-face interviews (Wrightsman, 2001), it is widely used by police psychologists and recommended in the Preemployment Psychological Evaluation Guidelines (IACP, 1998). The clini-cal interview has been criticized as lacking validity as a valid predictor of job per-formance. A second concern is the general lack of agreement on interview format. Some clinicians prefer a standardized interview, whereas others may wish to freely probe areas he or she feels are most relevant to the screening process. A third concern is the reality that in-dividuals attempt to portray themselves in a positive light during an in-terview, which may not be an accurate depiction of the candidate's usual behavior. Finally, there is no consensus as to what is an adequate or good interview performance versus an unsuitable presentation. Thus, the judgment of job suitability based on an interview may be unreli-able. Despite these drawbacks, interviews are one of the most common forms of assessment techniques. The criticisms of the clinical interview are typical of the clinical–actuarial debate regarding prediction of human behavior among clinicians and researchers (Weston & Wein-berger, 2004). Despite this debate in the literature, it is unlikely that the interview will be excluded in the evaluative process. Rather, many clinicians would suggest that psychological testing is an important com-ponent of the preemployment screening process, but is insufficient to render an opinion regarding psychological suitability (Borum et al., 2003). Clini-cians tend to employ both actuarial and clinical methods in their forensic work.

IACP Preemployment Guidelines direct that "individual, face-to-face interviews with candidates should be conducted before a final psychological report is submitted" (Guideline #12). The interview should follow a semi-structured format and cover rel-evant historical and background information. A semi-structured interview allows the psychologist to explore pertinent areas as information is revealed and also ensures con-sistency across interviews and makes it less likely that any particular area will be omit-ted. See Table 5.10 for a list of areas typically covered in a preemployment interview

Figure 5.2

Although there are some drawbacks, interviews are one of the most commonly used assessment techniques.
© 2009 icyimage. Used under license from Shutterstock, Inc.

**Topic Areas Covered in a Psychological Preemployment Interview**  **Table 5.10**

- Family History
  - Birthplace, where raised
  - Siblings: ages and gender, relationships
  - Mother: status, background, relationship
  - Father: status, background, relationship
  - Family problems: history of abuse, neglect, substance abuse, mental illness
  - Marital status
  - Children
- School History
  - Elementary school performance: special classes, held back, suspended or expelled, grades
  - High school performance: grades, date graduated, extracurricular activities, relationships with teachers and students
  - Coursework: strengths and weaknesses
  - School discipline problems
  - College or vocational education
- Work History
  - Military service
    - Type of discharge
    - Military occupational specialty
    - Rank obtained, length of service
    - Disciplinary action
    - Reserve status
  - Private sector work history
    - Past employment: position, length, reason for leaving
    - Career performance
    - Disciplinary problems
    - Relationships with supervisors and coworkers
- Behavioral History
  - Legal issues: juvenile and adult contact with law enforcement, arrest, etc.
  - Driving record: accidents, violations, insurance claims
  - Mental health history: treatment, medications, symptoms
  - Alcohol and drug use: age first started drinking, frequency, quantity, associated problems, illicit drug use
  - Medical history: surgeries, hospitalizations, chronic illnesses, medications
- Job-specific questions
  - Reasons for seeking the position
  - Perception of job and role
  - Strengths and weaknesses related to the position
- Possible job-related scenarios

(Borum et al., 2003). As with other types of forensic evaluations discussed in this text, the interview should occur after all the testing has been completed and scored so that the psychologist can use the test results to generate hypothesis to explore with the candidate as well as to clarify any concerns raised by the test results.

Once the testing and interview are completed, the police psychologist must determine the applicant's psychological suitability for the position. Suitability is loosely defined as the degree of "fit" between requirements of the position and the candidate's capabilities (Grisso, 1986). Any information obtained through testing, the interview, or third-party sources that call into question the candidate's ability to safely perform the essential duties of the position need to be considered. For example, the presence of severe pathology such as delusions or extreme mood swings could interfere with judgment and behavior. More subtly, sexist or racist attitudes could interfere with an officer's ability to treat individuals fairly. The determination of psychological suitability is not an all-or-none decision but rather is usually offered in three categories such as hire, marginal, do not hire, or in terms of suitability (suitable, marginally suitable, and unsuitable). Currently, there are no standard definitions for these ratings. Preferably, a police psychologist involved in preemployment screening would develop operational definitions of the three ratings. The use of operational definitions would increase the rater's consistency across applicants and enhance communication with the hiring agency. Examples of operational definitions for the three ratings are offered in Table 5.11 (Borum et al., 2003).

The structure of the final report varies based on the needs of the particular department. Most reports will include identifying information such as age, date of birth, gender, race, position sought, and so on. Reports should also include the sources of information, instruments used, date and length of interview with the candidate, the consent procedure, a brief narrative of background information, behavioral observations of the candidate during the interview, test results and interpretation, and con-

**Table 5.11** Operational Definitions for Psychological Suitability Ratings used in Preemployment Screening

- Suitable: Candidate appears to have the psychological capabilities to perform the essential functions of the position. There was no evidence of pathology or behavioral problems that would interfere with the performance of his or her duties.
- Marginally Suitable: There was evidence of potential psychological or behavioral problems that could result in job-related difficulties. However, the problem does not warrant exclusion for the position due to either
  1. the type of problem,
  2. the severity of the problem,
  3. current treatment indicating success in overcoming the problem, or
  4. the evidence for the problem. There were no indications of severe pathology or behavioral problems that would justify exclusion from the position.
- Unsuitable: Clear evidence of pathology or severe behavioral problems that would prevent the candidate from safely fulfilling the essential duties of the position. Either numerous areas of concern or the severity of symptoms indicates a strong likelihood for future job-related difficulties.

clusions. Screening reports should avoid using clinical diagnoses or psychiatric labels. Rather, the report should provide a suitability rating along with the relevant information to support that decision. This approach is similar to most forensic evaluations. Forensic evaluations should address the referral question and avoid the use of psychological jargon.

In addition to psychological screening, police agencies use other methods to evaluate police recruits. These additional screening procedures include background checks, polygraph testing, medical exams, and other assessment instruments. An example of an additional assessment instrument developed by psychologists is the National Police Officer Selection Test (POST). This is a battery of aptitude tests covering eight areas:

1. Reading Comprehension,
2. Vocabulary,
3. Memory,
4. Situational Judgment and Reasoning,
5. Directional Orientation,
6. Report Writing and Grammar,
7. Spelling, and
8. Mathematics.

The POST has been adopted by three states and is recommended by state police chief associations in 20 other states as an entry-level written test for their police officer applicants. The test appears to have adequate validity (Rafilson & Sison, 1996).

Aamodt (2004) provides a comprehensive meta-analytic review of techniques used in law enforcement selection. He provides meta-analysis of techniques used as predictors of police performance. His book covers education requirements, cognitive ability, background variables, personality inventories, interest inventories, physical agility tests, assessment centers, and interviews. Below is a list of various techniques frequently used along with the percentage of police agencies reporting their use (Bureau of Justice Statistics, 1999):

| | |
|---|---|
| Criminal-record checks | 99% |
| Background investigations | 98% |
| Driving-record checks | 98% |
| Medical exams | 97% |
| Psychological screening | 91% |
| Aptitude tests | 84% |
| Physical-agility tests | 78% |

# Fitness-for-Duty-Evaluations

Unlike preemployment screening to screen out candidates before employment, **fitness-for-duty evaluations** (FFDEs) are used to screen individuals currently on duty. An FFDE is requested to evaluate an officer whose behavior, performance, or communications have raised some concern about safety and/or job performance (Borum et al., 2003; Stone, 2002). The concerns about the officer's psychological fitness can be triggered by a life-threatening incident, stress, a series of problems or injuries, excessive use of force, substance abuse, repeated poor judgment, or domestic violence (Stone, 1990). The referral question is whether the officer is "fit for duty." Previously, a fitness-for-duty evaluation referred to the officer's physical fitness. When there was doubt about the officer's physical ability to perform the essential functions of the job, the officer was required to obtain a medical exam. More recently, FFDE evaluations focus on psychological issues

■ **Psychopathology**
Any form of a mental illness.

that may make an officer not fit to continue duty. Stone (1990) reports that the most common referral reason for an FFDE was **psychopathology**. Psychopathology refers to mental illness such as depression, anxiety, or even more severe symptoms, such as delusions or hallucinations. There are two principle reasons an agency will refer an officer for FFDE (Borum et al., 2003):

1. There exists a reasonable cause to suspect that an individual may pose a risk of harm to self or others, or
2. there is a reasonable cause to suspect that the employee has a psychological or substance use disorder that significantly interferes with his or her ability to perform the essential functions of the position.

An FFDE evaluation can pose ethical and legal difficulties for everyone involved. The officer who has been a member of the agency past the probationary period typically has legal rights and protections granted by the collective bargaining unit. The officer may have the right to restrict access to certain information or the right to refute the report. The police psychologist needs to be aware of the agency's and officer's legal rights as well as departmental policy and rights granted by the collective bargaining agreement. Administrators are reluctant to refer an officer for an FFDE since it indicates serious doubts about the officer's ability to perform his or her job. Administrative and legal difficulties can result from a referral for an FFDE. Officers are in a quandary when they are referred for an FFDE. It is not clear to the officer if they should cooperate and disclose potentially damaging information. If they disclose information, they could jeopardize their job; but if they hide problems, they could miss the opportunity for receiving treatment. Additionally, there is the issue of confidentiality. The psychologist performing the FFDE needs to be sensitive to the privacy concerns of the officer but still is obligated to reveal information obtained in the course of the evaluation.

The first legal issue to be addressed is whether the employer has a legal right to order an officer to submit to a psychological evaluation to determine his or her fitness to remain on duty. A police lieutenant sued his police chief for requiring him to submit to a psychiatric evaluation. In *Conte v. Horcher* (1977), the courts ruled that the police chief has the legal right to order an officer to submit to a physical or mental exam to determine the officer's ability to perform the requirements of the job. Soon after, in the case of *Bonsignore v. City of New York* (1982), the court ruled that the police agency has both a right and an *obligation* to ensure the psychological fitness of its officers. The court ruled that agencies employing individuals in high-risk positions should have official policies and procedures in place for monitoring the psychological health of its employees. This ruling applies to law enforcement agencies as well as other occupational groups. Therefore, not only sworn officers can be mandated to submit to a psychological evaluation, but also unsworn employees such as administrative staff and dispatchers.

The courts have also ruled on the issue of confidentiality of the evaluation. As with the other evaluations discussed in this text, the examinee is not the client. Rather, the courts have upheld that the employing agency that ordered the evaluation is the client and holds the right of confidentiality (*David v. Christian*, 1987). Finally, the courts have addressed the issue as to whether the examinee has a right to have a representative present during the evaluation, such as a union representative, an attorney, or another mental health professional. In *Vinson v. The Superior Court of Alameda County* (1987) the Court ruled that legal counsel would pose a distraction and would not provide a benefit to the examinee. The court stipulated that the examiner should "have the freedom to probe deeply into the plaintiff's psyche without interference by a third party" (p. 412).

Thus, regarding FFDEs, case law has generally sided with the employing agency. The agency has a right and an obligation to require personnel suspected of being psychologically unfit for duty to submit to a psychological evaluation. Case law dictates that the agency has the right to the confidentiality of the information and that the examinee does not have the right to have a representative present during the evaluation.

The Police Psychologists Services Section of the International Association of Chiefs of Police has published guidelines for psychologists who conduct fitness-for-duty evaluations (IACP, 1998). As with all forensic assessments, the examinee should grant informed consent to the evaluation. In an FFDE, the officer should be informed of the purpose of the evaluation, who requested it, and to whom the results will be provided along with a clear understanding of the implications of the evaluation. The examinee should be informed that they may refuse to participate or refuse to disclose any information they wish. However, it should also be clear to the examinee that such refusals will be noted in the report. The evaluation is designed to answer specific questions related to the particular facts of the case. Assessment instruments will vary depending on the circumstances of each case and the reason for the referral. IACP Guidelines recommend the following procedures:

1. Review of background information such as performance ratings, disciplinary actions, preemployment psychological evaluation, internal affairs investigations, citizen complaints, and so on.
2. Psychological testing using objective measures that have been validated. Borum et al. (2003) recommend including a broad measure of pathology such as the MMPI-2 and a measure of normal personality traits, such as the CPI.
3. A clinical interview including mental status exam, current functioning, and psychosocial history.
4. Interviews with third-party informants who may have particular knowledge about the officer's psychological fitness.

The FFD evaluation determines the degree of fit between the employee's current capacities and the essential requirements of the position (Stone, 1995). The determination is generally one of four conditions (Borum et al., 2003):

1. *Fit for duty*: Employee does not have psychological disorder that causes significant impairment in his or her ability to perform their job or that poses a threat of harm.
2. *Fit for duty with mandatory treatment*: Some psychological problems exist that may interfere with job functioning. However, employee does not pose an immediate threat and the nature of the problem is not sufficient to classify the employee as unfit for duty. The psychological problem can be remedied within a reasonable time frame with proper treatment. The report includes specific treatment recommendations and recommendations for any temporary change in duty assignments during treatment.
3. *Temporarily unfit for duty; mandatory treatment*: Employee has a psychological problem that causes significant impairment in their ability to perform the requirements of the job or it poses an immediate threat of harm. The severity of the impairment or risk of harm is sufficient to classify the employee as unfit for duty. However, it is likely that with treatment the condition can be remedied within a reasonable time frame.
4. *Permanently unfit for duty*: The individual has a psychological disorder that causes significant impairment in their ability to perform the requirements of the job or it poses an immediate threat of harm. The psychological problem is judged not to be remediable within a reasonable time frame. It is of sufficient severity to classify the individual as unfit for duty.

If the officer is found unfit for duty, the examiner should make recommendations regarding the potential benefits of treatment. The recommendations may include psychological treatment as well as other remedies. For example, if the psychologist is familiar with law enforcement procedures, the psychologist may recommend the officer review departmental procedures regarding firearm safety and is later evaluated by a firearms safety instructor (Blau, 1994). The psychologist conducting the evaluation should not provide psychological treatment. This dual role as evaluator and treatment provider may become blurred with pressure from supervisors wishing to know how treatment is progressing. If an officer is found temporarily unfit for duty pending treatment, a second FFDE will be required at some point during or after treatment to evaluate if the officer is fit to return to duty. The use of third-party information as well as information from the treatment provider is important for determining what changes have occurred since the first FFDE (Borum et al., 2003).

# Special Assignment Assessments

Policing is a high-stress job that can be dangerous and unpredictable. However, special units, typically in the larger police departments, can be distinguished by being more dangerous and/or stressful than daily routine police operations. The Commission on Accreditation for Law Enforcement Agencies (1989) recommends psychological testing as part of the screening process for individuals assigned to special units in particularly high-risk areas. The Accreditation Standards recommend the identification of selection criteria for special units, such as the voluntary nature of the assignment, law enforcement experience, physical fitness, and psychological screening. Along with selection criteria, the Accreditation Standards recommend ongoing annual testing by a licensed psychologist or psychiatrist to identify any symptoms associated with long-term high levels of stress. Members of special units are exposed to higher levels of stress than officers involved in routine police work. For example, research has found that the incidence of psychological problems is highest among active undercover agents (Girodo, 1991). Other research has highlighted the stress involved in undercover assignments (Farkas, 1986). These studies highlight the need for annual assessment of officers involved in these special assignments. Annual psychological testing is an attempt to identify psychological issues before they develop into serious problems that interfere with job performance.

Most police psychologists agree that preliminary screening and ongoing assessment of officers involved in these high-stress roles can be beneficial. However, to

**Table 5.12** Types of Special Assignments

- Special Weapons and Tactics (SWAT)
- Undercover Operations
- Decoy Operations
- Bomb Disposal Units
- Hostage Negotiations
- Juvenile Crime
- Sex Crimes
- Protection at Special Events

date very few studies have looked at which tests are reliable and valid for the specific referral question. The most commonly used instruments are the MMPI-2 and the CPI (Blau, 1994). Research is needed to identify valid psychological assessment instruments for selection and monitoring of officers assigned to special units (Blau, 1994; Super, 1999).

# Psychological Counseling

Most staff psychologists in police departments are expected to provide psychological counseling to police personnel and their families. Research indicates that the majority of a police psychologist's time is spent in preemployment assessment and provision of psychological counseling (Bartol, 1996). One important consideration for ensuring that police personnel and their families seek out consultations with the police psychologist is a clear-cut policy on confidentiality. A public policy stating the client's right to a confidential consultation and the limits of confidentiality is necessary to gain the trust of department personnel. Individuals need to know that what is discussed in treatment remains confidential and will not cause them embarrassment within the department or jeopardize their careers. Distrust of psychologists and concerns regarding confidentiality limits have been obstacles to treatment for law enforcement personnel. Some departments address these concerns by providing opportunities with outside agencies in the form of Employee Assistance Programs (EAPs). One survey found that nearly 60% of the police agencies surveyed provided in-house counseling services, whereas slightly over 80% offered referrals to outside agencies (Blau, 1994).

Common reasons for a referral to a mental health professional include marital and family problems, substance use problems, and mental health problems such as depression and anxiety. Many of these problems can be indirectly traced to the stress of police work. There is a wealth of literature on the sources of stress in police work and the effect stress has on the officers and their families. In fact, the most frequently requested type of training is for stress awareness and stress management. Interestingly, one study found that officers cite departmental politics as the largest source of stress (Toch, 2002). In discussing departmental disciplinary actions, one officer is quoted as saying, "the call of duty is not stress. Robbery, fighting, and so forth are part of the job. The worst stress comes from lack of respect and neglect" (Toch, 2002, p. 75). Readers may find it interesting that it is not the job of policing that is stressful but rather policies that can be controlled. Officers cited internal departmental politics, the department's leadership, inadequate information, and witnessing child abuse as the four most frequent sources of stress. These officers' self-reports confirm a review of the literature (Finn & Tomz, 1997, p. 7) that listed the following issues as the most common sources of stress for the police officer:

- Unproductive management styles
- Inconsistent discipline and enforcement of rules
- Equipment deficiencies and shortages
- Perceived excessive or unnecessary paperwork
- Perceived favoritism by administrators regarding assignments and promotions
- Lack of input into policy and decision making
- Second-guessing of officers' actions and lack of administrative support
- Inconsistent or arbitrary internal disciplinary procedures and review
- Lack of career development opportunities (and perceived unfairness of affirmative action) resulting in competition among officers
- Lack of adequate training or supervision
- Lack of reward and recognition for good work

The consequences of police stress are the same as for many occupations, including increase absenteeism, physical illness, substance abuse, and marital and family problems. A relatively recent review ("On-the-Job Stress in Policing," 2000, p. 20) found the most commonly reported consequences of occupational stress among police officers include:

- Cynicism and suspiciousness
- Emotional detachment from various aspects of daily life
- Reduced efficiency
- Absenteeism and early retirement
- Excessive aggressiveness
- Alcoholism and other substance abuse problems
- Marital or other family problems
- Posttraumatic stress disorder
- Heart attacks, ulcers, weight gain, and other health problems
- Suicide

Another study by the National Institute of Justice (1999) found that police officers reporting high levels of stress were three times more likely to abuse their partners, five times more likely to report alcohol problems, and 10 times more likely to experience depression than their counterparts.

Research has also shown that police work causes stress for the officer's family (DeAngelis, 1991). This creates the need for counseling for family members as well as the officer. In addition to individual counseling for family members, police psychologists also provide family counseling. The survey of police agencies reported by Blau (1994) indicated that over 70% of the agencies provided mental health services to family members as well as sworn and civilian employees. Perhaps the most common referral problem for psychologists who work with police is dissatisfaction between the husband and wife regarding the work situation, finances, the children, and the marital relationship (Blau, 1994). Borum and Philpot (1993) have identified factors associated with high-risk occupations that contribute to family problems. These factors include

- irregular schedules and shift work,
- the presence of weapons in the home,
- anxiety for family members due to the dangers associated with the job,
- authoritarianism,
- marital infidelity, and
- cohesion with coworkers to the exclusion of family members.

Police officers frequently complain about not knowing how much of their work to share with family members and the sense that they are not understood by persons not engaged in police work. The police officer has been socialized on the job to control situations and to remain emotionally detached (Southworth, 1999). Children of police officers resent having to compete with their parent's job for attention (Wester & Lyubelsky, 2005). The irregular shifts and emotional distance required of police work can cause problems in the marital relationship and interpersonal availability within family relationships.

These difficulties associated with "taking the job home" may be particularly salient for male police officers. The confusion created between the role of the strong, stoic police officer and the warm, caring, supportive spouse and father can lead to *male* **gender role conflict** (Wester & Lyubelsky, 2005). Gender role conflict (GRC) occurs when traditional gender role socialization results in behaviors that are inappropriate for the current situation. Males are socialized to be independent, self-reliant, tough,

■ **Gender role conflict (GRC)**

Traditional gender role socialization resulting in behaviors that are inappropriate for the current situation, such as a man's inability to express a weakness.

aggressive, and to restrict emotional expression. The socialization of males is reinforced and continued in law enforcement training (Gerber, 2001). Police officers are taught to be first-responders, with the expectation that the officer can take charge of a situation. The ability to take charge of a situation, particularly when life is threatened and the use of deadly force may be required, entails many of the socialized male traits, such as restriction of emotional expression, toughness, decisiveness, and the ability to react physically to the situation. The same characteristics that are rewarded on the job can lead to marital and family problems, even to the point of contributing to domestic violence (e.g., Sheenhan, 2000). Police psychologists need to understand the socialization and expectations of police officers to be effective therapists. Police officers have left therapy complaining that their therapist did not understand police work (Chamberlin, 2000). To address the confusion caused by GRC, some clinicians have developed gender-sensitive therapy for work with male police officers (Wester & Lyubelsky, 2005). These authors proposed helping male officers understand work and family conflicts within the context of police work expectations and masculine gender role expectations. The degree to which the individual officer accepts society's assigned gender role and the competing demands between family life expectations and career expectations becomes the focus of therapy.

Another topic unique to counseling police officers is diversity issues. Minorities now constitute over 20% of local police officers in the United States (Reaves, 1996). Women make up nearly 12% of the total number of police officers (IACP, 1999). The increase in diversity among police officers is clearly an improvement. However, minorities and women still face difficulties in the police work setting. These officers still suffer a certain degree of rejection and therefore suffer additional job stress (Daum & Johns, 1994; Norvell, Hills, & Murrin, 1993). The police psychologist working with women and minority officers needs to understand and address diversity issues. Similarly, gay and lesbian police officers experience a certain degree of rejection. Despite prejudice triggered by homophobia, gay and lesbian police officers are competent and accepted by many of their police colleagues (Blumenthal, 1993). This is an issue not commonly addressed in most textbooks on police work (e.g. Territo et al., 2004). In New York City, over 800 sworn officers openly acknowledge their homosexual orientation. The New York Police Department has a policy of zero tolerance of any harassment because of sexual lifestyle (Blau, 1994). Gay and lesbian officers, whether they openly acknowledge their sexual orientation or prefer privacy, experience some rejection and discrimination in police work. These individuals experience additional stress as a result and may seek counseling. The police psychologist needs to recognize the distinctive issues confronting gay and lesbian police officers (Blau, 1994).

Figure 5.3

Diversity among police officers is improving, although minorities and women still face difficulties.

© 2009 JupiterImages Corporation.

# Health and Wellness Counseling

As discussed above, police work can be extremely stressful. It is one of the few jobs where an individual is asked to risk their life at any given time. Due to the socialization process of police training, police can frequently feel isolated from the rest of society. This can contribute to the stress police officers experience. It should be noted that all workers can experience stress regardless of the occupational duties. Nearly 45% of all salaried workers in the United States report the experience of excessive stress as a direct result of their job (DeAngelis, 1993).

The effects of stress can be ubiquitous. Obviously, stress can affect performance on the job. Additionally, stress can take its toll on the individual's physical and mental health. Occupationally related stress has been found to be associated with cardiovascular, sexual, muscular, and gastrointestinal problems (DeAngelis, 1993). In addition to somatic complaints, stress is associated with marital problems, alcohol and drug use, as well as emotional and physical outbursts and suicidal behavior (Blau, 1994). Numerous authors have examined the role of stress and stress reduction programs for police officers. Several recommendations from the literature are provided for ways in which the police psychologist can help departments and officers reduce the impact of stress.

1. *Administrative and organizational changes*: stabilize work schedules, reduce workload, create guidelines regarding career security, career planning, more input in decision making from line officers, and decrease autonomy among superior officers.
2. *Stress management and stress inoculation training*: short training programs teaching officers about the sources of stress, impact of stress on health and behavior, and preventative measures.
3. *Brief stress counseling*: four or five stress counseling sessions provided to officers annually to address effects of stress on the job and family life.
4. *Retirement counseling*: brief counseling sessions for officers approaching retirement devoted to retirement planning, benefits, insurance, job-search skills, nurturing social relationships in retirement, financial management, and the psychology of retirement.
5. *Relaxation training*: traditional muscle relaxation techniques taught to officers that can be used during a 20-minute break or at the end of the day.
6. *Health and wellness education*: provide education regarding proper diet, nutrition, exercise, sleep, and recreation. Education can be through brief workshops, short 10-minute presentations after roll call, or part of an ongoing stress management campaign.
7. *Problem-specific workshops*: present workshops targeting specific health issues such as weight loss, smoking cessation, alcohol misuse, substance use, communication skills, marital retreats, and anger management.

# Critical Incident Counseling

A **critical incident** is a psychologically distressing event outside the range of usual human experience (Blau, 1994, p. 164). Well stated by Blak (1990), "it would appear that certain tragic events are so dramatic, shocking and disturbing to our collective psyches that we agree that they are 'stressful' and therefore 'critical incidents'" (p. 40). One unique aspect of police work is the potential exposure to traumatizing experiences. It has been estimated that 90% of law enforcement personnel are affected by one or more critical incident stress situations during their career (Conroy, 1990). Critical incidents are such a common aspect of police work that the second major police psychology conference hosted by the Behavioral Science Unit at the FBI Academy was titled *Critical Incidents in Policing* (Reese, Horn, & Dunning, 1990).

Definitions of critical incidents in policing usually refer to situations in which an officer is subjected to sudden serious jeopardy that poses a threat to the officer's or someone else's life (Gentz, 1990). Critical incidents in police work can include a variety of situations. Some examples include a line-of-duty death or serious injury of a coworker, an officer-involved shooting, a life-threatening assault, a police suicide, a death or serious injury caused by an officer, an incident involving multiple deaths, a traumatic death of a child, a hostage situation, a high-profile media event, or other incidents that appear critical (Kureczka, 1996). It is important to note that what affects one individual may not have the same affect on another officer. Psychological and behavioral reactions to critical incidents can be aggravated or mitigated by a variety of factors such as the officer's personality; circumstances surrounding the event; how the department, peers, family, and the media respond to the event; as well as any prior preparation for dealing with critical incidents. Common characteristics of critical incidents include (Blau, 1994, pp. 165–166):

1. The event is sudden and unexpected.
2. The event may include an element of loss (partner, physical ability, position).
3. The event is a threat to life or well-being.
4. The event may result in a change in the officer's values, confidence, ideals, etc.

Some critical incidents are unique to law enforcement. The most widely cited critical incidents for law enforcement personnel involve a shooting, either of officers or by officers. About 80% of officers who are involved in a shooting leave their departments shortly thereafter (Blau, 1994). Although statistics are difficult to obtain, best estimates indicate that police officers kill slightly fewer than 400 subjects annually. On the other hand, 100–150 police officers are killed annually in the line of duty. When we consider the population of sworn officers to be approximately 600,000 and the United States civilian population to be over 240 million, it appears that the civilians are taking a greater toll (Blau, 1994).

Other critical incidents common in police work include injury or death to a partner or colleague, hostage negotiation, being the first-responder to an accident involving death or injury, witnessing child abuse, and even witnessing a fellow officer accept a bribe (Toch, 2002). See Table 5.14 for a list of critical incidents unique to law enforcement. It should be noted that critical incident stress is not restricted to law enforcement personnel. A number of occupations are routinely exposed to potential critical incidents, including emergency service workers (Kureczka, 2002), firefighters (Vernon, 2006), military personnel (Sheehan & George, 2004), school personnel (J. Miller, 2001), and occupational health and safety inspectors (Moser, 1994), to name just a few. It is important to note that the stress of a critical incident does not just affect the witnesses and immediate responders. The stress from the incident can emanate outwardly, affecting others just as drastically. Some authors have coined the phrase "remote rescuers" to identify these individuals (Moser, 1994).

Figure 5.4

About 80% of officers who are involved in a shooting leave their departments shortly thereafter.
© 2009 Stephen Mulcahey. Used under license from Shutterstock, Inc.

## Common Characteristics of a Critical Incident — Table 5.13

- Event is sudden and unexpected
- Event may include an element of loss (partner, physical ability, position)
- Event is a threat to life or well-being
- May result in change in officer's values, confidence, ideals, etc.

## Table 5.14    Critical Incidents Unique to Law Enforcement

- Use of Deadly Force Incidents
  - Officers who are wounded, killed, beaten: affects both the individual and those close to him or her
  - Officers whose partner is subjected to deadly force
  - Officers who use deadly force: "failure to control situation"
    - "**suicide by cop**"–relevant also in hostage situations
- Participation of investigation of ghastly crimes or disaster

■ **Suicide by cop**

Person acts in a deliberate manner to provoke a lethal response from a law enforcement officer.

Although every individual responds to a critical incident differently, officers go through three phases of reaction following a critical incident: the *impact phase*, the *recoil phase*, and the *posttraumatic phase* (Blau, 1994).

The **impact phase** begins with the critical incident and continues until the stressor no longer has a direct effect. The length of the impact phase can be extended by a continued focus on the incident, as with an investigation after the use of deadly force or media coverage. The officer may feel stunned or confused. There can be a blurring of attention, restricted emotional expression, and automatic behavior.

The **recoil phase** follows the impact phase and may range from several days to several months. This phase is marked by strong emotional reactions such as depression, anger, withdrawal, anxiety, sleep disturbances, and nightmares. The phase is characterized by a need for support from other officers and retelling of the event to help gain some sense of emotional control over the incident. The end of this phase coincides with when the officer can return to active duty and routine living.

The final phase is the **posttraumatic phase**. This phase appears after the officer has returned to his or her regular routine. The phase can be characterized by an appearance of normalcy with periodic episodes of feelings of hopelessness, sleep problems, depression, and reexperiencing the critical incident (Wells, Getman, & Blau, 1988).

Many of the psychological reactions to critical incidents are characteristic of acute stress disorder and posttraumatic stress disorder. Acute stress disorder (ASD) is the development of a pattern of anxiety and dissociative symptoms within 4 weeks after exposure to a traumatic event, such as a critical incident. The symptoms need to resolve within the 4-week period, otherwise a diagnosis of posttraumatic stress disorder (PTSD) is considered. In both diagnoses, the individual must be exposed to a traumatic event that involves actual or threatened death or serious injury and the person's response involved intense fear, horror, or helplessness. Additionally, the individual must experience dissociative symptoms as well as reexperiencing the traumatic event, avoiding reminders of the trauma, or symptoms of hyperarousal. A detailed description of the diagnostic criteria for PTSD is provided in Table 7.10 in Chapter 7. The distinction between ASD and PTSD is that for ASD the symptoms resolve within 4 weeks after the traumatic event, whereas the diagnosis for PTSD is only given if the symptoms persist for more than 4 weeks.

The police psychologist should play a major role in the response to a critical incident. Everyone in the field agrees that early intervention is crucial in treating stress or trauma from critical incidents. Ideally, counselors should arrive at the scene of a critical incident to provide immediate support and start the intervention process. All law enforcement departments as well as other first-responders, such as fire departments and emergency medical services, should have a procedure in place to respond to a critical incident. Examples of programs include the Bureau of Alcohol, Tobacco, Firearms and Explosives (ATF) Peer Support/Critical Incident Stress Management program established in 1989; the Cop 2 Cop program established in 2000, serving law enforcement communities in New York and New Jersey; the Federal Law Enforcement Training Center's Critical Incident Stress Management and Peer Support Program, established in 1999; the U.S. Marshals Service (USMS) Critical Incident Response Team, established in 1991; and the U.S. Secret Service's Critical Incident Peer Support Team, established in 1985 (Sheehan, Everly, & Langlieb, 2004).

The police psychologist can play an active role in establishing a department's procedures for responding to a critical incident. As noted above, many departments have established critical incident response teams. In police departments, these teams consist of mental health professionals and police officers trained as peer counselors. It is a common feature of many law enforcement stress programs for mental health professionals to train police officers to work as peer counselors (Finn & Tomz, 1997). Patrol officers should be members of the team since they are some of the first persons to learn of a critical incident and can immediately alert other team members. Peer counseling training is initially characterized by idealism, enthusiasm to help, and a sense of a mission that binds the team members (Toch, 2002). This enthusiasm is difficult to maintain over long periods and can be strengthened by periodic training meetings (Nielson, 1990). The police psychologist can play an ongoing role in training and support for peer counselors. Some associations have established standardized debriefing models for handling critical incidents. For example, the International Critical Incident Stress Foundation, with over 3,000 members, has developed a model for debriefing persons involved in critical incidents (Robinson & Mitchell, 1995). However, there is some debate in the literature regarding the effectiveness of critical incident stress debriefing (Envoy, 2005; Look, 2004). Before we discuss this debate, it is important to define some of the terminology. Unfortunately, in the literature the terms are often used interchangeably, adding confusion to the findings. Debriefing is a generic term that is used for a wide range of counseling activities after a crisis. Critical Incident Stress Debriefing (CISD) is a small-group, seven-phase crisis intervention procedure developed by the International Critical Incident Stress Foundation, and Critical Incident Stress Management CISM) is a multicomponent crisis intervention that incorporates CISD as one of the 10 core elements of the procedure (Myers & Wee, 2005). Recent research has suggested that debriefing is not effective in preventing or lessening symptoms of PTSD (Van Emmerik, Kamphuis, Hulsbosch, & Emmelkamp, 2002). Some writers have even suggested that CSID may interfere with the natural processing of a traumatic event or with using other support systems (Look, 2004) or worsen symptoms of anxiety, depression, and PTSD (McEvoy, 2005). Myers and Wee (2005) recognize the mixed research findings for the effectiveness of CISD and CISM, yet conclude that both protocols have demonstrated sufficient success when used appropriately.

A recent recommendation has been the use of Psychological First Aid as an alternative to CISD (McEvoy, 2005). Psychological First Aid (PFA) consists of three components: (1) recreate a sense of safety, (2) establish meaningful social connections, and (3) reestablish a sense of efficacy. Both the National Institutes of Mental Health and the World Health Organization have endorsed PFA as a set of interventions proven to help first-responders.

The training of peer counselors is instrumental in the management of critical incidents but is important for addressing other mental health concerns as well. Police officers are much more likely to confide in a fellow officer than a civilian when they are experiencing difficulties. Fellow police officers have instant credibility in that they can empathize with the officer seeking help. Anecdotal evidence suggests officers will seek help sooner when a peer support network is in place. Peer counselors can serve a "bridging" function, referring difficult cases to mental health professionals when appropriate (Toch, 2002).

Another intervention that can mitigate the psychological effects of critical incidents is *preincident training* (Sheehan et al., 2004). Preincident training can help manage an officer's expectations regarding the outcome of a critical incident. Research in the military has shown that soldiers' expectations of their therapeutic outcome from war neurosis predicted their recovery. Currently, the FBI offers preincident training to new agents. As Sheehan and colleagues (2004) note, "Critical incident education provides one of the best inoculations available to law enforcement officers facing toxic situations. If they expect something, they are better able to cope with it" (p. 12).

# Training

Law enforcement agencies operate under a paramilitary structure and emphasize continual training (Blau, 1994). Training can occur at different times in the officers' careers. Most police officers have completed anywhere from 300 to 1,000 hours of training before graduation from the police academy. Although much of the training focuses on police work, such as firearms training, probable cause and arrest procedures, and securing a crime scene, police officers also need to know how to interact with people. Psychologists can teach courses on human behavior at the police academy. Topics offered by psychologists include responding to people with mental illness, juvenile delinquency, stress management, intervening in domestic violence disputes, and communication skills. Textbooks and manuals for developing these courses are commercially available. For example, the Police Executive Research Forum (PERF) develops training manuals on various topics for police training. PERF is a national organization consisting of law enforcement agencies across the country. An example of PERF's work is the development of a training curriculum and model policy on responding to people with mental illness. The curriculum includes a trainer's manual, a two-part training video, a brochure, and handouts for course participants (PERF, 1997).

A current trend in law enforcement is the professionalization of policing (Territo et al., 2004). Part of the movement toward professionalization is the call for higher education for police officers. A PERF study argued that a college degree could be a bona fide occupational qualification (BFOQ) for police (Carter, Sapp, & Stephens, 1988). The police academy cannot offer all the courses and provide all the skills that a police officer needs. The courses at the academy cover police work and there is neither the time nor the staff to educate officers about conflict and human behavior (Territo et al., 2004). The PERF studied suggest that college-educated police offers will be more flexible in decision making, more tolerant of diversity, and have enhanced communication skills. Research has found that officers with a 4-year degree tend to use significantly less physical force and any college education resulted in less verbal force in encounters with citizens (Paoline & Terrill, 2007). Police officers who are college educated also tend to use deadly force less often than officers with no college education (Mcelvain & Kposowa, 2008).

Psychologists can provide this type of training to police on a continuing education basis as well as through local colleges and universities that offer degrees in criminal justice. Nearly all police agencies require officers to receive a specific number of continuing education hours per certifying period. Psychologists can provide these continuing education workshops to local agencies. When providing continuing education to law enforcement agencies, the course material must be tailored to the specific population, recognizing differences in laws and policies among different jurisdictions. The workshop should not be a generic curriculum with the hope that "one size fits all." A recent welcome addition to the literature is a book titled *Improving Police Response to Persons with Mental Illness: A Progressive Approach* (Jurkanin, Hoover, & Sergevin, 2007). This is one of the first books to address police officers' response to mental illness. Although this has been a problem recognized by the law enforcement professionals for some time, it is only now that the scholarly literature is starting to offer some guidance (Cotton, 2008).

Table 5.15 presents a list of continuing education and coursework that a police psychologist can provide to law enforcement.

| Illustrative List of Training Topics a Police Psychologist May Provide | Table 5.15 |
| --- | --- |

- The offender with a mental disorder
- Stress management: prevention, inoculation, and treatment
- Restraint and sensitivity in policing
- Health and wellness
- Community mental health services
- Juvenile delinquency
- Techniques for interviewing children
- Psychological profiling
- Issues of insanity, competence, and criminal intent
- Effective interviewing and listening skills
- Suicide prevention
- Domestic violence: prevention and identification
- Effective report writing regarding the offender with mental illness
- Communication skills
- Gender-sensitivity training
- Diversity training

# Consultation

Psychologists can use their training in the behavioral sciences to assist police in law enforcement work. The police psychologist can fill the role of consultant by helping police catch criminals. Applying behavioral science methods to investigative work has been termed **investigative psychology**. The term investigative psychology was initially coined by David Canter, the director of the Centre for Investigative Psychology at the University of Liverpool in England. Initially defined as the application of psychological principles to the investigation of criminal behavior, Bartol and Bartol (2004) use a slightly expanded definition to include psychological autopsies, forensic hypnosis, and **criminal profiling**. These investigative techniques along with the role of the forensic psychologist are discussed in detail in Chapter 10 of this text. Below, several investigative areas are briefly introduced in the discussion of the police psychologist as consultant to law enforcement. The police psychologist consults with the department on topics such as hostage negotiation, psychological profiling, investigative hypnosis, and psychological autopsies.

■ **Investigative psychology**
The application of behavioral science methods to criminal investigative work.

■ **Hostage negotiation**
Mediation between hostage-taker and law enforcement personnel.

**Hostage Negotiation.** A hostage situation involves an individual or group of people being held prisoner by a person or persons. Once the hostages are seized, the hostage taker creates a barricade to defy law enforcement and may begin issuing demands. In the past, the primary method of dealing with a hostage situation was either a direct or an indirect assault on the barricade. More recently, the method of choice has been negotiation. The hostage negotiator is a person who mediates between the hostage-taker and law enforcement personnel. The negotiator does not have the power of decision making; rather, the negotiator's role is to buy time (Gallagher & Bemsberg, 1978). The negotiator should create a climate of negotiation and calm the hostage-taker (Myron & Goldstein, 1979). Police psychologists do not serve as hostage negotiators. Rather, they consult with the hostage-negotiation commanders and the officer-negotiators.

McMains (1988) has suggested that there are three roles for the police psychologist in hostage situations:

1. the professional,
2. the consultant, and
3. the participant observer.

As the professional, the psychologist can provide a wealth of applicable social science information. For example, in a hostage situation in which the perpetrator is trying to arrange a "cop-suicide," the psychologist can inform the police that the best way to diffuse the situation is to have the subject verbalize their intent to commit suicide. As a consultant, the psychologist can provide specialized knowledge to the trainers and administrators. The consulting psychologist can help develop a training program and work with administrators and trainers in designing and implementing selection and training procedures. Police psychologists are usually involved in the psychological screening and annual testing of members of the Hostage Negation Team (HNT). The third role is as a participant/observer. The psychologist is not in charge of the situation and must defer to the authority of law enforcement personnel in charge. A willingness to be on call 24/7 and trust between the psychologist and hostage-negotiation team is essential for this role to work.

The majority of police psychologists function in the role of consultant, and do not appear at the hostage scene. As consultants, psychologists assist with the selection of police negotiators. Research suggests that successful negotiators need better than average verbal skills, reasoning ability, self-image, flexibility under pressure, a belief in the power of verbal persuasion, and sensitivity to others. Detrimental traits include authoritarianism and intolerance of ambiguity (Blau, 1994). The psychologist can also consult on the negotiation strategy. For example, the strategy with an emotionally disturbed hostage-taker might utilize emotional techniques such as reflection of feelings, whereas a strategy with a criminal hostage-taker might utilize problem-solving techniques and compromise. Finally, the psychologist should be available to debrief individuals involved in the crisis once it is over. The individuals needing to be debriefed can include officers involved in the incident, hostages, and survivors of officers or hostages who were wounded or killed.

One unique aspect of hostage situations is the "**Stockholm syndrome**," so named after a hostage situation that occurred in Stockholm, Sweden. After spending a considerable amount of time with their captors, hostages identify with the hostage-takers or the hostage-takers' positions. Hostages who experience the Stockholm syndrome are usually surprised at their reaction. Victims usually require counseling to help resolve the emotional conflicts associated with the "identification with the aggressor" (Blau, 1994).

■ **Stockholm syndrome**
Hostage identifying with the hostage-takers; named after a hostage situation in Stockholm in which the hostages agreed with their takers after the incident.

■ **Psychological profiling**
A technique used in investigative psychology to identify the characteristics of unknown criminal suspects related to a specific crime. It is the process of inferring distinctive personality characteristics of individuals using physical and/or behavioral characteristics of a crime scene.

**Psychological Profiling.** Also called criminal profiling or offender profiling; this procedure refers to the process of inferring distinctive personality characteristics of individuals responsible for committing criminal acts from physical and/or behavioral evidence (Turvey, 2002). Criminal profiling is a method of helping to identify an offender based on an analysis of the nature of the offense and the manner in which the crime was committed. The process involves trying to determine aspects of the unknown criminal's personality based on the criminal's behavior before, during, and after the crime. This personality information is then combined with other details about the case, including physical evidence, and compared with characteristics of known personality types and mental abnormalities (Blau, 1994). This helps to develop a working description of the offender. Criminal profiling has been used with cold cases but has also been used to predict who may commit crimes (Hagaman, Wells, Blau, & Wells, 1987) as well as to identify individuals who may pose a threat to those protected by the Secret Service (Heilbrun, 1992). Criminal profiling is discussed in detail in Chapter 10 of this text.

**Investigative Hypnosis.**  In law enforcement, hypnosis is used as a tool to help enhance a victim's recollection of a crime (Blau, 1994). Victims of a crime may be traumatized by the event and report little or no memory of the details surrounding the crime, termed dissociative amnesia (Scheflin, Spiegel, & Spiegel, 1999). When hypnotized, individuals experience an enhancement of concentration and a lowering of peripheral awareness, the so-called hypnotic trance. Hypnosis is considered a shift in concentration with a relative suspension of critical judgment (Spiegel & Spiegel, 1987). Law enforcement has used hypnosis for more than 100 years (Wrightsman, 2001). The use of hypnosis grew in popularity in the 1970s due to its admissibility in courts. Reiser (1980), a prolific police psychologist in Los Angeles, started the Law Enforcement Hypnosis Institute to train police officers as forensic hypnotists (Wrightsman, 2001). Numerous psychologists have expressed concern about the reliability of information obtained through hypnotically enhanced memories (Hibler, 1988; Orne et al., 1985). The widespread use of hypnosis in law enforcement has diminished due to concerns regarding the reliability of the information obtained. Some research suggests that hypnosis increases one's *confidence* in their memory but not necessarily the accuracy of the recollection (Sheehan & Tilden, 1983). Investigative hypnosis is discussed in detail in Chapter 10 of this text.

**Psychological Autopsy.**  The term *psychological* autopsy was first coined by Shneidman (1981) and refers to a retrospective examination of the social and psychological events prior to an individual's death. The psychological autopsy is conducted when the *manner* of death is equivocal, or uncertain (La Fon, 2002). The cause of death is what caused the person to die and is usually determined by the medical examiner. The manner of death refers to the circumstances that led up to the cause of death. There are four accepted manners of death identified by the **NASH** acronym: natural, accident, suicide, and homicide.

■ **Investigative hypnosis**
A tool used to help enhance a victim's recollection of a crime.

■ **Psychological autopsy**
A retrospective examination of social and psychological events prior to an individual's death

■ **NASH**
NASH classification indicates that the manner of death is Natural, Accidental, Suicide, or Homicide.

## Four Accepted Manners of Death (NASH)                Table 5.16

- N – natural causes
- A – accidental death
- S – suicide
- H – homicide

The goal of a psychological autopsy is to establish the deceased's activities, interpersonal relations, attitudes, and behaviors for 30 days prior to the death (Blau, 1994). There are various approaches to conducting a psychological autopsy, with little research to suggest one way is superior to the other. Some authors have offered a thorough list of areas to explore as psychological autopsy guidelines (Ebert, 1987). The psychological autopsy is discussed in detail in Chapter 10 and only briefly presented here as one example of a police psychologist's opportunities as consultant.

# Management Consultation

In addition to providing consultation to law enforcement for solving crimes, police psychologists can also provide organizational consultation to the agency. Most large police agencies could benefit from the services of an industrial/organizational psychologist. Police departments are large bureaucratic agencies that are frequently managed by supervisors with little administrative training. Psychologists can assist management with a number of organizational tasks including administrative decision making, team building, organizational development, strategic planning and research, and program evaluation.

# Careers in Police Psychology

A career as a police psychologist generally requires the terminal degree (PhD) in psychology along with a license to practice. For example, the IACP guidelines for police officer evaluations recommend the use of psychiatrist or licensed psychologist. Most police psychologists are trained as clinical or counseling psychologists (Kuther & Morgan, 2004). Essential clinical skills include assessment, diagnosis, treatment, and crisis intervention. Due to the wide variety of roles a police psychologist is asked to fill, it is better to be trained as a generalist with strong foundation skills than to specialize in any one particular area. Additional skills for consultation require understanding the legal system along with courses in research, statistics, and industrial/ organizational psychology (Bartol, 1996). Coursework on organizational behavior, theories of management and leadership style, and organizational communication would prove to be valuable to the police psychologist. Training and supervision on topics specific to police work would include criminal profiling consultation, investigative hypnosis, hostage negotiation, and performing a psychological autopsy. A civilian police psychologist should participate in ride-alongs and orientation programs teaching psychologists about police work (Chamberlin, 2000). In addition to the academic training, it is important for an individual hoping to work as a police psychologist to have a clean criminal record so that they are not disqualified by foolish mistakes made in the folly of youth.

Police psychologists can work either in-house, usually in larger departments, or as a consultant to several smaller agencies. Psychologists working alone as consultants to several agencies have the opportunity to network with numerous police psychologists through professional associations devoted completely or in part to police psychology. See Table 5.17 for a list of professional organizations in police psychology. Police psychologists spend the majority of their time in counseling and screening and selection of police officers (Bergen et al., 1992). Police psychologists responding to a survey reported very high levels of job satisfaction (Bergen et al., 1992). Due to the wide variety of their duties, some police psychologists complain that they are asked to provide services beyond their expertise or to be all things to all people (Super, 1999). On the other hand, as Dr. Debra Glaser, Chief Police Psychologist of the LAPD, stated, "It's never boring" (personal communication, May 2, 2005). Average starting income is in the low $40,000s (Kuther & Morgan, 2004) and experienced police psychologists report a median annual salary of $53,000 (Bartol, 1996). However, these salary ranges need to be adjusted for annual raises to be comparable to current salaries.

## Professional Organizations for Police Psychologists    Table 5.17

- The Council of Police Psychological Services
- Academy of Police Psychologists
- Division 18 of APA–Division of Psychologists in the Public Sector: Police Psychology Section
- Law Enforcement Behavioral Sciences Association (LEBSA)

- Police Psychological Services Section of the International Association of Chiefs of Police
- Commission on the Accreditation of Law Enforcement Agencies
- Society for Police and Criminal Psychology
- FBI Behavioral Science Unit

## Summary

This chapter introduced the specialty of police psychology. Police psychology is the application of psychological principles to the investigation of criminal behavior. Police psychologists work with law enforcement personnel, not with criminal defendants. Police psychologists provide four general services to law enforcement: assessment, counseling, training, and consultation. The psychologist spends most of his or her time providing assessment and counseling. Assessment consists of the screening of new recruits, fitness-for-duty evaluations, and selecting and testing police officers assigned to special units such as SWAT and HNT assignments. All of these evaluations are associated with particular legal and ethical issues related to confidentiality and test use. The second major component of police psychology is the provision of counseling services to law enforcement personnel and their families. The stress of police work can take a toll on both the officer and his or her family. Police psychologists need to convey their policy of confidentiality so that officers do not fear for the security of their job when they seek help. The stress of the job can also cause marital and family relationship difficulties. Psychologists can provide counseling and stress management and inoculation training to officers and their families. One particular area where the police psychologist can play an important therapeutic role is counseling after a critical incident, such as the use of deadly force.

Police psychologists provide consultation and training to law enforcement agencies. Training for police officers in understanding human behavior starts in the academy and continues throughout their careers. Psychologists can teach in the police academies as well as provide continuing education on a wide range of topics, such as responding to individuals with a mental illness to developing effective and sensitive communication skills. Consultation can help with investigative work, as in criminal profiling, investigative hypnosis, and psychological autopsies. Psychologists also provide organization consultation on issues such as administrative decision making, strategic planning, and program evaluation.

Police psychology appears to be a growth field. There has been a steady increase in the number of departments using psychologists. Though some large departments, such as the LAPD, employ staff psychologists, many use psychologists on a contractual basis. This trend will continue into the future. Despite the demands of the job, police psychologists report a high level of job satisfaction. The wide variety of tasks appears to be what attracts many to the position. Students planning to pursue careers as police psychologists should learn strong assessment and clinical skills along with a solid understanding of police work.

# TEST YOUR KNOWLEDGE

1. With regard to police officer selection,
   a. the client has confidentiality regarding the results of the evaluation
   b. the candidate does not necessarily have access to the results of the evaluation
   c. the psychologist must receive permission to release the results of the evaluation to the candidate
   d. all of the above

2. Which instrument was specifically designed to select law enforcement personnel?
   a. MMPI-Police
   b. Correctional Officer and Police Screener (COPS)
   c. Inwald Personality Inventory
   d. California Personality Inventory

3. Which of the following are *not* true regarding fitness-for-duty evaluations (FFDEs)?
   a. Agency has a right to order an evaluation
   b. Officer has a right to know the results of the evaluation
   c. Agency has an obligation to order FFDE
   d. Officer may not have legal counsel available during the evaluation

4. One of the most commonly used psychological testing instruments for screening candidates is
   a. the California Psychological Inventory
   b. the Minnesota Multiphasic Personality Inventory–2
   c. the Law Enforcement Assessment Survey
   d. the Inwald Personality Inventory

5. Officer Wendy Holmes is involved in apprehending a child kidnapper. She is able to arrest the suspect but only after a gunfight in which her partner is wounded and she shoots an innocent bystander. Her commanding officer decides to refer her to the police psychologist. The referral is *most likely* for
   a. a fitness-for-duty evaluation
   b. Critical Incident Debriefing
   c. training
   d. none of the above

Answer Key: (1) d, (2) c, (3) b, (4) b, (5) b

# Chapter Six

# Correctional Psychology

## Learning Objectives

- What are the two definitions presented in the text for a correctional psychologist?
- What is meant by deinstitutionalization and what are the factors that contributed to it?
- What are some of the reasons given for the growth in the prison population?
- Approximately how many people are incarcerated in the United States?
- Approximately what percentage of the inmate population suffers from mental illness?
- What are the goals of incarceration presented in the text?
- What types of crimes have the highest recidivism rates?
- Distinguish between specific deterrence and general deterrence.
- What are some of the limits to confidentiality for inmates in counseling?
- Be able to describe the distinction between treatment and rehabilitation.
- What are the roles or duties of a correctional psychologist?
- What is the typical training of a correctional psychologist?
- Know the significance of the following court decisions: *Washington v. Harper* (1990), *McKune v. Lile* (2002), *Ford v. Wainwright* (1986), and *Estelle v. Gamble* (1976).
- Be able to define selective incapacitation and how this concept has evolved.
- Be able to cite relevant court cases upholding the constitutionality of selective incapacitation.
- What is restorative justice and give an example presented in the text.
- What is the job outlook for correctional psychologists and how does the majority rate their job satisfaction?

## Key Terms

- Actuarial prediction
- American Association of Correctional and Forensic Psychology
- Assessment
- Clinical prediction
- Coercion
- Community mental health movement
- Confidentiality
- Correctional psychologist
- Correctional psychology
- Correctional treatment programs
- Criminogenic needs
- Criminology
- Crisis intervention
- Deinstitutionalization
- Deterrence
- *Estelle v. Gamble* (1976)
- *Ford v. Wainwright* (1986)
- General deterrence
- Incapacitation
- Jail
- Jury nullification
- *Kansas v. Hendricks* (1997)
- Mandatory sentencing laws
- *McKune v. Lile* (2002)
- Mental health services
- Mental health treatment programs
- Multiple relationship
- Noncriminogenic needs
- N.W. theory of punishment
- *Penry v. Lynaugh* (1989)

*(continued)*

## Key Terms *(continued)*

- Prison
- Privilege
- Questionable validity generalization
- Rare risk or protective factors
- Recidivism
- Rehabilitation
- Restorative justice
- Retribution

- Selective incapacitation
- Social psychology
- Sociology
- Specific deterrence
- Statistical prediction
- Suicide screening
- Treatment
- *Washington v. Harper* (1990)

This chapter examines the role of psychologists who work in correctional facilities such as jails and prisons. Although the duties of correctional psychologists are similar to the work done by other clinical/counseling psychologists in community settings, there are also differences that are unique to the correctional environment and inmate population. Many other mental health professionals also work with offenders who are on probation or parole and are living in the community. However, these psychologists may or may not consider their profession to be that of a correctional psychologist, particularly if they are engage in this type of clinical work on a part-time basis.

The chapter begins by offering a definition for the title correctional psychologist. As with many emerging fields, opinions vary as to the correct definition. The field of correctional psychology has seen a tremendous amount of growth, corresponding with the increase in the number of individuals incarcerated in correctional facilities. There has also been a rise in the number of inmates who suffer from a mental illness. This rise in the prison population and inmates with a mental illness has made the need for psychological services in correctional facilities even more urgent. Reasons for the increase in the number of individuals incarcerated and the large increase of the number of mentally ill individuals in correctional facilities are presented. The goals of incarceration are then discussed along with the roles correctional psychologists can play in helping prisoners return to the community. Some of the unique challenges of providing mental health services in correctional facilities are covered, including a discussion of inmates' rights regarding treatment. The chapter presents a conceptual framework for clinical practice in correctional facilities. The lack of a treatment focus in forensic psychology has been identified as a shortcoming in the profession. Finally, training and job opportunities in correctional psychology are presented.

# Definition of Correctional Psychology

**Correctional psychology** is the work of psychologists working in correctional settings. These correctional settings include jails and prisons, although it may also be a halfway house or "boot camp" for juveniles. A psychologist working in a correctional facility is frequently referred to as a **correctional psychologist.** Some authors make a distinction between correctional psychologist and a psychologist who works in a correctional facility. Althouse (2000) suggests that correctional psychologists are psychologists who have specific training in forensic issues related to corrections. However, the majority of psychologists working in correctional facilities do not have this type of specific training (Bartol & Bartol, 2008). In fact, this type of specific training in correctional psychology is not readily available nor has the availability of training opportunities kept pace with the huge demand for psychologists in correctional settings (Magaletta & Boothby, 2003). Currently, there are a fair number of predoctoral internships in cor-

**■ Correctional psychologist**

A psychologist working in a correctional facility who may or may not have specialized training in correctional psychology.

rectional psychology, many in federal prisons with the Federal Bureau of Prisons. However, fewer than ten postdoctoral fellowships provide intensive training in correctional psychology (Ax & Morgan, 2002; Richardson, 2003). The numerous job opportunities for psychologists in correctional facilities has surpassed the number of training opportunities As a result, specific training in forensic psychology related to corrections may be desirable for applicants but is not typically a prerequisite for the majority of positions in correctional facilities. With that in mind, throughout this text all psychologists who work in correctional facilities, regardless of specific training in corrections, will be referred to as correctional psychologists. However, it is important to realize that clinical practice of psychology in correctional facilities is not the same as simply the practice of psychology with individuals who just happen to be incarcerated (Travis & Lawrence, 2002). There are unique aspects to the practice of psychology in correctional facilities and with inmate populations that the correctional psychologist must learn. These distinctions are presented later in the chapter.

The field of correctional psychology is considered a subspecialty of forensic psychology. The majority of psychologists working in correctional facilities are licensed psychologists with doctoral degrees in either clinical or counseling psychology. Nearly 50% of their time is spent in providing direct clinical services either in the form of treatment or assessment (Boothby & Clements, 2002). As correctional psychologists, they are forensic psychologists working in a specific type of forensic setting. This identification as forensic psychologists conforms to the recent name change of the American Association for Correctional Psychology to the American Association for Correctional and Forensic Psychology (*www.eaacp.org*). This classification of correctional psychology as an area within forensic psychology conforms to the definitions of forensic psychology and legal psychology presented earlier in the text.

# Recent Growth in the Field of Correctional Psychology

Correctional psychology has undergone tremendous growth in the past three decades for a number of factors. The field has been referred to as a "growth industry" (Richardson, 2003). Membership in the American Association for Correctional and Forensic Psychology has doubled in the past year alone and now totals over 500 members. Although estimates vary based on who is included, Boothby and Clements (2000) estimate that over 2,000 psychologists work in corrections. Naturally, the growth in the field of correctional psychology has paralleled the explosive increase in the prison population. The growth in correctional psychology has also benefited from a recent shift in philosophy regarding the purpose of incarceration. The past decade has seen a shift away from the goals of punishment and segregation back to the goal of **rehabilitation** of the offender (Ward & Stewart, 2003). One recent article reported, "The lock them up and leave them approach, in which corrections means little more than warehousing people, is a political agenda that has failed" (Nink, 2008, p. 1). Psychologists and mental health professionals can play a key role in the rehabilitation of offenders. Correctional psychologists can provide mental health treatment and rehabilitation services to assist with the inmate's successful transition back into the community. Although psychologists are now considered essential in correctional facilities (Morgan, Beer, Fitzgerald, & Mandracchia, 2007), the degree of success that psychologists have in correctional settings will largely depend on their efforts in promoting the value of mental health and rehabilitation services (Ax et al., 2007).

An additional factor that has contributed to the growth in correctional psychology is the process of **deinstitutionalization**. Deinstitutionalization resulted in the

■ **Deinstitutionalization**

The process of releasing mental health patients in the 1970s from large mental health hospitals after the discovery of antipsychotic medications and reform that sought to place individuals in the least-restrictive environment.

release of thousands of patients from psychiatric hospitals back into the community. Due to deinstitutionalization, there has been a large increase in the number of inmates with a mental illness, which has led to a need for more mental health services in correctional facilities.

We review each of the above issues in more detail throughout the chapter. However, it is important to note that correctional psychologists are not the only professionals providing mental health services in correctional facilities. Many of the mental health units in correctional facilities use an interdisciplinary team approach involving psychiatrists, psychiatric nurses, social workers, and mental health counselors in addition to psychologists.

Perhaps the most urgent problem facing the criminal justice system today is the overcrowding of the prison system (Territo et al., 2004). Over 2 million people are incarcerated in prisons, with an additional 250,000 people held in jails. The United States has the highest percentage of its population incarcerated for any developed country. In the first edition of this book in 2006, it was reported that one of every 142 U.S. residents is incarcerated. However, as of February 2008, the United States has the dubious record that for the first time in history, more than one of every 100 adults is in jail or prison, according to a report released by the Pew Center on the States. This is more than any other nation, whether in raw numbers or per capita. To put this number in perspective, approximately 9 million people are incarcerated worldwide, with more than 2 million in the United States (Ax et al., 2007). Note that this statistic cites residents; over 28% of the inmates held in federal prisons are not U.S. citizens. In addition to the number of people incarcerated, approximately 4–5 million people are on some form of community control such as house arrest, probation, or parole. The United States spends nearly $50 billion annually on corrections, according to the Pew Center report.

This steady increase in the prison population began nearly three decades ago during the early 1970s and is attributed to a fundamental change in attitudes regarding the goals of incarceration. Prior to the early 1970s, the consensus among professionals in the criminal justice system was that the primary goal of incarceration was rehabilitation with the intent of returning the offender back to the community. However, recidivism rates did not suggest that efforts at rehabilitation were effective. In fact, for many nonviolent crimes, such as theft and burglary, over 70% of the inmates discharged tend to reoffend.

It is important to realize when viewing statistics related to criminal behavior that there is a great deal of *discretion* within the criminal justice system. For example, when a police officer stops an individual for exceeding the speed limit, the officer can decide

## Table 6.1    Recidivism Rates for Various Crimes

- Grand theft auto, 78.8%
- Possessing or dealing in stolen property, 77.4%
- Larceny, 74.6%
- Burglary, 74%

- Dealing in illegal weapons, 70.2%
- Rape, 2.5%
- Murder, 1.2%

(Bureau of Justice Statistics, 2002)

either to give a warning or to write a ticket. This decision is left up to the officer's discretion. When someone is arrested for drug possession charges, the prosecutor can decide to offer the suspect a plea bargain with probation and mandatory substance abuse counseling or press charges seeking a prison sentence. Once convicted, the jury can decide to find the defendant guilty, or even in rare cases, overlook the evidence and acquit the defendant. When a jury ignores the evidence and acquits a defendant, it is known as **jury nullification.** Even after a defendant is found guilty by the jury, the judge can change the verdict. This occurred in 1997 when a jury found 19-year-old Louise Woodward, a British nanny in Boston, guilty of second-degree murder in the shaking death of an 8-month-old baby. The second-degree murder charge carried a mandatory life sentence. The judge changed the verdict to involuntary manslaughter and Ms. Woodward was released from prison and returned to the UK. Finally, even after a defendant is sentenced to prison, the parole board can exercise discretion in regards to early release. If discretion is taken away from one source, as in the dilemma judges face with **mandatory sentencing laws** for drug offenses, it is then squeezed to another source. Prosecutors may be reluctant to pursue a minor drug violation knowing that the defendant could be sentenced to a 5-year prison term.

Prior to the late 1970s, parole boards were tasked with determining when a prisoner had been rehabilitated and thus ready for release. If prison conditions were crowded, they could become slightly more liberal in their decisions and release a larger number of inmates. In this way, the parole boards were able to use their discretion to prevent overcrowding in the prisons (Territo et al., 2004). As the public gradually lost faith with the ability of correctional facilities to rehabilitate criminals, citizens expressed concern about inmates being released before they completed their sentences. This led to a "get tough on crime" approach and the adoption of mandatory sentencing laws (Benson, 2003). Mandatory sentencing laws removed discretion away from judges, juries, and parole boards. Once convicted of a crime, there were sentencing guidelines that dictated minimal sentences that the defendant would need to serve. This is particularly true of drug crimes, violent crimes, and for habitual offenders. Nearly half of the inmates in state prisons were convicted of violent crimes, with the remaining inmates convicted of drug, property, and "other" crimes (Costanzo, 2004). In federal prisons, 58% of the inmates were convicted of drug offenses and only 14% were convicted of a violent crime (Mauer, 1999). This philosophical shift in the late 1970s was indicative of the change toward a punitive approach regarding incarceration as opposed to a rehabilitative approach.

A second factor that has contributed to the increase in the prison population is age demographics in the United States. The postwar population growth known as the baby boom hit a peak in 1957. This large age cohort was entering their mid-20s during the 1980s, the same time mandatory sentencing laws were starting to fill the prisons. This is the age range when people are most likely to be incarcerated. Therefore, even if there had not been a shift in sentencing laws, it is likely that prison populations would have increased simply due to age demographics. This trend is not likely to change. The "baby boom echo," which started in 1977, hit its peak in 1990 with no significant drop in birth rate predicted for the remaining decade (National Center for Educational Statistics, 1997). Many college students are familiar with the recent glut of applications to colleges and high schools. This large increase in applications reflects the growing number of young adults, a result of the baby boom "echo." The "echo" refers to the children of the baby boomers who are now starting to hit their mid-20s. As a result, we will continue to se a high number of individuals at risk for incarceration. This poses a unique opportunity for correctional psychologists to develop intervention and prevention programs, an issue we return to later in this chapter.

A third factor, *deinstitutionalization*, also contributed to the growth in correctional psychology. Prior to the early 1960s, individuals with severe mental disorders

■ **Jury nullification**
Occurs when a jury ignores the evidence and acquits the defendant. The jury essentially finds a guilty defendant innocent. This may occur if the jury does not agree with the law or the enforcement of a particular law in a specific situation.

were confined to large psychiatric hospitals. Frequently, individuals with schizophrenia suffered from command hallucinations. Patients may hear voices commanding them to engage in behavior that at times can be violent and disruptive. The discovery of antipsychotic medications, such as the major tranquilizers, had a significant impact on the more severe symptoms of schizophrenia, such as auditory hallucinations. These new psychotropic medications helped patients to better control their disruptive behavior.

The 1960s also witnessed the **community mental health movement.** Due to overcrowded psychiatric facilities and new medications, professionals wanted to place patients with chronic, severe mental illness for treatment in the "least restrictive environment." Mental health professionals gradually recognized that large state psychiatric hospitals were antitherapeutic. The antipsychotic medications offered the possibility of an alternative to simply "warehousing" patients. This led to a dramatic reduction of the number of people hospitalized in state mental psychiatric facilities. Many of these patients were released into the community with plans for follow-up treatment to be provided by community mental health centers (CMHCs). This process of releasing patients from state hospitals with the intent of helping them to transition back into the community, called "deinstitutionalization," refers to deinstitutionalizing the patient and giving him or her their life back. In addition to the therapeutic arguments, there were also financial incentives. Many states saw this movement as a chance to reduce their hospital budgets. Indicative of this change, the number of patients in state psychiatric institutions dropped from a high of 559,000 in 1955 to 69,000 in 1995 (Butterfield, 1998).

Unfortunately, the funds never materialized for adequate follow-up care and the initial programs that were set up to help patients were insufficient to handle the large number of people with severe chronic mental illness. Medications only worked when patients were compliant and CMHCs were never funded sufficiently to address the complex treatment issues associated with severe mental illness. Many of the mentally ill ended up homeless and living on city streets. Another large percentage of these discharged patients found their way into the criminal justice system. Estimates of the percentage of mentally ill and developmentally disabled inmates have ranged from 6% to over 65% of the prison population, depending on the study and the type of facility surveyed. The U.S. Department of Justice estimates somewhere from 15 to 20% of people in prison are mentally ill (Benson, 2003). This estimate indicates that from 150,000 to 200,000 inmates suffer from a mental illness. To exacerbate the situation, individuals with mental disorders are likely to remain incarcerated four to five times longer than similarly charged individuals without a mental illness (American Psychiatric Association, 2000b).

As is emphasized throughout this chapter, correctional facilities in the United States are now the primary mental health facilities in the nation (American Psychiatric Association, 2004). The three largest psychiatric facilities in the nation in 2006 were the Los Angeles County Jail (17,000), New York City Rikers Island (13,500), and the Cook County Jail in Chicago (9,000) (Adams & Ferrandino, 2008). Research suggests, "both the size of the mentally ill population and the seriousness of their illnesses are increasing" (Adams & Ferrandino, 2008, p. 913). There is little doubt that rehabilitation and treatment in prisons needs to catch up to current conditions. With regard to rehabilitation of offenders, the practices of risk assessment, identification of inmate needs, and assessment of the inmates' responsivity to treatment are considered integral to successful offender intervention (Wormith et al., 2007). Additional recommendations from these authors include the use of cognitive-behavioral interventions and positive psychology. The treatment of the men-

**Figure 6.1**

Due to lack of funds and insufficient programs to handle the large number of deinstitutionalized patients, many of the mentally ill end up homeless.

© 2009 Jon le-bon. Used under license from Shutterstock,Inc.

tally ill offender needs to become more sophisticated, progressing from simple control to using expanded therapeutic options, broader role definitions for correctional staff, and a focus on individualizing treatments for the mentally ill inmate (Adams & Ferrandino, 2008). The increase in the population of mentally ill offenders has also led to the need for correctional psychologists to appreciate the wide range of legal issues that affect inmates with mental illness (Cohen, 2008).

To summarize the preceding discussion, three factors have contributed to a growth in correctional psychology:

1. a change in sentencing laws with longer sentences being applied, mandatory sentences, three-strikes laws, and a reduction in the use of parole;
2. an increase in the number of people who are in the highest risk age group for incarceration;
3. the deinstitutionalization of people with severe mental illnesses from state psychiatric hospitals.

The first two factors led to an increase in sheer numbers of the prison population. The third factor, deinstitutionalization, led to an increase in the number of inmates with mental illness. In the past decade, prison officials have come to realize the need for mental health services within the correctional system. The courts and federal government have mandated the provision of psychological services due to the unmet need (Cohen, 1998). Because of the federal mandate, correctional psychology now is a growth industry with a lot to offer the criminal justice system.

## Therapy in Correctional Settings: Can I Leave?

Dr. Bernadette Jackson is a correctional psychologist and treats patients at the state correctional facility using group and individual therapy. Dr. Jackson is treating Andy K., an inmate with an Axis I diagnosis of depression and an Axis II diagnosis of antisocial personality disorder. Andy was sentenced to 10 years in prison for strong-arm robbery. He has served 6½ years and goes before the parole board in 6 months for the possibility of early conditional release.

Andy requested individual psychotherapy sessions approximately 3 months ago with a presenting complaint of symptoms related to depression. Andy attributes his depression to news that his estranged mother has been diagnosed with stage-four cancer and has been told by her doctors that she has approximately 1 year left to live. In therapy, Andy expresses his desire to make amends with his mother and indicates his desire to care for her during her final days.

During a therapy session, Andy mentions that he has private information from inmate Zackman regarding a previous sexual offense. Inmate Zackman was sentenced to 3 years on a drug-related charge. However, Andy reports that Zackman bragged about a child abduction, which has never been solved.

The warden has requested that Dr. Jackson prepare a report on Andy's progress in therapy and offer a prediction regarding his risk to reoffend for Andy's upcoming parole hearing.

Should Dr. Jackson reveal Andy's information in therapy regarding inmate Zackman, considering the source of the information? Andy's parole hearing will be completed before the information can be confirmed.

What are the ethical implications of releasing information obtained in therapy? Also, should Dr. Jackson provide a report on Andy's progress in therapy and provide a risk assessment for the parole hearing?

What are the ethical implications and ramifications for future therapy with Andy, as well as with other inmates, if his request for early release is denied, particularly if Dr. Jackson provides a negative report or risk assessment?

How should Dr. Jackson proceed?

| Table 6.2 | Factors Contributing to the Growth in Correctional Psychology |
| --- | --- |

- An increase in sheer numbers of the prison population, due to
  - (1) a change in sentencing laws with longer sentences being applied, mandatory sentences, three-strikes laws, and a reduction in the use of parole; and
  - (2) an increase in the number of people who are in the highest risk age group for incarceration.
- The deinstitutionalization of people with severe mental illnesses from state psychiatric hospitals led to an increase in the number of inmates with a mental illness.

Until only recently, much of the scientific literature on the effectiveness of correctional treatment has come from a variety of fields, including psychology, criminology, and sociology, lacking a unifying conceptual framework (Correia, 2001). The disciplines of psychology, criminology, and sociology have progressed separately, without informing the others as well as could have been hoped concerning the correctional practice literature (Magaletta & Verdeyen, 2005). In the 1970s, as the fundamental shift discussed above was occurring in the correctional system, there was very little empirical research to support one treatment program over another. The different professions use different languages, publish in their own scholarly journals, and oftentimes do not keep up with the scholarly literature outside of their own discipline (McGuire, 2001). However, the empirical research in correctional psychology is no longer lacking. Now, 30 years later, psychologists can point to research indicating what works in terms of treatment and can push for better treatment programs in correctional facilities as well as postrelease community-based services.

# Theories of Punishment and the Goals of Incarceration

■ **Criminology**

The study of crime from a sociological perspective.

■ **Sociology**

The study of social institutions and groups in society.

■ **Social psychology**

The study of how people influence others' behavior and attitudes; the study of the individual within a group.

Much of the literature regarding theories of punishment and the goals of incarceration derives from the disciplines of criminology and sociology. **Criminology** is the study of crime from a sociological perspective. Criminologists study social influences on crime, such as the effects poverty, unemployment, or drug use have on the crime rate. An example of criminology research is a study designed to determine if adult businesses in an area increase the amount of criminal activity in that area. Another example would be to examine what effect mandatory sentencing laws have on recidivism rates for particular crimes. **Sociology** is the study of social institutions and groups in society. Sociologists study societal issues. A sociologist may design a study to understand the relationship between sex education in the schools and teenage pregnancy. Sociology differs from **social psychology**, which is the study of the individual within a group. A social psychologist may conduct research to understand how individual jurors are influenced by persuasive arguments during the trial. Although these are the general distinctions among the disciplines of social psychology, sociology, and criminology, scholars from the different disciplines will examine similar areas. The more apparent difference between the disciplines is how the researcher attempts to understand the problem and the methodology that is used. Sociologists and criminologists seek to understand crime through social problems such as poverty, substance abuse, lack of economic opportunities, and so on. These disciplines typically do not study ways to change individuals. "Simply stated, the professionals with sociology and criminology are students of crime, not necessarily students of change" (Magaletta & Verdeyen, 2005, p. 39). Psychologists more frequently look to change human behavior. Correctional psychologists can use the sociological literature to help frame solutions to behavior change.

Traditionally, criminologists have cited four goals for incarceration:

1. retribution,
2. deterrence,
3. incapacitation, and
4. rehabilitation/treatment

A recent addition to the first four approaches is termed "reintegration into the community" or *restorative justice*. These five terms have been referred to in the literature interchangeably as both goals of incarceration and theories of punishment. Each of the five approaches are presented below. Although borrowed from the criminology literature, it is equally important for a correctional psychologist to appreciate theories of punishment and to understand the current approach toward punishment within the American correctional system.

## Goals of Punishment and Incarceration  Table 6.3

- Retribution: a "just-deserts" approach in that a person gets a punishment equal to their crime
- Incapacitation: prevents offender from reoffending
  - Selective incapacitation: sentencing based on presumed dangerousness
- Deterrence
  - General deterrence: broad threat of punishment
  - Specific deterrence: experience of punishment prevents individual from reoffending
- Rehabilitation/Treatment
  - Treatment: treating psychological disorders, sex offenders, etc.
  - Rehabilitation: change in behavior patterns; can be psychological interventions, also include education and vocational training programs
- Restorative Justice—aim is to restore both the community who was the victim of the crime and reintegrate the offender back into the community

# Retribution

■ **Retribution**
Punishing people for violating
the rights of others.

**Retribution** has been called the "law of just deserts." The concept of retribution, or punishing people for violating the rights of others, makes a great deal of common sense to most people and has always been popular among the public. Someone who has been hurt or wronged usually wants revenge. Rather than allow individuals to mete out their own revenge, society empowers the criminal justice system to enact the punishment. Victims of a crime have the opportunity for revenge in our criminal justice system during the sentencing phase of a trial. Frequently, victims will have the opportunity to testify during the sentencing phase to inform the court how the defendant wronged them. The court can use this information to dole out the appropriate amount of punishment. Ideally, the punishment should fit the crime as in the biblical statement, "an eye for an eye, a tooth for a tooth." The American Psychological Association's Task Force on the Role of Psychology in the Criminal Justice System (1978) originally endorsed the policy of incarceration as retribution. However, given the current crowded conditions of the prison system today, perhaps the APA would prefer to promote a more humane approach to punishment.

# Incapacitation

■ **Incapacitation**
One of the goals of
incarceration based on the
premise that the offender is
unable to reoffend as long as
they are incarcerated.

The **incapacitation** approach argues that incarceration is justified since the offender is unable to reoffend as long as they are incarcerated. The assumption behind the theory is that as long as the courts can lock up the few "bad apples" of society, crime will be held in check. Unfortunately, there are several problems with this assumption. First, due to the current overcrowding in the prison system, the courts are unable to incarcerate every individual indefinitely. Decisions need to be made regarding the options of incarceration versus house arrest and community control. The cost of incarceration is approximately five times the cost of house arrest. However, the Justice Department claims that releasing repeat offenders early will simply lead to more crime (Langan & Conniff, 1992). In addition, there is evidence to suggest that time spent incarcerated may actually lead to an increase in criminal behavior among adolescents (Vachss & Bakal, 1979). There is certainly evidence to indicate that procedures in jails and prisons are detrimental to the psychological well-being of those incarcerated (Busch & Shore, 2000). Finally, as the criminal population increases, the need for more prison space increases. Some authors have estimated the cost of building sufficient prisons to be as high as $100 billion (Territo et al., 2004).

A new twist on the incapacitation approach is termed selective incapacitation. **Selective incapacitation** is the confinement of individuals based on *presumed* dangerousness. Individuals are not confined for violations of the law that they have committed; rather, they are *civilly* confined for violations that they may commit in the future. The practice of selective incapacitation, based on case law, assumes that mental health professionals can accurately predict how someone will behave in the future. The courts have such faith in the assumption that they have been willing to incarcerate individuals indefinitely based on predictions of future dangerousness made by mental health professionals.

■ **Selective incapacitation**
The confinement of an
individual based on presumed
dangerousness.

The courts' support for selective incapacitation serves as an example of how case law can gradually expand the precedent set from one legal question (i.e., death penalty) to another (i.e., sexual predators). The initial ruling regarding prediction of future dangerousness is based on a death penalty case. In 1978, Thomas Barefoot was convicted of killing a police officer in Texas. To hand down the death penalty under Texas law, the jury needed to consider the probability that the defendant would commit future acts of violence that would constitute a threat to society. Two psychiatrists testified that Barefoot did pose a danger, though neither psychiatrist had personally examined Barefoot. The jury sentenced Barefoot to death. Barefoot appealed his death penalty sentence, challenging the experts' testimony on a number of grounds including the lack of scientific validity (Cunningham & Goldstein, 2003). The case eventually reached the U.S. Supreme Court. The Court ruled in a 6 to 3 decision that it was constitutional to rely on clinical predictions of violence for making decisions regarding the death penalty (*Barefoot v. Estelle*, 1983). Although three judges dissented from the majority opinion, the majority did accept the experts' testimony despite the fact that neither psychiatrist actually interviewed Barefoot. The dissenting judges expressed doubt regarding the accuracy of predictions regarding future dangerousness. In an interesting side note, Dr. James Grigon, one of the psychiatrists, testified that there was a "100% and absolute chance that Barefoot would commit future acts of violence that would constitute a continuing threat to society." Dr. Grigon was expelled from the American Psychiatric Association in 1995 for a pattern of similar testimony in death penalty cases (Cunningham & Goldstein, 2003).

With the *Barefoot v. Estelle* (1983) decision, the Supreme Court ruled that a mental health professional's expert opinion regarding the prediction of dangerousness met the criteria for the Daubert standard regarding admissibility of evidence. Recall from Chapter 2 the four criteria for scientific expert testimony under the Daubert standard: have the methods used been tested, have the methods been subjected to peer review, is the error rate acceptable, and is there general acceptance in the scientific community. The American Psychiatric Association submitted an *amicus curiae* brief to the U.S. Supreme Court indicating that psychiatrists were likely to be wrong two out of three times in predicting dangerousness. Despite evidence to the many flaws associated with predicting future behavior, the courts have generally allowed expert testimony by mental health professionals predicting dangerousness based solely on clinical judgment (Conroy, 2003). The *Barefoot* ruling also indicated that testimony on future dangerousness was constitutional. This ruling opened the doors for psychologists and psychiatrists to testify for the prosecution and defense on this issue as well as to serve as rebuttal witnesses. In a related case, the U.S. Supreme Court later ruled that a juvenile could be held without probable cause while awaiting trial based on the prediction that the juvenile would engage in criminal behavior if released (*Schall v. Martin*, 1984). This ruling by the Court overturned decisions by the district court and the Second Circuit Court of Appeal. Again, the Supreme Court was indicating its belief that mental health professionals are capable of accurately predicting future behavior. The initial decision by the court in the *Barefoot* case addressed the sentencing phase of a trial. The second decision addressed the pretrial phase, indicating that the criminal justice system could incarcerate presumably innocent defendants based on a mental health professional's opinion regarding future behavior.

These two cases, among others, established the legal precedent for what has become known as the sexually violent predator (SVP) statutes. Sixteen states have enacted SVP statutes and nearly the same number of states has proposed similar legislation (Janus & Walbek, 2000). These statutes enable the state to involuntarily commit an individual for an indefinite period. Typically, an individual would need to have a history of violent behavior, a mental disorder suggesting lack of control over their behavior, and an opinion by a mental health professional that the individual was likely to reoffend. Individuals meeting these criteria could be civilly committed against their will for an indeterminate sentence. The individual will then be reevaluated by a mental health professional, typically a psychologist, to determine if they continue to pose a threat to society. Although most SVP statutes suggest that the individual needs to have a mental disorder to be civilly committed, a large percentage of the individuals committed under

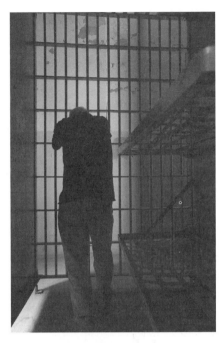

Figure 6.2

Evidence suggests that procedures in jails and prisons are detrimental to the psychological well-being of those incarcerated.
© 2009 Lou Oates. Used under license from Shutterstock, Inc.

these statutes do not have mental disorders related to sexual deviations (Janus & Walbek, 2000). In addition, treatment is infrequently provided (Janus, 2000).

It is important to note that this confinement is not based on crimes that defendants have committed. Rather, the involuntary commitment is only initiated after the offender has completed his or her prison sentence. Some authors suggest that these laws are simply ways of extending punishment (La Fond, 2000). This form of confinement can lead to an indeterminate sentence. One study found that individuals committed under a SVP statute rarely are released (Janus & Walbek, 2000). Since the confinement is in the form of civil commitment and not criminal confinement, advocates of the approach claim it is not double jeopardy. Double jeopardy includes being punished twice for the same crime. The U.S. Supreme Court upheld this practice as constitutional in the landmark ruling, *Kansas v. Hendricks* (1997). The Supreme Court emphasized that a risk assessment of Hendricks predicted that he was at a high risk for reoffending (Monahan, 2003). It is estimated that 1,300–2,200 individuals are held under these sexually violent predator statutes (La Fond, 2003). The U.S. Supreme Court appears to have more faith in the ability for mental health experts to predict future behavior than many of the experts in the profession (Monahan, 2003).

Although selective incapacitation clearly prevents individuals who are civilly committed from reoffending, there are constitutional and ethical concerns that need to be addressed. The lack of treatment along with the lengthy commitment periods may contribute to a precedent that could eventually extend to other criminal offenses.

## Deterrence

■ **Deterrence**

The notion that the threat of punishment will deter individuals from committing a crime.

**Deterrence** is the theory that the simple threat of incarceration will deter potential criminals from offending. The literature distinguishes between two types of deterrence: general deterrence and specific deterrence (Andenaes, 1968). **General deterrence** is the belief that the broad threat of punishment for all individuals keeps most people on the good side of the law. For example, the majority of motorists do not excessively exceed the speed limit due to the perceived threat of a speeding ticket. The general deterrence approach posits that the threat of incarceration will prevent would-be criminals from committing crimes. The argument for **specific deterrence** states that the experience of punishment prevents the convicted individual from reoffending. The individual who recently received a speeding ticket will be less inclined to exceed the speed limit having experienced recent punishment for a similar offense. Specific deterrence is designed to prevent convicted criminals from engaging in future offenses due to the fear of a subsequent prison sentence. The notion of specific deterrence is the backbone of so-called "three strikes" laws. These laws usually require a lengthy, mandatory sentence for felons convicted of a third violent crime. The belief is that the threat of a lengthy prison sentence will serve as a specific deterrent for would-be repeat offenders.

Although it is difficult to judge the effectiveness of general deterrence, it is possible to evaluate the effectiveness of specific deterrence by examining recidivism rates. **Recidivism** refers to the rate at which individuals convicted of a crime are arrested again. Recidivism rates are high for crimes of theft such as burglary (74%), grand theft auto (78.8%), possessing or dealing in stolen property (77.4%), and larceny (74.6%), suggesting a negligible effect of specific deterrence (Bureau of Justice Statistics, 2002). Contrary to popular belief, recidivism rates for violent crimes like rape (2.5%) and murder (1.2%) are relatively low.

In order to be effective, deterrence needs three components: speed, severity, and certainty of punishment (Territo et al., 2004). Psychologists can cite numerous studies indicating that for punishment to be effective it must occur shortly after the act, it must be severe enough to discourage the behavior, and it must be consistent and impartial. Unfortunately, due to overcrowded courtrooms, none of these three is possible in today's criminal justice system. Trials usually do not take place for up to a year or more after the defendant is arrested. Prosecutors simply cannot prosecute all of the cases and frequently must compromise with plea bargains and dismissed charges. Nearly 90% of cases result in a plea bargain. The criminal justice system is neither swift nor severe for the vast majority of offenders. As a result, the punishment of incarceration is ineffective. Nearly two-thirds of released inmates are rearrested within 3 years and about 50% are returned to prison (Cassel & Bernstein, 2001; U.S. Department of Justice, 2002). In theory, deterrence as a goal of incarceration could serve as an effective tool to control crime, in practice; it is currently not a possibility.

## Rehabilitation/Treatment

Correctional psychologists make a distinction between rehabilitation and treatment. However, over time the distinction has blurred and often the terms are used interchangeably. **Treatment** generally refers to the provision of psychological services to an individual who has been diagnosed with a mental disorder with the purpose of helping the individual attain improved functioning. Rehabilitation initially had as its goal the "moral redemption of the offender" and even shaped the vocabulary of criminal punishment; prisons were correctional institutions and reformatories were used to confine young adults (Territo et al., 2004). The intent was to rehabilitate individuals so that they could return to society. Concerning current usage, rehabilitation is not geared as much toward the treatment of a mental illness as it is toward changing behavior patterns. To this end, vocational and psychological training programs were introduced into correctional life. Rehabilitation programs can include a wide variety of services designed to help the offender succeed as a law-abiding citizen upon release from prison.

There was a great deal of public disenchantment with the success of rehabilitation programs throughout the 1970s and 1980s. This pessimism toward the rehabilitation of inmates help fueled the "get tough on crime" policies of the 1990s and prompted the so-called **"N.W." theory of punishment** (Benson, 2003, Territo et al., 2004). The "N.W." theory stands for "nothing works" with the solution for controlling crime to be punitive prison conditions and the warehousing of inmates. There is now some research to suggest that treatment programs are successful and recent court decisions have mandated treatment for inmates. Due to empirical evidence gathered over the past two decades regarding the effectiveness of treatment programs in reducing recidivism, there has been a gradual shift away from the punitive model of incarceration used by correctional institutions and toward the rehabilitative model. Some researchers have argued that this shift back to the rehabilitative model is one of the most significant events in modern correctional policy (Ward & Stewart, 2003).

There is considerable overlap in the types of services provided under the terms treatment and rehabilitation. Correctional psychologists are involved in the provision of both services. Some authors do not make a distinction between the two types of programs, whereas others do (Bartol & Bartol, 2004). Magaletta and Verdeyen (2005) proposed a conceptual framework of clinical practice in corrections that distinguished among three types of psychology services provided. This framework appears to describe more adequately the types of activities in which correctional psychologists are engaged rather than the treatment/rehabilitation distinction. The three psychology services identified are:

1. **mental health services** (MHSs)
2. **mental health treatment programs** MHTPs)
3. **correctional treatment programs** (CTPs).

We return to this classification when we discuss the clinical activities of correctional psychologists.

## Restorative Justice

Some authors have added a fifth goal of incarceration, termed restorative justice (Braithwaite, 1999; Presser & Van Voorhis, 2002). **Restorative justice**, also termed *reintegration*, is an approach aimed at "restoring" the community that was the victim of the crime and reintegrating the offender back into the community. The assumption behind reintegration is that the offender's behavior is the result of both the individual and the community from which he or she came. The approach extends beyond the rehabilitation model by assuming that both the individual and particular aspects of the individual's environment must be addressed in order for the inmate to make a successful transition to life on the outside. This model utilizes community-based programs such as halfway houses that assist the inmates upon release from prison. An example would be the Multisystemic Therapy program for serious juvenile offenders. The program provides intensive 24/7 treatment for the family, the youthful offender, and the system, such as the school and the community, simultaneously (DeAngelis, 2003). This program exists in 30 states and eight countries and boasts reductions in recidivism from 25 to 70%.

# Correctional Facilities: Jails and Prisons

Although many individuals both within and outside of the criminal justice profession use the terms **jail** and **prison** interchangeably, there are several important distinctions between the two terms. One important distinction for forensic psychology is that jails typically do not offer the kinds of mental health services that are available in prisons (Steadman & Veysey, 1997). Thus, many of the career opportunities for correctional psychologists are found in prisons.

*Jails* are typically run by the local government and are often situated in populated areas. Jails are used to hold defendants temporarily as pretrial detainees waiting to post bail or are used to confine people found guilty of misdemeanors, usually serving sentences of less than a year. Due to the nature of confinement, jails have a high turnover rate, with the population changing frequently. Detainees either make bail or complete their sentences. Jails tend to be small and have a smaller inmate population than prisons. Conversely, *prisons* are operated by the federal or state government and are usually located in rural areas. Prisons have large inmate populations who are serving sentences of more than 1 year, having been convicted of a felony. Prison populations are relatively steady, though inmates may be transferred to another facility at the discretion of the prison administrators.

The above comments are not meant to imply that jails provide no psychological services at all. The types of services provided vary by the size of the jail and the funding available. Some small county jails are no larger than a few jail cells in the back of the police station, whereas others facilities in larger metropolitan areas can easily resemble a prison. Due to the transient nature of the inmate population in a jail along with the types of charges, treatment is often short term and focused on specific misdemeanor offenses. For example, jails may provide domestic violence classes to inmates charged with domestic violence or Alcoholics Anonymous /Narcotics Anonymous meetings for inmates with an alcohol or drug problem. Frequently, enrollment in a suitable group program may be part of the probation requirement upon release from the jail

Research suggests that nearly 73 percent of U.S. jails assess inmates to determine appropriate treatment or rehabilitative goals. Mental health workers in jails are frequently asked to assess the new inmate and make a recommendation for appropriate treatment. As stated above, jails frequently provide self-help groups such as Alcoholic Anonymous (AA) and Narcotics Anonymous (NA) for individuals with alcohol or substance abuse problems. Jails may also offer group classes for anger management or domestic violence. Perhaps one of the largest services provided by jails is educational programs (Camp & Camp, 1995). While incarcerated, inmates without a high school degree can work toward obtaining their general equivalency diploma (GED) and may take vocational classes to learn a trade such as welding or carpentry.

# Psychologists' Duties in Correctional Facilities

The **American Association of Correctional and Forensic Psychology** (AACFP) revised their standards for psychological services in correctional facilities in 2000. The original standards were first published in 1980 (Althouse, 2000). The standards of practice are seen as an addition to the APA Ethical Standards and Code of Conduct and the Specialty Guidelines for Forensic Psychologists. The AACFP increased the number of standards from an original of 57 in 1980 to 66 standards in the 2000 revision. As with all ethical codes, the standards are not legal documents and do not protect one from liability issues. However, failure to follow the standards may result in civil and/or criminal proceedings (Althouse, 2000).

The 66 standards provide guidelines for the provision of psychological services to inmates in correctional facilities (Standards Committee, 2000). These standards, published in the Association's journal, *Criminal Justice and Behavior*, address ethical and procedural issues related to work in correctional facilities. All correctional psychologists are expected to adhere to the standards whether they are a dues-paying member of the Association or not. Sections covered by the standards include the following (Bartol & Bartol, 2004):

- Roles and Services: consultation, screening of staff, classification of inmates for services, training, assessment, diagnosis and treatment of mental illness, **crisis intervention**
- Staffing Requirements: recommendation that each facility employs at least one doctoral-level, licensed mental health professional with correctional psychology experience.
- Documentation: all documentation is to be maintained in compliance with professional and legal standards.
- Confidentiality: inmates and staff are informed verbally and in writing regarding limits of confidentiality.
- Informed Consent: all screenings, assessments, and treatments are preceded by an informed consent procedure.
- Employer and Ethical or Practice Standards Conflicts: there should be a documented policy for resolving conflicts between the facility and psychological staff.
- Screening/Evaluation: screening is provided by qualified personnel and psychological data is handled in a secure manner and is not available to inmate workers.
- Inmate Treatment: treatment is provided to inmates and staff and facilities exist for those needing close supervision.
- In-service Training: procedures exist for in-service training of facility and community staff regarding psychological services.
- Research: psychology staff are encouraged to conduct applied research or basic research aimed at improving the delivery of services.

More recently, the organization has changed its name to the International Association for Correctional and Forensic Psychologists (IACFP) and released new bylaws in 2008. Student memberships are available. Interested students or professionals can join through the organization's website, *www.ia4cfp.org*.

Psychologists working in correctional facilities spend the majority of their time in administrative tasks (Boothby & Clements, 2000). This is particularly relevant for training since only 13% of correctional internships offer any administrative experience (Ax & Morgan, 2002). In fact, nearly half of all doctoral-level psychologists end up in administrative or managerial roles, but the majority receive no formal training for these types of skills (O'Donohue & Fisher, 1999). Administrative work involves program coordination including development, implementation, and evaluation of effectiveness, training and supervision of other staff, report writing, and consultation with the administration. In regards to amount of time spent in particular tasks, after administrative duties (30%), correctional psychologists report that the rest of the bulk of their time is spent in provision of direct services (26%) and assessment (18%; Boothby & Clements, 2000). We now turn to the duties of assessment and treatment.

# Assessment in Correctional Facilities

**Assessment** has been emphasized throughout this text as a crucial area for forensic psychologists. Among mental health professionals, psychologists are uniquely trained in the administration, interpretation, and development of assessment instruments. It is not surprising that they are called upon in correctional facilities to answer questions regarding the initial screening of an inmate, the appropriateness of release (parole), and the prediction of future risk. Psychologists in correctional facilities are also involved in other types of assessment such as competency assessments (competency to stand trial, competency to be executed) and criminal responsibility evaluations.

Assessment can occur at several times during an inmate's journey through the correctional system. Prisons and the vast majority of jails assess inmates upon entry into the facility. This initial assessment is conducted to determine appropriate housing, special needs, and any potential problems. During the course of incarceration, an inmate who develops a psychological disorder or experiences an emotional crisis may be evaluated to determine risk level and to determine any diagnosis based on the *Diagnostic and Statistical Manual of Mental Disorders* (American Psychiatric Association, 2000a). Finally, in discharge planning, an inmate can be assessed to predict risk of dangerousness or recidivism and to determine if any community-based treatment programs would be warranted. Day reporting centers (DRCs) have become an increasingly utilized alternative to jail and prison sentences. DRCs, as part of community pretrial release programs, help reduce overcrowding in jails and provide programming to help facilitate the rehabilitation of offenders. An essential part of placement in a DRC requires an assessment of the risk level of convicted offenders before they are released back into the community (Kim, Joo, & McCarty, 2008).

The purpose of the initial assessment when an inmate first enters the correctional facility is to determine what programs might benefit the inmate, what level of custody security is required, and what special needs the inmate may have, such as medical or psychological treatment needs. This assessment fits within both the Mental Health Treatment Programs and Correctional Treatment Programs conceptual framework presented above (Magaletta & Verdeyen, 2005). The assessment involves assessing both *risks* and *needs*. Much of the research on risks and needs comes from the disciplines of sociology and criminology. Mental Health Treatment Programs (MHTPs) are the middle ground between traditional mental health services and Correctional Treatment Programs (CTPs). MHTPs target psychological conditions that are related to criminogenic need and risk factors. Criminogenic factors are factors demonstrated to be directly related to criminal behavior. For example, substance abuse and impulsivity are related to criminal activity and are targeted for change by MHTPs (Magaletta & Verdeyen, 2005). CTPs address the inmates' adjustment to the correctional facility including the likelihood that they will follow the facility's rules and attempt to reduce criminal recidivism. Examples of **criminogenic needs** addressed by CTPs include antisocial attitudes and criminal associates.

The correctional practitioner will find the literature on *dynamic criminality risk factors* to be most relevant (Magaletta & Verdeyen, 2005). Dynamic factors are those most likely to be malleable to change through treatment (Andrews & Bonta, 1998). Examples would include substance abuse, work skills, or attitudes toward the use of violence. These have been termed *criminogenic* in that these factors are related to criminal behavior. Changing these dynamic, criminogenic factors through treatment will lead to a reduction in the rate of recidivism (Gendreau, Cullen, & Bonta, 1994). The **noncrimonogenic needs** are factors that need to be addressed but are not seen as playing a role in criminal behavior, such as depression or anxiety (Bartol & Bartol, 2004). The *risk* factors are based on the concept that treatment services need to be matched to the inmate's assessed level of risk. Inmates who are at a high level of risk would be offered the greatest number of interventions (Hannah-Muffat & Maurutto, 2003). There is a wide variety of assessment instruments available to predict risk and to assist in the classification of treatment need (Andrews & Bonta, 1998).

The assessment of mental health disorders or crisis intervention falls into the Mental Health Services (MHS) conceptual framework of psychology services provided in correctional settings (Magaletta & Verdeyen, 2005). MHSs comprise the traditional treatment services provided by psychologists. These services include the diagnosis and treatment of inmates with mental health disorders and the reduction of frequency and intensity of symptoms. Inmates may be referred by correctional staff or may be self-referred. The majority of inmates express a willingness to seek psychological treatment and the majority are self-referred (Morgan, Rozycki, & Wilson, 2004). The goal of assessment is to identify individuals with mental health disorders and to assist in stabilizing individuals in a psychological crisis (Morgan, 2003). Assessment may also help identify areas to be the focus of treatment. The delivery of MHSs is perhaps the area with which psychologists are most familiar. Assessment instruments include the standard personality instruments discussed in Chapter 3 of this text, including the MMPI-2, the MCMI-III, and the Personality Assessment Screener.

Correctional psychologists are also involved in crisis intervention in correctional facilities. Suicide is the leading cause of death among inmates in jails (Clear & Cole, 2000). Jails have a much higher rate of suicide than prisons, possibly a rate five times higher than in prisons (Cohen, 1998). Often suicides occur within the first 24 hours of incarceration. Researchers have identified suicide prevention as one of the nine core bodies of knowledge for correctional psychologists (Magaletta, Patry, Dietz, & Ax, 2007).

It appears that jail suicides are triggered by two primary environmental circumstances. First, individuals in jail are typically facing a crisis in their life. Second, unique aspects of the jail environment exacerbate the crisis. Inmates are faced with numerous unknowns. Most likely, they trust no one and fear everyone, including the other jail inmates. They feel that they have no control over their future, both short and long term. They may be ashamed of the charges against them; they may lack social support, having been separated from family and friends; and they distrust the authority figures that contributed to their arrest and subsequent incarceration.

Suicide assessment in correctional facilities should be conducted by a trained mental health counselor. Unfortunately, this is often not the case in many jails. Suicide prevention could be increased by proper screening of individuals when they are first admitted since the majority of suicides occur within the first twenty-four hours of incarceration (Hayes, 1995). However, suicide can occur at any time during an inmate's stay. Ideally, a **suicide screening** can involve a brief interview assessing potential for suicide and lethality. One common myth surrounding suicide is the concern that speaking about suicide will "put ideas into someone's head." The reality is that asking someone about any *suicidal ideation* (thoughts of suicide) provides them with the opportunity to speak about their fears and to seek help. Table 6.4 provides a list of suicide-risk indicators (Sanchez, 2001) and sample questions. Many jails and prisons

| **Table 6.4** | Screening Items for Potential Suicide along with Possible Sample Questions |
| --- | --- |

- Suicidal ideation
  - With things going so bad right now, have you ever thought of hurting yourself?
- Detailed and feasible plan
  - If you were to hurt yourself, how would you do it?
- Prior suicide attempts
  - Have you ever tried to hurt yourself in the past?
- Family history of suicide attempts
  - Has anybody in your family ever tried to hurt him- or herself?
- Prior treatment for mental health problems
  - Have you ever been in any form of counseling or on any medications for emotional problems like depression or anxiety?
- Recent significant losses
  - What has been going on in your life? Have there been any recent major problems in your life?
- Signs of intoxication or drug use
  - In addition to obvious signs of substance use: Have you had anything to drink recently? Have you ingested drugs? Are you on any medications?
- Mental illness associated with suicidal behavior (e.g., depression, schizophrenia, substance abuse)
  - Have you been feeling down or depressed lately? Do you hear voices that other people do not hear? How often do you drink? Do you use any drugs?
- An offense that would create embarrassment or shame for most people
  - You have been charged with "name of offense," how do you think your friends or family will react to this news?
- Social support group
  - Do you have any family or friends that you can call?
- Major medical problems, especially chronic, incurable, or painful conditions
  - Are you on any medications? Do you have any medical problems?
- Childhood abuse or history of violent behavior
  - Have you ever been arrested before? What was your childhood like?
- Unattached, unemployed
  - Tell me about yourself. Are you married? Do you work?

Any responses that may indicate potential suicide risk should be more closely evaluated. Individuals thought to be at risk for suicide should be immediately referred to a mental health professional for further evaluation and observation.

use a screening checklist to determine suicide potential and refer individuals identified to be at risk to a mental health professional for further evaluation and observation (e.g., Rowan & Hayes, 1995). The use of a checklist allows psychologists to conduct suicide assessments in a systematic and consistent manner, reducing the chance of missing an important risk factor (Sanchez, 2001).

Finally, psychological assessments are used to assist in the release decision-making process. These prerelease assessments evaluate potential risk factors for recidivism. This use of risk assessment instruments fits into the CTPs' conceptual framework of psychological services in correctional facilities. Clinicians must make judgments regarding an inmate's potential for recidivism, particularly regarding violence, dangerousness, and potential to commit a sexual offense. The latter is particularly true due to recently enacted sexually violent predator statutes. As discussed earlier, these laws enable states to initiate civil commitment proceedings against individuals deemed to be at risk for committing a sexual offense.

Although there are a wide variety of risk assessment instruments on the market, many of them do not have the empirical support desirable for such decision making. In addition to the standard personality measures discussed, such as the Personality Assessment Inventory, the MMPI-2, and the MCMI-III, clinicians can also use measures aimed more specifically at predicting future behavior. On example is a measure used to assess psychopathy, or behaviors characteristic of antisocial personality disorder, the Hare Psychopathy Checklist—Revised (PCL-R; Hare, 2003). The PCL-R was the only instrument recommended by more than half of surveyed diplomats in forensic psychology for assessment of an individual's risk of violence (Lally, 2003). It is assumed that an individual who scores high on measures of psychopathy will continue to engage in criminal behaviors (Kraemer et al., 1997). *Antisocial personality disorder* (APD) is defined primarily in behavioral terms in the DSM. Behavioral characteristics of APD include irritability and aggressiveness, deceitfulness, impulsivity, recklessness, lack of remorse, and failure to conform to social norms (American Psychiatric Association, 2000a). However, not all individuals with APD meet the criteria for psychopathy (Cunningham & Reidy, 1998). Psychopathy includes characteristics of APD along with personality traits such as superficial charm, egocentricity, insincerity, shallow affect, and grandiosity (Conroy, 2003). Other instruments that have been developed to predict risk for postrelease include the Violence Risk Appraisal Guide (VRAG; Harris, Rice, & Quinsey, 1993; Rice, 1997), the HCR-20 (Douglas & Webster, 1999), and the MacArthur Violence Risk Assessment Study (Monahan et al., 2001). Monahan (2003) provides a review of the literature on violence risk assessment.

Researchers have debated the superiority of clinical versus statistical risk assessment for quite some time (Westen & Weinberger, 2004; Swets, Dawes, & Monahan, 2000). Meehl (1954) was the first to raise the issue and suggested that statistical formulas were better than clinical judgment for making diagnostic and treatment decisions. **Clinical prediction** has come to mean both how the data or information is collected and how decisions are made using the collected information. Clinical observation is considered unstructured and subjective. Clinical interpretation of the data is assumed to be impressionistic and informal (Westen & Weinberger, 2004). **Statistical prediction** uses an actuarial formula to make predictions. The *clinical versus statistical* debate can be viewed within the larger picture as a reflection of the tension between researchers and clinicians (Westen & Weinberger, 2004).

Some researchers have argued that the "empirical literature has consistently supported the superiority of actuarial data over clinical predictions of human behavior" (Bartol & Bartol, 2004, p. 273), although others have not been so quick to discount the role of clinical judgment (Monahan, 2003; Mossman, 1994). A few researchers have suggested that clinicians should, when warranted, use their judgment to revise actuarial violence risk assessment estimates. Most clinicians are not willing to use actuarial data to the exclusion of clinical judgment (Heilbrun et al., 2002). Hart (1998) has even suggested that exclusive reliance on actuarial decision making is unacceptable. Campbell (2003) suggests that adjusting the actuarial risk assessment using clinical judgment does not improve the accuracy of the prediction. However, Monahan (2003) offers two reasons to support clinicians using clinical judgment to adjust actuarial estimates: **questionable validity generalization** and **rare risk or protective factors**. Questionable validity generalization refers to the possibility that the actuarial model was developed on a population very different from the individual being evaluated. Only a few instruments exist and most were developed on very specific populations, such as white Canadian men in a maximum-security hospital. A clinician may want to use the estimate as advisory rather than conclusive when using the instrument to assess risk in individuals who are dissimilar from the normative group. The second issue refers to the identification of rare risk or protective factors that may not have been taken into account when developing the actuarial model. For example, in the *Kansas v. Hendricks* (1997) Supreme Court ruling, Hendricks, a convicted sex offender, conceded that he could not control his urges to molest children when he felt stressed. Regardless of the score on an actuarial measure, it would be imprudent for an evaluator not to consider an offender's admission of lack of control.

The VRAG is an actuarial instrument used to predict violent behavior. The VRAG is generally considered an acceptable measure to use for evaluating an individual's risk of violence (Lally, 2003). Initially, approximately 50 predictor variables culled from over 600 inmates' files in a maximum-security hospital were coded into the regression model. After a series of regressions, 12 variables from the initial 50 were included in the VRAG. The 12 variables that comprised the VRAG are:

1. score on the PCL-R ( a measure of psychopathy);
2. elementary school maladjustment;
3. age at the time of the offense;
4. diagnosis of a personality disorder;
5. separation from parents when under the age of 16;
6. failure on a prior conditional release from prison;
7. criminal history of property offenses;
8. marital status;
9. diagnosis of schizophrenia;
10. injury of victim in the prior offense;
11. history of alcohol abuse; and
12. a male victim in the prior offense (Rice, 1997).

All of the above factors are positively related to violent recidivism except age, diagnosis of schizophrenia, and victim injury, which are negatively related. The items are weighted and individuals receive a score that indicates their risk for violent recidivism. The correlation between scores on the VRAG and violent recidivism was .44. A cutoff score at the 80th percentile accurately classifies 74% of the individuals who reoffend (Rice, 1997).

It should be obvious that using such a scale reduces the role of clinical judgment when determining risk. Recent research questions the utility of weighting the risk factors, indicating that weighted factors do not improve predictive accuracy over that of a nonweighted reference. It is quite possible that these prediction models simply do not include true causal factors. For example, causal factors can change, such as employment status. Employment status can be affected by the efforts of the offender or through intervention. An actuarially derived score may fail to consider this when assessing risk. The authors conclude that, "Risk assessment research in the forensic mental health field should continue to take input from theoretical and clinical perspectives and not be restricted to empirical data" (Grann & Langstrom, 2007). It may also be useful to include clinical measures such as personality types in risk assessment (Listwan et al., 2007).

In the future, the field of risk assessment will continue to move toward the use of actuarial instruments combined with clinical judgment. The use of actuarial methods, including risk assessment software (e.g., Monahan et al., 2001), will allow for the identification of specific risk factors for violence among specific types of people. Rice, one of the developers of the VRAG, suggests, "The field of violence prediction research has advanced to the point where **actuarial predictions** about serious criminal violence by men who have already committed one violent offense can be made with a considerable degree of accuracy" (1997, p. 421). However, on a more guarded note, in evaluating the admissibility of expert psychological testimony on violence risk assessment, Monahan remarks, "No one questions that the state of the science is such that the prediction of violence is subject to a considerable margin of error" (2003, p. 529). It should not be surprising with such divergent views on the issue that the courts are sometimes frustrated by the conflicting expert testimony.

# Treatment in Correctional Facilities

After administrative duties, direct delivery of psychological treatment occupies the next largest amount of time for correctional psychologists. In comparison to assessment activities, correctional psychologists spend slightly more time providing treatment services (18% vs. 26% of their time). The role of the correctional psychologist is to rehabilitate and reintegrate the inmate back into the community (Hawk, 1997). Psychologists receive a great deal of training in the delivery of psychological services and typically feel most comfortable providing these services in the correctional environment. However, as noted earlier, the delivery of services in a prison to an inmate population is not the same as the provision of psychological services in a community setting (Travis & Lawrence, 2002). There are numerous factors unique to the field that makes working in corrections both challenging and rewarding.

In terms of MHSs, correctional psychologists diagnose and treat mental disorders, provide basic mental health services, and prevent the development of mental disorders that develop in response to incarceration (Milan, Chin, & Nguyen, 1999). Many inmates are treated for depression upon initial entry into the prison system. Treatment services consist of primarily individual and group treatment using a variety of theoretical approaches (Kratcoski, 1994). Recent surveys have found that clinicians use cognitive-behavioral approaches, behavioral approaches, rational-emotive therapy, and reality therapy. Correctional psychologists report that they spend approximately 60% of their treatment time conducting individual therapy and nearly 15% of their time providing group treatment (Boothby & Clemens, 2000).

Below is an overview of the general types of mental health treatment programs that are available in many correctional facilities:

- *Therapeutic communities*: Therapeutic communities use an entire unit or cell block to instill proper social skills as well as addressing particular problems such as substance abuse or antisocial behavior patterns.
- *Self-help substance abuse programs*: Many facilities will allow self-help groups such as the 12-step programs of Alcoholics Anonymous, Narcotics Anonymous, and Gamblers Anonymous to conduct groups within the facility. Though based on a self-help model, these programs work closely with mental health professionals.

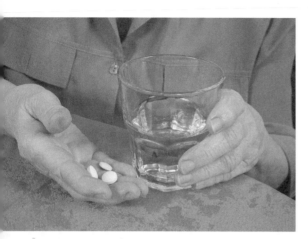

■ *Therapy:* Therapy can take many forms and utilize a variety of theoretical models. Therapy can be individual, couple, family, or group. Therapy typically involves developing a therapeutic relationship between the client and the clinician, usually a psychologist or psychiatrist. Group therapy tends to be psychoeducational in nature with a focus on specific problems, such as addressing attitudes toward women or impulse control problems. Family therapy will involve the inmate's family in the therapeutic sessions. Couple therapy includes the inmate's spouse or partner in the therapeutic process.

■ *Counseling:* The distinction between therapy and counseling is usually one of intensity. Counseling may be provided by a vocational or mental health counselor and focuses on developing problem-solving skills. Therapy focuses on mental health problems such as depression, anxiety, or sexual disorders.

■ *Medication:* Psychotropic medications are frequently prescribed by a psychiatrist or an advanced registered nurse practitioner (ARNP) to treat severe psychological illnesses or behavioral disorders. Psychological disorders can include depression, anxiety, or psychotic symptoms such as hallucinations and delusions. Behavioral problems can include restlessness and violent outbursts. Although only two states currently allow psychologists with the proper training to prescribe medications (New Mexico and Louisiana), psychologists need to understand the role of psychotropic medications in the treatment of their clients. Prescription privileges for properly trained psychologists is an ongoing debate within the profession as more psychologists lobby for prescription privileges (Fagan et al., 2004; Heiby, DeLeon, & Anderson, 2004; McGrath et al., 2004).

These general mental health services presented above are also supplemented with treatment programs that address specific populations or problems. To illustrate these supplemental services, a list of psychology services offered in federal correctional facilities by the Bureau of Prisons appears below (Office of the Inspector General, 2004).

■ Drug Abuse Education Program–an educational program about risks associated with drug use; provides skills training to stay drug-free; encourages participation in the residential treatment program.

■ Residential Drug Abuse Treatment Program–intensive drug treatment for up to 12 months in separate unit or cell block; incorporates assessment, planning, and group and individual therapy.

■ Nonresidential Drug Abuse Treatment Program–provides individual and group counseling as follow-up to residential treatment program and to inmates who do not choose the residential treatment program.

■ Transitional Drug Abuse Treatment Program–a community-based treatment program for inmates who successfully completed drug treatment while in prison or who are subsequently identified to be in need of drug treatment.

■ Sex Offender Management Plan–a comprehensive management strategy for all incarcerated sex offenders; designed to increase security and facilitate transition of inmates back to the community.

■ Sex Offender Treatment Program–a residential program offered at FCI Butner; designed to reduce recidivism; focuses on controlling criminal sexual behavior through a combination of treatment and intensive supervision.

■ Challenge, Opportunity, Discipline, and Ethics (CODE) Program–a residential treatment program offered in high-security facilities; designed for inmates whose psychological problems interfere with adjustment to incarceration. The program teaches inmates basic core values aimed at developing better interpersonal skills.

- E-CODE Program–an intensive, multiphase nonresidential and residential treatment program for maximum-security inmates; teaches inmates self-discipline, prosocial values, and strategies to change negative thoughts and behaviors that lead to legal difficulties. The program is designed to manage and treat violent and predatory inmates housed at USP Marion.
- Impulsive–Aggressive CODE Pilot–a residential program designed to identify and treat inmates with impulsive–aggressive disorders.
- Bureau Responsibility and Values Enhancement Program (BRAVE)–the program is designed to assist in the adjustment of medium-security inmates entering prison for the first time; improve institutional adjustment and reduce incidents of misconduct; and identify and treat psychological disorders that may lead to criminal activity and poor institutional adjustment.
- Skills Program–specialized treatment program for inmates with significant learning and social skills deficits; uses an interdisciplinary approach including staff from the unit, education, recreation, and psychology; the program consists of assessment and orientation, intensive treatment, and transitional planning.
- New Pathways Program–a program designed to treat the trauma resulting from sexual, psychological, or physical abuse for female inmates and to develop skills to facilitate a successful transition to the community.

Successful treatment outcome measures may include a range of indicators including stabilization of symptoms, improved psychosocial or occupational functioning, and a reduction in recidivism rates. Professionals working together from the different disciplines differ with regard to the goals of treatment and outcome measures. One of the problems in the scholarly literature is the different outcome measures used by psychology, criminology, and sociology (Magaletta & Veryden 2005) as well as the relative lack of the use of outcome measures in clinical practice (Lambert & Hawkins, 2004).

# Unique Challenges for the Correctional Psychologist

There are unique environmental challenges that serve as obstacles to effective psychological treatment outcomes in the correctional environment. First, the *physical environment* of the correctional facility can hinder effective treatment. Prisons are overcrowded, oftentimes with few if any adequate therapy rooms. Effective therapy rooms should convey a sense of tranquility and privacy, conditions usually not found in a correctional facility. Many jails and prisons are old with poor physical environments that contribute to a sense of hopelessness and futility. In addition, inmates are separated from their family and friends and have few support groups to assist in any meaningful behavior change. Finally, due to the nature of the correctional institution, mental health appointments are usually not a priority and can often be cancelled or missed due to a variety of reasons including security concerns, conflicting appointments such as a court appearance, disciplinary problems, or transfers to other facilities.

Another issue related to treatment in correctional facilities that has received attention in the literature is the issue of coercion (Bartol & Bartol, 2004). **Coercion** refers to forcing inmates into treatment programs. The amount of coercion can range from direct threats of loss of privileges to subtle hints or even small benefits for inmates who participate in treatment. Frequently, inmates are in treatment either against their wishes or simply as a way to avoid a less unpleasant situation. Inmates may not be explicitly coerced to participate in treatment in order to feel forced to comply. Inmates may feel that if they do not participate in treatment their decision will be negatively evaluated by the same individuals who can grant early release and parole (Stone, 1984). Upon release, many inmates are required to participate in treatment as a condition of release. Approximately 20% of inmates are mandated to either receive mental health services in the community or while incarcerated (Morgan et al., 2004). The postrelease requirement to remain in treatment is particularly true for sex offenders (Becker & Murphy, 1998), who may be expected to remain in treatment indefinitely (Conroy, 2003). There exists in the profession an untested conventional wisdom that individuals in therapy have to *want* to change for treatment to be effective. Some research suggests that treatment is effective even with initially noncompliant participants (Becker & Murphy, 1998; Prendergast, Farabee, Cartier, & Henkin, 2002). However, a recent meta-analysis of offender coercion in treatment suggests that mandated treatment, particularly in custodial settings, is ineffective (Parhar, Wormith, Derkzen, & Beauregard, 2008). These authors note that voluntary treatment appeared to be effective regardless of the treatment setting. Despite contradictory findings, it is reasonable to expect that offenders in prison and on conditional release will continue to be coerced, at some level, to participate in treatment.

Another unique obstacle to treatment that is frequently found in forensic psychology is the limitations placed on **confidentiality**. The limits to confidentiality between the therapist and inmate in a correctional facility include the typical limits that exist in most therapeutic relationships. There is a distinction between confidentiality and privilege. *Confidentiality* can be conceptualized as the mental health professional's ethical and legal obligations to the client to keep communications between the client and therapist confidential. **Privilege** is the law's recognition of the confidentiality in legal proceedings that protects the communications from disclosure (Petrila & Otto, 1996). For example, in a typical mental health setting, a client *may claim privilege*. Clients can refuse to disclose and can prevent others from disclosing in a legal proceeding any communications or records made for the purpose of diagnosis or treatment of mental disorders (Petrila & Otto, 1996). However, most states have enacted mandatory reporting laws for suspicion of child or elder abuse or neglect. When abuse or neglect of a child or older adult is suspected, the mental health professional must make a written report to the appropriate authorities. The mental health professional's obligation to report supersedes any guarantee of confidentiality or privilege granted by law. Mental health professionals can break privilege under a few circumstances addressed by case law, statute, and ethical obligations. For the correctional psychologist, additional reporting requirements exist that are unique to the correctional setting. These conditions include plans to commit a crime in the facility, plans to escape, and possession of contraband (Morgan, Winterowd, & Ferrell, 1999). Another obstacle to treatment is the inmate's legitimate fears that information he or she discloses in therapy may be used against him or her. Inmates disclosing prior crimes during the course of therapy that the criminal justice system is unaware of may receive additional prosecution or extended confinement (Kersting, 2003).

Another dilemma for the correctional psychologist is the potential for multiple relationships. The ethical issues regarding **multiple relationships** have been discussed in Chapter 2 of this text as well as elsewhere in the literature (Lamb et al., 2004). The APA's Ethics Code (2002) cautions against psychologists being involved in a multiple relationship with a client. As presented in Chapter 2 of this text, a *multiple relationship* occurs when a psychologist who is in a professional role or relationship with a client or student finds him- or herself in a second role or relationship with that individual (Lamb et al., 2004). Multiple relationships occur when a psychologist has a professional role with a client and then enters into a second relationship in one or more of the following three forms:

1. sexual relationships,
2. nonsexual social or professional relationship, or
3. financial–business relationship.

In correctional settings, due to the need for security, a psychologist may be pressured to interact with inmates in professional roles other than that of clinician. In an emergency in a federal prison, the psychologist's primary duty is to serve as a correctional officer (Federal Bureau of Prisons, 1993). In one situation reported in the literature, a psychologist was asked to assist in an inmate count when there was a shortage of staff. The psychologist was then enlisted to assist with a contraband search of the inmates (Weinberger & Screenivasan, 1994). The role of therapist and the role of correctional worker create a multiple relationship that could undermine the therapeutic relationship. Inmates can develop a view of the psychologist as simply another "prison guard" and not as an agent of therapeutic change. This type of multiple relationship has the potential to impair the psychologist's effectiveness in performing his or her functions as a psychologist and could be construed as an ethical violation (American Psychiatric Association, 2000a). Psychologists in correctional facilities need to be aware of the potential ethical conflicts inherent in their duties and to make their supervisors aware of the APA Ethics Code as well as potential ethical violations when they occur.

# Court Decisions Regarding the Rights of Inmates

Inmates have a number of rights that are guaranteed by the constitution. In this section, we review the rights and case law that are most relevant to the practice of correctional psychology. Correctional psychologists rarely serve as advocates for inmates' rights, having neither the legal expertise nor administrative authority to do so. However, as health care providers in the criminal justice system, correctional psychologists should be informed of basic rights regarding treatment along with court decisions. These rights include the following:,the right to receive adequate medical treatment, the right to refuse treatment, and the right to be competent to be executed.

Inmates have the right to receive adequate medical treatment. In *Estelle v. Gamble* (1976), the U.S. Supreme Court ruled that inmates have the constitutional right to receive adequate medical treatment. This ruling has been subsequently interpreted to include adequate mental health treatment. However, the real issue arises in determining what comprises "adequate" treatment. Clearly, there are differing standards of care in different facilities and even geographic locations. As stated earlier, correctional facilities have large inmate populations in need of mental health services. However, many of these facilities do not have the necessary resources to address the mental health needs of the inmates. The *Estelle v. Gamble* ruling required the inmate to prove that prison officials were "deliberately indifferent" to the health needs of the inmate. These rulings were extended to include psychiatric care (*Joseph v. Brierton*, 1984; *Wellman v. Faulker*, 1983).

Inmates also have the right to refuse treatment. Refusal of treatment is typically an issue in regards to the use of psychotropic medications, though it can also involve refusal to participate in psychological treatment. An inmate may desire to refuse psychotropic medications for a variety of reasons. Correctional psychologists are most interested in rulings related to the refusal of psychoactive medications and psychological treatment. Two recent U.S. Supreme Court rulings addressed these issues. In a ruling related to the refusal to participate in psychological treatment, the U.S. Supreme

Court ruled that a prison could withdraw privileges if an inmate refused to participate in a treatment program (*McKune v. Lile*, 2002). Mr. Lile was a sex offender convicted of rape. Mr. Lile refused to participate in a sex-offender treatment program that would require disclosure of past behavior, possibly exposing him to future prosecution. Mr. Lile refused to participate in the psychological treatment because he feared his participation would incriminate him for further prosecution. The prison administration took away privileges that Mr. Lile had enjoyed, such as canteen access and work duties, and threatened to transfer him to a more dangerous prison (Bartol & Bartol, 2004). The decision by the Court to allow the removal of privileges allows prison administrators to "punish" inmates who do not participate in treatment.

Inmates have the right to refuse medications, though this right can be overridden. Inmates may wish to avoid psychotropic medications for a variety of reasons. Inmates may wish to remain incompetent to stand trial, or may want to have their symptoms appear obvious during an insanity plea trial. Inmates may also wish to avoid the unpleasant side effects of some psychotropic medications or avoid execution. The U.S. Supreme Court has addressed the issue of the right to refuse medications. In *Washington v. Harper* (1990), the U.S. Supreme Court sided with the state of Washington, stating that an administrative hearing, as opposed to a more stringent independent judicial review, is sufficient to administer psychoactive drugs to an inmate against his or her will. Harper had sought to have an independent judicial review with counsel present to determine if he needed to be medicated to control his disruptive behavior.

The U.S. Supreme Court has ruled that it is unconstitutional to execute an inmate who does not appreciate what is happening to them due to a mental illness (*Ford v. Wainwright*, 1986). However, in Penry v. Lynaugh (1989), the U.S. Supreme Court ruled that the execution of an individual with mild mental retardation did not violate constitutional safeguards since Penry had been found competent to stand trial. The question remains as to whether the courts can force an inmate to take psychoactive medications in order to become competent to be executed. In 2003, a federal appeals court ruled that death row inmates do not have the right to refuse medications. Understandably, mental health professionals must evaluate their own personal values regarding the death penalty prior to participating in the treatment or evaluation of inmates on death row when the purpose of the treatment or evaluation is to facilitate the inmate's execution.

# Unique Aspects of Working in a Correctional Facility: Tips for the Beginning Clinician

Working in a correctional facility is not the same as working in a mental health clinic or other facility in the community. Clinicians, including student interns, should be aware of the special considerations inherent in the correctional environment. Below are a few tips for clinicians or students who will begin work in a correctional facility.

Security is the first priority in any correctional facility. Concerns for security will always take precedence over any mental health treatment services. It is important for the clinician to become aware of the facility's procedures for entering the facility, moving about within the facility, and exiting the facility. It is usually necessary to show proper identification, to obtain a pass that is worn at all times while in the facility, and to sign in and sign out according to proper procedures, returning the pass upon departure. Individuals entering a correctional facility should not have any contraband or items that may threaten the security of the facility, such as sharp objects but also cameras, tape recorders, and so on. Clinicians should be prepared to have their briefcase and/or handbag searched as well as the possibility of stepping through a metal detector. It is important to allow sufficient time for the check-in procedure, particularly on visitation days, as there may be a number of people going through the process. Finally, mental health professionals should be conscious of their own personal safety. When working with an inmate, a private, but not secluded, therapy room is preferred. A treatment room with a window in the door enabling the facility staff to monitor for any threatening behavior is preferable to a secluded room. Clinicians should always place themselves closest to the exit and not allow themselves to be blocked from leaving a room quickly should they so desire. Mental health staff should also recognize behavioral signs indicating that an inmate is becoming agitated and learn techniques to help diffuse the situation as well as recognizing when it is simply best to leave the situation.

In addition to understanding the facility's security procedures, it is also helpful to know the facility's schedule for daily routines. For example, it is important to know when the correctional officers change shifts. During a shift change, most facilities will not allow anyone to enter the facility until the shift change is complete. Even if a clinician is already in the facility, it is unlikely that an inmate will be escorted to an appointment during a shift change. The incoming correctional staff must be briefed and receive their assignments before attending to other activities. Meal times are another period that can cause disruption for mental health services. The clinician should know the mealtime schedule for their inmate's unit. It is best to avoid interfering with the mealtime schedule as that may prevent an inmate from being served a meal if it conflicts with a mental health appointment. Many facilities will also conduct a daily inmate count of the entire population. During an inmate count, movement within the facility is not permitted. It is also best to avoid scheduling an appointment during normal visitation hours. Inmates may have an appointment with an attorney or family member and would usually prefer to meet with either of the two as opposed to a mental health professional. Finally, it is preferable to avoid scheduling a mental health appointment during the inmate's scheduled recreation. Recreation provides an important opportunity for the inmate to socialize and leave their housing area. When possible, it is best not to interfere with the inmate's recreation period.

Clinicians should know the rules and policies of the facility as well as the rules for inmates. Inmates are usually given a written copy of the facility's rules; a clinician should ask for a copy of these rules. Sometimes a simple request from an inmate such as mailing a letter could be illegal. Seek the advice of the shift supervisor if there is uncertainty about a behavior or request from an inmate. Clinicians should also become familiar with the state laws and rules regarding mental health professionals' work in a correctional facility. States may have specific laws regarding the conduct of mental health professionals that would behoove the clinician to know. The clinician should also understand the facility's inmate classification system. At the time of intake, most facilities will classify inmates for purposes of determining appropriate housing assignments, overall level of security risk, and medical and mental health needs.

It is important to nurture effective working relationships with individuals throughout the criminal justice system. Many clinicians are seen as outsiders and can be viewed with skepticism by correctional staff and inmates. Inmates may believe the counselor is working on the side of the courts and the correctional staff may believe the counselor is an advocate for inmates. Counselors should attempt to make rounds and get to know inmates on an informal basis to help establish rapport. Visits to the units can help establish credibility in the eyes of the staff as well as the inmates. Psychologists should make efforts to get to know correctional staff including the medical personnel at the facility. Additionally, getting to know the prosecutor, public defender, judges, and probation officers will also help in the provision of mental health services to the appropriate inmates. It is also important to become familiar with community-based after-care treatment programs so that inmates can be referred to appropriate treatment programs upon release. Correctional staff should be politely addressed and referred to as officers rather than guards. Professional attire should be worn and jewelry and other fashion accessories should be avoided.

| Table 6.5 | Tips for the Beginning Clinician Working in a Correctional Facility |
|---|---|

- Security is the first priority
  - Do not carry contraband or items that threaten the security of the facility
  - Know the procedures for entering, working within, and exiting the facility
  - Carry a photo ID and be prepared for searches and delays
  - Be aware of one's own personal security
- Know the facility's schedule–avoid scheduling conflicts with the daily routine
  - Change of shift
  - Mealtimes
  - Visitation days
  - Inmate counts
  - Recreation period
  - Court appearance and appointments with lawyers
- Understand the rules and policies of the facility
  - Obtain the written rules of conduct for inmates
  - Know state laws for mental health professionals working in correctional facilities
  - Understand the facility's classification system
- Establish effective working relationships
  - Routinely make rounds to get to know inmates and correctional staff
  - Become acquainted with facility administrator, medical personnel, and correctional staff
  - Become acquainted with other criminal justice personnel such as prosecutors, public defenders, judges, probation officers, and staff at community-based treatment programs
  - Dress and act like a professional and treat others as such

# Careers in Correctional Psychology

As stated earlier in this chapter, there are numerous career opportunities for correctional psychologists. According to Edith King, a forensic psychologist in Oklahoma, "Nationwide, the jails have become the No.1 holding stop for the mentally ill" (Smith-Bailey, 2003, p. 55). The field of correctional psychology appears to be a growth industry that will continue to expand for some time. Optimism over effective treatment approaches coupled with the dramatic increase in the prison population suggests the need for correctional psychologists will persist. In the 1940s there were fewer than 100 correctional psychologists, today there are nearly 2,500 correctional psychologists in practice (Magaletta & Verdeyen, 2005).

Unlike other areas in forensic psychology, individuals interested in working in the mental health unit of a correctional facility can enter with either a master's degree or a doctoral degree. Obtaining a doctoral degree in either clinical or counseling psychology provides one with the greatest flexibility in duties as well as opportunities for advancement. More than 90% of the psychologists working in the Federal Bureau of Prisons hold doctorate degrees, whereas individuals in jails and state prisons tend to have master's degrees or certificates indicating advanced training (Bartol & Bartol, 2008). Although there has been a trend in corrections to hire non-doctoral-level clinicians to provide direct services (Morgan et al., 1999), a recent survey of inmates found a reluctance to seek services from non-doctoral-level providers (Morgan et al., 2004).

Regardless, one can still find rewarding career opportunities in corrections with a master's degree. It is best not to limit professional options by obtaining a specialist degree, such as a degree in forensic psychology. It is generally more desirable to obtain a master's degree or doctoral degree in either clinical or counseling psychology. This type of degree will prepare a student with the necessary foundation skills needed to enter the specialty training of correctional psychology. Correctional psychologists need to work as generalist clinicians since they will be treating a wide variety of presenting problems (Morgan et al., 2004). Students can then obtain focused training in correctional psychology during the internship experience or postdoctoral fellowship (Ax & Morgan, 2002). This training can be supplemented with attendance at continuing education workshops and membership in appropriate organizations, such as the **American Association for Correctional and Forensic Psychology**. Even students who may not have access to specialized training in correctional settings usually gain experience with related clientele, such as clients with a history of juvenile delinquency, criminal behavior, a history of incarceration, or clients who meet the criteria for antisocial personality disorder. Indeed, graduate students in psychology report generally favorable attitudes to working with inmate populations (Morgan et al., 2007).

In addition to the basic graduate psychology courses, students entering the profession should pursue additional training in assessment skills. Students may also wish to enhance both their undergraduate and graduate coursework with courses from criminology, law, sociology, and social work. Another beneficial area in light of correctional psychologists' administrative workload would be the addition of courses in management, administration, and organizational behavior. Some graduate programs are attempting to incorporate training in administrative skills into the curriculum (e.g., Zvolensky, Herschell, & McNeil, 2000). Correctional psychologists tend to function as a member of an interdisciplinary team consisting of a psychiatrist, social worker, and mental health workers. Training in these areas can facilitate communication with other members of the team.

Magaletta et al. (2007) surveyed psychology service providers in all the Federal Bureau of Prisons institutions asking for a list of the administrative and clinical bodies of knowledge characterizing an effective psychology department within the correctional setting. From the responses ($n = 309$, or 52% of surveys sent out), the researchers established a list of nine core bodies of knowledge relevant for psychological practice in corrections. The nine core bodies of knowledge are:

1. Knowledge of psychopathology
2. Suicide prevention
3. Environmental issues, in particular understanding secure housing units, which are 23-hour lockdown units
4. Interdepartmental communications/relations
5. Safety issues
6. Confrontation avoidance
7. Ethical issues

8. Medical/psychopharmacology
9. Clinical psychopathy

These authors recognized that some of these core bodies of knowledge are learned in graduate school, such as psychopathology, suicide prevention, and clinical psychopathy, other areas are acquired through on-the-job training.

In 2000, the average salary for doctoral-level correctional psychologists in the Federal Bureau of Prisons was $61,800 and in state correctional facilities, the average salary was $53,400 (Boothby & Clements, 2000). These figures should be adjusted for inflation in order to make current comparisons. Counselors with a master's degree reported an average salary of $40,100. The salary for master's-level clinicians is generally higher in correctional facilities than that found in other areas of psychological practice for individuals with a master's degree. In addition to satisfactory wage levels, correctional psychologists report high levels of job satisfaction. However, one comment on a job satisfaction survey was that there were few opportunities for advancement beyond prison administration (Boothby & Clements, 2002). In addition, correctional psychologists report little opportunity to spend time conducting research, a common complaint among practitioners.

## Summary

This chapter introduced the field of correctional psychology. Correctional psychologists are psychologists who work in correctional facilities. The chapter traced the increase in both the field of correctional psychology and the prison population over the past three decades. The contributions of the deinstitutionalization of the mentally ill and the shift away from rehabilitation to the "get tough on crime" approach in the criminal justice system played in the increase in the prison population and number of mentally ill inmates was reviewed. The differences between jails and prisons along with the five goals of incarceration were presented. Goals of incarceration include retribution, incapacitation, deterrence, rehabilitation, and restorative justice. The correctional psychologist's role in assessment and treatment was discussed. Assessment opportunities included suicide screening, assessment at entry into the correctional facility, ongoing assessment for mental health problems, and assessment prior to discharge. The area of risk assessment was briefly presented along with a discussion of the debate on clinical versus statistical prediction. A variety of treatment programs available in correctional facilities were presented as well as the unique challenges faced by correctional psychologists working in correctional facilities. The rights of inmates regarding health care and mental health treatment were covered and specific case law was presented when relevant. Some tips for working or interning in a correctional facility were discussed. In addition, nine core bodies of knowledge for correctional psychologists was presented. Finally, career opportunities for correctional psychologists were covered including education and training requirements.

## TEST YOUR KNOWLEDGE

1. Identify the Supreme Court ruling that found it was unconstitutional to execute a mentally ill person who was unable to appreciate what was happening.
   a. *Washington v. Harper*, 1990
   b. *McKune v. Lile*, 2002
   c. *Ford v. Wainwright*, 1986
   d. *Estelle v. Gamble*, 1976

2. Sentencing based on presumed dangerousness of the individual is referred to as
   a. mandatory sentencing laws
   b. selective incapacitation
   c. "just-deserts" sentencing
   d. retribution

3. One goal of incarceration is deterrence. What does *general deterrence* mean?
   a. The experience of punishment keeps the individual from reoffending.
   b. The threat of punishment keeps people from offending.
   c. General laws without specific sentencing guidelines are more effective as deterrents than mandatory guidelines.
   d. Incarceration among the general prison population is more effective than isolated incarceration.

4. What are the risks of an inmate disclosing prior crimes to a therapist of which the criminal justice system is unaware?
   a. The disclosure can result in additional prosecution and extended confinement.
   b. There are no risks since the inmate possesses privilege regarding the disclosure.
   c. There are no risks since self-disclosures to a therapist cannot be used as evidence in court.
   d. The inmate cannot be held accountable, although accomplishes may be pursued.

5. The Department of Justice estimates _____ of incarcerated inmates are mentally ill.
   a. less than 5%
   b. nearly 85%
   c. 15–20%
   d. The Department of Justice refuses to release this information stating that it violates the privacy rights of inmates.

Answer Key: (1) c, (2) b, (3) b, (4) a, (5) c

# Chapter Seven

# Assessment of Psychological Injury

## Learning Objectives

- Define a tort, identify the two parts to any tort, and be able to name the five necessary elements of a tort.
- Which burden of proof is required in civil law? Which court (criminal or civil) has the more restrictive burden of proof?
- What is the distinction between negligent infliction and intentional infliction of harm?
- Be able to identify examples of compensable psychological injuries.
- Describe the different models used by the courts regarding compensable injuries: Impact Rule, Zone of Danger Rule, Bystander Proximity Rule, and the Full Recovery Rule.
- What are the requirements for a tort claim for the intentional (and negligent) infliction of emotional distress?
- Define a directed verdict and define the distinction between a claim that is dismissed with prejudice and a claim that is dismissed without prejudice.
- What is the process of discovery?
- What are the five tasks confronting a forensic psychologist conducting a personal injury evaluation?
- What are the five conceptual parts of the examination for emotional injuries?
- What is the role of the forensic psychologist in personal injury cases?
- Briefly describe the Federal Rules of Civil Procedure.
- List types of compensable emotional damages.
- Describe the history of Title VII of the Civil Rights Act.
- What are the differences among discrimination, discriminatory effects, and discriminatory treatment?
- What is disparate impact?
- What groups are protected by Title VII of the Civil Rights Act?
- What is the role of race-norming in psychological testing and why was it initiated? What is the current status of race-norming?
- Define the two types of sexual harassment: *quid pro quo* and hostile work environment.
- Be able to briefly describe the significance of the court rulings in the *Meritor Savings Bank v. Vinson* (1986) case, the *Harris v. Forklift Systems* (1993) case, and the *Oncale v. Sundowner Offshore Services, Inc.* (1998) case.
- What are some examples of types of employment litigation for tort claims?
- What are the different types of damages the courts may award?

*(continued)*

## Key Terms

- Acute battering incident
- Battered woman syndrome
- Burden of proof
- Bystander proximity rule
- Civil law
- Contrite phase
- Criminal law
- Cycle of violence
- Damages
- Defamation
- Directed verdict
- Discrimination
- Discriminatory effects
- Discriminatory treatment
- Dismissal: with prejudice; without prejudice
- Disparate impact
- Domestic violence
- Eggshell plaintiff
- Emotional distress
- Employment litigation
- Full recovery rule
- General damages
- Hedonic damages
- Hostile work environment
- Impact rule
- Intentional infliction of emotional distress
- Intimate partner violence
- Liability
- Libel
- Loss of consortium
- Malingering
- Negligent infliction of emotional distress

*(continued)*

## Key Terms *(continued)*

- Nominal damages
- Pain and suffering
- Personal injury lawsuit
- Physical injury rule
- Plaintiff
- Posttraumatic stress disorder (PTSD)
- Preponderance of evidence
- Professional malpractice
- Proximate cause
- Psychological damages
- Punitive damages
- *Quid pro quo*
- Race-norming
- Rape trauma syndrome

- Reasonable person standard
- Sequella
- Sexual harassment
- Slander
- Specific damages
- Standard of persuasion
- Syndrome evidence
- Tension-building phase
- Title VII of the Civil Rights Act of 1964
- Tort
- Trier of law
- Wrongful death
- Zone of danger rule

## Learning Objectives *(continued)*

- Be able to briefly describe the assessment process for psychological injuries in discrimination and harassment claims.
- Distinguish between a disorder and a syndrome.
- Be able to describe battered woman syndrome and assess its legitimacy as a defense.
- What are some of the symptoms associated with battered woman syndrome?
- Describe and define posttraumatic stress disorder and its role in civil trials.

There is a general misconception that personal injury cases only involve individuals who have suffered physical injury from some form of an accident, such as a motor vehicle accident. Personal injury cases can involve any case in which an individual is injured either physically and/or psychologically in which damages occur. The physical or psychological injury can result from accidents, medical malpractice, discrimination, sexual abuse, or sexual harassment. Personal injury cases involve two aspects: **liability** and **damages**. Damages refer to how much damage has been caused by the injury, whereas liability refers to who is responsible for the damages.

This chapter discusses personal injury cases and the assessment of psychological injuries. Forensic psychologists typically become involved in personal injury cases on the damages side. Psychologists are asked to conduct an evaluation on the **plaintiff** (the person claiming injury) to determine the extent of the damages. Psychologists can also become involve in a case on the liability side when the suit arises from a claim of **professional malpractice**. The psychologist may be asked to address the liability of another mental health professional when the professional's behavior is called into question. The issue may be behavior of an unethical nature, such as a sexual relationship with a client or failure to provide the appropriate standard of care.

Although it is not the role of the forensic psychologist to make legal decisions, it is helpful for the psychologist to understand the legal process and the laws that form the basis for their role as the expert witness. Personal injury cases are based in civil law as opposed to criminal law. The chapter presents differences between criminal law and civil law. The civil court system is briefly reviewed followed by a discussion of the law of torts (lawsuits). The role of the forensic psychologist in conducting the examination is covered, as well as the format of the evaluation. The chapter then covers employment litigation with a focus on sexual harassment cases related to emotional damages. Finally, we examine the use of syndrome evidence (e.g., battered woman syndrome) as a defense due to its relationship with a demonstration of emotional damages.

# Criminal Law versus Civil Law

There are two types of laws in our society. There is **criminal law**, which deals with offenses committed against the safety of society or acts against the state. The other type of law is **civil law**, which deals with infringement upon the civil rights of other individuals or organizations. The distinctions between the two types of laws include the party harmed, who has the authority to proceed or drop the charges, the types of punishment that can be imposed, and the burden of proof required to win a case. Below we briefly consider the distinction between criminal and civil law. We then discuss the civil court system before delving into the area of personal injury evaluations for psychological damages.

■ **Criminal law**
The area of law that deals with offenses committed against the safety of society or acts against the state.

■ **Civil law**
The area of law that deals with the infringement upon the civil rights of an individual or organization; noncriminal law.

## Distinction Between Criminal and Civil Law
### Table 7.1

| Distinction | Criminal Law | Civil law |
|---|---|---|
| Injured Party | Society | Individual |
| Authority | State | Plaintiff |
| Punishment | Fines, incarceration, death | Financial awards |
| Burden of Proof | Beyond a reasonable doubt | Preponderance of the evidence |

# Criminal Law

Criminal law addresses crimes that are considered to threaten the safety and order of society and therefore are prosecuted by the government. The decision as to whether to proceed with the prosecution of a crime or to "drop the case" lies entirely with the government. For example, an individual alleging domestic violence cannot decide to drop a domestic battery charge once it has been "picked up" by the state. It is this author's experience in conducting court order evaluations that many people are dismayed that the state attorney has decided to prosecute their spouse even after they have asked to have the charges dropped. Victims of a crime do not have the authority to prosecute or drop criminal charges, regardless of the injured party's decision. Once criminal charges have been filed, the right to proceed with litigation belongs exclusively to the state. The very nature of criminal charges is that the crime is seen as a threat to society and must be dealt with by the state. Although an individual may have been injured, it is not that individual's right to have the charges dismissed. Criminal

■ **Tort**
A lawsuit.

■ **Punitive damages**
Financial awards that serve as punishment.

■ **Preponderance of the evidence**
The evidence for one side is more convincing than the evidence for the other side; the lowest burden of proof. Used in competency evaluations as well as civil court.

crimes are punishable by a fine, incarceration, or even death. If a fine is paid, the funds go to the state treasury. In criminal law, the state must prove its case *beyond a reasonable doubt*. Criminal law carries the highest **standard of persuasion** (*burden of proof*). Recall that there are three levels of burden of proof:

1.  preponderance of the evidence,
2.  clear and convincing evidence, and
3.  beyond a reasonable doubt.

Criminal offenses include charges such as murder, rape, theft, assault, battery, domestic violence, possession of controlled substances, robbery, burglary, grand theft, and so on. Individuals can also be charged with aiding and abetting someone who has committed such crimes or for failure to notify authorities when they have knowledge of such crimes.

# Civil Law

Civil law involves noncriminal violations of an individual's civil rights. Civil law involves lawsuits (**torts**) including malpractice lawsuits, breaches of contracts, divorce, contested wills, trusts, property contests, insurance claims, disability claims, and workman's compensation. Civil law is enforced by the individual who is injured or harmed (*the plaintiff*) bringing a lawsuit against the violator (*the defendant*) in a court of law. Therefore, in civil law, one or a group of individuals alleged that they have been harmed, unlike in criminal law, in which society as a whole is threatened. As a result of this distinction, the plaintiff has the choice whether to initiate or continue with litigation. Plaintiffs in civil suits may decide at any time to "settle out of court" and drop the charges. In civil cases, the only type of punishment that can be levied is a fine. Thus, even though monetary damages can run into the hundreds of millions, civil penalties can not include incarceration. Additionally, the exorbitant jury awards for monetary damages are unusual. Financial awards serve to compensate the victim for the harm they suffered and at times, as punishment, called **punitive damages**, for the defendant when the harm is considered malicious and bordering on criminal behavior. Finally, another distinction between criminal and civil court is that the burden of proof is lower in a civil court. Whereas the state must prove a criminal case beyond a reasonable doubt, civil law only requires *a* **preponderance of the evidence** for a burden of proof.

In many cases, criminal law and civil law can overlap. Because of this overlap, an individual can be tried for the same offense in both criminal and civil courts. Many torts can also be crimes. For example, an assault on another individual is a crime that threatens the safety of society and is prosecuted by the state. However, the assailant can also be sued in civil court for physical and emotional damages caused to the victim. This is what occurred in the highly publicized O.J. Simpson case. The famous football player and actor, O.J. Simpson, was charged in criminal court for the murders of Nicole Brown Simpson and Ronald Goldman. After 4 months of testimony, O.J. Simpson was acquitted (found innocent) of the charges. He was subsequently sued by the families of the two murder victims in civil court. After fewer than 45 days of testimony, O.J. Simpson was found liable for the deaths of Nicole Brown Simpson and Ronald Goldman and ordered to pay monetary damages. The inconsistency between the two verdicts is due in large part to the differing standard of persuasion (also called burden of proof) required in civil court versus criminal court. Remember, in criminal court the states must prove its case *beyond a reasonable doubt*. In civil court, the plaintiff must prove the case by a *preponderance of the evidence*, also referred to as the "more likely than not standard."

Preponderance of the evidence means that one side has more evidence in its favor than the other side, or that the weight of evidence for one side outweighs the weight of evidence for the other side. It does not mean that one side simply has more evidence (such as documents, experts, witnesses, etc.) than the other side. Rather, the evidence for one side is more convincing than the evidence offered by the other side. In civil court, liability can translate into the equation that 51% of the evidence indicates liability and 49% of the evidence indicates innocence, or rather, not liable. With this equation, the individual would be found liable in civil court but "not guilty" in criminal court. In civil court, defendants are found to be liable or not liable; in criminal court, defendants are found to be guilty or not guilty. One exception to the standard of proof required criminal courts is the issue of competence to stand trial. Recall from Chapter 4 that the preponderance of the evidence standard is used in criminal court when the state requires a defendant to prove that they are incompetent to stand trial.

The standard of persuasion used in civil court also applies to expert witness testimony (Greenberg, 2003). The expert may form his or her opinion based on a preponderance of the evidence he or she used to reach that opinion. In deciding admissibility of the expert's testimony, the expert must testify that the testimony is supported by a preponderance of the evidence that the expert used to reach the decision. The expert does not need to be 100% certain, or even 75% certain, that the opinion he or she offers is correct. The expert only needs to be reasonably certain that the opinion offered is more probably true than other alternative conclusions.

Forensic psychologists conducting personal injury evaluations are assessing **psychological damages**. Depending on the jurisdiction, psychological damages are referred to as

- emotional distress,
- emotional harm,
- emotional damages, or
- **pain and suffering**.

Psychological damages can occur in a variety of situations, including, though not limited to, cases that involve physical damages, therapeutic malpractice, and sexual harassment. It is important to note that psychologists are not qualified to assess the nature or extent of physical injuries. All cases alleging psychological injuries involve a *plaintiff* filing a *tort* (lawsuit) against a *defendant* for the alleged emotional injury. In a survey of judges and attorneys, medical and mental health professionals were the most frequently cited category of experts used, comprising over 40% of all expert witnesses presented (Krafka, Dunn, Johnson, Cecil, & Miletich, 2002). Before we discuss the necessary components of a tort action and the types of assessments conducted by forensic psychologists, we briefly review the civil court system.

Figure 7.2

Civil law includes lawsuits such as contested wills.
© 2009 Gina Sanders. Used under license from Shutterstock, Inc.

# The Civil Court System

In the United States there is a dual court system consisting of state courts and federal courts. There are different criteria used to determine in which court, state or federal, a civil case may be filed. Note that this discussion applies to civil cases; though there are similarities with criminal cases, there are also important differences. In both the state and federal systems, cases originate in the *trial court*. Parties may appeal the trial court's decision; the case is then brought through the appellate process. *Appellate courts* review the case and how the law was applied to the facts of the case. Appellate courts review

the case for any legal errors that may have been made by the trial court that would deem sending the case back to the trial court for additional findings of fact, or overturning the trial court's ruling. The judge, as the **trier of law**, is responsible for ensuring that the legal proceedings are in accordance with the requirements of the law. A judicial error could result in a successful appeal of a court's decision. The judge functions somewhat as a referee in a sporting event. However, the judge is not there to assist attorneys. The judge has the discretion to rule on legal proceedings only if an attorney raises the issue, such as in an objection to opposing counsel's questioning or use of evidence.

## Federal Courts

In order to bring a lawsuit to federal court, one of two conditions must be met. First, the case may involve a law of the United States or a question regarding federal law (federal question jurisdiction). The second option is when a case involves plaintiffs from different states and the amount of money in question exceeds $50,000. These are the only two options that a plaintiff has to file a case in the Federal District Court (federal trial court). A plaintiff who meets either of these criteria may decide to file in state or federal court. The federal court system is divided into four separate, hierarchical groups. The bottom or base of the hierarchy is formed by the U.S. *magistrate courts*. The U.S. *District Courts* comprise the second level and the third level is the U.S. *Courts of Appeal*. At the top of the hierarchy is the U.S. Supreme Court, the only federal court specifically mandated by the Constitution.

## State Courts

Most state courts are patterned after the federal system. However, there are numerous differences among the states, so it is difficult to make too many generalizations. Most states have trial courts, a middle-level appellate court, and a supreme court. However, the hierarchy in any given state may include two, three, four, or more levels of courts. Names of courts vary from state to state, adding to the confusion. Regardless, the function of the state courts is to rule on state and federal laws that affect the residents of the state. These rulings are final unless overturned by a higher court in the state or by a federal court. Each state has an appellate tribunal that serves as the court of last resort and is the final arbiter involving issues of state law. These courts have different names depending on the state and include the Court of Appeals, the Supreme Court of Appeals, Supreme Judicial Court, and Supreme Court of Errors.

## Appellate Process

At both the state and federal level, cases are originally heard in the trial court. Both sides have an opportunity to present evidence, call witnesses, and present their legal arguments. Depending on the court, either a judge or jury will hand down the decision with the appropriate remedy for the two adversaries. In both civil and criminal cases, parties may appeal the decision to intermediate-level appeals courts. In the 36 most heavily populated states, there is an intermediate-level appellate court that corresponds to the U.S. Court of Appeal. In the federal system, the intermediate-level appellate courts consist of the 13 U.S. Circuit Courts of Appeals. These courts review how the law was applied to the facts of the particular case. These courts review the trial decision for judicial error. They do not question the facts of the case, nor can they hear new evidence. The appellate court cannot reverse the factual findings of a trial court unless the trial court made a judicial error. The review is made on the trial record, not a new trial. If judicial error is cited, an appeals court may overturn a decision by the trial court, may reverse the decision, or can send it back to the trial court for additional findings of fact.

After the intermediate-level appellate courts, the losing party still has recourse to the state or federal Supreme Court. The purpose of the intermediate-level courts is to lessen the burden on the supreme courts. A state supreme court as well as the U.S. Supreme Court may refuse to hear a case. Refusing to hear a case typically implies that the court has upheld the lower court's decision. Cases that have been decided by the highest state court may be brought to the federal system through a *writ of certiotari*, requesting that the case be forwarded to the Supreme Court. The Supreme Court can use its discretion in deciding to grant the writ and typically refuses many times the number of cases it reviews. For example, the state appellate courts hear approximately 30,000 cases a year; the U.S. Supreme court hears fewer than 200 cases a year. For most citizens, the state appellate courts are the court of last resort. The U.S. Supreme Court will review cases involving laws that have caused confusion in the lower courts. For example, if the lower courts in different jurisdictions have ruled inconsistently on similar cases, the Supreme Court may accept a case to help clarify the constitutional issues involved.

# The Law of Torts

The area of civil law that determines the legal rules for personal injury cases is the law of torts. A lawsuit is formally known as a *tort*. The word tort derives from the Latin word *tortus*, meaning crooked or twisted. In Old French, the word tort meant a harm or wrong. A tort is a legal claim or complaint filed by the plaintiff against the defendant in civil court. It is a wrong that one commits against another. A general misconception exists that people can sue one another for almost anything. Although it is true that American society is a litigious society, with over 18 million lawsuits filed annually (Myers & Arena, 2001), there are requirements for a lawsuit to be legally viable. A tort requires demonstrating that an individual (the defendant) violated a legal responsibility owed to another individual (the plaintiff) and that the breach of that legal duty resulted in damage to the plaintiff (Greenberg, 2003). A **personal injury lawsuit** is for damages to the person, their feelings, or reputation. These damages can be in the form of physical injury, emotional injury, or injury to the person's reputation, as in a libel case. This is distinguished from damages to the person's property, such as damage to a person's residence by a construction crew working on a neighbor's home. As stated previously, there are two parts to every personal injury lawsuit: damages and liability.

There are five essential elements or requirements for a lawsuit to be viable (Greenberg, 1999).

■ **Personal injury lawsuit**
A lawsuit seeking compensation for damages to the person, their mental health, or reputation.

## Five Necessary Elements of a Tort — Table 7.2

1. The existence of a duty that is legally owed by a defendant to a plaintiff
2. the dereliction or breach of which,
3. directly or proximately causes an injury that would not have occurred had the duty not be breached
4. the injury causes the actual damage resulting in a significant impairment in a plaintiff's functioning
5. that is of the type, by definition, compensable under the law

The first legal requirement of a tort claim is the existence of a *duty* that is legally owed to the injured party by the defendant named in the lawsuit. For example, an amusement park has a legal responsibility to ensure that the amusement rides in the park, such as the roller coaster, are safe for patrons of the park. With regard to a professional malpractice case, a psychologist has a legal duty to meet a reasonable standard of care when treating his or her clients. Failure to provide a reasonable standard of care is a breach of the legal duty to the client. Although the parties involved may not explicitly articulate these duties, the duty nevertheless exists.

For a tort to proceed, the plaintiff must show that the defendant failed to uphold their duty. The plaintiff must prove that there was a *dereliction* or *breach* of the duty owed to him or her. In our example above, the plaintiff would need to show that the amusement park owners failed to keep the rides safe for the park's patrons. In the second example, the client would need to show that the psychologist breached his or her duty to the client by failing to provide treatment at the appropriate standard of care. It is not necessarily a breach of duty if the psychologist is not successful in treating the client. The psychologist would need to have failed to provide treatment that other mental health professionals would deem *reasonable* given the circumstances.

■ **Proximate cause**

Refers to the event closest to the injury, which had it not occurred the injury would not have occurred; also consider legal cause.

The third requirement for a tort is **proximate cause**. This requires that the breach of duty either directly or proximately results in injury to the plaintiff that would otherwise not have occurred. The requirement is for the plaintiff to demonstrate that any injuries were directly due to the breach of duty by the defendant. For example, if a child is thrown from a roller coaster and suffers life-threatening injuries, it is relatively obvious that the unsafe roller coaster caused the physical injuries. However, if the mother of the child witnessed her child's accident, she may experience emotional harm. Her emotional state may be such that she is unable to return to work due to depression and severe anxiety attacks. The courts require that there is an unbroken chain of events. The mother, as a plaintiff, may sue for lost wages (back pay), lost future earning (front pay), and family enjoyment (hedonic damage). These losses (damages) would not have occurred for the mother had it not been for witnessing a serious accident to a close relative caused by the unsafe roller coaster. In this example, the courts would need to determine if any *reasonable person* who witnessed his or her son in a similar accident would experience the psychological damages the mother suffered. We will return to the concept of a reasonable person later in this chapter. In our second example, the client would need to demonstrate that the psychologist's failure to provide an appropriate standard of care directly resulted in his or her damages. Nearly all psychologists and all professional associations would agree that engaging in a sexual dual relationship with a client is a failure to provide an appropriate standard of care. If a client can demonstrate that she experienced emotional distress, humiliation among friends and family, and an increase in her psychological symptoms due to this relationship with her therapist, she could meet the proximate cause requirement for a professional malpractice lawsuit.

The fourth requirement is to show actual existence of damage along with the severity of the damages. Only injuries that cause a substantial impairment in the plaintiff's functioning are likely to qualify. According to the law, *no harm, no foul* (Greenberg, 1999). However, one exception to the requirement to demonstrate psychological damages is in cases of sexual harassment in the workplace. We return to this issue later in the chapter. If the existence of damage is proven, then the defendant may be entitled to *damages*. Damages, when used in the plural form in the court, refer to the financial compensation rendered to the plaintiff. This may be a bit confusing in that damage is what happens to the plaintiff and damages are what the defendant pays to the plaintiff (Greenberg, 1999). In the examples above, the mother of the child injured on the roller coaster would need to prove the existence of emotional harm. Similarly, the client of the therapist would need to demonstrate that she experiences emotional harm or pain and suffering.

The fifth requirement states that the law must indicate that this type of damage is *compensable*. The law states that plaintiffs will be compensated for some types of injuries and not for other types. There are four theories or models adopted by the courts for determining what emotional injuries are compensable (Greenberg, 1999). These models, cited by the courts, are presented below.

The **Impact Rule** states that damages are awarded for emotional injury provided that there is some physical contact. For example, a person injured in an automobile accident may experience symptoms of anxiety and panic any time they are confronted with traveling by car. The injured person can sue for compensation for their pain and suffering provided he or she can prove it was caused by the automobile accident and the accident was the fault of the other driver. The second model, the **Zone of Danger Rule**, states that absent any physical contact, a plaintiff can sue for damages if the plaintiff was threatened with physical harm as a result of the defendant's negligence. For example, during an air show, two planes performing acrobatic maneuvers collide in midair above the grandstand. One plane crashes into the grandstand, injuring several people in the stands. Though not injured, Mr. Still is seated next to a man who suffers severe burns from the plane crash. Mr. Still becomes depressed and suffers symptoms of posttraumatic stress disorder (PTSD). He subsequently sues the organization that sponsored the air show for damages. The third model, the **Bystander Proximity Rule**, states that a plaintiff is entitled to damages if they personally observe an accident that injures someone to who they are closely related, such as an immediate family member. A mother who witnesses her child struck by a car and subsequently suffers emotional pain and suffering that leads to impaired functioning can sue the driver for pain and suffering. Finally, the **Full Recovery Rule** allows damages for emotional distress in circumstances in which a *reasonable person* would have experienced emotional distress as a result of the incident. Thus, if most normally constituted individuals would have experienced emotional distress as a result of the defendant's actions, then the plaintiff would be allowed to seek compensation for emotional damage.

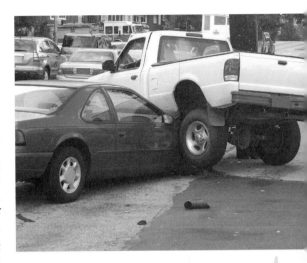

**Figure 7.4**

A person injured in this car accident can sue for compensation for their pain and suffering, provided another driver was at fault.
© 2009 Katherine Welles. Used under license from Shutterstock, Inc.

| Models Recommended by the Courts for Recovery of Emotional Injuries: | Table 7.3 |
| --- | --- |

1. Physical injury or Impact Rule: permitting "recovery for emotional injury provided there is some physical contact."
2. Zone of Danger Rule: providing recovery for emotional injuries absent any physical contact, which result "from the witnessing of peril or harm to another if the plaintiff is also threatened with physical harm as a consequence of the defendant's negligence."
3. Bystander Proximity Rule: permitting "recovery, even if one is not in the zone of danger, provided the complainant: (1) is physically near the scene of the accident, (2) personally observes the accident, and (3) is closely related to the victim."
4. Full Recovery Rule: allowing recovery in a negligence action for infliction of serious emotional distress where "a reasonable person, normally constituted, would not be able to cope adequately with the mental distress occasioned by the circumstances."

Some plaintiffs may be especially vulnerable to specific types of stressors. For example, a woman who was sexually assaulted as a teenager may be particularly vulnerable to sexual harassment on the job. Although the woman has recovered from the assault and does not demonstrate any psychological symptoms, persistent and unwanted sexual advances by her employer may cause her a greater amount of emotional distress than it would for most people. A plaintiff who is especially vulnerable to certain types of stressors is referred to as an **"eggshell" plaintiff** (Greenberg, 2003). The law regards the plaintiff as fragile as an eggshell. Typically, eggshell plaintiffs are entitled to compensation for all their emotional distress, not just that which would be expected of the average person.

There exist two major types of torts for psychological damages:

1. negligent infliction of emotional distress and
2. intentional infliction of emotional distress.

Recall from the discussion above the five basic elements of a tort:

1. duty,
2. dereliction or breach,
3. proximate cause,
4. actual damage, and
5. compensability.

A tort for the **negligent infliction of emotional distress** must meet the basic five elements of a tort plus two additional elements. In addition to the five basic elements, a claim for negligent infliction of emotional distress must prove by a preponderance of the evidence that the breach of the duty by the defendant was *negligent* on the defendant's part and that the *emotional distress was severe*. The law considers negligence as a *careless error* or *omission*. The incident is recognized to have occurred as an accident without intention. The issue of negligence is frequently the ultimate issue in a personal injury case and is decided by the trier of fact. A psychologist may testify in

---

**Table 7.4    Tort Claim for the Negligent Infliction of Emotional Distress**

- Plaintiff must prove by a *preponderance of the evidence*
  - i.  Five basic elements of a tort
    1. duty
    2. dereliction of breach
    3. proximate cause
    4. actual damage
    5. compensability
  - ii. Plus that the breach by the defendant was
    1. negligent (careless)
    2. caused the plaintiff emotional distress that was severe (would have damaged the normally constituted person)

a malpractice case regarding the standard of care and what actions the defendant, a therapist, should have taken. However, whether the defendant's actions amount to negligence is up to the jury to decide.

The *severity of emotional distress* refers to whether the actions of the defendant would have injured most people. The forensic psychologist can offer an opinion as to whether the psychological injuries suffered by the plaintiff are what most normally constituted people would have experienced, given the circumstances. The psychologist will be asked to distinguish between psychological injuries that most people would have experienced given the circumstances and any additional injuries suffered by the plaintiff. The plaintiff may have a preexisting condition or previous life experience that makes them particularly vulnerable to a particular stressor. For example, a mother who recently lost her son in combat may be particularly vulnerable to psychological injury due to the death of her remaining child in a motor vehicle accident.

The other type of tort for psychological damage is a claim of **intentional infliction of emotional distress**. In addition to the five basic elements of a tort, the plaintiff must prove three additional elements. The plaintiff must show that the breach of duty by the defendant was

1. intentional,
2. extreme or outrageous, and
3. that the emotional distress was severe.

The law considers foreseeable acts as intentional. If the defendant knew or should have known that his or her actions would reasonably result in harm to the plaintiff, then the action is considered intentional. A forensic psychologist may be asked for an opinion on whether the defendant had the capacity to foresee the potential harm of his or her actions to the plaintiff. The question of capacity may be raised in light of the defendant's emotional state or cognitive abilities at the time of the incident. The second element of a tort for intentional infliction of emotional damages is whether the defendant's behavior went beyond the bounds of the community's sense of decency.

**Tort Claim for the Intentional Infliction of Emotional Distress**    **Table 7.5**

- Plaintiff must prove by a *preponderance of the evidence*
  i. Five basic elements of a tort
    1. duty
    2. dereliction of breach
    3. proximate cause
    4. actual damage
    5. compensability
  ii. Plus that the breach by the defendant was
    1. intentional (foreseeable)
    2. extreme or outrageous (violated the community's sense of decency)
    3. caused the plaintiff emotional distress that was severe (would have damaged the normally constituted person)

The defendant's behavior needs to be considered extreme or outrageous to meet this criterion. Similar to a tort for negligent infliction of emotional harm, the tort for intentional infliction of emotional harm must demonstrate that the breach of duty was severe enough to cause emotional harm to the normally constituted individual.

These elements of a tort are used to establish liability and damages. "Damages without liability or liability without damages will render a personal injury legal action moot" (Ackerman, 1999, p. 58). Questions of liability are addressed by the proximate cause requirement. The question is whether the plaintiff's emotional distress and consequent impairment in functioning would not have occurred but for the wrongful action of the defendant (Greenberg, 1999). The issue of liability is also addressed by the severity of the circumstances element. The question to the court is whether the severity of the circumstances was such that no reasonable person could be expected to experience the circumstance without emotional damage. The degree of damage to the plaintiff determines the compensation. The current impairment experience by the plaintiff, minus any impairment from preexisting conditions, determines the amount of psychological damage and is the basis for determining the amount of compensation (Greenberg, 1999).

After a claim is filed, the defendant may file a motion to dismiss the claim for a variety of reasons, such as an untimely filing or failure to meet the basic elements of the tort (Greenberg, 2003). The case can be dismissed by the judge with or without prejudice. If a case is **dismissed with prejudice** then the matter is permanently decided. If the case is **dismissed without prejudice**, the court leaves open the possibility that the plaintiff may refile the case after addressing the problems that caused the suit to be dismissed. Even after trial and before jury deliberations, the judge, as the trier of law, may end the process. In what is called a **directed verdict**, a judge can rule that the plaintiff has failed to present sufficient evidence to support the basic elements of the tort claim and prevent the case from going to jury deliberation. Judges may even overrule a jury decision, as is also the case in criminal court.

# Role of the Forensic Psychologist as Examiner

Personal injury evaluations are somewhat similar to criminal responsibility evaluations discussed in Chapter 4. As Melton et al. (1997) suggest, evaluations of mental injury require determining the plaintiff's mental state prior to the injury. In this regard, the evaluation of mental injury is retrospective since the examiner must determine the plaintiff's functioning prior to the injury. However, the evaluation of mental injury is also prospective in that the forensic examiner must offer an opinion regarding the plaintiff's future functioning. Issues to be addressed include the likelihood that the plaintiff will return to their earlier level of functioning prior to the accident, what sort of treatment, if any, will be needed, and for how long. As with other forensic evaluations, the forensic psychologist utilizes an extensive range of information in forming his or her opinion. Sources of information include psychological testing, clinical interviews, collateral information from third parties as well as historical records, and a review of all records from both attorneys related to the case.

In all forensic examinations, the psychologist's primary role is that of expert to the court (Greenberg, 2003; Shuman & Greenberg, 2003). The psychologist must provide an impartial and nonpartisan opinion to the court to assist the trier of fact in the decision-making process. The role of the psychologist in conducting forensic examinations is very different from the role of therapist. The psychologist should examine the plaintiff with the same thoroughness and objectivity regardless of the side of the

■ **Dismissed with prejudice**
Refers to a judge's decision to dismiss a case and the case cannot be brought before the court again.

■ **Dismissed without prejudice**
Refers to a judge's decision to dismiss a civil case but allows for the possibility of refiling the case at a later date; associated with tort law.

retaining lawyer. The psychologist needs to be aware that any records related to the case, including notes from interviews, tests results, and written reports, are all open to discovery by the opposing side. *Discovery* is a process in which lawyers have the right to ask for and receive all relevant information including any information that will be submitted as evidence before the case goes to trial (Swenson, 1997). Both the plaintiff and the retaining lawyer need to understand the limits of confidentiality. There is no therapist–patient privilege regarding information disclosed in the course of the evaluation. The psychologist should obtain informed consent in writing from both the plaintiff and the retaining attorney.

Five basic tasks confront the forensic psychologist conducting a personal injury evaluation (Greenberg, 2003). The psychologist must assess the plaintiff's

1. functioning prior to the injury,
2. the nature and extent of any psychological harm,
3. the resulting impairments caused by the psychological harm,
4. the probable cause of each impairment, and
5. the type of treatment necessary to enable the plaintiff to return to their original level of functioning.

## Five Tasks Confronting the Psychologist Conducting a Personal Injury Evaluation     Table 7.6

- The baseline state of mental health functioning prior to the injury
- The nature and extent of the psychological harm suffered by the injured party
- The nature and extent of impairments or injuries to the plaintiff's functioning
- The likely psychological cause of each impairment or injury
- The nature of any psychological treatment that may help the plaintiff to return to the level of baseline functioning prior to the injury

The forensic examination is conducted under Rule 35 of the Federal Rules of Civil Procedure, referred to as CR35. Initially, the law did not compensate for psychological damages. Therefore, the original purpose of a CR35 exam was an examination by physicians for physical problems and was routinely referred to as an Independent Medical Examination (IME). However, the law was amended in 1988 to include a "mental examination" by a "physician or psychologist" and subsequently amended in 1991 to indicate that a "suitably licensed or certified examiner" perform the examination. Since the plaintiff in a psychological personal injury case is claiming psychological injury, the court will typically order the plaintiff to undergo a CR35 examination performed by an expert of the defendant's choosing. The plaintiff has a right to know, or discover, the results of the CR35 examination conducted on behalf of the defense. However, the plaintiff must also release to the defense the results of any psychological evaluations and treatment records the plaintiff has accumulated in preparation for the trial. A CR35 examination is only conducted in preparation for trial. Therefore, only information relevant to the case is within the proper scope of the CR35 (Greenberg, 1999).

Rule 35 of the Federal Rules of Civil Procedure consists of two main parts. Part A, *Order of Examination*, addresses the conditions of the examination, such as what circumstances need to exist for the motion of an examination, who may conduct the examination, and the scope of the examination, such as tests used and general area of inquiry.

Part B, *Report of the Examiner*, addresses who is entitled to the written report, the reciprocal nature of discovery such that opposing counsel must release any such evaluations upon receipt of the report, and the fact that if no report is offered the testimony may be excluded at trial. The written report is only generated at the retaining attorney's request. If the examination fails to support the plaintiff's claim, the plaintiff's attorney may prefer that the expert's testimony be excluded from trial. If the report is not produced, then obviously it cannot be discovered by opposing counsel. Furthermore, as stated above, failure to produce a report could exclude the expert's testimony from trial. It is good practice for the examining psychologist to discuss with the attorney the proposed findings for the report to clarify if the attorney wishes the report to be produced. This practice does not violate the impartiality of the expert. Rather, it allows the expert to present an objective opinion. In this approach, the expert does not need to feel compelled to form an opinion based on the attorney's case.

As previously discussed, the forensic evaluation for psychological damages is comparable to other forensic evaluations. The attorney is considered the client, the purpose of the evaluation is not therapeutic, and the information is likely to be made public with no therapist–client privilege. The psychologist will collect information from a variety of sources, including two or more interviews with the plaintiff, legal documents and historical records, psychological testing, and third-party interviews. There is no standard format in the field for the evaluation of psychological injury. Different examiners use different tests and interview formats (Boccaccini & Brodsky, 1999; Lees-Haley, 1992).

Examiners should use tests in which they are competent in the administration, scoring, and interpretation. Generally, an examiner should utilize a test battery consisting of several "core" tests that are routinely used along with any specialty tests selected for the case at hand. Selection of tests should include a consideration of the test normative sample and the plaintiff's cultural background, reading ability, and language skills. A "core" test battery will generally consist of a measure of intellectual assessment, objective and perhaps projective personality measures, and measures of trauma or psychological symptoms. The most frequently used measures of intellectual functioning in forensic settings are the Wechsler scales, either the most current version of the WAIS or WISC (Lally, 2003). The most frequently used personality measures include the MMPI-2 and the Millon Clinical Multiaxial Inventory–II (Greenberg, 2003; Greenberg & Greene, 2000). Projective personality measures include the Rorschach Inkblot, Bender Gestalt and the Sentence Completion Test, and the Thematic Apperception Test (Archer, Maurish, Imhoff, & Piotrowski, 1991; Lees-Haley, 1992). Specialized instruments typically assess the results of trauma and focus on symptoms of PTSD along with other psychological disorders, such as depression and anxiety. Instruments used to assess symptoms associated with PTSD include the Trauma Symptom Inventory (Briere, 1995) and Posttraumatic Stress Diagnostic Scale (Foa, 1995) as well as the semi-structured interview and Clinician-Administered PTSD Scale (CAPS; Blake et al., 1990). The CAPS consists of 30 items assessing all 17 symptoms of PTSD. Originally developed at the National Center for PTSD in Boston, it has been successfully used in noncombat populations. The CAPS also assesses areas associated with occupational and social functioning, areas particularly relevant to personal injury claims. Although some authors have suggested that the CAPS is the "gold standard" for the assessment of PTSD (Huss, 2009), other authorities discuss a variety of reliable and valid measures (Barlow, 2004). A review of the first 10 years of research on the CAPS is offered by Weathers and his colleagues (2001).

The MMPI-2 also has two PTSD scales, the PK scale (Keane, Malloy, & Fairbank, 1984) and the PS scale (Schlenger & Kukla, 1987). Other frequently used specialized instruments developed to assess psychological symptoms include the Beck Depression Inventory and the Symptom Checklist 90—Revised. Despite the controversy surrounding the use of projective techniques in forensic settings, the Rorschach Inkblot Test appears to be one of the more frequently used instruments by psychologists who assess emotional injury, ranking as the fourth most frequently used test overall (Boccaccini & Brodsky, 1999). Indeed, research indicates that the Rorschach is accepted in the courtroom (Piotrowski, 1996; Weiner, 1996). More importantly, a survey of psychologists who conduct emotional injury evaluations found that psychological test results were never denied admittance into evidence (Boccaccini & Brodsky, 1999). Results from psychological testing should form the basis of hypotheses to be explored during the assessment interviews. Therefore, the testing needs to be administered and scored prior to the assessment interviews.

In addition to psychological testing, the examiner will conduct two or more interviews with the plaintiff. There is a variety of reasons to conduct more than one assessment interview with the plaintiff. First, the repeated exposure to the examiner allows the plaintiff to develop rapport and feel less anxious regarding the evaluation process. Second, testing and interviews can be tedious and breaking the process up into several sessions avoids any fatigue effects, particularly for someone who may be suffering from acute depression, cognitive impairment, or elevated anxiety. Third, meeting with the plaintiff over several sessions allows the examiner to see the plaintiff on different occasions, providing a more complete view of the plaintiff's psychological functioning as opposed to a single snapshot from one interview. Finally, the additional meetings provide a chance for the examiner to clarify any questions or potential misunderstandings prior to formulating an opinion and submitting a report.

No standard exits in the literature for the evaluation of psychological injury. Greenberg (2003) has proposed a model consisting of five conceptual parts to the examination process (see Table 7.7). This model helps to guide the interview process. The examiner, after conducting collateral interviews, a review of all pertinent records, and psychological testing, can meet with the plaintiff and walk through the five stages of the evaluation. It is recommended to routinely use a structured or semi-structured interview in order not to miss any crucial information (Greenberg, 2003; Vasquez et al., 2003). The routine use of a structured interview also prevents the appearance of any possible bias regardless if the evaluation is ordered by the attorney for the plaintiff or the defendant.

The first part of the evaluation involves the plaintiff's preallegation history. This consists of exploring what the plaintiff's life was like prior to the incident. The psychologist should ask about both strengths and vulnerabilities that may have existed prior to the incident. Particular note should be made of any preexisting conditions. Preexisting conditions do not necessarily diminish any damage caused by the incident, but may indicate a vulnerability to specific stressors. Recall the earlier discussion of an "eggshell" plaintiff with specific vulnerabilities due to earlier life stressors. It is helpful to document any supporting evidence for claims regarding prior functioning. For example, did the plaintiff frequently dine out, travel, and engage in vocational hobbies, all of which have been curtailed since the incident. Credit card statements can usually substantiate lifestyle as well as any changes in a person's routine.

Next, the examiner should ask the plaintiff about the incident in question. The goal is to assess the plaintiff's experience of the stressor. It is necessary to ascertain the plaintiff's perceived severity of the stressor along with the plaintiff's reaction to the event. The psychologist is likely to be asked on the witness stand if the plaintiff's

| Table 7.7 | Five Conceptual Parts of the Examination for Emotional Injuries |
|---|---|

- Preallegation History
  - Strengths and competencies, resilience
  - Lifestyle: social, occupational, vocational
  - Vulnerabilities due to history
  - Preexisting conditions or prior treatment
- The Incident
  - What was the plaintiff exposed to; focus on plaintiff's perception of the stressor
- **Sequella**
  - Psychological or cognitive impairments since the stressor
  - Changes in lifestyle: occupational, social, vocational
  - Strengths demonstrated by plaintiff
- Proximate Cause
  - Impairments or changes that occurred as a result of the trauma
  - Impairments or changes that were likely to occur regardless of the trauma
- Prognosis
  - Prognosis regarding future impairments and likelihood of recovery with treatment
  - Treatment or other necessary accommodations required

reaction to the stressor was similar to how other, normally constituted individuals would respond. If this is not the case, the examiner should discuss with the plaintiff the reasons why he or she may have responded differently.

The third area of inquiry documents the plaintiff's functioning since the incident. A chronology of functioning from the time of the incident to the present enables the examiner to form opinions about any improvements along with a prognosis for further improvement. This discussion should include any treatment and the perceived value of that treatment. Additionally, the examiner should ask specifically about any positive outcomes that resulted from the incident. An example of a positive outcome occurred in a recent case involving a man in a motor vehicle accident. Mr. Speed raced cars as a hobby and lived with his girlfriend for a number of years. During one race, he was involved in an accident resulting in life-threatening injuries and an extended hospital stay. During his hospital stay and subsequent convalesce, his "significant other" was constantly by his side and helped nurse him back to health. He realized his good fortune and her devotion, and they finally married after living together for over 10 years. He states that the accident and his near brush with death helped him to realize the importance of making a commitment to his long-time girlfriend. Some traumas can have an unseen benefit and it is important to explore that possibility with the plaintiff. The presence of some good from a trauma does not mitigate any damage that is done. Rather, it provides perspective for the examiner and the plaintiff.

The next focus of the evaluation is on the *proximate cause* of the impairments. The psychologist can form an opinion as to whether the plaintiff's current impairments are likely to be the result of the experienced stressor. Finally, the forensic examiner should form an opinion as to the plaintiff's prognosis. The psychologist can evaluate the potential for future damages such as the loss of future earnings or diminished earning capacity. The evaluator can also determine the likelihood that the plaintiff will remain impaired and require continued treatment. This opinion is based on the plaintiff's response to any treatment, need for occupational training or schooling, and any need for special accommodations in the home and workplace. It is important to note that the courts do not compensate a plaintiff based on a diagnosis. Rather, the court needs to understand the type of impairment and how the impairment affects the plaintiff's quality of life.

There is a range of possibilities leading to tort claims of emotional pain and suffering. As noted above, claims can be for the negligent or intentional infliction of emotional distress. In addition to exposure to a traumatic event, other actions can lead to claims for emotional pain and suffering. For example, the cause of the psychological harm may be due to **wrongful death**, such as when an accident or medical procedure causes the death of a person's family member. The surviving family member can sue for wrongful death and the pain and suffering associated with the loss. As discussed earlier, tort claims for emotional damages can also be pursued in professional malpractice cases. This could include medical malpractice as well as psychological malpractice cases. Additionally, individuals who feel others have tarnished their reputation can sue for damages. **Defamation** of character involves harming the reputation of another by publicizing untrue statements. **Libel** is the harming of an individual's reputation through the written word, such as on the Internet or in a newspaper; **slander** is the harming of an individual's reputation through the spoken word, as might be the case on television or on the radio. Table 7.8 presents a brief list of examples of actions leading to claims for psychological injury. This is not a comprehensive list but is provided to give the reader an

**Figure 7.5**

A surviving family member can sue for wrongful death when an accident or medical procedure is the cause of death.

© 2009 Fara Spence. Used under license from Shutterstock, Inc.

## Examples of Personal Injury Cases Involving Psychological Damages                Table 7.8

- Medical malpractice resulting in psychological damages such as an inferior cosmetic surgery, childbirth resulting in physical injury to the mother or child, unnecessary surgery, a disability preventing enjoyment in life, etc.
- Sexual abuse, sexual harassment, or sexual misconduct occurring in the workplace, school, or home environment.
- Accidents resulting in psychological injury, typically in the form of PTSD.
- Mental health malpractice resulting in psychological damages including sexual relationships between therapist and client, implanting of false memories, failure to inform a client about alternative therapies, and failure to report child or elder abuse.
- Spousal abuse, physical assault, and battery resulting in psychological trauma.
- Injury cases resulting in neuropsychological impairment, often seen in closed-head injury cases.
- Wrongful death of a family member resulting in loss of consortium (e.g., time with the person).
- Defamation of character such as slander or libel hurting the plaintiff's reputation and causing embarrassment.
- Employment litigation including discrimination, harassment, and retaliation.

appreciation of the wide range of possible circumstances leading to claims for psychological damages.

As discussed earlier, some types of claims are compensable, whereas others are not. Compensation for pain and suffering is called damages in the legal arena. Thus, if a claim is compensable, the plaintiff will be entitled to damages, or a monetary award. Damages can be classified in a variety of ways, such as future damages if a plaintiff is unable to work in the future or unable to earn what he or she could have earned if it were not for the impairment. Psychologists have no special expertise in determining damages, which is better left to experts such as economists or accountants. Table 7.9 provides a list of the types of damages for tort claims (Greenberg, 1999),

## Table 7.9      Types of Damages

- **Nominal Damages**: the minimal award for vindication where no real loss or injury occurs
- Compensatory or Actual Damages: losses suffered by the plaintiff
  - **General Damages**: restitution for the natural, necessary, and usual result of the wrongful act (e.g., pain and suffering and emotional distress)
    - **Loss of Consortium**: restitution for losing the love and companionship of a family member
    - **Hedonic Damages**: restitution for diminished enjoyment in life
  - Special Damages: restitution for damages that are the actual result of the injury, but not inevitable from the injury but apply in the current matter for reasons special to the case (e.g., out-of-pocket costs including medical bills, therapy bills, etc.)
    - Future Damages: plaintiff unable to work or has diminished earning capacity
    - Consequential Damages: for injury that is indirectly or secondarily caused by the defendant (e.g., a subsequently caused injury)
  - Punitive Damages or Exemplary Damages: punishment for outrageous conduct and to deter future transgressions

# Employment Litigation Involving Psychological Injury

State and federal laws protect employees from discrimination and harassment at the workplace. When harassment or discrimination results in significant emotional distress, workers may have claims under unemployment law, workman's compensation law, and civil rights statutes (Vasquez et al., 2003). This section examines employment litigation with a particular focus on violations of a worker's civil rights under the Civil Rights Act of 1964. State jurisdictions vary widely with regard to whether violations of an individual's civil rights that result in only psychological damages without evidence of physical assault are compensable. Similarly, torts filed under workman's compensation claims and unemployment claims vary widely among jurisdictions. Because of this variability among states, this section restricts the discussion to federal civil lawsuits. It is not necessary for the forensic psychologist to have a lawyer's understanding of the complex laws regarding employment litigation. However, a basic understanding of the history and the basis for claims will help guide the assessment process to address information relevant to the legal issues.

## Title VII of the Civil Rights Act of 1964

Prior to 1964, there existed a wide range of discriminatory employment practices of which many students today would have a hard time imagining. Classified want ads listed employment opportunities by sex. Help wanted sections of the newspapers divided jobs into "men's work" and "women's work" and even further divisions based on race. These practices systematically limited non-whites and females to the lowest paying jobs. Additional laws "protecting" women by restricting work hours and stating weight lift limits further prevented women from numerous job opportunities. The Civil Rights Act passed in 1964 and became law on July 1, 1965. Title VII of the Civil Rights Act addresses employment and forbids discrimination based on race, color, religion, national origin, and sex. An interesting footnote is that sex was only added as an amendment by legislators hoping to defeat the passage of the bill (Vasquez et al., 2003). There is currently no federal law banning discrimination based on sexual orientation.

**Discrimination** is defined as acting unreasonably or with bias because of a person's status as a member of a protected class. Litigation based on discrimination can be filed stating either **discriminatory effects** or **discriminatory treatment**. The major difference is whether the case can show discrimination against an entire group, termed discriminatory effects, or discrimination against a single individual, called discriminatory treatment. Title VII prohibits discrimination at the workplace and entitles the victim harmed by discrimination to monetary damages. The compensation is for loss of wages and benefits as well as psychological pain and suffering. If the behavior is particularly egregious, punitive damages may also be awarded. Monetary damages are usually granted when the employee can demonstrate that the discrimination was intentional.

The 1960s and 1970s saw a flourish of lawsuits challenging long-held discriminatory practices in employment. These lawsuits led to reform and eventually, affirmative action. One example is a company that hired only one African American, as a janitor, in the 7-year period after Title VII became law (*Jones v. Tri-County Electric Cooperative*, 1975). After the initiation of the lawsuit, the company hired several more African Americans, but at a percentage far below the local population census statistics. The company hired approximately 19% African Americans from a local population of 40% African Americans. The company was found to be in violation of Title VII due to discriminatory effects of the hiring practices. Recall that discriminatory effects, also called **disparate impact**, is required to show that an entire group was adversely affected by the hiring practice of the company.

Employers also used job qualifications or test scores to discriminate against non-Whites and females (Wrightsman, 1999). In 1971, the U.S. Supreme Court ruled that when qualifications for employment (such as test scores) discriminated against women or minorities, the qualifications violated Title VII unless the employer could prove that the practice was a business requirement (*Griggs v. Duke Power Company*, 1971). If the employer could demonstrate that a test score was necessary for employment, the employer could continue to exclude minorities. As a result, the United States Department of Labor instituted a process of changing the norms on the General Aptitude Test Battery by using

**■ Discrimination**

Acting with bias because of a person's race, color, religion, national origin, or sex.

**■ Discriminatory effects**

Discrimination against a protected group, as in employment law, where the entire group suffers.

**■ Discriminatory treatment**

Discrimination against an individual in a protected group.

**■ Disparate impact**

Occurs when an entire protected group (sex, race, or age) is adversely affected by discrimination.

Figure 7.6

Prior to the Civil Rights Act of 1964, none of these five people would have had any recourse for suffering discrimination on the job.
© 2009 iofoto. Used under license from Shutterstock, Inc.

■ **Race-norming**
An individual's scores are compared to norms for their ethnic group.

a within-group procedure called **race-norming** (Wrightsman, 1999). An individual's score is based on norms for their ethnic group. Whites, African Americans, and Hispanics all have different normative groups. Consequently, individuals from the three groups may score differently on the test but all score within the same percentile for their group and the scores would be reported as such to an employer. However, this controversial procedure was later banned by Congress in 1991 with the Civil Rights Act of 1991 that prohibited score adjustments based on race, sex, color, religion, or national origin.

## Sexual Harassment

■ **Sexual harassment**
Unwelcome, sex-based advances; requests for sexual favors or verbal or physical conduct of a sexual nature that renders harm to an individual.

One specific type of discrimination is harassment. The courts have determined that the employer has a duty to provide the worker with a workplace free from "hostility, intimidation, or insult based on race, sex, color, religion or national origin" (EEOC Compliance Manual, 1994). An employee does not need to demonstrate that the harassment was intentional discrimination, as harassment by its nature is considered hostile. The employee must show that the harassment altered the workplace conditions, such as resulting in an adverse evaluation, disrupting performance, or causing psychological harm. A specific type of harassment is sexual harassment. **Sexual harassment** is defined as unwelcome, sex-based advances, requests for sexual favors, or verbal and physical conduct of a sexual nature that renders harm to the individual. Specifically, the law states that such conduct is harassment when:

1. Submission to such behavior is explicitly or implicitly a condition of employment
2. Submission or rejection of such behavior can result in employment decisions
3. Such behavior interferes with the employee's job performance or creates a hostile work environment (Vasquez et al., 2003).

Psychology has an important role in educating the court regarding the perception of sexual harassment, conditions under which it can occur, and the effects of harassment. For example, research shows that men and women have differences with regard to what they consider sexual harassment. Women are more likely to perceive a wider range of behaviors as harassment (Pryor, Giedd, & Williams, 1995). Although men and women tend to agree that the more blatant behaviors such as sexual bribery are harassment, women tend to perceive the more ambiguous behaviors, such as flirting and nonsexual touching, as harassment when compared to men (Frazier, Cochran, & Olson, 1995). Furthermore, research shows that women are more likely to encounter sexual harassment, particularly when employed in traditionally male-dominated professions, such as firefighter, police officer, physician, or the armed services. Research suggests that over half of the women in the military experienced unwanted sexual attention (Seppa, 1997). The phenomenon of sexual harassment of female employees is not restricted to male-dominated professions. Although females are more likely to experience unwanted sexual advances at the workplace, men also report sexual harassment along with similar consequences, such as negative job outcomes (Magley, Waldo, Dragow, & Fitzgerald, 1999). Media reports suggest that approximately 10% of sexual harassment complaints are made by men against female bosses (Wrightsman, 1999). Nevertheless, the majority of sexual harassment occurs against women. Swisher (1994) reports that between 40 and 60% of women in the workplace state they have been sexually harassed. Sexual harassment is not only an issue in the workplace. The law also protects against sexual harassment at school. One survey found that 60% of female graduate students reported some form of sexual harassment by male faculty

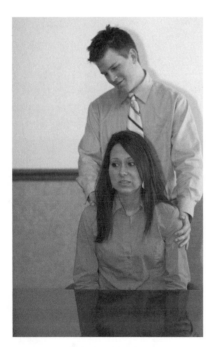

**Figure 7.7**

Unwelcome, sex-based advances in the workplace are considered sexual harassment.
© 2009 Steve Adamson. Used under license from Shutterstock, Inc.

(Schneider, 1987). Industry and universities have established policies regarding sexual harassment due to the widespread attention sexual harassment has received in the media. In a similar vein, the new APA ethical standards adopted in 2002 prohibit dual sexual relationships between faculty and students as well as between clients and therapists.

Sexual harassment can take two different forms, as defined by the law: hostile work environment and *quid pro quo*. **Quid pro quo** is perhaps the more obvious type of sexual harassment and amounts to sexual bribery in which the harasser makes sexual relations contingent on some outcome such as job retention, promotion, or a raise. In the academic environment, a professor may make passing a course or receiving a higher grade in a course contingent upon sexual relations with the student. Most people agree that this type of sexual bribery is sexual harassment.

In a **hostile work environment**, plaintiffs need to demonstrate that "an intimidating, hostile, or offensive working environment" was created through the use of harassment. Exactly what constitutes this type of harassment has been more difficult to define in the courts. In contrast to other forms of harassment, such as racial harassment, sexual harassment requires demonstrating that the alleged conduct was unwelcome. A hostile environment can include unwanted sexual advances, lewd comments, or pornographic materials at the work site. In one of the first cases heard by the Supreme Court, the Court ruled that demand for sexual conduct absent the explicit threat of adverse employment action can create a hostile environment (*Meritor Savings Bank v. Vinson*, 1986). The court distinguished between "welcomeness" and "voluntary" behavior. Ms. Vinson worked at Meritor Savings Bank for approximately 4 years, gradually advancing from bank teller to assistant manager. She was discharged due to excessive sick leave. Ms. Vinson filed a sexual harassment complaint against her supervisor. She claimed that she felt pressure to engage in sexual relations with her supervisor over a period of several years. She claimed that she felt coerced due to his supervisory role and stated that she agreed to have sexual relations with him out of fear of an adverse employment action. The relationship lasted several years and Ms. Vinson estimated that she and her supervisor had sexual relations 40–50 times, sometimes during the day at a nearby hotel. The initial court case favored the defendant, ruling that Ms. Vinson voluntarily engaged in sexual relations. The case eventually was heard by the U.S. Supreme Court. The Court ruled that an employee who willingly accepts a supervisor's request for a date could claim sexual harassment if it is known that such behavior is the only way to get a promotion or retain one's job. The court stated that the issue was not voluntary behavior, but rather whether the sexual advances were unwelcome. This case set the initial standards for demonstrating a hostile environment. The U.S. Supreme Court held that a hostile work environment could be the basis of a sexual harassment claim if the harassment was sufficiently severe to affect the conditions of employment and create an abusive environment. It is important to note that the reason for Ms. Vinson's termination, excessive sick leave, is a possible consequence of sexual harassment (Magley et al., 1999).

A second important ruling by the Supreme Court further addressed what constitutes a hostile workplace required in a harassment complaint. Teresa Harris was the only female employee in her job classification as a rental manager at Forklift Systems, Inc. of Nashville, Tennessee. She alleged that her supervisor repeatedly made demeaning and humiliating comments that forced her to leave her job after 2 years of employment. Ms. Harris stated that her employer, the owner of the company, suggested they go to a local hotel to negotiate her pay raise, asked her to retrieve coins from his front pants pocket, and asked if her success at sales was due to the granting of sexual favors. She sued for lost wages, claiming that his behavior had created a hostile environment. The Sixth Circuit Court rejected Ms. Harris's claims, stating that there was no evidence she had suffered a serious psychological injury but did note that

■ *Quid pro quo*

Tit for tat; used to describe sexual harassment when job retention, promotion, or raises are contingent on sexual relations.

■ **Hostile work environment**

An intimidating, hostile, or offensive working environment due to sexual harassment.

her boss's behavior was crude and offensive and characterized him as a "a vulgar man who demeans the female employees at his workplace" (Plevan, 1993, p. 20; cited in Wrightsman, 1999). The U.S. Supreme Court rejected the Sixth Circuit ruling and stated that even when there is no evidence of psychological trauma, evidence of discriminatory conduct against an individual based on race, gender, religion, or national origin violates Title VII. The APA filed an *amicus curiae brief* in this case, stating that the plaintiff should not have to demonstrate psychological damages to prove a hostile environment. The argument the APA presented was that requiring the demonstration of psychological damages places the responsibility on the victim as opposed to the perpetrator. For example, a highly resilient person may not experience any psychological trauma despite an extremely hostile environment; on the other hand, an "eggshell" plaintiff may experience trauma in situations unlikely to cause problems for most persons. The decision that the plaintiff did not have to prove psychological damages was a victory for employees since psychological trauma may develop long after the harassment has started.

The Court ruled that determinations of sexual harassment must be based on "the record as a whole and at the totality of the circumstances." The *Harris* decision established two criteria for determining that a hostile environment existed:

1. the conduct is sufficiently severe to be offensive to a reasonable person, and
2. the plaintiff must have been subjectively offended (Vasquez et al., 2003).

Although the Court did not accept all of the arguments in the APA's amicus brief, it did adopt a position consistent with a view used by many psychologists who study sexual harassment. Psychologists in this area agree that context is important in determining if a hostile environment existed. An important determination by the court was the use of a **reasonable person standard** in deciding if the behavior is offensive. The Court rejected the use of a *reasonable woman standard*, which had been used by a lower court, the Ninth Circuit Court, in deciding harassment cases (Wrightsman, 1999). The Ninth Circuit Court wished to view the harassment from the perspective of the victim. Others have argued that the use of a reasonable woman standard further diminishes women by suggesting that they are more vulnerable than men and need special accommodations in order to be protected at work.

A third Supreme Court ruling addressed the issue of same-sex sexual harassment. This issue resulted in conflicting rulings among various jurisdictions of the U.S. Federal Courts of Appeals. For example, the Fifth Circuit Court ruled that an employee could not claim sexual harassment for male-on-male harassment (*Oncale v. Sundowner Offshore Oil*, 1996). Other courts ruled that the harasser had to be homosexual for a claim of same-sex sexual harassment (*McWilliams v. Fairfax County Board of Supervisors*, 1996), and other courts ruled that anyone could claim sexual harassment if subjected to offensive behavior of a sexual nature (Vasquez et al., 2003). In order to address the issue, the Supreme Court heard the *Oncale v. Sundowner Offshore Oil* appeal in 1998. Mr. Oncale was a worker on an oil crew who alleged that he was threatened with rape and was assaulted by male crew members in a sexual manner. The Supreme Court reversed the Fifth Circuit Court's ruling, stating that persons of one group may well discriminate against others of the same group. In this case, group referred to sexual "group" and therefore a claim of sexual discrimination would be supported. The Court also ruled that nothing in Title VII bars a claim by a plaintiff against a harasser of the same sex (*Oncale v. Sundowner Offshore Oil*, 1998). The ruling that persons of one group can discriminate against members of the same group could also apply to any group status, such as race or religion. That suggests that an African American could successfully sue another African American for discrimination based on race.

In addition to discrimination based on sex, employees may seek compensation for other forms of discrimination and adverse employment actions. Employees are protected from discrimination based on race, sex, age, religion, and national origin. Employees are also protected from retaliation for filing a complaint against an employer or for filing a complaint regarding alleged employer misconduct (whistleblower protection).

■ **Employment litigation**
Any injury at the workplace or caused by work responsibilities not covered by workman's compensation.

## Types of **Employment Litigation** for Tort Claims        Table7.10

- ■ Wrongful Discharge: terminating employment without just cause
- ■ Discrimination: acting unreasonably or with bias because of a person's status as a member of a protected class
  - • Sexual Discrimination: discrimination based on sex
    - ○ Hostile Environment Sexual Harassment: offensive and damaging work environment based on sexually related offensive material
    - ○ *Quid Pro Quo* Sexual Harassment: welcome required sexual performance in order to obtain, keep, or advance in employment
  - • Racial Discrimination: discrimination based on race
  - • Age Discrimination : discrimination based on age
- ■ Retaliation: vindictive, unjustified reaction to punish a legitimate action by employee for:
  - • Filing a Personal Complaint: in response to previous wrongful act directed at employee
  - • Whistleblower: in response to employee complaint about employer misconduct

## Assessment of Psychological Injuries in Discrimination and Harassment Claims

The psychological assessment process in a harassment or discrimination claim is similar to other forensic assessments discussed in the book, particularly personal injury evaluations for emotional pain and suffering. The assessment involves three main tasks. The claim of harassment or discrimination raises the following issues:

1. did the alleged events occur,
2. what caused the alleged events to occur, and
3. what are the nature and extent of effects of the events on the plaintiff (Vasquez et al., 2003).

The first issue, whether the harassment or discrimination occurred, is for the jury to decide. Whether or not the events occurred is an *ultimate issue* and an expert may not testify as to whether the defendant or plaintiff is telling the truth. Rather, the trier of fact, typically the jury, must make the decision on this issue. The psychologist can provide testimony that the plaintiff is capable of distinguishing reality from fantasy. For example, a plaintiff may have a *delusional disorder* and suffer from delusions that he or she is being persecuted or romantically pursued by a coworker. A delusional

# The Eggshell Plaintiff

Marilyn Hall has had several episodes of clinical depression, the first one when she was 16 years old and the most recent 1 year ago. She is currently 34 years old and takes an antidepressant at a prophylactic dose to prevent a fourth clinical depression. Marilyn spends one day a week volunteering at her community library. The library was renovating one of the reading rooms and asked volunteers to help out with minor construction, painting, and clean-up. One of the county employees used a glass pitcher to store a caustic cleanser used to remove glue and paint from wood surfaces. During the busy clean-up, a young child asked Marilyn for a drink of water. Unknowingly, Marilyn thinks the pitcher of cleanser is actually water and pours the child a glass. The child suffers serious burns throughout her mouth and down her throat.

Marilyn is not held liable for the mistake, but the city is sued since the cleanser was placed in the pitcher by a city employee. The family of the child wins a $2 million law suit against the city. After the incident, Marilyn experienced an episode of clinical depression and

blamed herself for the accident. The city has a law that requires the city to seek compensation from individuals whose actions result in a financial loss to the city. Based on this law, the city initiates a lawsuit against Marilyn. The burden of defending against the lawsuit and reliving the experience causes Marilyn severe emotional distress. Her attorney initiates a countersuit against the city for causing Marilyn emotional harm.

The attorney contracts with Dr. Andrew Bronco to conduct a personal injury evaluation. What are some of the issues Dr. Bronco faces in this evaluation? Do the facts of the case suggest that Marilyn has a claim against the city? Identify the breach of contract as well as what caused the harm. Also, identify what harm that Marilyn suffered is compensable. What standard for compensable damages would be applicable to this case? How should Dr. Bronco conduct the evaluation? What instruments should he use and what collateral sources of information, if any, should he pursue? (Adapted from Greenberg, 2003)

disorder is characterized by the presence of a persistent, though not bizarre, delusion. Otherwise, the person's behavior is relatively normal. A delusion is an incorrect belief that is maintained despite evidence to the contrary. Delusional disorder is believed to be relatively rare (Sarason & Sarason, 2005). The forensic psychologist can assist the court on understanding the plaintiff's prior and current mental state.

With regard to the second question, what caused the event to occur, psychologists can address the issues of voluntary behavior and unwelcome sexual advances. Recall that there is no need to address this issue with discrimination in that discrimination is assumed to be hostile. However, in sexual harassment cases, a defendant may claim that the plaintiff was the pursuer. The plaintiff must demonstrate that the conduct was unwelcome. The *Vinson* decision established that voluntary behavior does not necessarily mean the conduct was welcomed. The examiner should consider any evidence to indicate that the behavior was welcomed and any evidence to indicate that the behavior was not welcomed. The examiner must also form an opinion as to whether the conduct was so severe that it would affect any reasonable person in the same circumstance. This type of opinion requires the psychologist to be familiar with the scientific literature on the effects of discrimination and harassment as well as case and statutory law in the jurisdiction in which the case is being tried.

Finally, the psychologist must determine what harmful effects, if any, the alleged conduct had on the plaintiff. This evaluation is similar to the assessment of psychological injury in personal injury cases and the reader is referred to the previous discussion. The evaluation requires an assessment of the plaintiff's behavior prior to the harassment or discrimination and an assessment of any impairment in his or her functioning caused by the harassment or discrimination. This assessment of former, current, and future psychological functioning requires information from a variety of sources, including interviews, historical records, third-party informants, psychological testing, and all attorney records relevant to the case.

The assessment should include an attempt to distinguish between the psychological effects of the harassment or discrimination and the psychological effects of participation in the lawsuit (Vasquez et al., 2003). The effects of dispositions, testifying on the witness stand, and defense strategies alleging that the behavior did not occur or the behavior was the plaintiff's fault can all exacerbate the plaintiff's psychological pain and suffering. However, the psychological effects of participation in the lawsuit are not compensable, only the effects due to the alleged behavior resulting in the harassment or discrimination complaint. Vasquez et al. (2003) suggests attempting to distinguish if the plaintiff's condition would be different if the defendant had initially agreed to all claims by the plaintiff.

The issue of **malingering** or exaggerating symptoms must always be considered in a personal injury case due to the financial incentive (Kane, 1999b). Indeed, the DSM-IV-TR specifically warns of malingering in personal injury evaluations (American Psychiatric Association, 2000a). Malingering is the voluntary falsification or fabrication of psychological symptoms (Shuman, 1994). Although the number of plaintiffs who present with malingered symptoms is unknown, it has been suggested that there are relatively few fakers in court (Scrignar, 1996). A malingerer would need to fool plaintiff and defense attorneys, private investigators, mental health professionals, physicians, and others before they would find their way into the courtroom. Other researchers have suggested that malingering occurs in 15–17% of all forensic cases, including both criminal and civil cases. However, the majority of studies have looked at malingering in forensic criminal cases (Rogers, 1998).

It is possible that a plaintiff will exaggerate symptoms for a variety of reasons. Some plaintiffs with valid psychological disorders may exaggerate their symptoms, seeking justice for harm caused by the employer or to demonstrate the pain and suffering they initially experienced even though they may have improved in their mental state (Resnick, 1997). Lawyers may encourage plaintiffs, intentionally or unintentionally, to exaggerate symptoms or to perceive him- or herself as more disabled than he or she actually is (Kane, 1999b). Lawyers may also try to influence plaintiffs to exaggerate or feign symptoms in an unethical manner and possibly coach plaintiffs on test-taking procedures (Lees-Haley, 1997; Victor & Abeles, 2004). However, a plaintiff who exaggerates his or her symptoms is not malingering and exaggeration of symptoms does not indicate that actual psychological injuries do not exist (Rogers, 1997). Malingering and mental psychological injuries are not mutually exclusive and the clinician cannot rule out real injury based on evidence of malingering or exaggeration (Rogers & Bender, 2003). Comparison of collateral information with the plaintiff's self-report can help substantiate claims of injury. In addition, many objective tests have validity scales used to detect defensive response sets or overreporting or unlikely symptoms. For example, the Trauma Symptom Inventory has three validity scales and the MMPI-2 has validity scales to assess response set. If an objective measure suggests feigning of symptoms, the psychologists can conduct a more thorough assessment of malingering with an instrument designed to assess malingering. The Structured Interview of Reported Symptoms is a structured interview designed to assess feigning and related response styles (SIRS; Rogers, 1998; Rogers, Bagby, & Dickens, 1992). The determination of malingering should not be based solely on an assessment interview (Rogers & Shuman, 2000). Nor should malingering or exaggeration of symptoms be considered an all-or-none determination; plaintiffs can have real injury and malinger or exaggerate other symptoms for a variety of reasons. Malingering should always be assessed as a possibility in civil forensic cases but cannot be used by itself to dismiss a plaintiff's claim of psychological injury.

# Legal Psychology's Contribution to Discrimination and Harrassment Claims

In addition to evaluating plaintiffs for personal injuries, psychologists can play a lead role in educating the courts regarding the causes and consequences of harassment. Legal psychologists have demonstrated that two conditions generally lead to sexual harassment. The factors that lead to sexual harassment are both personal and situational. Persons who have a high likelihood of sexually harassing subordinates tend to be sexually aggressive males with a macho image of themselves (Pryor et al., 1995). Pryor (1987) developed the Likelihood to Sexually Harass Scale (LSH) as a measure of personality factors associated with individuals who harass. Personality characteristics include

- hostility
- cynicism toward relationships
- sexual aggressiveness
- avoidance of stereotypically feminine occupations
- toughness
- hypermasculinity

However, these men need to perceive that the organization allows such behavior to occur. If work leaders appear to condone such behavior, these individuals are more likely to engage in sexually offensive actions (Vasquez et al., 2003). Legal psychologists can also research the effects of harassment. Issues to be studied include similarities and differences in the consequences to harassment between men and women and the phenomenon of same-sex harassment. Similarly, differences between men's and women's perception of what constitutes harassment needs to be further explored. Research suggests men and women agree on blatant forms of harassment but tend to disagree on the more ambiguous forms, such as flirting (Frazier et al., 1995). A meta-analysis of over 90 studies suggests that male–female differences in perception of harassment are reliable, though comparatively small (Blumethal, 1998). Research on the above issues can help inform the court and lead to policy based on sound scientific data.

# PTSD and the Use of Syndrome Evidence

**■ Battered woman syndrome**
Collection of symptoms and behaviors that are believed to occur in women who are the victims of repeated physical and psychological abuse.

Attorneys have used **syndrome evidence** in both criminal cases and civil cases claiming psychological injury. The presence of psychological injury has been presented as exculpatory evidence for guilt or as mitigating circumstances at sentencing hearings in criminal cases. For example, **battered woman syndrome** has been used as a defense for women who have injured or killed their abusive partner. Other syndromes have also been suggested in criminal trials, such as **rape trauma syndrome** and *child sexual abuse accommodation syndrome*. These latter two syndromes have been used to clarify a victim's response to the alleged crime, such as explaining why a woman who was raped did not contact the police until the following morning. This section focuses on battered woman syndrome and how public policy, though with good intentions, has ignored psychological research.

**Domestic violence** includes violence between siblings, adolescents, and their parents, or violence between adult partners (Dutton & McGregor, 1992). There is little doubt that domestic violence between adult partners, also called **intimate partner violence** (IPV), is a major problem in the United States. Estimates of abuse vary depending on the survey, although some researchers have suggested that anywhere from 30% (Plichta, 1996) to 50% (Walker, 1992) of all women will be abused at some point in their lives. A recent national survey of over 8,000 women found that lifetime prevalence for physical assault by a male partner was 25% (Tjaden & Thoennes, 2000a, 2000b). Although female aggression against men also occurs at disturbing rates (Magdol, Moffitt, Caspi, & Silva, 1998), male violence against women is much more likely to result in injury or death. In fact, women are much more likely to be killed by their partners than by a stranger and nearly 30% of all women murdered are killed by their partner (Kellerman & Mercy, 1992). A survey in the state of Washington found that nearly 22% of women reported injury as a result of IPV as compared to 8% of men (Washington State Department of Health, 2000) and a national survey found that of people injured as a result of IPV, 73% were women and 27% were men (Zlotnick, Kohn, Peterson, & Pearlstein, 1998). Despite these alarming statistics, prevalence figures most likely underestimate the extent of the problem. Surveys tend to miss the very poor, homeless, incarcerated, hospitalized, and those living on military bases (Samuelson & Campbell, 2005). Also missing from these surveys are those unwilling to disclose experiences regarding IPV. One study found higher rates of IPV among military versus civilian couples by querying adolescents about their parents' behavior, suggesting certain circumstances make it more likely the women will underreport incidences of IPV (Cronin, 1995). These high incidence rates make the routine assessment of IPV among health care providers a practice whose time has come (McCloskey & Grigsby, 2005; Samuelson & Campbell, 2005).

Figure 7.8

Battered woman syndrome is a collection of symptoms and behaviors that occur in women who are the victims of repeated physical and psychological abuse.
© 2009 JupiterImages Corporation.

## Battered Woman Syndrome

Battered woman syndrome is a phenomenon said to be present in women who have been victims of IPV. First identified nearly 25 years ago (Walker, 1979, 1984), a great deal of research has questioned the validity of this concept in recent years. In fact, Diane Follingstad has stated, "The careful analyses of the problems surrounding the battered woman syndrome as a concept, irrespective of whether it is a useful explanatory mechanism for court cases, have shown that it is difficult to conclude anything other than that the syndrome is virtually unsupportable as a well-defined and valid concept" (2003, p. 502). Despite this lack of scientific validity, testimony on battered woman syndrome is accepted in most jurisdictions and has been called the most successful syndrome in terms of acceptance in the history of the courts (Downs, 1996). Twelve states have legislated the acceptance of battered woman syndrome testimony and the Battered Woman's Testimony Act of 1992 encouraged state officials to accept testimony on battered woman syndrome based on the acknowledgment that women are frequently the victims of IPV (Follingstad, 2003). It should be noted that casting doubt on the scientific validity of battered woman syndrome does not diminish the harmful effects of IPV nor does it imply that women who retaliate against their abusers should not be vigorously defended in court. Rather, as Slobogin (1994) has suggested, time-honored legal principles should be used in courts as opposed to basing legal policy on dubious syndrome evidence, reflecting in part the court's wish to protect sympathetic victims.

As initially conceptualized by Walker (1979), *battered woman syndrome* is a collection of symptoms and behaviors that occur in women who are the victims of repeated physical and psychological abuse. Walker suggested that a **"cycle of violence"** exists in abusive relationships consisting of three phases. The **tension-building phase** is the result of disappointments or disagreements in the relationship and signals the inevitability of a battering episode. This leads to the second phase in the cycle, an **acute battering incident**, followed by the third stage, the **contrite phase**. During the contrite phase, the male partner is remorseful for his behavior and showers his spouse with affection and apologies. According to Walker, the woman, who can recognize the tension-building phase in her partner, lives in constant fear of the inevitable violence. As a result, the woman develops battered woman syndrome, characterized by the following behaviors and characteristics (Walker, 1984):

- Learned helplessness, believing there is nothing she can do to change her life circumstance or escape the abusive behavior
- Low self-esteem
- Depression
- Self-blame
- Hypervigilant to subtle cues of impending abuse
- Social isolation
- Traumatic bonding, or the process of becoming more attached to her abuser
- Cognitive distortions, such as poor problem-solving skills and failure to see alternatives

However, research on these behaviors has been inconclusive at best. Although some studies have found support for some of the characteristics, other studies have failed to find support or have even found contrary evidence. For example, the majority of studies has found depression and low self-esteem among battered women, but has failed to find self-blame or social isolation. Other studies have even found battered women to be more sociable than control groups (see Follingstad, 2003, for a review of the literature). Similarly, no research has supported the cycle of violence as a pervasive pattern in all abusive relationships. Walker (1984) failed to identify the phases in over one-third of the 400 women she interviewed. Follingstad reports "the cycle of violence has been considered by numerous commentators to be so flexible and limitless (i.e., no time intervals are ever specified) as to be useless for predicting behavior" (2003, p. 503).

A syndrome is defined as a group of subjective symptoms and objective signs that occur together and characterize a disease (Morse, 1978; Wrightsman, 2001). Medical syndromes are typically distinguished by a collection of symptoms co-occurring and indicating a pathological condition, as with acquired immune deficiency syndrome (AIDS), eventually discovered to be caused by a specific virus, HIV. In medicine, the co-occurring symptoms are first identified, followed by a search for the cause of the disease. In the identification of behavioral syndromes, the process has usually taken place backward (Follingstad, 2003). Rather than identifying associated symptoms and looking for the cause, commentators first identify the common experience, and then the investigation for similar co-occurring symptoms or characteristics begins. For example, researchers have searched for similar characteristics of children who have been sexually abused or children who were raised by an alcoholic parent. The methodology ignores the immense individual differences people display in reaction to trauma and disregards the vast amount of literature on people's ability to overcome adversity (Masten, 2001; Newman, 2005). There is no evidence to indicate that all women who are battered developed behaviors associated with battered woman syndrome. Furthermore, the suggestion of battered woman syndrome implies that women who have been battered are pathological in that evidence of a behavioral syndrome implies psychological impairment. The conceptualization of battered woman syndrome as indicating a psychological impairment has actually been used against women in family court in child custody cases, an unfortunate irony that can be attributed to junk science. In summarizing the research on battered woman syndrome, Diana Follingstad states:

> The battered woman syndrome appears to fail all tests of a true syndrome: specific criteria are lacking; the required etiology is unclear; the syndrome does not explain why some women develop symptoms and others do not; it is unclear whether all women with the syndrome would exhibit all of the suggested characteristics; it is difficult for the syndrome to prove that the present symptoms are uniquely different from related entities (i.e., would not have been produced by other sources); and it has not been established that professionals can reliably "diagnose" women as suffering from battered woman syndrome. (2003, p. 503)

Despite the controversy surrounding the validity of battered woman syndrome, testimony on it has rarely been rejected as admissible evidence based on the Frye or Daubert standard. Blowers and Bjerregaard (1994) reviewed 72 cases involving the admissibility of expert testimony on battered woman syndrome. Although at times the testimony was not allowed, only 15 of the cases indicate that the court even considered the scientific validity of battered woman syndrome. Moreover, since 1985, only one court rejected the testimony due to concerns regarding the scientific validity of the syndrome.

Other researchers have suggested using already-in-place legal precedents to defend women who have killed or injured their abusers. Possible affirmative defenses include the insanity plea or self-defense. Although most cases would not meet the strict criteria for the insanity defense as discussed in Chapter 4, many of the cases would meet the criteria for self-defense. A person can claim self-defense if the individual reasonably believed that he or she was in imminent danger of death or great bodily harm and the person had no other means of avoiding the harm (i.e., escape, use of less force, etc.). However, not all cases involving women who killed their abuser occurred during episode of violence. In fact, some court cases have involved women who killed or injured their partners while they slept (Wrightsman, 2001). Even so, the jury could consider the woman's behavior in light of knowledge regarding the history of her partner's abusive and violent behavior. This kind of knowledge would enable the jury to understand the woman's subjective evaluation of imminent danger. The Supreme Court in the state of Washington ruled that the jury should have knowledge of the woman's prior experiences in order to rule if her actions were reasonable from a subjective standpoint (Follingstad, 2003).

## Posttraumatic Stress Disorder

If the scientific community dismisses battered woman syndrome as a valid syndrome, what is left to describe the emotional difficulties experienced by women who have been abused? Many women who suffer IPV demonstrate symptoms of **posttraumatic stress disorder** (PTSD). Walker (1992) originally viewed battered woman syndrome as a subcategory of PTSD. The development of PTSD appears to be related to severity and frequency of physical and sexual abuse by male partners. PTSD is a severe

■ **Posttraumatic stress disorder (PTSD)**

A severe anxiety disorder resulting from exposure to a traumatic event outside the range of usual human experience.

anxiety disorder resulting from exposure to a traumatic event. The fourth edition of the *Diagnostic and Statistical Manual of Mental Disorders* (DSM-IV), published by the American Psychiatric Association (2000a), identified the traumatic event as involving "actual or threatened death or physical injury, or a threat to the physical integrity of self or others" (pp. 427–428). Physical assault is not necessary to qualify as a traumatic event. Threat of physical assault is sufficient for the development of PTSD. Physical partner abuse and the threat of physical abuse would certainly meet DSM criteria for the trauma required in PTSD. Researchers have identified symptoms of PTSD in battered women and have suggested the use of PTSD as part of understanding women's response to battering. PTSD is frequently used as a diagnosis in cases claiming psychological damage (Ackerman, 1999) and certainly meets the Frye and Daubert standards for scientific acceptance. Table 7.11 provides the diagnostic criteria used to identify PTSD (American Psychological Association, 2002).

Ewing (1990) has argued for *psychological self-defense* as a justification for women who kill their abusers. He suggests that the use of deadly force would be justified if necessary to prevent infliction of serious psychological injury. On the other hand, it would be difficult to demonstrate that a person could reasonably foresee the imminent infliction of psychological injury. Perhaps the best defense would be an affirmative self-defense allowing the jury to hear information regarding the history of abuse and thus able to view the situation from the woman's subjective vantage point. Nonetheless, it appears that despite the lack of scientific validity, testimony on battered woman syndrome will continue to be readily accepted by courts hoping to address a repugnant social ill.

| Table 7.11 | Diagnostic Criteria for Posttraumatic Stress Disorder (PTSD) |
|---|---|

- A severe anxiety disorder
- Person was exposed to a traumatic event
- Traumatic event is persistently reexperienced in the following ways:
  - Recurrent and intrusive distressing recollections of the event
  - Recurrent distressing dreams of the event
  - Acting or feeling as if the event was recurring (flashbacks, hallucinations)
- Intense distress to situations similar to the event
- Persistent avoidance of similar situations
  - Efforts to avoid thoughts, feelings, and conversations associated with the trauma
  - Efforts to avoid activities, people, and places that remind one of the event
  - Inability to recall aspect of the trauma
  - Loss of interest in activities
  - Restricted affect
  - Sense of a foreshortened future
- Persistent symptoms of increased arousal
  - Difficulty sleeping
  - Irritability or outbursts of anger
  - Difficulty concentrating
  - Hypervigilance
  - Exaggerated startle response
- Symptoms last longer than 1 month and cause significant distress or impairment

# Summary

This chapter discussed the assessment of psychological injuries, also termed emotional pain and suffering. The assessment of psychological injury was presented within the context of personal injury cases. Personal injury cases are based on civil law, and the distinction between criminal law and civil law was reviewed as well as a brief overview of the civil court system. The law of torts is the civil law that provides for lawsuits by a plaintiff against a defendant. The necessary elements for a legally viable lawsuit were outlined, including lawsuits for negligent and intentional infliction of emotional harm. A model for the assessment of emotional harm was presented along with a review of appropriate assessment instruments. The chapter then examined several specific forms of psychological harm including discrimination and harassment (employment litigation) and battered woman syndrome. Employment litigation focused on sexual harassment and **Title VII of the Civil Rights Act of 1964**. The courts have categorized sexual harassment at the workplace into two forms: *quid pro quo* and hostile environment. *Quid pro quo*, or sexual bribery, is easily recognizable. The definition of a hostile environment has been harder for the courts to pin down and several cases that have helped clarify the meaning were reviewed. A brief review on the assessment of the psychological effects of sexual harassment was provided. Legal psychology's contribution to educating the courts about the causes, effects, and perception of sexual harassment was covered. Finally, the use of battered woman syndrome in criminal and civil cases was presented as an example of how the courts have ignored scientific evidence in an attempt to rectify the social problem of intimate partner violence and women who strike back.

# TEST YOUR KNOWLEDGE

1. A tort is a
   a. legal claim in the form of a lawsuit
   b. evidence that there has been a dereliction that has caused harm
   c. a matter for criminal courts to prosecute
   d. a and c

2. In a tort, what burden of proof does the plaintiff need to reach?
   a. Preponderance of the evidence
   b. Clear and convincing
   c. Beyond a reasonable doubt
   d. The burden of proof rests on the defendant, not the plaintiff

3. Sexual discrimination in which the individual is offered employment or advancement in exchange for sexual performance is termed:
   a. hostile environment sexual harassment
   b. *quid pro quo* sexual harassment
   c. retaliation
   d. hedonic damages

4. Posttraumatic stress disorder is typically caused by
   a. a chemical imbalance in the brain
   b. a combination of genetic and childhood experiences
   c. exposure to a traumatic event
   d. a comorbid anxiety disorder

5. In a tort, the individual filing the claim is called the
   a. defendant
   b. plaintiff
   c. prosecutor
   d. suspect

Answer Key: (1) a, (2) a, (3) b, (4) c, (5) b

# Chapter Eight

# Child Custody Evaluations

## Learning Objectives

- Be able to list the five reasons child custody evaluations are considered so difficult to perform by forensic psychologists.

- Explain the reasons why child custody evaluations pose a high liability risk for forensic psychologists and what measures some states have taken to protect evaluators.

- How do good faith immunity laws protect forensic psychologists who perform child custody evaluations?

- What are some of the roles a psychologist can perform with regard to child custody decisions?

- What are advantages and disadvantages to mediation?

- What is the current state of affairs about child custody cases? What is the divorce rate and what percentage of couples with children under age 18 pursue child custody litigation?

- What does the research suggest regarding the types of custody arrangements and the best interests of the child?

- Be able to trace the development of the current standard for deciding child custody from the initial "tender-years doctrine" to the current "best interests of the child" standard.

- Be able to discuss the research about the legal relevance of child custody recommendations.

- Distinguish between legal parental authority and physical authority.

- List and explain the various types of custody arrangements.

- The text presents guidelines for forensic child custody evaluators published by three different professional organizations. Be able to identify the organizations and give a brief overview of their guidelines. Also, discuss the advantages and disadvantages of these guidelines.

- Discuss the evaluation process. Specifically, name the sources of information; the evaluator's relationship to the participants; who should be contacted; what testing, if any, is used; and the format of the report.

- Describe the type of training required for psychologists to perform competent child custody evaluations.

## Key Terms

- Ackerman-Schoendorf Scales for Parent Evaluation of Custody Test (ASPECT)
- Alternative dispute resolution
- Best interest of the child standard
- Bricklin Perceptual Scales
- Collaborative law
- Court-appointed evaluator
- Divided custody
- Dual relationship
- Forensic assessment instruments
- General guidelines
- Good faith practice
- Guidelines for Child Custody Evaluations in Divorce Proceedings (American Psychological Association)
- Immunity laws
- Joint custody
- Least detrimental standard
- Legal parental authority
- Limited joint custody
- Mediator
- Minnesota Multiphasic Personality Inventory–2
- Model Standards of Practice for Child Custody Evaluations (Association of Family and Conciliation Courts)

*(continued)*

## Key Terms *(continued)*

- Multiple relationships
- Orienting guidelines
- Physical authority
- Practice Parameters of Child Custody Evaluation (American Academy of Child and Adolecent Psychiatry)
- Procedural guidelines

- Same-sex parenting
- Social framework testimony
- Sole custody
- Split custody
- Tender-years doctrine
- Uniform Marriage and Divorce Act of 1979

This chapter explores one of the more complex areas of forensic practice, the area of child custody evaluations. Child custody evaluations are governed by civil law as opposed to criminal law. Custody evaluations are typically ordered in contested divorce cases, although a psychologist may also be asked to conduct a *termination of parental rights* evaluation for the state when issues of abuse or neglect have been documented. These state-ordered assessments have a variety of terms depending on the jurisdiction, including *assessments of minimal parenting*, *child protection evaluations*, *dependency evaluations*, and *parenting capacity assessments* (Carr, Moretti, & Cue, 2005). The chapter reviews the numerous pitfalls associated with child custody evaluations, making this area of work laden with professional liability issues. The possible roles a psychologist can play in the process of divorce and custody decisions are discussed, along with the potential conflict of dual relationships. The current state of divorce and custody agreements in the United States is presented, as well as laws and models used by the courts to guide custody decisions. The child custody evaluation process is presented with particular attention to guidelines for these evaluations that have been recommended by various professional associations. Included in this discussion is a brief overview of the types of arrangements psychologists may recommend. Legal psychology's contribution to child custody decisions is presented. Psychologists can educate the courts on issues such as child development, parenting behaviors, and the impact of various custody arrangements on children's adjustment. The chapter ends with a brief discussion on the training and skills necessary to conduct child custody evaluations.

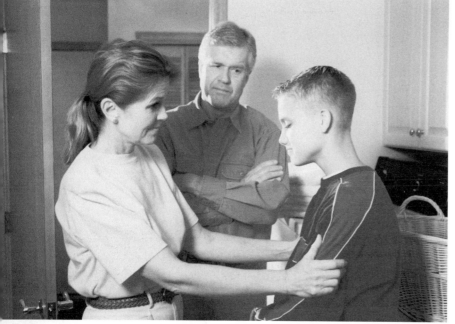

Figure 8.1

Most parents who divorce are able to amicably come to an agreement about child custody arrangements.
© 2009 JupiterImages Corporation.

# The Challenge of Child Custody Evaluations

Child custody evaluations have been termed the "most complex, difficult, and challenging of all forensic evaluations" (Otto et al., 2003, p. 179). Most authors agree that child custody evaluations are difficult and work-intensive, but highly satisfying (Benjamin & Gollan, 2003; Bow & Quinnell, 2001). The majority of parents who divorce are able to amicably negotiate child custody arrangements without the court's intervention. Courts only intervene in disputed custody arrangements in about 6–20% of all divorcing couples with children under 18 years old (Melton et al., 1997). Many parties referred for custody evaluations have attempted and failed less adversarial means of compromise (Benjamin & Gollan, 2003). Most jurisdictions have statutory laws that give judges the power to determine child custody arrangements if the parents are unable to reach a solution (Sales, Manber, & Rohman, 1992). When the courts must serve as the final arbiter of children's custody arrangements, the court will seek the advice of mental health professionals, although this advice is often not entirely heeded (Horvath, Logan, & Walker, 2002; Settle & Lowery, 1982). Among mental health professionals, psychologists conduct the majority of child custody evaluations (Mason & Quirk, 1997).

The reasons for the complexity and challenge of child custody evaluations are multifaceted. First, unlike many other forensic evaluations in which one individual is to be evaluated, a child custody evaluation can involve multiple individuals, all with conflicting agendas. Second, the assessment is not within the normal expertise of a psychologist and the scientific literature used to guide decisions is, at best, tenuous. Although the identification of psychopathology may be relevant to the legal question, more important for the decision maker are issues of parenting capacity, family relationships, and individuals' needs and interests. A third complicating matter is the lack of an agreed-upon standards for the assessment process and the paucity of relevant assessment instruments. A fourth complicating factor is the highly-adversarial nature of the process and the psychologist's exposure to licensing complaints and litigation. Finally, a fifth factor contributing to the difficulty of the evaluation is the scorn and disrespect a psychologist is likely to encounter in the courtroom, both from opposing attorneys and judges. Table 8.1 summarizes the factors that contribute to the complexity of child custody evaluations. The attitudes and biases of judges, attorneys, families, and psychologists all shape the custody evaluative process. Each of these areas is presented in more detail below.

## Multiple Participants

The forensic psychologist conducting a child custody evaluation must assess, at minimum, two parents who are contesting custody and their child. However, frequently there is

## Factors Contributing to the Complexity of Child Custody Evaluations     Table 8.1

- Multiple participants
- Lack of clarity and scientific support regarding the psycholegal question
- Lack of agreed-upon standards for the assessment process and validated assessment instruments
- Adversarial nature of the process and high risk of liability suits and licensing complaints
- Attitudes and biases of those involved in the decision-making process

more than one child involved in the custody dispute. The assessment of multiple individuals is in contrast to most forensic evaluations that involve only one individual. Frequently, child custody evaluations involve other individuals who also need to be assessed, such as potential stepparents and stepsiblings. Grandparents may also be involved in the custody litigation. Clark (1995) has recommended that the evaluator interview any party living in the custodial or visited home, school personnel (teachers, coaches, etc.), physicians, childcare workers, and any other adults directly responsible for care of the children. These evaluations include testing, interviews, and observations. Interviews with the children may be conducted alone and again with each child interacting with each parent individually. Interviews with the adults may occur in the clinician's office, although it may be useful to conduct the interviews with young children in the home. Clark recommends observing the child and adults interacting and suggests that school visits may be warranted if further information is needed. Regardless, a home visit to the two potential homes may help provide valuable information to the decision maker. It should be obvious that arranging assessment interviews with so many family members is labor-intensive and time-consuming. Ackerman and Ackerman (1997) reported that the average child custody evaluation took approximately 26.4 hours and a more recent survey found that average time to complete an evaluation ranged from 24.5 to 28.5 hours (Bow & Quinnell, 2001), depending on the number of parties involved. Bow and Quinnell (2001) report a range of 5–90 hours for evaluations involving two parents and one child, with an average of 24.5 hours and a range of 6–90 hours for an evaluation involving two parents and two children, with an average of 28.5 hours. The extreme variability around the average suggests some evaluations are conducted within a minimal amount of time, whereas others require an exorbitant amount of time. The average time frame reported in the Bow and Quinnell study was 9.27 weeks from beginning to end.

Not all practitioners routinely follow the above model and interview all interested parties. Several surveys have been conducted over the years in an attempt to determine the actual practices of child custody evaluators. The first survey queried 82 mental health professionals, the majority being psychologists, on the procedures used in child custody evaluations (Keilin & Bloom, 1986). Ackerman and Ackerman (1996, 1997) replicated the study 10 years later and surveyed 201 psychologists. LaFortune and Carpenter (1998) asked 165 mental health professionals, the majority being psychologists, about their custody evaluation practices. Bow and Quinnell surveyed 198 psychologists involved in child custody proceedings to determine the state of the field in 2001. The first study on evaluation practices (Keilin & Bloom, 1986) was before the APA published guidelines for child custody evaluations. Guidelines from the APA were first published in 1994. The other surveys were completed after both the publication of the guidelines and organized efforts within the field to educate evaluators on best practices. Taken together, these surveys can be viewed as a snapshot of the maturing of the practice of custody evaluations. We return to the results of these studies throughout the remainder of the discussion.

Horvath et al. (2002) conducted a content analysis of 60% of the child custody evaluations in one circuit court over a 2-year period. The authors distinguished between court-appointed social workers and private practitioners. They report a wide variety of practices among evaluators, with many of the assessments not meeting the expected standard of care. For example, fewer than 10% of the privately retained evaluators interviewed schoolteachers and only 33% of the court-appointed evaluators interviewed teachers. Only 12% of the private practitioners visited the home, whereas nearly 40% of the court-appointed evaluators conducted a home visit. Despite the fact that court-appointed evaluators appeared to provide a more comprehensive assessment than the privately retained evaluators, the overall low compliance with recommended guide-

**Figure 8.2**

It would be potentially harmful to ask this child to choose which parent he would like to live with.
©2009 Dmitry Shironosov. Used under license from Shutterstock, Inc.

lines is still startling. The labor-intensive nature of evaluations involving multiple individuals can jeopardize the quality of the work, as suggested by the above studies indicating nonadherence to guidelines and evaluations conducted in 5 hours.

## The Psycholegal Question Involved in Child Custody Evaluations

Another factor that adds to the complexity of the evaluation is determining what the specific psycholegal question to be answered is and what process should be used to form an expert opinion. Over the years, the rules the courts have used for determining custody have evolved. Currently, all 50 states mandate that the child's best interests be the primary consideration in determining custody arrangements (Keilin & Bloom, 1986). However, opinions regarding determining what the child's best interest is and how to meet this goal vary widely. The task of the evaluator is to determine what the best interests of the child are. The evaluator needs to weigh educational goals, social adjustment, geographic location, economic resources, both parents' parenting skills, and contact with friends and family in determining the child's best interests. Most commentators agree that younger children should not be asked their preferences regarding custody, although there is some debate about asking older adolescents (Rohman, Sales, & Lou, 1987). It is considered potentially harmful to place a younger child in the position of choosing favorites. As a result, young children may only have minimal input into the decision process (Szaj, 2002). Additionally, there is very little solid research on determining what types of custody arrangements are best in terms of the children's adjustment. Studies report various levels of adjustment for children based on joint versus sole custody arrangements (e.g., Emery, Laumann-Billings, Waldron, Sbarra, & Dillon, 2001; Gunnoe & Braver, 2001; Kelly, 2000). A similar debate exists in the research literature regarding parental behavior and child development (e.g., Collins, Maccoby, Steinberg, Hetherington, & Bornstein, 2000). Defending expert opinions based on this area of social science research during a hostile cross-examination can challenge the most conscientious clinician. Furthermore, determining the child's best interests assumes that the custodial parent at the time of the evaluation will meet the child's best interests for the remainder of the child's life with that parent. It is possible that a child's needs will predictably change (e.g., educational opportunities) and one parent may be better able to meet the child's needs in the future than the other parent.

In addition to the conflicting social science data, the evaluator must know how the jurisdiction applies the **best interest of the child standard**. Statutory laws regarding custody decisions vary widely across states and judges have wide discretion in weighing each factor when determining the child's best interests (Krauss & Sales, 2000). A critique expressed in the literature is that the entire process "is little more than subjective value judgment dressed up as expert opinion or social science data" (Otto et al., 2003, p. 203). Connell (2004, p. 1) has suggested that the question is no longer, "What is in the child's best interest?" but has now changed to "What parenting plan would work best for this child and these parents?" We return to this topic later in the chapter. The overly broad notion of a child's best interests, the various ways that this standard is interpreted, and the conflicting data on many of the potentially relevant constructs all contribute to the complexity of the child custody evaluation.

■ **Best interest of the child standard**
The standard used in child custody disputes that suggests custody decisions should be made with regards to the best interests of the child, as opposed to parental rights.

## Confusion Regarding the Assessment Process and Instruments

Another complication of child custody evaluations is the lack of a standard evaluation procedure as well as appropriate assessment instruments. Several professional organizations have published guidelines for child custody evaluations. The American Psychological Association (1994), the Association of Family and Conciliation Courts (n.d.), and the American Academy of Child and Adolescent Psychiatry (1997) have all published practice recommendations for conducting child custody evaluations. However, even these recommendations are at times conflicting (e.g., regarding the use of psychological assessment instruments) and although somewhat helpful, have been criticized as overly broad and failing to provide much direction with regards to substantive areas of inquiry (Otto et al., 2003). Psychologists conducting custody evaluations should be familiar with all the guidelines as well as other relevant literature. Despite the wealth of literature on the topic of child custody evaluations, there continues to be a wide range of standard of care, with many commentators expressing reservations about the current state of the profession.

Horvath, Logan, and Walker (2002) examined child custody evaluation practices in a circuit court over a 2-year period. The study examined adherence to the American Psychological Association practice guidelines as well as recommendations by Clark (1995). The authors conclude, "On the basis of this review of custody evaluations and others . . . we found that there are clearly a few areas frequently neglected by evaluators, including assessment of domestic violence and child abuse, adequate assessment of parenting skills, assessment of health status, formal psychological testing, and using multiple methods of information gathering" (Horvath et al., 2002, p. 563). Other reviews (Bow & Quinnell, 2001, p. 267) have painted a more optimistic appraisal of current practices, suggesting, "the present study indicates improvements in the scope and nature of child custody evaluations conducted by psychologists since publication of the Keilin and Bloom (1986) study. The type and range of data reportedly collected by psychologists was found to be diverse and thorough, as was the comprehensiveness of the process". Bow and Quinnell (2001) further state, "Overall, the practices and procedures used by the present study's group of psychologists closely follow APA Guidelines" (p. 267). The conflicting conclusions from these two reviews may be due to methodology. The Bow and Quinnell study, as well as earlier studies (e.g., Ackerman & Ackerman, 1977; Keilin & Bloom, 1986), were based on self-report surveys. The Horvath et al. (2002) study was based on content analysis of actual custody evaluations submitted to the court. It is possible that respondents completing surveys overestimate or exaggerate their practices with regard to custody evaluations, or simply indicate what they believe to be best practices and then perform differently given the perceived nuances of each particular evaluation (Horvath et al., 2002; Otto et al,, 2003).

Regardless of the reasons, there continues to be confusion regarding the appropriateness of various procedures used in custody evaluations. For example, authors have expressed concerns about the involvement of children in the decision process (Connell, 2004; Kuehnle, Connell, & Otto, 2004), the role of psychological testing (Krauss & Sales, 2000; National Interdisciplinary Colloquium on Child Custody, 1998; Otto et al., 2003), and even the level of competence and ethics among child custody evaluators (Benjamin & Gollan, 2003). Some professionals recommend home visits for the observation of children and parents (Collins, 1995; Gould, 1998). Other experienced clinicians state, "Home visits are to be avoided, if at all possible, because they lack standardization that could influence clinical judgment and require more evaluator time than in-office observations" (Benjamin & Gollan, 2003, p. 71). Based on the above discussion, it appears that there is no "standard of practice" for child custody evaluations (Bartol & Bartol, 2004).

In addition, clinicians do not appear to agree on appropriate assessment instruments. Indeed, not only do clinicians have a difficult time agreeing on appropriate tests, but also researchers have even disagreed on conclusions based on the same data sample used to report on testing practices. Two studies reported on the same survey data regarding psychological testing in child custody evaluations. Ackerman and Ackerman (1996) replicated one of the first studies looking at child custody evaluation practices (Keilin & Bloom, 1986). In the 10 years between the two studies, several changes occurred with regard to testing. The Ackerman and Ackerman study only examined the practice of doctoral-level psychologists. They found that 58% of the respondents reported using measures of intellectual functioning in their evaluations. The results also indicated that 92% of the psychologists used the MMPI/MMPI-2 in evaluations and the Rorschach Inkblot was the second most widely used test with adults. They noted a number of other tests used in evaluations such as the Bricklin Perceptual Scales (BPS; Bricklin, 1990) for children and the **Ackerman–Schoendorf Scales for Parent Evaluation of Custody** for adults (ASPECT; Ackerman & Schoendorf, 1992). Ackerman and Ackerman (1997) reported, "In conclusion, the Ackerman and Ackerman study demonstrated that psychologists have become more sophisticated in the custody evaluation process in that they utilize more test results, review more materials, and are less likely to make recommendations based on a single variable" (p. 144). Subsequent writers suggested that the study was quickly "becoming the standard of practice" with regard to child custody evaluations (Ackerman, 1999, p. 28).

However, Hagen and Castagna (2001) analyzed the same data used in the Ackerman and Ackerman (1997) study and arrived at decisively different conclusions. Rather than the percent of respondents who reported that they had ever used a test, Hagen and Castagna reported the percentage of evaluations in which a test had ever been used. Of the 43,195 evaluations performed in the nearly 20-year period, only the MMPI was used in more than one-third of the evaluations. The second most frequently used instrument, the Rorschach Inkblot, was used in 31% of the evaluations. The researchers concluded that "nothing approaching a *standard of practice* for test use in custody evaluations exists other than an estimated 84% frequency of use of the Minnesota Multiphasic Personality Inventory in the assessment of adults" (Hagen & Castagna, 2001, p. 269). They further state that "it would be highly misleading to represent to the public on the basis of existing data that there exists at the present time anything approaching a usual and customary practice much less an actual standard of practice for use of psychological tests in custody evaluations" (p. 271).

The above discussion highlights the lack of agreement in the profession regarding the use of psychological tests in child custody evaluations. The lack of consensus and questions regarding the value of testing in child custody evaluations makes the process all the more difficult for clinicians entering into this area of practice. The differing professionals' opinions can result in apparent incompetence of evaluators who are searching for mandated procedures or methods (Benjamin & Gollan, 2003). Perhaps what appears to be a reasonable suggestion is that a psychological test can only be used when specific issues related to what the test was designed to assess appear to be related to the custody decision (Melton et al., 2007). For example, an intellectual assessment may be conducted on a child who appears to have a learning disability that would require special educational needs. Or perhaps if a parent appeared to be suffering from a mental illness, such as depression, then a diagnostic test may be appropriate. The debate on psychological testing increases the potential for a battle of the experts in courtroom testimony, with one side criticizing the opposing side's expert for the use or nonuse of psychological tests.

## Adversarial Nature of Child Custody Evaluations

It is safe to assume that the vast majority of forensic psychologists understand the adversarial nature of the courtroom. Lawyers have an ethical responsibility to zealously protect their client's best interest. However, this adversarial role can become highly inflated by the emotionally charged win–lose outcome of child custody disputes. As stated above, the majority of divorcing couples with children under the age of 18 can negotiate custody arrangements without intervention by the courts. It is a minority of cases, perhaps as few as 10%, who wind up settling child custody disputes in court (Maccoby, Mnookin, Depner, & Peters, 1992; Melton et al., 1987). Frequently, these couples have tried and failed at reaching a compromise using mediation or other less adversarial methods. Custody disputes can be emotionally charged and disruptive to the families involved. Even the majority of cases heard by the courts typically do not involve testimony from a mental health expert (Melton et al., 2007). Evaluators are likely to come across hostile and combative parents, overinvolved and adversarial lawyers, and distressed children (Benjamin & Gollan, 2003). The evaluator needs to consider that he or she is observing a family in crisis and under a great deal of stress. The presentation of the parents and children may not at all be typical of the individuals' normal functioning.

Families involved in custody disputes exhibit high levels of hostility, ineffective problem-solving skills, and poor communication skills (Maccoby et al., 1992). Couples are hostile and express contempt and criticism toward each other. Frequently, there are allegations of parental misconduct exchanged between couples. These allegations can include restricting access to the children, domestic violence, child abuse, child neglect, and child sexual abuse (Benjamin & Gollan, 2003; Gardner, 1992; McIntosh & Prinz, 1993). The evaluator needs to distinguish between true and false accusations of child sexual abuse (Gardner, 1992; Kuehnle, 1996) along with other allegations of mistreatment (Oberlander, 1998). The evaluator may need to have a sexual abuse specialist investigate allegations of sexual abuse before the child custody evaluation can proceed, depending on the evaluator's expertise and local legal requirements.

Benjamin and Gollan (2003) provide standardized allegations forms for couples to use to list and document allegations regarding the other parent. The bulk of the evaluation may involve assessing the unresolved allegations of each parent. Evaluation of the parents frequently becomes a process in which each parent attempts to present him- or herself as the better parent while denigrating the parenting skills of the other. Licensing complaints against the evaluator may occur because of a perceived impartiality on the part of the evaluator. Evaluators must strive at all times to project the image of objectivity and impartiality. It is important for the evaluator to remember that parents are literally fighting for custody of their children and the stakes could hardly be higher.

Lawyers will also attempt to pull the evaluator into an adversarial position. Dr. Lenore Walker, a respected forensic psychologist, started the introduction to a symposium on child custody evaluations with the following comment: "No area in forensic psychology requires more skills than child custody. It is my least favorite area. Psychologists are treated with the greatest disrespect in Children's Court" (as cited in Wrightsman, 2001). Otto et al. (2003, p. 180) provide the following quote from an article written for attorneys working with clients in child custody disputes (Oddenino, 1994):

> Once the report comes out in your client's favor all you have to do is convince the court that this evaluator is truly an expert whose recommendations must be followed or the well-being of the client will be imperiled. Then again, if the evaluation is against your client, it is all psychobabble, erroneous data, and dangerous conclusions and clearly the court should not abdicate its responsibility to do what is right for the children because of the temptation to follow the specific recommendations of this charlatan.

Due to the intensity of the parents' emotions and zealotry of the lawyers' defense, it should be no surprise that child custody cases were second only to sexual misconduct cases with regards to the likelihood of licensing board complaints and malpractice lawsuits (Montgomery, Cupit, & Wimberly, 1999). One study found that 7–10% of ethics complaints filed are against child custody evaluators (Glassman, 1998). Frequently, formal complaints to the licensing board are without merit and result from a vengeful parent who lost in the custody hearing. In fact, out of 2,413 complaints filed in 34 states over a 10-year period, only 27 cases, or approximately 1%, resulted in disciplinary actions by the board (Kirkland & Kirkland, 2001). Most licensing boards use a screening process to determine if a complaint should move on to a full investigation (Van Horne, 2004). Nonetheless, a frivolous complaint can cause emotional and financial stress to the evaluator who must defend him- or herself before the licensing board. Nearly three out of four psychologists surveyed who had a complaint filed reported the experience as unpleasant or very unpleasant and indicated that their work was adversely affected by the complaint. A complaint, unfounded as well as valid, can affect malpractice insurance rates as well as ability to be on a provider list for certain managed-care companies.

Recently, two states have passed **immunity laws** that protect psychologists who conduct child custody evaluations from frivolous lawsuits. Both West Virginia and Florida have laws that allow psychologists to provide "**good faith**" custody evaluations without fear of being sued by a disgruntled parent. The laws no longer allow anonymous board complaints against a court-appointed evaluator and also stipulate that the complainant must pay for all legal fees for both parties if the judge rules that the suit is frivolous (Greer, 2004). If the evaluation was performed in "good faith," then the judge can rule the suit frivolous. For both states, good faith constitutes following the APA's *Guidelines for Child Custody Evaluations in Divorce Proceedings* (1994).

## Attitudes and Biases of Those Involved in the Decision-Making Process

The last complicating factor associated with child custody evaluations is the attitudes and biases of those involved in the decision-making process, including those of the evaluator. Everyone involved may approach the decision with their own biases and prejudices regarding childrearing and child custody. For example, an earlier assumption by the courts was that women are more capable than men at raising children. Although statute law has replaced this assumption, anecdotal evidence suggests that some judges and attorneys still hold the belief that women are better parents than men are (Otto et al., 2003). This perception of advantage to women in custody battles appears to be supported in that the majority of children are placed with the mother in custody proceedings (U.S. Bureau of the Census, 1989). This high rate of placement with the mother is in variance with wishes expressed by the father. Maccoby and Mnookin (1988) found that nearly one-third of the fathers reported that they had wanted to be the custodial parent, yet less than half of these fathers sought custody. Another study found that nearly 60% of the fathers had wanted custody, but only about one-third discusses their wishes with the children's mother (Weitzman, 1985).

Other issues that are affected by attitudes and prejudices are decisions involving mixed-race couples and same-sex couples. Wrightsman (2001) cites two cases in which judges overstepped their authority to support their own prejudices. In one example, a judge awarded custody of a 2-year-old child to the child's grandmother, citing the mother's homosexual orientation as a valid reason for losing custody. In another case, a judge transferred the custody of a white child from her white mother to the father because the mother had married an African American. It is reassuring to note that both decisions were eventually overturned.

With reference to mixed-race couples, some judges assume that the child's best interests are in placing him or her with the parent whom the child most closely resembles in terms of racial attributes (Sales et al., 1992). Attitudes can also influence judges' decisions regarding same-sex couples and a parent's sexual orientation. The evaluator needs to be familiar with the literature on sexual orientation, parenting, and child development (American Psychological Association, 1995; Falk, 1989; Patterson, 1995). Falk (1989) has identified erroneous assumptions held by judges regarding a mother's sexual orientation and child development. Among these assumptions are the unproven notions that children raised by homosexual parents are more likely to become homosexual themselves, children raised by homosexuals will have a difficult time establishing a gender identity, children raised by homosexuals are more likely to be victims of sexual molestation, and homosexuality is associated with mental illness. No research supports any of these uninformed assumptions. Rather, research suggests that children raised by same-sex couples are comparable to children raised by heterosexuals (American Psychological Association, 1995).

The political landscape surrounding divorce also poses some ethical and clinical complications (Melton et al., 2007). Writers have argued that mothers should retain custody of the children and argue that a mother who loses custody suffers more so than fathers. Others groups, such as the American Association of Retired Persons, have argued for greater involvement of the grandparents in custody decisions. Still others suggest children, the center of custody battles, should have more protections, such as making divorce more difficult for the parents.

The psychologist conducting the evaluation also needs to be aware of his or her own prejudices and misconceptions. These biases can also include assumptions regarding the presence of mental illness, substance abuse, or violent behavior in one of the parents, as well as the issues discussed previously. No single issue or fact should be routinely considered dispositive (deciding the final outcome of the case) in terms of custody unless it can be demonstrated that it is clearly detrimental to the child's well-being.

As previously mentioned, child custody evaluations can be some of the most complex work faced by a forensic psychologist. The involvement of multiple participants with conflicting agendas, lack of clarity and scientific support regarding the psycholegal question, lack of a standard of practice and appropriate assessment instruments, the intense, adversarial nature of the process, and the attitudes and prejudices of those involved all come together to make the child custody evaluation professionally challenging for the forensic psychologist. However, helping families to navigate successfully through an exceedingly difficult time can be quite rewarding. The skilled clinician who is aware of the potential pitfalls can avoid many missteps and assist families to move on after the divorce. We now turn to the roles psychologists can perform during the custody decision process.

# Psychologist's Roles

The psychologist may enter the arena of child custody evaluations from a variety of roles. A psychologist may be working with a couple in counseling that decides to divorce and seek assistance with custody arrangements. Similarly, a therapist may be treating a child whose parents are in the process of filing for a divorce. It appears logical to attorneys and judges that a psychologist treating a couple or child would be in an ideal position to offer an opinion on custody arrangements. However, such a role places the clinician in a **dual relationship**. It is nearly impossible for a treating therapist to offer an objective, impartial opinion regarding a client. A treating therapist who serves as an expert witness for the courts does a disservice to both his or her client and the courts. The therapeutic relationship is jeopardized by the clinician appearing as an impartial, objective expert and the impartiality of the therapist is easily called into question by an opposing attorney. The conflict of interest, or at least the appearance of a conflict of interest, should prevent clinicians from serving as both a therapist and evaluator (Strausburger, Gutheil, & Brodsky, 1997). The *Ethical Principles of Psychologists and Code of Conduct* (American Psychological Association, 2002) prohibits psychologists from functioning in **multiple relationships**. Some states prohibit psychologists from conducting custody evaluations in cases where they have treated the child (e.g., Petrila & Otto, 1996).

Psychologists may also function as a **mediator** for couples seeking to resolve differences on custody arrangements. Although training as a mediator varies, both attorneys and psychologists have served as mediators (Emery & Wyer, 1987). Frequently, a mediator will have training in either the legal or mental health professions along with specialized training in family and couple conflict and dispute resolution. Mediation, also termed **alternative dispute resolution**, gives couples the opportunity to resolve their differences in a more collaborative atmosphere than the adversarial tone of the courtroom. Mediation has received increased attention for a variety of reasons. As a practical alternative to expensive, drawn-out, and overscheduled family court proceedings, mediation attempts to reduce the tension of the custody dispute and increase compliance to custody arrangements. There is a movement among family law attorneys, called **collaborative law**, which attempts to have conflicted parties work together to avoid the adversarial nature of the legal system (Tesler, 1999). One survey of 161 family lawyers found positive attitudes toward divorce mediation as a desirable alternative to litigation (Lee, Beauregard, & Hunsley, 1998). As mentioned earlier, families in custody disputes have poor communication skills and reduced problem-solving abilities. Mediation strives to educate families on conflict resolution and communication skills, facilitate cooperation and negotiation, and develop a practical custody arrangement (Benjamin & Gollan, 2003).

There appear to be several advantages to mediation when compared to the traditional family court custody battle. Outcomes based on mediation have some advantages to court-mandated decisions, although there are also some drawbacks (Beck & Sales, 2001). For example, mediation offers the advantages of confidentiality and active participation by all parties in developing a workable plan. Mediation also appears to resolve disputes quicker and parents seem more satisfied than parents who used the courts. However, mediation is not focused on establishing the child's best interest. Rather, mediation attempts to find common ground between two disputing adults' positions, which may not represent the best interests of the child (Garber, 2004). Mediators cannot force parties to participate or disclose information relevant to the decision. The success of mediation has been questioned (Melton et al., 1997) and mediation does not appear to be particularly effective with highly conflicted couples (Garber, 2004; Ratner, 2001). Finally, individuals who choose mediation may surrender their legal and financial rights (Hysjulien, Wood, & Benjamin, 1994). Despite its shortcomings, it appears that compulsory mediation will continue to be an alternative to help alleviate the workload of the courts (Tondo, Coronel, & Drucker, 2001; Wrightsman, 2001).

Perhaps the most desirable role a psychologist can play in the child custody process is that of **court-appointed evaluator**. Child custody evaluators prefer to serve in an impartial capacity. One survey found that nearly 100% of psychologists surveyed indicated a preference to serve as a court-appointed evaluator or to be retained by both parents (Ackerman & Ackerman, 1997). The psychologist is appointed by the court to gather information for the decision maker, typically a judge (although some jurisdictions, such as Texas, use a jury). The psychologist has the opportunity to work impartially and is not beholden to either side. Custody evaluations are part of the legal system and are used

■ **Mediator**
Someone who helps opposing sides in a dispute come to an agreement; does not have the authority to make decisions. See Arbitrator.

■ **Court-appointed evaluator**
Mental health professional who is appointed by the court to gather information for the court.

by the trier of fact to determine legal outcomes (Benjamin & Gollan, 2003). The need for impartiality and appearance of objectivity cannot be overemphasized. In a "how-to" manual on custody evaluations, the authors recommend:

> The evaluator asks open-ended questions, takes detailed notes, and minimizes eye contact and other empathic contact. In addition to the reminder that no party confidences are permitted, the parents are told at the beginning of the interview that no feedback, advice, support, or discussion of known information or sources will occur. These prohibitions prevent the incidental confusion of role boundaries and sustain the practice of equitable time and process. (Benjamin & Gollan, 2003, p. 54)

The authors further suggest the use of a laptop computer during the interview to enter responses made by each party. They advise, "This approach allows for a further impersonalized stance and a detached objectivity" (Benjamin & Gollan, 2003, p. 60).

Aside from the impartiality of the court-appointed evaluator, there is another practical advantage to court-appointed evaluators. A recent survey of child custody evaluators found that the average cost of an evaluation for a family with two parents and two children was $3,335, with the range from $600 to $15,000 (Bow & Quinnell, 2001). This cost reflected an increase of 245% from a survey conducted 15 years earlier (Keilin & Bloom, 1986). Many families cannot afford to cover the cost of the evaluations. Because of the financial inaccessibility of private evaluators for families who may need assistance in resolving disputes, judicial systems employ mental health professionals to provide services to the court. Some jurisdictions appoint parenting coordinators to serve as mediators-arbiters resolving visitation issues and compliance (Garber, 2004).

Opportunities to work with child custody decisions are not only open to clinicians or counselors conducting therapy, mediation, or evaluations. Legal psychologists serve in custody decisions as expert witnesses testifying on social science research. **Social framework testimony** presents conclusions based on social science research to assist the trier of fact in reaching a decision (Monahan & Walker, 1988). The legal psychologist may testify on a wide range of issues regarding child custody disputes. For example, research on how a child's adjustment is affected by various child custody

■ **Social framework testimony**
Expert testimony that presents conclusions based on social science research to assist the court in making a decision.

**Table 8.2**  **Areas in Which Legal Psychologists May Testify as Expert Witnesses**

- Impact of parents on child development
  - Mental disorder of a parent
  - Parenting practices
- Effects of divorce on child development
- Parental/marital conflict and children's adjustment
- Economics and remarriage
- Additionally, issues such as assessing child allegations of abuse and children's testimony

arrangements, being raised by same-sex couples or mixed-race couples, and the effects of divorce on children would all be fodder for expert witness testimony in custody evaluations. For example, a developmental psychologist may testify how different custody arrangements, such as joint or sole custody, influence a child's emotional adjustment postdivorce. A clinician could inform the court about research documenting the negative impact domestic violence has on children. Table 8.2 presents a few examples of research areas on which legal psychologists may be asked to testify to educate the trier of fact.

# Current State of Child Custody in Divorce Proceedings

The rate of divorce has increased dramatically over the past 40 years, nearly doubling since 1960 (Hughes, 1996). Relationships with children tend to have an even higher rate of discord, with nearly 64% of all relationships with children ending in separation (Castro-Martin & Bumpass, 1989). Due to the increase number of divorces, numerous children are growing up in families marked by parental hostility and separation. Fifty to sixty percent of children born in the early 1980s will live with only one parent before they turn 18 (Glick, 1984). Estimates indicate approximately 1.4 million divorces occur per year in the United States (National Center for Health Statistics, 2001). Studies suggest that between 36 and 48% of divorcing couples report having children under 18 years old (Clark, 1995). However, anywhere from 70% (Maccoby & Mnookin, 1988) to 85% (McIntosh & Prinz, 1993) of divorcing couples are able to agree on custody arrangements. Mothers become the primary parent in the vast majority of divorces, with over 84% of the children living with the mother postdivorce (U.S. Bureau of the Census, 1989). However, there has been an increase in the number of single-father families in recent years, although the norm continues to be single-mother families, comprising over four-fifths of all one-parent families (Hernandez, 1993; U.S. Bureau of the Census, 1998).

Approximately 10% of families going through divorce are unable to negotiate custody arrangements and resort to litigation (Maccoby et al., 1992). Still, nearly one-third of families that reach a mediated resolution report continued hostility and conflict regarding care of the children (Wallerstein & Lewis, 1998). Disagreements over child-care, discipline, visitation arrangements, and parental access interfere with maintaining a positive parent–child relationship. Continued conflict between parents after the divorce places the children at risk for serious and long-term emotional harm (Amato, 2001; Kelly, 2000). Even parents who are able to separate cordially may experience impaired parenting skills during the divorce process that can affect the emotional and physical well-being of the children (Kalter, Kloner, Schreier, & Okla, 1989). Research indicates that conflict during the divorce process can have long-lasting negative effects persisting into young adulthood (Frost & Pakiz, 1990; Sorenson & Goldman, 1990). On the other hand, positive parental behavior increases the chances for a successful adjustment to divorce by children (Buchanan, Maccoby, & Dornbusch, 1991; Hetherington, 1989). Custody arrangements appear to interact with level of parental conflict regarding children's adjustment. In low-conflict families, adolescents in joint physical custody appear better adjusted than adolescents in joint physical custody in high-conflict families (Maccoby & Mnookin, 1992). In high-conflict families, sole custody appears to be a preferred alternative to joint custody (Johnston, 1995). Parental conflict, both before and after divorce, plays a fundamental role in children's adjustment. The level of interparental conflict needs to be considered when formulating custody recommendations and parenting plans (Otto et al., 2003).

In families with a high amount of conflict, sole custody appears to be in the best interest of the child. © 2009 Andresr. Used under license from Shutterstock, Inc.

■ **Tender-years doctrine**
Assumes the mother is the most appropriate parent for young children.

■ **Same-sex parenting**
The belief that a boy living with his father and a girl living with her mother was necessary for the adjustment of the child; was an early consideration regarding child custody decisions.

Recently, some states have attempted to change custody laws as an effort to reduce the animosity between parents. For example, Florida enacted a new law effective October 2008. The new law has done away with terms such as custodial and noncustodial parent as well as primary residential and secondary residential parent. Additionally, the term "visitation" has been replaced with *time-sharing*. Custody arrangements will now be referred to as the *parenting plan*. Some attorneys and parents have argued that changing terms will do little to change the process. Only an evaluation of changes as the law starts to have an impact will clarify whether this new terminology will have a significant impact.

# Child Custody Laws

At the beginning of the 19th century, children were considered property and women were not allowed to own property. Thus, in cases of divorce, children were awarded to the father. However, the **tender-years doctrine** was introduced around the mid-19th century and was gradually adopted in all jurisdictions. The tender-years doctrine assumes that the mother is the most appropriate parent for young children, and particularly female children, since the mother can provide the tender care children need (Wyer, Gaylord, & Grove, 1987). The father could only gain custody by demonstrating that the mother was an unfit parent, effectively placing the burden of proof on the father.

A number of factors converged in the 1960s that led to significant changes in family law. The 1960s witnessed an emergence in fathers' rights, equitable division of assets and property, no-fault divorce, and challenges to sexist presumptions regarding the superiority of mothers as better caretakers based solely on sex (Otto et al., 2003). Additionally, research was accumulating documenting the negative effects of divorce on children. Lawmakers searched for ways to minimize the deleterious effects of divorce on children, moving toward a more child-oriented approach to custody decisions (Benjamin & Gollan, 2003). The tender-years doctrine was replaced with the best interests of the child standard upon passage of the **Uniform Marriage and Divorce Act** (1979). The best interest standard dictates that the custody arrangements of children should be made in the children's best interests as opposed to the individual interests of the parents. The best interests of the child standard is the prevailing standard in all U.S. jurisdictions (Rohman et al., 1987). Table 8.3 summarizes the various standards that have been used to resolve child custody cases.

As interpreted in state laws, the best interest of the child standard provides greater weight to evidence from the following domains:

1. the wishes of the parents;
2. the children's wishes regarding their preferred custodial parent, assuming that the children are mature enough to offer an opinion;
3. relationships and interactions of the children with parents, siblings, and others who significantly affect the children's lives;
4. the children's adjustment to home, school, and the community; and
5. the psychological and physical health of all individuals (Benjamin & Gollan, 2003).

There was a brief period when commentators felt that **same-sex parenting** (boys living with their fathers and girls living with their mothers) was necessary for good adjustment. This assumption was based mainly on a study with a rather small sample size (Santrock & Warshak, 1979). A larger study with over 20,000 participants found very little difference between the adjustment of children living with the same-sex parent and the opposite-sex parent (Powell & Downey, 1997).

States have attempted to operationalize the best interests standard to assist decision makers and custody evaluators. However, jurisdictions differ widely in how they interpret the best interest standard. Some states list factors related to each parent's capacity and skills including psychological health and ability to successfully coparent and support each child's attachment to each parent (Benjamin & Gollan, 2003). Despite the differences among jurisdictions, there also appears to be important consistencies from state to state (Schutz, Dixon, Lindenberger, & Ruther, 1989). For example, most states will consider a history of spousal abuse, substance abuse, child abuse, or mental illness when deciding custody arrangements. Some commentators have suggested that the best interests standard has functioned as the "best parent" standard. Although the law is child-focused, the breadth of the law allows for a review of parental attributes. The custody evaluation becomes a process of each parent parading their parenting skills and healthy relationships with the children to the evaluator while at the same time denigrating the other parent's skills (Benjamin & Gollan, 2003).

Judges, as the fact finder, have wide discretion in how they weigh the evidence in custody decisions. Due to the breadth of the law, judges can be guided by their own idiosyncratic beliefs regarding a child's best interest and parenting skills when deciding on custody arrangements. For example, a number of states have used Michigan's 1970 Child Custody Act as a model to develop legislation identifying factors to consider when determining the child's best interest. This approach attempts to operationalize and define the best interests standard legislatively (Otto et al., 2003). One of the factors proposed is the "moral fitness" of the parties involved. Still, how moral fitness, as well as many of the other factors, is defined can vary from jurisdiction to jurisdiction. As an example, see Table 8.4 for factors the state of Florida considers in determining the best interest of the child (Petrila & Otto, 1997, p. 156).

One difficulty with the best interest standard is the lack of consensus as to what constitutes important parenting skills. Researchers have the opportunity to educate the courts by identifying what factors lead to parental success and what factors contribute to parental failure (Benjamin & Gollan, 2003). It is also necessary for the

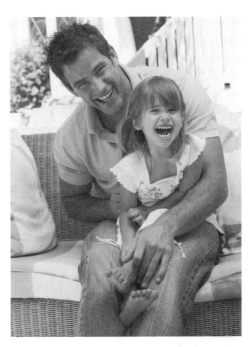

**Figure 8.5**

There is very little difference between the adjustment of children living with their same-sex or opposite-sex parent.
© 2009 Monkey Business Images. Used under license from Shutterstock, Inc.

## Standards for Resolution of Child Custody        Table 8.3

- *Tender-years doctrine*: presumes that the best interests of young children and the best interests of girls of any age is awarding custody to the mother, assuming she is fit
  - Puts the burden of proof on the father to show that the mother is unfit
- *Best interests of the child standard*–Uniform Marriage and Divorce Act (1979)
  - Mental and physical health of all involved
  - Child's adjustment to his or her home, community, and school
  - Each parent's ability to provide care
  - Relationship of child with parents and other individuals
  - Wishes of the parents and child

■ **Least detrimental standard**
A standard used in child custody evaluations that attempts to identify the custody resolution that does the least amount of harm to the children.

evaluator to know how the jurisdiction in which he or she is functioning interprets the law. The **least detrimental standard** has been proposed as an alternative to the best interest standard. This alternative proposal presumes that all children are harmed by divorce to some extent. The aim is to identify the resolution that appears to do the least amount of harm to the children (American Academy of Child and Adolescent Psychiatry, 1997).

| **Table 8.4** | **Considerations in Determining Best Interests of the Child in Florida** |
|---|---|

- The parent who is more likely to allow the child frequent and continuing contact with the nonresidential parent
- The love, affection, and other emotional ties existing between the parents and the child
- The capacity and disposition of the parents to provide the child with food, clothing, medical care, and other material needs
- The length of time that the child has lived in a stable, satisfactory environment and the desirability of maintaining continuity
- The permanence, as a family unit, of the existing and proposed custodial homes
- The moral fitness of the parents
- The mental and physical health of the parents
- The home, school, and community record of the child
- The reasonable preference of the child, if the court considers the child to be of sufficient intelligence, understanding, and experience to express a preference
- The willingness and ability of each parent to encourage a close and continuing parent–child relationship between the child and the other parent
- Any other factors that may be relevant

# The Legal Relevance of Mental Health Professionals' Recommendations

There appears to be some confusion in the literature regarding the importance judges and attorneys place on custody evaluations when making custody decisions. Some commentators have suggested that judges and attorneys cautiously consider the input from custody evaluations when making their decisions (Otto, Edens, & Barcus, 2000). Custody evaluations by mental health professionals appear to play an important role as an independent information-gathering tool (Settle & Lowery, 1982). However, several studies found more skepticism among the decision makers regarding the value of custody evaluations. One survey study reported that expert testimony was no more than occasionally useful in custody decisions (Melton, Weithorn, & Slobogin, 1985) and another study reported that only 2% of judges surveyed identified mental health professionals' recommendations as one of the top five factors in reaching a decision (Felner, Rowlison, Farber, Primavera, & Bishop, 1987). Based on these and other

## Child Custody Decisions: A King Solomon's Solution?

Jack K. and Sally L. met at a "Parents without Partners" picnic. Jack was 2 years past a divorce and had his three children, all girls under 7 years old, for the weekend. A friend suggested attending the picnic so that the children might have some friends around and Jack could interact with other adults. Sally had a 2-year-old son and was never married. She was dating a man and had an unplanned pregnancy. She did not want to marry the father and decided to raise the child on her own. The father of the boy has not been involved in his life.

Jack and Sally hit it off and married 18 months after meeting. Both Jack and Sally love children and decided to have more children. Sally gives up her career as a pharmacist with the decision to raise the children. Jack owns a construction business and can easily support the family. Jack and Sally have another two children over the next 5 years. Jack continues to have weekend custody with his three children from his previous marriage and his children from the previous marriage spend 1 month during the summer with the new family.

However, after 7 years of marriage to Sally, Jack decides he wants a divorce and wishes to remarry his first wife. Sally is taken totally by surprise and learns that Jack has been having an affair with his ex-wife for the past 3 years of their marriage. Jack wants to have full custody of the two children he had with Sally along with Sally's first son. Her first son developed a strong attachment to Jack and thinks of Jack as his biological father. Jack and his first wife file for full custody of all the children and threaten a long, drawn-out court battle. Sally wants full custody of all of her biological children and does not want to separate her family. She also countersues for shared custody of Jack's three girls as she and the girls have established a family bond.

The court appoints Dr. Evelyn King, a forensic psychologist, to make child custody recommendations to the court.

Please decide who should have custody of whom; and what type of custody arrangements should be made based on the information above.

What other information would be important to gather? How did you reach your decisions?

What standard(s) did you consider in reaching your decisions? Did you noticed any personal biases swaying your decision?

The children involved include: Jack's three girls from his previous marriage, Sally's first son from her earlier relationship, and Jack and Sally's two children.

studies, some commentators have suggested that "mental health professionals are not routinely consulted by judges" and "only a few judges include evaluation by a mental health professional" in the decision-making process (Wrightsman, 2001, p. 296).

On the other hand, Horvath et al. (2002) compared mental health professionals' custody recommendations to the judges' custody rulings in a circuit court over a 2-year period. They report, "it appeared that judges and attorneys frequently considered recommendations of the evaluators, as reflected in the similar rulings of the court; however, final rulings were rarely exactly as recommended" (pp. 562–563). Indeed, the rulings were exactly as recommended by the evaluator in 27.3% of the cases and quite similar with minor modifications in 63.6% of the cases. In only 9.1% of the cases did the judge's ruling go completely counter to the evaluator's recommendation. Horvath et al. conclude, "This suggests that in the majority of the cases in this study, judges, parents, and attorneys rely heavily on evaluator recommendations when deciding arrangements for child custody" (p. 562).

There are several possible reasons for the conflicting results. Many of the studies indicating a low reliance on the evaluations were self-report surveys. Judges and attorneys may perceive their decisions as independent from the mental health professionals' recommendations and not realize how heavily they rely on the evaluator's opinion. Alternatively, judges and attorneys may wish to present the appearance of independence and respond accordingly in self-report surveys. In fact, during a presentation at the annual meeting of the American Psychological Association, a judge emphatically pointed out to psychologists, "*You* are not making the custody or visitation decision: I am" (Freedman, 1995, original emphasis). Another possibility for the differing conclusions is that the data reflect how the decision-making process is conducted in different jurisdictions. All the studies were conducted in different localities and may reflect the norms of the family court for that particular jurisdiction. An interesting study would be to survey judges and attorneys regarding the value of custody evaluations and then to compare the judges' ruling to the evaluators' recommendations in the same jurisdiction. It would then be possible to compare judges' self-reports regarding the use of the evaluation with their final decision. Although this would not indicate if the judge used the mental health professional's evaluation to make the decision, a finding similar to the Horvath et al. (2002) study would suggest that mental health professionals' evaluations do indeed play a significant role in the decision-making process. It is possible that judges and attorneys, inundated with a plethora of information and the burden of a difficult decision, are simply not cognizant of the significant impact mental health professionals' recommendations have on their rulings.

# Types of Custody Arrangements

An assortment of custody arrangements exists, with no clear research to suggest that one form of custody is superior to the other. Laws regarding custody address both decision-making authority and physical residence of the children. Decision-making authority, referred to here as **legal parental authority**, refers to who has the decision-making role regarding the child's long-term welfare. For example, legal parental authority addresses issues such as which school the child will attend, what religion the child will adopt, and issues related to medical care. **Physical authority**, addressing the children's physical residence or placement, involves decisions affecting the child's daily activities. Physical authority deals with decisions such as where the child goes to play during the day, curfew times, dating rules, and participation in extracurricular activities after school. The courts make rulings on the living arrangements and visitation rights of the noncustodial parent as well as the parents' decision-making rights regarding their children's long-term welfare. The courts can mix these decisions, giving one parent legal authority and splitting physical authority between the two parents. The various combinations are discussed below and are presented in Table 8.5 (Bartol & Bartol, 2004).

The custody arrangements address both legal parental authority and physical authority. **Sole custody** means that one parent has both physical and legal authority over the children. **Joint custody** requires that the parents share legal authority but the children reside predominantly with one parent. For example, the children may live with the mother during the week and spend alternate weekends along with several weeks during the summer with the father. However, the children would tend to view their primary residence as the mother's home. Both the mother and the father, sharing legal authority, would need to cooperatively work together to make decisions regarding long-term issues, such as which school to attend, religious practices, and health care concerns. Joint custody has gradually become the preferred form of custody in family court. However, as mentioned above, the research on custody arrangements is equivocal at best. Joint custody requires successful co-parenting between the mother and the father. In highly conflicted couples, this may not always be possible. Evaluators need to consider the likelihood of the parents cooperatively participating in the rearing of the children (Connell, 2004).

Other types of arrangements, though less common, include **divided custody**, **limited joint custody**, and **split custody**. Divided custody alternates both physical and

■ **Legal parental authority**
The decision-making role regarding the child's long-term welfare; used in child custody decisions.

■ **Physical authority**
The decision-making role affecting daily activities and with whom the child lives; used in child custody evaluations.

■ **Sole custody**
One parent has both physical and legal authority over the child; used in child custody decisions.

■ **Joint custody**
In child custody cases the parents share legal authority but the children reside predominantly with one parent.

■ **Limited joint custody**
A child custody arrangement in which both parents share legal authority, but one parent has exclusive physical authority.

legal authority between parents on a rotating basis. A child may live with one parent during the school year or while attending middle school, and then reside with the other parent during the summer, or during high school, respectively. Limited joint custody allows parents to share legal authority but one parent maintains exclusive physical authority over the children. Lastly, split custody involves custody disputes with more than one child. In a Solomon-like solution, legal and physical custody of one or more children are awarded to one parent and legal and physical authority of the remaining children are awarded to the other parent.

There have been numerous studies comparing types of custody arrangements and children's adjustment. However, the research results do not provide a definitive answer as well-designed studies offer different conclusions (Krauss & Sales, 2000). Part of the problem is the complexity of the question. One cannot simply ask whether joint custody is preferable to sole custody. Many other factors need to be considered, such as the age and sex of the children; the level of hostility between the parents; the economic resources of each parent; presence of spousal, child, or substance abuse by either parent; the personality characteristics of the children and adults; and the quality of the relationship among the children and adults (parenting styles, capabilities, etc.). Although a few truisms exist, such as the deleterious effects of witnessing domestic violence or parental substance abuse (Otto et al., 2003), many custody decisions need to be decided on a case-by-case basis absent any more definitive research data.

## Types of Custody Arrangements

**Table 8.5**

- Legal parental authority—concerns the decision-making authority of the child's long-term welfare
- Physical authority—involves decisions affecting only the child's daily activities
- Sole custody—one parent has both legal and physical authority
- Divided custody—each parent has legal and physical decision-making powers on an alternate basis
- Joint custody—both parents share legal authority but the children live predominantly with one parent
- Limited joint custody—both parents share legal authority but one parent is given exclusive physical authority
- Split custody—legal and physical authority of one or more children is awarded to one parent and legal and physical authority of the remaining children to the other

# Professional Organizations' Guidelines for Child Custody Evaluations

Although the law determines the decision-making process in child custody evaluations, guidelines and standards published by professional organizations provide the examiner with some direction regarding the evaluation process (Otto et al., 2003). To date, three professional organizations have developed guidelines for conducting child custody evaluations. See Table 8.6 for the list of professional organizations' guidelines for child custody evaluations. The different organizations' guidelines are an attempt to standardize the process of custody evaluations. However, the standards have been criticized as being both too broad and lacking in direction or conflicting with one another, only adding to the confusion (Otto et al., 2003). The American Psychological Association (1994), the Association of Family and Conciliation Courts (n.d.), and the American Academy of Child and Adolescent Psychiatry (1997) have all published practice recommendations for conducting child custody evaluations. Most practitioners agree that a forensic psychologist's failure to perform an evaluation in accord with the APA's guidelines would amount to substandard practice (Otto et al., 2003). Although psychologists may not be required, in the strictest sense, to adhere to the other professional organizations' guidelines, it is recommended that an evaluator is familiar with all published guidelines.

## Table 8.6   Professional Organizations' Guidelines for Child Custody Evaluations

1. Guidelines for Child Custody Evaluations in Divorce Proceedings
     American Psychological Association
2. Model Standards of Practice for Child Custody Evaluations
     Association of Family and Conciliation Courts
3. Practice Parameters of Child Custody Evaluation
     American Academy of Child and Adolescent Psychiatry

Perhaps the most comprehensive guidelines are the recent practice parameters for custody evaluations published by the American Academy of Child and Adolescent Psychiatry (AACAP; 1997). These guidelines address both the process as well as substantive issues involved in the evaluation. For example, the guidelines address areas of inquiry for the evaluator as well as evaluation techniques (Otto et al., 2003). See Table 8.7 for an overview of areas covered by the AACAP guidelines. Interestingly, these guidelines have been criticized for minimizing the usefulness of psychological testing in the evaluation process. Otto et al. (2003) suggest that this recommendation reflects guild concerns more so than a valid appraisal of the role of testing in custody evaluations. As you may recall from previous chapters, one area of expertise that distinguishes psychologists from other mental health professionals is training in psychological assessment. Psychiatrists, on the other hand, receive little if any training in psychological testing. Guidelines published by a psychiatric association that admonish against testing may be politically motivated as opposed to scientifically based. Students should note that publications such as practice guidelines are, to some extent, political documents protecting guild interests (Otto et al., 2003). With that caveat in mind, we turn to the American Psychological Association's *Guidelines for Child Custody Evaluations in Divorce Proceedings* (1994).

The APA *Guidelines for Child Custody Evaluations in Divorce Proceedings* address the format and the process of the evaluation. The Guidelines are divided into three

## Summary of AACAP Practice Parameters for Child Custody Evaluations
**Table 8.7**

- Conceptual Models
  - Tender-years standard
  - Best interest of the child standard
  - Least detrimental alternative standard
  - Mediation
- Role of the Evaluator
  - Distinction between forensic and clinical work
  - Avoidance of dual relationships
  - Ethical considerations
- Issues in Child Custody Disputes
  - Continuity of care
  - Parent–child attachments
  - Child preferences (children older than the age of 12)
  - Parental alienation from a child
  - Children with special needs (handicap, illness, etc.)
  - Educational plans for the child
  - Gender issues (same-sex parenting)
  - Sibling relationships
  - Parents' physical and emotional health
  - Parents' employment schedules
  - Parenting skills and discipline styles
  - Conflict resolution skills among family members
  - Child's social support system
  - Cultural issues
  - Evaluator's own ethical and value issues
  - Religious upbringing
- Special Issues in Custody Disputes
  - Infants
  - Homosexual parents
  - Stepparents' and grandparents' rights
  - Parental kidnapping
  - Relocation problems
  - Allegations of sexual abuse
  - Reproductive technology (frozen embryos, etc.)
- The Evaluative Process
  - Referrals
  - Parent interviews and issues to be discussed
  - Child interviews and issues to be discussed
  - Collateral information
- Written report
- Courtroom testimony

sections: Orienting guidelines, General guidelines, and Procedural guidelines (see Table 8.8). **Orienting guidelines** address the approach the psychologist takes toward the evaluation process. This includes the purpose of the evaluation, the best interest standard, and a focus on parenting capacity. The **General guidelines** address ethical issues regarding the general practice of forensic psychology and the explicit practice of child custody evaluations. These guidelines specify that the evaluator has specialized knowledge in the area of custody evaluations, avoids multiple relationships, serves as an impartial expert to the court, and is aware of potential biases. The **Procedural guidelines** address the process of the evaluation, although they do not offer specific suggestions as to which techniques to use. Rather, the Procedural guidelines reinforce the issue of obtaining informed consent and stressing the lack of confidentiality in forensic assessments. The Procedural guidelines do recommend the use of multiple methods to obtain information, such as interviews, collateral sources of information, and testing. The guidelines also stress that opinions are offered only on individuals who were evaluated. Thus, an evaluator should not offer an opinion on a person's parenting ability if that parent was not interviewed. Finally, guidelines stress the importance of financial arrangements as well as record keeping. As has been stated, the guidelines appear to be obvious and therefore, not objectionable. However, they are fairly broad and do not provide much guidance concerning the substantive areas of inquiry (Otto et al., 2003).

**Table 8.8** APA Guidelines for Child Custody Evaluations in Divorce Proceedings

- Orienting Guidelines
  - Purpose of evaluation is to assess best psychological interests of the child
  - Child's interests and well-being are paramount
  - Focus is on parenting capacity, developmental needs of the child
- General Guidelines
  - Psychologist is an impartial, objective expert
  - Psychologist has specialized competence
  - Psychologist is aware of personal and societal biases
  - Psychologist avoids multiple relationships
- Procedural Guidelines
  - Scope of evaluation determined by evaluator
  - Informed consent is obtained
  - Participants understand limits of confidentiality
  - Multiple methods are used to gather information
  - Evaluator does not go beyond the data
  - Opinions offered only on individuals who were evaluated
  - Recommendations are based on best psychological interests of the child
  - Clarifies financial arrangements
  - Maintains written records/documentation

# The Evaluation Process

It should be apparent that there is no standard of practice in the field regarding custody evaluations. Some experts recommend home visits, others caution against home visits; some experts suggest psychological testing, others state that testing is useless. Even the research is equivocal regarding child custody evaluation procedures and placement recommendations. The following discussion is restricted to a brief outline of what must be accomplished in an evaluation. The goal is to provide the student with an overview of the process, and not to provide a "how-to" manual for child custody evaluations. For the interested reader, there are several texts that provide detailed suggestions on conducting child custody evaluations (e.g., Benjamin & Gollan, 2003; Schultz et al., 1989; Stahl, 1994).

Despite conflicting suggestions on assessment procedures, there are a few procedures consistently recommended. All commentators recommend informed consent for all parties involved, including lawyers, parents, children, and any collateral sources of information, such as teachers and daycare workers. Although children under 18 years old cannot provide consent, they can provide their assent to the process. Informed consent should be written, signed, and a copy provided to each participant. The consent should indicate the limits of confidentiality of the information, the purpose of the evaluation, to whom the information will be released, and the impartiality of the evaluator. The informed consent should also document fee structures, what occurs when one of the parties fails to comply with the evaluation, how the evaluation process will proceed, a time line for the various procedures to be used, and that there will be no feedback from the evaluator during the process. The evaluator should make clear at the beginning of the process to all parties involved his or her role as the evaluator and not as a therapist or mediator. Everyone should understand that the evaluator is impartial and is not on "someone's side." Additionally, parties should understand that the role of the evaluator is to complete an assessment and report to the court. The evaluator is not functioning in a therapeutic role and cannot affirm or provide information to either side. Any procedure completed with one parent should also be completed with the other parent. For example, if the evaluator conducts a home visit with the mother, then a home visit with the father should also be conducted. This consistency among all parties helps to standardized the assessment as well as limit any appearance of partiality.

Another broadly agreed-upon recommendation is the need for the use of multiple data sources. Multiple data sources would include interviews with all parties involved and third-party collaterals, observations, review of relevant records (e.g., medical, legal, academic, and occupational files), and psychological testing. Evaluators should plan to interview all individuals involved, such as parents, children, and any stepparents or stepsiblings. The two parents should be interviewed together, if possible. In addition, each parent should be interviewed alone and together with each child. If the children are over the age of 3, they too may be interviewed individually, with the interview content adjusted to the child's age group. Most commentators recommend against asking younger children their preference for the custodial parent. There is debate regarding asking older children, usually the age of 12 and older, regarding their preference. Evaluators also need to be alert to children who have been coached by a parent to respond in a particular way.

A cautious approach would be to also interview other significant adults in the child's life, such as daycare workers, schoolteachers, physicians, and so on, particularly if interviews with the parents or children raise any unanswered questions. Some state laws require that psychologists conducting evaluations attempt to make contact with all parties involved including medical or mental health professionals who are treating the child. All individuals interviewed should be informed that no information is private

and any information revealed in the course of the interview can and may become part of the official public record.

## Assessment Interviews

Interviews should be thorough and cover a wide range of issues. Benjamin and Gollan (2003) provide a semistructured interview for adults and for adolescents. Prior to the interview, each parent is asked to complete the Parenting History Survey (PHS; Greenberg & Humphreys, 1998), a 32-page, 107-item questionnaire. This instrument covers a wide range of topics using checklists and a short-answer format. It provides an economical and efficient way to collect a wealth of information prior to the first interview. See Table 8.9 for a list of topics covered in the interview with parents and Table 8.10 for topics covered during the interviews with children (adapted from Benjamin & Gollan, 2003; Otto et al., 2003). It is not uncommon to interview the parents and children on more than one occasion. Good practice recommends a closing interview after all the information is gathered, including any psychological testing and collateral reports, to clarify any discrepancies and to allow the parents to present any additional information that they feel will assist the evaluator to form an opinion.

## Direct Observation

Most commentators recommend observing the children and parents interact. Ideally, the evaluator can observe the children interacting with each parent separately in some form of structured activity. Evaluators with an observation room and a one-way mirror may have the parent and child interact in the room while observing behind the mirror. On the other hand, the evaluator may watch unobtrusively while in

## Table 8.9   Topics for the Parental Inquiry During Child Custody Evaluation

- Demographics
- Mental status
- Family history
- Social history
- Educational history
- Occupational history
- Medical history
- Mental health history
- Substance use history
- Legal history
- Financial status
- Health status
- Dating and sexual history
- Current dating activity
- Description of marital history and family structure
- Developmental status of all the children
- Description of parenting strengths and weaknesses
- Prior and current relationship with the children and role in raising the children
- Current and anticipated living and working arrangements
- Current emotional functioning and reaction to the divorce and custody dispute
- Concerns regarding the other parent, including any allegations of misconduct
- History of child abuse, neglect, and interparental violence
- Document all allegations

| Topics for the Child Inquiry During Child Custody Evaluation | Table 8.10 |
| --- | --- |

- Mental status exam
- School history
- Extracurricular activities
- Feelings toward parents, current living situation, future living arrangements, and visitation with non-custodial parent
- Description of relationship with each parent including discipline, mutual activities
- Feelings toward siblings
- Emotional and physical health
- Prior or current substance use
- Legal history
- Allegations of abuse or neglect or interparental hostility/violence

the room, or record the interaction on videotape to be observed later. Commentators recommend the videotaping of interactions for review later to garnish additional information that may be missed during a live observation.

For the interaction, the evaluator may ask the parent and child to play a game or have the parent teach the child material slightly above their current grade level. Interactions are designed to observe the nature of the parent–child relationship, parenting skills, and the parent's responsiveness to the child's needs. Benjamin and Gollan (2003) recommend interrupting the parent–child interaction for the parent to complete a behavioral checklist about the child, such as the Achenbach Child Behavior Checklist (Achenbach, 1991). These authors suggest that the interruption provides an opportunity for the evaluator to observe the parent's flexibility and ability to manage multiple tasks simultaneously. Regardless of the structure of the interaction, the evaluator's goal is to gain information regarding the parent–child interactions and the relationship between the two. Unfortunately, most clinicians receive very little formal training in observing parent–child interactions and forming opinions about the relationships based on these observations. As previously noted, professionals disagree on the value of a home visit. Some authors recommend home visits as a way to put children at ease and allow them to interact with the parent in a familiar environment. Others caution against home visits, partly due to the time investment required for travel and observation.

## Collateral Sources

In addition to interviews with relevant third-party individuals discussed previously, the evaluator should attempt to obtain other relevant collateral information. For example, in addition to speaking with schoolteachers, the evaluator should review academic records. If allegations of spousal abuse are present, any legal or medical records that document abuse should be obtained. Failure of legal or medical documentation of spousal abuse does not indicate the allegation is false, however, since arrests for domestic violence vary due to a number of factors (Hall, 2005). Regardless, the evaluator should review any information that supports or contradicts allegations. There are no set standards regarding types of third-party information that should be gathered. This decision is up to the discretion of the psychologist and requires thinking like a private investigator regarding what sorts of information to request.

Third-party information should be used judiciously in forming opinions. First, information may be confidential and only accessible through formal release by interested parties. As such, information available to the evaluator may be biased or slanted to influence the evaluator's opinion. Other third-party information, though not confidential or privileged, may only be released by the third party with the parent's consent. For example, a daycare owner may be unwilling to release childcare records to the evaluator without the parent's permission. Furthermore, some information may be illegally obtained and not permissible as evidence. Examples would include audio- or videotapes made without the parties' consent. A hypothetical example is the clandestine videotaping of a father–daughter interaction by the mother to obtain images that harm the father's petition for custody. Alternatively, the father may have stolen personal notes the mother wrote to a current romantic partner and present these notes to the evaluator as evidence of the mother's moral fitness. If the evaluator believes third-party information may have been obtained illegally, he or she should consult with the attorneys involved before reviewing the information (Otto et al., 2003).

All third parties supplying information should know how the information is to be used. Collaterals should understand that they are providing information that will be used in a child custody decision and that the information is not private and anything they reveal may be included in a report to the court as well as in testimony before the court. This includes interviews with third parties as well as requests for information from third parties. For example, a schoolteacher or childcare worker should know the purpose of any records released to the evaluator.

## Psychological Testing

As previously discussed, there is a debate about the value of psychological testing in child custody evaluations. Many of the instruments traditionally used by psychologists do not address issues related to the custody decision. For example, measures of intellectual assessment have little relevance to the best interests of the child standard. The clinician must infer from the rather global construct of intelligence to a more specific behavior relevant to child custody decisions (Otto et al., 2003). Additional confusion is created by the lack of agreement about current testing practices. Despite at least four surveys of child custody evaluators (Ackerman & Ackerman, 1997; Bow & Quinnell, 2001; Keilin & Bloom, 1986; LaFortune & Carpenter, 1998), there continues to be confusion regarding testing procedures used in evaluations. A reexamination of the Ackerman and Ackerman data by Hagen and Castagna (2001) further contributed to the confusion. Finally, content analysis of actual child custody evaluation reports by Horvath et al. (2002) indicated wide variability in terms of testing by professional degree (PhD, EdD, or MSW). Rather than attempt to muddle through the confusing statistics regarding what tests are used and how often, a brief list of tests is provided as illustrative of tests mentioned in the literature.

This discussion on psychological testing in custody evaluations presents several consistencies found in the literature regarding the utility of psychological testing in custody evaluations. First, we discuss the role of psychological testing in custody evaluations, attending to the few constant reservations expressed in the literature. We then briefly examine the current development of forensic assessment instruments related to custody decisions. The interested reader is directed to several review articles regarding psychological testing trends for adults and children. These articles provide a starting point for students to begin to understand the complexity of testing in clinical and forensic practice (Budd, Felix, Poindexter, Naik-Polan, & Sloss, 2002; Cashel, 2002; Camara et al., 2000; Kamphaus, Petoskey, & Rowe, 2000).

The MMPI-2 has been consistently reported as the most frequently used psychological test in child custody evaluations. The MMPI-2, discussed in detail in Chapter 3 of this text, has three validity scales and 10 clinical scales along with numerous supplemental scales. The validity scales can detect a test-taker's response set, such as trying to "fake bad" or "fake good." Most research with high-conflict families indicates that psychological test results are skewed by the tendency of respondents to present themselves in a positive light (Bagby, Nicholson, Buis, Radovanovic, & Fidler, 1999). Researchers reliably report elevated measures of positive self-presentation on the MMPI-2 among parents embroiled in a custody evaluation. This finding should be expected given the high stakes involved and the parents' interest in retaining or obtaining custody rights. The clinical significance of these elevations on the validity scales is uncertain (Medoff, 1999). Some researchers have found no effect on the clinical scales of the MMPI-2 despite indications of positive self-presentation (Bagby et al., 1999), whereas others have found a significant suppressive effect on the clinical scales due to positive self-presentation (Carr et al., 2005). A few commentators have suggested that the only value of the MMPI-2 is to generate hypotheses about the respondents' response set (honest and open or defensive and minimizing difficulties) and possible personality traits that would interfere with parenting (Benjamin & Gollan, 2003). However, since much of the research suggests that parents in custody litigation use a positive self-presentation response set, the "faking good profiles should be accepted as normal" (Carr et al., 2005, p. 194). Regardless of which psychological instruments are used, literature on the MMPI-2 suggests that any test utilized in custody valuations will need to have robust validity scales (Carr, Moretti, & cue, 2005). Psychological instruments lacking such validity indicators should be avoided in forensic settings.

Due to the lack of **forensic assessment instruments** available for child custody evaluations, researchers and test publishers have started to fill the niche with a small avalanche of new instruments.[1] Several of these instruments have been cited in surveys by child custody evaluators. These instruments include measures such as the **Bricklin Perceptual Scales** (Bricklin, 1990), the Ackerman–Schoendorf Parent Evaluation of Custody Test (Ackerman & Schoendorf, 1992), the Adult–Adolescent Parenting Inventory (Bavolek, 1984), Parent–Child Relationship Inventory (Gerard, 1994), and the Parenting Stress Index (Abidin, 1995). Nearly all forensic assessment instruments that have been developed to date for custody evaluations have been criticized for lacking minimal psychometric properties and as having significant conceptual limitations related to the psycholegal question (Otto et al., 2000).

Based on the above discussion, it would not be surprising if evaluators used only the MMPI-2 or simply did not incorporate testing into the evaluation. However, that does not appear to be the current practice. Psychologists are the largest group of child custody evaluators and tend to use psychological tests. The use of tests appears to be increasing along with the use of instruments specifically developed for custody evaluations, despite reservations expressed by many writers. As such, clinicians and consumers of custody evaluations need to be reminded of the limitations of testing. The results of psychological tests should only be used to generate hypotheses that can be tested using additional information, such as third-party report, review of records, or a structured interview. Evaluators should also include a statement in the custody report indicating the limited value readers should attribute to psychological test results (Benjamin & Gollan, 2003). Tables 8.11 and 8.12 briefly list psychological tests used with children and adults, respectively, in child custody evaluations (Ackerman & Ackerman, 1997).

---

[1]For a discussion of forensic assessment instruments (FAIs), the reader is referred to Chapter 3 of this text on assessment in forensic psychology.

| Table 8.11 | Psychological Assessment Instruments Used in Custody Evaluations–Child |
|---|---|

- Wechsler Intelligence Scale for Children
- Children's Apperception Test or Thematic Apperception Test
- Rorschach Inkblot Test
- An academic achievement test
- A sentence completion test (e.g., Rotter's Sentence Completion Blank)
- Bricklin Perceptual Scales

| Table 8.12 | Psychological Assessment Instruments Used in Custody Evaluations–Adult |
|---|---|

- Wechsler Adult Intelligence Scale
- Minnesota Multiphasic Personality Inventory–2
- Millon Clinical Multiaxial Inventory–III
- Rorschach Inkblot
- Thematic Apperception Test
- Ackerman–Schoendorf Scales for Parent Evaluation of Custody Test (ASPECT)

## The Custody Report

Child custody reports can range from 4 to 80 pages (Bow & Quinnell, 2001). Clearly, this wide range suggests great variability in the thoroughness and scope of the report. Though reports can vary based on the nuances of each custody evaluation, there are several factors the psychologist needs to consider when preparing the report.

- All reports written for the court should avoid psychological jargon, using language and concepts understood by nonprofessionals (Otto et al., 2003).
- The report should thoroughly explain the process used to reach the opinion including all sources of information.
- The psychologist should provide the reader with an understanding of the information used to reach each decision including the resolution of any contradictory findings.
- Psychological testing should be discussed within the limitations described above and collateral sources of information should be documented.
- The report should reflect the evaluator's neutrality in the process and ideally present a balanced view of each parent's concerns.

Whether or not the evaluator provides an opinion on the ultimate issue is partly due to the psychologist's inclinations and the norm within the specific jurisdiction. If the psychologist chooses not to recommend a specific parenting plan, the report can:

1. summarize the parents' parenting plan suggestions along with data to support or refute each plan,
2. summarize the child's perspective on parenting plans,
3. discuss the current relationships among the parents and children along with the relevant psychological literature,
4. discuss the child's cognitive capacity for expressing a preference, and
5. provide recommendations for a strategy that might assist the family to develop a mutually agreed-upon parenting plan (Connell, 2004).

Otto et al. (2003) suggest that the report fails to serve its purpose if it does not describe the evaluator's understanding of the unique family situation, including a conceptualization of the parents and children, and describe the process on how the evaluator's opinions were formed.

# Training

The complexity of child custody evaluations requires extensive training in a wide range of topics to function competently and ethically. Evaluators may obtain either a master's or doctoral degree in a mental health–related profession, such as counseling, clinical psychology, or social work. Generally, the evaluator would need to be licensed by the state to practice. Clinicians have typically completed graduate education with core courses in child development, child psychopathology, adult development, adult psychopathology, family therapy, interviewing skills, and assessment of adults and children. Additional coursework should include topics in family law, domestic violence, child sexual and physical abuse, substance abuse, and methods of legal and social science research (Benjamin & Gollan, 2003). The duties of report writing and testifying in court would be bolstered by courses in writing and public speaking. One study found that written custody reports ranged in length from 4 to 80 pages, with an average length of 21 pages. Even with excellent graduate school preparation, graduate coursework alone would be insufficient to prepare a recent graduate for the challenge of conducting child custody evaluations.

Most practicing professionals in the field received graduate and postgraduate supervision working with adult and child populations. A survey of mental health professionals who conduct child custody evaluations provides some insight on the training of child custody evaluators (Bow & Quinnell, 2001). Professionals reported an average of 9 years of clinical work and 2 years of forensic work before beginning custody evaluations. Psychologists received most of their training in performing child custody evaluations at seminars after graduate school, not surprising given the lack of formal training in universities focusing on child custody. The majority of participants in the survey reported receiving their training in child custody evaluations by attending postgraduate seminars, ranging from 1 to 75 seminars, with an average of 8.7. Nearly half of the respondents reported receiving supervision, with an average of 241 hours. Fewer than 20% of the respondents indicated having taken a graduate forensic course, reflecting the lack of specialized graduate courses in forensic psychology as well as suggesting that such preparation is not a prerequisite for entering the field.

The *Ethical Principles of Psychologists and Code of Conduct* (American Psychological Association, 2002) requires that psychologists maintain competency in the areas in which they work. This is particularly relevant for child custody evaluators as research continues to shed light on issues of family law, parenting practices, and child development. Child custody evaluators will need to continually update their skills through participation in workshops such as those offered by the American Psychological Association, American Bar Association, the Association of Family Court and Community Professionals, and the American Academy of Forensic Psychology. Practitioners also need to remain current with changes in local laws affecting custody decisions. Many mental health professionals tend to neglect following shifts in the legal landscape due to fluctuating legal and judicial standards. Child custody evaluators are encouraged to attend continuing legal education workshops and conferences related to family law to stay abreast of recent developments (Benjamin & Gollan, 2003).

## Summary

This chapter explored the complex area of child custody evaluations. Child custody evaluations present a challenge to the forensic psychologist for a variety of reasons, including the multiple participants who must be evaluated, the adversarial nature of the process, the lack of a standard procedure or assessment instruments, the influence of personal biases among decision makers, and the vague psycholegal constructs used by the courts to decide custody. These five complicating factors were examined in some detail. This area of forensic psychology is fraught with inconsistencies and debate regarding current practices, usefulness of the mental health professional's role in custody evaluations, and recommendations based on social science research. Even though the rate of divorce has increased dramatically in the past 40 years, most couples are able to amicably negotiate custody arrangements without the court's intervention. For the 10–20% of couples who pursue litigation, custody evaluations by mental health professionals have proven useful to judges tasked with deciding custody arrangements. Most jurisdictions currently use the best interests of the child standard, though previous and recommended standards were discussed, including the tender-years doctrine and least detrimental alternative. Concerns regarding how to operationalize the best interests of the child standard along with attempts by the courts to do so were summarized. Possible custody arrangements were presented with an emphasis on the lack of research to support any one particular arrangement over another. The distinction between legal authority and physical authority was reviewed along with a description of the various custody combinations. The many factors that affect arrangements, such as age and sex of the children, parenting capacity, and level of conflict between the parents, were identified as confounding variables in determining the optimal custody arrangements. Currently, most jurisdictions have a proclivity to award joint custody. The custody evaluation process was presented. The process was separated into interviews, direct observation, collateral or third-party information, psychological testing, and the written report. Finally, a review of training and qualifications was offered so that the interested student can tailor their educational and professional experience to be equipped to conduct child custody evaluations.

## TEST YOUR KNOWLEDGE

1. Good faith immunity laws require that the forensic psychologist
    a. exercise "good faith" when testifying regarding the ultimate issue
    b. follow guidelines established by the APA in conducting forensic evaluations
    c. notify all parties of ethical limitations and their immunity from prosecution for cooperating
    d. none of the above; immunity laws have not been adopted

2. A dual relationship would exist when a child's therapist also serves as
   a. his parent's therapist
   b. the child custody evaluator
   c. the marriage counselor for the child's parents
   d. all of the above

3. Which doctrine states that young children, particularly girls, should be placed with the mother?
   a. Tender-years doctrine
   b. Unfit or ill-equipped parent doctrine
   c. Best interests of the child standard
   d. No doctrine stated that children should be placed with the mother

4. In child custody decisions, who typically makes the final decision regarding the ultimate issue: where should the child be placed?
   a. The jury
   b. The expert witness
   c. The parents
   d. The judge

5. Decisions affecting the child's daily activities refers to
   a. legal custody
   b. physical custody
   c. divided custody
   d. joint custody
   e. sole custody

Answer Key (1) b, (2) d, (3) a, (4) d, (5) b

# Chapter Nine

# Trial Consultation

## Learning Objectives

- What educational background do trial consultants have?
- Is trial consultation part of forensic psychology or legal psychology?
- Be able to identify some of the numerous areas involved in trial consultation.
- Define voir dire and the trial consultant's role in jury selection.
- Define peremptory challenge, challenge for cause, and a Batson challenge and how these procedures are used by defense and prosecution attorneys.
- Be able to explain the courts rulings in *Batson v. Kentucky* (1986) and *J.E.B. v. Alabama ex rel T.B.* (1994).
- Define evaluation anxiety and demand characteristics and their role in a potential juror's responses during voir dire.
- What is a stealth juror?
- Contrast traditional jury selection to scientific jury selection.
- What is a change of venue and under what circumstances is it appropriate?
- What effect can pretrial publicity have on the outcome of a trial?
- What is the community survey? List the key components of a community survey.
- Be able to discuss characteristics used to predict verdicts including demographic variables, personality traits, and attitudinal variables. Be sure to identify which variables are effective.
- Define death-qualified juror.
- What is the work product doctrine?
- What role does the trial consultant play in witness preparation?
- What is a shadow jury?
- Be able to discuss some of the ethical concerns regarding the use of a trial consultant.
- What training is required to be an effective trial consultant?

## Key Terms

- American Society of Trial Consultants
- Attitudinal predictors
- Authoritarianism
- Batson challenge
- *Batson v. Kentucky*, 1986
- Belief in a just world
- Big Five Personality Factors
- Challenge for cause
- Change of venue request
- Community survey
- Death-qualified jurors
- Demand characteristics
- Evaluation anxiety
- Extended *voir dire*
- Internal locus of control
- *J.E.B. v. Alabama, ex rel T.B.*, 1994
- Jury consultant
- Jury selection
- Legal psychology
- Litigation consultants
- Minimal *voir dire*
- Mock jurors
- Peremptory challenge
- *Powers v. Ohio*, 1991
- Scientific jury selection
- Shadow juries
- Small group research
- *State v. Lozano*, 1993
- Stealth jurors
- Traditional jury selection
- Trial consultants
- Venire
- Witness preparation
- Work product doctrine

| Table 9.1 | A Real-Life Vignette |
|---|---|

In 1996, Oprah Winfrey had a guest on her show from the Humane Society who discussed the practice of feeding cows ground-up meat from dead livestock. This practice, now banned by the Food and Drug Administration in the United States, is believed to have contributed to the spread of bovine spongiform encephalopathy, commonly known as "mad cow disease." Oprah, after hearing of the risks associated with this practice, pronounced on her show that she would not eat another burger. The resultant "Oprah Crash" of 1996 sent beef prices and cattle futures tumbling downward by nearly 10%. Cattle ranchers were convinced that Oprah's comments led to the decline in prices, the public's concerns regarding the safety of beef and the heightened fear of mad cow disease. Oprah Winfrey was sued in 1998 by the cattle industry for $12 million in damages and losses. The ranchers sued under a Texas law, the False Disparagement of Perishable Food Products Act of 1995. The trial was held in the heart of the cattle industry, Amarillo, Texas. About 350 miles away sat Dr. Phil McGraw, a clinical psychologist and president of Courtroom Sciences, Incorporated of Irving, Texas. Oprah Winfrey's legal team hired Courtroom Sciences as a trial consultant for the civil defamation case filed by the cattle ranchers. Oprah won the case with the judge ruling that the plaintiffs would need to show that her comments were made with malice toward the cattle industry. Oprah was so impressed with Dr. Phil's assistance in preparing her as a witness that she invited him to be on her show as a "life strategist." The rest is Hollywood history. Now, Dr. Phil, the clinical psychologist turned trial consultant, turned celebrity, has his own television show, second only to Oprah in daytime ratings, several bestsellers, an endorsement contract for nutritional supplements sold in thousands of retail stores, and millions of fans. Obviously, this is an unusual case and should not be construed as representing either the typical client of trial consultants or the typical success of a trial consultant.

This chapter provides an overview of the work of trial consultants. Based on the definition used in this text, trial consultation falls under the realm of legal psychology and not forensic psychology. **Trial consultants** are retained by attorneys to assist on a case. Trial consultation is a relatively young profession and is in the process of identifying areas of expertise, training, and ethical guidelines. Trial consultants, also know as **litigation consultants**, can provide a variety of services to lawyers and come from a range of educational and experiential backgrounds. Trial consultants can work on criminal and civil cases, though their services are more commonly utilized in civil lawsuits. This chapter describes the current state of the field for trial consultants.

We begin by examining the qualifications of trial consultants. We review the services a consultant can provide, focusing in some detail on jury selection, request for a change of venue, and witness preparation. We then explore the ethical issues related to work as a trial consultant and the use of trial consultants in the courtroom. Finally, we review training opportunities and job prospects for students wishing to enter the field.

# Qualifications of Trial Consultants

Not all trial consultants are psychologists. Since trial consultants perform a variety of services, it also happens that consultants have a wide range of educational and experiential qualifications. Some consultants will have advanced degrees in the social sciences, such as psychology and sociology. Other consultants may have an advanced degree in speech communication, computer graphics, or a background in theater. Some consultants will have a law degree with an advanced degree in another area, such as the social sciences. However, most professionals in the field consider a master's degree in the social sciences as the minimal entry-level educational requirement, with many expressing a strong preference for the doctorate or terminal degree (C. Morris, personal communication, 2005).

Currently, the largest percentage of trial consultants are trained as either psychologists (Streier, 1999) or in the field of communications (C. Morris, personal communication, 2005). Psychologists' training in research methodology and understanding of human behavior and social science makes individuals in the profession uniquely prepared to work as trial consultants (Myers & Arena, 2001). As is true with many areas of work discussed in this text, some professionals work full time as trial consultants while many are employed full time in other roles, such as university professors, and only consult on a part-time basis. There is no state regulation of the profession and no licensing requirements, so practically anyone can call him- or herself a trial consultant. Some commentators have expressed concerns regarding the lack of professional regulation for trial consultants (Fulero & Wrightsman, 2009; Nietzel & Dillehay, 1986; Posey & Wrightsman, 2005; Streier, 1999). On the other hand, although anyone can hang a shingle to practice, the marketplace would quickly eradicate from the profession the incompetent individual.

The professional organization for trial consultants is the **American Society of Trial Consultants** (ASTC). ASTC was first formed in 1982 with only a small group of members. Today, membership in ASTC is over 500 members from a variety of professional fields including communication, psychology, sociology, theater, marketing, linguistics, political science, and law. The organization holds both regional and national meetings offering workshops and opportunities for networking. One workshop routinely offered at the annual meeting, which may be of interest to students entering the profession, is titled *Trial Consulting 101*. The ASTC publishes an online newsletter, *CourtCall*, as well as a monthly trade publication, *The Jury Expert*. The *Jury Expert* is designed to help attorneys improve their courtroom communication skills. The newsletter, geared toward the legal profession, presents articles on topics such as jury selection, focus groups, mock trials, storytelling, cross-examination, instructions, and courtroom technology. Articles from a recent edition addressed the patterning of questions at voir dire, how to start the opening statement with a "silver bullet," and suggestions on how to effectively communicate to jurors the extent of damages in a personal injury case. As listed on the web site (ASTC, 2005b), the organization's goals are:

- Provide an opportunity for networking and dialogue among individuals who share professional interests in trial consulting, trial-related research, and teaching.
- Encourage and assist in the professional growth and training of Society members and provide a forum for the exchange of ideas, opinions, techniques, experiences, and research results in the area of trial consulting.
- Encourage the development and refinement of appropriate methods for the application of research techniques to trial practice.
- Promote the effective and ethical use of trial consulting techniques by attorneys.
- Encourage awareness of and provide accurate information about trial consulting.

Initially disparaged as having a "brief, one-page Code of Professional Standards" (Wrightsman, 2001, p. 169), the organization now publishes a 37-page Professional Code that includes Ethical Principles, Professional Standards, Practice Guidelines, and Commentary. Currently, its membership has approved and adopted Practice Guidelines in the areas of Witness Preparation, **Small Group Research**, and Motion for a Change of venue. **Jury Selection** and Post-trial Interview Practice Guidelines are pending approval (C. Morris, personal communication, 2005). Membership to ASTC is open to professionals and to students at a discounted rate. The web site (*www.astcweb.org*) also features a link to job postings and internship opportunities.

One sign that the field is rapidly maturing is the significant growth in the professional organization, with an almost 2000% increase in membership in 23 years. The practice of trial consultation is not limited to members of the ASTC, making it somewhat difficult to get an accurate estimate of the number of trial consultants currently practicing. Membership is voluntary, as with most professional organizations, and not all practitioners decide to affiliate with the guild organization. In 1999, Streier estimated that there were over 700 trial consultants in the United States and the ASTC website currently lists over 400 firms offering trial consultation services. Law firms have also turned to establishing in-house departments of trial consultants (Stolle, Robbennolt, & Weiner, 1996). It is not surprising that in a changing marketplace (Newman, 2004) psychologists have focused their attention on opportunities to work as trial consultants (Myers & Arena, 2001).

Moreover, the career opportunities appear to be nearly infinite. Although the profession of trial consultation was practically unheard of 30 years ago, some lawyers have recently suggested that it would now be considered malpractice not to hire a trial consultant in a big case (Posey & Wrightsman, 2005). There are nearly 18 million lawsuits filed annually in the United States. Furthermore, there are over 900,000 practicing lawyers with 40,000 new lawyers added to the ranks annually (Myers & Arena, 2001). In light of these numbers, it would be premature to suggest that the field of trial consultation is saturated. Rather, the future promises steady growth and further professionalization of the discipline. Authors have also noted the financial benefits associated with the profession, citing the "multimillion dollar trial consulting industry" (Kovera, Dickinson, & Cutler, 2003, p. 168). Fees are comparable to psychologists' and attorneys' fees and range from $75 to $300 an hour (Myers & Arena, 2001), although most firms appear to offer services as a package. For example, one trial-consulting firm advertises on its web site use of a mock jury to evaluate a trial strategy for approximately $12,000. The use of two mock juries, which is preferable, would be approximately double the cost. However, this is on the low end of the fee structure for small group research (C. Morris, personal communication, 2005). Costs can easily exceed $50,000 for the use of **mock jurors**. Another firm charges $7,500 per day for one associate to assist with voir dire in court. Costs for a community survey range from $15,000 to $50,000 and charges for witness preparation run as high as $500 per hour. The ASTC has proposed a *Pro Bono Initiative* that would require pro bono work as a condition of membership in the organization. However, this initiative has yet to be finalized and still does not address the issue of accessibility to trial consultants for all litigants, an issue discussed later in this chapter. Some trial consultants also work on a contingency basis, a practice prohibited by the APA ethics code.

Figure 9.1

A trial consultant with a public relations background may assist a law firm with a case that involves extensive media coverage. © 2009 Milos Jokic. Used under license from Shutterstock, Inc.

# Services Offered by Trial Consultants

The consulting services offered by trial consultants are as varied as their professional backgrounds. Consultants with a background in graphic arts may consult on how best to present graphic representations of evidence to juries. The consultant can provide attorneys with various graphic representations for the presentation of evidence during the trial. Consultants with a background in theater may assist attorneys in preparing witnesses for courtroom testimony. Witness preparation is an area fraught with misunderstanding and ethical concerns, which is addressed in more detail later in this chapter. A consultant with a background in public relations may assist a law firm with a case that involves extensive media coverage. For example, high-interest trials can spark excessive media coverage. The attorney who can help quash negative publicity early on may have an advantage in the trial and would theoretically benefit from the assistance of an effective trial consultant skilled in public relations. Research has demonstrated the harmful effects of negative pretrial publicity for a defendant.

The possibilities for trial consultation services appear to be limited only by the professional imagination of experts in the field. Trial consultants, sometimes narrowly defined in the role of **jury consultant**, assist attorneys in voir dire and the selection of jurors. Consultants may also assist with case presentation, witness preparation, conducting community surveys for change of venue petitions, and rehearsing a case with mock jurors. Notwithstanding the diversity in types of services offered, a few areas can be considered the core domain of trial consultation. These areas include *jury selection* during the process of *voir dire*, request for a *change of venue*, and *witness preparation*. Table 9.2 presents a list of consulting activities offered by firms holding membership in the American Society of Trial Consultants. This chapter focuses on several select areas including jury selection, request for a change of venue, and witness preparation. Although trial consultants can work on either a criminal or civil case, nearly 80% of their work is on civil cases and approximately 5% of the caseload is criminal cases (Posey & Wrightsman, 2005). There are several reasons for this distribution. First, nearly 95% of criminal cases are settled with a plea bargain. Second, the vast majority of criminal defendants cannot afford the services of a trial consultant. On the other hand, many civil lawsuits involve large sums of money such that law firms and corporations are willing to use all their available resources to prepare for trial.

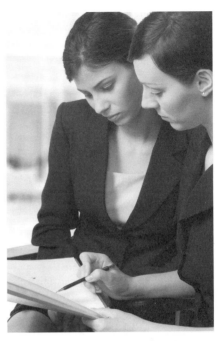

### Figure 9.2

One of the duties of a jury consultant is to assist with with witness preparation.

■ **Jury consultant**

A trial consultant who assists an attorney during voir dire and the selection of jurors, as well as other activities such as witness preparation and a change of venue request.

# Voir Dire and Jury Selection

Voir dire, from French meaning to *speak the truth*, is a pretrial legal proceeding used to assemble a jury. Voir dire is used in both civil and criminal trials, though the process varies somewhat between the two. During voir dire, the judge and/or the attorneys for both sides may question the potential jurors from the jury pool, known as the **venire**. The process of voir dire varies between state court and federal court and across jurisdictions. The judge has wide latitude in how the process proceeds and can allow a **minimal** *voir dire*, with limited or no participation from the attorneys, or an **extended** *voir dire*, allowing attorneys ample time and leeway regarding the questioning of the venire (Moran, Cutler, & Loftus, 1990). Research suggests that an extended voir dire conducted by attorneys in a personable, open-ended questioning manner solicits more open and honest responses from prospective jurors than a minimal voir dire conducted by the judge (Kovera et al., 2003).

The primary purpose of the voir dire is to identify any bias prospective jurors might have that would prevent them from forming a fair and appropriate verdict (McCarter, 1999). For example, a prospective juror may have lost a loved one to a drunk driver, and thus not feel capable of weighing the evidence fairly in a criminal trial of an intoxicated driver involved in a hit-and-run accident. Although voir dire is a

## Table 9.2     Areas Involved in Trial Consultation

- Theory and Presentation
- Change of Venue Studies
- Community Attitude Surveys
- Continuing Legal Education Seminars
- Damages Analysis
- Deposition Preparation
- Expert Testimony
- Focus Groups
- Graphics and Demonstrative Evidence
- Initial Case Assessment
- Interviewing and Counseling
- Jury Selection
- Language and the Law
- Media Relations
- Mediation and Arbitration (ADR)

- Mock Jury Trials
- Negotiations
- Opening Statement and Closing Argument Writing
- Posttrial Juror Interviews
- Presentation Strategy
- Pro Bono Services
- Psychological Evaluation
- Shadow Juries
- Strategy Development and Research
- Trial Simulations
- Trial Technology
- Voir Dire Strategy
- Witness Evaluation Research
- Witness Preparation

pretrial process, for all essential purposes, the proceeding marks the beginning of the trial. Lawyers may use the process to educate jurors about aspects of the case as well as relevant law (McNulty, 2000), as an opportunity to develop rapport with the jurors (Levine, 2001; Liotti & Cole, 2000), and as an opportunity to inoculate potential jurors against negative evidence to be presented by the other side (Kovera et al., 2003).

Voir dire, the process of jury selection, is considered by some to be the most important act lawyers perform during a trial (Stapp, 1996). Though not typical, in rare cases, lawyers will spend hundreds of thousands of dollars preparing for voir dire, polishing their questions with mock jurors. For example, in a personal injury case in St. Petersburg, Florida, attorneys spent 4 days and exhausted the entire jury pool of 104 potential jurors, unable to agree on six jurors and three alternates (Thompson, 2005). The plaintiff was seeking $20 million in compensation and $100 million in punitive damages from a physical therapy clinic. The failure to seat a jury after 4 days of voir dire resulted in a mistrial. Many of the jurors were dismissed because they indicated that they would not be able to serve on jury duty for 3–4 weeks, the expected length of the trial. However, the plaintiff's attorney dismissed others because they admitted that it would be difficult to award $120 million. Even the 83-year-old judge stated that she "never had a jury take so long to be picked" (Thompson, 2005). The attorney for the plaintiff readily admitted that his firm has spent hundreds of thousands of dollars preparing for the voir dire. Although unusual, this case illustrates the importance of selecting a jury that is receptive to the case being tried.

Trial consultants and lawyers hope for extended voir dire in which the trial judge permits thorough questioning of the prospective jurors. The term *jury selection* is actually a misnomer because lawyers cannot select jurors from the venire, but only eliminate biased jurors. The goal is to retain jurors who will be most sympathetic to the attorney's case and strike jurors who possess an obvious bias. Attorneys have two mechanisms in which they can eliminate a prospective juror:

1. a **peremptory challenge** and
2. a **challenge for cause.**

A peremptory challenge is the removal of a prospective juror from the group for no stated reason. Attorneys are able to remove jurors who may be reluctant to admit their prejudice during questioning or who the attorney may have inadvertently offended during voir dire (Kovera et al., 2003). The number of peremptory challenges varies by jurisdiction, although each side is frequently permitted three in civil trials. Judges can also grant additional peremptory challenges at their discretion, as may be the case in a trial preceded by intense pretrial publicity. Additional peremptory challenges may be necessary to seat an impartial jury (Kovera et al., 2003). In criminal cases, the number of peremptory challenges increases with the severity of the crime and usually the defense is granted as many if not more challenges than the prosecution. The use of peremptory challenges is part of the trial strategy and is utilized by attorneys and trial consultants to retain jurors receptive to the case while eliminating jurors who may possess a bias against issues in the case. For example, trial consultant Donald Vinson urged Marcia Clark to use her peremptory challenges to dismiss black women from the O.J. Simpson jury pool. Research from surveys and focus groups suggested that black women were sympathetic to O.J. Simpson. Marcia Clark did not accept his advice and the jury had eight African American women (Wrightsman, 2001). After 4 months of testimony, O.J. Simpson was acquitted of murdering his ex-wife, Nicole Brown Simpson, and Ronald Goldman.

However, in 2008 O.J. Simpson was found guilty on 12 charges including kidnapping and robbery. Several members of this jury reported after the verdict that they thought O.J. Simpson should have been found guilty in the original murder trial. This belief may have influenced their vote, despite the fact that they all claimed they were able to objectively judge the case without any prejudice.

It is interesting to note that the consultant suggested striking jurors who were African American females. The U.S. Supreme Court has ruled that peremptory challenges may not be used to exclude people based solely on their membership in a recognizable group. In 1986, the Court ruled that prospective jurors could not be excluded in criminal trials based solely on race (*Batson v. Kentucky*, 1986). This ruling was extended to civil trials in 1991 (*Powers v. Ohio*, 1991). The court later ruled that gender also could not be used as the sole criterion for a peremptory challenge (*J.E.B. v. Alabama*, ex rel *T.B.*, 1994). However, anecdotal evidence suggests that a clever lawyer can fabricate reasons for striking a prospective juror from the jury pool, circumventing the goal of the law (Kovera et al., 2003; Rose, 1999).

Most trial consultants and attorneys would agree that fabricating reasons to strike a juror is unethical. An opposing attorney can challenge a peremptory strike, called a **Batson challenge**. The striking attorney must present a race- or gender-neutral reason for exercising the strike. If the judge agrees that race or gender was not the sole reason for the peremptory challenge, then the strike stands and the Batson challenge is defeated. The role of the trial consultant is to assist the attorney in identifying non-race- or gender-based reasons to exercise strikes wisely. Race or gender may contribute

■ **Peremptory challenge**
Removal of a prospective juror for no stated reason during voir dire. This is distinguished from for-cause challenges, which requires a reason to remove a potential juror.

■ **Challenge for cause**
Removal of a prospective juror during voir dire because of a prejudice the juror holds that would interfere with rendering a fair verdict.

■ **Batson challenge**
A claim that opposing counsel's use of a peremptory strike during voir dire is based solely on race or gender.

Figure 9.3

These jurors survived both peremptory challenge and challenge for cause to end up on this jury.
© 2009 BXP.

to certain life experiences that make bias on a particular issue more likely, and factors such as life experience, attitudes, and opinions are legal reasons for elimination from the panel by peremptory challenge (C. Morris, personal communication, 2005).

The second mechanism attorneys can use to strike a prospective juror is a challenge for cause. If questioning during voir dire reveals that a juror holds a prejudice that would interfere with rendering a fair verdict, the attorney can ask that the juror be removed from the panel. Potential jurors may be dismissed using a challenge for cause if the juror holds a prejudicial attitude, fails to meet state requirements for jury duty, or disagrees with the fundamental principles of due process (Kovera et al., 2003). If the juror admits to a prejudicial view, the judge can asked the juror if he or she could set aside their view and still arrive at a fair and just verdict. Numerous pressures exist in the courtroom that increase the likelihood that a juror so questioned by a judge will answer affirmatively. The demand characteristics of the situation along with evaluation anxiety increase the likelihood that the juror will answer in a socially desirable manner. **Evaluation anxiety** is the desire to be judged positively by others. The juror certainly wishes to be perceived in a favorable light by the judge, the individual with the most authority in the courtroom, but also by the attorneys, other members of the venire, the bailiff, court stenographer, and so on. **Demand characteristics** are usually associated with experiments in social sciences, particularly psychology. Demand characteristics refer to how the situation influences participants to respond. In voir dire, the demand characteristics of the courtroom increase the likelihood that the prospective juror will answer questions as he or she believes they are *expected* to answer the question. Research has indicated that both demand characteristics and evaluation anxiety increase the social desirability and decrease the honesty of responses of prospective jurors (Kovera et al., 2003). If the juror answers the judge's query regarding the ability to set aside prejudicial feelings affirmatively, then the juror will remain on the panel. There is no limit to the number of challenges for cause that an attorney can use. However, a challenge for cause is frequently denied by the judge.

In addition to jurors who may be pressured to answer less than candidly due to evaluation anxiety and demand characteristics, there are other jurors who may deliberately lie to get onto a jury. **Stealth jurors** are individuals who deliberately misrepresent themselves to get on a jury to further their own agenda. In criminal cases, a stealth juror can have a significant impact due to the requirement that the verdict must be unanimous. Thus, a lone juror can block a verdict in a criminal trial. Stealth jurors attempting to get on criminal cases may feel that the criminal justice system is ineffective and wish to dole out their own vigilante justice. A retired municipal worker was accused of being a stealth juror in the Scott Peterson murder trial and was subsequently dismissed from the jury by the judge. The juror was alleged to have told a travel companion on a bus to Reno that Scott Peterson was "guilty as hell" and he was "going to get what's due to him" (Abrams, 2005). In civil cases, stealth jurors may wish to punish corporations and hand out large monetary damages awards. Additionally, with all the recent media hype surrounding trials, both celebrity and notorious cases, stealth jurors may see jury service as an opportunity for their own 15 minutes of fame. Some individuals fantasize about a book deal or being interviewed on television after participating in a highly publicized case and see jury service as their pathway to celebrity status. In a survey by DecisionQuest, a large trial-consulting firm, 14% of respondents indicated that they would hide information to get on a jury (Abrams, 2004). There is even a book on how to hide information during voir dire and secretly work to acquit a defendant. The book, titled, *Stealth Jurors: The Ultimate Defense Against Bad Laws and Government Tyranny*, has recommendations on how to be seated on a jury and how to influence fellow jurors in deliberations (Hammerstein, 2002). It is difficult for attorneys to identify a stealth juror during voir dire since the presumption is that prospective jurors are truthful. The identification of deception is difficult and unreliable at best.

■ **Evaluation anxiety**

Anxiety caused by the desire to be judged positively by others.

■ **Demand characteristics**

The aspects of a situation may influence a participant to respond in a particular manner. For example, the demand characteristics of a courtroom may convince a potential juror to affirm that they can offer an impartial verdict in a case even when the juror may hold a bias.

■ **Stealth jurors**

Individuals who misrepresent themselves to get on a jury in order to further their own goals.

Trial consulting firms are aware of the potential for stealth jurors and are developing techniques to identify individuals who use deception to be seated as a juror. Currently, the most effective tool is to watch for inconsistencies in responses. As Mark Twain once quipped, "If you tell the truth, you don't have to remember anything." A stealth juror may forget or confuse responses on a questionnaire or to earlier questioning and betray him- or herself with an inconsistency.

# The Technique of Jury Selection

Perhaps of all the services trial consultants provide, the work of jury selection is the role most frequently associated with the profession. With the mention of trial consultant, attorneys envision the professional who formulates jury questionnaires or voir dire questions, developing profiles of who to strike and who to keep on the jury panel (Gabriel & Fenyes, 2003). Some find this role objectionable, suggesting that jury consultants use social science and market research to "stack" the jury in order to render the desirable verdict (e.g., Kressel & Kressel, 2002). We return to the issue of ethical guidelines for the work of trial consultants later in this chapter.

Trial consultants distinguish between traditional jury selection and scientific jury selection. **Traditional jury selection** is "any strategy that has traditionally been used by attorneys to identify jurors who are favorable (or unfavorable) to their case" (Kovera et al., 2003, p. 165). Attorneys tend to rely on their own court experience, advice from other attorneys, and information gleaned from trial manuals. These sources usually result in stereotypes and mistaken preconceptions regarding how certain traits, such as style of dress and belief in law and order, are related to one another. These implicit personality theories have created a folklore of jury selection strategies that is contradictory and somewhat amusing (Fulero & Penrod, 1990). For example, some strategies suggest that women are desirable as jurors in criminal cases, unless the defendant is an attractive woman. Poor jurors are good for the defense in a civil case since they are unfamiliar in dealing with large sums of money. On the other hand, poor jurors may live the "Robin Hood" fantasy, taking from the rich to give to the poor due to their own resentment about their financial hardships. Others have suggested attorneys should select jurors who are similar to their client because they will be able to empathize with the defendant's predicament. Alternatively, some have offered the "black sheep hypothesis," arguing that attorneys should strike similar members from the panel since they may wish to punish in-group members who reflect poorly on the group (Kovera et al., 2003). Most of these implicit theories have not been empirically tested and appear to reflect a rather unsophisticated approach to juror selection. Studies have demonstrated that attorneys fare no better than college sophomores in strategies used to identify favorable jurors (Olczak, Kaplan, & Penrod, 1991). These approaches tend to include stereotypes, hunches, guessing the meaning of body language, and implying attitudes based on style of dress, grooming, economic status, and occupation (Fulero & Penrod, 1990). However, attorneys do appear to be able to identify the *most* biased jurors against the defense or prosecution (Zeilsel & Diamond, 1978).

**Scientific jury selection** attempts to identify which characteristics will be associated with a favorable verdict. Researchers have examined both demographic as well as broad personality characteristics as predictors of verdicts and juror behavior. Scientific jury selection uses the methods of social science to select jurors. The advent of scientific jury selection marked the beginning of trial consultation and is traced back to a high-profile case in the early 1970s. Numerous observers have cited the "Harrisburg

■ **Traditional jury selection**
Any traditional strategy used by attorneys to identify jurors who are favorable, or unfavorable, to their case.

■ **Scientific jury selection**
Attempting to identify characteristics that will be associated with a favorable verdict using scientific methods such as community surveys, questionnaires, etc.

Figure 9.4

Some traditional jury selection strategies suggest that this woman would be a desirable juror in a criminal case, unless the defendant is an attractive woman.
© 2009 Simone van den Berg. Used under license from Shutterstock, Inc.

Seven" case as the beginning of scientific jury selection (Myers & Arena, 2001; Posey & Wrightsman, 2005; Streier, 1999; Wrightsman, 2001). During the height of the Vietnam antiwar protests, seven activists, priests and nuns, were charged with, among other things, conspiracy to kidnap Secretary of State Henry Kissinger, blow up steam tunnels under Washington, D.C., and raid draft boards. Jay Shulman, a sociologist sympathetic to the antiwar movement, offered to assist the defense for free. He and his colleagues used social science methods to prove that the venire was not representative of the Harrisburg community. The judge ordered a new venire. The academics then conducted an extensive survey to establish profiles of desirable and undesirable jurors. The case eventually ended in a mistrial due to a hung jury—the jury could not reach a unanimous verdict. The prosecution did not retry the case. This first successful use of social science methodology in jury selection offered pro bono ironically sparked the beginning of a multimillion-dollar industry, now mostly used by large corporations to defend against individual plaintiffs.

The main tool of jury selection is the community survey. The **community survey** is built around the particular case and involves five key components (Kovera et al., 2003). The survey consists of a synopsis of the case along with a summary of the evidence. Questions on the survey assess case-specific attitudes, attitudes toward the legal system in general, respondents' belief about the guilt or innocence of the defendant, and basic demographic information. The survey is randomly administered to jury-eligible individuals in the locality where the trial will be held. Individuals are selected using the same criteria for assembling the venire, usually either voter registration or driver's license lists. The survey may be administered door-to-door, or more economically, over the telephone and typically requires approximately 25 minutes to complete. The presumption is that prospective jurors who are similar along various demographic variables (variables that can be assessed during voir dire such as race, age, education, etc.) as well as attitudes toward case-relevant issues will be similar in their verdict tendencies (Myers & Arena, 2001). The consultant, using the community survey, collects information on the respondent's demographic information, case-relevant attitudes, and how he or she would decide in reaching a verdict. Statistical analysis using a regression equation weights the various factors to identify what variables best predict verdict tendencies. The consultant can then develop profiles of favorable and unfavorable jurors to be used by the attorney during voir dire. Research on the effectiveness of scientific jury selection has examined the predictive value of demographic variables, personality traits, and attitudinal measures.

Another technique available to trial consultants is database analysis. Database analysis allows consultants to access, compare, and contrast the numerous databases in existence that explore the attitudes and opinions of laypersons (Anthony, Kidd, & Daniel, 2005). For example, numerous organizations have developed databases on the attitudes and opinions of ordinary citizens on a variety of topics relevant to litigations. Examples of these organizations include the Gallop Poll, ABC News, CNN, the University of Michigan Center for Survey Research, the *Wall Street Journal*, and *Time* magazine. This information can be culled from the electronic databases to

1. obtain a general sense of a community, useful in identifying a particular venue;
2. understand the general knowledge of a particular topic of the litigation;
3. gauge attitudinal views of the likely jurors to a specific issue; and
4. form hypothesis about how jurors may respond to particular trial strategies.

The use of existing electronic databases can be more cost-effective and time-efficient than community surveys.

■ **Community survey**

A randomly administered survey of jury-eligible individuals that collects information on demographics, case-relevant attitudes, and potential verdict decisions. A community survey is commonly used in change of venue requests and jury selection by trial consultants.

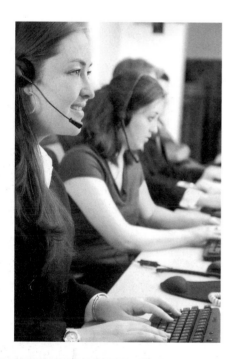

Figure 9.5

A community survey, usually done over the phone, is an important way to assess case-specific attitudes and beliefs.
© 2009 Andresr. Used under license from Shutterstock, Inc.

## Key Components of the Community Survey          Table 9. 3

- Synopsis of the case including summary of the evidence and then questions assessing
  - Case-specific attitudes
  - Attitudes toward the legal system
  - Defendant culpability
  - Demographic information

It is perhaps an artificial distinction to suggest that the process of voir dire is conducted using either traditional jury selection or scientific jury selection. Rather, the actual practice by a trial consultant may be a blend of the two approaches. Trial consultants who have been in the business for years have gained experienced from small-group research that can be relevant to new cases. The consultant has developed experience in formulating voir dire questions and can assist attorneys with their communications skills to solicit candid responses from prospective jurors. The consultant may not conduct a community survey due to cost or time constraints, but nonetheless can apply their knowledge of social science to eliminate jurors with obvious biases.

■ **Death-qualified jurors**

Jurors who are not opposed to deliberating the death penalty, in capital cases jurors must all be death-qualified jurors.

# Characteristics Used to Predict Verdicts
## Demographic Variables

The possibility of predicting jurors' verdict inclinations based on demographic variables is certainly attractive to trial lawyers. Attorneys could readily discern most demographic variables even in a minimal voir dire (Kovera et al., 2003). These variables include race, gender, age, and socioeconomic status. However, the results concerning demographic variables and verdict inclinations suggest that the relationship between the two is weak at best. The relationships that do exist appear to be based on a relationship between demographic variables and issues specific to the case. For example, gender does not appear to be a reliable predictor of verdict inclinations in a wide range of cases. However, gender may be a useful variable in jury selection in specific types of cases. Research evidence suggests that female jurors are more likely to convict in rape cases and child sexual abuse cases. Additionally, female jurors are more likely to find defendants guilty in sexual harassment cases and less likely to convict battered women who murdered their abusive partners (Kovera et al., 2003).

Death penalty attitudes are also related to demographic variables. However, jurors in capital cases need to be death-qualified. **Death-qualified jurors** are jurors who do not oppose the death penalty. Research has shown that death-qualified jurors are conviction prone (Wrightsman, 2001). Demographic variables do appear to be related to death penalty attitudes, an example of demographics being related to

Figure 9.6

Males with a high socioeconomic status are often chosen as the jury foreperson, and may be able to influence the other jurors.
© 2009 Katrina Brown. Used under license from Shutterstock, Inc.

case-specific attitudes. Research suggests that being white, Republican, and male are all related to pro–death penalty attitudes compared to being African American, female, or a Democrat (Kovera, et al., 2003.

Demographic variables may also be used to predict which jurors will be able to influence the other members of the jury during deliberations. Males with a high socioeconomic status tend to be selected as the foreperson more often than females and individuals with a low socioeconomic status. The attempt to retain a high socioeconomic status male who is receptive to the attorney's case may be a useful strategy by the trial consultant for ensuring that a particular opinion is expressed during deliberations (Kovera et al., 2003). Another technique used by the trial consultant is the "poison pill" strategy (Posey & Wrightsman, 2005). If the defendant is clearly guilty with the weight of the evidence against him or her, the consultant might decide the best alternative is to go for a mistrial. The trial consultant attempts to retain jurors whose personalities would clearly clash during deliberations. When the jurors' personalities clash, it is less likely that they will be able to render a unanimous verdict in a criminal trial. The result would be a mistrial with the possibility that the prosecution will not retry the case.

## Personality Traits and Attitudinal Predictors

With a supplemental questionnaire, trial consultants may be able to collect information about potential jurors' personality traits and attitudes toward specific topics. Research on personality traits has produced inconsistent results. Similar to the research on demographic variables, the relationships between verdict inclination and personality traits appears weak at best. Several personality traits have been explored including **internal locus of control**, **belief in a just world**, and **authoritarianism**. Individuals with a high internal locus of control tend to believe that their actions affect the outcomes in their life. On the other hand, individuals with an *external locus of control* tend to believe that they can do very little to affect change in their lives and outcomes are determined by events beyond their control. For example, an individual with an internal locus of control is likely to attribute their success at landing a job to their own interviewing skills and qualifications. Alternatively, an individual with an external locus of control may attribute their success at landing the job to the luck of being at the right place at the right time. Individuals with an internal locus of control tend to hold defendants responsible for their actions when the evidence is weak and tend to hold plaintiffs responsible for their injury if the plaintiff's behavior contributed in any way toward the injury (Kovera et al., 2003).

People who subscribe to the *belief in a just world hypothesis* believe that bad things happen to bad people. Research results on this trait have been inconsistent, suggesting that individuals with this belief may either hold victims responsible for their situation or feel punitively toward defendants. Perhaps the only personality trait that has been consistently related to verdict inclinations is authoritarianism. Authoritarian individuals "endorse conventional values, respect authority, and act punitively toward people who defy authority or conventional norms" (Kovera et al., 2003, p. 170). Individuals with high scores on measures of authoritarianism, such as the Legal Attitudes Questionnaire (Kravitz, Cutler, & Brock, 1993), are more likely to vote for conviction and recommend harsher sentences compared to nonauthoritarian jurors.

Due to these relatively small effects of personality traits as predictors of juror selection and jury decisions, it appears that investigators have discontinued this line of research (Greene, Sommerville, Nystrom, Darley, & Cohen, 2002). Rather, researchers have more recently focused on how the information is presented during trial as well as how attitudes regarding legal issues impact jurors' decisions (Robbennolt, Groscup, & Penrod, 2006). However, a recent study looked at personality traits among 764 actual venire members using the Big Five Inventory. The **Big Five personality** traits in-

■ **Internal locus of control**
The belief that your actions affect the outcomes in your life, in contrast to an external locus of control, which is characterized by the belief that regardless of what you do, you cannot control situations. This is a personality trait sometimes considered in jury selection.

■ **Belief in a just world hypothesis**
A belief that bad things happen to bad people and good things happen to good people; attitude sometimes used in jury selection.

■ **Authoritarianism**
A personality trait characterized by endorsement of conventional values, respect for authority, and acting punitively toward people who defy authority or conventional norms; individuals high in authoritarianism are generally more willing to convict defendants in criminal trials.

■ **Big Five personality factors**
Personality trait theory suggesting individuals can be described using five personality factors: openness, conscientiousness, extraversion, agreeableness, and neuroticism (OCEAN).

clude openness, conscientiousness, extraversion, agreeableness, and neuroticism (OCEAN). The results suggest that attorneys do not appear to use personality traits to guide decisions during the jury selection process. Rather, the researchers report that attorneys tend to base their decisions during jury selection on demographic variables, such as juror sex and race, particularly in criminal cases (Clark, Boccaccini, Caillouet, & Chaplin, 2007). It appears that the prosecution more frequently excused younger, African American male and employed venire members, whereas the defense excused white jurors more frequently. It is interesting to note that these authors indicate that the criminal prosecutors used 47.5% of their peremptory challenges on African American venire members and the defense used only 9.9% of their peremptory challenges on African American venire members, suggesting that these challenges were based on race, despite case law to the contrary. Recall that *Batson v. Kentucky* (1986) dictates that peremptory challenges cannot be based on race alone.

The authors did report a relationship between jurors high on the trait of extraversion and the tendency for not-guilty verdicts in criminal cases. In two cases that went to trial, the foreperson for the jury that delivered not-guilty verdicts was high on the trait of extraversion. Extraversion was associated for being selected as the jury foreperson as well as the jury spending a longer amount of time deliberating the case. Clark et al. (2007) suggest longer deliberation times allow for a deeper examination of the evidence and may lead to acquittal in criminal cases. However, this study highlights one of the difficulties of conducting research in this area. From an initial pool of 764 venire members, 18 juries deliberated in 12 civil and six criminal trials. Of the criminal trials, four found the defendant guilty and two found the defendant not guilty. Thus, the conclusion is based on two juries from the initial pool of over 700 participants, limiting the generalizability of the results.

Studies on **attitudinal predictors** have been somewhat more successful in predicting verdict inclinations than either personality or demographic variables. In particular, attitudes relevant to a specific case have been shown to be related to verdict inclinations. Attitudinal measures tend to assess rather specific beliefs related to issues in the case, more so than either personality traits or demographic variables. For example, individuals who favor tort reform tend to side with the prosecution in criminal trials and with the defense in civil trials (Moran, Cutler, & De Lisa, 1994). Additionally, attitudes toward psychiatrists predict verdict inclinations in insanity cases (Cutler, Moran, & Narby, 1992) and attitudes toward drugs predict verdict inclinations in drug cases (Moran et al., 1990). Taken together, the research on case-relevant attitudes suggests that this information may provide a clue as to how a juror will vote during deliberations (Kovera et al., 2003). It is important to note that much of the research is conducted with simulated trials (i.e., Narby & Cutler, 1994) or after the verdicts have been rendered (Moran & Comfort, 1986). However, attitudinal research may assist attorneys to strike jurors who are biased against their case. Wrightsman, Batson, and Edkins (2004) have published a book of questionnaires assessing attitudes toward issues in the legal arena. The book is not meant for use in jury selection as many of the instruments lack the necessary psychometric properties necessary for valid research. Rather, the book is intended for use in forensic and **legal psychology** courses to assess students' attitudes toward issues discussed in class.

# Effectiveness of Scientific Jury Selection

There is not a great deal of evidence assessing the effectiveness of either traditional or scientific jury selection. Indeed, due to the uniqueness of each case, venue, and jury, very little evidence exists to support the effectiveness of trial consultants, though

■ **Attitudinal predictors**
Attitudes relevant to a particular case that are related to verdict inclinations among jurors.

■ **Legal psychology**
The scientific study of the effect of the law on people, and the effect people have on the law. Areas of legal psychology discussed in the text include eyewitness identification and investigative psychology.

some authors claim that the use of social science methods is superior to traditional jury selection (Myers & Arena, 2001). There are generally two approaches to studying the effectiveness of scientific jury selection. The first approach is to examine the statistical relationship, expressed in the form of a correlation coefficient, between the variables (demographic, personality traits, or attitudes) and participants' self-reported verdict inclination. The second approach is to examine the predictive strength, using a regression equation, of these same variables to predict verdicts in trial simulations.

The success of jury selection has been measured by the ability to identify biased jurors. However, this assumes that biased jurors cannot set aside their biases and weigh the evidence fairly. Kovera et al. (2003) suggest that a better measure of successful jury selection would be to ask if jury selection results in an increase in jurors' ability to assess the quality of the evidence presented. If the goal was to achieve a more informed jury, voir dire might be used to educate jurors about matters of the law, such as due process and the presumption of innocence. For example, research indicates a prevalent belief among jurors that those charged with a crime are probably guilty (Myers & Lecci, 1998).

Regardless of jury composition, the most important determinant of jury verdict is the quality of the evidence; the side with the most convincing evidence wins the case (Visher, 1987). Nevertheless, in particularly close cases where the evidence can go either way, trial attorneys want every possible edge and the use of a trial consultant may be justified (Wrightsman, 2001). The trial consultant can also work with the attorney on the *process* of voir dire. The consultant may decide that a survey of prospective jurors is unnecessary. The consultant can provide assistance to the attorney on constructing good questions for the voir dire, training in communication skills, and learning the "art" of conducting a voir dire. This assistance can result in a much more

## Guilty or Not Guilty: Does It Matter?

Dr. Jennifer Bauer, a trial consultant, has been asked by the defense attorney to assist in jury selection. The defendant is a battered wife who has been accused of murdering her abusive husband one night after he had been drinking and became verbally abusive. Dr. Bauer agrees to do the work pro bono because of her concern about the plight of battered women.

The defense attorney has also hired a prominent psychiatrist who suggested that the defense attorney use battered woman syndrome as the defense strategy. Dr. Bauer thinks that this is a poor decision since syndrome evidence has not been very successful in court cases and thinks that the argument would be more successful using PTSD as a defense. However, she was hired to assist with jury selection and not to help develop the defense strategy. Additionally, the psychiatrist retained by the attorney has developed a career arguing syndrome evidence in courts and is not very receptive to criticism.

In preparation for voir dire, Dr. Bauer reads through the discovery materials including the evidence provided by the defense and prosecution. Despite her empathy for battered women, Dr. Bauer feels that the weak defense strategy along with the strong evidence against the defendant will lead to a guilty verdict for the defendant. In fact, after weighing all the evidence, Dr. Bauer thinks that the defendant is guilty of manslaughter.

During the voir dire process, Dr. Bauer concludes that many of the potential jurors are not sympathetic toward the defendant. She decides that the only possibility is to hope for a mistrial by employing the *poison pill strategy*. She hopes to select jurors with strong personality differences so that they clash during the deliberations and are unable to come to a unanimous verdict.

How should Dr. Bauer proceed? Should she offer her advice regarding syndrome evidence? Should she pursue the poison pill strategy? What are the ethical implications of Dr. Bauer's decision?

open-ended and qualitatively rich jury selection process. Both the attorney and consultant can then feel confident that they have eliminated prospective jurors with obvious bias from the jury (C. Morris, personal communication, 2005).

Lieberman and Sales (2006) offer a comprehensive review of scientific jury selection. They review the effectiveness of voir dire, including the influence of demographic, personality, and attitudinal factors in jury decisions. They examine in-court questioning of prospective jurors as well as the utility of in-court observations of nonverbal behavior. The overall effectiveness of jury selection is evaluated and ethical and professional issues as well as future directions for scientific jury selection are presented.

# Change of Venue Requests

Another service a trial consultant may provide is the research to support a change of venue request. A **change of venue request** occurs when the attorney, usually for the defense, requests that the trial be moved to a different jurisdiction. Previous studies have demonstrated the harmful effects of pretrial publicity on the impartiality of jurors (Steblay, Besirevic, Fulero, & Jimenez-Lorente, 1999; Studebaker & Penrod, 1997). In a meta-analysis of 44 tests of the effects of pretrial publicity involving over 5,700 participants, Steblay et al. (1999) found that respondents who were exposed to negative pretrial publicity were more likely to judge the defendant guilty than respondents who were not exposed to pretrial publicity. Defense attorneys may feel that negative pretrial publicity will substantially harm their chances of obtaining an impartial jury and request a change of venue.

Trial consultants can assess the impact of pretrial publicity by conducting surveys in the community If a large percentage of people in the community are familiar with the case *and* also have already decided that the defendant is guilty, a change of venue is warranted (Myers & Arena, 2001). The trial consultant conducts the survey in the county where the trial will be held, and preferably another county away from the trial location. The survey is typically a 15-minute telephone survey based on an analysis of the media publicity in the locality (Wrightsman, 2002). The consultant prepares an affidavit for the court explaining the literature regarding effects of pretrial publicity on juror bias, the survey methodology, and conclusions. Testimony by the consultant regarding the methodology and results of the survey are subject to cross-examination. For a change of venue request to be successful, the survey will need to demonstrate that:

1. many potential jurors in the county where the trial is to be held are familiar with the case and the publicity surrounding the case,
2. potential jurors familiar with the case through pretrial publicity are likely to believe that the defendant is guilty, and
3. respondents in the other county are less likely to be aware of the case and surrounding publicity and less likely to have prejudged the defendant as guilty (Myers & Arena, 2001).

The methodology behind the survey is crucial to the success of the request. The consultant should have impeccable credentials in research methodology and statistical analysis, bolstered by a PhD in a social science discipline, to withstand the scrutiny of cross-examination. Many trial consultants without these credentials avoid this type of work and subcontract this work out to firms more skilled in survey methodology (C. Morris, personal communication, 2005). However, even the best methodology does not guarantee that a change of venue request will be granted. Change of venue requests are expensive, time-consuming, and inconvenient (Wrightsman, 2002).

■ **Change of venue request**
The process in which an attorney requests that a trial be moved to a different jurisdiction, usually based on concerns that the defendant could not get a fair trial in the presiding jurisdiction.

The change can substantially alter the composition of the venire. The courts have ruled that a when a change of venue is granted, the new location must have similar demographic characteristics to the original venue (*State v. Lozano*, 1993). The costs and political implications appear to conspire against a successful change of venue request. However, even if the request is unsuccessful, the community survey can be of assistance to the attorney during voir dire.

# Witness Preparation

An important aspect of preparing for trial is the preparation of witnesses. This area of trial consulting has come under the most scrutiny from the courts. Critics have argued that practiced testimony by witnesses affects their perceived credibility and that jurors should know about such assistance. However, the U.S. Court of Appeals for the Third Circuit ruled that a trial consultant's meetings with witnesses are shielded under the **work product doctrine**. Chief Judge Anthony J. Scirica wrote, ""Litigation consultants retained to aid in **witness preparation** may qualify as nonattorneys who are protected by the work product doctrine." The judge further ruled, "Moreover, a litigation consultant's advice that is based on information disclosed during private communications between a client, his attorney, and a litigation consultant may be considered 'opinion' work product, which requires a showing of exceptional circumstances in order for it to be discoverable" (*In re Cendant Corp. Securities Litigation*, 2003). This appellate court ruling protects the work of consultants in preparing witnesses for testimony from discovery (Bureau of National Affairs, 2003).

■ **Work product doctrine**
Maintains the privacy of a trial consultant's meetings with witnesses.

Trial consultants can examine both the stylistic and substantive aspects of mock testimony offering feedback on speech patterns, expressions of arrogance or defensiveness, and so on (Wrightsman, 2001). Nietzel and Dillehay (1986) identified five topics on which the psychologist can contribute expertise on witness preparation:

■ The facts to which the witness will testify
■ Witnesses' feelings associated with the case
■ The courtroom environment
■ Direct examination
■ Cross-examination

Consultants argued that the success of a trial depends heavily on the strength of the witnesses' confidence, credibility, and clarity in both disposition or on the witness stand (Gabriel & Fenyes, 2003). Consultants can help prepare witnesses to present a credible testimony, improving both their listening and communication skills. A consultant can educate the witness about their role in the trial and help them to provide an understandable and concise testimony without offering unnecessary or confusing information. Small-group research can evaluate a witness's testimony and provide insight into credibility and clarity. A recent example of a flawed witness discussed in the media is the mother who alleged that the pop star Michael Jackson sexually abused her son. While on the witness stand, the mother snapped her fingers at the jury during her testimony. Posttrial interviews of jurors indicated that her finger-snapping behavior came across as arrogant and hurt her credibility. Jackson was subsequently acquitted of all charges.

Most fact witnesses have not had experience testifying in court and may be intimidated by the experience. Proper preparation can help alleviate some of the anxiety associated with the experience and ensure that the testimony is both clear and credible. Gabriel and Fenyes (2003) offer a series of suggestions on how lawyers can prepare their witnesses for testimony. The following is a brief summary of their recommendations, illustrating the role of the trial consultant in witness preparation:

- Prepare witnesses to be cooperative and clear and to give complete answers without volunteering additional information beyond the scope of the question.
- Make sure they understand that their role is to tell their part of the story, and that they are not there to advocate a case or position. Advocacy can lead to a loss of credibility, for both a fact witness and an expert witness.
- Witnesses need to understand their audience. They should be familiar with the courthouse and courtroom environment, the opposing counsel's examination style, the judge, and the jury.
- Outline key trial themes or strategy for the witness, if appropriate.
- Use videotape of practice testimony so that the witness can see how he or she appears to others. Use reactions from small-group research participants (also referred to as mock jurors in the literature) to give feedback on mannerisms, eye contact, dress, facial expressions, gestures, and voice.
- Obtain feedback from small-group participants to provide feedback on substantive issues in the testimony including credibility and clarity.
- Instruct witnesses on basic presentation skills including dress, posture, enunciation, and eye contact.
- Take time to address witnesses' concerns or questions. Jurors can sense and usually negatively interpret a witness's hidden agenda. If you do not address these questions and concerns prior to their testimony, often the witness's uncertainty, confusion, or emotional state will affect how they listen to questions and respond on the stand.
- Practice cross-examination with the witness, teaching him or her about objections and responses to various question formats: compound, hypothetical, vague, or buildup. Instruct the witness to listen to questions and to control the pace of the cross-examination by pausing to form an accurate response as well as to allow counsel to object if necessary.

# Other Activities the Trial Consultant May Perform

Table 9.2 provided an extensive list of services provided by trial consultants. Not all consultants provide all services. Rather, consultants tend to specialize in a particular area. Since a high percentage of the membership of ASTC have training in communication (C. Morris, personal communication, 2005), it should come as no surprise that many trial consultants train lawyers on communications skills. Trial lawyers need to hold the attention of the jury and persuade jurors of their story. An example is Gillian Drake, a theater director and voice instructor turned trial consultant. She offers a class titled Acting for Lawyers, aimed at teaching lawyers how to express themselves to juries (Klyce, 1994). Drake also teaches lawyers how to present to an appellate court, arguing that presentation to a panel of judges requires substantially different skills than presentations to a jury of laypersons.

In addition to teaching lawyers effective communication skills, trial consultants also assist attorneys with developing trial strategy. Research suggests that assistance with case theory and presentation is one of the more common functions of a trial consultant (Streier & Shestowsky, 1999). Attorneys develop a strategy prior to the trial and attempt to tell a "story" to the jury throughout the process. Strategic decisions involve what evidence to present, when to present the evidence, order of witnesses, and content of testimony, as well as to what story the jury will be most receptive. Consultants use small-group research to evaluate effective arguments, credibility of witnesses, presentation of evidence, and so on. Attorneys develop their "story," or trial strategy, based on the evidence and law. Consultants develop the story based on the audience. It is very much an instance of marketing to a particular audience. A famous husband and wife consulting team[1] stated it succinctly in their popular text on jury selection and trial dynamics. The trial consultants write, "Like it or not, you are selling a product, and it is important to know what real people, in this instance the jury, think of your goods and your sales pitch" (Bennett & Hirschorn, 1993, p. 47). An attorney would probably not change his or her trial strategy based on jury composition. On the other hand, a jury consultant shapes the trial story based on jury composition. For example, if a jury was replaced and a new jury assembled, the consultant's approach might differ substantially from the initial strategy (Streier & Shestowsky, 1999).

Consultants may also use a shadow jury to evaluate the trial as it progresses. **Shadow juries** consist of participants similar in demographics to the seated jury who watch the trial as it progresses. Each evening they provide their feelings and reactions to the evidence and trial as it progresses. The consultant can use this feedback to help the attorney fine-tune the trial strategy. High tech has even invaded the courtroom with shadow jurors sending text messages of their reactions in real time to a consultant or even attached to biofeedback monitors that supply the consultant with information on the shadow jurors' physiological responses.

Consultants also help with the presentation of evidence. The use of small-group research can help determine how well the jury understands the evidence along with what specific issues need clarification. Small-group research can guide the selection and order of evidence presentation. For example, an attorney may decide that it is best to present negative evidence about his or her client before the opposing attorney has the opportunity, essentially stealing the thunder from the opposing counsel.

**■ Shadow jury**
Group of individuals similar in demographics to the seated jury who watch the trial as it progresses and provide feedback to the attorney.

# Ethical Issues in Trial Consultation

The practice of trial consulting is a relatively young field that has experienced rapid growth since its beginnings in the early 1970s. However, the field has not been without its critics, some of whom are psychologists with experience as trial consultants (Posey & Wrightsman, 2005) or attorneys (Streier & Shestowsky, 1999). Although a variety of ethical concerns have been expressed in the literature (Wrightsman, 2001), the majority of the issues have focused on the fairness of trial consulting and the lack of regulation in the industry (Myers & Arena, 2001). Concerns of fairness address two main issues. First, does the use of consultants threaten our system of justice by substantially altering the composition of the jury, rendering the jury no longer a representative sample of the community, as contemplated under the Constitution? Second, is it fair if one side has access to a jury consultant and the other side does not? Concerns with the lack of industry regulation also address primarily two issues. First, since the field is not regulated, anyone can hang a shingle as a trial consultant, with no minimum educational or professional requirements. Second, lack of regulation also means a lack of enforceable professional standards, allowing for the possibility of unethical behavior and outright charlatanism. Each of these concerns is explored in the following paragraphs.

The first question of fairness asks if trial consultants, specifically jury consultants, can so stack the jury that the members of the jury are no longer representative of the community as envisioned by the Constitution. Some critics have suggested that scien-

---

[1]It is perhaps appropriate now to point out that nothing in this chapter is meant to disparage the work of trial consultants or individuals involved in the field. Rather, it is the hope that this discussion contributes to students' understanding of the profession and controversies within the field.

tific jury selection is no more than high-tech jury-rigging. Indeed, a recent book on jury consulting is cynically titled, *Stack and Sway: The New Science of Jury Consulting* (Kressel & Kressel, 2002). Some constitutional scholars have suggested that the basic methods of scientific jury selection threatens the constitutional right to an impartial jury and that the basic goal of scientific jury selection is not to eliminate biased jurors but rather to seat unrepresentative and unbalanced juries (Streier & Shestowsky, 1999). However, until there is stronger evidence than currently exists regarding the ability of consultants to affect jury composition, the argument that consultants can "stack and sway" jury members is hard to support. Proponents of scientific jury selection have argued that jury consultants actually help to restore fairness to a process that can be inherently unfair. These authors cite the many prejudicial attitudes and mistaken beliefs that prospective jurors hold that threaten the seating of a "fair and impartial jury" (Myers & Arena, 2001). Examples include the belief held by many jurors that it is the duty of the defendant to prove his or her innocence, or the negative attitudes many jurors hold toward corporations in civil cases. Proponents argued that consultants help to eliminate biased jurors and educate others to be better impartial jurors. Consultants are quick to note that they cannot select favorable jurors, but only eliminate obviously biased jurors (C. Morris, personal communication, 2005).

The second issue of fairness concerns the imbalance of power between the two parties involved in the adversarial process when one side can afford a trial consultant and the other side cannot. The cost of trial consultants can easily run into the tens of thousands of dollars and in a large case can reach six-figure fees. The first jury consultants offered pro bono work to represent indigent criminal defendants in the case of the Harrisburg Seven. Now, the majority of trial consultants indicate that their work is in civil cases, typically representing large corporations in liability litigation. The criticism is that the extra cost of trial consultants widens the imbalance of resources between the rich and the not so rich. The wealthy clients can already afford the better attorneys, the better expert witnesses, and the better investigators. Adding the extra costs of trial consultants only increases the disparity between opposing sides in the courtroom. This criticism assumes equal resources and equal litigation skills for the two sides, which is never the case, nor an assumption of the law. Court cases have concluded that equality of counsel is not attainable and the court does not presume that the two opposing sides are equal in skills or resources (Wrightsman, 2001).

One recommendation that has been offered as a remedy for this criticism is to make trial consultants available to both sides. The suggestion is that if both sides have access to jury consultants, then scientific jury selection would make the goal of seating an impartial jury more feasible than ever before (Saks, 1987). In the spirit of this suggestion, some authors have suggested that the courts appoint trial consultants for indigent defendants who cannot otherwise afford the services. In a few cases, the courts have agreed. The attempted murder trial of Reginald Denny is a recent example. On Wednesday, April 29, 1992, Reginald Denny, a white truck driver stopped at a traffic light, was dragged from his truck by a crowd of angry black youths and was severely beaten as news helicopters hovered above recording the assault, including footage of youths dropping a cinder block on the head of the prostrate Denny. This assault occurred after outrage from the acquittal of four white police officers involved in the beating of motorist Rodney King. The two indigent defendants in the attempted murder trial of Reginald Denny had a consultant from Litigation Sciences, Inc. appointed by the court to assist in their defense. The court paid for a $175-per-hour consultant to assist the defendants (Cox, 1993). The two defendants were subsequently found guilty of lesser misdemeanor charges of assault and not the "willful, deliberate, and premeditated attempted murder" felony charges of which they were initially charged.

The precedent of the court paying for litigation assistance for indigent defendants was set in other trials in which the courts appointed expert witnesses, such as psychologists in insanity plea cases. However, court funding for trial consultants continues at the court's discretion (Streier & Shestowsky, 1999). The membership and Board of Directors of ASTC are currently reviewing an initiative to require pro bono work of all ASTC members. Although a laudable idea, not all trial consultants belong to ASTC and due to the number of lawsuits filed every year, a pro bono requirement of ASTC members is unlikely to balance the scales of inequity between the wealthy and the not so wealthy.

The second major criticism of the field is the lack of professional regulation. Concerns include an absence of minimum educational requirements to practice as well as weak and nonenforceable ethical principles. Currently, there are no university training programs geared to prepare students to become trial consultants. Despite what many practitioners may claim, the lack of standardized educational programs and entry-level requirements contributes to tremendous diversity regarding the quality of practice. Proponents argued that the free market place would ferret out incompetent practitioners. In professions where public safety is at risk, such as medicine, psychology, and the law, members are required to be licensed by the state and to obtain continuing education in their profession. Some commentators argue that trial consulting does not jeopardize public safety and should not have the unnecessary burden and costs of state regulation. In addition, the extra costs of regulation including licensure fees and maintenance of a professional regulatory board would only tend to increase costs. Proponents for licensure suggest that regulation would create minimal educational standards for entry into the profession. In a survey of the ASTC membership, 55% were against licensure, 30% favored licensing, and 15% were uncertain (Streier & Shestowsky, 1999).

Regulation could also ensure adherence to an enforceable code of ethical standards as well as continuing education requirements. Critics suggest that the current ASTC Professional Code is weak and unenforceable. Trial consultants, regardless of membership in ASTC, are expected to abide by the ethical code of their profession. For example, psychologists who work as trial consultants are expected to adhere to the APA's Ethical Standards for psychologists. Attorneys are expected to abide to their own profession's ethical guidelines, published by the American Bar Association. Some authors have pointed out that the ASTC's Professional Code is in conflict with the APA's code and more lax than either the APA or ABA ethical standards. The ASTC has recently strengthened the Professional Code and has provided Practice Guidelines for a number of areas in consulting work. The ASTC currently publishes Professional Standards and Practice Guidelines for Motions for a Change of Venue, Witness Preparation, and Small-Group Research. Practice guidelines for Jury Selection and Post Trial Juror Interviews are pending approval. The organization continues to revise the ethical standards and currently is reviewing a pro bono initiative. Regardless of these recent attempts, if history is to be a lesson, the organization will need to police itself or the government will regulate the profession.

Recent recommendations regarding professional ethics include suggestions already in the ASTC's Code. These 10 recommendations, summarized by Streier and Shestowsky (1999), are:

1. Trial consultants must possess a thorough knowledge of the legal system and an expertise in the research methodologies used in behavioral sciences
2. Trial consultants must respect the legal system
3. The privacy and sensibilities of jurors and prospective jurors must be respected
4. It is the responsibility of the trial consultant to assist in the seating of fair and impartial juries
5. Trial consultants must strive to ensure that the testimony of witnesses is truthful and accurate

6. The rights of clients must be protected
7. Trial and settlement scientists must provide objective and reasoned opinions
8. Trial consultants shall contribute to the amicable resolution of disputes
9. Trial consultants shall accurately and truthfully present their credentials to the bar and judiciary
10. Trial consultants shall keep current with research and theory in the field and advance and share their knowledge

Many of these recommendations have been incorporated into the revised ASTC Professional Code. However, the current code is relatively brief and broad concerning ethical principles. The Code addresses Competence, Integrity, Professional Responsibility, and Social Responsibility in fewer than nine sentences. See Table 9.4 for the Ethical Principles from the ASTC Professional Code (ATSC, 2005a). It is likely that more rigorous standards in training and practice will be established as the field continues to develop (Myers & Arena, 2001). It is also likely that licensure and state regulation will eventually become the norm for the practice of trial consultation. Although this development may limit some excellent practitioners from the profession, it will likely increase the quality and accountability of services provided.

## American Society of Trial Consultants Ethical Principles — Table 9.4

### I. Competence

Trial consultants strive to maintain high standards of competence in their work. They recognize the boundaries of their particular competencies and the limitations of their expertise. When in the role of trial consultant, the member does not practice law but seeks to enhance the practice of law by facilitating the skills of the legal practitioner. Trial consultants are dedicated to providing the legal community with information on litigation-related behavior and communication. They provide only those services and use only those techniques for which they are qualified by education, training, or experience. They maintain knowledge of relevant professional information related to the services they render.

### II. Integrity

Trial consultants conduct themselves at all times with professional integrity, personal dignity, and respect for the legal system.

### III. Professional Responsibility

Trial consultants uphold professional standards of conduct and clarify their professional roles and obligations.

### IV. Social Responsibility

Trial consultants comply with the law and encourage the development of law and social policy that serve the interests of their clients and the public generally.

# Training

Unlike other areas mentioned in this text, there are no set professional or educational requirements required for entering the field. The diversity of professional opportunities is a reflection of the diverse educational experiences people bring to the profession. Trial consultants may or may not have a law degree. There are different schools of thought on the value of a law degree. Some attorneys are interested in consulting with individuals who can offer a nonlegal but informed perspective on the case. Some trial consultants do have law degrees, although they frequently will also have another advanced degree to assist in the role of consultant. Nearly all trial consultants have advanced degrees in a discipline related to their work. Trial consultants come from a variety of academic backgrounds including clinical or counseling psychology, organizational psychology, sociology, anthropology, speech communication, drama and theater, and graphic design. Regardless of degree, consultants should possess some of the basic skills acquired in social science training. These skills include:

- Understanding the processes that shape and motivate human behavior
- Ability to observe and analyze human behavior
- Ability to conduct social science research, such as developing and analyzing community surveys
- Quantitative and qualitative data analysis
- Excellent public speaking and writing skills

| **Table 9.5** | **List of Continuing Education Workshops Presented at the ASTC Annual Meeting in 2005** |
|---|---|

- ADR and the Vanishing Jury Trial
- Trial Consulting 101: The Nuts and Bolts of the Profession
- Celebrity on Trial: The Prosecution of Martha Stewart
- Courtroom Technology for the 21st Century
- The ASTC Pro Bono Initiative
- Examining the ABA's Jury Trial Initiatives: What are the Implications for Trial Consultants?
- Understanding Media's Influence and the Impact on Trials in the 21st Century
- Electronic Evidence: Getting it Admitted and Making an Impact
- When the Media Comes Knocking
- Emerging Ethical Issues: Witness Preparation
- Jury Selection in the 21st Century
- The American Jury on Trial
- The American Jury
- Trial Consultants Beware: The Mock Trial Has Been Patented!
- Professional Standards and Practice Guidelines: Posttrial Juror Interviews
- The Corner of 1st and 6th- America's Most Dangerous Intersection
- A Logical Way to Evaluate a Cause of Action and Predict Its Verdict
- Vision and Reality: The Twilight of the American Jury and the Rise of Executive Constitutionalism

In addition to the educational requirements, a consultant needs excellent interpersonal and communications skills. Any type of consulting requires networking with potential clients to develop business for the consulting company. Professional presentations and publications help to develop credibility among clients. The ability to be organized, work efficiently, and under strict deadlines as well as with a diverse team of professionals are all crucial to success. Translating abstract academic concepts into practical suggestions, which lawyers and their clients can follow, are an important aspect of the work. Finally, the willingness to put in long hours before and during a trial is all part of the job.

One of the best ways to break into the profession is through experiential learning. Students enrolled in a relevant academic discipline, such as psychology, communication, or a related social science field, should look for an internship with a trial-consulting firm. The search for an internship will be the initial practice in networking and developing personal connections in the field. Students may also network at the annual meeting of the ASTC. Students can attend workshops and meet other professionals in the field. Table 9.5 provides a list of workshops offered at the 2005 annual meeting of the ATSC. The ASTC web site lists internship sites as well as employment opportunities along with a directory of consulting firms. Students at the undergraduate or graduate level may want to contact trial consultants in their local area to establish an internship or even to volunteer their time to assist with research and case preparation. Emphasize what you can bring to the firm, such as a willingness to work weekends and late hours, data analysis techniques, and participation in focus groups and mock juries, also referred to as small-group research. Trial consultation is a fast-paced and demanding profession. Frequently, the monetary stakes are quite high, running into the millions of dollars, and the expectations are that the consultant will work diligently to assist the client.

# Summary

This chapter provided an overview of the practice of trial consultation, an area of legal psychology. Although a relatively young profession, the field has experienced exponential growth and has won respect among attorneys and clients, although skeptics continue to question the legitimacy of the consultant's role in the courtroom. Trial consultants come from a variety of educational backgrounds, the majority appearing to be trained in psychology or speech communication. Partly due to their diverse training, consultants are able to offer attorneys a wide range of services. Trial consultants, also known as litigation consultants, assist attorneys with preparation for voir dire and jury selection, witness preparation, change of venue requests, trial strategy, communication skills, and the effective graphical presentation of evidence, among other services. The chapter provided an overview of three specific areas of trial consultation: jury selection, request for a change of venue, and witness preparation. The American Society of Trial Consultants (ASTC) was introduced as the professional guild organization. The ethical issues and concerns regarding trial consultation were reviewed along with the ASTC Professional Code, consisting of Ethical Principles, Professional Standards, and Practice Guidelines. Finally, qualifications to work as a trial consultant were presented along with training recommendations. Students interested in the field are encouraged to pursue an advanced degree in the social sciences or communication. Regardless of the degree, students will need strong research and analytic skills along with a dynamic personality and willingness to work long hours. One of the best ways to break into consulting is through an internship with a trial consulting firm. Another networking and educational opportunity is attendance at ASTC regional and national meetings.

# TEST YOUR KNOWLEDGE

1. Trial consultants do all of the following *except*:
   a. pretrial publicity assessment
   b. evaluation of trial strategy
   c. witness preparation
   d. jury selection
   e. they do all of the above

2. The request to relocate a trial to a different jurisdiction is termed a _____ request.
   a. voir dire
   b. change of jurisdiction
   c. change of venue
   d. peremptory challenge
   e. none of the above

3. The removal of a juror from the prospective panel for no avowed reason is referred to as:
   a. voir dire
   b. challenge for cause
   c. peremptory challenge
   d. no avowed reason challenge

4. The ruling that prohibits the use of peremptory challenges based solely for the purpose of striking individuals from specific groups including race was:
   a. *J.E.B. v. Alabama* ex rel *T.B.* (1994).
   b. *Batson v. Kentucky* (1986)
   c. *Rose v. United States* (1999)
   d. Civil Rights Act

5. Jury selection based on hunches, stereotypes, implicit personality theories, dress, etc. has been termed
   a. voir dire
   b. scientific jury selection
   c. traditional jury selection
   d. attitudinal selection process

Answer Key (1) e, (2) c, (3) c, (4) b, (5) c

# Chapter Ten

# Criminal Investigative Techniques

## Learning Objectives

- In which area, legal or forensic psychology, do criminal investigative techniques fall and why?
- Define criminal profiling and three approaches to criminal profiling presented in the text.
- What are the goals of criminal profiling?
- What type of training do most criminal profilers have?
- What types of crimes are most likely to benefit from the use of a profiler?
- Be able to describe the three approaches to criminal profiling and give an example of each.
- Identify recent real-world uses of criminal profiling.
- Define racial profiling and the rationale that has been offered for its use. Is this rationale appropriate?
- Describe crime scene analysis and be able to identify all the components of crime scene analysis.
- Distinguish between *modus operandi* and signature behaviors.
- What are the goals of criminal profiling and how do the goals differ depending on whether profiling is done during the investigative phase or the trial phase?
- Evaluate the effectiveness of criminal profiling and explain the concepts of transtemporal and transsituational consistency.
- Describe some of the current approaches to the detection of deception.
- Be able to describe the theory behind the polygraph and the physiological measures related to increased anxiety.
- What are some of the typical uses of the polygraph?
- What is the status of the polygraph for use in court?
- What did the National Research Council conclude regarding the validity of the polygraph?
- Describe the three approaches to use of the polygraph: relevant/irrelevant questions, control questions, and guilty knowledge test.
- How is hypnosis used in criminal investigation?
- Be able to briefly describe alternatives to the polygraph for detecting deception.
- Define PET, MRI, and fMRI.
- What are the courts' views on the use of hypnotically refreshed memories?

*(continued)*

## Key Terms

- Academy of Behavioral Profiling
- Autoerotic asphyxia
- Autonomic measures
- Behavioral evidence analysis (BEA)
- Behavioral Science Unit
- Cause of death
- Concealed information test
- Control question technique (CQT)
- Countermeasures
- Crime analysis
- Crime scene characteristics
- Criminal profile
- Criminal profiling
- Deception cues
- Demeanor
- Direct investigation
- Dissociative amnesia
- Dissociative theory
- Employee Polygraph Protection Act of 1988
- Equivocal death psychological autopsy
- Facial Action Coding System (FACS)
- Galvanic skin response (GSR)
- Guilty knowledge test (GKT)
- Hypnosis
- Hypnosis: role theory
- Hypnosis: state theory
- Hypnotic susceptibility
- Hypnotically refreshed memories
- Integrity tests

*(continued)*

## Key Terms *(continued)*

- Investigative phase
- Investigative psychology
- Legal psychology
- Lie detection
- Magnetic resonance imaging (MRI)
- Manner of death
- Minnesota Multiphasic Personality Inventory–2
- *Modus operandi*
- NASH
- Offender description
- Offender profiling
- *Per se* exclusionary rule
- Polygraph
- Positron emission tomography (PET)

- Psychological autopsy
- Racial profiling
- Relevant/irrelevant technique
- Serial crimes
- Signature behaviors
- Sphygmomanometer
- Stim test
- Suicide psychological autopsy
- Totality of the circumstances test
- Toxicology
- Transsituational consistency
- Transtemporal consistency
- Trial phase
- Voice stress analysis

## Learning Objectives *(continued)*

- What are the three general theories used to explain hypnosis?
- What are the per se exclusionary rule and the totality of the circumstances test?
- Define the two types of psychological autopsies and list the four distinctions between the two.
- What agency is responsible for developing training guidelines for psychological autopsies?
- What is the NASH classification?

■ **Legal psychology**
The scientific study of the effect of the law on people, and the effect people have on the law. Areas of legal psychology discussed in the text include eyewitness identification and investigative psychology.

■ **Criminal profiling**
Any process used to infer distinctive personality traits, behavioral tendencies, physical and demographic characteristics, or even geographic locations of individuals responsible for committing criminal acts from physical and/or behavioral evidence

It is important to note that the activities discussed in this chapter more appropriately belong to the area termed **legal psychology** than the area of *forensic psychology*. Recall, based on the narrow definition of the field of forensic psychology as proposed by the American Psychological Association and adopted by this text, forensic psychology is the applied aspect of psychology to legal questions. Legal psychology, on the other hand, is the application of psychological knowledge and principles to solving legal questions. In this chapter we review several areas in which psychological knowledge is used to solve legal questions. These areas include criminal profiling, lie detection including the use of the polygraph, the use of hypnosis, and constructing psychological autopsies. Many of the professionals involved in these activities are not psychologists at all but rather have their training and backgrounds in law enforcement.

# Criminal Profiling

This is perhaps one of the most popular and most misunderstood areas in the field. Many students taking forensic psychology courses indicate that their career goal is to become a criminal profiler. The popularity of television shows and movies romanticizing the profession certainly contribute to the allure of criminal profiling. Some authors have even questioned whether the topic of criminal profiling should be included

---

## Criminal Investigative Techniques                    Table 10.1

---

- Criminal Profiling
- Lie detection
    - The polygraph
    - Alternative autonomic measures
    - Demeanor
    - Direct investigations
- Hypnosis
- Psychological autopsies

---

in a textbook on forensic psychology. Wrightsman (2001) presents five arguments on why the topic of criminal profiling is not an area within the domain of either forensic or legal psychology. The five reasons for excluding criminal profiling from forensic or legal psychology proposed by Wrightsman are

1. The majority of criminal profilers in the United States are not psychologists nor do they possess graduate training in psychology. Rather, profilers have traditionally come from law enforcement backgrounds, primarily the FBI.
2. Training in criminal profiling has largely occurred at the **Behavioral Science Unit** of the FBI Academy at Quantico, Virginia. The Behavioral Science Unit (BSU) was started in 1972 when the federal government opened the new FBI Academy. The BSU was at the forefront of training criminal profilers for several decades. Currently, the FBI's profiling unit operates under the National Center for the Analysis of Violent Crime at the FBI Academy. The Behavioral Science Unit continues as one of the instructional components of the Academy, providing training, consultation, and research in the behavioral sciences for the law enforcement community. It should be noted that the recently named current director of the Behavioral Science Unit is a psychologist. Although the FBI has led the field in training profilers, there has been a recent increase in the number of universities offering graduate programs in criminal **investigative psychology** and criminal profiling. As discussed in Chapter 1 of this text, students should investigate all graduate training programs thoroughly before committing to a year or more of advanced study.
3. The number of job opportunities for criminal profilers is extremely limited. The BSU at the FBI Academy typically employed fewer than a dozen or so profilers. A former profiler with the FBI told this author that there are fewer than 26 profiler positions in the entire United States with the FBI, although with the increase in popularity and training opportunities, more employment openings may develop. However, it is unlikely that the demand will ever meet the potential supply of profilers as indicated by the number of students who express an interest in the profession. It is interesting to note that there are private companies and organizations involved in criminal profiling casework and research. However, criminal profiling is not a career in itself but rather a skill developed by law enforcement personnel.

■ **Investigative psychology**
The application of behavioral science methods to criminal investigative work.

4. Many professionals question the validity of criminal profiling, suggesting it is more art than science. In a recent survey, over 70% of police psychologists indicated that they neither felt comfortable developing a criminal profile nor were convinced of its usefulness (Bartol, 1996). However, in 1999, the **Academy of Behavioral Profiling** (ABP; *www.profiling.org*) was founded partly in response to the "rapid de-professionalization" of the field (Turvey, 2002, p. 18). The ABP now offers a code of ethics, written criminal profiling guidelines, and a profiling general knowledge exam.

5. The expert testimony by criminal profilers is *not* likely to meet the Daubert standards for admissibility in a courtroom proceeding. In fact, that is exactly what happened in the case of *The Estate of Sam Shepard v. State of Ohio* (2000). The judge ruled that a former FBI profiler would need to limit his expert testimony and could not testify that the Sheppard murder had been staged. The judge ruled that such testimony would amount to profiling evidence and profiling testimony did not meet the standards of Daubert or the U.S. Supreme Court's ruling in the *Kumbo Tire Co. v. Carmichael* (1999) regarding admissibility of expert opinion.

| Table 10.2 | Five Reasons for Excluding Criminal Profiling from a Textbook on Forensic Psychology |
|---|---|

- Majority of criminal profilers have little or no background in psychology
- The majority of training to be a profiler is within the FBI's Behavioral Science Unit
- There are an extremely limited number of job opportunities for profilers
- There is a great deal of controversy within the field regarding the validity of profiling
- Expert testimony by profilers is infrequently admissible in court

Despite the above-cited caveats regarding the suitability of criminal profiling in a textbook on forensic psychology, we discuss it here as part of our presentation of criminal investigative procedures. First, we need to define criminal profiling, highlighting the distinction between it and other areas of forensic science. We discuss the process of profiling, recommended training, and briefly present career opportunities.

# Definition of Criminal Profiling

**Criminal profiling**, or **offender profiling**, is a general term that describes any process used to infer distinctive personality characteristics, behavioral tendencies, physical and demographic characteristics, or even geographic locations of individuals responsible for committing criminal acts from physical and/or behavioral evidence. Different terms have been used interchangeably to describe profiling, including psychological profiling, sociopsychological profiling, or criminal investigative analysis. The latter term was adopted by FBI profilers to distinguish their procedures from those used by mental health professionals. The numerous terms and lack of clear definitions has led to confusion both in the field and among the general public. Part of this confusion can be attributed to the relatively recent attempts to increase the professional standards in the field. Though the concept of inferring behavioral characteristics of perpetrators from crime scene evidence has existed for centuries, it is only relatively recent that scientific principles have been used to test and develop these theories. This text uses the term criminal profiling as defined here.

Today there are many fictional accounts of profilers and forensic scientists in the media and the two are frequently confused. *Forensic pathology* is the field of medicine that applies medical knowledge and procedures to solving problems in the legal arena. A forensic pathologist is responsible for understanding the victim's interaction with his or her environment that led to his or her injury and/or death. The forensic pathologist is in charge of the body of the deceased and the related forensic evidence. It is the forensic pathologist's responsibility to understand the crime scene and related issues such as wound patterns, blood splatter, decomposition of the body, and so on. A criminal profiler may use this information to develop an **offender description**.

The goal of criminal profiling is to develop an offender description. An *offender description* can include psychological variables such as personality traits, psychopathologies, and behavior patterns, as well as demographic variables such as age, race, or geographic location (Winerman, 2004). This helps to narrow the range of potential suspects down to a manageable number. It is important to note that a criminal profile does not indicate the specific individual who committed the crime. Rather, it can provide some statistical probabilities that the perpetrator may possess specific behavioral, demographic, or psychological characteristics.

Wrightsman (2001) presents three approaches to criminal profiling: profiling historical and political figures, profiling criminals' common characteristics, and profiling criminals from crime scene analysis. These three approaches are briefly reviewed. However, we will spend the majority of our discussion on *crime scene analysis*, the use of evidence from the crime scene to generate an offender description.

> ■ **Offender description**
> A general description that can include personality traits, psychopathologies, behavior patterns, and demographic variables of the offender, which is arrived at through the process of criminal profiling.

## Historical Approach

The historical approach relies on historical records for the data used to generate an offender description. This might be the case when an attempt is made to develop a profile of the individual responsible for the Whitechapel (a.k.a., Jack the Ripper) murders that occurred in Great Britain in 1888. Also, this approach may be used to predict how a specific individual will behave, as with political leaders such as Adolf Hitler, Fidel Castro, and Saddam Hussein. Henry Murray, a Harvard psychologist who worked with the Office of Strategic Services (OSS), a predecessor of the CIA, completed a psychological profile of Adolf Hitler in 1943 (Murray, 1943). This profile was based on Hitler's book *Mein Kampf*, along with books about Hitler and collateral information from people who knew Hitler. Although Murray predicted Hitler's suicide should Germany be defeated, he guessed that Hitler might kill himself in a dramatic, explosive way.

As an interesting footnote, Theodore Kaczynski, a student at Harvard, was a participant in research conducted by Murray after the war. The research exposed participants to a stress test similar to one used by the OSS to evaluate recruits. At his trial as the Unabomber, Kaczynski's defense lawyers argued that some of his emotional problems were related to his participation in this research while at Harvard (Myers, 2005). The failure of the FBI to identify Kaczynski as the Unabomber is often cited as a failure of criminal profiling. The FBI was led to Kaczynski when his brother recognized his style of writing in the Unabomber's "manifesto" published in national newspapers. Wrightsman (2001) states that the "eventual identification of the Unabomber was not a sterling example of the usefulness of profiling" (p. 78).

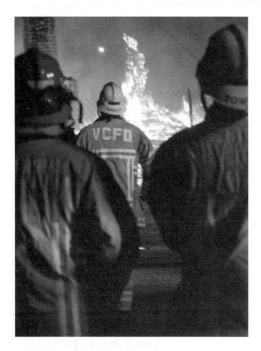

**Figure 10.1**

A profiler would attempt to identify similarities between individuals who commit arson.

There has been very little success in predicting how individuals will behave under future circumstances based on psychological profiles developed from archival data (Wrightsman, 2001). It is difficult to predict how individuals will behave in the future, even when one has access to the individual and can use the full armamentarium of clinical skills and measures. It is even more difficult to make accurate predictions based on archival and anecdotal data.

The case of David Koresh, leader of the besieged Branch Davidain cult that ended in the tragic loss of life in Waco, Texas, is a prime example of the difficulty in predicting human behavior. The 51-day siege of the Branch Davidian compound ended when the compound was gassed by the FBI. A fire ensued and over 80 people died in the resulting gun battle and blaze. Reports suggest that FBI profilers had reassured Attorney General Janet Reno that the use of tear gas was the only way to end the standoff peacefully. However, other profilers on the case accused the FBI of providing slanted information to the Attorney General and ignoring memos indicating that the Branch Davadians "would rather die than surrender" (Hancock, 2000). Whether the information was wrong, conflicting, or ignored, the expertise of the profilers did not help to avoid a tragedy or predict the behavior of individuals. Perhaps the best lesson to learn is that one should not place too much credence on psychological profiles of specific individuals until research suggests otherwise.

## Profiling Criminals' Common Characteristics

In this approach, the profiler attempts to identify similarities among individuals who commit the same or similar crimes. This is therefore an attempt to categorize criminals. For example, we would want to know if all individuals who commit a particular crime, such as arson, have similar personality, behavioral, or demographic characteristics. Researchers have examined the background of convicted offenders to identify similarities, such as a history of childhood sexual abuse.

There are several problems with this approach to profiling. First, the bulk of the research is conducted with convicted offenders. If in fact individual characteristics can predict criminal behavior, it is also possible that these characteristics predict behavior that leads to arrest versus avoiding arrest. Second, it is quite possible to misunderstand baseline rates. For example, let's say that we interview 50 convicted rapists and find that 45 of the rapists (90%) report having been sexually abused as a child. We may then assume that childhood sexual abuse leads to becoming a sex offender. However, the reality is that the vast majority of individuals sexually abused as children do not commit crimes as adults (Murphy & Peters, 1992). Therefore, we find that only a small percentage of people abused as children later become sex offenders.

More importantly, despite popular belief that such typologies are accurate, there is no evidence to support these types of claims. This type of misinformation is particularly true for commonly held beliefs regarding sex offenders. Several authors have proposed boilerplate typologies for the motivations of rapists and these "profiles" have gained popular acceptance among the general public. Examples include the Groth (1979) Rapist Motivational Typologies and a typology of seven rapists' motivations (Baker, 1997).

Despite scientific evidence to the contrary regarding the accuracy of these typologies, a naive belief in the validity of these criminal typologies continues. A recent survey found that over two-thirds of judges believed that sex offenders abused others because they were sexually abused as children and nearly 50% of the judges surveyed believed that mental health professionals could present "sex offender profiles" in court (Bumby & Maddox, 1999). Again, it is necessary to point out that the majority of individuals who were sexually abused as children do not become sex offenders.

Researchers have also turned to the use of the **Minnesota Multiphasic Personality Inventory–2** (MMPI-2) as a way to identify common characteristics of offenders. As discussed in the chapter on assessment, the MMPI-2 is one of the most frequently used objective personality measures. Therefore, it is understandable that a number of studies would attempt to use the MMPI-2 to identify similar personality characteristics among offenders. Although some studies have claimed to find specific scales on the MMPI-2 elevated among child molesters (i.e., Hall, 1989; Swenson & Grimes, 1969), most researchers would conclude that there are no valid psychological assessment instruments for profiling sex offenders nor do any accurate sex offender classification systems exist (Prentky & Burgess, 2000). In fact, Federal courts have ruled that forensic psychologists may not testify as to whether an individual could or could not have committed a crime based on these sorts of typologies (*United States v. Robinson*, 2000).

Another concern with the use of looking for similar characteristics among offenders is the development of racial profiling. **Racial profiling** is the use of racial or ethnic background that leads law enforcement to suspect an individual is engaged in illegal activity. Again, these assumptions based on one characteristic ignore baseline rates in that the vast majority of individuals are not engaged in any criminal activity. Racial profiling has been used to initiate "pretext" traffic stops of members of ethnic minority groups. Pretext stops occur when an individual is pulled over for a minor infraction simply as a way to further the police officers' visual search of the vehicle. Racial profiling has been banned in some jurisdictions.

## Crime Scene Analysis

Contemporary criminal profilers use crime scene analysis to develop an offender description. It is important to note that developing an offender description does not specify any particular individual as the likely suspect. Rather, as stated above, it provides statistical probabilities that the individual will have certain characteristics. However, these probabilities are simply statistical predictions and can frequently be wrong. Recent examples of inaccurate criminal profiles include the false identification of Richard Jewel as the Atlanta Olympic bomber and the profiles suggesting an unmarried white male as the Washington, D.C., sniper in fall of 2002. Both times the criminal profiles were wrong. The FBI settled a civil lawsuit brought by Richard Jewel in the Atlanta bombing case. The profile suggesting a white male as the D.C. sniper certainly did not facilitate the subsequent arrest of two African American males. As Bartol and Bartol (2004) suggests one area that would certainly benefit from empirical research is criminal profiling. Researchers need to examine the accuracy of profiling methods and search for ways to improve criminal profiling and how to apply profiles in law enforcement.

The following discussion focuses on key concepts used in developing an offender description, the process of crime scene analysis, guidelines for criminal profiling, and the research on the accuracy of criminal profiles. Criminal profilers use **crime analysis** to develop a criminal profile (Beaza, Chisum, Chamberlin, McGrath, & Turvey, 2000). Crime analysis is the process of examining evidence from a crime, including any tests or examinations conducted, in order to develop the offender description. Crime analysis includes examining **crime scene characteristics**, which include the physical and behavior features of a crime scene. Crime scene characteristics include

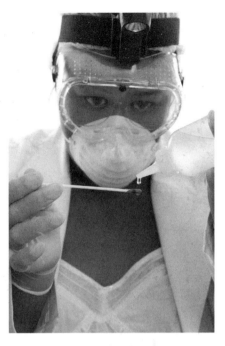

Figure 10.2

Crime scene analysis is used by criminal profilers to develop an offender description.
© 2009 Leah-Anne Thompson. Used under license from Shutterstock, Inc.

■ **Racial profiling**
Suspecting an individual of illegal activity because of ethnic background, such as pulling over an African American male driver simply because of his race. Racial profiling has been ruled illegal in many states.

- location type,
- crime scene type,
- point of contact,
- primary scene,
- secondary scene,
- intermediate scene,
- dumpsite/disposal site,
- location of the scene,
- method of approach,
- method of attack,
- use of force,
- methods of control,
- weapons, victim resistance,
- planning/preparation,
- precautionary acts,
- items taken, and
- opportunistic elements.

Table 10.3 provides a brief list of major crime scene characteristics.

## Table 10.3    Crime Scene Characteristics

- Location Type
  - Indoor crime scenes
  - Vehicle crime scenes
  - Outdoor crime scenes
  - Underwater crime scenes
- Crime Scene Type
  - Point of contact
  - Primary scene
  - Secondary scene
  - Intermediate scene
  - Dumpsite/disposal site
  - Location of the scene
- Method of Approach
  - Surprise
  - Con
- Method of Attack
- Use of Force
- Methods of Control
  - Control-oriented force
  - Verbal threat of controlling, punishing, sexual, or lethal force
  - Unarticulated presence of the physical threat of controlling, punishing, sexual, or lethal force
- Weapons
- Victim Resistance
  - Victim compliant
  - Passive resistance

- Verbal resistance
- Physical resistance
- Nature and Sequence of Sexual Acts
- Planning/Preparation
- Precautionary Acts
  - Clothing/Disguise
  - Alteration of voice
  - Blindfold
  - Time of day
  - Location selection
  - Victim selection
  - Use of gloves
  - Use of condom
  - Use of fire
  - Disposing of the victim's clothing
  - Looking at or collecting victim identification
- Items Taken
  - Evidentiary
  - Valuables
  - Personal
    o Trophy
    o Souvenir
- Opportunistic Elements
- The Body
- Verbal Behavior/Scripting
- Motive
- Victim Selection
  - Availability
  - Location
  - Vulnerability
  - Relationships
  - Symbolic criteria
  - Fantasy criteria

(Adapted from Turvey, 2002)

Partly as a result of a thorough crime scene analysis, profilers will identify the offender's **modus operandi**. *Modus operandi* (MO) is a Latin term that roughly translates to method of operating. The MO refers to the manner in which a crime was committed and reflects choices and behaviors by the criminal in order to assist in the completion of the crime. Not all criminals have a particular MO. However, a sufficient number of criminals do have a characteristic MO that makes it worthwhile as an investigative tool (Weston & Wells, 1974). The MO can evolve over time as the criminal gains more experience and confidence or can deteriorate due to mental condition or substance use (Turvey, 2000).

The important point to recall is that the MO consists of learned behaviors that the criminal uses to successfully complete the criminal act. The MO does not reflect the criminal's motive for committing the crime. Motive refers to the reason the individual committed the criminal act. It is possible to infer an offender's motive from their **signature behaviors**. A criminal's signature behavior reflects personal aspects of the

■ *Modus operandi*
Latin for "method of operating" or the choices and behaviors by the criminal in order to commit the crime; a term used in criminal profiling.

■ **Signature behavior**
Personal aspects of criminal behavior carried out to satisfy emotional and psychological needs.

criminal act and is carried out in order to satisfy emotional and psychological needs, not to successfully complete the crime. The offender signature represents the emotional or psychological themes that the offender satisfies when he commits a crime and can include the general motivational categories of profit, anger, reassurance, assertiveness, and sadistic (Turvey, 2002). The *signature behaviors* are acts committed by the criminal that are not necessary to successfully commit the crime. Rather, these behaviors reflect the emotional and psychological needs of the offender. The difficulty for the criminal profiler is to identify what constitutes MO behaviors and what behaviors are signature behaviors. Further complicating the distinction is the complexity of human behavior. Behaviors can be multidetermined and serve more than one purpose (Turvey, 2002). For example, a rapist may blindfold his victim in order to fulfill a fantasy of bondage. The behavior would then serve as a signature behavior, satisfying the offender's psychological needs. Another rapist may blindfold his victim in order to prevent her from accurately identifying him should he be apprehended. This behavior would then serve to successfully complete the crime and would be considered part of the offender's MO. Finally, a third rapist may blindfold victims to satisfy both psychological needs and the need to successfully complete the crime. This behavior would then be both part of the offender's MO and his signature.

Whereas the MO may change over time with increased knowledge, experience, and confidence, the signature behaviors may reflect more stable psychological characteristics of the offender and remain consistent over time (Bartol & Bartol, 2004). If this assumption is accurate, the offender's signature may be more useful to criminal profilers than the offender's MO. Regardless, it is crucial to always remember the two important axioms regarding criminal profiling and behavioral evidence analysis discussed by Turvey (2002, p. 280):

- Different offenders do similar things for different reasons.
- Individual offender behaviors are multidetermined; they can be the result of multiple motivations and multiple external influences.

# The Process of Generating a Criminal Profile

The process of generating a criminal profile can be thought of as an investigative process that culminates in an offender description. A **criminal profile** is a written report that describes the offender characteristics based on a thorough crime analysis and victimology. A *crime analysis* is a report that examines behavioral evidence for a crime and makes interpretations of the behavioral evidence. This behavioral evidence includes victim behaviors, offender behaviors, and environmental circumstances related to the crime. The crime analysis includes an examination of the crime scene with documentation of any and all crime scene characteristics. When possible, the crime analysis includes opinions as to the motivation of the offender based on crime-related behaviors. Profilers must be careful in inferring motivations and behaviors and only do so strictly in accordance with the evidence in the case. All inferences must be supported by the evidence and include supporting argumentation in the report. *Victimology* refers to a thorough study of all the available information regarding the victim of the crime. In addition to basic demographic information, this includes information regarding the victim's lifestyle, personal habits, and any background information including educational, criminal, medical, and vocational histories.

Once the profiler has completed a thorough crime analysis and victimology, the criminal profile, or a description of the offender characteristics, can be completed. The criminal profile can include any characteristics that the profiler can attribute to the unknown offender. These characteristics may include physical descriptions as well as psychological attributes, social habits, patterns or preferences, geographical habits, and/or relational characteristics. For example, physical characteristics in a profile may indicate the gender, approximate age, approximate height and weight including any disabilities, and dominant hand. Social habits may include descriptions that lead to an individual who frequents nightclubs, smokes a particular brand of cigarette, and engages in "one-night stands." Geographical characteristics may include where the offender frequently goes to find victims along with where the offender lives. A relational attribute would be the offender's prior relationship with the victim. In addition to these predictions, a criminal profile may include predictions about the offender's behavior prior to, during, or after the commission of the crime. For example, a profile may predict whether an offender will return to the crime scene (Turvey, 2002). The Academy of Behavioral Profiling has established the first written guidelines for criminal profiling. Though relatively brief, they do attempt to establish a scientific basis for this emerging field.

# The Effectiveness of Criminal Profiling

Before we can determine the effectiveness of criminal profiling, we need to understand the goal of profiling. **Behavioral evidence analysis** (BEA), another term for criminal profiling, is the "process of analyzing behavior patterns in the physical and behavioral evidence, then inferring (deducting) offender characteristics from them" (Turvey, 2002, p. 43). This process has two phases with separate goals: the investigative phase and the trial phase.

The investigative phase has received the most attention in the media and the scientific literature. The **investigative phase** of criminal profiling involves the analysis of behavioral evidence in order to develop an offender description of an unknown offender for a known crime. Profilers are typically involved in cases that are extremely violent, sexual or predatory in nature and tend to receive a lot of media coverage. According to Turvey (2002), there are five goals of the investigative phase:

- To help reduce the number of potential suspects and to prioritize the investigation of suspects into the smaller potential suspect pool.
- To facilitate the linkage of potentially related crimes by examining and identifying similar crime scene characteristics and patterns, such as the MO of an offender.
- To provide investigators with relevant leads and strategies.
- To assess the potential for the escalation of crimes (i.e., stalking to sexual assault).
- To help keep the investigation on track and focused.

The **trial phase** uses BEA for cases in which there is already a suspect or defendant. Profiling techniques are used in preparation for trials including criminal trials, appeals, or the sentencing phase of a criminal trial. The goals of the trial phase differ from the investigative phase. Turvey (2002) lists five primary goals of profiling during the trial phase:

- To assist in evaluating the nature and value of the forensic evidence.
- To assist in developing interrogative strategies.
- To assist in developing insight into offender psychological motivations.
- To assist in developing insight into the offender's state of mind before, during, and after the offense.
- To facilitate crime scene linkage issues through examining MO and signature behavior.

**■ Investigative phase**
Analysis of behavioral evidence in order to develop an offender description; used during the process of criminal profiling.

**■ Trial phase**
Analysis of forensic evidence and the offender to assist in various aspects of a trial.

The psychological profile has been used in court testimony to

1. prove the defendant committed the crime,
2. to prove the defendant did not commit the crime, and
3. to solidify the credibility of the defendant (Arrigo, 2003).

However, very little research exists as to its effectiveness and possible detrimental effects in the trial phase.

Based on the two different phases of profiling with their differing goals, it is first necessary to establish what questions to answer when evaluating the effectiveness of profiling. A potential problem with criminal profiling during the investigative phase is that an investigation may lock in to the wrong suspect based on a profile. This is what happened in the case of the Atlanta Olympic Park bomber in 1996. A FBI criminal profile mistakenly indicated that a security guard, Richard Jewell, matched the profile as the prime suspect in the case. Mr. Jewell worked as a security guard at Olympic Park and was the subject of an intense investigation by the FBI and the police as well as the object of public scorn. His name and photograph were released to media outlets as the prime suspect and subsequently appeared in newspapers and television reports across the country. After 3 months of investigation, the FBI admitted that they had no evidence linking Mr. Jewell to the bombing and eventually settled a civil lawsuit filed by him claiming damages. Two years later, the FBI charged Eric Randolph, an antiabortion activist, with the Olympic bombing (Costanzo, 2004).

The major difficulty with evaluating the effectiveness of criminal profiling is the dearth of empirical research. Few studies assess the accuracy of the technique and whether or not the police are actually assisted by profilers any more than by other forensic consultants. The few studies that do exist are usually after-the-fact surveys comparing trained police profilers' predictions pf apprehended offenders to those of nonprofilers, such as college students. Richard Kocsis, former chief of the Criminal Profiling Research Unit in Australia, has published extensively on profiling (Kocsis, 2003; Kocsis & Cooksey, 2002; Kocsis, Cooksey, & Irwin, 2002). Kocsis's research suggests that profilers outperform other groups in prediction accuracy.

Bartol and Bartol (2004) have argued that profiling is inaccurate since it is based on two questionable assumptions:

■ **Transtemporal consistency**
The proposition that behavior is consistent over time.

1. that behavior is consistent over time (**transtemporal consistency**), and
2. that behavior is consistent across situations (**transsituational consistency**).

■ **Transsituational consistency**
The proposition that behavior is consistent across situations.

They point to evidence that indicates most criminal behavior is dependent upon characteristics of the situation (e.g., Merry & Harsent, 2000).

Regardless of the empirical evidence, or lack thereof, the difference in opinion also reflects a clash in culture between the "investigative experience" of law enforcement and the scientific rigor that psychologists expect. Researchers and law enforcement personnel will interpret the data as they see fit based on their preconceived notions (Winerman, 2004). A forensic psychiatrist compares the practice of medicine to the practice of profiling: "Profiling currently is, at best, an art and some may show proficiency in this area, while others will not. The 'scientific' basis of profiling is clearly less well established than in a field such as medicine, but the practice of medicine remains an art" (McGrath, 2000). Hopefully, the future will see more psychologists contributing the scientific method to evaluating and developing the practice of profiling. Collaborative studies between psychology and law enforcement will certainly enhance our understanding of profiling.

# The Polygraph

The **polygraph** test has also had its share of fame in the mass media. It is easy to find a crime story movie with a suspect strapped to a chair, electrodes connected to his head and arms, and the suspect sweating bullets in a dimly lit (one 60-watt bulb please) interrogation room. The cop, wearing a white shirt with the shirt-sleeves rolled up, gun tucked away in a shoulder holster, paces the room firing questions at the nervous suspect. A man, wearing black-rimmed eyeglasses, sits behind our suspect at a large polygraph, reams of paper rolling off as ink-needles dance across the lines on the paper. Our interrogator barks a question at the shaking suspect, "Where were you on the night of the murder?" The suspect replies, fumbling for words, searching for an alibi. The man behind the machine looks at out interrogator and shakes his head to say that was a lie. Our cop pounds his fist on the table and gets in the face of our suspect and whispers, "That's a lie, and we know it."

The above scenario is great for television and movies, but not at all the reality of the polygraph test. The polygraph test is also known as the "lie-detector test," a misnomer at best. In addition, as with most everything else in our lives, technology has drastically changed both the look and validity of the polygraph test. Finally, although the instrument used is fairly standard, there are a variety of ways that the test can be conducted. As such, it perhaps makes more sense to speak about the polygraph tests as a series of tests as opposed to one singular test. The choice of one technique over another relates as much to the purpose of the test as well as to the examiner's training and preferences. The polygraph can be used in a variety of situations that may call for different techniques. The use of the test to screen a potential law enforcement candidate may call for a different technique than assessing a postconviction sex offender regarding probation violations (Holden, 2000). Some of the potential uses of a polygraph test are listed in Table 10.4.

## List of Typical Uses of the Polygraph Technique — Table 10.4

- Assess honesty of exculpatory statements given by criminal suspects
- Screening of law enforcement applicants and individuals involved in intelligence work
- Post-conviction sex offender evaluation for probation violations
- Conviction appeals
- Assist in interrogations

# The Polygraph Instrument

The polygraph is no longer the large, bulky machine that spewed off reams of paper with ink-needles madly dancing on the charts when a suspect told a lie. The large apparatus has been replaced by the laptop computer, the graph paper replaced by the computer screen. The contemporary polygraph consists of a laptop computer and several devices that connect to the computer and are used to measure various physiological responses. As a result, the polygraph is a rather compact assessment instrument that can easily fit into a briefcase.

The devices that attach to the computer record various physiological measures of the examinee. The premise behind the polygraph is that physiological changes are related to arousal, and that the arousal is indicative of lying. It is important to note that a polygraph does not measure whether an individual is telling the truth or lying. Rather, the polygraph examiner compares the pattern of physiological arousal that occurs to the examinee while answering a series of questions. The assumption is that examinees will be more aroused when they are telling a lie than when they are telling the truth. It is important to note that there is no known physiological response pattern that would indicate deception. Therefore, the term "lie detector" is really a misnomer. The suggestion that someone is lying is an *inference* based on changes in arousal. The comparison of arousal patterns from one question to the next is also done by computer software that uses algorithms to suggest truth or deception.

Typically, anywhere from three to four physiological measures of arousal are taken. Pneumographs are strapped around the examinee's chest and abdomen and record breathing rate and depth of respiration. This makes it possible to obtain a record of a sigh or when an examinee attempts to hold his or her breath. A **sphygmomanometer,** or pressure cuff, is placed around the upper arm and records changes in blood pressure. Electrodes are attached to the fingertips to record changes in the **galvanic skin response** (GSR). The GSR has also been referred to as the skin conductance response or the electrodermal response. The GSR is a measure of perspiration; as an individual perspires there is better conductance of an electrical current through the skin. Finally, some examiners will have a subject sit on a sensor that detects any movement. Although movement is not used to measure physiological arousal or infer deception, it is used to detect any attempts at countermeasures. **Countermeasures** are any efforts used by the examinee to "beat" the test. The record of the interview stored in the computer can indicate all the physiological responses and when they occurred in relation to when each question was asked.

The actual testing procedure can use several different techniques. However, most testing procedures can be broken down into three steps:

1. the pretest interview,
2. the polygraph examination, and
3. the posttest interview.

The entire procedure can last between 1 and 3 hours. However, it is important to note that much of the procedure is the pretest and posttest interview. Contrary to popular portrayals of the polygraph procedure in the media, all questions are typically brief and require a yes–no response. Questions are not open-ended.

The pretest interview is an opportunity for the examiner to develop rapport with the examinee. It is also important to explain to the examinee their legal rights regarding participation and to obtain their signed informed consent. At this time it is also necessary to inquire about any physical limitations or medical conditions that may interfere with the accuracy of the procedure. For example, medications such as barbiturates will tend to lower physiological reactivity and can adversely influence the results. The examiner also wants to create an optimal testing response set in which the examinee understands the procedure and believes that the polygraph will readily detect a lie. (Anecdotally, some polygraphists have stated to me that the true value of the procedure lies in the fact that subjects with something to hide believe they will be caught and readily confess before the procedure even begins.)

Finally, during the pretest interview the examiner will review all the questions to be asked with the examinee to ensure that there in no misunderstanding regarding the meaning of each question. An ambiguous question that can be interpreted in several different ways will only make the inference of deception or truthfulness all the more difficult. Recall that all questions require a yes–no response. An example of an ambiguous question would be one that allows interpretation, such as, "Did you leave the bar prior to the murder?" A "yes" response could indicate that the examinee left the bar to retrieve something from their car (such as a weapon) and then entered back into the bar to commit the offense, or it could mean the subject left the bar and was not present at the time of the offense. The skill of the examiner lies in developing specific questions that address the issue in question. The examinee should understand all the questions fully prior to the start of the procedure. There are no surprise questions during the testing. Any ambiguous questions are rephrased so that both the examiner and examinee agree on the meaning of the question.

Once the pretest interview is completed, the subject is hooked up to the equipment and baseline data is collected. Since having various sensors connected to one's body can cause some anxiety in even innocent subjects, it is reasonable to allow a few moments for the subject to acclimate to the equipment.

Once the subject is acclimated to the equipment, the examiner may wish to record what is termed a "known lie." Various procedures exist for obtaining this measure. A simple example is to ask the subject to pick a number from 0 to 10 and to keep that number in mind. The examiner will then tell the subject to answer "no" to the following questions. The examiner will then ask, "Is the number 0?" "Is the number 1?" The examiner will proceed up to the number 10. Ideally, the examiner will note a change in arousal for the number on which the examinee lied. This is known as a "stimulation" or "**stim**" **test** and serves to further convince the examinee of the accuracy of the test (Office of Technology Assessment, 1983). The testing procedure then commences and the examiner will ask the participant all the questions previously discussed. Once all the questions have been answered, the examiner will typically repeat the procedure two to three times. Therefore, each question is asked multiple times to compensate for any error in measurement and to be sure that physiological responses are consistent. Individuals may have exaggerated physiological responses to a question for reasons other than deception.

After the testing procedure is completed the examiner will conduct the posttest interview. This involves reviewing with the examinee their responses. Thus, if a response to a question suggests deception, the examiner can give the examinee an opportunity to clarify their response, which may help elicit a confession. This type of questioning can also occur during the testing procedure whenever a response on the polygraph raises suspicions. The examiner can explain to the examinee that their physiological response suggests that they may be attempting to be deceptive in their answers. The examiner who has established rapport with the examinee can typically elicit more information from the participant at this time.

Several different questioning procedures can be used. We review here three typical questioning procedures:

1. the relevant/irrelevant technique,
2. the control question technique, and
3. the **concealed information test** or guilty knowledge test.

The technique used depends on the purpose of the polygraph examination. The **relevant/irrelevant technique** lends itself to preemployment screening, whereas the **control question technique** is typically used in criminal investigations (Office of Technology Assessment, 1983). Furthermore, these techniques may be combined or altered depending on the examiner.

■ **Control-question technique**
A technique used in polygraph examinations in which the comparison of physiological responses is between relevant questions and control questions. Control questions are questions about possible past infractions that should elicit anxiety in all examinees.

## Table 10.5 — Three Polygraph Questioning Techniques

- The relevant/irrelevant technique (R/I)
- The control question technique (CQT)
- The concealed information or guilty knowledge test

# The Relevant/Irrelevant Technique (R/I)

The relevant/irrelevant technique was one of the first widely used procedures with the polygraph (Wrightsman, 2001). The relevant questions deal directly with the topic of investigation and specifically address the alleged offense. An example of a relevant question is, "Did you embezzle money from your employer, the ABC Company, by writing fraudulent checks?" Another example of a relevant question is to ask a defendant, "Did you murder your wife on the day of December 5, 2001?" Relevant questions may also be broad, particularly when the polygraph is used for screening purposes. An example of a broad question is, "Have you ever stolen anything of greater than $10 from your employer?" Another example of a broad question that may be used in a private consultation would be, "Have you ever engaged in an extramarital affair?"

In contrast to relevant questions, irrelevant questions are used as a control or comparison. Irrelevant questions have nothing to do with the investigation or screening. Rather, they may be fairly innocuous questions dealing with trivial, factual matters. An example of an irrelevant question is, "Is the month February?" Another example of an irrelevant question is to ask a male, "Are you a male?" An irrelevant question should not elicit any fear of detection or reason for deception. The purpose of an irrelevant question is to provide a comparison for the physiological responses to the relevant questions. The assumption is that a guilty person will have a stronger or more pronounced physiological response to the relevant questions as opposed to the irrelevant questions. Likewise, it is assumed that an innocent person will have the same physiological responses to the relevant questions as to the irrelevant questions. However, questions about crime scenes and criminal offenses may in fact cause more anxiety and thus a stronger physiological response than questions about the date or one's name even if the individual is innocent (Bull, 1988).

To briefly summarize, relevant questions can be either broad or specific and are directly about the issue under investigation. Relevant questions are assumed to elicit a physiological response in guilty individuals. Irrelevant questions are used as a comparison and are designed to elicit no physiological response.

# The Control Question Technique (CQT)

The control question technique (CQT) also relies on the comparison of physiological responses to different questions. In the CQT, the comparison is between responses to relevant questions and control questions. Relevant questions are questions about the specific topic under investigation. However, control questions are also questions about possible past infractions or crimes and are intended to elicit anxiety. Thus, a control question should trigger anxiety in an individual. The assumption is that an innocent person will respond to the control question with as much anxiety as to the relevant questions. For example, the control question "As a teenager, did you ever steal anything of value?" may generate as much anxiety in an innocent person as the relevant question, "Did you steal $1,000 from the cash register?" An innocent person may wish to lie to the control question since they would not want the examiner to think that they are a thief. So, they may in fact respond "no" to both questions, but have the same or even stronger physiological response to the control question. On the other hand, a guilty individual may also respond "no" to both questions, but it is assumed that they would have a stronger response to the relevant question than to the control question. Therefore, the control question provides a baseline of emotional reactivity for both guilty and innocent persons. The innocent person will respond with the same reactivity to the relevant questions. The guilty person will respond with a stronger physiological response to the crime-related (relevant) questions. The assumption is that although a guilty individual will be concerned about control questions, they will have more concern and a greater physiological response to relevant questions.

It should be obvious from the above discussion that control questions must be developed with care. Control questions must elicit a physiological response from innocent persons and ideally should prompt an innocent person to lie. The control question should not include the act under investigation, as that may, from the examinee's perspective, constitute a relevant question. For example, a control question that is inclusive, such as "Did you ever steal anything of value?" may include, in the guilty person's mind, the crime under investigation. So there would be no distinction between the guilty person's physiological reactivity to the control and relevant question.

# The Concealed Information or Guilty-Knowledge Test

The guilty-knowledge test (GKT) was developed by Lykken (1981) and is considered to be one of the more accurate procedures (Swenson, 1997). The GKT works on a different premise than the two previously discussed techniques. The GKT does not ask the examinee whether or not they have committed a crime of transgression. Rather, the questions attempt to determine if the examinee has particular knowledge about a crime that only a guilty individual would know. The GKT can also be used to elicit specific information that only the guilty party would know. For example, an examinee can be asked about the specific details of the crime scene such as the use of a weapon, whether sexual assault was involved, or even clothing worn by the victim. Another difference between the GKT and the two previously mentioned approaches is that questions may be of the multiple-choice type rather than the yes–no response type. For example, an examiner may ask the following question: "The murderer hid the body at the crime scene. Was it hidden in the freezer, buried in the yard, covered with rags in the garage, or in the trunk of the car?

The GKT can also be used to elicit information that only the guilty party knows and is unknown to law enforcement. The following example was related to the author by a veteran polygraph examiner. A woman had claimed that her children were abducted in a car-jacking incident. The police started to suspect the veracity of her claims and asked if she would submit to a polygraph examination. Since she claimed innocence she really had no alternative. The police reasoned that the children were somewhere within the state. Police did not believe that the mother had the time to take the children across state lines. The investigating officers took a map of the state and sectioned it off into four quadrants. The examiner pointed to the upper corner and asked, "Are your children anywhere in this area of the state?" naturally, she responded with the anticipated, "I don't know." The examiner then asked her about each of the other quadrants in the same manner. The premise was that if she knew where the children were, she would show physiological activity when questioned about that specific area. She in fact did show heightened arousal when questioned about one of the four quadrants. That section of the map was then divided into four new quadrants and the procedure was repeated, asking the mother if her children were in one of the four sections. She again showed heightened arousal on one of the sections. This procedure was continued and eventually narrowed the location down to an area with a lake. At this time, the mother confessed to drowning her children. Whether or not this example is accurate, as I have read conflicting reports about this case, it does illustrate how previously unknown information can be gathered using the GKT.

The results of a polygraph are typically one of three outcomes; deception was detected, no deception was detected, or inconclusive. The decision is based on the difference score between physiological reactivity to control or irrelevant questions and the physiological reactivity to relevant questions. The greater the difference in reactivity between the two types of questions, the more likely the result will be interpreted as one of deception.

# The Uses and Accuracy of the Polygraph

The polygraph is primarily used by people in law enforcement and security work. The Federal Government uses the polygraph examination for screening purposes in sensitive job positions in agencies including the National Security Agency, the Central Intelligence Agency, and the Department of Defense, the Department of Energy, the Treasury, and the U.S. Postal Service. In the private sector, the polygraph was routinely used for preemployment screening for all sorts of jobs including retail sales. Nearly 3 million polygraph exams were administered annually. However, the U.S. Congress barred the use of polygraph examinations for testing employees with the **Employee Polygraph Protection Act of 1988**. The law ended the routine testing of employees but does allow testing of employees by government agencies, in cases of drug theft and cases involving national security.

The polygraph examination has had an interesting relationship with the courts. William Marston originally developed the polygraph, or lie detector, as he coined it, back in the early 1900s. Marston (1917) claimed that he could detect deception by changes in systolic blood pressure. It was Marston's instrument that eventually led to the landmark *Frye v. United States* (1923) ruling regarding the admissibility of scientific expert testimony. James Frye was convicted of murder, though he claimed Marston's lie detector proved his innocence. His appeal was denied by the U.S. Supreme Court and set the standard known as the *Frye test*, which states the "admissibility of scientific evidence depended on it being sufficiently established to have gained general acceptance in the particular field to which it belongs." Since Marston's lie detector was not generally accepted in the field of psychology, it was deemed inadmissible.

Currently, the majority of courts do not allow the admission of polygraph evidence. Twenty states will allow polygraph examiners to testify regarding a particular test result if both the prosecution and defense agree to admit the evidence. A few states do allow polygraph evidence to be admitted. The U.S. Supreme Court again recently ruled on the admissibility of polygraph evidence. Airman Edward Scheffer had a urine analysis that tested positive for methamphetamine use. He claimed "innocent ingestion" and passed a polygraph examination administered by the Air Force Office of Special Investigations. The court denied the admissibility of the polygraph results at his court martial. He subsequently appealed his conviction and the case eventually came before the U.S. Supreme Court. The U.S. Supreme Court ruled by an 8-to-1 decision that polygraph evidence was inadmissible due to continuing questions in the scientific community regarding the reliability and validity of polygraph results (Wrightsman, 2001).

The validity of the polygraph examination was recently reviewed by the prestigious National Research Council (Committee to Review the Scientific Evidence on the Polygraph, National Research Council, 2003). The conclusions from the Council state that the evidence for the scientific validity of the polygraph is "scanty and scientifically weak." The report noted the lack of scientific rigor in evaluating the effectiveness of the test for detecting deception. The authors of the report do suggest that the polygraph is more effective at detecting deception related to specific incidents than to screening of applicants for sensitive jobs in the government. However, they dismiss the polygraph as a valid tool and recommend developing a research program exploring alternative methods of detecting deception. This has supported claims made by psychologists about the lack of scientific validity for the polygraph (Adelson, 2004).

The authors of the National Research Council also note the controversy within the profession regarding the accuracy of the polygraph. The majority of individuals who administered the polygraph are trained in law enforcement. Most polygraphists will state that the test is accurate 80–90% of the time. Some will admit that that percentage does not justify its use in court since research indicates that polygraph evidence can sway a jury (Swenson, 1997). Perhaps the best use of the polygraph is in obtaining confessions. Many "guilty" suspects, when faced with the perceived credible threat of being caught, will confess to transgressions.

Despite anecdotal claims to the contrary, the polygraph is not the highly accurate "lie detector" that many individuals in law enforcement and intelligence work claim it to be. It is perhaps best to think of the polygraph as another tool that can be used in detecting deception. In fact, it may not be that any one measure of deception is accurate for every lie and for every individual. For example, it is reasonable to think that some people are better liars than others. Furthermore, it may be easier to tell some lies, depending on the level of threat experienced or the consequences of being caught, than other lies. We would not assume that an individual would show the same type of physiological response when deceiving their 3-year-old child about the existence of Santa Claus as they might when telling a state trooper at a traffic stop that they have nothing to hide when in fact they have 20 kilos of cocaine stashed in the trunk.

The detection of deception is not an either–or phenomenon; rather, there are a variety of factors that need to be considered. These issues include but are not limited to the skill of the deceiver, the perceived seriousness of the threat of detection, the opportunity to rehearse the lie beforehand, and the strength of the motivation to deceive. Also, it is equally important to note the limitations of research in this area. Frequently, research participants are asked to lie about a trivial issue. Their motivation to successfully deceive along with their apprehension regarding being caught in a lie may differ significantly from the real-world phenomenon of deception. Finally, the detection of deception is big business with a large market in law enforcement, the government, and the private sector. Frequently, claims about the success of an instrument or technique are inflated in order to sell a product and are not justified by the scientific literature. In fact, one manufacturer of a product also publishes a "scientific" journal related to research on the product. This obvious conflict of interest should be sufficient to warrant skepticism. The consumers of these products frequently do not have the background in basic research so as to understand the scientific literature and tend to base their purchasing decisions on a few testimonials. This is one of the many reasons why students entering the field should have a basic understanding of research and statistics. Armed with basic research and statistical knowledge, professionals can become informed consumers able to evaluate the research on their own. So, with these caveats in mind, we now turn to other measures that researchers and practitioners have used to attempt to detect a lie.

Several alternative approaches to the use of the polygraph have been explored for detecting deception. However, research on these alternative approaches pales in comparison to the amount of research that has been conducted on the polygraph. Therefore, evidence for the accuracy of any of the alternative approaches is minimal at best. Some of the approaches have shown very little success, whereas some show promise in terms of future possibilities. Currently, none have outperformed the polygraph in regards to accuracy, suggesting that the polygraph will continue to be the benchmark to which other techniques are compared for the near future.

| Table 10.6 | Four Possible Alternatives to the Traditional Polygraph |
|---|---|

- Brain activity
- Autonomic measures
- Demeanor
- Direct investigation

The possible alternatives to the traditional polygraph can be categorized into four areas:

1. brain activity,
2. autonomic measures,
3. demeanor, and
4. direct investigation.

The first two measures work on the same premise as the traditional polygraph. The assumption is that there are specific physiological changes associated with deception. With new technology that enables researchers to more accurately measure brain activity and autonomic responses, the search is on for physiological changes that indicate deception. The third alternative approach, **demeanor**, is something that humans have been doing since the first lie was told. This approach attempts to detect deception from careful observation of the individual's behavior, such as their facial expression, eye gaze, choice of words, body language, and so on. Finally, the fourth approach is based on **direct investigation** using standard techniques such as background checks and employment questionnaires.

# Brain Activity

Newer technologies have allowed researchers to look directly at brain activity during deception. Theoretically, this would allow for a direct examination of psychological phenomena related to deception. This area of research is in the developing field of cognitive neuroscience, which combines the experimental discipline of cognitive psychology with the emerging technologies used to study brain function. Potential candidates in this area include modern functional imaging techniques such as **positron emission tomography** (PET) and **magnetic resonance imaging** (MRI), and the examination of EEG patterns and specifically, event-related potentials. Each of these measures are briefly discussed below.

PET scans can localize brain cell activity, identifying specific brain regions that are active during certain psychological states. For example, studies have shown that specific brain regions become activated when people observe fearful facial expressions (Morris, et. al., 1998). PET scans work by detecting the concentration of radioactive substances in a particular region of the brain. Radioactive substances are first injected into the bloodstream. The scan then records images from the brain, noting the concentration of radioactive substances as the brain performs the particular functions under study, such as engaging in deception. (For a comprehensive general review of PET research, see Carson, Daube-Witherspoon, & Herscovitch, 1997.) The PET scan traces blood flow, which coincides with cellular activity in that region of the brain. Thus, as cells in a particular region of the brain become more active during a task, blood flows to that area, and the radioactive substance measured by the PET scan will concentrate in that brain region.

The PET scan can measure changes in activity in regions of the brain. The MRI, on the other hand, can provide a structural picture of the brain. The MRI exposes the brain to a magnetic field and measures the radio-frequency waves. This provides an image of the anatomical structures of the brain. (For a review of research on magnetic resonance imagining, see Buxton, 2002.) A combination of the PET and MRI can provide an ongoing picture of neuronal activity. As stated above, the PET uses a measure of blood flow. These changes in blood flow coincide with changes in oxygen consumption. The MRI signal intensity is sensitive to the amount of oxygen, such that changes in blood oxygen content can be detected by the MRI at the site of changes in brain activity. This combination of PET and MRI technology has become known as functional MRI (fMRI).

The use of these techniques to study brain activity is in its infancy. Only recently have researchers begun to use fMRI studies to look for localized activity changes in brain regions that may be associated with deception (Langleben et al., 2002; Lee et al., 2002). Other fMRI studies have examined brain activity associated with other emotions, such as love (Bartels & Zeki, 2000), moral reasoning (Greene et al., 2001), and even racial bias (Cunningham et al., 2004) and racial differences (Eberhardt, 2005). Much more work remains to be done to identify specific brain activity uniquely associated with deception and to understand individual differences in brain activity. Furthermore, fMRI is expensive and time-consuming, making the practical application for detecting deception unlikely in the near future. The complexity of brain function and its relationship to emotion and behavior suggests potential benefits for this line of research, adding to the theoretical understanding of cognitive changes associated with deception.

■ **Magnetic resonance imaging (MRI)**

Exposes the brain to a magnetic field and measures the radio frequency waves, providing an image of the anatomical structures of the brain.

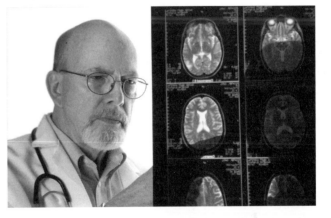

Figure 10.3

The emerging field of cognitive neuroscience presents the possibility of relating changes in brain activity to behavior.

© 2009 forestpath. Used under license from Shutterstock, Inc.

A new approach that has been receiving some attention in the criminal justice field as well as the mass media is the idea of brain fingerprinting. Although relatively new, the science on which this approach is built has been around for a long time. As you may know, researchers can use electrodes placed on an individual's scalp to measure electrical activity in the brain. This is a noninvasive procedure as it only entails electrodes on the scalp and is called an electroencephalograph, also known as an EEG. The EEG cannot measure localized activity but rather gives a fairly broad view of what is going on in the brain. Researchers have studied brain wave patterns for years and how these brain wave patterns respond to various stimuli.

One particular pattern that has been well documented is an event-related potential termed the P300. The P300 is measured best by electrodes placed on the parietal lobe of the brain, which is roughly near the top of the head. The P300 is considered to be an indication of cognitive function during decision-making processes in the brain. The P300 is a spike in brain wave activity that occurs within 300 milliseconds after the individual sees a recognizable stimulus. The stimulus must be recognizable and noteworthy for the P300 spike to occur. If the stimulus is not of any relevance, the P300 does not appear. Researchers have used the presence of the P300 to identify differences between normal functioning and impaired cognitive functioning. For example, there appears to be a decrease in the intensity of the P300 in individuals with schizophrenia as well as among alcoholics. There are also gender differences, with females showing higher-amplitude P300s than males. Additionally, the P300 appears to diminish with age. The research on the P300 event-related potential dates back to the 1960s. See Polich and Kok (1995) and Polich (2007) for extensive reviews of the research on the P300 and implications for theory and applications.

A recent use for the P300 has been in the area of **lie detection**. And, since the P300 has been in the scientific literature for decades, the use of the P300 for lie detection has been admissible in court. Recall the Daubert standard requiring scientific evidence to meet the general acceptance rule. Although the use of the P300 as a measure of lie detection is relatively new, research supporting the P300 is unequivocal.

One researcher, Dr. Lawrence Farwell, has identified a use for the P300 in detecting deception. He has also identified event-related potentials that occur between 800 and 1,400 milliseconds after the presentation of relevant information, which he terms the memory- and encoding-related multifaceted electroencephalographic response, or MERMER for short. Dr. Farwell has termed this approach brain fingerprinting. The P300 is used as a **guilty knowledge test**. In a guilty knowledge test, it is assumed that only the person guilty of a crime would have knowledge about details of the crime unknown to the general public (Farwell & Donchin, 1991).

In the procedure of brain fingerprinting, the individual wears a headband with electrodes placed on the scalp. The suspect is presented with slides showing pictures of relevant objects and irrelevant objects. For example, a suspect is presented with information that only an individual familiar with a crime would know, such as the weapon used in a murder or the location of a body. If the individual knows information related to the crime that only the perpetrator would know, they will demonstrate a P300 as well as the rest of the event-related potential referred to as a MERMER. The guilty knowledge test assumes that only a guilty individual would have this particular knowledge. The attractiveness of using EEG patterns to detect deception is that most scientists agree that EEG patterns cannot be manipulated, whereas the psychophysiological measures associated with the polygraph may be susceptible to manipulation.

This is indeed an exciting area of research and has already been used to set an innocent man free as well as to catch a serial killer. The Iowa Supreme Court released Terry Harrington after serving years in prison for a murder that he did not commit (*Harrington v. Iowa*, 2000). Brain fingerprinting is also credited with obtaining a confession and guilty plea from serial killer J.B. Grinder, as cited on Farwell's web site.

It is important to note that brain fingerprinting also has limitations. Currently, brain fingerprinting only detects whether or not an individual has knowledge of an event. It does not assess guilt or innocence. Also, it cannot assess intent. The issue of intent is important in murder cases as well as when rape is alleged in that frequently in rape cases the question is not whether the act occurred but rather whether it was consensual.

Finally, brain fingerprinting is not without is skeptics. Farwell left academia and patented the technology and now markets the procedure to law enforcement agencies. Unfortunately, his company web site (see *www.brainwavescience.com*) makes some fairly dubious claims, citing "100% accuracy" and that the "technology is fully developed and available for application in the field." Rosenfeld (2005) provides a detailed review of the research on brain fingerprinting and arrives at a less-than-favorable opinion of the evidence. Rosenfeld refutes claims made by the web site regarding the United States government's interests in brain fingerprinting. A U.S. General Accounting Office (2001) report suggests the scientific validity of the procedure has not been sufficiently demonstrated. As Rosenfeld points out, claims on the web site may simply be Internet marketing tools. However, excessive claims used in marketing can diminish the serious research currently conducted on brain-based deception-detection methods.

## Autonomic Measures

The traditional polygraph uses **autonomic measures** associated with arousal to detect deception. The standard polygraph assesses heart rate, respiration, blood pressure, and the galvanic skin response (GSR). The GSR is a measure associated with increased perspiration. However, all of these autonomic responses are influenced by a wide range of factors other than deception, which are both internal (psychological factors) and external (environmental factors) to the participant. With new technologies it may be possible to develop accurate measures of autonomic activity that are more closely related to deception. Now, researchers can noninvasively measure cardiac output, myocardial contractility, respiratory sinus arrhythmia, and thermography (skin temperature) (Cacioppo, Tassinary, & Berntson, 2000). One area that has recently received attention is facial thermography (Pavlidis, Eberhardt, & Levine, 2002; Pollina & Ryan, 2002). *Facial thermography* utilizes a device that measures radiant energy emitted from a subject's face. The advantage of this approach is that it would be quicker, easier, and less invasive than a polygraph. It is even possible that it could be conducted without the participant's knowledge or consent. Though a detailed discussion of the ethical implications of measuring deception without consent is not appropriate for this text, it should be noted that obtaining physiological measures without an individual's informed consent does raise some ethical and legal issues. Although facial thermography is an intriguing possibility for detecting deception, there is currently insufficient scientific evidence to support the use of facial thermography for the detection of deception.

Figure 10.4

Body movements, facial expressions, eye gaze, and posture are all behaviors that can indicate deception.
© 2009 Marcin Balcerzak.
Used under license from
Shutterstock, Inc.

## Demeanor

This approach to detecting deception relies on observing subtle changes in specific behaviors emitted by the individual engaging in deception. These changes can include body movements, facial expressions, eye gaze, posture, sound of the voice, and even choice of words. These subtle changes can be observed by other individuals, especially if they have received training, but may also be measured by scientific devices. These observations can be used by themselves as a single measure of deception, or combined with one another or as a supplement to other traditional measures of deception. Some of these behaviors assumed to be associated with deception are held in conventional wisdom, such as avoidance of eye contact or stuttering over words when lying. However, these changes commonly associated with lying have not always been supported in scientific studies.

It is important to note that many jurors will scrutinize the non-verbal behavior of witnesses to attempt to identify lying. Many people, professionals as well as lay people, assume specific nonverbal behaviors are indicative of deception. For example, it is nearly universally assumed that avoiding eye contact, or gaze aversion, is associated with lying. Additionally, the majority of people believe that nonverbal behaviors increase while lying. Research indicates that nonverbal behaviors actually decrease during deception (Sporer & Schwandt, 2007). These researchers found no relationships between gaze aversion and lying. Only three nonverbal behaviors were found to be *negatively* correlated with deception: nodding and foot and leg movements. This meta-analysis found that these behaviors decrease while lying, but the authors caution practitioners against using nonverbal behaviors as indicators of deception.

As with other areas previously discussed, the research is limited and often cannot be generalized to crime investigation. Laboratory studies frequently enlist college students to "lie" about a "crime" that they committed. Lykken (1988) has suggested that these studies do not instill guilt or a fear of being caught and thus have little to do with evaluating techniques for detecting deception when the stakes are high. The limitations in terms of external validity for much of this research are related to the relatively low stakes and lack of negative consequences for being caught in a lie. Research suggests that detection of deception is somewhat improved when the stakes are high (DePaulo et al., 2003).

Ekman and his colleagues (1991) have developed a facial coding system that has yielded a hit rate better than chance alone in detecting lies. There is now a large body of literature relating deception to changes in demeanor (Ekman, 2001). In fact, there are scoring systems sold over the Internet to allow individuals to develop skills to distinguish facial movements, such as the **Facial Action Coding System**. However, the development of these skills and accurate measurement of facial expressions is labor-intensive, although computer imaging may facilitate automated measurement of facial movements (Bartlett, Hager, Ekman, & Sejnowski, 1999).

In addition to facial and body movements, researchers have looked at **voice stress analysis** as a way to detect deception. The assumption is that a liar under high stakes will experience a greater deal of stress than someone telling the truth. This stress is experienced throughout the body and expressed in autonomic measures as well as in the voice. Studies have consistently shown an association between vocal tension and deception (DePaulo et al., 2003). This finding has led to the manufacture of a variety of devices purported to detect deception in the voice. These instruments attempt to identify deception by measuring changes in pitch, intensity, frequency, harmonics, and tremors (National Research Council, 2003). One can easily purchase a range of "voice stress" detectors on the Internet. Many of the advertisements for these devices make unsubstantiated claims such as "100% accuracy" using "scientific principles." These devices are sold as instruments that you can use over the telephone to tell if someone is deceiving you. In reality, the reliability (Waln & Downey, 1987) and validity of this method is not supported by the research (O'Hair & Cody, 1987).

One device that has been adopted by a number of law enforcement agencies is the Computer Voice Stress Analyzer manufactured and marketed by the National Institute for Truth Verification (NITV). These devices start at nearly $10,000. The National Institute for Truth verification has a web site that "exposes" the failures of the polygraph and also offers training to become a "certified" user of their instrument. The

NITV also publishes its own "journal," which consists primarily of success stories in the use of the device in solving crimes. However, a number of studies completed by the U.S. Department of Defense Polygraph Institute (DoDPI) do not support the use of computer voice stress analyzers for the detection of deception (Janniro & Cestaro, 1996; Meyerhoff, Saviolakis, Koenig, & Yourick, 2000; Palmatier, 1996). The National Research Council (2003) report states that the "practical performance of voice stress analysis for detecting deception has not been impressive" (p. 168).

So why, if the NITV web site is accurate, do over 1,500 law enforcement agencies purchase these devices? Part of the answer may lie in the disconnect between law enforcement and science. Frequently, law enforcement personnel may rely more on their own experience and anecdotal evidence as opposed to being consumers of the scientific literature. Researchers do not try to improve this situation by making their research more accessible to individuals outside of the discipline. Scholarly articles are frequently difficult to decipher, full of jargon and statistical procedures that are confusing to the majority of the readers. However, it does serve as a lesson as to why basic research skills and an understanding of statistics is important for the majority of individuals graduating from college. In order to make use of the research, one needs to know how to get the information and how to understand what the studies show.

It does seem that it is possible for some individuals to detect deception from measures that have been included in the category of demeanor. Evidence suggests that individuals can be trained to be better at observing these subtle cues. The use of these cues in combination with other measures may prove to be of benefit. It seems reasonable that individual differences will account for much of the variance in research results. These differences are not only among observers attempting to detect deception but also in the skill of those who are attempting to deceive.

# Direct Investigation

The use of direct investigation refers to some of the more traditional methods used such as face-to-face interviews and background checks. Background checks have been widely used for screening potential job candidates for a wide variety of government positions. Background checks are readily available on the Internet from a variety of sources. This wide availability reflects one of the problems regarding their use. There is no standardized format or way to measure quality assurance. Frequently, individuals who conduct background checks receive very little training in conducting the investigative process and discerning the accuracy of the information they uncover. In addition to evaluating the accuracy of the information, another disadvantage with background checks is the cost and time involved. Very few organizations can afford to conduct a background check on every applicant. Rather, a due diligence background check may be conducted once an individual has reached a certain stage in the hiring process in which they have a reasonable chance of being hired. Finally, very little research exists to support the scientific validity and value of background checks. However, sufficient anecdotal evidence is available to support the continued use of this technique.

In searching for more cost-effective approaches to detecting deception, or the potential for deception, psychologists have turned to developing "pencil-and-paper" **integrity tests**. Integrity tests are standardized tests that are used to assess personality traits such as conscientiousness, dependability, and honesty. Many students may have had experience in completing an integrity test when applying for a job as a retail sales clerk. Integrity tests usually assess information in one or more of the following four areas: admission of illegal behaviors, opinion regarding illegal and /or questionable behavior, attitudes or traits believed to be related or predictive of dishonest or illegal behavior, and personal reactions to hypothetical scenarios involving illegal or questionable behavior.

■ **Integrity tests**
Standardized tests that are used to assess personality traits such as conscientiousness, dependability, and honesty.

| Table 10.7 | Four Areas Assessed by Integrity Tests |
|---|---|

- Admission of illegal behaviors
- Opinion regarding illegal and /or questionable behavior
- Attitudes or traits believed to be related or predictive of dishonest or illegal behavior
- Personal reactions to hypothetical scenarios involving illegal or questionable behavior

As noted above, the U.S. Congress passed the Employee Polygraph Protection Act of 1988 barring the use of the polygraph for screening the majority of job applicants. The only exceptions were for individuals applying for jobs in the federal government or security personnel. Prior to this law, numerous individuals were required to take a polygraph test for a wide range of jobs. I recall as a 17-year-old youth when a friend had to travel to Philadelphia to take a polygraph exam before he could get a job as a sales clerk in a hardware store. We joked about all the hammers and nails he had presumably stolen in his past incarnations as a hardware sales clerk. The Employee Polygraph Protection Act put an end to the routine assessment (and some would argue, harassment) of job applicants.

The new law also created a vacuum that psychologists promptly filled. Although integrity tests existed prior to the Congressional ban on polygraph testing, these tests tended to flourish after the enactment of the ban. Today, well over 3 million such tests are administered each year by prospective employers. The use of integrity tests is typically concentrated in the food service, retail sales, and banking industries. Initial reviews of the literature regarding integrity tests were less than favorable (Goldberg, Grenier, Guion, Sechrest, & Wing, 1991). However, this may have been partly a result of the rush to meet the new demand created by the law barring routine polygraph testing. Regardless of the reasons for the initial less than favorable reviews, later reviews cite research to support the relationship between test scores and measures of job performance and counterproductive behavior on the job (Ones, Viswesvaran, & Schmidt, 1993). Although these tests have correlated well with measures of job performance, they have not been successful in identifying deception. As such, these instruments are best considered one aspect of the screening process for employment and/or intelligence work.

In summary, a wide variety of approaches have been investigated for detecting deception. The preceding discussion is not meant to be an exhaustive list of all potential methods for detecting deception. There are other areas that were not discussed, such as handwriting analysis, known as graphology (Ben-Shakhar, Bar-Hillel, Bilu, Ben-Abba, & Flug, 1986), analysis of brain wave patterns and event-related potentials (Bashore & Rapp, 1993; Farwell & Smith, 2001), or linguistic analysis (Pennebaker, Francis, & Booth, 2001), which is the analysis of language use patterns. The standard against which most approaches for detecting deception are compared is the traditional polygraph. None of the approaches appear to be superior to the polygraph and the polygraph is far from 100% accurate. It may be possible to add incremental validity to any one approach by combining two or more of the methods. For example, the use of the polygraph in combination with trained observers monitoring facial and postural changes may increase the accuracy of detection beyond either that obtain when using a single measure. Future research will need to examine the possibility of detecting deception using multiple methods.

# Hypnosis

Hypnosis has been used in forensic settings by mental health professionals and law enforcement personnel primarily to help "refresh" the memories of witnesses or victims. It is not used to elicit a confession or to detect deception. Although hypnosis has been used in one form or another since at least the late 1700s starting with the work of Franz Anton Mesmer (mesmerism), there is still debate as to defining what hypnosis is. For our purposes, we define **hypnosis** as an altered state of consciousness characterized by varying degrees of willingness to engage in changes in behavior or conscious experience, usually brought on by special techniques.

Not all people can be hypnotized. It is possible to evaluate the **hypnotic susceptibility** of individuals using various tests. Approximately 10% of the adult population is difficult to hypnotize. Typically, a stage hypnotist will solicit volunteers from the audience. The hypnotist will then perform a few tests to evaluate the hypnotic susceptibility of the volunteers before selecting one or two of the more susceptible participants to assist with the remainder of the performance. Several factors related to hypnotic susceptibility include ability to focus attention, ability to ignore distractions, and positive attitudes toward hypnosis. Perhaps one of the major factors related to hypnotic susceptibility is the willingness to be hypnotized. An individual cannot be hypnotized against his or her will. Also, an individual cannot be compelled to do something while hypnotized that they would not otherwise do in a nonhypnotized state.

Once while attending a workshop on hypnosis as a graduate student, a distinguished professor agreed to perform a hypnosis demonstration. He asked for a volunteer from the group. An attractive female medical student agreed to be hypnotized. He had her seated in front of the audience and went through the usual trance induction procedure beginning with suggestions that she feel relaxed and sleepy. After approximately 10 minutes of the procedure during which he had her follow simple commands, his pager beeped and he was required to leave the workshop. Before exiting, he asked a young male student who had apparently been in his seminar to continue with the demonstration. The student agreed and asked the hypnotized female to sing her ABC's, which she did. He then asked her to take off her blouse. At this point, she stood up, slapped the male student across the face, and stormed out of the workshop. Oh, the seductive power of hypnosis![1]

■ **Hypnosis**
An altered state of consciousness characterized by varying degrees of willingness to engage in changes in behavior or conscious experience.

---

[1]Actually, this event did not occur but is presented to humorously make the point that one will not act against their own will when hypnotized.

## Three General Theories Used to Explain Hypnosis — Table 10.8

- The role theory
- The state theory
- The dissociation theory

■ **Dissociative amnesia**

Inability to recall a traumatic event that is not attributable to head injury or drug use.

There are three general theories used to explain hypnosis: the role theory, the state theory, and the dissociation theory. Before we discuss these theories, it is worthwhile to mention a few of the uses for hypnosis. Hypnosis has been successfully used to block pain from dental and surgical procedures (Van Sickel, 1992) as well as chronic pain from burns, migraine headaches, cancer, and arthritis (Patterson, Goldberg, & Heed, 1996). As stated above, in the forensic setting, hypnosis is typically used to refresh a victim's or witnesses' memory of an event. When a victim or witness has been traumatized by an event, they may experience a **dissociative amnesia**. A dissociative amnesia is an inability to recall a traumatic event that is not attributable to a head injury or drug use (Scheflin et al., 1999). The police may wish to use hypnosis to help the victim recall events surrounding the crime. With the above uses of hypnosis in mind, we now turn to the three possible explanations.

**Role theory** posits that hypnosis is simply nothing more than a social role being played by the "hypnotized" subject. The subject is giving in to the social demands of the situation and going along with the expectations. As stated above, it is not possible to hypnotize someone against his or her will. One of the strongest predictors of hypnotic susceptibility is the willingness to be hypnotized. Also, positive attitudes toward hypnosis increase a person's susceptibility. If role theory is correct, then using hypnosis to refresh memories could have unwanted consequences. If a victim feels that they are expected to have better recall under hypnosis, once hypnotized they may feel compelled to make up details that they actually do not recall. Furthermore, if they believe hypnosis helps them to remember facts, they may feel more confident in the memory after being hypnotized.

**State theory** proponents argue that hypnosis is an altered state of consciousness that has specific changes in experience. One important characteristic of this altered state is the heightened level of suggestibility the person experiences. The argument continues that while in this altered state, an individual can do things that they would not normally be capable of doing, such as recall events from very early in life, as with "age-regression" hypnosis. Or, the person can be instructed not to feel pain during a surgical procedure.

The third theory, **dissociative theory**, is a combination of the role theory and state theory. Hilgard (1992) suggests that hypnosis is a general condition in which the hypnotized participant makes an implicit contract with the hypnotist, surrendering partial control of his or her conscious experience to the suggestions of the hypnotist. This blending of the two above theories argues that it is a role played by the participants, but that it can also lead to changes in conscious awareness.

The role of hypnosis in forensic psychology is used primarily to refresh a witness's memory. The value placed on hypnosis as a forensic tool that can refresh memories that are lost due to dissociative amnesia depends on which theory of hypnosis is accepted. If hypnosis is merely a social role acted out by participants, then the possibility that hypnosis can help with memory retrieval seems limited. However, if hypnosis is in fact an altered state, then perhaps it does provide for the ability to do mental gymnastics that would not be possible without the use of hypnosis. Finally, it is necessary to look at the current understanding of memory. Memory is not conceived of as a videotape or file that can be accessed at any point and played forward or backward. Rather, memory appears to be reconstructive in nature, building each active memory from schemas or scripts that we know well. For example, if you wanted to recall attending a friend's wedding, you would naturally use your schema of weddings to add information to your memory. You may recall the bride in a white dress, the groom in a tuxedo, and the wedding party all dressed similarly. Part of your recollection will be accurate; however, part of your recollection may be embellished because of what you simply expect to occur at a wedding. In one study, college students were asked to wait in the office of a graduate student. Now, imagine what the office of a graduate student may look like. When the students were asked to recall what they saw in the office, the majority of the students recalled seeing books. However, no books were in the office. Students used a schema of what they believed to be in a "graduate student's office" and constructed a memory (Brewer & Treyens, 1981).

Based on the above discussion regarding explanations for hypnosis, we now look at the forensic use of hypnosis to generate admissible evidence. Clearly, the stakes in criminal court can be fairly high and evidence should not be based on junk science or controversial studies. The Daubert standard cites the importance of peer review and acceptance within the scientific community. Research indicates that memories generated under hypnosis may be less accurate than those of nonhypnotized participants (Lynn, Myers, & Malinoski, 1997). Furthermore, research indicates that hypnosis is not likely to help victims or witnesses recall details about a crime (Lynn et al., 1997). Finally, as discussed above under the role theory, individuals' expectations and beliefs about the benefits of hypnosis appear to cause them to have a higher degree of confidence in the accuracy of their testimony. This is complicated by the finding that confidence in the recall and susceptibility to hypnosis are related (Steblay & Bothwell, 1994), suggesting that confidence has more to due with expectations about hypnosis than actual recall of the event.

Few states allow unlimited admissibility of testimony based on **hypnotically refreshed memories**. Prior to the early 1980s, the *open admissibility rule* enjoyed popularity in the courts. This principle allowed for the admissibility of any hypnotically refreshed memory. However, due to research focusing attention on problems with confabulation and distortion of hypnotically refreshed memories, most states adopted a more restrictive approach, with only a few states using the open admissibility rule (Knight & Meyer, 2007). A minority of the state courts and the federal courts allow testimony based on hypnotically refreshed memories if a number of safeguards have been followed in the procedure. This approach is called the **totality of circumstances test** (Wrightsman, 2001) and was adopted in a New Jersey ruling (*State v. Hurd*, 1981). Psychologists (Speigel & Speigel, 1987), as well as the courts, have suggested a variety of guidelines that should be followed before, during, and after the hypnosis. If these guidelines are not followed, the courts may decide to limit or prohibit the testimony based on the hypnotically refreshed memory. The remainder of the states prohibit all testimony based on hypnotically refreshed memories regardless of the procedures used. This prohibition on all uses of hypnosis for witness or victim testimony is termed the *per se* **exclusionary rule** (Wrightsman, 2001).

Hypnosis has also been used to evaluate a defendant's alibi, as in the infamous Hillside Strangler case of the late 1970s. Kenneth Bianchi was arrested in Washington State for the murder of two university students in Bellingham, WA. The murder pattern was similar to a series of murders that occurred in the Los Angeles area, dubbed the Hillside Strangler because the victims' nude bodies were conspicuously left on hillsides. Under hypnosis, Bianchi displayed behaviors characteristic of dissociative identity disorder (multiple personality disorder) and appeared to have several different personalities. One of the personalities, Steve Walker, confessed to the killings in Washington as well as the Los Angeles murders. Bianchi claimed ignorance of any wrongdoing and his defense lawyers filed the insanity plea. As you may recall from an earlier chapter, the insanity plea is typically a last resort defense once a suspect has no other alternative since the suspect must admit to the crime. In all insanity plea cases, it is crucial to assess the possibility of malingering. The police had several experts hypnotize Bianchi to assess the veracity of his claims of multiple personalities. Two experts agreed that he met the diagnostic criteria for dissociative identity disorder and was not responsible for his actions.

A third expert on forensic hypnosis, Martin Orne was not convinced and tricked Bianchi during a forensic interview while Bianchi was supposedly hypnotized. One way to catch a person who is malingering is to suggest that "individuals with this type

■ **Hypnotically refreshed memories**
Memories that have been enhanced under hypnosis; used to help victims or witnesses recall details of a crime; not admissible as evidence in many jurisdictions.

■ **Totality of circumstances test**
Used by courts to determine if a hypnotically refreshed memory can be admitted into testimony; usually depends on whether a variety of guidelines were followed before, during, and after the hypnosis.

■ *Per se* **exclusionary role**
The prohibition of all testimony based on hypnotically refreshed memories.

of disorder often display these types of symptoms" and then to detail symptoms that are not associated with the disorder. A person who is malingering may then produce those symptoms. That is exactly how Dr. Orne concluded that Bianchi was malingering and doing so while "under hypnosis." Bianchi pled guilty to the murders and will remain incarcerated for the remainder of his life, having avoided the death penalty through the plea bargain.

The other experts who were fooled by Bianchi were surprised that he could have known as much as he did about psychology and hypnosis. They believed that it would not be possible for a lay person without graduate study in the field to have known so much. However, information on disorders and how to feign disorders as well as how to "beat" the polygraph is readily available and clients may even be coached on how to successfully malinger (Guriel et al., 2004).

The ethical practice of forensic hypnosis requires proper training in hypnosis, understanding the legal standards regarding hypnotically refreshed memories in the jurisdiction, staying abreast of relevant research, and following appropriate guidelines (Knight & Meyer, 2007). Guidelines have been established from the *Hurd* case mentioned previously. Additional guidelines have been developed by the American Society for Clinical Hypnosis as well as the FBI (Knight & Meyer, 2007).

# Psychological Autopsies

■ **Psychological autopsy**
A retrospective examination of social and psychological events prior to an individual's death.

Perhaps fittingly, we end this chapter on investigative techniques by looking at the **psychological autopsy**. The term *psychological autopsy* was first coined by Shneidman (1981) and refers to a retrospective examination of the social and psychological events prior to an individual's death. The psychological autopsy is conducted when the **manner of death** is equivocal, or uncertain (La Fon, 1999), or in cases of a suicide. It is necessary to distinguish between the **cause of death** and the *manner* of death. The medical examiner can often ascertain the cause of death. The cause of death is the "pathological process that results in the physical body's death" (La Fon, 2002, p. 157). On the other hand, the manner of death refers to the circumstances that brought about the cause of death. For example, if we have a dead body with a gunshot wound to the head, then we know the cause of death was the hemorrhaging of the brain due to the bullet entering the cranium. However, the manner of death is not certain. The individual may have been purposely shot (murder), may have self-inflicted the wound with the intent of death (suicide), or may have been cleaning what they thought was an empty chamber when the gun accidentally fired (accident). Finally, they could have been loading the gun when they had a fatal stroke, causing them to discharge the gun (natural). There are four accepted manners of death are identified by the **NASH** acronym: natural, accident, suicide, and homicide.

## Table 10.9    Two Types of Psychological Autopsies

■ Suicide psychological autopsy
■ Equivocal death psychological autopsy

As mentioned above, there are two occasions when a psychological autopsy may be performed: the **suicide psychological autopsy** and the **equivocal death psychological autopsy** (La Fon, 2002). Although both types of psychological autopsies utilize similar procedures, the purposes and goals of each distinguish between the two. Typically, a psychologist or a psychiatrist conducts a psychological autopsy, ideally someone with experience in forensic psychology and/or death investigation (La Fon, 2001). More recently, the Department of Defense has established some general guidelines for training individuals who conduct psychological autopsies (Ritchie & Gelles, 2002).

The suicide psychological autopsy is conducted when the manner of death was clearly suicide. The Centers for Disease Control (CDC) has established guidelines for determining that the manner of death was suicide (Jobes, Berman, & Josselson, 1987). These guidelines by the CDC classify the manner of death as a suicide if there is evidence to support two specific conditions. First, the injury or cause of death must be self-inflicted. Second, there has to be evidence to suggest that the intent of the inflicted injury was to die. This is an important distinction. Some self-inflicted injuries that result in death may not be deemed suicide since the intent to die was never there. For example, autoerotic asphyxia can often be mistaken for either suicide or homicide (McGrath & Turvey, 2002). **Autoerotic asphyxia** is the deliberate induction of hypoxia (restriction of oxygen to the brain) in order to increase sexual arousal.

Suicide psychological autopsies are conducted to help better understand why the individual committed suicide and to gain a better understanding of suicide in general. A better understanding of suicide would ideally lead to prevention and intervention techniques. The U.S. Army has routinely investigated all suicides for the past 20 years (Ritchie & Gelles, 2002) in an attempt to learn from each suicide. Demographic information and motivations of those who completed suicide are collected and form a database for suicidologists.

The second type of autopsy is the equivocal death psychological autopsy. The equivocal death autopsy is performed when the manner of death cannot be ascertained with any degree of certainty. Suppose a 25-year-old man drives his car over a guard rail on a steep hill and crashes to his death. We would want to know if the death was an accident, a suicide, a mechanical failure, or perhaps caused by another vehicle, which is no longer at the scene of the accident. Although a psychological autopsy cannot rule out all possibilities, it should help to distinguish between an accident and a suicide. The manner of death can have significant psychological, criminal, and civil implications for any survivors. For example, if a death was ruled to be accidental as opposed to suicide, that information may help alleviate feelings of guilt and loss among the deceased's family and friends. Additionally, some insurance policies my not pay death benefits in the case of a suicide. An accident caused by mechanical failure may result in a lawsuit in civil court.

Both the suicide psychological autopsy and the equivocal death psychological autopsy are conducted in the same manner. As stated above, the distinction between the two applications is the goal or purpose of each. The psychological autopsy involves a thorough review of the individual's psychosocial history in an attempt to reconstruct the deceased individual's psychological state leading up to and at the time of their death.

Since there are no established guidelines regarding a psychological autopsy, the procedure varies based on the individual conducting the autopsy. Generally, the process would include interviews with individuals who knew the deceased individual, including friends, family, coworkers, personal physician, and so on. The autopsy would also include a thorough review of any personal documents that might shed light on motivations for suicide along with any suicide notes or videotapes. It is also important to review the police report and the medical examiner's report. La Fon (2002, p. 162) provides a list of over 50 "empirically based core set of components" to be included in an equivocal death psychological autopsy. The inclusive list established by surveying experts in the field includes the components presented above (interviews, etc.) to less obvious items such as contents of the deceased's medicine chest.

Psychological autopsies are a relatively new development with very little empirical support regarding their validity. Researchers are only starting to identify the type of training for individuals who conduct reports, what components should be included in the process, and what information should be conveyed in the report. Partly as a result of the much publicized *U.S.S. Iowa* incident, the U.S. Inspector General mandated that the military services perform psychological autopsies in a uniformed manner.

The *U.S.S. Iowa* incident involved an explosion onboard that resulted in the deaths of 47 sailors. An equivocal death analysis that was conducted by the FBI and facilitated by the Naval Investigative Service concluded that Gunner's Mate Clayton Hartwig had caused the explosion in order to commit suicide. It should be noted that an equivocal death analysis is not the same as a psychological autopsy. There are four major distinctions between a psychological autopsy (PA) and an equivocal death analysis (EDA): the professional conducting the procedure, the theoretical background, the collection of data, and the timing of the procedure (La Fon, 2002). An EDA is conducted by law enforcement personnel and is used to assist in the inquiry in a legal death investigation. A PA is conducted by a mental health professional such as a forensic psychiatrist or forensic psychologist to help determine the manner of death. Due to the different nature of the training that mental health professionals receive compared to law enforcement personnel, the skills used to conduct the two evaluations differ. The PA is grounded in psychological theory, whereas the EDA is based on law enforcement techniques such as crime scene analysis and criminology. Third, the mental health professional conducting the PA gathers their own data, whereas the FBI usually uses data collected by the referring agency. In the *U.S.S. Iowa* incident, the Naval Investigative Service collected the data and passed it on to the FBI for analysis. Finally, the PA is usually conducted close to the time of death in order to assist in determining the manner of death. The EDA is a law enforcement technique in a legal death inquiry and may not be used until all other leads fail, which could be well after the time of death.

| **Table 10.10** | Four Distinctions between a Psychological Autopsy (PA) and an Equivocal Death Analysis (EDA) |
|---|---|

- The professional conducting the procedure
- The theoretical background
- The collection of data
- The timing of the procedure

The U.S. House of Representatives Armed Services Committee asked the American Psychological Association to independently review the FBI's report and the Navy's conclusion regarding the actions of Hartwig. A panel of 14 psychologists reviewed the report and came to, at best, an equivocal decision regarding the Navy's conclusion

(Wrightsman, 2001). Four of the 14 psychologists felt that Hartwig did not commit suicide, three of the 14 felt that he did commit suicide, and the others were uncertain. The procedures used by the FBI in generating the report have been criticized (Darkes, Otto, Poythress, & Starr, 1993; Poythress, Otto, Darkes, & Starr, 1993).

Perhaps the most important lesson is that a panel of expert psychologists was unable to come to a unanimous decision. The majority of psychological autopsies are not conducted by a panel of experts, but rather by one individual who submits the final report. Frequently, this report may be accepted at face value as the final conclusion from an expert. It is important for forensic psychologists to point out the limitations of conducting reconstructive psychological evaluations. The conclusions from psychological autopsies, as well as many forms of assessments that forensic psychologists conduct, need to be presented as probability statements. The level of probability would reflect the professional's confidence in the decision and would ideally reflect the reliability and validity of the technique. Research data regarding the reliability and validity of psychological autopsies are scant and inconclusive. "The conclusions and inferences drawn in psychological reconstruction are, at best, informed speculations or theoretical formulations and should be labeled as such" (Poythress et al., 1993, p.12). Despite the lack of empirical evidence to validate the psychological autopsy, it should not be considered useless or invalid. Rather, research needs to be carried out to determine the role psychological autopsies can play in forensic psychology. The psychological autopsy can assist in determining the manner of death and also provide insight into the mental status and personality of the deceased (La Fon, 2002).

An initial step in establishing an empirical database on the reliability and validity of psychological autopsies was recently taken by the Department of Defense. As a result of the mandate from the U.S. Inspector General calling for uniformed procedures in psychological autopsies among the military services, the Department of Defense has begun to establish guidelines. Although a "work in progress," these guidelines address standardized training of individuals who conduct psychological autopsies as well as a program of quality assurance to credential mental health professionals to conduct psychological autopsies (Ritchie & Gelles, 2002). The training model calls for an interdisciplinary approach with training in basic mental health, crime scene investigation, **toxicology**, and forensic pathology. Table 10.11 shows a proposed sample didactic curriculum from Ritchie and Gelles (2002).

## Proposed Sample Curriculum for Training in Psychological Autopsies          Table 10.11

- The psychological autopsy in criminal investigations
- Doing a psychological autopsy
- The autopsy process and death investigation
- Crime scene investigation
- Equivocal death investigation

- Postmortem changes and time of death
- Firearm injury
- Basics of toxicology
- Asphyxial deaths
- Autoerotic deaths

Another use of psychological autopsies has been in the area of risk assessment.

Some researchers have used the psychological autopsy methodology to identify factors that led to the death. A review of completed suicides, using a standardized protocol, can help shed light on the link between factors such as family history and physical and mental health along with other major life events and suicide. Unfortunately, this area of research has numerous methodological problems, such as lack of control subjects, the complexity of suicide, and questionable reliability of assessment instruments (White, 2008).

However, White (2008) has suggested that the methodology of the psychological autopsy, which can be standardized, could be developed as an institutional risk management strategy. Using a standardized data collection protocol, a large number of variables associated with suicide deaths could be tracked over time. These variables could include clinical, demographic, institutional, and environmental policies that may have played a role in the suicide. The information gained could be used to evaluate existing policies and perhaps lead to screening and assessment instruments to help establish suicide prevention programs. Large institutions such as the military, medical and psychiatric hospitals, residential care facilities, and correctional facilities would be ideal for such a long-term project.

## Status of Expert Testimony for Psychological Autopsies

Ogloff and Otto (1993) reviewed the status of expert testimony on psychological autopsies over a decade ago and found very few criminal cases that allowed expert testimony based on a psychological autopsy. Recall that the trial judge has the discretion to admit expert testimony based on the Federal Rules of Evidence and the *Daubert* decision discussed earlier in the text. The psychological autopsy has been introduced into criminal and civil court to challenge or support death determinations. Due to the numerous methodological problems associated with the procedure, psychological autopsies have experienced minimal acceptance, particularly in U.S. Federal Court (White, 2008). The introduction of a psychological autopsy in a trial typically shifts the focus of attention from the forensic report onto the qualifications and training of the expert witness. Courts are generally reluctant to accept the psychological autopsy at face value without first scrutinizing the training, experience, and expertise of the psychologist testifying as the expert (White, 2008).

Recent developments in the area suggest that expert testimony of this nature will find its way into the courtroom. There is a growing body of literature regarding the use of psychological autopsies, the training of individuals who conduct the autopsies, and appropriate peer review procedures for quality assurance. This body of literature will enable judges to evaluate the experience and training of the individual presenting as an expert witness along with the quality of the psychological autopsy itself. This literature does not as of yet speak to the scientific reliability and validity of the technique. That type of information will be necessary before expert testimony on psychological autopsies can routinely be admitted without restrictions.

# TEST YOUR KNOWLEDGE

1. Crime scene analysis would include all of the following *except*:
   a. analysis of the crime scene
   b. interviews with the victims and witnesses
   c. interviews with the offender
   d. study of the nature of the crime

2. The polygraph uses all of the following to identify deception *except*:
   a. changes in respiration
   b. changes in blood pressure
   c. changes in pupil diameter
   d. changes in heart rate
   e. all of the above are used

3. The *per se exclusionary rule* regarding the use of hypnotically refreshed memories as testimony states that
   a. hypnotically refreshed memories may be introduced if they are directly related to the crime
   b. hypnotically assisted memories are prohibited in all cases
   c. courts will consider the admissibility of the evidence if certain safeguards were followed
   d. hypnotically refreshed memories are always permissible (hence "per se") as evidence

4. A psychological autopsy is conducted
   a. by doing a thorough medical examination of the corpse
   b. to determine if the manner of death was suicide
   c. through interviews with the deceased
   d. all of the above

5. When conducting a polygraph interview,
   a. the suspect should not be aware of the questions prior to the interview in order to prevent them from using countermeasures
   b. the suspect is asked only yes–no questions
   c. the suspect is asked each question only once to prevent the use of countermeasures
   d. all of the above
   e. none of the above

Answer Key (1) c, (2) c, (3) b, (4) b, (5) b

# Chapter Eleven

# Eyewitness Memory and Recovered Memory

## Learning Objectives

- What role does eyewitness evidence play in jury decisions?
- Be able to discuss the accuracy of eyewitness testimony.
- Define social framework testimony.
- Distinguish between direct and circumstantial evidence.
- What is the status of the admissibility of expert testimony on the accuracy of eyewitness testimony and who determines the admissibility of the expert testimony?
- What are some of the reasons stated for allowing or disallowing expert testimony on eyewitness accuracy?
- Researchers who studied the accuracy of eyewitness testimony typically have what type of training?
- Distinguish between estimator variables and system variables and give examples.
- Compare the chronological categorization of factors that influence the accuracy of memory to the estimator/system categorization.
- What is the difference between a lineup and a showup?
- What are some differences between a lineup and a photo array?
- Define the following terms: unconscious transference, relative judgment process, weapon focus, postevent variable, foil, imagination inflation, optimality hypothesis, match-to-description strategy.
- What is the inaccuracy rate associated with a lineup?
- What are some of the common errors associated with the procedure of a lineup? What are some recommendations to improve the procedure?
- What is the relationship between accuracy and level of confidence in identifying a suspect in a lineup?
- What effect do hypnosis and postidentification feedback have on the accuracy of eyewitness identification? What effect do hypnosis and postidentification feedback have on the witness's level of confidence?
- Be able to discuss the Lineups White Paper.
- Be able to discuss the importance of the following cases: *Neil v. Biggers* (1972), *Stovall v. Denno* (1967), *United States v. Ash* (1973).
- What criteria did the Supreme Court recommend for establishing the accuracy of a witness's identification?
- Be able to provide a definition for false memory, repressed memory, and recovered memory.
- What is the APA's position on recovered memories and false memory syndrome?

## Key Terms

- Chronological category
- Composite images
- Confirmation bias
- Constructive memory
- Delayed reporting statutes
- Detractors
- Episodic memory
- Estimator variables
- Event characteristics
- Experimenter bias
- False memory syndrome
- Foils
- Functional size
- Identification task variables
- Imagination inflation
- Known innocents
- Lineup
- Match-to-description strategy
- Memory
- Memory testimony
- Mug book
- *Neil v. Biggers*, 1972
- Optimality hypothesis
- Photo lineup
- Postevent factors
- Postidentification-feedback effect
- Recovered memory
- Relative judgment process
- Repressed memory
- Rosenthal effect
- Schema
- Semantic memory
- Sequential lineup
- Showup
- Simultaneous lineup
- Social framework testimony

*(continued)*

## Key Terms *(continued)*

- *Stovall v. Denno*, 1967
- System variables
- Technical Working Group for Eyewitness Evidence

- Unconscious transference
- *United States v. Ash*, 1973
- Witness characteristics

This chapter discusses the role psychologists can play in assisting law enforcement on assessing and improving the accuracy of memory testimony. Memory plays a critical role in courtroom proceedings and is routinely entered as part of the evidentiary record. Victims are asked to recall their assailant and the circumstances surrounding the attack. Witnesses are asked to pick out the suspect from a police lineup, frequently months after the event occurred. Even months later, the same witness may be subpoenaed to identify the suspect in court and to describe details regarding the crime. Research in this area falls under our definition of legal psychology, which is the application of psychological principles and methods to solving legal questions. This

## Table 11.1 Eyewitness Testimony: A Case Scenario

Imagine that you have been summoned to jury duty. The case involves the abduction, molestation, and murder of an 11-year-old boy. The boy was last seen playing in the arcade room of a hotel where his parents were vacationing. When the body is found, there is no retrievable DNA evidence due to the amount of time that has elapsed and conditions where the body had been placed. The only evidence linking the defendant to the missing boy is three eyewitnesses who all claim to have seen the defendant in the arcade room with the boy or leaving the hotel with the boy. As each witness sits on the stand, the prosecutor asks if he or she saw the missing boy in the company of a man shortly before the time of the boy's disappearance. Each witness responds that he or she did see the boy with a man at the time in question. When asked if the man is in the courtroom, each witness answers affirmatively. When asked to point to the man in the courtroom, each witness points directly at the defendant and states that he or she is certain they saw the boy with that man at the time in question. Although there is no other direct evidence linking the defendant to the boy, it is hard to believe that three independent eyewitnesses could all be wrong. The defense calls a cognitive psychologist to the stand who refutes the eyewitness accounts. She explains how memory works and how it is very easy for witnesses to be influenced by pre- and postevent factors that can alter the accurate recollection of the facts. The defense attorney questions witnesses regarding their testimony and suggests that the witnesses are all mistaken in recalling the defendant in the child's company. Then the prosecution and defense rests. As a juror, you must now decide if there is sufficient evidence to convict the defendant of kidnapping, child sexual assault, and murder. How would you weigh the evidence?

chapter explores two areas of memory research: accuracy of eyewitness testimony, and the debate regarding repressed/recovered memories and false memory syndrome. Cognitive psychologists, testifying as expert witnesses, can educate the court about important aspects of memory and recall. This chapter first discusses the accuracy of eyewitness memory. It will be necessary to briefly describe how memory works. We then cover recommendations for improving eyewitness testimony.

The second area to be covered is the controversy regarding repressed memories and false memory syndrome. Some professionals in the profession suggest that victims of child sexual abuse frequently repressed the memory of the abuse into their unconscious. These clinicians argue that only through treatment and recollection of the abuse can the emotional scars start to heal. Partly due to therapeutic techniques aimed at recovering repressed memories, there was a rash of lawsuits and criminal trials in which accusers cited as evidence recovered memories of childhood abuse. States altered many of the statute of limitation laws to allow prosecution several years after the memory was recovered, *not* several years after the incident occurred. Researchers and practitioners have hotly debated the veracity of memories that were lost and later recovered through therapy. One side of the debate suggests these memories are false memories planted by suggestive therapeutic techniques. The other camp argues that repression of trauma is normal and these memories need to be retrieved in therapy to alleviate symptoms. Either way, both recovered memories and false memories appear to exist and can cause irreparable harm to the families involved. A case involving Rutherford of Missouri is a classic example of the damage done by false memories. Beth Rutherford, through therapy with a church counselor, came to believe that she had been repeatedly raped and twice impregnated by her father, himself a clergyman, only to abort the fetuses with a coat hanger. The father had to resign his post once the allegations were made public. However, medical examination revealed that the daughter was a virgin at the age of 22 and had never been pregnant. The daughter sued her therapist and was awarded a $1 million settlement. How to distinguish between true and false memories of childhood abuse is the legal question confronting cognitive psychologists. Related to this question is the need to understand how false memories can be implanted into people's memories and how it is that these individuals frequently place a great deal of confidence in the accuracy of these false memories.

Figure 11.1

The victim or witness to this crime may be asked to pick these men out of a lineup months after the crime has taken place.
© 2009 BXP.

# Eyewitness Memory Fallibility

The majority of physical trace evidence retrieved from the crime scene in criminal trials is *circumstantial* evidence. For example, fingerprints do not necessarily prove that someone was at the crime scene at the time of the crime. Similarly, fibers from clothes may match a defendant's apparel, but these same fibers are likely to match numerous individuals' clothes. This type of circumstantial evidence does not directly place a suspect at the crime scene at the time of the offense. Unlike most circumstantial evidence, eyewitness testimony is *direct* evidence of guilt and can be the most damning for a defendant (Wells & Loftus, 2003). Eyewitness evidence directly places the suspect at the crime scene around the time of the offense. Eyewitness evidence assists both the investigation of a crime and the prosecution of the defendant. Information provided to the police by an eyewitness greatly increases the likelihood that a crime will be solved (Greenwood &

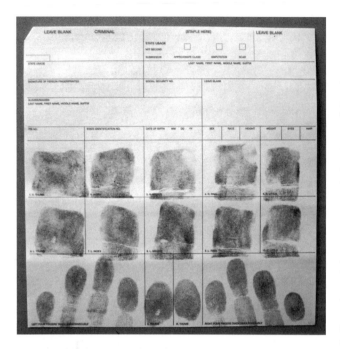

Fingerprints are considered circumstancial evidence and do not necessarily prove that someone was at the crime scene at the time of the crime.
© 2009 Kevin L. Chesson. Used under license from Shutterstock, Inc.

Petersilia, 1976) and that a defendant will be convicted (Loftus, 1979). As Loftus (1979) concluded, "All the evidence points rather strikingly to the conclusion that there is almost nothing more convincing than a live human being who takes the stand, points a finger at the defendant, and says 'that's the one!'" (p. 19). The account in Table 11.1 of the kidnapping and murder trial is an actual case that was played out in Las Vegas. The jury acquitted the defendant, Howard Haup, of all counts. There is no doubt that the acquittal was due in large part to the expert testimony on eyewitness identification provided by cognitive psychologist Dr. Elizabeth Loftus.

Research indicates there is a high degree of inaccuracy in eyewitness testimony (Wells, 1995). This inaccuracy is due to a number of factors including both perceptual factors, such as sensory deficiencies (Yarney, 1979), and social and cognitive factors (Wells, 1995). All of these factors can influence the accuracy of the identification. Witnesses may be tired or have poor eyesight. Alternatively, through suggestive questioning or perceived pressure to make an identification, witnesses may inaccurately identify a suspect. Mistaken eyewitness testimony is typically the primary evidence for the conviction of innocent individuals (Huff, Rattner, & Sagarin, 1986; Scheck et al., 2000). Frequently, these convictions are later overturned on physical evidence, such as DNA samples. In fact, some researchers have concluded that "mistaken eyewitnesses account for more convictions of innocent persons than all other causes combined" (Wells & Loftus, 2003, p. 149). A report by the National Institute of Justice titled *Convicted by Juries, Exonerated by Science: Case Studies in the Use of DNA Evidence to Establish Innocence After Trial* (Connors, Lundregan, Miller, & McEwen, 1996) found that the most compelling evidence for the majority of wrongly convicted defendants was eyewitness testimony presented at trial. As of 2003, over 100 innocent people wrongfully convicted of a crime have been released from prison after DNA or other evidence proved their innocence (Death Penalty Information Center, 2002). These innocent victims were convicted mostly based on faulty eyewitness testimony. One individual spent 18 years on death row, whereas another spent 20 years in prison for a rape he never committed. By February 2008, misidentifications accounted for more than 75% of the wrongful convictions of the 213 people exonerated through postconviction DNA testing in the United States (Innocence Project, 2007).

The popular television show, *Crime Scene Investigation* (CSI), portrays the scientific approach to collecting and evaluating physical evidence from the crime scene. Law enforcement has established optimal procedures for the collection and storage of physical evidence. These procedures are based on scientific principles established by forensic scientists (Technical Working Group on Crime Scene Investigations, 1999a). Particular caution is used so as not to contaminate or otherwise diminish the integrity of the physical evidence collected. However, no such practices are involved in the collection of memory evidence. Wells and Loftus (2003) have called for the criminal justice system to embrace a scientific approach to eyewitness evidence just as it has adopted a scientific approach to collecting and evaluating physical evidence. Cognitive psychologists argue for the application of the same methodical approach to evaluating eyewitness accounts. Typically, eyewitness evidence is collected by individuals who have no particular training in human memory. Since memory is easily influenced by external factors, law enforcement personnel can unwittingly contaminate memory evidence during the collection phase.

The recent advances in crime-scene evidence collection and preservation only serve to highlight the lack of scientific protocols for eyewitness evidence. Law enforcement has not adopted a scientific approach to eyewitness evidence for a variety of reasons. First, people often have their own theories and beliefs about how memory functions. Police officers, judges, and members of the jury may all believe they have at least some understanding of how memory functions. This common-sense approach to memory includes a belief that memory is like a videotape of an event that we can rewind and review later. Contrast this notion with the proposition that most people do not have any implicit theories on how physical evidence, such as a fingerprint or DNA sample, might implicate criminals. Although eyewitness testimony is given a great deal of weight in the courtroom, it is treated as common knowledge by law enforcement in the collection and preservation stages of crime scene evidence. Law enforcement personnel who collect eyewitness evidence have no special training in preserving the witness's memory for the event. For example, suggestive or leading questions by investigators and exposure to other witness statements can contaminate a witness's memory.

In addition to a lack of a theoretical framework for understanding memory, law enforcement may simply have failed to adopt scientific procedures due to tradition (Wells & Loftus, 2003). Law enforcement officers have been using eyewitness evidence since the beginning of crime investigations and well before the introduction of scientific procedures used to collect other types of evidence. Protocols for handling physical evidence such as DNA samples were developed by forensic scientists. Perhaps as Wells and Loftus (2003) suggest, if scientists had developed the suspect lineup procedure before it was adopted by the criminal justice system, it may have included a number of scientifically sound safeguards. However, the police lineup has been used for years prior to any research evaluating potential pitfalls and ways to improve the collection of eyewitness data. Because of tradition, law enforcement appears to underestimate the need for rigorous scientific procedures for collecting eyewitness evidence.

The cognitive psychologist can serve the role of the expert witness in courtroom proceedings to educate the jury about the high rate of inaccuracy of eyewitness testimony. **Social framework testimony** presents results of social science research to the jury to assist the trier of fact in coming to a decision (Monahan & Walker, 1988). This approach supports the use of qualified experts in the conduit-educator role, discussed in Chapter 2 of this text. The psychologist as expert witness can provide an impartial representation of the psychological science knowledge base. However, as noted earlier in the text, judges decide on the admissibility of expert testimony using four criteria based on the *Daubert* ruling:

■ **Social framework testimony**
Expert testimony that presents conclusions based on social science research to assist the court in making a decision.

1. the scientific nature of the work,
2. the agreement among experts in the field regarding the reliability of the results,
3. relevance of the testimony to the case at hand, and
4. the extent to which the expert may unduly influence the jury.

Some judges have refused to allow expert testimony regarding the accuracy of eyewitness testimony. Wells and Loftus (2003) have petitioned for the criminal justice system to embrace a scientific approach to eyewitness evidence just as it has adopted a scientific approach to collecting and evaluating physical evidence. Treating eyewitness evidence with the same rigor and scrutiny that is applied to physical evidence would clearly encourage the use of expert testimony regarding the collection and preservation of that evidence.

The U.S. Department of Justice has acknowledged the potential fallibility of eyewitness testimony. Janet Reno, as Attorney General, noted, "Recent cases in which DNA evidence has been used to exonerate individuals convicted primarily on the basis of eyewitness testimony have shown us that eyewitness evidence is not infallible" (**Technical Working Group for Eyewitness Evidence** [TWGEYEE], 1999b, p. iii). As a result, the Department of Justice established a technical working group to develop procedures for the collection and preservation of eyewitness evidence, published in a guide for law enforcement personnel (TWGEYEE, 1999b). Though the guide only provides recommendations on the collection of eyewitness testimony and is not mandatory, it is an initial success by cognitive psychologists involved in eyewitness memory research. As Janet Reno commented in the preface to the Guide, "This issue has been at the heart of a growing body of research in the field of eyewitness identification over the past decade" (TWGEYEE, 1999b, p. iii). Thus, although it may have been too late for some wrongly convicted individuals, psychological research has had very practical applications for law enforcement as well as a significant impact on innocent persons' lives.

Before discussing ways to improve eyewitness accuracy, we review a theoretical model on how memory works. Memories of events are called **episodic memories**. This is in contrast to memories of facts, called **semantic memories**. For example, your memory of your high school graduation or wedding is an episodic memory. Most likely, you can recall people, sounds, and perhaps even smells from the event. On the other hand, your memory of facts, such as the multiplication tables or how to spell a word, are simply facts and do not possess the richness and vividness of episodic memories. Most eyewitness testimony is related to episodic memories.

Many people believe that memory works like a videotape, and we can replay that tape at any time and observe details from the event. However, recent research suggests that memory does not work like a tape that stores all the details of the event. Rather, we *construct* memory from schemas. **Schemas** are mental representations that we have for people, objects, places, and events. For instance, if I mentioned that I attended a wedding last week, you would immediately think of a bride and groom walking down the aisle with the traditional Justice of the Peace or minister overseeing the ceremony. Similarly, if I stated that I left an important paper in my office at the university, you may picture a cluttered office littered with papers and books on the desk, bookshelves, and floor. These mental representations are *schemas* that we use to construct or add details to our memories.

For example, in a study on how memories are constructed from schemas, college students were asked to wait for several minutes in the office of a graduate student (Brewer & Treyens, 1981). Before reading on, create in your mind's eye a mental picture of the office of a typical graduate student. What would you expect to see? Later, the students who waited in the office were asked to recall everything they saw in the office. Nearly all of the research participants recalled seeing books in the office. However, no books were actually in the office. Most of us would expect books to be in a graduate student's office. The research participants' schemas representing what they believed would typically be in a graduate student's office

■ **Episodic memories**

Memories of events such as a wedding or graduation, as compared to memories of facts (semantic memory).

■ **Semantic memories**

Memories of facts.

■ **Schema**

Mental representations for people, objects, places, and events.

Figure 11.3

The memory of your high school gradutation is an episodic memory.
© 2009 Larry St. Pierre. Used under license from Shutterstock, Inc.

caused them to mistakenly "remember" books in the office. The idea that we used schemas to construct memories of events can account for many memory errors, such as the mistaken recall of objects or people. An eyewitness account of a bank robbery may include the presence of a gun since people typically expect a gun to be used when "holding up" a bank.

In addition to the **constructive memory** process that can lead to inaccurate eyewitness testimony, research has also shown how postevent misinformation can distort recollections of an event. Research in this area uses a straightforward paradigm. Study participants are asked to witness a complex crime scene, such as a violent crime or an automobile accident (Wells & Loftus, 2003). After witnessing the event, half of the participants are randomly selected to receive misleading information about the event. The remaining 50% of the participants do not receive any misinformation. The crime scene is typically a simulated event on videotape and the misinformation is in written format. Participants are then asked to recall details of the simulated event that they witnessed. For example, in one experiment, participants witnessed an automobile traffic accident involving an intersection with a stop sign. Later, half of the participants were given misinformation that the traffic sign at the intersection was a yield sign. When asked to indicate the type of traffic sign at the intersection, participants given the false information tended to adopt it as real and stated that they had observed a yield sign. Research has shown that the performance differences between groups given misinformation and groups given no information can be as high as 30–40% (Wells & Loftus, 2003). Loftus (1997b) reports having conducted over 200 experiments involving over 20,000 participants demonstrating how exposure to misinformation can lead to memory errors.

It is not only the deliberate exposure to misinformation that can distort memory, but also incidental exposure to new information about a crime or even the wording of questions posed to the witness. Exposure to new information about a crime, including information included in a lawyer's question, has been shown to alter a witness's memory (Belli & Loftus, 1996). Postevent information, such as an event or object being mentioned after the crime, can be incorporated into the witness's memory (Dodson & Reisberg, 1991). In a now classic experiment, Loftus and Palmer (1974) showed that the phrasing of a question could influence a witness's memory of the event. Witnesses of a simulated traffic accident who were asked how fast the cars were going when they "smashed into" each other recalled a higher speed than witnesses who were asked how fast the cars were going when they "hit" each other.

This line of research suggests that memory distortion and inaccuracy are common (Schmolck, Buffalo, & Squire, 2000) and can occur in a variety of ways. New information may interfere with the recall of the original memory (Tversky & Tuchin, 1989) or new information may become part of the original memory, making the distinction between the original memory and new information nearly impossible (Loftus, 1992). For example, repeated exposure to a potential suspect's face in a photo lineup may cause an eyewitness to mistakenly place the suspect at the crime scene due to familiarity with the face. **Unconscious transference** is the process of confusing a person seen in one situation as having been seen in another situation. This usually only occurs with people seen for brief periods of time. For example, a witness who briefly notices another patron at the Starbucks where they purchase coffee in the morning may mistakenly identify that person as someone they saw at the hotel where a crime occurred.

Constructive memories can account for misidentification or inaccurate recollection of the details of an event, such as the presence of a weapon used in the commission of a crime. However, constructive memories would not account for the

■ **Unconscious transference**
The process of confusing a person seen in one situation as having been seen in another situation.

recollection of events that never actually occurred. In addition to studies demonstrating how facts and details can become distorted, another similar line of research has shown that false memories can also be implanted. Cognitive psychologists attempted to answer the question of just how far memories can be distorted using suggestion and misinformation (Wells & Loftus, 2003). Researchers have been successful in implanting a variety of false memories by simply using suggestion and false information. These false memories include being lost in a shopping mall at the age of 5 (Loftus & Ketchum, 1994), being hospitalized overnight for a high fever and possible ear infection as a child (Hyman, Husband, & Billings, 1995), having been the victim of a vicious animal attack as a child (Porter, Yuille, & Lehman, 1999), and even having witnessed demonic possession as a child (Giuliana, Mazzoni, Loftus, & Kirsch, 2001). One participant in the Hyman et al. (1995) study even recalled a male doctor, a female nurse, and a friend from church who came to visit (Loftus, 1997a). This line of research demonstrates the malleability of memory and shows how easily false memories can be created.

To illustrate the technique used for implanting memories, a detail description of one study is provided. Elizabeth Loftus and her research associate, Jacqueline Pickrell, attempted to implant the memory of being lost in a shopping mall at about the age of 5 (Loftus, 1997a; Loftus & Pickrell, 1995). The memory included phony details such as being lost for an extended period, crying, being comforted by an elderly woman, and then being reunited with the family. The researchers asked participants ranging in age from 18 to 53 to recall events from their childhood that had already been related to the researchers by a friend or close relative. Each participant received a booklet relating three stories that had actually occurred. A fourth story that had not occurred was also included. To make the story plausible, information provided by a relative was incorporated into the false story. The participants were asked to read the booklets and then to write any information they remembered about the event. If they could not recall the event, participants were instructed to write that they did not remember this event. Two subsequent follow-up interviews were conducted under the pretense of wishing to determine how much detail the participant could remember and how well their memory matched the memory of their relative. After the first reading of the booklet, participants recalled 68% of the actual events. However, 29% of the participants recalled partially or fully the factitious event after the initial reading, and 24% continued to recall the factitious event after the two follow-up interviews. Other studies have obtained similar results using the same paradigm (Hyman & Billings, 1998; Hyman & Pentland, 1996).

Taken together, this research indicates that memory is not as static as most people believe it to be. In particular, investigators need to recognize the dangers of using suggestive techniques when attempting to dig up faded or forgotten memories from victims, suspects, and witnesses (Wells & Loftus, 2003). Unfortunately, many individuals believe in the accuracy of memory and eyewitness testimony. As the research indicates, it is quite easy for our memories to become distorted. Undoubtedly, you have had the experience of being at an event with a friend, but the two of you may have conflicting recollections regarding details of the event. More likely than not, you attribute the discrepancies between your report and your friend's report to your friend's poor memory. Most of us want to believe that our memories are accurate representations of the past. Jurors and judges tend to believe otherwise honest and impartial witnesses would not distort or provide inaccurate eyewitness testimony. Cognitive psychologists working in the legal arena can educate jurors and judges about memory research through expert testimony, if permitted to do so.

# Admissibility of Expert Testimony on the Fallibility of Eyewitness Memory

As previously noted, some judges will allow psychologists to testify as expert witnesses on eyewitness testimony, whereas other judges have ruled against the admissibility of such testimony. Wells (1995) has argued that this variation in admissibility rulings is more a reflection of judges using their own idiosyncratic views on the testimony, ambiguity of criteria for determining admissibility, and characteristics related to the jurisdiction. Judges have argued that the inaccuracy of eyewitness testimony is common knowledge and does not add any new information for the jurors (Leippe, 1995). Expert witness testimony would thus infringe on the work of the jury as the trier of fact. Judges have been skeptical of the general acceptance among the scientific community regarding the validity of the results. Judges also fear the potential for a "battle of the experts" with conflicting testimony regarding memory research that would only confuse the jury (Wrightsman, 2001). Finally, expert testimony questioning the accuracy of eyewitness testimony may lead to juror skepticism regarding all eyewitness testimony (Woocher, 1986).

Nevertheless, increasing skepticism among jury members regarding an eyewitness's testimony may be a good thing, as advocated by Hall and Loftus (1985), "In view of the sometimes devastating and tragic consequences of unreliable eyewitness testimony, it behooves us to search for ways of not only increasing juror skepticism, but simultaneously increasing juror wisdom" (p. 433). Additionally, Wrightsman (2001) cites four different surveys suggesting that jurors are not aware of memory research and the information provided by an expert witness on the topic would potentially educate jurors about important technical information that would need to be considered during deliberations. Additional survey research among 63 memory experts indicates a high "general acceptance" on a number of issues related to the accuracy of eyewitness memory (Kassin et al., 1989). These two arguments, lack of knowledge among prospective jurors regarding memory's fallibility and consensus among memory experts, support the admissibility of expert testimony on the fallibility of eyewitness memory. However, the reality is that even when admitted into court, hiring an expert witness to contest eyewitness accuracy is an expensive proposition that is available to only a few individuals and is thus infrequently employed in the courts (Wells et al., 1998).

# Recommended Procedures to Improve Eyewitness Memory

When discussing evidence based on memory, researchers in the field distinguish between **memory** and **memory testimony** (Wells, 1995). Memory is what the witness recalls about the event. It is important to recognize that the memory can be influenced by a variety of factors. Memory testimony is the witness's statement of what he or she recalls about a prior event. Memory testimony can also be influenced by a wide variety of events and processes. As a result, we have two processes that are susceptible to outside influences.

Factors that can influence memory can be divided into various categories depending on when they influence memory (**chronological category**) or whether they are something that the criminal justice system can control, termed the system-variable versus estimator-variable distinction (Wells, 1978; Wells & Loftus, 2003). **System variables** are variables introduced by police procedure and are preventable (Wells, 1993). These include the nature of the **lineup**, the presence of videotaping

■ **Memory**
What the witness recalls about the event.

■ **Memory testimony**
A witness's statement of what he or she recalls about a prior event.

■ **System variables**
Preventable variables introduced by police procedure.

■ **Estimator variables**

Factors out of police control that typically occur before the police arrive on the scene and can affect eyewitness accuracy.

during the procedure, instructions given to witnesses during a lineup, interviewing techniques such as poorly worded and/or leading questions, and so on. **Estimator variables** refer to factors out of police control and typically occur before the police arrive on the scene (Wrightsman, 2001). These include factors such as the view the witness had of the offender, lighting at the scene, visual acuity of the witness, and so on. Whereas estimator variables are out of the investigative team's control, legal psychologists can help law enforcement improve procedures related to system variables.

## Table 11.2 — System Variables and Estimator Variables Affecting Eyewitness Testimony

- ■ System Variables: introduced by police procedure and are preventable
  - The nature of the lineup
  - Presence of videotaping the procedure
  - Instructions given during a lineup
  - Interviewing technique to include poorly worded and/or leading questions
- ■ Estimator Variables: factors out of police control
  - The view the witness had of the offender
  - Lighting at the scene
  - Visual acuity of the witness

In addition to the system-estimator variable distinction, psychologists can also categorize variables based on the chronology or time frame as to when the variable may influence memory. The chronological category looks at factors that influence memory based on when they occur in the collection and preservation of the memory. Factors that influence eyewitness memory prior to the event involve **witness characteristics**, such as sex, age, intelligence, personality variables, visual acuity, impairment due to alcohol or drug use, and other sensory impairments. Factors influencing eyewitness memory during the event include variables such as length of exposure to the perpetrator, use of a disguise, same-race versus other-race identification, lighting, view the witness had of the perpetrator, and weapon focus. Law enforcement does not typically have much influence over these variables, although the use of surveillance cameras has increased the amount of control law enforcement can have over event variables.

The opportunity to use procedures that will enhance recollection of events and increase accuracy of eyewitness testimony occurs after the event. **Postevent factors** can include suggestions from others, including law enforcement personnel interviewing witnesses, exposure to sketches or photo arrays that may bias a witness, and the amount of time between the event and the recall of details. Factors can affect eyewitness memory during the identification process as well as after the identification has been made. **Identification task variables** include how the lineup is conducted, including prelineup instructions, the similarity of **foils** (known innocents used in the lineup), and suggestive behavior or "hints" provided during the identification procedure. Postidentification variables include feedback given after the identification is made. Juries tend to believe eyewitnesses who express confidence in their identification. Feedback

## Examples of the Chronological Categorization of Factors Affecting Eyewitness Identification | Table 11.3

- Witness characteristics: sex, intelligence, age, drug use, personality
- Event characteristics: exposure duration, weapon focus, view, disguise, same-versus other-race identification, stress
- Postevent factors: suggestions from others, exposure to sketches, retention interval
- Identification task variables: lineup, showup, prelineup instructions, foils, suggestive behaviors during lineup, simultaneous versus sequential procedure
- Postidentification variables: feedback regarding identification

given to an eyewitness after the identification procedure can increase the witness's confidence but has little effect on accuracy. Naturally, there is some overlap between the chronological distinction and the system-estimator category. Concerning the chronological category, witness characteristics and **event characteristics** refer to estimator variables.

Ways to improve the identification procedure obviously must occur with the system variables; these are the variables that the police can control. Psychologists can work with law enforcement to develop and validate procedures that improve the accuracy of eyewitness identification. The psychological community can then educate law enforcement on the use of these techniques. This is precisely the effort that led to the research report from the U.S. Department of Justice titled *Eyewitness Evidence: A Guide for Law Enforcement*. Recommendations from the report are reviewed below. A multidisciplinary team of experts from the United States and Canada put these recommendations together. The 34 members of the team represented lawyers, police chiefs, psychologists, district attorneys, prosecutors, sheriffs, and police officers. Recommendations include procedures for the initial report of the crime, use of mug book and composite images, interviewing techniques, showups, and lineups. The following recommendations are augmented by recent developments in the research literature.

Figure 11.4

## Initial Report of a Crime

Initial responders must collect as much information as possible and disseminate this information to other law enforcement personnel as quickly as possible. The actions of the first-responder can affect the safety of others involved as well as the integrity of the investigation. Information from witnesses and victims should be obtained after establishing rapport with the individual. Initial questions should be open-ended followed by closed-ended questions. For example, "Can you tell me anything about the car?" might be followed by "Was the car a two-door or four-door model?" Responders

Someone witnessing this crime would be affected by estimator variables such as lighting and whether they had a clear view.
© 2009 Lisa F. Young. Used under license from Shutterstock, Inc.

should avoid asking suggestive or leading questions and all information from the witness/victim should be documented. The information obtained from the witness should be paraphrased or clarified with the witness before disseminated to other law enforcement personnel. The witness should be encouraged to avoid contact with media sources, other witnesses, and any media accounts of the crime to prevent contamination of their memory from postevent information.

# Mug Books and Composite Images

**Mug books** are collections of photographs of previously arrested individuals. Mug books are used when all other reliable sources have been exhausted and no suspect has been identified. Photos in a mug book should be grouped by format so that no one photo stands out. For example, all black and white photographs should be together. Photos should be relatively recent and only one photo of each individual should be in the mug book. Photos for any one particular mug book should be uniform with regard to general characteristics such as race, age, sex, and so on. Photos may be grouped according to specific crime, such as gang activity, robbery, assault, and so on. When instructing the witness with regard to the mug book, no other witnesses should be present. The mug book should simply be described as a "collection of photographs." The witness should know that if they are unable to identify a suspect, the police will continue the investigation regardless. The witness should also be informed that the person who committed the offense may or may not be present in the mug book and he or she should not feel compelled to make an identification. The witness should be told that they will be asked to indicate how certain they are of the identification.

**Composite images** are reconstruction of faces by witnesses. Composites can be beneficial as investigative tools but do not rise to the level of probable cause and cannot be used as stand-alone evidence. Facial composites are constructed with the assistance of a police sketch artist or commercially available kits such as Identikit or Photofit (Bartol & Bartol, 2004). These kits consist of photos of facial features that the witness can piece together like a puzzle to obtain a facial composite. Computer-based systems also exist with facial features stored in memory that can be manipulated and placed together to form a composite. One computer system, the Mac-a-Mug Pro, can generate nearly 100 times the number of facial composites of a noncomputerized kit (Davies, van der Willik, & Morrison, 2000). Along with facial features, most kits include accessories such as hats and eyeglasses. To improve identification using a composite, witnesses should:

- avoid seeing any mug photos prior to developing the composite to prevent interference effects or potential contamination through suggestion;
- construct a composite separately to prevent any potential influence one witness may exert on another;
- each should be provided with instructions to the procedure without other persons present.

Despite the investigative value of these techniques, it is important to recognize the limitations of developing facial composites. Facial recognition is a complex task that is generally accomplished by perceiving the whole face. Most individuals would be hard pressed to accurately recognize a friend's nose or chin. Imagine the task of selecting your father's chin from an array of 30 different chins. Now, imagine the difficulty of selecting a chin that you may have observed once during the commission of a crime, when both your arousal and attention were considerably taxed due to the circumstances. The difficulty of the task of describing a face by piecing together various facial features can lead to inaccurate facial composites. Although very little empirical evidence exits, some researchers have suggested that the use of an artist sketching based on open-ended descriptions is the best approach (Bartol & Bartol, 2004).

Regardless of the approach used, it is necessary for the individual conducting the procedure to document the process in order to preserve an accurate record of the results obtained from each witness. Documentation should include the procedure used (e.g., mug book, artist, computer-generated image, etc.), the witness's own words regarding confidence in the identification, and all items used as well as any composites generated.

# Lineup Procedures

Many readers are familiar with the lineup procedure from watching the popular television series *Law and Order*. The possible suspect, along with **known innocents** (also termed nonsuspects, fillers, **detractors**, or foils), stand behind a one-way mirror and are viewed by the witness. The witness is asked to identify the suspect from the lineup. A **simultaneous lineup** is when the suspect and known innocents appear together. In a **sequential lineup**, the witness views the suspect and the known innocents one at a time. The lineup can be conducted live, with individuals behind a one-way mirror, or with a photo array, known as a **photo lineup**.

Research suggests there is no difference in the effect on eyewitness accuracy between a live lineup and a photo lineup (Cutler, Berman, Penrod, & Fisher, 1994). A live lineup does allow the witness to observe the suspect's behaviors, such as voice, facial expressions, and gait. However, a photo lineup offers other advantages over the live lineup. The use of a photo lineup is easier since it precludes the need to gather together individuals who are similar in appearance to the description of the suspect as provided by the witness. In addition, courts have ruled that the suspect has the right for a lawyer to be present during a live lineup but does not have the right for a lawyer to be present during a photo lineup (*United States v. Ash*, 1973). Other advantages to the photo lineup include its portability, immediate availability, ability to be repeatedly examined and for extended periods of time, and potential for reducing anxiety among victims who may feel threatened when viewing the alleged criminal through a one-way mirror (Cutler et al., 1994).

A recent development is the use of videotaped lineups. A videotaped lineup offers the advantages of a mug book along with additional possibilities using technology. Videotaped images can be enlarged, paused, and observed moving in slow motion.

Regardless of which technique is used, these identification procedures are vulnerable to bias and error, both blatant and unintended (Bartol & Bartol, 2004). Errors can occur due to the instructions the police give to witnesses, the way the lineup is conducted, and the composition of the lineup, as well as any feedback provided to the witness by the police after an identification is made. This is an area where

■ **Simultaneous lineup**
Suspect and known innocents appear together.

■ **Sequential lineup**
The suspect and known innocents appear one at a time.

■ **Photo lineup**
The use of photos instead of live people in a lineup. This technique is used in eyewitness identification.

**Figure 11.5**

What are some of the errors present in this photo lineup?
© 2005 JupiterImages Corporation.

---

## Table 11.4    Common Errors in Lineup Procedures

- Nonsuspects in the lineup do not closely resemble the suspect
- Implying that the criminal is definitely in the lineup
- Pressuring witness to make a choice
- Confirmation bias (asking questions about the suspect but not about known innocents)

- Giving obvious cues to the eyewitness as to the police officer's suspicion
- Confirming the eyewitness's selection, thus increasing their level of confidence in their "memory"
- Accepting a loose recognition threshold

---

■ **Relative judgment**
Selecting the individual in a lineup that most closely resembles the witness's recollection.

■ **Match-to-description strategy**
The known innocents should match the witness's prelineup description of the suspect.

■ **Functional size**
Used in research on the validity of a lineup; it is the number of members in a lineup who physically match the suspect, plus the suspect.

research from the social sciences can make major contributions to improving the accuracy of eyewitness identification.

Common errors that occur in lineup procedures can occur before, during, or after the identification. Errors that occur prior to the identification procedure are mainly due to the composition of the lineup. Individuals in the lineup should all have similar physical characteristics, such as age, race, hair color, height, weight, and so on. Any distinguishing features, such as scars or tattoos, should either be concealed or artificially added to all individuals in the lineup. The suspect should not stand out among the known innocents. Finally, there should be a minimum of five nonsuspects per identification procedure.

Witnesses will attempt to identify individuals who most closely match the initial physical description he or she reported to the police. Thus, if the witness reported that the perpetrator was a "tall white male with long blond hair and an angular face," then the known innocents should be all tall white males with long blond hair and angular faces. Clearly, a live lineup or a photo lineup consisting of only one white male with long blond hair would bias the witness's judgment. A witness will select the individual in the lineup who *most* closely resembles the witness's recollection of the perpetrator. This process of selecting the best possible fit is termed the **relative judgment process** (Wells, 1984). This can be effective if the real perpetrator is in the lineup. However, if the lineup consists of only innocent individuals, the relative judgment process is likely to result in an innocent individual being identified as the culprit (Wrightsman, 2001). Researchers have recommended a **match-to-description strategy** in selecting nonsuspects for the lineup (Wells et al., 1998). This strategy recommends that the foils match the witness's prelineup description of the guilty party. Wells (1984) has argued that the **functional size** of the lineup (number of members who physically match the suspect plus the suspect) should approximate the *nominal size* (number of persons in the lineup). Regardless of the number of persons present in the lineup (nominal size), the value of the investigation is restricted to the number of persons who resemble the witness's prelineup description of the offender. Witnesses feel pressure to assist the police in the identification process. Lineups are conducted after the police have a definite suspect. The witness has been called to the police station.

The police have summoned together a number of individuals and they clearly hope that the witness can assist in the investigation by providing a positive identification. There is a great deal of implicit pressure on the witness to identify a suspect. Research suggests that nearly 80% of witnesses will select someone from the lineup even when the guilty individual is not present in the lineup (Malpass & Devine, 1981). Even when witnesses are informed that the guilty individual may not be in the lineup, nearly one-third of the witnesses still identify an innocent person as the offender (Wells, 1993). However, explicit warnings to the witness that the perpetrator may not be present do reduce the rate of incorrect identifications (Steblay, 1997).

During the lineup procedure, police may inadvertently cause an inaccurate identification through their instructions, subtle cues, or feedback. The police should indicate that the person who committed the crime may or may not be present in the lineup and it is just as important to clear innocent persons from suspicion as to apprehend the guilty individual. All individuals in the lineup should be treated the same. If the police ask the witness questions about the suspect but not about the other individuals in the lineup, they may sway the witness to select the suspect. This process is termed **confirmation bias**. The police should treat all individuals in the lineup similarly, asking questions about each of them and having each engage in any requested behaviors, and so forth. The police should avoid pressuring the witness to make a identification and assure the witness that the investigation will continue regardless if an identification is made.

It is particularly important for the police to avoid giving any subtle cues as to who they believe is the suspect. The possibility of inadvertently providing cues to the witness is so powerful that researchers in the field recommend that the police officers conducting the lineup procedure do not know who the suspect is (Wells et al., 1998). The possibility that the police can inadvertently lead the witness to identify the individual the police believe to be the suspect is similar to the phenomenon in psychology called experimenter bias. **Experimenter bias**, also called the **Rosenthal effect**, demonstrates how influential our expectations can be on another's behavior. The effect is named after Robert Rosenthal, a psychologist who conducted a frequently cited series of studies starting in the early 1960s. In the initial study, he gave teachers at an elementary school a list of students who, based on testing, were predicted to blossom academically. At the end of the academic year, students on the list did well academically compared to students not on the list. The reality is the names on the list were randomly selected, although the teachers did not know this fact. It was the teachers' expectations for the students that appeared to make the difference in the students' academic performance. Rosenthal and his colleague, Lenore Jacobson, extended this research to the behavior of lab rats (Rosenthal & Jacobson, 1968). The researchers asked graduate students to teach two sets of laboratory rats how to run a maze. One set of rats were labeled "fast learners," whereas the other set were labeled "slow learners." In actuality, the rats were randomly labeled and were all from the same litter. Remarkably, the fast learners mastered the mazes more quickly than the slow learners and were described by the graduate students as smarter and more "likable" than the "dull" rats. Again, the evidence suggests that the graduate students' expectations about the rats' behavior somehow influenced the rats' performance. Rats expected to learn quickly did so, and rats expected to perform poorly did so. If the behavior of rats can be influenced by graduate students' expectations, it is reasonable to assume that a police officer's expectations could sway a witness's identification of a possible suspect. The optimal procedure for the lineup is for the person conducting the live lineup or photo lineup to not know which individual in the lineup is the suspect. Along this line, the police should not encourage a loose recognition threshold for the identification (Wrightsman, 2001).

■ **Confirmation bias**
The deliberate or inadvertent use of subtle cues to bias an eyewitness's identification.

■ **Experimenter bias**
Research indicating that the expectations of the experimenter can influence the behavior of research participants in a study.

Another potential error is providing feedback to the eyewitness regarding their identification prior to assessing the eyewitness's confidence in the identification. The issue of witness confidence is an important consideration, as juries tend to rely upon how confident the witness feels about his or her identification. A witness testifying that he or she is 100% certain of their identification of the suspect as the offender is bound to have a stronger influence on the jury's decision-making process than a witness who admits that he or she could be mistaken. However, research has shown that an eyewitness's level of confidence can be influenced by postevent variables such as police feedback or even the use of investigative hypnosis (Sheehan & Tilden, 1983; Wells & Bradfield, 1998). Feedback provided to the witness regarding an accurate the identification of the suspect increases the witness's confidence in their identification. In one study, witnesses watched a videotape from a store security camera of a man entering a store (Wells & Bradfield, 1998). Participants were asked to pay attention to the videotape, as they would be questioned about details later. They were then asked to identify the man from a photo lineup that did not include a picture of the man. Some participants were given positive feedback ("Good, you identified the suspect") and others were told that they were wrong. The positive feedback not only increased witness's confidence in the identification, but these participants also reported being more willing to testify about their identification, having paid greater attention to the videotape, and having a better view of the man than participants who did not receive the positive feedback. To minimize the **postidentification-feedback effect**, witnesses should be asked to state in their own words how certain he or she is of any identification. The statement should be documented in writing, and preferably, by videotape (Kassin, 1998). The witness's statement of certainty should be obtained prior to giving any feedback to the witness regarding the identification. Certainty of the eyewitness has been shown to be a poor indicator of the accuracy of the identification (Wells & Loftus, 2003).

A **showup** is a field investigative procedure that is used when circumstances require the prompt identification of a single suspect by a witness (TWGEYEE, 1999b). Essentially, a showup is a lineup with only one person, the suspect. Many psychologists in the memory field believe that a showup increases the risk of misidentification (Kassin et al., 1989; Wells, Leippe, & Ostrom, 1979; Yarney, 1979; Yarney, Yarney, & Yarney, 1996). Even the courts and law enforcement personnel recognize the inherent suggestiveness of using only one person in a lineup (*Stovall v. Denno*, 1967; TWGEYEE, 1999b). Although the U.S. Supreme Court has ruled a showup as suggestive, it did not find the showup to be "unnecessarily" suggestive that it should be ruled inadmissible. Other researchers have argued that the showup is superior to a lineup, claiming that witnesses are less likely to identify innocent persons in the showup when compared to the use of a lineup procedure. Law enforcement recommends the use of procedural safeguards to limit the inherent suggestiveness of a showup (TWGEYEE, 1999b). These safeguards include:

- obtaining a description of the perpetrator prior to the showup,
- cautioning the witness that the person may or may not be the offender,
- documenting the witness's statement of certainty regarding the identification, and
- if a positive identification is made with one witness, to use other identification procedures, such as a lineup, with other witnesses.

Gary Wells, an expert in the field of eyewitness memory, and his colleagues have proposed four rules for increasing the accuracy and fairness of a lineup (Wells et al., 1998; Wells & Seelau, 1995). Some of these recommendations were later used in the preparation of the National Institute of Justice guide, *Eyewitness Evidence: A Guide for Law Enforcement* (TWGEYEE, 1999). Kassin (1998) published an

**■ Postidentifications feedback effect**

Giving positive feedback regarding the identification increases a witness's level of certainty.

**■ Showup**

A lineup with only one suspect presented to the eyewitness(es).

article in the same issue of the journal in which the Wells et al. (1998) paper appeared, recommending a fifth rule for improving the fairness of lineup procedures. The original four rules along with other recommendations were published by the American Psychology-Law Society (AP-LS) in a paper known as the Police Lineups White Paper (Wells, 2001). The four rules along with Kassin's fifth recommendation are described below.

1. "The person who conducts the lineup or photospread should not be aware of which member of the lineup or photospread is the suspect" (Wells et al., 1998, p. 627). (This rule was not adopted in the National Institute of Justice guide.)
2. "Eyewitnesses should be told explicitly that the perpetrator might not be in the lineup or photospread and therefore eyewitnesses should not feel that they must make an identification" (p. 629).
3. "The suspect should not stand out in the lineup or photoarray as being different from the distractors based on the eyewitness's previous description of the culprit or based on other factors that would draw extra attention to the suspect" (p. 630).
4. "A clear statement should be taken from the witness at the time of the identification and prior to any feedback as to his or her confidence that the identified person is the actual culprit" (p. 635).
5. Kassin's (1998) fifth recommendation is for the entire identification process to be videotaped to ensure the integrity of the process. Kassin (2005) has recently argued that interviews and interrogation of suspects be videotaped. He notes that all sessions are videotaped in Great Britain and four states presently mandate videotaping suspect interviews. He cites numerous advantages to videotaped records. These same advantages apply to eyewitness identification procedures as well as interrogations. The presence of a camera is likely to deter the use of suggestive or leading questions by law enforcement personnel. A videotape record will also deter frivolous claims by the defense regarding an abuse of power or use of coercive techniques. Judges and juries would be able to evaluate the fairness of the procedure.

The Innocence Project (2007) has also released a resource guide for reform of eyewitness identification procedures. The Innocence Project is a public policy and litigation organization that works to free wrongfully convicted individuals through postconviction DNA testing. As of February 2008, they have helped secure the release of 213 people who were wrongfully convicted, including 17 individuals who were serving time on death row. The average length of time served for the people exonerated was 12 years. Over 75% of the individuals exonerated were convicted due to faulty eyewitness identification.

The *Eyewitness Identification Resource Guide: A Primer for Reform* (Innocence Project, 2007) provides five recommendations as well as a sixth *optional* recommendation for reforming eyewitness identification procedures. The five recommendations are:

1. *Blind Administration*: The person administering the eyewitness procedure does not know which photo in a photo array or which individual in a live lineup is the suspect. A blind administration can also be accomplished if, although the person administering the procedure knows who is suspected by the police, the person administering the procedure does not know which lineup member or photo in the array is being viewed by the eyewitness. Blind administration is used to prevent the eyewitness from tailoring their responses to meet the expectations of the administrator. Blind administration will prevent the administrator from inadvertently leading the eyewitness towards the suspect and/or leading

the eyewitness away from a foil. Blind administration will also prevent post-identification feedback from occurring. In order to assist small police departments with limited officer power or off-site identifications, the Folder System was developed. Basically, six photos (one of the suspect and five foils) are placed in six numbered folders. Four additional empty folders are also numbered. The folders are shuffled so that the administrator does not know which folder contains the suspect. Folders are individually handed to the eyewitness one at a time and then returned to the administrator, with the order of presentation maintained. The empty folders are to prevent the witness from knowing when he or she has seen the last photo.

2. *Recommended Instructions to Eyewitnesses*: Recommendations provided by the Innocence Project are similar to recommendations provided by the Technical Working Group for Eyewitness Identification discussed earlier. These recommendations include (1) instruct the eyewitness without other persons present, (2) describe the photo array as a "collection of photographs," (3) indicate that the suspect may or may not be present in the identification procedure, (4) suggest to the eyewitness to think back to the event, (5) instruct the eyewitness to select a photo or member in a lineup if he or she can and to indicate how he or she knows the person, (6) assure the individual that the investigation will continue regardless of their ability to make an identification, (7) ask the eyewitness to state in his or her own words how confident he or she is of the identification, (8) inform the eyewitness that the administrator does not know who the suspect is, and (9) instruct the eyewitness not to discuss the procedure with others involved in the case and the media.

3. *Composition of the Photo Array and Live Lineup Members*: The suspect should not unduly stand out when compared with the foils. When using a photo, it should be contemporary and resemble the appearance of the suspect at the time of the offense. If there is more than one eyewitness, the suspect should be placed in a different position in the lineup or photo array for each eyewitness. No information about the suspect should be provided to the eyewitness. With regard to foils, the recommendation is that at least five additional foils be used in a photo array and at least four additional foils be used in a lineup. The foils should resemble the description of the suspect from the eyewitness and should not have any significant differences from the suspect, such as weight, height, scars, and so on. If the eyewitness views several lineups attempting to identify multiple suspects, different foils should be used.

4. *Confidence Statements*: It is recommended that a confidence statement is taken at the time of the identification and before any postidentification feedback is given. Research indicates that the confidence statement should be secured at the time of the identification (Douglas & Stabley, 2006).

5. *Electronic Recording of the Identification Procedure*: A video recording of the identification procedure is preferred over an audio recording or simple written documentation. The recording should include all persons present including foils, suspects, administrators, and eyewitnesses, and photographs when a photo array is used. Any erroneous identification of foils should be recorded as well as the order of presentation if a sequential format is used in the identification procedure.

6. *A Sequential Presentation*: This is offered as an optional reform since research suggests it can decrease the likelihood of a correct identification when a blind administrator is not used. A sequential format simply implies that the eyewitness views members in a live lineup or photographs from a photo array one by one. As stated, the sequential format should only be used with a blind administrator. The superiority of sequential lineup with a blind administrator has not been

adequately demonstrated to warrant recommendations on sequential versus simultaneous lineups (McQuiston-Surret, Malpass, & Tredoux, 2006). Indeed, a recent study using a policy analysis approach based on decision theory examined the utility of sequential and simultaneous lineup (Roy, 2006). The author concludes that simultaneous lineups are superior to sequential lineups overall. The study examined identification outcomes and their probabilities.

The similarity of the above recommendations suggests that there is ample scientific evidence to reform eyewitness identification procedures. The incarceration of innocent individuals due to faulty eyewitness identification can be minimized by following these simple procedures. Not only are falsely identified individuals harmed, but incorrect eyewitness identifications hamper the ability of law enforcement officials to investigate the crime. Any delay in investigation can reduce the potential for apprehending the perpetrator. A misidentification distracts the police from further investigation. The courts have recognized the importance of accurate identification procedures and have ruled on the admissibility of eyewitness identification.

## Can You Point Out the Person You Saw in the Park Here Today in the Courtroom?

In March 2007, a 10-year-old boy vacationing with his family at a large amusement park is reported missing. Due to confusion between the parents, with each parent thinking that the other parent was with the boy, the child was missing for approximately 45 minutes before authorities were notified. Once notified, park officials placed security at all the park exits. Security watched for the boy as well as questioned patrons leaving the park regarding any unusual behavior they may have witnessed. Nearly 20 patrons reported seeing a young boy who fit the child's description with a man leaving the park. These individuals are asked for contact information. As the day ends and the park closes, the boy is still missing. Park officials conduct a thorough search of the park and find the boy's body in a dumpster in a remote section of the park near a service entrance. It appears that the boy was sexually molested.

Police contact patrons who offered earlier information in hopes of developing a composite sketch of the suspect. Of the 20 patrons who were contacted, only three were able to accurately identify the boy in a photo array with a photograph supplied by the parents. Eight of the patrons reported that the suspect appeared to be a Hispanic male, whereas four suggested the suspect was African American. The police artist, using computer software, generates a sketch. Fifteen of the patrons agree that the sketch resembles the man they saw. The police publicize the sketch on the evening news asking for any information. Within the following 3 weeks, they received approximately 200 leads. Only five of the leads result in individuals who were at the park on the day of the crime based on surveillance videos at the entrance/exit of the park.

The detective in charge of the case recognizes that the only evidence they have is eyewitness evidence, as no DNA or other physical evidence was obtained. The detective also realizes that the eyewitnesses presented conflicting information. She decides that in order to obtain a conviction of the guilty individual, she will need to meticulously handle any eyewitness accounts placing any of the five subjects with the boy on the day of the disappearance. She contacts Dr. Shayleigh Cooper, a well-known cognitive psychologist who specializes in eyewitness testimony. The detective asks Dr. Cooper to consult on the case and offer suggestions as to how to obtain the most accurate and convincing eyewitness identification.

What procedures should Dr. Cooper recommend to the detective? Discuss how the eyewitness identification should be conducted including format, number and appearance of foils, feedback, individuals present, and interaction among witnesses. Also, how should Dr. Cooper prepare for testifying in court if she is called by the prosecution and/or the defense?

# Supreme Court Rulings on the Admissibility of Eyewitness Identifications

The U.S. Supreme Court has ruled on the admissibility of eyewitness identifications. As mentioned earlier, in the *Stovall v. Denno* (1967) trial, the Court ruled that a showup was suggestive, but not "unnecessarily" suggestive (Wrightsman, 2001). If law enforcement had other options available, such as a lineup, then the showup could be ruled unnecessary. In the *Stovall* case, the use of the showup was considered necessary since the survival of the witness was uncertain. Stovall, the suspect, was transported to the hospital bedside of the lone witness, the wife of a man Stovall was accused of murdering. Her wounds from the attack were so severe that doctors could not guarantee her surviving through the night. Stovall was taken to the hospital under police escort and in restraints. Stovall was convicted of the murder and the Supreme Court upheld the use of the showup to identify him as the perpetrator. However, the National Institute of Justice guide, *Eyewitness Evidence: A Guide for Law Enforcement*, recommends transporting the witness to the suspect when feasible. The Connecticut Supreme Court ruled that when a showup results in a positive identification, in an absence of instructions to the eyewitness that "the perpetrator may not be present," the jury must be informed that failure to provide such instructions increased the probability of a false identification (*State v. Ledbetter*, 2005). This ruling highlights the importance of the reforms discussed above and that these recommendations are being considered by the courts.

In a second ruling relevant to eyewitness identification, the Supreme Court articulated criteria to be used when considering the likelihood of an accurate identification (*Neil v. Biggers*, 1972). The Court ruled that even if the police used suggestive techniques in obtaining an eyewitness identification, these criteria could be used to determine if the identification was accurate and not unduly influenced by the police (Wrightsman, 2001). Some of these criteria are related to witness characteristics, and are estimator variables. These include the witness's view of the criminal at the crime scene and the witness's level of attention during the event. The Court reasoned that if the witness had a good view of the criminal during the commission of the offense, it is more likely that the identification is accurate. Similarly, if the witness was highly attentive at the time of the offense, as opposed to intoxicated or half-asleep, then the accuracy would be increased. Other criteria discussed by the Court can be considered system variables, the kind that can be influenced by the police. One criterion is the accuracy of the witness's description of the culprit. This description needs to be col-

**Table 11.5** **Supreme Court Criteria Used to Consider the Likelihood of an Accurate Identification**

- Witness's view of the perpetrator at the time of the crime
- Interval between the event and the recollection
- Witness's level of attention during the crime
- Accuracy of witness's description of the culprit
- Level of confidence that the witness expresses regarding the identification

lected from the witness using open-ended questions prior to any identification. The use of suggestive or leading questions by the police can influence a witness's description (e.g., "Other witnesses stated that the perpetrator was about 6 feet tall and probably weighed 180 pounds. Is that the same as what you saw?"). Likewise, feedback after the identification can influence a witness's confidence level in his or her identification.

Wrightsman (2001) has raised three important issues regarding how the Supreme Court's decision conflicts with empirical psychological evidence.

1. The Supreme Court ruled that a showup, which is deemed "suggestive," was not "unnecessarily" suggestive to deem it inadmissible (*Stovall v. Denno*, 1967). Wrightsman (2001) points out that the Court failed to indicate guidelines for determining when suggestive procedures would not be admissible. However, the Court's decision was handed down in 1967. There now exists a large body of literature that can be incorporated into law enforcement investigations. The National Institute of Justice guide, *Eyewitness Evidence: A Guide for Law Enforcement*, appears to be an effort to incorporate research findings from psychological studies into law enforcement procedures.
2. Wrightsman further notes that the U.S Supreme Court suggests that the witness's level of confidence in the accuracy of their identification reflects a more accurate identification. However, as previously noted, research indicates a very low correlation between accuracy and confidence level (Bothwell, Deffenbacher, & Brigham, 1987). The **optimality hypothesis** suggests that the more optimal the conditions in which the offender was viewed, the stronger the relationship between confidence and level of accuracy (Deffenbacher, 1980).
3. Third, a witness's level of confidence can be inflated by feedback from the police, termed the *postidentification-feedback effect* (Wells & Bradfield, 1998). This can also distort how confident the witness believed he or she was at the initial time of the identification. This feedback can even influence the witness's recollection of the condition under which he or she observed the alleged offender. As noted above, participants in a research study who were given positive feedback believed that they had a better view of the criminal and paid more attention than witnesses who did not receive the positive feedback.

Although the courts have not incorporated much of the scientific findings regarding eyewitness accuracy into the decision-making process, the fact that the National Institute of Justice convened a working group to produce recommendations to law enforcement is promising. As stated, this working group of 34 individuals consisted of psychologists, attorneys, and law enforcement personnel from the United States and Canada. Psychologists on the panel included many of the researchers cited in this text, such as Gary Wells, Roy Malpass, and Solomon Fulero. These collaborative efforts between psychology and law enforcement are promising and appear to be increasing.

**Figure 11.6**

The Supreme Court has made several rulings on the admissibility of eyewitness identifications.
© 2009 Johnny Kuo. Used under license from Shutterstock, Inc.

■ **Optimality hypothesis**
A concept related to eyewitness testimony that posits that the more optimal the conditions in which the offender was viewed, the stronger the relationship between confidence of eyewitness identification and level of accuracy of the identification by the witness.

# Recovered Memory versus False Memory

Very few scholarly debates have triggered the emotional intensity as the debate surrounding recovered memories and false memories. This debate has generated scholarly articles with researchers calling each other "deceptive," "smearing," and accused of making "categorically false" claims (e.g., Karon & Widener, 1999; Lilienfeld & Loftus, 1999; Pendergrast, 1999). Needless to say, the debate over repressed memories and recovered memories is a controversial topic in psychology and law and has been played out in the media through news reports, coverage of lawsuits, and television specials. The "memory wars" debate is far from resolved, although there are several areas where a consensus has been reached. Perhaps as Knapp and VandeCreek (2000) suggest, "Focusing on the areas of consensus may reduce unnecessary acrimony in the field and facilitate research into the areas of uncertainty where knowledgeable authorities respectfully disagree" (p. 365). This section defines several of the terms used in the debate, discusses legal implications, and presents areas of consensus and disagreement.

■ **Repressed memory**

The unconscious psychological process of keeping the memory of an event out of awareness for an extended period of time.

**Repressed memory** refers to the unconscious psychological process of keeping the memory of an event out of awareness for an extended period of time. Repression refers to the unconscious motivated forgetting of unpleasant material (Holmes, 1990). Others have used the terms "dissociative amnesia" and "psychogenic amnesia." Some clinicians have argued that repressed memories of trauma linger in the unconscious and can cause "neurotic" symptoms, such as those associated with posttraumatic stress disorder (PTSD) (Pope, 1997). It is important to note that not all forgetting or failing to report abuse can be attributed to repression. Failure to report early traumatic events may be attributed to ordinary forgetting, childhood amnesia, or even an unwillingness to disclose personal information (Knapp & VandeCreek, 2000; Lilienfeld & Loftus, 1999). Perhaps the main reason the repressed memory debate is characterized by such emotional intensity and rancor is due to the focus on early childhood sexual abuse. Some authors who have questioned the veracity of recovered memories of early childhood sexual abuse have been accused in the literature of condoning the sexual abuse of children (e.g., Pendergrass, 1999). These kinds of comments appear to go well beyond the scholarly enterprise. Rather, there is little doubt that all responsible parties on both sides of the debate certainly agree that child abuse is prevalent and harmful (APA Working Group on Investigation of Memories of Childhood Abuse, 1998; Knapp & VandeCreek, 2000).

The repressed memory of the trauma is later recalled, often through the process of psychotherapy. Some clinicians believe that the memory of childhood trauma, particularly childhood sexual abuse, once repressed, can only be recovered through the process of psychotherapy. The theory proposes that the repressed memory will cause neurotic symptoms and only by recovering the memory of the trauma can the patient experience alleviation of the symptoms (Herman, 1992; Karon & Widener, 1998, 1999). Psychologists have recommended the cautious use of memory recovery techniques when working with adults who were possibly abused as children and have repressed the memory of the abuse (Courtois, 1997; Enns et al., 1998). Others argue that the recovery of repressed childhood memories of abuse is neither sufficient nor necessary for successful treatment (Terr, 1994). Likewise, although some clinicians have argued that the confrontation of the abuser can be therapeutic (Clute, 1993), there is no empirical evidence to support this claim (Knapp & VandeCreek, 2000).

As discussed earlier, most memory researchers argued that memory is constructive in nature and can be readily influenced by a wide array of factors. These researchers contend that the majority, though not all, of these recovered memories are actually false memories. The false memories have been implanted inadvertently through suggestive therapeutic techniques, such as hypnosis and imagination inflation. False memories that patients adhere to has led to the term **false memory syndrome**. Patients with false memory syndrome experience false memories of childhood abuse that they adamantly believe to be real. Their belief in these memories has prompted lawsuits and criminal investigations of the alleged abuser.

■ **False memory syndrome**

False memories that have been implanted inadvertently through suggestive therapy techniques but the individual believes the memories to be real.

Experts need to consider a variety of factors when assessing the credibility of re-covered memories of childhood sexual abuse. This is particularly important when there has been a significant delay in recall. Factors contributing to the difficulty of the assessment include the individual's account of how they forgot the abuse and how they came to recall the abuse and whether and how the abuse originated in therapy (Ali-son, Kebbell, & Lewis, 2006). These authors comment that it is difficult to general-ize from the empirical evidence to specific cases and suggest that practicing forensic psychologists need to maintain a case-specific focus when addressing **recovered mem-ory** testimony in court.

Many states have altered the laws regarding the statute of limitations for filing a law-suit regarding alleged child abuse. Generally, civil lawsuits must be filed within a certain period dating from the alleged occurrence of the act that caused physical or emotional harm. However, many states passed legislation allowing victims of childhood sexual abuse to bring tort actions against the alleged perpetrator well after the abuse is claimed to have occurred. These **delayed reporting statutes** allow victims to file suit against their attackers within 3 years *after* the memory is recovered (Wrightsman, 2001).

The American Psychological Association convened a working group of experts in the field representing both sides of the debate to review the relevant scientific litera-ture. The goal of the group was to clarify issues related to the debate regarding re-pressed memories and childhood sexual abuse. The group consisted of six members from differing areas of expertise and was able to reach agreement on five key points, summarized below (APA Working Group, 1998, p. 933):

■ **Delayed reporting statues**
A law that allows a victim of alleged abuse to file a claim within a set time period after the abuse is remembered. The statute of limitations is not linked to when the crime occurred but is linked to when it is recalled.

1. Controversies regarding adult recollections should not be allowed to obscure the fact that child sexual abuse is a complex and pervasive problem in America that has historically gone unacknowledged.
2. Most people who were sexually abused as children remember all or part of what happened to them.
3. It is possible for memories of abuse that have been forgotten to be remembered. The mechanism, or mechanisms, by which such delayed recall occurs is not cur-rently well understood.
4. It is also possible to construct convincing false memories for events that never oc-curred. The mechanism, or mechanisms, by which these false memories occur is not currently well understood.
5. There are gaps in our knowledge about the processes that lead to accurate and inaccurate recollections of childhood abuse.

Since the publication of the APA Working Group report, others have attempted to identify additional areas of consensus and disagreement (Gore-Felton et al., 2000; Knapp & VandeCreek, 2000; Palm & Gibson, 1998). The controversy hinges on adults who claim to have lost memories of childhood sexual abuse and then later re-gained these memories. The debate does not involve continuous memories of child-hood abuse. Adults who recall having been abused as a child and who do not claim to have ever forgotten the memory are usually not questioned about the veracity of their allegations (Berliner & Loftus, 1992). Most psychologists recognize that some persons may lose memories of abuse only to later recall the memory as an adult. Evidence indicates that some trauma victims later have no recollection of the traumatic occurrence (e.g., Karon & Widener, 1997; Knapp & VandeCreek, 1997). It appears that most psychologists agree that memories of traumatic experience can be forgotten and later recalled.

One area of disagreement is the frequency of how often this occurs. Some re-searchers report a relatively frequent rate of amnesia for childhood abuse and the memory being recalled later. For example, Pope (1996) cites survey research indicating that 40% of clinicians who had been abused as children report having lost the memory of the abuse only to recall it later. This survey was unique in that approximately half of the reports of abuse were collaborated. Pope and Tabachnick (1995), in a national survey of therapists, cite 73% of the therapists reported seeing a client with a recovered memory of abuse. Despite the apparent frequent occurrence from the Pope and Tabachnick survey, the therapists in this survey reported that fewer than 1% of their clients had a recovered memory of childhood sexual abuse. Other studies have found very few therapists reporting clients with recovered memories, prompting some authors to suggest the low rates may reflect a failure of clinicians to adequately address the pervasive problem of childhood sexual abuse among their clients (Palm & Gibson, 1998)

Another area of consensus regards very early childhood memories. Most psychologists agree that memories from infancy are highly unreliable and that most children have a very poor memory of events until about the age of 4 (British Psychological Society, 1995). Most clinicians agree that screening for a history of childhood sexual or physical abuse should be a routine part of the initial assessment. Considering the frequency of childhood abuse, it is wise for therapists to seek training and develop competence in the assessment and treatment of abuse (Enns et al., 1998). It is unlikely that questioning adults about a history of abuse would lead to a false memory of abuse. As the APA Working Group stated, "The mechanism, or mechanisms, by which these false memories occurs is not currently well understood" (1998, p. 933). Some authors have suggested that "repeated suggestion, confrontations, or the use of highly suggestive 'memory recovery' techniques could cause the creation of memories that are not true" (Knapp & VandeCreek, 2000, p. 367). False memories occur as the result of combining actual memories with the suggestions of content provided by others. Loftus (1997a) cites three conditions can contribute to the development of false memories.

1. There is social pressure to recall an event. The pressure can be exerted by the demand characteristics of an experiment when a researcher encourages a participant to remember as much as he or she can about a childhood event. Alternatively, the social pressure can be exerted by law enforcement personnel or a lawyer, encouraging a witness to recall details or make an identification, or by a therapist encouraging a client.
2. The construction of false memories can be explicitly encouraged when people are having difficulty recalling details by allowing them to imagine events, as may be done in therapy. **Imagination inflation** is the process whereby a person comes to believe that a fictitious event occurred after imagining the event.
3. Individuals can be told not to worry about the accuracy of their recollections. This technique is also used in some therapy settings.

■ **Imagination inflation**
The process whereby a person comes to believe that a fictitious event actually occurred as a result of imagining the event.

Enns et al. (1998) and Courtois (1997) provide an overview of techniques used to retrieve repressed memories. Techniques include hypnosis, expressive therapeutic techniques, and seeking corroboration.

Some clinicians have suggested that a pattern of symptoms may reliably indicate a history of childhood abuse. However, this appears to be the minority opinion. The majority opinion is that one cannot infer childhood abuse based on any particular set of symptoms (APA Working Group, 1998; Enns et al., 1998). Rather, psychological symptoms can be caused by a variety of factors. The majority of psychologists believe that false memories can be treated. Clients who have "recovered" memories but later retracted the memories can be helped to understand the process that led to the false memory (de Rivera, 2000). However, some clients may need to learn to live with the uncertainty regarding the accuracy of the recovered memory (Knapp & VandeCreek, 2000).

Finally, despite the intense media attention to criminal trials and lawsuits arising from recovered memories, it appears that the majority of patients do not wish to pursue legal action (de Rivera, 2000) nor is there any evidence that confrontation and litigation is therapeutic. Nearly all psychologists agree that therapists should not encourage litigation or provide legal advice. Additionally, ethical considerations require psychologists to think of the effects of their actions on third parties, such as the client's family of origin.

Areas of disagreement include the psychological effects of childhood abuse, the proper treatment of adults with histories of abuse, and the relationship between childhood abuse and adult disorders. There is also considerable disagreement about the mechanisms underlying repression, recovery of memories, and the creation of false memories. Part of the problem with regard to the memory literature is a fundamental difference of opinion between the two camps regarding methodology. Practitioners suggest that experimental studies implanting ordinary childhood memories, such as the previously discussed study involving being lost in a shopping mall, have little relevance to the creation of memories of childhood sexual abuse. Researchers argue that anecdotal evidence of repression and recovered memories shed little scientific light on the underlying mechanisms. Perhaps as more researchers increase the ecological validity of their studies and practitioners embrace methodological rigor in their clinical work, a bridge can be built bringing the two sides closer together (Knapp & VandeCreek, 2000).

## Figure 11.7

Most psychologists would agree that this 3-year-old will have a very poor memory of events that occur during this time in his life.

© 2009 Felix Casio. Used under license from Shutterstock, Inc.

# Summary

This chapter described the area of legal psychology that researches memory and the accuracy of eyewitness identification. The focus was on how psychological science can help improve the collection and preservation of eyewitness evidence. Law enforcement routinely uses standard protocol for the collection of trace evidence from a crime scene. However, it has only been relatively recent, primarily due to the accumulation of empirical literature, that the law enforcement community has recognized the need to develop procedures for collecting and preserving eyewitness evidence.

The research into memory in the legal system has focused on two different, though not mutually exclusive, lines of inquiry. One approach has been to demonstrate the fallibility of memory. Researchers have attempted to debunk the popular notion that memory works like a videotape, allowing the individual to rewind and play scenes in their mind's eye, picking out details. Rather, researchers have shown the constructive nature of memory with the use of schemas to fill in the details of an episode. Additional research has shown how pre- and postevents, including phrasing of questions and provision of feedback, can easily influence memory. This line of research has been utilized by legal psychologists testifying as expert witnesses to educate judges and juries on the inaccuracy of eyewitness identification. Inaccurate eyewitness identification has been cited as the largest single cause for the wrongful conviction of innocent persons.

The second approach in the area of memory research has been the development of procedures for improving the collection of eyewitness evidence. The focus of this research has been on improving identification of suspects from a lineup, whether a live lineup or a photo lineup. Common errors in the use of a lineup include the composition of the lineup, confirmation bias, the possibility of the Rosenthal effect, providing the witness with feedback, failing to ascertain the witness's level of certainty, and poor documentation of the procedure. Five specific recommendations were provided to improve the accuracy and fairness of eyewitness identification from lineups.

Finally, the debate on repressed memory/recovered memory was introduced. The concept of false memory syndrome was discussed along with an overview of the contentiousness of this scholarly debate. Areas of consensus were presented as well as areas on which both sides of the debate continue to disagree. This debate is important for legal psychologists to understand, as recovered memories have resulted in criminal prosecution and civil lawsuits. These lawsuits have been against perpetrators of the alleged abuse as well as malpractice suits against clinicians who implanted or facilitated the creation of false memories. States have responded to this issue by altering the statute of limitations on filing civil suits against alleged abusers.

# TEST YOUR KNOWLEDGE

1. Psychologists can improve eyewitness identification procedures by assisting with
   a. witness characteristics
   b. event characteristics
   c. system variables
   d. estimator variables

2. Some researchers claim that more innocent individuals have been wrongly convicted due to _____ than all other causes combined.
   a. DNA
   b. polygraph
   c. eyewitness testimony
   d. expert witness testimony

3. Psychologists have testified on the accuracy of eyewitness testimony. Typically, these psychologists have a background in
   a. clinical psychology
   b. forensic psychology
   c. law enforcement
   d. cognitive psychology

4. What term is used to describe the following factors that can influence memory: lighting at the crime scene, visual acuity of the witness, view witness had of the offender, etc.?
   a. estimator variables
   b. system variables
   c. cognitive variables
   d. environmental variables

5. Approximately how many witnesses select an *innocent* person in a lineup *even when they are informed* that the perpetrator may not be present?
   a. 80%
   b. fewer than 5%
   c. nearly 33%
   d. 50%

Answer Key (1) c, (2) c, (3) d, (4) a, (5) c

# Chapter Twelve

# Emerging Trends in the Field of Forensic Psychology

## Learning Objectives

- Briefly describe the four emerging trends in forensic psychology discussed in the text.

- What are some reasons given for the continued growth in the field of forensic psychology?

- What are some indicators presented as evidence of increased sophistication within the field of forensic psychology?

- What are some examples of increased collaboration between psychology and law?

- What is an *amicus* brief and how has the American Psychological Association used it? Be able to provide some examples.

- Distinguish between an advocacy brief and a science translation brief.

- What occurred at the Villanova Conference in 1995?

- What are the three proposed levels of training for forensic psychologists? Be able to describe each level in some detail.

- What is the status of training standards for forensic psychologists?

- What are some obstacles to establishing a credentialing process?

- What are some likely future changes to training for forensic psychologists?

- What is board certification and what does the term "vanity board" mean?

- What function does the American Board of Professional Psychology perform?

- Define therapeutic jurisprudence and be able to provide some examples.

- What is a psycholegal soft spot?

## Key Terms

- Advocacy brief
- American Board of Forensic Psychology
- American Board of Professional Psychology
- American Psychology-Law Society
- *Amicus curiae* brief
- Association of State and Provincial Psychology Boards
- Board certification
- Brandeis brief
- Diplomate
- Division 41 of APA
- Dual degree programs
- Entry level
- FBI Behavioral Science Unit
- Friend of the court
- Generalist
- Legal psychology
- National Invitational Conference on Education and Training in Law and Psychology
- Preventive law
- Professional psychology
- Proficiency level
- Psycholegal soft spots
- Restorative justice
- *Roper v. Simmons* (2005)
- Science-translation brief
- Specialty level
- Standards for Educational and Psychological Testing

*(continued)*

## Key Terms *(continued)*

- Therapeutic jurisprudence
- Therapeutic lawyering
- Tier-one specialties
- Tier-two delimited specialties
- Treatment compliance

- Two-tier specialty training
- Vanity boards
- Villanova Conference

In this chapter, we review four areas identified as emerging trends in the field of forensic psychology. The four areas reviewed are: (1) the increased growth and sophistication within forensic psychology; (2) the increased cooperation between professionals in psychology and law; (3) future training models for forensic psychologists; and (4) therapeutic jurisprudence. These trends are not an exhaustive list of future changes in the field; in any specialty or discipline there are numerous changes occurring. The rapid development of technology, the ease of access to information, and increased educational opportunities all are major influences on any scientific discipline. These four areas are presented because of the particular impact they will have on students entering the discipline.

| Table 12.1 | Four Emerging Trends in Forensic Psychology |
|---|---|

- Increased growth and sophistication within the specialty
- Increased cooperation between law and psychology
- Future training models for forensic psychology
- Therapeutic jurisprudence

# Increased Growth and Sophistication

As stated in the first chapter of this text, there has been an exponential increase in interest among students, professionals, and the public in the area of forensic science. This interest in forensic science is exemplified in the huge success of the television drama *CSI*, which has spawned numerous offshoots. This interest in forensic science has also fueled popular interest in forensic psychology, initially sparked by films such as *Silence of the Lambs* and *Seven*. Since much of what the public knows about forensic psychology comes from the mass media, it is not surprising that there are many misconceptions about the field. The mass media is market driven with the public wanting to see bigger-than-life characters who lead intense, action-packed careers solving problems on a daily basis that deal with life and death issues. It is ironic to the practitioner that you never see the television forensic psychologists at their desk toiling over a 15-page report or involved in the drudgery of administrative paperwork. Some professionals, who work as consultants to television or TV show hosts, appear to endorse, or at the least do very little to discourage, the public's misperception of forensic psychology (Turvey, 2002). In fairness, professionals serving as consultants or hosts to television shows tend to have very little influence on reducing these fictitious portrayals of the profession.

Along with the public's increased interest in forensic psychology, there has been a substantial increase in the number of students interested in taking forensic psychology courses and pursuing a career in the field. The fictional and nonfictional accounts of forensic psychology in the media have stimulated interest at the undergraduate level (Otto, 2003). There has also been an increased interest in forensic psychology at both the graduate and postgraduate and professional levels. A number of events have prompted this spark in interest in forensic psychology among graduate students and professionals. Certainly, the formal recognition of forensic psychology as a specialty by the American Psychological Association in 2001 granted the specialty increased credibility and exposure among practitioners. The formal recognition by APA also placed the burden upon practitioners within the specialty to help advance the professional and ethical development of the field.

Prompted by student demand, graduate programs now provide specialized training in forensic psychology. Some of these programs offer a doctoral degree in clinical psychology with a concentration in forensic psychology, whereas other programs offer a degree in forensic psychology or clinical–forensic psychology. A small number of graduate programs now offer specialty training in **legal psychology**. Students can complete a predoctoral internship that offers a concentration in forensic psychology. Over 50 predoctoral internships indicate they offer training in forensic psychology. Students can pursue specialized training in forensic psychology at the postdoctoral level. Postdoctoral fellowships allow a recent graduate of a doctoral program to receive a year or more of intensive training and supervision in a specialized area. Although still relatively few in number, postdoctoral fellowships in forensic psychology can be expected to produce some of the most highly trained individuals in the field (Packer & Borum, 2003).

In addition to students expressing an interest in the specialty of forensic psychology, others have noted the increased interest among professionals wishing to pursue forensic work (Otto, 1998). This interest in forensic work among practitioners has been attributed, in part, to economic and administrative changes in the health care system. These so-called "economically driven experts" enter the specialty of forensic psychology to compensate for diminished financial opportunities attributed to restrictions imposed by managed care companies (Otto & Heilbrun, 2002). Many health care professionals are acutely aware of restrictions on income and fee-for-service opportunities created by the managed care companies. Health care professionals in all specialties complain of oversight by bureaucrats, limits on reimbursement, and the difficulty of negotiating the paperwork hurdles for filing a claim. As a result, health care professionals in a multiple of areas have looked for alternative ways to earn a living or have simply abandoned the industry altogether to pursue new careers.

Undoubtedly, some psychologists have turned to the forensic arena as a safe refuge from the bureaucracy of managed care. Typically, health insurance does not reimburse for forensic services, allowing the provider to avoid the paperwork of filing a claim. For example, if a divorcing couple has a child custody dispute and requests a child custody evaluation, one or both of the parents will need to pay for the evaluation. The client directly pays for all expert testimony without any third-party reimbursement. Similarly, a defendant who uses the insanity plea in a criminal trial will need to cover the costs of the evaluation. Sometimes the state will cover costs for certain forensic evaluations, such as a competency to stand trial evaluation or a termination of parental rights evaluation. However, even with this "third-party payer," fees are set and payment is usually prompt without the paperwork burden customary of many managed care companies. Clearly, forensic work, along with other areas in psychology, such as coaching, does open the door for alternative financial opportunities without the "HMO blues."

As noted by Otto (2002), the fact that professionals turn to the specialty in part due to financial incentives is not necessarily a problem. Actually, with the increased interest in the specialty, it appears that positions that went previously unfilled now have a number of qualified applicants (Otto, 1998). The main concern is that individuals who do not possess adequate specialty training and supervision to practice at a professional standard will enter into the forensic arena without adequate preparation (Otto & Heilbrun, 2002). However, this author has noted an increase in the number of postgraduate training opportunities in the form of continuing education workshops along with an increase in attendance at these workshops. It is the responsibility of the profession to ensure the quality of services offered by forensic psychologists.

In fact, there should be little doubt that the increased interest and recognition of the specialty has helped to push for higher standards and more sophistication within the specialty. It is relatively recent that the *Specialty Guidelines for Forensic Psychologist* was adopted (Committee on Ethical Guidelines for Forensic Psychologists, 1991). However, Otto and Heilbrun (2002) have already suggested updating these guidelines to help advance the development of the profession. In addition to broad practice guidelines, the profession has adopted more specific practice guidelines such as the *Guidelines for Child Custody Evaluations in Divorce Proceedings* (American Psychological Association, 1994). The term *guidelines* refers to statements regarding recommended professional behavior or conduct. Guidelines are not the same as professional *standards*. Standards of practice are mandatory and can be enforced through sanctions when they are not followed. Guidelines, on the other hand, are aspirational. Ideally, they help professionals to evaluate their own skills and to identify areas in which the professional may wish to pursue further training. Guidelines are intended to "facilitate the continued systematic development of the profession and to help assure a high level of professional practice by psychologists" (American Psychological Association, 2004, p. 238). The APA has established *General Guidelines for Providers of Psychological Services* along with the APA's *Ethical Principles of Psychologists and Code of Conduct* that included a section titled "Forensic Activities" in the 1992 version. However, the revised version of the APA Ethics Code no longer contains special sections for specialties in psychology, having abolished the special section on forensic psychology (Knapp & VandeCreek, 2003). The ethical principles present standards of practice and are enforceable by the APA. Recently, some authors have suggested ways to approach colleagues who practice forensic psychology unethically (Brodsky & McKinzey, 2002).

A revision of the *Specialty Guidelines for Forensic Psychologists* would most likely lead to the identification of specific areas of practice in forensic psychology. Once identified, it would then be possible to establish practice guidelines for additional areas, such as competency evaluations. It is notable that this area has not been addressed since it is the most common form of forensic assessment conducted by forensic psychologists. Obviously, other professional organizations also establish practice guidelines. Other professional organizations have developed practice guidelines relevant to the practice of forensic psychologists. For example, the Police Psychological Services Section of the International Association of Chiefs of Police developed guidelines for preemployment psychological screening of law enforcement personnel (International Association of Chiefs of Police, 1999). The Department of Defense is developing guidelines for the training of individuals who conduct psychological autopsies (Ritchie & Gelles, 2002). Other professions outside of psychology have also developed relevant forensic guidelines, such as the American Academy of Psychiatry and Law and the American Academy of Child and Adolescent Psychiatry. If psychologists can identify specific practice areas that would benefit from published guidelines, it would behoove the profession to take an interdisciplinary approach with other professions in developing such guidelines.

The lack of guidelines for many common forensic evaluations continues to impede the advancement of the field. The field is only gradually starting to identify a standard of care for forensic assessments. A *standard of care* specifies the appropriate procedures of treatment, based on scientific evidence, which would be used in specific situations. For example, a standard of care for child custody evaluations would go beyond the current aspirational guidelines currently published by the APA. Some authors have argued for the need to have minimum standards of practice for specific forensic services, such as child custody evaluations (Kirkpatrick, 2004). Others have expressed concern that the field of forensic assessment has grown rapidly in the past two decades with no regulation of poor practice (Heilbrun, DeMatteo, Marczyk, & Goldstein, 2008). These authors suggest legal regulation that would define a standard of care in forensic mental health assessment. The authors identify the need for a clear standard of practice that could then lead to an operational definition of a standard of care for forensic assessment services. A recent contribution to the field is an 800-page compendium of areas of practice in forensic psychology (Goldstein, 2007). Goldstein, the editor of the text, suggests that this sourcebook for practitioners presents the "current state of the field in terms of law, ethics, research and practice" (2007, p. xiv).

Goldstein (2007) states that the standard of care in forensic psychology is composed of a number of elements:

> ethical conduct, knowledge of the legal system and the statutes and case law that drive forensic assessments; use of appropriate methodology, including, when appropriate, traditional psychological tests, forensic assessment instruments, and forensically relevant instruments; the integration of information from a variety of date sources to formulate opinions; an awareness of empirical research relevant to the psycholegal question being evaluated and the use of results of such studies to inform the forensic decision-making process; and the preparation of written reports and presentation of expert testimony in court that is objective and thorough and that honestly reflects *all* findings, not only those advanced by the retaining attorney. (p. 6)

With more individuals entering into the field of forensic psychology, there will be an increase in the sophistication of the profession. The need for services provided by forensic psychologists will likely expand over the next decade or longer. However, with the increase in training opportunities at all levels and the establishment of guidelines for specific practice areas, competition for job opportunities should be intense. As the role of psychology continues to gain acceptance in the legal arena, higher expectations will be placed on the quality of services provided. This is particularly true of forensic psychology since many of the activities of a forensic psychologist are performed under the scrutiny of professionals engaged in an adversarial process. The profession as a whole can help to ensure high standards of practice by individual forensic psychologists by educating the consumers of forensic psychological services (Grisso, 1987; Otto & Heilbrun, 2002). Informed judges and attorneys who are aware of the practice guidelines and limitations of forensic psychologists will be able to identify an unethical or incompetent practitioner. An excellent example of educating attorneys and judges is a series of texts written by the late forensic psychologist Jay Ziskin and his colleague, David Faust, that question the scientific basis of psychological testimony (e.g., Ziskin, 1995). This three-volume set provides a wealth of ammunition for an adversarial cross-examination on a variety of forensic topics. I have successfully used these texts to help educate attorneys in preparation for questioning opposing council's expert witness.

Other examples of educating the consumers of forensic psychological services include training programs provided free of charge to judges and attorneys by the members of the American Academy of Forensic Psychology on issues of interest (Otto & Heilbrun, 2002). Increased collaboration among attorneys and psychologists has also led to training seminars co-sponsored and attended by both psychologists and attorneys. A recent example is a collaborative workshop between attorneys and psychologists at the annual meeting of the American Psychological Association in Hawaii. This workshop presented an initial draft document titled *Assessment of Older Adults with Diminished Capacity: A Handbook for Attorneys* and was coauthored by members of the American Bar Association and the American Psychological Association (2005). In 2008, the ABA/APA Assessment of Capacity in Older Adults Working Group published their third handbook, *Assessment of Older Adults with Diminished Capacity: A Handbook for Psychologists*. These types of collaborative educational efforts will help to ensure the quality of forensic psychological services provided to the courts.

In addition to educating consumers of forensic psychology about the scope and limitations of the field there has been a recent emphasis on policing the quality of forensic assessment instruments (Otto & Heilbrun, 2002). As stated previously in this text, there has been a relative explosion of the introduction of new psychological assessment instruments into the forensic arena. Many of these instruments lack adequate psychometric properties to be considered either reliable or valid and few meet the **Standards for Educational and Psychological Testing** (American Educational Research Association, American Psychological Association, & National Council on Measurement in Education, 1999). As attorneys and judges become familiar with psychometric test properties and the use of specific tests, it is likely that psychologists who are using poorly developed instruments will face an unpleasant time defending the use of such a test under cross-examination. To this end, manuals on the use of psychological tests in legal issues have been published to assist psychologists and attorneys (e.g., Pope, Butcher, & Seelen, 2000).

As forensic psychology continues to expand in both scope and number of practitioners, there will be increased scrutiny of the services provided and an increase in the quality of the services provided. More and more, psychological expert testimony is finding its way into the courtroom. Expert psychological testimony can summarize the results of years of social science research and expertise to help solve legal issues. It is likely that there will always be the infrequent expert witness playing the role of the "hired gun." However, judges and attorneys will identify and challenge incompetent and unethical practices as they become more knowledgeable about the profession of forensic psychology. As the consumer of forensic psychology becomes more educated, the "hired gun" will simply be shooting blanks. This will help the public and the continued professional development of the specialty.

# Increased Cooperation between Law and Psychology

With the increased sophistication in the field of forensic psychology, there has been a comparable increase in collaboration between psychology and representatives from the legal system. This increased collaboration is apparent in hiring practices, clinical workshops, and collaborative scholarly works. As Ogloff stated in his Presidential Address of the **American Psychology-Law Society**, "The fact is that, without a doubt, law and psychology is 'bigger and better' now than ever" (2000, p. 464).

Law schools have started to hire psychologists on their faculty and psychology departments have faculty with law degrees (Ogloff, 1997). There are also postdoctoral fellowships available with joint appointments in the psychology department and law school at certain institutions. Not only does the **FBI Behavioral Science Unit** employ clinical psychologists on its staff but the Chief of the Unit is also a psychologist (Winerman, 2004). The American Bar Association's Center on Children and the Law sponsors a biennial conference on children and the law that attracts attorneys, judges, child advocates, and mental health professionals. The theme of the 11th National Conference on Children and the Law held in 2004 was "Lawyers and psychologists working together" and was for the first time co-sponsored by APA. Guest speakers at the American Psychology-Law Society annual meeting in 2005 include, among others, Janet Reno, former Attorney General, and Robert Grey, president of the American Bar Association. There are also numerous collaborative continuing education workshops co-sponsored by psychologists and lawyers at the annual meetings of the professional associations. Finally, there are a number of collaborative texts and articles authored by psychologists and lawyers (e.g., Petrila & Otto, 1996; Weissman & DeBow, 2003).

These examples reflect the increased mutual professional acceptance among the disciplines and illustrate the recognition that psychology can make contributions to resolving legal questions (Ogloff, 2000).

Part of the increased cooperation is due to the large number of individuals with a mental illness entering the legal system. A report by the U.S. Bureau of Justice Statistics in 2006 stated that nearly a quarter of state prisoners and jail inmates who stated that they had a mental illness had been incarcerated on three or more separate occasions. This suggests that individuals with mental illness are cycling through the courts and correctional facilities. A national project, the Chief Justices' Criminal Justice/Mental Health Leadership Initiative, will examine ways to improve how the criminal justice system serves the needs of people with mental illnesses. Four states, Delaware, Idaho, New Hampshire, and Wisconsin, have been selected to participate in the project. The four chief justices from these states will gather state leaders to address the problem.

## Influencing Public Policy

Partly due to the increased collaboration between psychology and the legal system, it is inevitable that psychologists will attempt to influence public policy. As psychologists become familiar with the legal system and its unique methods of change, they will feel more comfortable promoting their professional agenda. Psychologists can influence public policy in a variety of ways. Perhaps one of the more obvious ways is by entering the political arena. A number of psychologists hold elected office in the U.S. Congress and state legislatures (Sullivan, 1999). Work on a legislature gives psychologists direct opportunity to influence state laws and government policy (Blanchard, 2002; Miller, 2002). Legislators have been able to identify mental health needs in their states and then push for reform. Examples of areas include adequate funding, mental health parity legislation, better understanding by legislators of the nature and impact of mental illness, and more effective advocacy (Miller, 2002).

Psychologists can also make their voice heard on Capitol Hill through rallies, petitions, and letter-writing campaigns. The APA sponsored a recent Web-based petition urging congress to support biomedical and behavioral research using science to inform public policy (Mumford, 2004). Psychology as a profession has also become involved in class action lawsuits. These lawsuits are usually against managed care companies and are used to pressure the companies to change prohibitive policies toward mental health care. A recent case saw the APA Practice Organization file a class action lawsuit, along with other litigants, against CIGNA using the Racketeer Influenced Corrupt Organization Act (RICO; Holloway, 2005). RICO was originally created to prosecute organized crime and signals the use of aggressive legal measures in such class action cases. Additionally, the APA Practice Organization and the Association for the Advancement of Psychology have united and formed a political action committee, Psychologists for Legislative Action Now (PLAN).

Another way the APA can influence public policy is with an *amicus curiae brief*. A professional organization may file, on behalf of its membership, an ***amicus curiae* (friend of the court) brief** in appellate court. The organization's members (interested parties) have an interest in the outcome of the trial but do not participate directly in the trial. The interested parties either have a stake in the outcome of the trial or have knowledge to offer the appellate courts (Saks, 1993). For example, members of the APA certainly have a stake if the appellate court is ruling on whether clinical psychologists have the expertise to make diagnostic decisions. Similarly, psychology has much to offer the court in terms of social science research regarding the competency of juveniles to be executed.

The intent of an *amicus* brief can be placed along a continuum regarding how impartial the brief appears (Roesch, Goulding, Hans, & Reppucci, 1991). In the first example given above, psychologists have much to lose should the courts rule that only psychiatrists can offer a diagnosis of mental illness. The issue at stake is a guild issue and threatens the profession of psychology. The second example has less to do with the financial livelihood of the profession. Rather, psychologists feel that they can offer social science evidence to assist the court. Even though the second example is not a guild issue, the APA is still trying to influence public policy.

The first example is an **advocacy brief** attempting to produce a specific outcome of the case. These briefs could be viewed by the courts as partisan attempts to sway the court's decision and, therefore, may lack credibility.

The second example presented above is a **science-translation brief**. A science-translation brief provides the court with an objective, neutral summary of social science evidence relevant to the issues in the case at hand. The assumption is that the science-translation brief is not an attempt to sway opinion but rather an attempt to inform the decision makers. However, science-translation briefs may also appear to advocate a particular outcome, jeopardizing their credibility and usefulness.

Since the early 1960s, the American Psychological Association has submitted over 100 *amicus* briefs to the courts on a wide variety of topics. In 2004 alone, the APA submitted five *amicus* briefs to various courts. The briefs submitted by the APA provide research relevant to public policy issues being considered by the courts. The positions the APA took on the issues addressed in 2004 included:

- supporting same-sex marriage,
- allowing the use of race-based decisions regarding promoting diversity in education,
- banning the juvenile death penalty, and
- allowing online access to information previously available only in print form.

The APA provides the courts with relevant behavioral research on the issues involved. For example, the U.S. Supreme Court recently ruled on the constitutionality of capital punishment for juveniles (*Roper v. Simmons*, 2005). In the brief, the APA cited brain-imaging research demonstrating that the brain continues to mature through the late teens and into the early 20s. In particular, areas that control decision-making skills and those that help to inhibit impulsive behavior are not developmentally mature in the adolescent. The APA cited this research as evidence to suggest that adolescents have diminished responsibility for their behavior and thus should not be subjected to capital punishment. This is an example of how the APA uses science and the empirical method to guide decisions. In ruling on the case, the Court noted juveniles' diminished culpability and reasoned that the death penalty was not justified as retribution or deterrence. In the opinion, the Court noted the brain-imaging data as well as the difficulty for psychologists to distinguished entrenched antisocial behavior and reck-

■ **Advocacy brief**
Letter to the court advocating for a specific outcome of the case.

■ **Science-translation brief**
Provides the court with an objective, neutral summary of social evidence relevant to the case.

lessness and immaturity in youth under the age of 18. Justice Kennedy, writing for the majority, said, "Retribution is not proportional if the law's most severe penalty is imposed on one whose culpability or blameworthiness is diminished, to a substantial degree, by reason of youth and immaturity" (*Roper v. Simmons*, 2005, p. 17). Not only did Justice Kennedy cite APA's position in the majority opinion, Justice Scalia, who wrote the dissenting opinion, also cited the APA brief. In an earlier brief to the Supreme Court, the APA argued that 14- and 15-year-olds are capable of making moral and medical decisions (*Hodgson v. Minnesota*, 1989). The *Hodgson* case involved mandated parental notification of adolescents seeking an abortion. The APA argued that adolescents are capable of making these decisions and involving parents through a legal mandate frequently creates more difficulties for the adolescent. The adolescent would not need a legal mandate to inform a supportive parent of her decision. On the other hand, the *Simmons* case looked at maturity at the time of the crime, as well as sentencing, which can occur years apart. In addition, many states require a prediction of future dangerousness for the death penalty. Predicting future dangerousness is difficult, if not impossible, when an adolescent is involved. The APA noted the differences in the two briefs before submitting the *Simmons* brief (Gilfoye, 2005). It is noteworthy that the two briefs submitted by APA received as much attention as they did, suggesting that the courts are taking notice of social science research.

However, not all members of the APA support its active role in attempting to influence public policy. In particular, some members have expressed dissent from the APA position on controversial topics such as the rights of gay and lesbian people and abortion. For example, most recently the APA provided evidence to the California Supreme Court supporting same-sex marriage. The California Supreme Court cited the brief filed by the APA in ruling that banning same-sex marriage was against the state's constitution. However, voters in November 2008 passed an amendment to the state constitution banning same-sex marriage.

Issues such as these are polarizing topics for many individuals who form their opinion based on religious, moral, and social convictions, unrelated to the results of scientific data. As such, it is not surprising that some individuals would disagree with positions advocated by the APA, regardless of the position adopted by the professional organization. As a result, some members have questioned the role of APA in attempting to influence public policy.

The issue of whether the APA should attempt to influence public policy through the courts is not simply an academic question. The APA is the largest professional organization representing psychologists. It is reasonable to put forth that the organization has a professional responsibility to disseminate social science research, much of which is funded thorough taxpayer dollars. Social science research touches on many aspects of life and can help influence public policy. Simply because an issue is controversial does not entitle an organization such as the APA to shirk its responsibility to the public. The question is not whether the APA should be involved in influencing public policy. Rather, the APA has an ethical obligation to present an objective explanation of empirical social science research findings to the courts. The courts can then use this information, along with other factors, in setting policy.

# Future Training Models for Forensic Psychology

There is little doubt that the field of forensic psychology will continue to grow. Many of the chapters in this text cited authors proclaiming various areas of forensic psychology as a "growth industry," including police psychology, correctional psychology,

| Table 12.2 | Issues of APA-Submitted *Amicus* Briefs |
| --- | --- |

Below is an alphabetized list of issues on which the APA has submitted *amicus* briefs. See the end of the chapter for a more detailed list along with a brief explanation of each brief submitted by the APA (*www.apa.org/psychlaw/amicus.html*).

Abortion
Affirmative Action
Animal Research
Antitrust
Battered Woman Syndrome
Child Abuse/Child Witnesses
Child Sexual Abuse
Civil Commitment
Competency
Confidentiality/Psychotherapist–Patient Privilege
Copyright
Criminal Defendants' Right to Mental Health Assistance (Psychiatric Evaluations)
Death Penalty
Defamation
Duty to Warn/Protect
Employment
Environmental Impact Analyses
ERISA
Expert Witnesses/Psychologists' Competency
Gay, Lesbian, and Bisexual Parenting
Hospital Privileges for Psychologists
Insanity Defense
Medicare
Medication (Right to Refuse)
Mentally Ill and Mentally Retarded (Rights of)
Neuropsychologists' Competency (Brain Injury Assessment)
Peer Review
Psychologists' Scope of Practice/Reimbursement for "Mental Health" Services
Residential Treatment
Sexual Harassment
Sexual Orientation
Scientific Research
Tests (Use, Validity, and Security of Psychological Tests and Test Data)

forensic assessments, and trial consultation. Membership in **Division 41 of the American Psychological Association** (the American Psychology-Law Society) has more than doubled from approximately 1,400 members in 1990 to 3,000 members in 2000 (Ogloff, 2000). The American Psychology-Law Society, perhaps the largest and most influential professional organization devoted to law and psychology, is interdisciplinary and covers a range of topics related to law and the social sciences. Due to the surge of interest in the field, there have been increased educational opportunities, including courses at the undergraduate, graduate, internship, postdoctoral fellowship, and postdoctoral continuing education level.

In an effort to develop effective training models for psychologists entering the larger area of law and psychology (includes forensic psychology as well as legal psychology), approximately 60 experts attended the **National Invitational Conference on Education and Training in Law and Psychology** at Villanova Law School in 1995 (Bersoff et al., 1997). The goal of the Villanova Conference was to develop an agenda for legal psychology training into the 21st century (Ogloff, 2000). Working groups discussed models of training for students at all levels of education, including the undergraduate level, graduate training in law and psychology, joint degree (JD/PhD or PsyD) programs, internship, postdoctoral, and continuing education programs. Although it is too early to assess the impact that the Villanova Conference will have on training in psychology and law, other professionals in the field have already endorsed one training recommendation from the conference. Otto and Heilbrun (2002) recommend three levels of training for practicing psychologists in forensic psychology modeled on the levels of training identified at the Villanova Conference. These three levels of training are the entry level, proficiency level, and specialty level.

## Three Levels of Training in Forensic Psychology From the Villanova Conference — Table 12.3

- *Entry level*–The legally informed clinician; develop a working knowledge of legal issues relevant to psychological practice (e.g., confidentiality, third-party reporting, etc.), recognition that legal issues have permeated traditional practice.
- *Proficiency level*–Establish forensic competence in one or more circumscribed areas related to some other major clinical specialty with which the psychologist has primary identification and expertise (e.g., child psychologist who performs custody evaluations as part of the general practice).
- *Specialty level*–Oriented toward the training of psychologists whose professional activities focus primarily on the provision of services to courts, attorneys, law enforcement, or corrections. Main professional identification is in forensic psychology. Involves intensive didactic and supervised experience in forensic work.

The **entry level** is the equivalent of the legally informed clinician. The practice of psychology is increasingly more complex with various legal hurdles that all practitioners must cross. The practitioner at this level needs to develop a working knowledge of legal issues relevant to psychological practice. A recent article by the Committee on Professional Practice and Standards (2003) addressed a variety of frequently asked legal questions pertinent to the practicing psychologist. The five sections of the article cover a range of issues that confront clinicians who encounter legal issues in the course of their general practice. Topics covered were

- differences between ethics and the law,
- professional relationships,
- confidentiality/privilege,
- requests for information regarding clients,
- record keeping,
- termination of services,
- business issues such as managing a private practice,
- issues related to legal settings such as responding to a subpoena, and
- privacy of records concerns.

This recommendation for the entry level of training reflects the recognition that legal issues have permeated all areas of traditional practice. Practitioners need to adopt a risk management approach (Welch, 1998a; Woody, 1988). Recent research suggests that many psychologists provide services without a full understanding of the laws and regulations affecting their practice (e.g., Renninger, McCarthy-Veach, & Bagdade, 2002).

There are numerous resources available to help the practicing psychologist understand his or her legal obligations. Most graduate programs offer a course on ethical, legal, and professional issues. In addition to frequent scholarly articles in the professional journals, a number of reference books are available for psychologists to turn to for legal advice. For example, Woody (1988), a practicing attorney and licensed psychologist, has published a guidebook for mental health professionals, *Fifty Ways to Avoid Malpractice*. The American Counseling Association publishes a similar resource, *The Counselor and the Law* (Anderson, 1996). The American Psychological Association is in the process of publishing a series of books, *Law and Mental Health Professionals*, for each state and the District of Columbia that reviews and integrates all of the laws that affect the work of mental health professionals in that jurisdiction (Petrila & Otto, 1996). Another recent addition to the clinician's legal library is a comprehensive introduction to the legal obligations and responsibilities of mental health professionals, recommended for graduate students and professionals (see Sales, Miller, & Hall, 2005).

The **proficiency level** indicates that the clinician has established forensic competence in one or more circumscribed areas related to some other major clinical specialty with which the psychologist has primary identification and expertise. This represents a degree of expertise beyond that of the general practitioner's forensic knowledge and skill level. A graduate student trained through a general professional program may take a "concentration" or "minor" in forensic psychology. A clinician interested in working at this level would gain the additional knowledge and skills through formal coursework, continuing education, and supervision in forensic work. The forensic "minor" is proposed as a possible certificate program within a general professional program. However, a graduate school would need several faculty with expertise in forensic psychology to staff such a component. Many departments do not have the kind of resources to staff specialties (Drum & Blom, 2001). Another option to achieve the proficiency level of training would be for currently licensed professionals to seek out additional training in continuing education workshops or postdoctoral work. Most licensed clinicians are unlikely to devote a year to a postdoctoral fellowship due to the reduced income one receives. There are fewer than 15 forensic postdoctoral programs in the United States. The majority of practicing clinicians who achieve this level of forensic expertise will most likely do so through continuing education and supervision.

An example of the proficiency level would be a child psychologist who performs child custody evaluations as part of the general practice. Although they primarily identify as a child therapist, they have also sought out the additional skills and knowledge base to perform competent and ethical child custody evaluations. Another example is the clinician who limits his or her forensic work to competency to stand trial and criminal responsibility evaluations. The primary clinical practice may be as a **generalist** treating adults. However, the clinician may conduct court-ordered evaluations as part of his or her clinical practice. Again, formal coursework, supervision, and continuing education would help develop and maintain the necessary forensic skills.

The **specialty level** is oriented toward the training of psychologists whose professional activities focus primarily on the provision of services to courts, attorneys, law enforcement, or corrections. Professionals trained at the specialty level would represent psychologists whose main professional identification is in forensic psychology. The specialty level forensic psychologist would have an in-depth understanding of legal procedures and law relevant to psychology. These individuals would work with a variety of populations, such as sex offenders, victims of sex offenders, criminal defendants, personal injury victims, defendants of sexual harassment suits, and so on. Their expertise is based on graduate coursework and a postdoctoral fellowship involving intensive didactic and supervised experience in forensic work. Psychologists at this level would have the highest expertise and ideally would be board certified.

It is too soon to know if the profession will formally adopt these three levels of training. As was noted in the first chapter of this text, although the APA has formally defined forensic psychology as the applied practice of psychology to legal issues, there continues to be debate about the definition of forensic psychology in textbooks (e.g., Bartol & Bartol, 2004) and the scholarly literature (e.g., Ogloff, 2000). Failure to obtain consensus regarding the scope of forensic practice will slow progress toward developing a standardized training curriculum. Related to the issue of specialty training, some authors have commented on the current two-tier model of specialization in professional psychology (Drum & Blom, 2001). Recall that the term **professional psychology** refers to the applied specialties within the discipline. This two-tier model has not been developed intentionally, but rather due to the forces of the marketplace and as a response to the expanded and differentiated knowledge base in psychology.

The first tier consists of the original four specialties recognized by the discipline as applied areas: clinical, counseling, school, and industrial/organizational. Graduate programs in clinical, counseling, and school psychology prepare individuals to be health service providers. These programs prepare graduates to function as generalists, able to obtain a generic practice license. Many states do not license individuals as clinical or counseling psychologists, but rather issue generic licenses (**Association of State and Provincial Psychology Boards**, 2000). The general professional training serves as a foundation or prerequisite training for entry into the newer, delimited specialties that comprised the second tier (Drum & Blom, 2001).

The second tier consists of the newer specialties in which the training is the development of in-depth competencies beyond the generalist skills acquired in the first tier. The APA's Board of Professional Affairs tasked the Subcommittee on Specialization to develop criteria to formally recognize a specialty (American Psychological Association, 1984). The **American Board of Professional Psychology** (ABPP) offers **board certification** in specialty areas. ABPP incorporated the APA's criteria into a broad set of requirements used to define new specialties eligible for board certification (Drum & Blom, 2001). The ABPP now recognizes and certifies practitioners in

Figure 12.1

Graduate programs in clinical, counseling, and school psychology prepare individuals to be health service providers.

© 2009 Monkey Business Images. Used under license from Shutterstock, Inc.

"second tier" specialties such as forensic psychology, family psychology, behavioral psychology, clinical health psychology, psychoanalysis, group psychology, clinical neuropsychology, and rehabilitation psychology. The proliferation of delimited specialties can lead to territorial conflicts among professionals across and within disciplines (Drum & Blom, 2001).

This two-tier model dictates that *generalist* training is offered to all graduates in the three applied tracks (clinical, counseling, and school) and that tier-two *specialty* training occurs at the postdoctoral level. Specialty training in forensic psychology is accumulated at the postdoctoral level under the current training model in professional psychology. The current model suggests that training in forensic psychology will continue to occur primarily at the postdoctoral level in the form of continuing education workshops. All states require licensed psychologists to maintain their skills by accumulating a specified number of continuing education (CE) hours per licensure period. For example, a professional may need to attend 40 hours of continuing education workshops every 2-year period. Although there have been a few **dual degree programs** (JD and PhD) or doctoral degrees with a focus on forensic psychology, it is unclear if this narrow focus would serve the long-term career goals of all students. There are several obstacles to pursuing the joint degree programs. First, only a handful of these programs are in existence. The additional time required to complete the degree along with the added financial expense of tuition payments to both a university and a law school can also serve as an obstacle to many students. In addition, some of the coursework may seem irrelevant to the practice of forensic psychology, such as required coursework on tax law (Bersoff et al., 1997). Finally, no evidence exists suggesting that graduate training in two disciplines results in any particular benefit to the profession (Roesch, Grisso, & Poythress, 1986). The narrowly focused doctoral degree in forensic clinical psychology may also limit a graduate's career options later in life. For example, individuals trained in correctional psychology may have a difficult time moving into a general practice outside of prison walls. Focusing on a delimited specialty during graduate training may be at the expense of developing the board generalist foundation skills expected of doctoral-level graduates. The forensic psychology specialty graduate programs that have recently developed may simply provide false claims of specialty training (Otto, 2005). Some of these graduate programs are tuition driven and follow poorly considered standards. There are currently no recognized standards for what constitutes proper training for a graduate degree in forensic psychology.

An alternative to obtaining a degree in a specialty area in psychology is to obtain board certification. Board certification was designed to distinguish between basic training and competence that comes with licensure and more advanced levels of training and competence. With the growth of the "delimited" specialties in psychology, there will be a need to identify professionals with the additional, postdoctoral skills. Some authors have suggested that board certification may eventually become a requirement of some employers in particular specialties, such as neuropsychology, clinical, health, and forensic psychology (Belar & Jeffrey, 1995). However, although some employers do offer incentives for board certification, the trend toward certification has been slow (Dattilio, 2002). Unlike other professions, psychology does not expect board certification of its members as the final step toward qualifying as a specialist practitioner (Bent, Packard, & Goldberg, 1999).

Numerous boards exist to certify professionals in both recognized and not so recognized exotic specialty areas. Many of these boards have seemingly sprung up overnight and lack credibility with the profession. These so-called **vanity boards** offer questionable credentials that can actually increase the risk of a malpractice action (Woody, 1988). Vanity boards have minimal or even nonexistent requirements for board certification. A board that awards certification based only on a qualifying de-

■ **Vanity boards**

Certification boards that have minimal or nonexistent requirements for board certification.

gree and a payment of a (substantial) fee is to be avoided. Similarly, single specialty boards that operate for a profit should be suspect. "Certification should come from a nonprofit governing board with multiple specialty board affiliates adhering to clear standards and peer review" (Bent et al., 1999, p. 72). Legitimate boards that offer the "Diplomate" or "Board Certified" credential require a rigorous review of education and training, a work sample reviewed by a panel of specialists, and an examination. Individuals touting credentials from vanity boards may be the recipient of the ire of a court in any legal proceeding. Courts "strain to uphold the professional" in any malpractice suits (Woody, 1988, p. 72). However, a vanity board credential can be viewed by the court as unethical behavior and an attempt to mislead the public regarding one's competence. Most state licensing boards mandate that psychologists do not promote themselves as having credentials without undergoing proper review and examination (Dattilio, 2002).

The oldest and perhaps most respected certifying board for psychology is the *American Board of Examiners in Professional Psychology*. Founded in 1947, the board shortened its name to the *American Board of Professional Psychology* (ABPP) in 1968 (Bent et al., 1999). This organization oversees 11 specialty boards in psychology: clinical, counseling, industrial/organizational, school, clinical neuropsychology, forensic, family, health, behavioral, psychoanalysis, and rehabilitation psychology. The ABPP then grants the ABPP diploma or board certification in 13 recognized specialties. The initials *ABPP* after the PhD in one's title signify **diplomate** status. The ABPP started awarding the diplomate in forensic psychology in 1985.

■ **Diplomate**
Recognition by a professional association that a member has advanced training, skills, and competence; commonly referred to as board certified.

## Specialties Recognized by the American Board of Professional Psychology

**Table 12.4**

| | |
|---|---|
| Clinical Psychology | Forensic Psychology |
| Clinical Child and Adolescent Psychology | Family Psychology |
| Cognitive and Behavioral Psychology | Clinical Health Psychology |
| Counseling Psychology | Psychoanalysis |
| Industrial/Organizational Psychology | Rehabilitation Psychology |
| School Psychology | Group Psychology |
| Clinical Neuropsychology | |

Despite the numerous calls for board certification by psychologists (e.g., Bent et al., 1999; Dattilio, 2001; Packard, 2002), a relatively small number of psychologists have pursued this process through the ABPP.[1] The estimated number of licensed psychologists in the United States and Canada is slightly over 100,000. However, fewer than 3.5% (approximately 3,300) were board certified by the ABPP in the year 2000

[1]The discussion regarding board certification will be restricted to certification by the ABPP. Although some of the other specialty boards offering credentialing may require more than a fee and basic credentials, the ABPP is certainly the most respected within the profession.

(Dattilio, 2002). This number represents board certification in all specialties recognized by the ABPP; only slightly over 200 psychologists are board certified in forensic psychology by the ABPP. There are several possible explanations as to why psychologists do not seek board certification. The process is time-consuming, costly, frustrating for a number of the applicants, and, as of yet, of questionable return for one's efforts.

In order to become board certified in forensic psychology by the ABPP, the candidate must meet a number of criteria. Only candidates with a doctoral degree in clinical or counseling psychology from an APA-approved program and with an APA-approved internship may apply. If the program was not APA-approved at the time, the candidate can still apply but must demonstrate that the program would have met APA requirements for accreditation. The candidate must also have 1,000 hours of forensic work experience over a 5-year period and 100 hours of formal coursework or continuing education in forensic psychology. If these requirements are met, the candidate may sit for a 200-item multiple-choice exam covering eight major topic areas in forensic psychology. If the written examination is passed, the candidate must submit two work samples related to forensic psychology that will be reviewed by a committee of experts in the field. The work samples can consist of peer review articles, forensic evaluations, forensic treatment protocols, or similar materials. Upon acceptance of the work samples, the candidate must pass a 3-hour oral examination administered by three diplomates covering ethics and the candidate's particular area of expertise in forensic psychology. The entire process can require from 2 to 3 years to complete. The cost of the application is approximately $1,000, not including travel and lodging to testing locations along with time missed from work.

**Table 12.5** Eight Topic Areas of the Written Examination for Board Certification in Forensic Psychology by the ABPP

- Ethics, Guidelines, and Professional Issues
- Law, Legal Precedents, Court Rules, and Civil and Criminal Procedure
- Testing and Assessment, Judgment and Bias, and Examination Issues
- Individual Rights and Liberties, Civil Competencies, Substitute Judgment
- Juvenile, Parenting, and Family/Matrimonial Matters
- Personal Injury, Civil Damages, Disability, and Workers? Compensation
- Criminal Competence
- Criminal Responsibility

Many professionals do not see the need for board certification and perceive it as having more of an intellectual or academic value than any practical value for practicing clinicians (Dattilio, 2002). Indeed, the requirement to prepare for and pass an examination on the eight broad areas of forensic practice may prevent many forensic psychologists from seeking board certification. Many psychologists who practice in forensic psychology specialize in one particular area, such as child custody evaluations or competency to stand trial evaluations. Although it may be a rewarding intellectual experience to understand case law related to personal injury evaluations, many clinicians fail to see the relevance to their particular area of practice if they are not directly involved in personal injury cases. In addition, the failure rate is 25–30% of all applicants applying for board certification through the ABPP. The arduous task of preparing for and passing the certification process coupled with the perceived lack of practical benefit suggests that it will be a gradual process for many practitioners to become board certified. A recent article by board-certified psychologists proposed, "It is not the exceptional specialist who should be board certified, but the specialist who is not board certified should be the exception" (Bent et al., 1999, p. 72). To encourage more psychologists to pursue board certification, the testing procedure has recently been simplified. Although board certification is proposed as the ideal qualification for specialists, it remains to be seen how many practitioners will pursue the process.

## Training in Legal Psychology

As stated in the beginning of the text, legal psychology is defined as the "scientific study of the effect of law on people, and the effect people have on the law" (Ogloff, 2000, p. 467). The majority of the current research literature in legal psychology focuses on eyewitness testimony and jury decision making (Wiener, Watts, & Stolle, 1993). However, there have been repeated calls for legal psychologists to broaden the focus of inquiry into additional areas of law (Ogloff, 2000). It is reasonable to assume that as the knowledge base of legal psychology expands, researchers will start to explore a wider variety of areas. Few programs currently exist to train graduate students in legal psychology. Most graduate programs only offer one or two courses in social science and the law (Bersoff et al., 1997). Graduate students can receive training in legal psychology by attending a graduate program that has a faculty member who is working in legal psychology. The student would need to recruit that faculty member as a mentor. It is uncommon to have more than one faculty member within a department involved in legal psychology (Ogloff, 2000).

The working group on graduate social science and law programs at the **Villanova Conference** addressed the lack of a coherent model for training future psycholegal scholars. Although no single training model was endorsed by this group, a consensus did emerge regarding training goals and core knowledge areas. These programs would train future scholars to apply social science and legal knowledge to legal problems. Although graduates of these programs could enter academia, they may also choose careers in the private sector or in public service. The working group identified five areas deemed crucial for the psycholegal scholar (Bersoff et al., 1997). These areas include

1. substantive psychology,
2. research design and statistics,
3. legal knowledge,
4. substantive legal psychology, and
5. scholarship and training.

The substantive areas in psychology include core knowledge areas basic to the study of the discipline, such as developmental, cognitive, abnormal, social, ethics, and professional issues. Along with this core knowledge, students should understand social and cultural influences and their impact on social policy. Researchers need a thorough understanding of research methodology and statistical procedures. Concerning research methods, students should understand a variety of approaches, such as observation, survey, experimental, and quasi-experimental design along with laboratory and field research. Students will also need sophisticated statistical skills. Legal psychologists will need to "think like a lawyer" (Melton, 1987, p. 293). The working group recommended that students learn the basic tools of law, sources of law, and the substance of law. Initially, students can take undergraduate and graduate courses in law-related disciplines. This advanced knowledge can even be obtained through a yearlong Master of Legal Studies at some law schools (Bersoff et al., 1997). The Villanova Conference working group also recommended that students acquire a basic education in law and psychology. This would include areas in legal psychology such as eyewitness testimony, jury decision making, expert testimony and admissibility of scientific evidence, competency and insanity evaluations, and so on. Finally, training should involve developing and conducting original research and presenting the research at professional meetings and publishing in scholarly journals.

## Summary Regarding Training

The profession is likely to witness an increase in training opportunities at all levels of the educational spectrum from the undergraduate on to the postdoctoral, continuing-education level. Students can also anticipate the standardization of training guidelines as more institutions start to offer training in forensic psychology and legal psychology. Hopefully there will not be a rush to adopt poorly thought-out guidelines (Otto, 2005), but rather a disciplined approach allowing empirical research to guide the process. An initial push in the direction of standardization of training was the Villanova Conference held in 1995. Additional efforts to standardized training in forensic psychology are ongoing. For example, the American Psychology-Law Society collects and distributes undergraduate and graduate syllabi for courses on psychology and law. It is also likely that new training opportunities will be met by increased competition for these opportunities. This in turn will lead to increased competition for job opportunities (Otto, 2005). Partly due to competition for diminishing resources, there will continue to be a push for practitioners to become board certified in forensic psychology as well as other specialties. Although not all practitioners may become board certified through the ABPP, there is the possibility of future credentialing of forensic psychologists. Some states certify psychologists and other mental health professionals to perform specific activities in the legal system. For example, a state agency may certify mental health professionals to perform competency evaluations, divorce mediation, or evaluation of allegations of child sexual abuse. This form of state certification would be awarded after intensive training on the psycholegal issues involved. Although the profession of psychology would not grant this type of certification, state certifications of this nature may eventually be a requirement to function in the courts.

# Therapeutic Jurisprudence

■ **Therapeutic jurisprudence**
Using social science to guide legal decisions so that all involved benefit psychologically or therapeutically.

Therapeutic jurisprudence is the final trend presented. **Therapeutic jurisprudence** uses social science to "study the extent to which a legal rule or practice promotes the psychological and physical well-being of the people it affects" (Slobogin, 1995, p. 767). This approach is a return to the original aspirations of psychology and law as formulated by Saleem Shah in 1978: "Perhaps a basic challenge for psychology in its interactions with legal and social processes is to bring relevant knowledge and skills to bear on major social inequities so that the policies and practices in our society can more truly comport with the deepest notions of what is fair and right and just" (as cited in Ogloff, 2000). Bruce Winick and David Wexler are considered the founders of therapeutic jurisprudence (Wexler & Winick, 1991). This area of enquiry initially grew out of mental health law and applies behavioral science methods to evaluate the therapeutic and antitherapeutic consequences of the laws and the legal system. The early focus of therapeutic jurisprudence on mental health law led to examining how civil commitment, criminal responsibility, and competency laws were antitherapeutic (Wexler, 1990). The early role of therapeutic jurisprudence was to suggest legal reform of existing mental health laws to make the outcome of enforcing the law more sensitive to the psychological well-being of defendants.

Therapeutic jurisprudence (TJ; Daicoff & Wexler, 2003) has expanded to examine how existing laws, procedures, and personal interactions among legal actors and clients can be modified to produce therapeutic outcomes. TJ focuses on how substantive law and legal proceedings affect the psychological well-being of the participants involved. Laws, legal proceedings, and individuals involved in these proceedings, such as attorneys and judges, can help to promote the psychological well-being of individuals by encouraging healthy behavior change. Examples include drug offender probation that mandates treatment, or domestic violence classes for offenders that facilitate a change in attitudes regarding aggressive behavior toward women. A divorce proceeding in family court that considers the psychological well-being of the divorcing couple as well as children and in-laws is also an example of TJ. Wexler (n.d.) identifies three categories where TJ can be applied:

Therapeutic jurisprudence focuses on how substantive law and legal proceedings affect the psychological well-being of the participants.
© 2009 BXP.

1. legal rules, or substantive law;
2. legal procedures, such as trials and hearings; and
3. the roles of the legal actors and the behavior of legal actors and therapists acting in a legal context.

Wexler (1996) looked at applying psychological principles to criminal law. Specifically, he looked at treatment adherence principles used in the health care field (e.g., Meichenbaum & Turk, 1987) and how these principles can be applied to facilitate a probationer's compliance with the terms of probation. Research from the mental health field on **treatment compliance** identified specific techniques that can enhance compliance. These techniques include involving significant others in the treatment discussion, use of a behavioral contract, an open dialogue between the patient and the health care provider exploring and paraphrasing all aspects of treatment, and a public commitment to comply to treatment recommendations. TJ encourages the use of these same techniques borrowed from the mental health care field and applied in the criminal courts. For example, a judge could engage in many of these compliance-enhancing behaviors with an insanity acquittee or criminal defendant (Wexler, n.d.) The judge could ask the defendant to sign a behavioral contract regarding the terms of probation. This would be after a lengthy dialogue between the defendant and the judge regarding the conditions of probation. Noncompliance sometimes is simply the result of miscommunication between the defendant and the courts. Family and/or friends of the defendant could be at the hearing to witness a public commitment by the defendant to adhere to the conditions of probation. All of these actions could result in a more therapeutic outcome for the defendant.

■ **Psycholegal soft spots**
Areas involving legal issues or procedures that may harm or help the psychological well-being of the parties involved.

In addition to therapeutic judging as discussed, lawyers can interact with their clients in ways that are more therapeutic. TJ can be combined with preventive law. **Preventive law** is an approach to lawyering that attempts to identify legal disputes before they occur with the goal of avoiding, preventing, or minimizing disputes (Daicoff & Wexler, 2003). Lawyers can be sensitive to a client's anxiety and emotional state surrounding the litigation and can interact in ways with the client to help ameliorate some of the stress. Examples include coaching clients through the trial process, role playing, anticipating questions from opposing counsel while on the witness stand and formulating possible replies, and thoroughly explaining the legal process and the court's decision. A therapeutically preventive approach would require the lawyer to consider what "**psycholegal soft spots**" may be of concern for his or her client(s). Psycholegal soft spots are areas involving legal issues or procedures that may harm or help psychological well-being (Daicoff & Wexler, 2003). The attorney needs to identify potential problems ahead of time and devise ways to reduce the unintended harmful effects of the legal action.

In this manner, TJ explicitly considers individuals' concerns and psychological well-being in addition to their strict legal rights and entitlements. This approach suggests ways that laws may be changed, or applied differently, to enhance the therapeutic effect. One significant aspect of therapeutic jurisprudence is the emphasis on the process rather than the outcome. Research indicates that legal disputants are more likely to feel that the procedure was fair, regardless of the outcome, if they feel that they had some degree of control over the process. For example, legal adversaries feel the procedure is fair if they have a chance to present their side of the story and feel that they were treated respectfully by the court (MacCoun, Lind, & Tyler, 1992). Due to the extralegal focus of TJ and consideration of the therapeutic goal, this approach tends to be more collaborative and less adversarial than traditional law.

TJ has been applied to a wide variety of areas including criminal law, personal injury law, employment law, and family law. TJ also expands upon the specialized court movement. Specialized courts have been established to treat drug and alcohol problems, domestic violence offenders, their victims, and the mentally ill (Rottman, 2000). These specialized courts recognize the need for psychological intervention for many of the individuals involved and frequently mandate treatment as part of the sentence.

Forensic psychologists can play a variety of roles in the therapeutic jurisprudence movement. Forensic psychologists can serve as consultants, educators, and researchers. As consultants to attorneys and the courts, forensic psychologists can make recommendations regarding ways to enhance the therapeutic outcome of legal proceedings. These recommendations can include substantive as well as procedural changes. For example, a family psychologist may recommend joint custody for a child custody case as a substantive issue. The psychologist may also recommend allowing the children to not be present in the courtroom during an adversarial fight between the two parents. Psychologists can also consult with attorneys and work as part of an interdisciplinary team for the client. The psychologist can monitor the psychological well-being of the client and evaluate the therapeutic outcomes of legal options with the attorney's client. As educators, psychologists can train law students, lawyers, and judges to be more empathic and attuned to clients' psychological concerns. Psychologists can also conduct research to evaluate the therapeutic outcome of legal disputes on the litigants and recommend changes. Popular interest in therapeutic jurisprudence is growing both nationally and internationally. For example, in May 2010, the Australian Institute of Judicial Administration along with Monash University will present a conference entitled *Nonadversarial Justice: Implications for the Legal System and Society*. Students with an interest in therapeutic jurisprudence have an opportunity to make a significant contribution to a promising new area of law and psychology.

# Summary

This chapter presented four emerging trends in the field of forensic psychology. These trends are likely to influence the careers of students considering forensic psychology as a profession. The chapter discussed the increased growth and sophistication within the specialty. The growth has triggered numerous course offerings in law and psychology at all levels of training. It is likely that as interest continues, competition for training sites and job opportunities will increase. The increased focus on forensic psychology will lead to better-informed consumers, such as attorneys and judges. This informed scrutiny will force the profession to provide high-quality services including scientifically sound assessment instruments and ethical and impartial expert testimony. More collaboration between the legal profession and psychology reflects the mutual professional acceptance. Psychologists and attorneys will continue to work together in applied and research settings, creating more opportunities for collaborative work. Psychology will continue to play a role in influencing public policy. The profession, due to its increased recognition, has an opportunity to apply social science research to social issues. Psychologists can influence public policy through their work with the legislature, as in petition writing campaigns, political rallies, and through legal means such as class action lawsuits and by running for public office. Psychology can also allow social science research to play a role in legal decisions through use of the *amicus* brief. Already, the APA has submitted over 100 briefs. The chapter also examined future training models in forensic and legal psychology. The impact of the Villanova Conference on training was discussed and levels of specialty training were presented. The current two-tier model of specialty training was discussed along with the proposed model of three levels of specialty training for forensic psychology. The issue of board certification was reviewed along with cautionary comments regarding vanity boards. Finally, therapeutic jurisprudence was presented. Included in the discussion of therapeutic jurisprudence were ways psychologists can assist the legal system to make laws and legal proceedings more psychologically beneficial for participants.

## *Amicus Curiae* Briefs Submitted by the American Psychological Association

Table 12.6

### *Ake v. Oklahoma* (1985)

[U.S. Supreme Court/brief filed 6/84]—Whether an indigent defendant has the constitutional right to the appointment of a mental health professional at the State's expense to help the defendant prepare an insanity defense and rebut evidence of future dangerousness.

### *Akron v. Akron Center for Reproductive Health, Inc.* (1983)

[U.S. Supreme Court/brief filed 8/82]—Whether the City of Akron's adoption of an informed consent requirement for abortions, which mandated that the individual providing pre-abortion counseling must be the woman's attending physician (as opposed to other qualified professionals) and specified the kind and substance of the information to be presented, was constitutional.

*(continued)*

*(Continued)*

### Alaska v. R. H. Wetherhorn (1984)

[Alaska Court of Appeals/brief filed 10/83]—Whether admissions of child abuse made during either voluntarily-obtained or court-ordered therapy are admissible in a criminal trial or protected by the state's privileged communication statutes and the right against self-incrimination under the state and/or federal constitution.

### Andersen v. King County (2006)

[Supreme Court of the State of Washington/brief filed 2/05]—addresses a challenge to the constitutionality of Washington's statutes limiting the right to marry to opposite-sex couples.

### Atkins v. Virginia (2002)

[U.S. Supreme Court/motion filed 11/19/01 to have McCarver v. North Carolina brief considered in this case]—addresses the question, "whether the execution of mentally retarded individuals convicted of capital crimes violates the Eighth Amendment."

### BenShalom v. Marsh (1989)

[U.S. Court of Appeals for the Seventh Circuit/brief filed 3/89]—Whether the U.S. Army may constitutionally deny reenlistment to any serviceperson who declares him/herself to have a homosexual orientation.

### Blue Shield of Virginia v. McCready (1982)

[U.S. Supreme Court/brief filed 1/82] Whether an insured patient receiving psychotherapy has standing to sue for treble damages under antitrust laws (i.e., the Clayton Act) when third party payors refuse to reimburse psychologists for mental health services unless those services are billed by physicians.

### Bodell v. Superior Court (2007)

[Court of Appeal of the State of California, 2nd Appellate District/letter in support of cert filed 1/07]—whether the Superior court may compel the production of psychiatric and medical records upon a mere showing of "relevance" and with no stated compelling public interest.

### Boswell v. Boswell (1998)

[Maryland Court of Appeals/brief filed 7/98]—Whether a gay father may be denied overnight visitation with his children and visitations in the presence of his male partner.

### Bottoms v. Bottoms (1995)

[Virginia Court of Appeals/brief filed 11/93 & Virginia Supreme Court/brief filed 12/94]—Whether a lesbian biological mother could be denied custody of her child on the grounds that her sexual orientation rendered her unfit as a parent.

### Bowen v. Kendrick (1988)

[U.S. Supreme Court/APA joined a brief filed 2/88]—Whether the 1981 Adolescent Family Life Act (AFLA) was constitutional, including whether it violated the constitutional rights of individuals to make informed reproductive decisions free of government coercion.

*(continued)*

*(Continued)*
### Bowers v. Hardwick (1986)
[U.S. Supreme Court/brief filed 1/86]—Whether Georgia's sodomy law which outlawed private sexual conduct between consenting adults was constitutional.

### Boy Scouts of America v. Dale, 530 U.S. 640 (2000)
[U.S. Supreme Court/brief filed 3/29/2000]—Whether the Boy Scouts' claim that the recent New Jersey Supreme Court's decision, that the Boy Scouts of America is subject to the State's Law Against Discrimination and violated the law in expelling an assistant scoutmaster because he stated publicly that he is gay, infringes upon its First Amendment right to freedom of association.

### Boy Scouts of America, National Capital Area Council v. Pool et al. (2002)
[D.C. Court of Appeals/APA brief filed 2/26/02]—Addresses the Boy Scout's claim that the decision of the District of Columbia's Commission on Human Rights that the BSA is subject to D.C. law against discrimination and violated the law in terminating all relationships with two gay former Eagle Scouts, is contrary to the Supreme Court precedent in *Dale v. Boy Scouts of America* and infringes on its First Amendment right to freedom of association.

### Bucy v. Bucy (1990)
[Connecticut Court of Appeals/brief filed 2/90]—whether expenses incurred in psychotherapy for the treatment of eating disorders are "medical expenses" within the meaning of a separation and support decree.

### California Association of Psychology Providers v. Rank (1990)
[California Supreme Court/brief filed 6/88]—Whether certain California regulations were inconsistent with legislation defining the scope of psychologists' practice in hospitals and permitting psychologists to provide services as independent practitioners "without discrimination."

### Campbell v. Sundquist (1996)
[Tennessee Court of Appeals/brief filed 10/95]—Whether a Tennessee "Homosexual Acts" statute prohibiting private sexual activity between consenting adults of the same sex violates the Tennessee Constitution's right to privacy.

### Chandler Exterminators, Inc. v. Morris (1992)
[Georgia Court of Appeals/brief filed 12/90 & Georgia Supreme Court/brief in support of petition for reconsideration filed 6/92]—Whether the lower court erred in rejecting the testimony of a neuropsychologist concerning the causes of brain damage as a result of exposure to the neurotoxic substance Aldrin and ruling that psychologists are not competent to testify as to the organic causes of psychological dysfunction by stating "Medical causation is not a subject within the scope of psychological expertise."

### Citizens for Equal Protection v. Bruning (2006)
[U.S. Court of Appeals for the Eighth Circuit/brief filed 11/05]—involves a federal challenge to a section of the Nebraska constitution that bans any legal recognition of same-sex couples.

*(continued)*

*(Continued)*

### City of Cleburne v. Cleburne Living Center, Inc. (1985)

[U.S. Supreme Court/APA signed onto brief filed 1984]—Whether zoning restrictions limiting the right of mentally retarded persons to establish group homes was unconstitutional.

### Clark v. Arizona (2006)

[U.S. Supreme Court/APA signed onto brief filed 1/06]—at issue is the scope of the constitutional duty of states to allow evidence of sanity to be used as a defense in criminal cases relevant to the intent element of a charged crime.

### Colorado v. Connelly (1986)

[U.S. Supreme Court/brief filed 3/86]—Whether an individual diagnosed as paranoid schizophrenic acting in response to "command hallucinations" is competent to waive Miranda rights and his subsequent confession is voluntary and admissible.

### Comfort v. Lynn (2005)

[Missouri Supreme Court/brief filed 6/98]—Whether a lesbian mother may be denied custody solely on the basis of her sexual orientation rather than on the basis of what is in the best interests of the child.

### Conaway v. Deane (2007)

[Maryland Court of Appeals/brief filed 10/06]—addresses a constitutional challenge to Maryland's refusal to issue marriage licenses to same-sex couples.

### Currie v. United States (1987)

[U.S. Court of Appeals for the Fourth Circuit/brief filed 1/87]—Whether a psychotherapist is liable under tort law for failure to institute involuntary commitment proceedings.

### Delong v. Delong (1998)

[Missouri Supreme Court/brief filed 6/98]—Whether a lesbian mother may be denied custody solely on the basis of her sexual orientation rather than on the basis of what is in the best interests of the child.

### Dept. of Human Services v. Howard (2006)

[Supreme Court of Arkansas/brief filed 12/05]—at issue is a challenge to an administrative regulation promulgated by the Arkansas Child Welfare Agency Review Board that prohibits anyone who has a "homosexual" adult household member from providing foster care for children.

### Dept. of Treasury, Bureau of Alcohol, Tobacco, & Firearms v. Galioto (1986)

[U.S. Supreme Court/brief filed 2/86]—Whether provisions of a federal crime statute which permanently prohibited any individual adjudicated as suffering from a mental defective or committed to any mental institution from receiving, transporting, or shipping a firearm or ammunition in interstate commerce or being sold a firearm was unconstitutional.

### Detroit Edison Co. v. National Labor Relations Board (1979)

[U.S. Court of Appeals for the Sixth Circuit/brief filed 1976 & U.S. Supreme Court/brief filed 1977]—Whether an order of the National Labor Relations Board that re-

*(continued)*

*(Continued)*

quired Detroit Edison to provide to a union with copies of an actual test battery and employees' raw scores and test papers without their consent should be enforced in light of confidentiality and test security concerns.

### *Emerich v. Philadelphia Center for Human Development, Inc.* (1998)

[Pennsylvania Supreme Court/brief filed 10/96]—Whether a mental health professional has a duty to warn a third party of a patient's threats to harm the third party and the scope of any such duty.

### *Equality Foundation of Greater Cincinnati, Inc. v. City of Cincinnati* (1995)

[U.S. Court of Appeals for the Sixth Circuit/brief filed 12/94]—Whether an anti-gay rights ballot initiative was constitutional.

### *Estate of Davis v. Yong-Oh Lhim* (1986)

[Michigan Supreme Court/brief filed 7/86]—Whether a psychotherapist is liable under tort law for the standard of care concerning the discharge of patients from mental hospitals and not a therapist's duty to warn of potential danger.

### *Ewing v. Goldstein* (2004)

[California Supreme Court/letter in support of petition for review filed 9/04]—addresses review of a decision that extends California's duty to warn statute from communications from the patient to the therapist to include communications about the patient from a third party.

### *Faulkner v. National Geographic Enterprises, Inc.* (2005)

[U.S. Court of Appeals for the Second Circuit/brief filed 6/04]—addresses the rights of scholarly publishers to digitize their present and past works.

### *Ford v. Norton*, 107 Cal. Rptr. 2d 776 (2001)

[Court of Appeal of the State of California/brief filed 1/6/00]—the case raises the issue of the scope of psychologists' practice (i.e., whether a clinical psychologist is authorized to order the early release of a patient who is hospitalized involuntarily).

### *Ford v. Wainwright* (1986)

[U.S. Supreme Court/brief filed 1/86]—Whether (1) it is unconstitutional to execute an incompetent person, and (2) the procedural issue of whether Florida's statutory scheme for evaluating the competency of a condemned prisoner meets the requirements of due process.

### *Forrest v. Ambach* (1983)

[NY Supreme Court/briefs filed 9/80, 7/81 & NY Supreme Court, Appellate Division/brief filed 12/82]—Whether the New York Commissioner of Education acted in an arbitrary and capricious manner in not permitting a school psychologist to challenge her employment termination for due disagreeing with the State Commissioner regarding the statutory requirements for services to handicapped children.

### *Goodman v. Georgia* (2006)

[U.S. Supreme Court/brief filed 7/05]—addresses whether the American with Disabilities Act applies to conditions under which the disabled are held in state prisons.

*(continued)*

*(Continued)*

### *Greenberg v. National Geographic Enterprises* (Pending)

[U.S. Court of Appeals for the 11th Circuit/brief filed 10/07]—Addresses the rights of scholarly publishers to digitize their present and past works.

### *Grutter v. Bollinger,* 539 U.S. 306, and *Gratz v. Bollinger,* 539 U.S. 244 (2003)

[U.S. Supreme Court/brief filed 2/18/03]—this case addresses whether the University of Michigan's consideration of race in student admissions violates the Equal Protection Clause of the 14th Amendment, Title VI of the Civil Rights Act, or 42 U.S.C. 1981?

### *Harris v. Forklift Systems, Inc.* (1993)

[U.S. Supreme Court/brief filed 4/93]—Whether a sexual harassment plaintiff must prove not only that the conduct complained of would have offended a reasonable victim, and that the plaintiff was in fact offended, but also that the conduct caused the plaintiff to suffer serious psychological injury.

### *Harris v. McRae* (1980)

[U.S. Supreme Court/APA signed onto a brief filed 7/80]—Whether (1) a state participating in the Medicaid program were required to pay for medically necessary abortions and (2) Whether the Hyde Amendment denying federal reimbursement for such abortions was unconstitutional.

### *Hartigan v. Zbaraz* (1987)

[U.S. Supreme Court/brief filed 2/87]—Whether the Illinois Parental Notice Abortion Act which required a physician to give 24-hour notice to both parents of a minor was unconstitutional.

### *Hawthorne v. State of Florida* (1985)

[Florida District Court of Appeals/brief filed 2/83]—Whether expert testimony on battered women's syndrome is admissible to help establish claims of self-defense in a murder case (Parallels the *New Jersey v. Kelly* case).

### *Hedlund v. Superior Court of Orange County* (1983)

[California Supreme Court/brief filed 10/83]—Whether a "foreseeable" bystander in a close relationship to the victim of an assault by a patient can bring a cause of action against the patient's psychotherapist for emotional injury resulting from a failure to warn.

### *Hernandez v. Robles* (2005)

[New York, Appellate Division, First Department/Brief filed 8/05]—addresses a constitutional challenge to New York's refusal to issue marriage licenses to same-sex couples.

### *Hertzler v. Hertzler* (1995)

[Wyoming Supreme Court/brief filed 12/94]—Whether the "best interests of the child" is served by restricting visitation rights to a minimum level due to a mother's sexual orientation as a lesbian.

*(continued)*

*(Continued)*

### Hodgson v. State of Minnesota (1988) & (1990)

[U.S. Court of Appeals for the Eighth Circuit/brief filed 3/87 & U.S. Supreme Court/brief filed 9/89]—Whether a Minnesota statute requiring physicians to notify the parents of all unemancipated minors under the age of 18 at least 48 hours before performing an abortion was unconstitutional (companion case to *Ohio v. Akron*).

### Horne v. Goodson Logging Co. (1986)

[North Carolina Court of Appeals/brief filed 8/86]—Whether a neuropsychologist is competent and credible to testify as an expert determining neurological disability for the purposes of awarding monetary compensation.

### Hudgins v. Moore (1999)

[Supreme Court of South Carolina/briefs filed 2/98 and 2/99]—Whether the prosecution could use raw MMPI-A test materials, administered to determine the defendant's competency to stand trial, to argue at trial that the defendant admitted to being a liar.

### Huntoon v. TCI Cablevision of Colorado (1998)

[U.S. Court of Appeals for the Ninth Circuit/brief filed 7/97 & Colorado Supreme Court/brief filed 2/98]—Whether a neuropsychologist is qualified to testify as to the causation of a head injury.

### Hutchinson v. Proxmire (1979)

[U.S. Supreme Court/brief filed 2/79]—Whether a research scientist is a "public figure" for the purposes of libel law if he is supported by public funds, thereby rendering it difficult for a scientist to sue for libel.

### In re Bryant (1988)

[District of Columbia Court of Appeals/brief filed 6/87]—Whether involuntarily committed mental patients have the right to refuse anti-psychotic medication.

### In re Adoption of Luke (2002)

[Nebraska Supreme Court/APA brief filed 9/01]—this case involves an adoption proceeding commenced by the lesbian partner of a child's natural mother. The case challenges the issue that second-parent adoptions must be denied when the co-parents are gay or lesbian.

### In re Marriage Cases (2008)

[Supreme Court of California/brief filed 9/07]—Whether prohibiting same-sex marriage discriminates on the basis of sexual orientation, rather than just imposing disparate burdens on gay people.

### In re R.A. & M.A. (2007)

[Maine Supreme Judicial Court/brief filed 10/06]— addresses a challenge to the Maine state law barring same-sex couples from legally adopting foster children for whom they are caring.

*(continued)*

*(Continued)*

### Insurance Board v. Muir (1987)

[U.S. Court of Appeals for the Third Circuit/brief filed 8/86]—Whether employee benefit plans issued by private employers but administered by fiscal intermediaries are subject to ERISA or constitute the business of insurance, thus saving the state benefits laws from preemption (the main issue for psychology was whether ERISA exempts insurance carriers from complying with psychologists' freedom of choice laws and mandated mental-health benefit laws.

### International Primate Protection League v. Institute for Behavioral Research (1986)

[U.S. Court of Appeals for the Fourth Circuit/APA joined 69 scientific organizations filing a joint *amici curiae* brief filed 1986—Whether animal rights organizations have standing to sue for custody of a laboratory under state anti-cruelty to animals.

### Jaffee v. Redmond (1996)

[U.S. Supreme Court/brief filed 1/96]—Whether a psychotherapist-patient privilege was recognized under Rule 501 of the Federal Rules of Evidence. The U.S. Supreme Court granted *certiorari* to review a decision of the Seventh Circuit that recognized the existence of a psychotherapist-patient privilege and held that confidential communications of a police officer with a licensed social worker were protected from compelled disclosure.

### Jegley v. Picado (2002)

[Arkansas Supreme Court/brief filed 10/01]—addresses the constitutionality of an Arkansas law that makes sodomy between same-sex couples a crime.

### Jenkins v. United States (1962)

[U.S. Court of Appeals for the District of Columbia/brief filed 2/62]—Whether a psychologist is competent to state professional opinions as an expert witness concerning the nature, and existence or non-existence, of mental disease and defect.

### Kentucky v. Stincer (1987)

[U.S. Supreme Court/brief filed 1/87]—Whether a defendant accused of sexually abusing a child has the right to be present at a pretrial hearing at which a child is questioned to determine competence to testify at trial.

### Kentucky v. Wasson (1992)

[Kentucky Supreme Court/brief filed 8/91]—Whether Kentucky sodomy laws are constitutional under the Kentucky Constitution.

### Kerrigan v. Commissioner of Public Health (2008)

[Connecticut Supreme Court/brief filed 1/07]—addresses a constitutional challenge to Connecticut's refusal to issue marriage licenses to same-sex couples.

### Landers v. Chrysler Corporation (1997)

[Missouri Court of Appeals/brief filed 8/97]—Whether a neuropsychologist is qualified to testify as to the causation of a head injury.

*(continued)*

*(Continued)*
## *Lawrence v. Texas,* 539 U.S. 558 (2003)

[U.S. Supreme Court/brief filed 1/16/03]—addresses the constitutionality of a Texas law that makes sodomy between same-sex couples a crime.

## *Levy v. Edelhofer* (2001)

[Fourth District Court of Appeal, State of California/briefs filed 11/13/00 & 12/4/00]—the case presents the questions of: (1) whether the client/therapist privilege applies to the communications of therapist to the client, (2) whether a court should evaluate communications in therapy to decide whether they are "therapeutic" before deciding whether they are privileged, and (3) whether psychotherapists owe a general duty of care to third parties, or whether psychotherapists owe a general duty of care to their patients' former therapists with whom they have no contractual relationship.

## *Lewis v. Harris* (2005)

[Superior Court of New Jersey, Appellate Division/brief filed 10/04]—whether the New Jersey Constitution compels the State to allow same-sex couples to marry.

## *Li v. Oregon* (2005)

[Supreme Court of the State of Oregon/brief filed 10/04]—addresses a challenge to Oregon's refusal to issue marriage licenses to same-sex couples.

## *Lockhart v. McCree* (1986)

[U.S. Supreme Court/brief filed 12/85]—Whether the use of a death-qualified jury in a capital case is unconstitutional.

## *Martin v. Benson* (1988)

[North Carolina Supreme Court/brief filed 4/97]—Whether a neuropsychologist is competent to testify as to whether the symptoms evidenced by a person are indications of a closed head injury.

## *Maryland v. Craig* (1990)

[U.S. Supreme Court/brief filed 3/90]—Whether certain procedural protections such as the use of one-way close circuit television may be afforded to the victims of child abuse when testifying against the accused individual.

## *McCarver v. North Carolina* (2001)

[U.S. Supreme Court/brief filed 6/8/01]—this case addresses whether the Eighth Amendment's ban against cruel and unusual punishment prohibits the execution of individuals with mental.

## *Menendez v. State of California* (1992)

[California Supreme Court/brief filed 10/91]—Whether patient-therapist communications lose their privileged status once a patient threatens others in a manner such that the therapist's Tarasoff duties are triggered and when a therapist-patient relationship is terminated.

*(continued)*

*(Continued)*

***Metropolitan Edison Co. v. People Against Nuclear Energy*** (and *United States Nuclear Regulatory Commission v. People Against Nuclear Energy*) (1983)

[U.S. Supreme Court/briefs filed 9/82 and 1/83]—Whether there are situations in which an environmental impact statement under the National Environmental Policy Act must consider the effects of a proposed action on psychological health.

***Metropolitan Life Insurance Co. v. State of Massachusetts*** (and *Travelers Insurance Co. v. State of Massachusetts*) (1985)

[U.S. Supreme Court/brief filed 1/85]—Whether a state law requiring mandatory minimal mental health benefits under which outpatient services could be provided by a licensed psychologist was preempted by the federal ERISA law.

***Miller v. City of Poughkeepsie*** (1991)

[New York Supreme Court, Appellate Division/brief filed 12/91]—Whether the State of New York and the federal government consider "medical treatment" to include services provided by a psychologist.

***Mills v. Rogers*** (1983)

[U.S. Supreme Court/brief filed 1/83 and Massachusetts Supreme Court/brief filed 9/81]—Whether a patient institutionalized in a state psychiatric facility has the right to refuse the administration of anti-psychotic medication.

***National Kidney Patients Association v. Sullivan*** (1993)

[U.S. Supreme Court brief in support of a petition for certiorari/brief filed 12/92]—Whether health care providers and Medicare beneficiaries may seek judicial review of HCFA regulations without first completing lengthy administrative review process by HCFA.

***New Jersey v. Kelly*** (1984)

[New Jersey Supreme Court/brief filed 4/83]—Whether expert testimony on battered women's syndrome is admissible to help establish claims of self-defense in a murder case (Parallels case of *Hawthorne v. Florida*).

***New York v. Uplinger*** (1984)

[U.S. Supreme Court/brief filed 12/83]—Whether a New York Loitering law that prohibited loitering for the purpose of engaging in "deviate" sexual intercourse was unconstitutional.

***Ohio v. Akron Center for Reproductive Health, Inc.*** (and *Hodgson v. State of Minnesota*) (1990)

[U.S. Supreme Court/brief filed 9/89]—Whether an Ohio statute which prohibited a physician from performing an abortion upon a minor unless notice was provided to one of the minor's parents.

***Olmstead v. L.C.*** (1999)

[U.S. Supreme Court/brief filed 3/99]—Whether the Americans With Disabilities Act compels a state to provide treatment for mentally disabled patients in a community

*(continued)*

*(Continued)*

placement rather than a state mental institution when that is an appropriate treatment option.

### Oregon v. Miller (1985)

[Oregon Supreme Court/brief filed 12/84]—Whether psychotherapist-patient privilege extended to a receptionist and to statements made to a psychiatrist that were not for the purpose of diagnosis or treatment.

### Panetti v. Quarterman (2007)

[U.S. Supreme Court/brief filed 2/07]—at issue is the appropriate standard for determining the level of mental illness that should preclude execution, as well as the issue of how to define the factors that should be assessed in such a case.

### Parents v. Seattle School District and Meredith v. Jefferson Co. Board of Education (2007)

[U.S. Supreme Court/brief filed 10/06]—the consolidated cases involve voluntary desegregation plans in Kentucky and Seattle K-12 public school systems that use race as a factor in some instances when assigning children to particular schools or programs within schools.

### Patrick v. Burget (1989)

[U.S. Supreme Court/brief filed 11/87]—Whether the conduct of hospital peer committees with the power to grant hospital privileges were absolutely immune from antitrust liability under the state action doctrine.

### Penry v. Lynaugh (1988)

[U.S. Supreme Court/brief filed 9/88]—Whether mentally retarded individuals possess the moral culpability to be subjected to the death penalty.

### People v. Gil (1998)

[New York Supreme Court, Appellate Division/brief filed 7/97]—Whether cognitive research evidence and expert testimony regarding laypersons' beliefs concerning physics was admissible in a murder trial.

### Planned Parenthood of S.E. Pennsylvania v. Casey (1992)

[U.S. Supreme Court/brief filed 3/92]—Whether (1) the challenged provisions of Pennsylvania's abortion statute are constitutional, and (2) the standard of review established under *Roe v. Wade* for regulations restricting abortion remained the law of the land.

### Price Waterhouse v. Hopkins (1989)

[U.S. Supreme Court/brief filed 6/88]—Whether social psychological research and expert testimony regarding sex-role stereotyping is sufficient to support a finding of sex-discrimination in a Title VII (mixed motivation) case.

### Progressive Animal Welfare Society (PAWS) v. University of Washington (1994)

[Washington Supreme Court/brief filed 7/93]—Whether unfunded grant proposals submitted to a federal agency are protected from disclosure by federal preemption and the researcher's First Amendment right of academic freedom.

*(continued)*

*(Continued)*

### Riese v. St. Mary's Hospital & Medical Center (1988)

[California Supreme Court/brief filed 8/88]—Whether civilly committed mental patients could refuse the administration of antipsychotic medication absent a judicial determination of incompetence.

### Rivers v. Katz (and Grassi v. Acrish) (1986)

[New York Court of Appeals/brief filed 2/86]—Whether involuntarily committed mental patients, who have not been formally adjudicated to be incompetent, can refuse antipsychotic medication.

### Romer v. Evans (1996)

[U.S. Supreme Court/brief filed 6/95]—Whether an enacted state constitutional amendment prohibiting the State and all local governmental entities from enacting, adopting or enforcing any law or policy protecting lesbians, gay men and bisexuals from discrimination violates the Equal Protection Clause of the Fourteenth Amendment because it burdens the fundamental right of lesbians, gay men and bisexuals to seek such legal protections.

### Rone v. Fireman (1979)

[U.S. District Ct., Northern District, Eastern Div./brief filed 1//78]—Whether the State had an obligation to treat persons confined to state mental hospitals in the least restrictive setting.

### Roper v. Simmons (2005)

[U.S. Supreme Court/filed 7/04]—Whether the imposition of the death penalty on an individual who was 17 years old when he committed a murder constitutes "cruel and unusual" punishment, and is thus barred by the Eighth and Fourteenth Amendments.

### Samuels v. New York State Department of Health (2006)

[New York Appellate Division: Third Department/brief filed 5/05]—addresses a constitutional challenge to New York's refusal to issue marriage licenses to same-sex couples.

### Schudel v. General Electric (1997)

[U.S. Court of Appeals for the Ninth Circuit/brief filed 7/95]—Whether neuropsychologists are competent to testify on issues pertaining to causation of an "organic" mental condition.

### Sell v. U.S., 539 U.S. 166 (2003)

[U.S. Supreme Court/brief filed 12/19/02]—this case addresses whether a criminal defendant should be involuntary medicated for the purpose of restoring the defendant to competency so that he can stand trial.

### Shields v. Madigan (2006)

[New York Appellate Division: Second Department/brief filed 7/05]—addresses a constitutional challenge to New York's refusal to issue marriage licenses to same-sex couples.

*(continued)*

*(Continued)*
### Smith v. Murray (1986)

[U.S. Supreme Court/brief filed 12/85 under *Smith v. Sielaff*]—Whether information the defendant provides to a mental health professional for the purpose of diagnosis or assessment incident to preparing a defense to a charge of a capital offense can be used against him by the State to establish an aggravating circumstance during the death penalty phase.

### Soroka v. Dayton Hudson Corp, d.b.a. Target Stores (1992)

[California Supreme Court/APA filed 1/92 letter in support of cert. petition. Although review was granted, the case was settled in 7/93 without an APA brief filed]—Whether certain portions of the MMPI and the California Psychological Inventory administered to job applicants (i.e., questions that facially and in isolation suggest they are related to religious and sexual matters) violate the privacy provisions of the California Constitution and certain anti-discrimination laws.

### Stogner v. California, 539 U.S. 607 (2003)

[U.S. Supreme Court /brief filed 2/18/03]—this case involves the validity of a California statute that retroactively expanded the statute of limitations for certain sex offenses (i.e., the rape and molestation of children by.

### Stover v. State of Georgia (1986)

[Georgia Supreme Court/brief filed 11/86]—Whether a state anti-sodomy law criminally prohibiting oral sex was constitutional.

### Texas v. Morales (1994)

[Texas Court of Appeals/brief filed 1/92 and Texas Supreme Court/brief filed 12/92]—Whether the equal protection and due process components of the Texas Constitution prohibit criminalization of consensual homosexual sodomy among adults in private.

### Thornburgh v. American College of Obstetricians and Gynecologists (1986)

[U.S. Supreme Court/brief filed 8/85]—Whether a Pennsylvania state law that required physicians to inform women contemplating an abortion of the detrimental physical and psychological effects was constitutional.

### U.S. v. Fields (2007)

[U.S. Court of Appeals for the Fifth Circuit/brief filed 4/05]—addresses the reliability of expert testimony in a death penalty case.

### U.S. v. Gomes (2002)

[U.S. Court of Appeals for the Second Circuit/brief filed 9/01]—addresses whether a criminal defendant can be involuntarily medicated in order to restore the defendant to competency.

### U.S. v. Leatherman (1984)

[U.S. Court of Appeals for the District of Columbia/brief filed 11/83] (case dismissed when Leatherman escaped from hospital in 2/84)—addresses whether a prisoner found not guilty by reason of insanity and committed for treatment can refuse antipsychotic medications.

*(continued)*

*(Continued)*

### U.S. v. Lyons (1984)

[U.S. Court of Appeals for the Fifth District/brief filed 11/83]—Whether evidence of drug addiction should be admitted when the defendant raises an insanity defense.

### United States v. Brawner (1972)

[U.S. Court of Appeals for the District of Columbia/brief filed 5/71]—Whether in insanity defense cases (1) the medical model should be abandoned, and (2) the results of psychological tests like the Rorschach should be admissible.

### United States v. Byers (1982)

[U.S. Court of Appeals for the District of Columbia/brief filed 10/81]—Whether a prosecution-requested, court-ordered clinical interview conducted in custodial confinement of a criminal defendant who was offering an insanity defense endangered the privilege against self-incrimination protected by the Fifth Amendment and the right to assistance of counsel protected by the Sixth Amendment.

### United States v. Charters (1988)

[U.S. Court of Appeals for the Fourth Circuit/brief filed 6/88]—Whether a hospitalized patient has a federal constitutional right to refuse antipsychotic drugs unless the patient has been found incompetent to make treatment decisions or is imminently dangerous to self or others.

### Varnum v. Brien (pending 2008)

[Iowa Supreme Court/brief filed 5/08]—Addresses a constitutional challenge to Iowa's refusal to issue marriage licenses to same-sex couples.

### Virginia Academy of Clinical Psychologists v. Blue Shield of Virginia (1980)

[U.S. Court of Appeals for the Fourth Circuit/brief filed 7/79]—Whether a health insurance company's refusal to provide direct payments to clinical psychologists for outpatient psychological services rendered to the company's subscribers unless those services were ordered, supervised, and billed by a physician violated the Sherman Act and "Virginia's "freedom of choice" legislation.

### Washington v. Harper (1990)

[U.S. Supreme Court/brief filed 6/89]—Whether a prisoner in a correctional facility has the right to refuse the administration of psychotropic drugs.

### Watkins v. United States Army (1989)

[U.S. Court of Appeals for the Ninth Circuit/brief filed 8/88]—Whether U.S. Army regulations requiring the discharge of lesbians and gay men and barring them from reenlisting were unconstitutional.

### Watson v. Fort Worth Bank and Trust (1988)

[U.S. Supreme Court/brief filed 9/87]—Whether the use of non-validated employment assessment tools violated Title VII of the 1964 Civil Rights Act.

### Webster v. Reproductive Health Services (1989)

[U.S. Supreme Court/brief filed 3/89]—Whether a state statute that comprehensively regulated abortion was unconstitutional.

*(continued)*

*(Continued)*

*Williamson v. Liptzen*, 539 S.E. 2d 313 (2000)

[Court of Appeals of North Carolina/brief filed 2/00]—Whether public policy supports the extension of the law of proximate causation to allow liability in this case concerning negligence by a mental health professional.

*Wright v. Pennsylvania* (pending 2008)

[Supreme Court of Pennsylvania/brief filed 11/08]—involves the lower courts' interpretation that the Post Conviction DNA testing statute (which governs when convicted felons can have potentially exonerating DNA tests performed) does not allow access to DNA testing, if there has been a "voluntary" confession in the case.

*Wyatt v. Aderholt* (1973)

[U.S. Court of Appeals for the Fifth Circuit/brief filed 11/72]—Whether (1) mentally impaired individuals who are involuntarily confined in state institutions have the right to treatment and (2) confinement without treatment deprives such individuals of their constitutional rights.

*Youngberg v. Romeo* (1982)

[U.S. Supreme Court/brief filed 9/81]—Whether mentally retarded residents of state hospitals have the constitutional right to be free from undue bodily restraint, the right to personal security and protection, and the right to adequate treatment.

# TEST YOUR KNOWLEDGE

1. The textbook discusses *increased sophistication in the field of forensic psychology* as one of the emerging trends. What is meant by increased sophistication?
   a. More training opportunities
   b. Greater recognition of the benefits that psychology has to offer in the legal arena
   c. Establishment of specific guidelines for assessment and other forensic activities
   d. All of the above

2. An *amicus* brief that attempts to objectively summarize a body of research for the court's benefit is called
   a. an advocacy brief
   b. a summary brief
   c. a science translation brief
   d. a veritas brief

3. What are the three levels of training recommended for a forensic psychologist?
   a. entry, proficiency, and specialty
   b. novice, practitioner, expert
   c. predoctoral, doctoral, postdoctoral
   d. nonpractitioner, part-time practitioner, full-time practitioner

4. The level of training recommended for *all* practicing psychologists is
   a. novice
   b. entry
   c. proficiency
   d. specialty

5. The use of social science to study the extent to which a legal rule or practice promotes the psychological and physical well-being of the people it affects is termed
   a. social framework theory
   b. legal psychology
   c. restorative justice
   d. therapeutic jurisprudence

Answer Key (1) d, (2) c, (3) a, (4) b, (5) d

# Case Law by Topic

■ **Competency to Stand Trial and Criminal Responsibility**

- *Durham v. United States* (1954) (Criminal Responsibility)
  The court ruled that when attempting to determine guilt there has to be both free will and intent to do harm.

- *Faretta v. California* (1975)
  Court ruled that competency to waive one's right to counsel had no relationship to the defendant's actual ability to legally self-represent.

- *Godinez v. Moran* (1993) (Competency to stand trial)
  The court ruled that no different or higher standard was required for the waiver of important rights than the Dusky standard.

- *Jackson v. Indiana* (1972) (Competency to stand trial)
  The U.S. Supreme Court ruled that if a defendant is determined incompetent, the state may involuntarily hospitalize and treat the defendant for a reasonable period of time to determine the probability that the person can achieve trial competency in the foreseeable future.

- *Pate v. Robinson* (1966) (Competency to stand trial)
  The U.S. Supreme Court ruled that a trial judge must raise the issue of competency if any evidence presented creates a "bona fide doubt" about the defendant's competency.

- *Riggins v. Nevada* (1992) (Competency to stand trial)
  The U.S. Supreme Court ruled that a defendant found incompetent could be administered medication against his or her will if the state can show that the medication is essential for the defendant's safety or the safety of others, or that there are no other less intrusive means to obtain an adjudication of guilt or innocence.

- *United States v. Brawner* (1972) (Criminal Responsibility)
  The court repealed the Durham rule and adopted a modified version of the Model Penal Code Rule (Brawner rule).

- *United States v. Duhon* (2000) (Competency to stand trial)
  The court ruled the release of a mentally retarded defendant who did not pose a danger to himself or society since he would never achieve trial competency.

- *United States v. Hinckley* (1982) (Criminal Responsibility)
  The U.S. Congress passed the Federal Insanity Defense Reform Act (1984). Defendants must prove insanity by clear and convincing evidence.

■ **Expert Witness and Expert Testimony**

- *Daubert v. Merrell Dow Pharmaceuticals* (1993)
  The court ruled that the Federal Rules of Evidence requires the judge, when ruling on the admissibility of scientific testimony, to determine if the evidence

is *relevant* to the case at issue, *reliable*, and likely to *assist* the trier of fact.

- *Frye v. United States* (1923)
  The court established the *general acceptance rule* regarding the admissibility of scientific testimony. The court ruled that for a scientific expert testimony to be admissible, it must be based on generally accepted scientific methods.

- *Jenkins v. United States* (1962)
  The court ruled that the training required for a PhD in clinical psychology qualifies an individual to testify regarding criminal responsibility and mental illness.

- *Kansas v. Hendricks* (1997)
  Court allowed for the postincarceration civil commitment of "any person who has been convicted of or charged with a sexually violent offense and who suffers from a mental abnormality or personality disorder that makes the person likely to engage in the predatory acts of sexual violence."

■ **Police Psychology**

- *Bonsignore v. City of New York* (1982)
  Court ruled that the police agency can be held liable for the actions of employees who were not properly screened.

- *Conte v. Horcher* (1997)
  Courts ruled that police agencies have a right to order an officer to submit to a physical or mental exam to determine the officer's ability to perform the requirements of the job.

- *David v. Christian* (1987)
  Courts upheld that the employing agency that requests an evaluation is the client and holds the right of confidentiality.

- *McCabe v. Hoberman* (1969)
  Courts ruled that police agencies have a right to include psychological evaluations in their screening process.

- *Vinson v. The Superior Court of Alameda County* (1987)
  The court ruled that the examiner should have the freedom to probe deeply into the plaintiff's psyche without interference by a third party.

■ **Correctional Psychology**

- *Barefoot v. Estelle* (1983)
  The U.S. Supreme Court ruled that a mental health professional's expert opinion regarding the prediction of dangerousness met the criteria for the Daubert standard regarding admissibility of evidence.

- *Estelle v. Gamble* (1976) (Right to treatment)
  Court ruled that an inmate must prove that prison officials were deliberately indifferent to the health needs of the inmate.

- *Ford v. Wainwright* (1986)
  The U.S. Supreme Court ruled that it is unconstitutional to execute an inmate who does not appreciate what is happening to him or her due to a mental illness.

- *Joseph v. Brierton* (1984) (Right to treatment)
  The ruling of *Estelle v. Gamble* was extended to include psychiatric care.

- *McKune v. Lile* (2002) (Coerced treatment)
  The U.S. Supreme Court ruled that a prison could withdraw privileges if an inmate refused to participate in a treatment program.

- *Penry v. Lynaugh* (1989)
  The U.S. Supreme Court ruled the execution of a mildly mentally retarded individual (Penry) did not violate constitutional safeguards if the individual was found competent to stand trial.

- *Washington v. Harper* (1990)
  The U.S. Supreme Court upheld that an administrative hearing is sufficient to administer psychoactive drugs to an inmate against his or her will.

- *Wellman v. Faulker* (1983) (Right to treatment)
  The ruling of *Estelle v. Gamble* was extended to include psychiatric care.

- **Personal Injury and Employment Law**

  - *Griggs v. Duke Power Company* (1971)
    The U.S. Supreme Court ruled that when qualifications for employment discriminated against women or minorities, the qualifications violated Title VII unless the employer could prove that the practice was a business requirement.

  - *Jones v. Tri-County Electric Cooperative* (1975)
    The court ruled that the company was in violation of Title VII due to discriminatory effects of the hiring practices, hiring a much smaller percentage of the adversely affected group than found in the local workforce.

  - *McWilliams v. Fairfax County Board of Supervisors* (1996)
    Court ruled that anyone could claim sexual harassment if subjected to offensive behavior of a sexual nature.

  - *Meritor Savings Bank v. Vinson* (1986)
    The court ruled that demand for sexual conduct absent the explicit threat of adverse employment action can create a hostile environment.

  - *Oncale v. Sundowner Offshore Oil* (1996)
    The Fifth Circuit Court ruled that an employee could claim sexual harassment for male-on-male harassment, setting the precedent for same-group discrimination.

- **Trial Consultation**

  - *Batson v. Kentucky* (1986)
    Court ruled that prospective jurors could not be excluded in criminal trials based solely on race.

  - *J.E.B. v. Alabama* (1994)
    The court ruled that gender could not be used as the sole criterion for a peremptory challenge.

  - *Powers v. Ohio* (1991)
    The *Batson v. Kentucky* ruling was extended to include civil trials.

  - *State v. Lozano* (1993)
    The court ruled that when change of venue is granted, the new location must have similar demographic characteristics to the original venue.

■ **Investigative Psychology**

- *The Estate of Sam Shepard v. State of Ohio* (2000)
  The judge ruled that a former FBI profiler would need to limit his expert testimony and could not testify. The judge ruled that such testimony would amount to profiling evidence, and profiling testimony did not meet the standards of Daubert.

- *U.S. v. Robinson* (2000)
  Federal courts ruled that forensic psychologists may not testify as to whether an individual could or could not have committed a crime based on typologies.

■ **Eyewitness Memory**

- *Stovall v. Denno* (1967)
  The U.S. Supreme Court ruled a showup, although suggestive, is not unnecessarily suggestive that it should be ruled inadmissible.

- *United States v. Ash* (1973)
  The courts ruled that a suspect has the right for a lawyer to be present during a live lineup but does not have the right for a lawyer to be present during a photo lineup.

# References

Aamodt, G. M. (2004). *Research in law enforcement selection.* Boca Raton, FL: Universal Publishers.

Abidin, R. R. (1995). *Parenting Stress Index.* Odessa, FL: Psychological Assessment Resources.

Abrams, D. (2004). Can "runaway jury" be real?: So-called "stealth jurors" could be sabotaging the justice system. *The Abrams Report.* Retrieved July 31, 2005, from http://msnbc.msn.com/id/4653700/

Achenbach, T. M. (1991). *Manual for the Child Behavior Checklist/4-18 and 1991 Profile.* Burlington: University of Vermont, Department of Psychiatry.

Ackerman, M. (1999). *Essentials of forensic psychological assessment.* New York: Wiley.

Ackerman, M. J., & Ackerman, M. C. (1996). Child custody evaluation practices: A 1996 survey of psychologists. *Family Law Quarterly, 30,* 565–586.

Ackerman, M. J., & Ackerman, M. C. (1997). Custody evaluation practices: A survey of experienced professionals (revisited). *Professional Psychology: Research and Practice, 28,* 137–145.

Ackerman, M. J., & Kane, A. W. (1998). *Psychological experts in divorce actions* (3rd ed.). New York: Aspen Law & Business.

Ackerman, M. J., & Schoendorf, K. (1992). *The Ackerman–Schoendorf scales for parent evaluation of custody (ASPECT).* Los Angeles, CA: Western Psychological Services.

Adams, K., & Ferrandino, J. (2008). Managing mentally ill inmates in prison. *Criminal Justice and Behavior, 35,* 913–927.

Adelson, R. (2004). The polygraph in doubt. *Monitor on Psychology, 35*(7), 71.

Ainsworth, P. B. (1995). *Psychology and policing in a changing world.* Chichester, UK: Wiley.

Althouse, R. (2000). AACP standards: A historical overview (1978–1980). *Criminal Justice and Behavior, 27,* 430–432.

Amato, J. M., Cornell, D. G., & Fan, X. (2008). Adolescent psychopathy: Factor structure and correspondence with million adolescent clinical inventory. *Criminal Justice and Behavior, 35,* 294–310.

Amato, P. (2001). Children of divorce in the 1990s: An update of the Amato and Keith (1991) meta-analysis. *Journal of Family Psychology, 15,* 355–370.

American Academy of Child and Adolescent Psychiatry. (1997). Practice parameters for child custody evaluations. *Journal of the American Academy of Child and Adolescent Psychiatry, 36,* 57S–68S.

American Association for Correctional Psychology. (2000). Standards for psychology services in jails, prisons, correctional facilities and agencies. *Criminal Justice and Behavior, 27,* 433–493.

American Bar Association. (2003). *Model rules of professional conduct—2004 edition.* Retrieved March 12, 2005, from http://www.abanet.org/cpr/mrpc/mrpc _toc.html

American Bar Association Commission on Law and Aging & American Psychological Association. (2005). *Assessment of older adults with diminished capacity: A handbook for lawyers.* Washington, DC: American Bar Association Commission on Law and Aging & American Psychological Association.

American Counseling Association. (1995). *ACA code of ethics and standards of practice.* Alexandria, VA: American Counseling Association.

American Educational Research Association, American Psychological Association, & National Council on Measurement in Education. (1999). *Standards for educational and psychological testing* (3rd ed.), Washington, DC: American Educational Research Association.

American Psychiatric Association. (2000a). *Diagnostic and statistical manual of mental disorders* (4th ed., text rev.) Washington, DC: American Psychiatric Association.

American Psychiatric Association. (2000b). *Psychiatric services in jails and prisons, a Task Force Report of the American Psychiatric Association.* Washington DC: American Psychiatric Association.

American Psychiatric Association. (2004). *Mental illness and the criminal justice system: Resources toward treatment, not containment.* Arlington, VA: American Psychiatric Association.

American Psychological Association. (1978). Report of the Task Force on the role of psychology in the criminal justice system. *American Psychologist, 33,* 1099.

American Psychological Association. (1984). *Specialization in psychology: Principles.* Washington, DC: American Psychological Association.

American Psychological Association. (1992). Ethical principles of psychologists and code of conduct. *American Psychologist, 47,* 1591–1611.

American Psychological Association. (1994). Guidelines for child custody evaluations in divorce proceedings. *American Psychologist, 49,* 677–680.

American Psychological Association. (1995). *Lesbian and gay parenting: A resource for psychologists.* Washington, DC: American Psychological Association.

American Psychological Association. (2000). *1998–1999 Survey of undergraduate departments of psychology.* Washington, DC: American Psychological Association.

American Psychological Association. (2002). Ethical principles of psychologists and code of conduct. *American Psychologist, 59,* 236–260.

American Psychological Association. (2004). Guidelines for psychological practice with older adults. *American Psychologist, 49,* 677–680.

American Psychological Association Committee on Professional Practice and Standards. (1998). *Guidelines for psychological evaluations in child custody matters.* Washington, DC: American Psychological Association.

American Psychological Association Committee on Professional Practice and Standards. (2003). Legal issues in the professional practice of psychology. *Professional Psychology: Research and Practice, 34* (6), 595–600.

American Psychological Association Working Group on Investigation of Memories of Childhood Abuse. (1998). Final conclusions. *Psychology, Public Policy, and Law, 4,* 933–940.

American Society of Trial Consultants. (2005a). *Ethical principles.* Retrieved August 4, 2005, from http://astcweb.org/content/File/AboutUs/ASTC_Code_Full.pdf

American Society of Trial Consultants. (2005b). *Goals.* Retrieved July 28, 2005, from http://www.astcweb.org/content.php?page=aboutus_goals

Anastasi, A. (1998). *Psychological testing* (4th ed.) New York: Macmillan.

Andenaes, J. (1968). Does punishment deter crime? *Criminal Law Quarterly, 11,* 76–93.

Anderson, B. S. (1996). *The counselor and the law* (4th ed.). Alexandria, VA: American Counseling Association.

Anderson, S. D., & Hewitt, J. (2002). The effect of competency restoration training on defendants with mental retardation found not competent to proceed. *Law and Human Behavior, 26,* 343–351.

Andrews, D. A., & Bonta, J. (1998). *The psychology of criminal conduct* (2nd ed.) Cincinnati, OH: Anderson.

Anthony, P., Kidd, J. E., & Daniel, J. E. (2005). New techniques in trial consulting and jury research. *Decision Points: Litigation Library.* Retrieved July 28, 2005, from http://www.decisionquest.com/litigation_library.php?NewsID=190

Appelbaum, P. S., & Grisso, T. (2001). *MacArthur Competence Assessment Tool for Clinical Research*. Sarasota, FL: Professional Resource Press.

Archer, R. P., Maurish, M., Imhoff, E., & Piotrowski, C. (1991). Psychological test usage with adolescent clients: 1990 survey findings. *Professional Psychology: Research and Practice, 22*, 247–252.

Ashford, J. B., Wong, K. W., & Sternbach, K. O. (2008). Generic correctional programming for mentally ill offenders. *Criminal Justice and Behavior, 35*, 457–473.

Ashkar, P. J., & Kenny, D. T. (2007). Moral reasoning of adolescent male offenders: Comparison of sexual and nonsexual offenders. *Criminal Justice and Behavior, 34*, 108–118.

Association of Family and Conciliation Courts. (n.d.). *Guidelines for court connected Child custody evaluations*. Madison, WI: Association of Family and Conciliation Courts. (Available from 329 Wilson Street, Madison, WI 53703)

Association of State and Provincial Psychology Boards. (2000). *Handbook of licensing and certification requirements for psychologists in the U.S. and Canada*. Montgomery, AL: Association of State and Provincial Psychology Boards.

*Atkins v. Virginia*, 260 Va. 375, 534 S.E. 2d 312 (2002).

Atkinson, M. J. (2003). California Psychological Inventory—Third Edition. In B. S. Plake, J. C. Impara, & R. A. Spies (Eds.), *The fifteenth mental measurement yearbook*. Lincoln, NE: Buros Institute of Mental Measurements.

Ax, R. K., & Morgan, R. D. (2002). Internship training opportunities in correctional psychology. *Criminal Justice and Behavior, 29*, 332–347.

Bagby, M. R., Nicholson, R. A., Buis, T., Radovanovic, H., & Fidler, B. J. (1999). Defensive responding on the MMPI-2 in family custody and access evaluation. *Psychological Assessment, 11*, 24–28.

Baker, K. (1997, January). Once a rapist? Motivational evidence and relevancy in rape law. *Harvard Law Review*.

Baker, R. R., Lichtenberg, P. A., & Moye, J. (1998). A practice guideline for assessment of competency and capacity of the older adult. *Professional Psychology: Research and Practice, 29*(2), 149–154.

Ballis, D., Darley, J., Waxman, T., & Robinson, P. (1995). Community standards of criminal liability and the insanity defense. *Law and Human Behavior, 19*, 425–446.

*Barefoot v. Estelle*, 463 U.S. 880 (1983).

Bartels, A., & Zeki, S. (2000). The neural basis of romantic love. *NeuroReport, 11*, 3829–3834.

Bartlett, M. S., Hager, J. C., Ekman, P., & Sejnowski, T. J. (1999). Measuring facial expressions by computer image analysis. *Psychophysiology, 36*, 253–263.

Bartol, C. R. (1996). Police psychology then, now and beyond. *Criminal Justice and Behavior, 23*, 70–89.

Bartol, C. R., & Bartol, A. M. (1999). History of forensic psychology. In A. K. Hess & I. B. Weiner (Eds.), *The handbook of forensic psychology* (2nd ed., pp. 3–23). New York: Wiley.

Bartol, C. R., & Bartol, A. M. (2004). *Psychology and Law*. Belmont, Ca: Wadsworth.

Bartol, C. R., & Bartol, A. M. (2008). *Introduction to forensic psychology: Research and application* (2nd ed.). Thousand Oaks, CA: Sage.

Bashore, T. R., & Rapp, P. E. (1993). Are there alternatives to traditional polygraph procedures? *Psychological Bulletin, 113*, 3–22.

*Batson v. Kentucky*, 106 S. Ct. 1712 (1986).

Bavolek, S. J. (1984). *Handbook for the Adult–Adolescent Parenting Inventory*. Schaumburg, IL: Family Development Associates.

Beaza, J., Chisum, W. J., Chamberlin, T. M., McGrath, M., & Turvey, B. (2000). Academy of Behavioral Profiling: Criminal profiling guidelines. *Journal of Behavioral Profiling, 1*(1).

Beck, C. J. A., & Sales, B. D. (2001). *Family mediation: Facts, myths, and future prospects.* Washington, DC: American Psychological Association.

Beck, S. J., Beck, A. G., Levitt, E. E., & Molish, H. B. (1961). *Rorschach's Test 1. Basic processes* (3rd ed.). New York: Grune & Stratton.

Becker, J. V., & Murphy, W. D. (1998). What we know and do not know about assessing and treating sex offenders. *Psychology, Public Policy, and Law, 4,* 116–137.

Bednar, R. L., Bednar, S. C., Lambert, M. J., & Waite, D. R. (1991). *Psychotherapy with high-risk clients: Legal and professional standards.* Pacific Grove, CA: Brooks/Cole.

Bekerian, D. A. (1993). In search of the typical eyewitness. *American Psychologist, 48,* 574–576.

Belar, C. D., & Jeffery, T. B. (1995). Board certification in health psychology. *Journal of Clinical Psychology in Medical Settings, 2*(2), 129–132.

Belli, R. F., & Loftus, E. F. (1996). The pliability of autobiographical memory: misinformation and the false memory problem. In D. C. Rubin (Ed.), *Remembering our past: Studies in autobiographical memory* (pp. 157–179). New York: Cambridge University Press.

Benjamin, G. A. H., & Gollan, J. K. (2003). *Family evaluation in custody litigation: Reducing risks of ethical infractions and malpractice.* Washington, DC: American Psychological Association.

Benjamin, L. T. (2001). American psychology's struggles with its curriculum: Should a thousand flowers bloom? *American Psychologist, 56,* 735–742.

Bennett, C., & Hirschorn, R. (1993). *Bennett's guide to jury selection and trial dynamics in civil and criminal litigation.* St. Paul, MN: West.

Bennett, G., & Kish, G. (1990). Incompetency to stand trial: Treatment unaffected by demographic variables. *Journal of Forensic Sciences, 35,* 403–412.

Ben-Shakhar, G., Bar-Hillel, M., Bilu, Y., Ben-Abba, E., & Flug, A. (1986). Can graphology predict occupational success?: Two empirical studies and some methodological ruminations. *Journal of Applied Psychology 71,* 645–653.

Benson, E. (2003). Rehabilitate or punish? *APA Monitor, 34*(7), 46–47.

Bent, R. J., Packard, R. E., & Goldberg, R. W. (1999). The American Board of Professional Psychology, 1947–1997: A historical perspective. *Professional Psychology: Research and Practice, 30,* 65–73.

Bergen, G. T., Aceto, R. T., & Chadziewicz, M. M. (1992). Job satisfaction of police psychologists. *Criminal Justice and Behavior Special Issue: Psychology of Policing, 9*(3), 314–329.

Berliner, L., & Loftus, E. (1992). Sexual abuse accusations: Desperately seeking reconciliation. *Journal of Interpersonal Violence, 7,* 570–578.

Bernstein, B. E., & Hartsell, T. L. (2005). *The portable guide to testifying in court for mental health professionals: An A–Z guide to being an effective witness.* New York: Wiley.

Bersoff, D. N., Goodman-Delahunty, J., Grisso, T., Hans, V. P., Poythress, N. G., & Roesch, R. G. (1997). Training in law and psychology: Models from the Villanova Conference. *American Psychologist, 52,* 1301–1310.

Bittner, E. (1990). *Aspects of police work.* Boston: Northeastern University Press.

Black, H. C. (1990), *Black's law dictionary* (6th ed.) St. Paul, MN: West.

Blak, R. (1990). Critical incident debriefing for law enforcement personnel. In J. T. Reese, J. M. Horn, & C. Dunning (Eds.), *Critical incidents in policing* (pp. 39–50). Washington, DC: Federal Bureau of Investigation.

Blake, D. D., Weathers, F. W., Nagy, L. M., Kaloupek, D. G., Gusman, F. D., Charney, D. S., & Keane, T. M. (2005). The development of a clinician-administered PTSD scale. *Journal of Traumatic Stress*, 75–90.

Blanchard, J. (2002). At home in a strange land! *Professional Psychology: Research and Practice*, 33(3), 285–288.

Blau, T. H. (1994). *Psychological services for law enforcement*. New York: Wiley.

Blowers, A. N., & Bjerregaard, B. (1994). The admissibility of expert testimony on the battered woman syndrome in homicide cases. *Journal of Psychiatry and Law*, 22, 527–560.

Blumenthal, J. A. (1998). The reasonable woman standard: A meta-analytic review of gender differences in perceptions of sexual harassment. *Law and Human Behavior*, 22, 33–57.

Blumenthal, R. (1993). Gay officers find acceptance on New York's police force. *New York Times* (p. 1).

Boccaccini, M. T., & Brodsky, S. L. (1999). Diagnostic test usage by forensic psychologists in emotional injury cases. *Professional Psychology: Research and Practice*, 30, 253–259.

Boccaccini, M. T., & Brodsky, S. L. (2002). Believability of expert and lay witnesses: Implications for trial consultation. *Professional Psychology: Research and Practice*, 33(4), 384–388.

Bonnie, R. (1992). The competence of criminal defendants: A theoretical reformulation. *Behavioral Sciences and the Law*, 10, 291–316.

Bonnie, R., & Grisso, T. (2000). Adjudicative competence and youthful offenders. In T. Grisso & R. Schwartz (Eds.), *Youth on trial* (pp. 73–103). Chicago: University of Chicago Press.

Bonnie, R., & Slobogin, C. (1980). The role of mental health professionals in the criminal process: The case for informed speculation. *Virginia Law Review*, 66, 427–522.

Boothby, J. L., & Clements, C. B. (2000). A national survey of correctional psychologists. *Criminal Justice and Behavior*, 27, 716–732.

Boothby, J. L., & Clements, C. B. (2002). Job satisfaction of correctional psychologists: Implications for recruitment and retention. *Professional Psychology: Research and Practice*, 33, 310–315.

*Borawick v. Shay*, 68 F.3d S97 (1995).

Borum, R., & Fulero, S. M. (1999). Empirical research on the insanity defense and attempted reforms: Evidence toward informed policy. *Law and Human Behavior*, 23, 375–394.

Borum, R., & Grisso, T. (1995). Psychological test use in criminal forensic evaluations. *Professional Psychology: Research and Practice*, 26, 465–473.

Borum, R., & Philpot, C. (1993). Therapy with law enforcement couples: Clinical management of the "high-risk" lifestyle. *American Journal of Family Therapy*, 21, 121–132.

Borum, R., Super, J., & Rand, M. (2003). Forensic assessment for high-risk occupations. In I. B. Weiner (Series Ed.) & A. M. Goldstein (Vol. Ed.), *Handbook of Psychology: Vol. 11. Forensic psychology* (pp. 143–147). New York: Wiley.

*Bosignore v. City of New York*, 683 F2d 635 (1982).

Bothwell, R. K., Deffenbacher, K. A., & Brigham, J. C. (1987). Correlation of eyewitness accuracy and confidence: Optimality hypothesis revisited. *Journal of Applied Psychology*, 72, 691–695.

Bow, J. N., & Quinnell, F. A. (2001). Psychologists' current practices and procedures in child custody evaluations" Five years after American Psychological Association Guidelines. *Professional Psychology: Research and Practice*, 32(3), 261–268.

Bow, J. N., Quinnell, F. A., Zaroff, M., & Assemany, A. (2002). Assessment of sexual abuse allegations in child custody cases. *Professional Psychology: Research and Practice, 33*(6), 566–575.

Braithwaite, J. (1999). Restorative justice: Assessing optimistic and pessimistic accounts. In M. Torry (Ed.), *Crime and justice: A review of research* (Vol. 25). Chicago: University of Chicago Press.

Brewer, W. F., & Treyens, J. C. (1981). Role of schemata in memory for places. *Cognitive Psychology, 13,* 207–230.

Bricklin, B. (1984). *Bricklin Perceptual Scales.* Furlong, PA: Village Publishing.

Bricklin, B. (1990). *Bricklin Perceptual Scales.* Furlong, PA: Village Publishing.

Briere, J. (1995). *Trauma Symptom Inventory professional manual.* Odessa, FL: Psychological Assessment Resources.

British Psychological Society. (1995). *Report of the Working Party of the British Psychological Society on recovered memories.* East Leicester, UK: British Psychological Society.

Brocato, J., & Wagner, E. F. (2008). Predictors of retention in an alternative-to-prison substance abuse treatment program. *Criminal Justice and Behavior, 35,* 99–119.

Brodsky, S. L. (1999).*The expert expert witness: More maxims for the expert witness.* Washington, DC: American Psychological Association.

Brodsky, S. L. (2004). *Coping with cross-examination and other pathways to effective testimony.* Washington, DC: American Psychological Association.

Brodsky, S. L., & McKinsey, R. K. (2002). The ethical confrontation of the unethical forensic colleague. *Professional Psychology: Research and Practice, 33*(3), 307–309.

Brown, D. R. (1992). A didactic group program for persons found unfit to stand trial. *Hospital and Community Psychiatry, 43,* 732–733.

Bryan, P. E. (2005). *Constructive divorce: Procedural justice and sociolegal reform.* Washington, D.C.: American Psychological Association.

Buchanan, C., Maccoby, E., & Dornbusch, S. (1991). Caught between parents: Adolescents' experiences in divorced homes. *Child Development, 62,* 1008–1029.

Budd, K. S., Felix, E. D., Poindexter, L. M., Naik-Polan, A. T., & Sloss, C. F. (2002). Clinical assessment of children in child protection cases: An empirical analysis. *Professional Psychology: Research and Practice, 33*(1), 3–12.

Bull, R. H. (1988). What is the lie detector test? In A. Gale (Ed.). *The polygraph test: Lies, truth and science* (pp. 10–18). London: Sage.

Bumby, K. M., & Maddox, M. C. (1999). Judges' knowledge about sexual offenders, difficulties presiding over sexual offense cases, and opinions on sentencing, treatment, and legislation. *Sexual Abuse: A Journal of Research and Treatment, 11,* 305–315.

Burchfield, K. B., & Mingus, W. (2008). Not in my neighborhood: Assessing registered sex offenders' experiences with local social capital and social control. *Criminal Justice and Behavior, 35,* 356–374.

Bureau of Justice Statistics. (1999). *Local police departments 1997.* Washington, DC: U.S. Department of Justice.

Bureau of National Affairs. (2003, September). Trial consultant's meetings with witness are shielded under work product doctrine. *ABA?/BNA Lawyers' Manual on Professional Conduct–Current reports Only, 19.* Retrieved July 28, 2005, from http://litigationcenter.bna.com/pic2/lit.nsf/id/BNAP-5RMMJJ?OpenDocument

Bureau of Prisons. (1993). *Psychology Services Manual.* Program Statement No. 5310.12. Washington, DC: U.S. Department of Justice, National Institute of Justice.

Busch, A. B., & Shore, M. F. (2000). Seclusion and restraint: A review of recent literature. *Harvard Review of Psychiatry*, 8, 261–270.

Bush, S. S., Connell, M. A., & Denny, R. (2006). *Ethical practice in forensic psychology: A systematic model for decision making*. Washington DC: American Psychological Association.

Butterfield, F. (1998, March 5). By default, jails become mental institutions. *New York Times*.

Buxton, R. B. (2002). *Introduction to functional magnetic resonance imaging: Principles and techniques*. New York: Cambridge University Press.

Cacioppo, J. T., Tassinary, L. G., &. Berntson, G. G. (Eds.). (2000). *Handbook of Psychophysiology* (2nd ed.). New York: Cambridge University Press.

Caldwell, M. F., McCormick, D. J., Umstead, D., & Van Rybroek, G. J. (2007). Evidence of treatment progress and therapeutic outcomes among adolescents with psychopathic features. *Criminal Justice and Behavior*, 34, 573–587.

Camara, W. J., Nathan, J. S., & Puente, A. E. (2000). Psychological test usage: Implications in professional psychology. *Professional Psychology: Research and Practice*, 31, 141–151.

Camp, C. T., & Camp, G. M. (1995). *The correctional yearbook, 1995: Jail systems*. South Salem, NY: Criminal Justice Institute.

Caplan, L. (1984). *The insanity defense and the trial of John W. Hinckley, Jr.* New York: Godine.

Carr, G. D., Moretti, M. M., & Cue, B. J. H. (2005). Evaluating parenting capacity: Validity problems with the MMPI-2, PAI, CAPI, and ratings of child adjustment. *Professional Psychology: Research and Practice*, 36, 188–196.

Carson, R. E., Daube-Witherspoon, M. E., & Herscovitch, P. (1997). *Quantitative functional brain imaging with positron emission tomography*. San Diego, CA: Academic Press.

Carter, D., Sapp, A., & Stephens, D. (1998). Higher education as a Bona Fide Occupational Qualification (BFOQ) for police: A blueprint. *American Journal of Police*, 7(2), 16–18.

Cashel, M. L. (2002). Child and adolescent psychological assessment: Current clinical practices and the impact of managed care. *Professional Psychology: Research and Practice*, 33, 446–453.

Cassel, E., & Bernstein, D. A. (2001). *Criminal behavior*. Boston: Allyn & Bacon.

Castro-Martin, T., & Bumpass, L. (1989). Recent trends and differentials in marital disruptions. *Demographics*, 26, 37–51.

Chamberlin, J. (2000). Cops trust cops, even one with a PhD. *Monitor on Psychology*, 31(1).

Chambers, M. (1993). Sua sponte. *National Law Journal* (pp. 21–22).

Chandler, J. T. (1990). *Modern police psychology: For law enforcement and human behavior professionals*. Springfield, IL: Thomas.

Charles, M. (1986). *Policing the streets*. Springfield, IL: Thomas.

Chibnall, J. T., & Detrick, P. (2003). The NEO PI-R, Inwald Personality Inventory, and MMPI-2 in the prediction of police academy performance: A case for incremental validity. *American Journal of Criminal Justice*, 27(2), 233–248.

Christy, A., Douglas, K. S., Otto, R. K., & Petrila, J. (2004). Juveniles evaluated incompetent to proceed: Characteristics and quality of mental health professionals' evaluations. *Professional Psychology: Research and Practice*, 35(4), 380–388.

Cirincione, C., Steadman, H., & McGreevy, M. (1995). Rates of insanity acquittals and the factors associated with successful insanity pleas. *Bulletin of the American Academy of Psychiatry and Law*, 23, 399–409.

Clark, B. K. (1995). Acting in the best interest of the child: Essential components of a child custody evaluation. *Family Law Quarterly*, 29, 20–38.

Clark, J., Boccaccini, M. T., Caillouet, B., & Chaplin, W. F. (2007). Five factor model personality traits, jury selection, and case outcomes in criminal and civil cases. *Criminal Justice and Behavior, 34,* 641–660.

Clark, S. C. (1995, March). Advance report of final divorce statistics, 1989 and 1990. In *Monthly vital statistics report, 43*(9). Hyattsville, MD: National Center for Health Statistics.

Clear, T. R., & Cole, G. F. (2000). *American corrections* (5th ed.). Belmont, CA: West/Wadsworth.

Clute, S. (1993). Adult survivor litigation as an integral part of the therapeutic process. *Journal of Child Sexual Abuse, 2,* 447–449.

Cochrane, R. E., Grisso, T., & Frederick, R. I. (2001). The relationship between criminal charges, diagnosis, and psycholegal opinions among federal defendants. *Behavioral Sciences and the Law, 19,* 565–582.

Cochrane, R. E., Tett, R. P., & VandeCreek, L. (2003). Psychological testing and the selection of police officers: A national survey. *Criminal Justice and Behavior, 30,* 511–527.

Cohen, F. (1998). *The mentally disordered inmate and the law.* Kingston, NJ: Civic Research Institute.

Cohen, F. (2008). *The mentally disordered inmate and the law* (2nd ed.). Kingston, NJ: Civic Research Institute.

Collins, W. A., Maccoby, E. E., Steinberg, L., Hetherington, E. M., & Bornstein, M. H. (2000). Contemporary research on parenting: The case for nature and nurture. *American Psychologist, 55,* 218–232.

Commission on Accreditation for Law Enforcement Agencies. (1989). *Standards for law enforcement agencies. The standards manual for the law enforcement agency accreditation program.* Fairfax, VA: Commission on Accreditation for Law Enforcement Agencies.

Committee on Ethical Guidelines for Forensic Psychologists. (1991). Specialty guidelines for forensic psychologists. *Law and Human Behavior, 15,* 655–665.

Committee to Review the Scientific Evidence on the Polygraph, National Research Council. (2003). *The polygraph and lie detection.* Washington, DC: The National Academies Press.

Connell, M. (2004, August). *Child custody and visitation: Have we forgotten the child?* Paper presented at the annual meeting of the American Psychological Association, Honolulu, Hawaii.

Connors, E., Lundregan, T., Miller, N., & McEwen, T. (1996). *Convicted by juries, exonerated by science: Case studies in the use of DNA evidence to establish Innocence after trial.* Washington, DC: U.S. Department of Justice, National Institute of Justice, NCJ 161258.

Conroy, M. A. (2003). Evaluation of sexual predators. In I. B. Weiner (Series Ed.) & A. M. Goldstein (Vol. Ed.), *Handbook of Psychology: Vol. 11. Forensic psychology* (pp. 463–484). New York: Wiley.

*Conte v. Horcher,* 365 N.E.2d 567 (1977).

Cook, W. G. H. (1921). *Insanity and mental deficiency.* London: Routledge.

Cooper, D., & Grisso, T. (1997). Five-year research update (1991–1995): Evaluations for competence to stand trial. *Behavioral Sciences and the Law, 15,* 347–364.

Cooper, J., & Neuhaus, I. M. (2000). The "hired gun" effect: Assessing the effect of pay, frequency of testifying, and credentials on the perception of expert testimony. *Law and Human Behavior, 24,* 149–171.

Correia, K. M. (2001). *A handbook for correctional psychologists.* Springfield: IL: Thomas.

Costanzo, M. (2004). Psychology applied to law. Belmont, CA: Wadsworth.

Cotton, D. (2007). [Review of the book Improving police response to persons with mental illness: a progressive approach]. Criminal Justice and Behavior, 35 (4), 536–538.

Courtois, C. A. (1997). Guidelines for the treatment of adults abused or possibly abused as children with attention to issues of delayed/recovered memory. *American Journal of Psychotherapy, 51,* 497–510.

Cowles, C. A., & Washburn, J. J. (2005). Psychological consultation on program design of intensive management units in juvenile correctional facilities. *Professional Psychology: research and Practice, 36*(1), 44–50.

Cox, G. D. (1993, May 3). Consultant appointed in *Denny* case. *National Law Journal* (p. 38).

Cronin, C. (1995). Adolescent reports of parental spouse abuse in military and civilian families. *Journal of Interpersonal Violence, 10*(1), 117–122.

Cunero, D., & Brejle, T. (1984). Predicting probability of attaining fitness to stand trial. *Psychological Reports, 55,* 35–39.

Cunningham, M. D., & Goldstein, A. M. (2003). Sentencing determinations in death penalty cases. In I. B. Weiner (Series Ed.) & A. M. Goldstein (Vol. Ed.), *Handbook of Psychology: Vol. 11. Forensic psychology* (pp. 407–436). New York: Wiley.

Cunningham, M. D., & Reidy, T. J. (1998). Antisocial personality disorder and psychopathology: Diagnostic dilemmas in classifying patterns of antisocial behavior in sentencing evaluations. *Behavioral Sciences and the Law, 16,* 333–351.

Cunningham, W. A., Johnson, M. K., Raye, C. L., Gatenby, J. C., Gore, J. C., & Banaji, M. R. (2004). Separable neural components in the processing of black and white faces. *Psychological Science, 15,* 806–813.

Curran, S. F. (1998). Revised IACP guidelines: Pre-employment psychological evaluation of law enforcement applicants. *The Police Chief, 65*(10), 88–95.

Cutler, B. L., Berman, G. L., Penrod, S. D., & Fisher, R. P. (1994). Conceptual, practical, and empirical issues associated with eyewitness identification test media. In D. F. Ross, J. D. Read, & M. P. Toglia (Eds.), *Adult eyewitness testimony: Current trends and developments* (pp. 163–181). New York: Cambridge University Press.

Cutler, B. L., Moran, G. P., & Narby, D. J. (1992). Jury selection in insanity defense cases. *Journal of Research in Personality, 26,* 165–182.

Dae-Young, K., Hee-jong, J., & McCarty, W. P. (2008). Risk assessment and classification of day reporting center clients: An actuarial approach. *Criminal Justice and Behavior, 35,* 792–812.

Daicoff, S., & Wexler, D. B. (2003). Therapeutic jurisprudence. In I. B. Weiner (Series Ed.) & A. M. Goldstein (Vol. Ed.), *Handbook of psychology: Vol. 11. Forensic psychology* (pp. 561–580). New York: Wiley.

Darkes, J., Otto, R. K., Poythress, N., & Starr, L. (1993). APA's expert panel in the Congressional Review of the *USS Iowa* incident. *American Psychologist,* 8–15.

Dattilio, F. M. (2002). Board certification in psychology: Is it really necessary? *Professional Psychology: Research and Practice, 33*(1), 54–57.

*Daubert v. Merrell Dow Pharmaceuticals,* 509 U.S. 579 , 113 S Ct. 2786, 125 L. Ed. 2d 469 (Supreme Court 1993).

Daum, J., & Johns, C. (1994). Police work from a woman's perspective. *Police Chief, 19,* 339–348.

*David v. Christian,* 520 N.Y.S.2d 827 (A.D. 2 Dept. 1987).

Davis, D. L. (1985). Treatment planning for the patient who is incompetent to stand trial. *Hospital and community Psychiatry, 36,* 268–271.

DeAngelis, T. (1991). Police stress takes its toll on family life. *APA Monitor, 22*(7), 38.

DeAngelis, T. (1993). Workplace stress battles fought all over the world. *APA Monitor, 24*(1), 22.

DeAngelis, T. (2003). Youth programs cut crime, costs. *Monitor on Psychology, 34*(7), 48–50.

Death Penalty Information Center. (2002). *The death penalty in 2002: Year end report.* Washington, DC: Death Penalty Information Center.

Deffenbacher, K. A. (1980). Eyewitness accuracy and confidence. Can we infer anything about their relationship? *Law and Human Behavior, 4,* 243–260.

DeLisi, M. (2005). *Career criminals in society.* Thousand Oaks, CA: Sage.

Delprino, R., & Bahn, C. (1988). National survey of the extent and nature of psychological services in police departments. *Professional Psychology: Research and Practice, 19,* 421–425.

DePaulo, B. M., Lindsay, J. J., Malone, B. E., Muhlenbruck, L., Charlton, K., & Cooper, H. (2003). Cues to deception. *Psychological Bulletin, 129,* 74–118.

de Rivera, J. (2000). Understanding persons who repudiate memories recovered in therapy. *Professional Psychology: Research and Practice, 31*(4), 378–388.

Detrick, P., & Chibnall, J. T. (2002). Prediction of police officer performance with the Inwald Personality Inventory. *Journal of Police and Criminal Psychology, 17*(2), 9–17.

Detrick, P., Chibnall, J. T., & Luebbert, M. C. (2004). The revised NEO personality inventory as predictor of police academy performance. *Criminal Justice and Behavior, 31*(6), 676–694.

Detrick, P., Chibnall, J. T., & Rosso, M. (2001). Minnesota Multiphasic Personality Inventory–2 in police officer selection: Normative data and relation to the Inwald Personality Inventory. *Professional Psychology: Research and Practice, 32*(5), 484–490.

Dodson, C., & Reisberg, D. (1991). Indirect testing of eyewitness memory: The (non)effect of misinformation. *Bulletin of the Psychonomic Society, 29,* 333–336.

Douglas, A. B., & Stabley, N. (2006). Memory distortion in eyewitnesses: a meta-analysis of the post-identification feedback effect. *Applied Cognitive Psychology. 20*(7), 859–869.

Douglas, K., & Webster, C. (1999). The HCR-20 Violence Risk Assessment Scheme: Concurrent validity in a sample of incarcerated offenders. *Criminal Justice and Behavior, 26,* 3–19.

Downing Hansen, N., & Goldberg, S. G. (1999). Navigating the nuances: A matrix of considerations for ethical–legal dilemmas. *Professional Psychology: Research and Practice, 30*(5), 495–503.

Downs, D. A. (1996). *More than victims: Battered women, the syndrome society, and the law.* Chicago: University of Chicago Press.

Drum, D. J., & Blom, B. E. (2001). The dynamics of specialization in professional psychology. *Professional Psychology: Research and Practice, 32*(5), 513–521.

Dunnette, N., & Motowidlo, S. (1976). *Police selection and career assessment.* Washington, DC: U.S. Department of Justice.

*Durham v. United States,* 214 F.2nd 862 (D.C. Cir. 1954).

*Dusky v. United States,* 362 U.S. 402 (1960).

Dutton, D. G., & McGregor, B. M. S. (1992). Psychological and legal dimension of family violence. In D. K. Kagehiro & W. S. Laufer (Eds.), *Handbook of psychology and law* (pp. 318–340). New York: Springer-Verlag.

Duwe, G., Donnay, W., & Tewksbury, R. (2008). Does residential proximity matter? A geographic analysis of sex offense recidivism. *Criminal Justice and Behavior, 35,* 484–504.

Eberhardt, J. (2005). Imaging race. *American Psychologist, 60*(2), 181–190.

Ebert, B. (1987). Guide to conducting a psychological autopsy. *Professional Psychology: Research and Practice, 18*(1), 52–56.

Ebert, B. (1991). Guide to conducting a psychological autopsy. In K. N. Anchor (Ed.), *Handbook of medical psychotherapy*. Lewiston, NY: Hofgrefe & Huber.

Egeth, H. E. (1993). What do we not know about eyewitness identification? *American Psychologist, 48*, 577–580.

Ekman, P. (2001). *Telling lies: Clues to deceit in the marketplace, politics, and marriage* (3rd ed.) New York: Norton.

Ekman, P., & O'Sullivan, M. (1991). Who can catch a liar? *American Psychologist 46*, 913–920.

Ekman, P., O'Sullivan, M., & Frank, M. G. (1999). A few can catch a liar. *Psychological Science, 10*(3), 263–266.

Emery, R. E., Laumann-Billings, L., Waldron, M. C., Sbarra, D. A., & Dillon, P. (2001). Child custody mediation and litigation: Custody, contact and coparenting 12 years after initial dispute resolution. *Journal of Consulting and Clinical Psychology, 69*, 323–332.

Emery, R., & Wyer, M. (1987). Divorce mediation. *American Psychologist, 42*, 472–480.

Enns, C. Z., Campbell, J., Courtois, C. A., Gottlieb, M. C., Lese, K. P., Gilbert, M. S., & Forrest, L. (1998). Working with adult clients who may have experienced childhood abuse: Recommendations for assessment and practice. *Professional Psychology: Research and Practice, 29*(3), 245–256.

Equal Employment Opportunity Commission. (1992). *Technical assistance manual on the employment provisions (Title I) of the Americans With Disabilities Act.* Washington, DC: Equal Employment Opportunity Commission.

*Equal Employment Opportunity Commission Compliance Manual.* (1994). N: 4072–4073, Harassment, Section 615. Washington, DC: Bureau of National Affairs.

*Estelle v. Gamble*, 429 U.S. 97 (1976).

Ewing, C. P. (1985). *Psychology, psychiatry, and the law: A clinical and forensic handbook*. Sarasota, FL: Professional Resource Exchange, Inc.

Ewing, C. P. (2000, June). *Criminal forensic assessment: exculpatory and mitigating defenses*. Workshop presented for the American Academy of Forensic Psychology, San Juan, Puerto Rico.

Ewing, C. P. (2003). Expert testimony: Law and practice. In I. B. Weiner (Series Ed.) & A. M. Goldstein (Vol. Ed.), *Handbook of psychology: Vol. 11. Forensic psychology* (pp. 55–66). New York: Wiley.

Exner, J. E. Jr. (1991). *The Rorschach: A comprehensive system: Vol. 2. Interpretation* (2nd ed.). New York: Wiley.

Fagan, T. J., Ax, R. K., Resnick, R. J., Liss, M., Johnson, R. T., & Forbes, M. R. (2004). Attitudes among interns and directors of training: Who wants to prescribe, who doesn't, and why. *Professional Psychology: Research and Practice, 35*(4), 345–356.

Faigman, D. L., Kaye, D. H., Saks, M. J., & Sanders, J. (1997). *Modern scientific evidence: The law and science of expert testimony*. St. Paul, MN: West.

Falk, P. (1989). Lesbian mothers: Psychosocial assumptions in family law. *American Psychologist, 44*, 941–947.

*Faretta v. California*, 422 U.S. , 806 (1975).

Farkas, G. (1986). Stress in undercover policing. In J. Reese & H. Goldstein (Eds.), *Psychological services for law enforcement*. Washington, DC: U.S. Government Printing Office.

Farwell, L. A., & Donchin, E. (1991). The truth will out: Interrogative polygraphy ("lie detection") with event-related potentials. *Psychophysiology, 28*, 531–547.

Farwell, L. A., & Smith, S. S. (2001). Using brain MERMER testing to detect knowledge despite efforts to conceal. *Journal of Forensic Science, 46*, 135–143.

Fass, T. L., Heilbrun, K., Dematteo, D., & Fretz, R. (2008). The LSI-R and the compass: Validation data on two risk-needs tools. *Criminal Justice and Behavior, 35*, 1095–1108.

Federal Bureau of Prisons. (1993). *Psychology service manual.* Washington, DC: U.S. Department of Justice.

*Federal Rules of Evidence Handbook 2000–2001.* (2000). Cincinnati, OH: Anderson.

Felner, R. D., Rowlison, R. T., Farber, S. S., Primavera, J., & Bishop, T. A. (1987). Child custody resolution: A study of social science involvement and impact. *Professional Psychology: Research and Practice, 5*, 468–474.

Ferrell, S. W., Morgan, R. D., & Winterowd, C. L. (2000). Job satisfaction of mental health professionals providing group psychotherapy in state correctional facilities. *International Journal of Offender Therapy and Comparative criminology, 44*, 232–241.

Finkel, N. J. (1980). *Therapy and ethics: The courtship of law and psychology.* New York: Grune & Stratton.

Finn, P., & Tomz, J. E. (1997). *Developing a law enforcement stress program for officers and their families.* Washington, DC: National Institute of Justice.

First, M. B., Spitzer, R. L., Gibbon, M., Williams, J. B. W., Davies, M., Borus, J., et al. (1995). The Structured Clinical Interview for DSM-III-R personality disorders (SCID-II) II: Multi-site test–retest reliability study. *Journal of Personality Disorders, 9*, 92–104.

Foa, E. (1995). *Post-traumatic Diagnostic Scale manual.* Minneapolis, MN: National Computer Systems.

Follingstad, D. R. (2003). Battered woman syndrome in the courts. In I. B. Weiner (Series Ed.) & A. M. Goldstein (Vol. Ed.), *Handbook of psychology: Vol. 11. Forensic psychology* (pp. 485–507). New York: Wiley.

*Ford v. Wainwright*, 477 U.S, 399 (1986).

Forester-Miller, H., & Davis, T. E. (n.d.). *A practitioner's guide to ethical decision making.* Alexandria, VA: American Counseling Association.

Fowler, R. (1976). *The clinical use of the automated MMPI.* Nutley, NJ: Roche Psychiatric Service.

Frazier, P. A., Cochran, C. C., & Olson, A. M. (1995). Social science research on lay definitions of sexual harassment. *Journal of Social Issues, 51*, 21–37.

Frederick, R. I., DeMier, R. L., & Towers, K. (2004). *Examinations of competency to stand trial: Foundations in mental health case law.* Sarasota, FL: Professional Resource Press.

Freeman, S. J. (2000). *Ethics: An introduction to philosophy and practice.* Belmont, CA: Wadsworth.

Frost, A., & Pakiz, B. (1990). The effects of marital disruption on adolescence: Time as a dynamic. *American Journal of Orthopsychiatry, 60*, 544–555.

*Frye v. United States*, 293 F. 1013 (D.C. Cir. 1923).

Fulero, S., & Finkel, N. (1991). Barring ultimate issue testimony: An "insane" rule? *Law and Human behavior, 15*, 496–507.

Fulero, S. M. & Penrod, S. D. (1990). The myths and realities of attorney jury selection folklore and scientific jury selection. What works? *Ohio Northern University Law Review, 17*, 229–253.

Gabriel, R. K., & Fenyes, J. (2003, Oct/Nov). What a trial consultant can teach you–even if you can't afford to hire one. *GPSolo Magazine: ABA General Practice, Solo and Small Firm Section, 20*(7), 1–5.

Gallagher, R., & Bember, C. (1978). *Hostage negotiation for police*. Schiller Park, IL: Motorola Teleprograms.

Garb, H. N., Wood, J. M., Lilienfeld, S. O., & Nezworski, M. T. (2002). Effective use of projective techniques in clinical practice: Let the data help with selection and interpretation. *Professional Psychology: Research and Practice, 33*(5), 454–463.

Garber, B. D. (2004). Directed co-parenting intervention: Conducting child-centered interventions in parallel with highly conflicted co-parents. *Professional Psychology: Research and Practice, 35,* 55–64.

Gardner, R. A. (1992). *True and false accusations of child sex abuse*. Cresskill, NJ: Creative Therapeutics.

Garimella, R., Plichta, S. B., Houseman, C., & Garzon, L. (2000). Physician beliefs about victims of spouse abuse and about the physician role. *Journal of Women's Health and Gender-Based Medicine, 9,* 405–411.

Gatowski, S. I., Dobbin, S. A., Richardson, J. T., Ginsburg, G. P., Merlino, M. L., & Dahir, V. (2001). Asking the gatekeepers: A national survey of judges on judging expert evidence in a post-*Daubert* world. *Law and Human Behavior, 25,* 433–458.

Gendreau, P., Cullen, F. T., & Bonta, J. (1994). Intensive rehabilitation supervision: The next generation in community corrections? *Federal Probation, 58,* 72–78.

*General Electric Company et al. v. Joiner et al.,* 522 U.S. 136 (1997).

Gentz, D. (1990). The psychological impact of critical incidents on police officers. In J. T. Reese, J. M. Horn, & C. Dunning (Eds.), *Critical incidents in policing* (pp. 175–181). Washington, DC: Federal Bureau of Investigation.

Gerard, A. B. (1994). *Parent-Child Relationship Inventory Manual* Los Angeles, CA: Western Psychological Services.

Gerber, G. L. (2001). *Women and men police officers*. Westport, CT: Praeger.

Gillespie, C. K. (1989). *Justifiable homicide: Battered women, self-defense, and the law*. Columbus: Ohio Sate University Press.

Gindes, M. (1995). Competence and training in child custody evaluations. *American Journal of Family Therapy, 23,* 273–280.

Girodo, M. (1991). Symptomatic reactions to undercover work. *Journal of Nervous and Mental Disease, 179* (10), 626–630.

Giuliana, A. L., Mazzoni, G. A. L., Loftus, E. F., & Kirsch, I. (2001). Changing beliefs about implausible autobiographical events: A little plausibility goes a long way. *Journal of Experimental Psychology: Applied, 7,* 51–59.

Glassman, J. B. (1998). Preventing and managing board complaints: The downside risk of custody evaluation. *Professional Psychology: Research and Practice, 29,* 121–124.

Glick, P. C. (1984). Marriage, divorce, and living arrangements. Prospective changes. *Journal of Family Issues, 5,* 7–26.

*Godinez v. Moran,* 113 S.Ct. 2680 (1993).

Goldberg, J. O., & Miller, H. R. (1986). Performance of psychiatric inpatients and intellectually deficient individuals on a task assessing the validity of memory complaints. Cited in R. Rogers (Ed.), *Clinical assessment of malingering and deception*. New York: Guilford Press.

Goldberg, L. R., Grenier, J. R., Guion, R. M., Sechrest, L. B., & Wing, H. (1991). *Questionnaires used in the prediction of trustworthiness in preemployment selection decisions*. Washington, DC: American Psychological Association.

Golding, S. L. (1993). *Training manual: Interdisciplinary Fitness Interview—Revised*. Salt Lake City: University of Utah, Department of Psychology.

Golding, S. (1999, August). *The voir dire of forensic experts: Issue of qualification and training*. Paper presented at the annual meeting of the American Psychological Association, Boston.

Golding, S. L., & Roesch, R. (1987). The assessment of criminal responsibility: A historical approach to a current controversy. In I. B. Weiner & A. K. Hess (Eds.), *Handbook of forensic psychology*. New York: Wiley.

Golding, S. L., Roesch, R., & Schreiber, J. (1984). Assessment and conceptualization of competency to stand trial: Preliminary data on the interdisciplinary fitness interview. *Law and Human behavior, 8,* 321–334.

Golding, S. L., Skeem, J. L., Roesch, R., & Zapf, P. A. (1999). The assessment of criminal responsibility: Current controversies. In I. B. Weiner & A. K. Hess (Eds.), *Handbook of forensic psychology*. New York: Wiley.

Goldstein, A. G., Chance, J. E., & Schneller, G. R. (1989). Frequency of eyewitness identification in criminal cases: A survey of prosecutors. *Bulletin of the Psychonomic Society, 27,* 71–74.

Goldstein, A. M. (2003a). *Handbook of psychology: Vol. 11. Forensic psychology*. New York: Wiley.

Goldstein, A. M. (2003b). Overview of forensic psychology. In I. B. Weiner (Series Ed.) & A. M. Goldstein (Vol. Ed.), *Handbook of psychology: Vol. 11. Forensic psychology* (pp. 3–20). New York: Wiley.

Goldstein, A. M. (2007). *Forensic psychology: Emerging topics and expanding roles*. Hoboken, NJ: Wiley.

Goldstein, A. M., & Weiner, I. B. (2003). Handbook of Psychology: Volume 11, Forensic Psychology, Hoboken, N.J.: John Wiley & Sons, Inc.

Goldstein, A. M., Morse, S. J., & Shapiro, D. L. (2003). Evaluation of criminal responsibility. In I. B. Weiner (Series Ed.) & A. M. Goldstein (Vol. Ed.), *Handbook of psychology: Vol. 11. Forensic psychology* (pp. 381–406). New York: Wiley.

Gore-Felton, C., Koopman, C., Thoresen, C., Arnow, B., Bridges, E., & Spiegel, D. (2000). Psychologists' beliefs and clinical characteristics: Judging the veracity of childhood sexual abuse memories. *Professional Psychology: Research and Practice, 31*(4), 372–377.

Gough, H. G. (1987). *California Psychological Inventory administrator's guide*. Palo Alto, CA: Consulting Psychologists Press.

Gould, J. W. (1998). *Conducting scientifically crafted child custody evaluations*. Thousand Oaks, CA: Sage.

Grann, M., & Langstrom, N. (2007). Actuarial assessment of violence risk: To weigh or not to weigh? *Criminal Justice and Behavior, 34,* 22–36.

Greenberg, L. A., & Gould, J. W. (2001). The treating expert: A hybrid role with firm boundaries. *Professional Psychology: Research and Practice, 32*(5), 469–478.

Greenberg, S. (1999, February). *Personal injury evaluation: Ethics, practice, instruments and case law*. Workshop presented at the Department of Mental Health Law & Policy, University of South Florida, Tampa, Florida.

Greenberg, S. A. (2003). Personal injury examinations in torts for emotional distress. In I. B. Weiner (Series Ed.) & A. M. Goldstein (Vol. Ed.), *Handbook of psychology: Vol. 11. Forensic psychology* (pp. 233–257). New York: Wiley.

Greenberg, S. A., & Greene, R. (2000, June). *Civil forensic applications of the MMPI-2*. Paper presented at the American Academy of Forensic Psychology, San Juan, Puerto Rico.

Greenberg, S. A., & Humphreys, L. (1998). *Parenting history survey*. (Available from S. Greenberg, Ph.D., 2815 Eastlake Avenue East, Suite 220, Seattle, WA 98102)

Greenberg, S. A., & Shuman, D. W. (1997). Irreconcilable conflict between therapeutic and forensic roles. *Professional Psychology Research and Practice, 28,*
50–57.

Greene, E., Chopra, S. R., Kovera, M. B., Penrod, S. D., Rose, V. G., Schuller, R.,
et al. (2002). Jurors and juries: A review of the field. In J. R. P. Ogloff (Ed.),
*Taking psychology and law into the twenty-first century* (pp. 225–284). New
York: Kluwer Press.

Greene, J. D., Sommerville, R. B., Nystrom, L. E., Darley, J. M., & Cohen, J. D.
(2001, September 14). An fMRI investigation of emotional engagement in
moral judgment. *Science, 293,* 2105–2108.

Greene, R. L. (2002). *The MMPI-2: An interpretive manual* (2nd ed.). Needham
Heights, MA: Allyn & Bacon.

Greenwood, P. W., & Petersilia, J. (1976). *The criminal investigative process.*
Washington, DC: Law Enforcement Assistance Association.

Greer, M. (2004). Ensuring that "good-faith" evaluations are safe. *Monitor on
Psychology, 35,* 25.

Gregory, R. J. (1999). *Foundations of Intellectual assessment: The WAIS-III and other
tests in clinical practice.* Needham Heights, MA: Allyn & Bacon.

*Griggs v. Duke Power Co.,* 401 U.S. 424 (1971).

Grisso, T. (1986). *Evaluating competencies: Forensic assessments and instruments.*
New York: Plenum Press.

Grisso, T. (1987). The economic and scientific future of forensic psychological assessment. *American Psychologist, 9,* 831–839.

Grisso, T. (1988). *Competency to stand trial evaluations: A manual for practice.*
Sarasota, FL: Professional Resource Exchange.

Grisso, T. (1991). A developmental history of the American Psychology-Law
Society. *Law and Human Behavior, 15,* 213–231.

Grisso, T. (1998). *Forensic evaluation of juvenile offenders: A manual for practice.*
Sarasota, FL: Professional Resource Press.

Groth, A. N. (1979). *Men who rape: The psychology of the offender.* New York:
Plenum Press.

Grove, W. M., & Barden, R. C. (1999). Protecting the integrity of the legal system.
*Psychology, Public Policy and Law, 2,* 224–242.

Gunnoe, M. L., & Braver, S. L. (2001). The effects of joint legal custody on mothers, fathers, and children controlling for factors that predispose a sole maternal
versus joint legal award. *Law and Human Behavior, 25,* 25–43.

Guriel, J., Yañez, T., Fremouw, W., Shreve-Neiger, A., Ware, L., Filcheck, H., &
Farr, C. (2004). Impact of coaching on malingered posttraumatic stress symptoms on the M-FAST and the TSI. *Journal of Forensic Psychology Practice, 4*(2),
37–56.

Hagaman, J., Wells, G., Blau, T., & Wells, C. (1987). Psychological profile of a family homicide. *The Police Chief, 54*(12), 19–23.

Hagen, M. A. (1997). *Whores of the court: The fraud of psychiatric testimony and the
rape of American justice.* New York: HarperCollins.

Hagen, M. A., & Castagna, N. (2001). The real numbers: Psychological testing in
custody evaluations. *Professional Psychology: Research and Practice, 32*(3),
269–271.

Hall, D. L. (2005). Domestic violence arrest decision making: The role of suspect
availability in the arrest decision. *Criminal Justice and Behavior, 32,* 390–411.

Hall, G. C. N. (1989). WAIS-R and MMPI profiles of men who have assaulted children: Evidence of limited utility. *Journal of Personality Assessment, 53,* 404–412.

Hammerstein, T. (2002). *Stealth juror: The ultimate defense against bad laws and
government tyranny.* Boulder, CO: Paladin Press.

Handelsman, M. M., Gottlieb, M. C., & Knapp, S. (2005). Training ethical psychologists: An acculturation model. *Professional Psychology: Research and Practice*, 36(1), 59–65.

Hannah-Moffat, K., & Maurutto, P. (2003). *Youth risk/need assessment: An overview of issues and practices*. Department of Justice, Canada. Retrieved March 8, 2005, from http://canada.justice.gc.ca/en/ps/rs/rep/rr03yj-4/rr03yj-4_0.html

Hanson, R. K., & Bussiere, M. T. (1998). Predicting relapse: A meta-analysis of sexual offender recidivism studies. *Journal of Consulting and Clinical Psychology*, 66, 348–362.

Hare, R. D. (2003). *Hare PCL-R Technical Manual* (2nd ed.). North Tonawanda, NY: Multi-Health Systems, Inc.

Hargrave, G., & Berner, J. (1984). *POST psychological screening manual*. Sacramento: California Commission on Police Officer Standards.

Hargrave, G., & Hiatt, D. (1989). Use of the California Psychological Inventory in law enforcement officer selection. *Journal of Personality Assessment*, 53(2), 267–277.

Hargrave, G. E., Hiatt, D., Ogard, E. M., & Karr, C. (1994). Comparison of the MMPI and MMPI-2 for a sample of peace officers. *Psychological Assessment*, 6, 27–32.

*Harris v. Forklift Systems*, 510 U.S. 17,114 S.Ct. 367, 63 FEP. (1993).

Harris, G. T., & Rice, M. E. (2007). Characterizing the value of actuarial violence risk assessments. *Criminal Justice and Behavior*, 34, 1638–1658.

Harris, G. T., Rice, M. E., & Quinsey, V. L. (1993). Violent recidivism of mentally disordered offenders: The development of a statistical prediction instrument. *Criminal Justice and Behavior*, 20, 315–325.

Hart, S. (1998). The role of psychopathy in assessing risk for violence: Conceptual and methodological issues. *Legal and Criminological Psychology*, 3, 121–137.

Hart, S. D., Cox, D. N., & Hare, R. D. (1995). *The Hare Psychopathology Checklist: Screening version*. North Tonawanda, NY: Multi-Health Systems, Inc.

Hatcher, C., Mohandie, K., Turner, J. & Gelles, M. G. (1998). The role of the psychologist in crisis/hostage negotiations. *Behavioral Sciences and the Law*, 16, 455–472.

Hawk, K. M. (1997). Personal reflections on a career in correctional psychology. *Professional Psychology: Research and Practice*, 28(4), 335–337.

Hayes, L. M. (1995, December). National study of jail suicides: Seven years later. *Prison Journal*, 75(4), 431–456.

Haynes, S. N., Richard, D. C. S., & Kubany, E. S. (1995). Content validity in psychological assessment: A functional approach to concepts and methods. *Psychological Assessment*, 7, 238–247.

Hecker, T., & Steinberg, L. (2002). Psychological evaluation at juvenile court disposition. *Professional Psychology: Research and Practice*, 33(3), 300–306.

Heiby, E. M., DeLeon, P. H., & Anderson, T. (2004). A debate on prescription privileges for psychologists. *Professional Psychology: Research and Practice*, 35(4), 336–344.

Heilbrun, K. (1992). Careers. *Psychology Law Society News*, 12(3), 5.

Heilbrun, K. (2000, July 20). *Petition for the recognition of a specialty in professional psychology*. Submitted on behalf of the American Board of Forensic Psychology and the American Psychology-Law Society to the American Psychological Association.

Heilbrun, K., DeMatteo, D., & Goldstein, A. M. (2008). Standards of practice and care in forensic mental health assessment: Legal, professional, and principles-based consideration. *Psychology, Public Policy and Law*, 14(1), 1–26.

Heilbrun, K., Marczyk, G. R., & DeMatteo, D. (2002). *Forensic mental health assessment: A casebook.* New York: Oxford University Press.

Heilbrun, K., Marczyk, G. R., & DeMatteo, D. & Mack-Allen, J. (2007). A principles-based approach to forensic mental health assessment: Utility and update. In A. M. Goldstein (Ed.), *Forensic psychology: Emerging topics and expanding roles* (pp. 45–72). New York: Wiley.

Heilbrun, K., Rogers., R., & Otto, R. (2002). Forensic assessment: current status and future directions. In J. R. P. Ogloff (Ed.), *Taking psychology and law into the twenty-first century* (119–146). New York: Kluwer Academic/Plenum Publishers.

Heilbrun, K., Warren, J., & Picarello, K. (2003). Third party Information in forensic assessment. In I. B. Weiner (Series Ed.) & A. M. Goldstein (Vol. Ed.), *Handbook of psychology: Vol. 11. Forensic psychology* (pp. 69–86). New York: Wiley.

Hemphill, J. F., & Hart, S. D. (2003). Motivating the unmotivated: Psychopathy, treatment, and change. In M. McMurran (Ed.), *Motivating offenders to change: A guide to enhancing engagement in therapy.* Chichester, UK: Wiley.

Herman, J. (1992). *Trauma and recovery.* New York: Basic Books.

Herman, R. M. (1997) Jury selection. *Trial, 33,* 60–63.

Hernandez, D. J. (1993). *America's children: Resources from family, government, and the economy.* New York: Russell Sage Foundation.

Hess, A. K. (1998). Accepting forensic case referrals: Ethical and professional considerations. *Professional Psychology: Research and Practice, 29*(2), 109–114.

Hess, A. K. & Weiner, I. B. (Eds.). (1999). *The handbook of forensic psychology* (2nd ed.). New York: Wiley.

Hetherington, E. M. (1989). Coping with family transitions: Winners, losers, and survivors. *Child Development, 60,* 1–14.

Hibler, N. (1988). Managing a forensic hypnosis program. In J. Reese & J. Horn (Eds.), *Police psychology: Operational assistance* (pp. 199–208). Washington, DC: U.S. government Printing Office, Federal Bureau of Investigation.

Hibler, N., & Kurke, M. I. (1995). Ensuring personal reliability through selection and training. In M. I. Kurke & E. M. Scrivner (Eds.), *Police psychology into the 21st century* (pp. 57–91). Hillsdale, NJ: Erlbaum.

Hilgard, E. R. (1992). Divided consciousness and dissociation. *Consciousness and Cognition, 1,* 16–31.

Hoge, S. K., Bonnie, R. J., Poythress, N., & Monahan, J. (1992). Attorney-client decision-making in criminal cases: Client competence and participation as perceived by their attorneys. *Behavioral Sciences and the Law, 10,* 385–394.

Holcomb, W. B. (2006). Thinking correctly about ethics. *Psyc Critiques, 51,* Article 6.

Holden, E. J. (2000). Special issue: Post conviction polygraph testing. *Polygraph, 29*(1).

Hollin, C. R., McGuire, J., Hounsome, J. C., Hatcher, R. M., Bilby, C. A. L., & Palmer, E. J. (2008). Cognitive skills behavior programs for offenders in the community. *Criminal Justice and Behavior, 35,* 269–283.

Holloway, J. D. (2005). Managed-care suit brings concessions. *Monitor on Psychology 36*(5), 32.

Holmes, D. S. (1990). The evidence for repression: An examination of sixty years of research. In J. L. Singer (Ed.), *Repression and dissociation* (pp. 85–102). Chicago: University of Chicago Press.

Hoover, L. (1989). Psychological service units. In W. G. Bailey (Ed.), *The encyclopedia of police science.* New York: Garland Publishing.

Horvath, L. S., Logan, T. K., & Walker, R. (2002). Child custody cases: A content analysis of evaluations in practice. *Professional Psychology: Research and Practice*, 33(6), 557–565.

Huff, R., Rattner, A., & Sagarin E. (1986). Guilty until proven innocent. *Crime and Delinquency*, 32, 518–544.

Hughes, R. (1996). *Demographics of divorce. Internet in-service on children and divorce*. Columbus: Ohio State University. Retrieved March 21, 2005, from http://www.hec.ohiostate.edu/famlife/divorce/index.htm

Huss, M. T. (2009). Forensic psychology: Research, clinical practice, and applications. Malden, MA: Wiley-Blackwell.

Huss, M. T., & Ralston, A. (2008). Do batterer subtypes actually matter? Treatment completion, treatment response, and recidivism across a batterer typology. *Criminal Justice and Behavior*, 35, 710–724.

Hyman, I. E., & Billings, F. J. (1998). Individual differences and the creation of false childhood memories. *Memory*, 6, 1–20.

Hyman, I. E., Husband, T. H., & Billings, F. J. (1995) False memories of childhood experiences. *Applied Cognitive Psychology*, 9, 181–197.

Hyman, I. E., & Pentland, J. (1996). The role of mental imagery in the creation of false childhood memories. *Journal of Memory and Language*, 35, 101–117.

Hysjulien, C., Wood, B., & Benjamin, G. A. H. (1994). Child custody evaluations: A review of methods used in litigation and alternative dispute resolution. *Family and Conciliation Courts Review*, 32, 466–489.

IACP Police Psychological Services Section. (1998). *Fitness-for-duty evaluation guidelines*. Alexandria, VA: IACP Police Psychological Services Section. *In re Cendant Corp. Securities Litigation*, 3d Cir., No. 02-4386, 9/16/03.

Insanity Defense Reform Act. (1984). Pub. L. 98-473, 18 U.S.C. 401–406.

International Association of Chiefs of Police. (1999). The future of women in policing: mandates for action. *Police Chief*, 66(3), 53–56.

Inwald, R. E. (1992). *Inwald Personality Inventory Technical Manual* (Rev. ed.). Kew Gardens, NY: Hilson Research.

IPAT Staff. (1972). *Manual for the 16 PF*. Champaign, IL: Institute for Personality and Ability Testing.

Jackson, N. (2003). Bankruptcy as it affects character and fitness. *The Bar Examiner*, 72, 6–13.

*Jackson v. Indiana*, 406 U.S. 715 (1972).

Janik, J. (1994). Why psychological screening of police candidates is necessary: The history and rationale. *Journal of Police and Criminal Psychology*, 10, 18–23.

Janniro, M. J., & Cestaro, V. L. (1996). *Effectiveness of detection of deception examinations using the computer voice stress analyzer* (Report No. DoDPI96-R-0005). Ft. McClellan, AL: U.S. Department of Defense Polygraph Institute.

Janus, E. S. (2000). Sexual predator commitment laws: Lessons for law and the behavioral sciences. *Behavioral Sciences and the Law*, 18, 5–21.

Janus, E. S., & Walbek, N. H. (2000). Sex offender commitments in Minnesota: A descriptive study of second generation commitments. *Behavioral Sciences and the Law*, 18, 343–374.

*J. E. B. v. Alabama ex rel.* T.B., 114 S. Ct. 1419, 62 U.S.L.W. 4219 (1994).

*Jenkins v. United States*, 307 F.2nd 637 (U.S. App. D.C., 1962).

Jensen, E. (1993). When "hired guns" backfire: The witness immunity doctrine and the negligent expert witness. *University of Missouri at Kansas City Law Review*, 62, 185–207.

Jobes, D. A., Berman, A. L., & Josselson, A. R. (1987). Improving the validity and reliability of medical–legal certifications of suicide. *Suicide and Life-threatening Behaviors*, 17(4), 310–325.

*Joseph v. Brierton*, 739 F.2d 1244 (1984).

Johnson, W. B. (2003). A framework for conceptualizing competence to mentor. *Ethics and Behavior, 13*, 127–151.

Johnson, W. B., & Campell, C. D. (2002). Character and fitness requirements for professional psychologists: Are there any? *Professional Psychology: Research and Practice, 33*, 46–53.

Johnson, W. B., & Campbell, C. D. (2004). Character and fitness requirements for professional psychologists: training director's perspectives. *Professional Psychology: Research and Practice, 35*(4), 405–411.

*Jones v. Tri-County Electric Cooperative*, 512 F:2d 13 (5th Cir. 1975).

Jurkanin, T. J., Hoover, L. T., & Sergevinin, V. A. (Eds.). (2008). Improving police response to persons with mental illness: A progressive approach. *Criminal Justice and Behavior, 35*, 536–538.

Kalter, N., Kloner, A., Schreier, S., & Okla, K. (1989). Predictors of children's post-divorce adjustment. *American Journal of Orthopsychiatry, 59*, 605–618.

Kamphaus, R. W., Petoskey, M. D., & Rowe, E. W. (2000). Current trends in the psychological testing of children. *Professional Psychology: Research and Practice, 31*, 155–164.

Kane, A. W. (1999a). Essentials of civil commitment assessment. In *Essentials of forensic psychological assessment* (pp. 136–164). New York: Wiley.

Kane, A. W. (1999b). Essentials of malingering assessment. *Essentials of forensic psychological assessment* (pp. 78–99). New York: Wiley.

*Kansas v. Hendricks*, 117 S. Ct. 2072 (1997).

Karon, B. P., & Widener, A. J. (1998). Repressed memories: The real story. *Professional Psychology: Research and Practice, 29*, 482–487.

Karon, B. P., & Widener, A. J. (1999). Repressed memories: Just the facts. *Professional Psychology: Research and Practice, 30*(6), 625–626.

Kaslow, N. J. (2004). Competencies in professional psychology. *American Psychologist, 59*(8), 774–781.

Kassin, S. M. (1998). Eyewitness identification procedures: The fifth rule. *Law and Human Behavior, 22*, 649–653.

Kassin, S. M. (2005). On the psychology of confessions: Does innocence put innocents at risk? *American Psychologist, 60*(3), 215–228.

Kassin, S. M., Ellsworth, P. C., & Smith, V. L. (1989). The "general acceptance" of psychological research on eyewitness testimony: A survey of the experts. *American Psychologist, 44*, 1089–1098.

Keane, T. M., Malloy, P. F., & Fairbank, J. A. (1984). Empirical development of the MMPI subscale for the assessment of combat-related post-traumatic stress disorder. *Journal of Consulting and Clinical Psychology, 52*, 888–891.

Keilin, W. G., & Bloom, L. J. (1986). Child custody evaluation practices: A survey of experienced professionals. *Professional Psychology: Research and Practice, 17*, 338–346.

Kellerman, A. L., & Mercy, J. M. (1992). Men, women, and murder: Gender-specific differences in rates of fatal violence and victimization. *Journal of Trauma, 33*, 1–5.

Kelly, J. B. (2000). Children's adjustment in conflicted marriage and divorce: A decade review of research. *Journal of the American Academy of Child and Adolescent Psychiatry, 39*, 963–973.

Kersting, K. (2003). New hope for sex offender treatment. *APA Monitor, 34*(7), 52–53.

Kim, D. Y., Joo, H. J., & McCarty, W. P. (2008). Risk assessment and classification of day reporting center clients: an actuarial approach. *Criminal Justice and Behavior, 35*, 792-812.

Kirkland, K., & Kirkland, K. L. (2001). Frequency of child custody evaluation complaints and related disciplinary action: A survey of the Association of State and provincial Psychology Boards. *Professional Psychology: Research and Practice*, 32(2), 171–174.

Kirkpatrick, H. D. (2004). A floor, not a ceiling: Beyond guidelines—an argument for minimum standards of practice in conducting child custody and visitation evaluations. *Journal of Child Custody: Research, Issues, and Practices*, 61–75.

Klein, M. (1986). Hypnosis in police work. In W. Bailey (Ed.), *The encyclopedia of police science*. New York: Garland Publishing.

Klobuchar, A., Steblay, N. K., & Caligiuri, H. L. (2006). Improving eyewitness identifications: Hennepin county's blind sequential lineup pilot project. *Cardozo Public Law, Policy and Ethics Journal*, 4, 381–413.

Klyce, J. (1994, July 24). Acting up in court. *The Montgomery Journal*. Retrieved August 2, 2005, from http://www.ontrialassociates.com/news/9.html

Knapp, S., & VandeCreek, L. (2000). Recovered memories of childhood abuse: Is there an underlying professional consensus? *Professional Psychology: Research and Practice*, 31(4), 365–371.

Knapp, S., & VandeCreek, L. (2001). Psychotherapists' legal responsibility to third parties: Does it extend to alleged perpetrators of childhood abuse? *Professional Psychology: Research and Practice*, 32(5), 479–483.

Knapp, S., & VandeCreek, L. (2003). An overview of the major changes in the 2002 APA Ethics Code. *Professional Psychology: Research and Practice*, 34(3), 301–308.

Knight, S. C., & Meyer, R. G. (2007). Forensic hypnosis. In A. M. Goldstein (Ed.), *Forensic psychology: Emerging topics and expanding roles* (pp. 734–763). New York: Wiley.

Kocsis, R. N. (2003) Criminal psychological profiling: Validities and abilities *International Journal of Offender Therapy and Comparative Criminology*, 47(2), 126–144.

Kocsis, R. N., & Cooksey R. W. (2002). Criminal psychological profiling of serial arson crimes. *International Journal of Offender Therapy and Comparative Criminology*, 46(6), 631–656.

Kocsis, R. N., Cooksey, R. W., & Irwin, H. J. (2002). Psychological profiling of offender characteristics from crime behaviors in serial rape offenses. *International Journal of Offender Therapy and Comparative Criminology*, 46, 144–169.

Koocher, G. P., & Keith-Spiegel, P. (1998). *Ethics in psychology: Professional standards and cases*. New York: Oxford University Press.

Kornfield, A. D. (1995). Police officer candidate MMPI-2 performance: Gender, ethnic, and normative factors. *Journal of Clinical Psychology*, 51, 536–540.

Kovera, M. B., & McAuliff, B. D. (2000). The effects of peer review and evidence quality on judge evaluations of psychological science: Are judges effective gatekeepers? *Journal of Applied Psychology*, 85, 574–586.

Kovera, M. B., Dickinson, J. J., & Cutler, B. L. (2003). Voir dire and jury selection. In I. B. Weiner (Series Ed.) & A. M. Goldstein (Vol. Ed.), *Handbook of psychology: Vol. 11. Forensic psychology* (pp. 161–175). New York: Wiley.

Kraemer, H., Kazdin, A., Oxford, D., Kessler, R., Jensen, P., & Kupfer, D. (1997). Coming to terms with the terms of risk. *Archives of General Psychiatry*, 54, 337.

Krafka, C., Dunn, M. A., Johnson, M. T., Cecil, J. S., & Miletich, D. (2002). Judge and attorney experiences, practices, and concerns regarding expert testimony in federal civil trials. *Psychology, Public Policy and Law*, 8, 309–331.

Kratcoski, P. C. (1994). *Correctional counseling and treatment* (3rd ed.). Prospect Heights: IL.: Waveland.

Krauss, D. A., & Sales, B. D. (2000). Legal standards, expertise, and experts in the resolution of contested child custody cases. *Psychology, Public Policy, and Law*, 6, 843–879.

Kravitz, D. A., Cutler, B. L., & Brock, P. (1993). Reliability and validity of the original and revised Legal Attitudes Questionnaire. *Law and Human Behavior*, 17, 661–667.

Kressel, N. J., & Kressel, D. F. (2002). *Stack and sway: The new science of jury consulting*. Boulder, CO: Westview Press.

Kuanliang, A., Sorensen, J. R., & Cunningham, M. D. (2008). Juvenile inmates in an adult prison system. *Criminal Justice and Behavior*, 35, 1186–1201.

Kuehnle, K. (1996). *Assessing allegations of child sexual abuse*. Sarasota, FL: Professional Resource Press.

Kuehnle, K., Connell, M., & Otto, R. (2004, August). *Child custody evaluations: Did we forget the child?* Paper presented at the annual meeting of the American Psychological Association, Honolulu, Hawaii.

*Kumbo Tire Company Ltd. et al. v. Carmichael et al.*, 526 U.S. 137 (1999).

Kupers, T. A. (2008). What to do with the survivors? Coping with the long-term effects of isolated confinement. *Criminal Justice and Behavior*, 35, 1005–1016.

Kureczka, A. W. (1996). Critical incident stress in law enforcement. *FBI Law Enforcement Bulletin*, 65, 10–17.

Kureczka, A. W. (2002). Perspective: surviving assaults—after the physical battle ends, the psychological battle begins. *FBI Law Enforcement Bulletin*, 71, 18–21.

Kuther, T. L. (2004). *Your career in psychology: Psychology and law*. Belmont, CA: Wadsworth.

Kuther, T. L., & Morgan, R. (2004). *Extending the boundaries of psychology: Career opportunities in a changing world*. Pacific Grove, CA: Wadsworth.

Ladd, M. (1952). Expert testimony. *Vanderbilt Law Review*, 5, 414–419.

Laddis, B., Convit, A., Zito, J., & Vitrai, J. (1993). The disposition of criminal charges after involuntary medication to restore competency to stand trial. *Journal of Forensic Sciences*, 38, 1442–1459.

Lafon, D. S. (1999). Psychological autopsies for equivocal deaths. *International Journal of Emergency Mental Health*, 3, 183–188.

Lafon, D. S. (2002). The psychological autopsy. In B. Turvey (Ed.), *Criminal profiling: An introduction to behavioral evidence analysis* (2nd ed., pp. 158–167). New York: Academic Press.

La Fond, J. Q. (2000). The future of involuntary civil commitment in the U.S.A. after *Kansas v. Hendricks*. *Behavioral Sciences and the Law*, 18, 153–167.

La Fond, J. Q. (2003). Outpatient commitment's next frontier: Sexual predators. *Psychology, Public Policy, and Law*, 9, 159–182.

LaFortune, K. A., & Carpenter, B. N. (1998). Custody evaluations: A survey of mental health professionals. *Behavioral Sciences and the Law*, 16, 207–224.

LaFortune, K., & Nicholson, R. (1995). How adequate are Oklahoma's mental health evaluations for determining competency in criminal proceedings? The bench and the bar respond. *Journal of Psychiatry and Law*, 23, 231–262.

Lally, S. J. (2003). What tests are acceptable for use in forensic evaluations?: A survey of experts. *Professional Psychology: Research and Practice*, 34(5), 491–498.

Lamb, D. H., & Catanzaro, S. (1998). Sexual and nonsexual boundary violations involving psychologists, clients, supervisees, and students: Implications for professional practice. *Professional Psychology: Research and Practice*, 29, 498–503.

Lamb, D. H., Catanzaro, S. J., & Moorman, A. S. (2004). A preliminary look at how psychologists identify, evaluate, and proceed when faced with possible multiple relationship dilemmas. *Professional Psychology; Research and Practice, 35*(3), 248–254.

Lambert, E. G., Hogan, N. L., & Griffin, M. L. (2008). Being the good soldier: Organizational citizenship behavior and commitment among correctional staff. *Criminal Justice and Behavior, 35,* 56–68.

Lambert, M. J., & Hawkins, E. J. (2004). Measuring outcome in professional practice: Considerations in selecting and using brief outcome instruments. *Professional Psychology: Research and Practice, 35*(5), 492–499.

Langan, P., & Conniff, M. (1992). Recidivism of felons on probation, 1986–1989. *Special report.* Washington, DC: U.S. Department of Justice.

Langleben, D. D., Schroeder, L., Maldjian, J. A., Gur, R. C., McDonald, S., Ragland, J. D., et al. (2002). Brain activity during simulated deception: An event-related functional magnetic resonance study. *NeuroImage, 15,* 727–732.

Langton, C. M., Barbaree, H. E., Harkins, L., Arenovich, T., McNamee, J., Peacock, E. J., et al. (2008). Denial and minimization among sexual offenders: Post-treatment presentation and association with sexual recidivism. *Criminal Justice and Behavior, 35,* 69–98.

Langton, C. M., Barbaree, H. E., Seto, M. C., Peacock, E. J., Harkins, L., & Hansen, K. T. (2007). Actuarial assessment of risk for reoffense among adult sex offenders: Evaluating the predictive accuracy of the Static-2002 and five other instruments. *Criminal Justice and Behavior, 34,* 37–59.

Lanyon, R. I. (2001). Psychological assessment procedures in sex offending. *Professional Psychology: Research and Practice, 32*(3), 253–260.

Leahey, T. H. (1997). *A history of psychology: Main currents in psychological thought.* (4th ed.). Upper Saddle River, N.J.: Prentice-Hall.

Lee, C. M., Beauregard, C. P. M., & Hunsley, J. (1998). Lawyers' opinions regarding child custody mediation and assessment services: Implications for psychological practice. *Professional Psychology: Research and Practice, 29,* 115–120.

Lee, G. P., Loring, D. W., & Martin, R. C. (1992). Rey's 15-item Visual Memory Test for the detection of malingering: Normative observations in patients with neurological disorders. *Psychological Assessment, 4,* 43–46.

Lee, T. M. C., Liu, H. L., Tan, L. H., Chan, C. C. H., Mahankali, S., Feng, C. M., et al. (2002). Lie detection by functional magnetic resonance imaging. *Human Brain Mapping, 15,* 157–164.

Lees-Haley, P. R. (1992). Psychodiagnostic test usage by forensic psychologists. *American Journal of Forensic Psychology, 10*(1), 25–30.

Lees-Haley, P. R. (1997). Attorneys influence expert evidence in forensic psychological and neuropsychological cases. *Assessment, 4,* 321–324.

Lees-Haley, P., Smith, H. H., Williams, C. W., & Dunn, J. T. (1996). Forensic neuropsychological test usage: An empirical study. *Clinical Neuropsychology, 11,* 45–47.

Lefkowitz, J. (1977). Industrial–organizational psychology and the police. *American Psychologist, 32*(5), 346–364.

Leippe, M. R. (1995). The case for expert testimony about eyewitness memory. *Psychology, Public Policy, and Law, 1,* 909–959.

Levine, M. (2001). Persuasion in advocacy: Conditioning the jury in voir dire and opening statement. *Trial Lawyers Quarterly, 30,* 141–146.

Levitt, E., & Webb, J. (1992). The MMPI is still preferred over the MMPI-2. *The National Psychologist, 1*(2).

Lezak, M. D. (1983). *Neuropsychological assessment.* New York: Oxford University Press.

Lieberman, J., & Sales, B. (2006). *Scientific jury selection.* Washington, DC: American Psychological Association.

Lilienfeld, S. O., & Loftus, E. F. (1999). A step backward in the recovered memory debate. *Professional Psychology: Research and Practice, 30*(6), 623.

Lilienfeld, S. O., Wood, J. M., & Garb, H. N. (2001). The scientific status of projective techniques. *Psychological Science in the Public Interest, 20,* 27–66.

Liotti, T. F., & Cole, A. H. (2000). Quick voir dire: Making the most of 15 minutes. *Journal of the New York State Bar Association, 72*(7), 39–42.

Lipsitt, P. D. (2007). Ethics and forensic psychological practice. In A. M. Goldstein (Ed.), *Forensic psychology: Emerging topics and expanding roles* (pp. 171 –189). New York: Wiley.

Lipsitt, P. D., & Lelos, D. (1970). Competency to stand trial assessment instrument. *Innovations in clinical practice: A source book* (pp. 278–284). Sarasota, Fl: Professional Resource Exchange.

Lipsitt, P., Lelos, D., & McGarry, A. L. (1971). Competency for trial: A screening instrument. *American Journal of Psychiatry, 128,* 105–109.

Listwan, S. J., van Voorhis, P., & Ritchey, P. N. (2007). Personality, criminal behavior, and risk assessment: Implications for theory and practice. *Criminal Justice and Behavior, 34,* 60–75.

Loftus, E. F. (1979). *Eyewitness testimony.* Cambridge, MA: Harvard University Press.

Loftus, E. F. (1992). When a lie becomes memory's truth: Memory distortion after exposure to misinformation. *Psychological Science, 3,* 121–123.

Loftus, E. F. (1993). Psychologists in the eyewitness world. *American Psychologist, 48,* 550–552.

Loftus, E. F. (1997). Creating false memories. *Scientific American,* pp. 71–75.

Loftus, E. F. (1997). Memory for a past that never was. *Current Directions in Psychological Science, 6,* 60–65.

Loftus, E. F., & Ketcham, K. (1994). *The myth of repressed memory.* New York: St. Martin's Press.

Loftus, E. F., & Palmer, J. C. (1974). Reconstruction of automobile destruction: An example of the interaction between language and memory. *Journal of Verbal Learning and Verbal Behavior, 13,* 585–589.

Loftus, E. F., & Pickrell, J. E. (1995). The formation of false memories. *Psychiatric Annals, 25,* 720–725.

Look, L. (2004). Critical incident stress debriefing: Some perspectives. *The Cost of Traumatic Stress.*

Loranger, A. W., Sartorius, N., Andreoli, A., Berger, P., Buchheim, P., Channabasavanna, S. M., et al. (1994). The international personality disorder examination: The World Health Organization/Alcohol, Drug Abuse and Mental Health Administration international pilot study of personality disorders. *Archives of General Psychiatry, 51,* 215–224.

Lovell, D. (2008). Patterns of disturbed behavior in a supermax population. *Criminal Justice and Behavior, 35,* 985–1004.

Low, P. W., Jeffries, J. C., & Bonnie, R. J. (1986). *The trial of John W. Hinckley Jr.: A case study in the insanity defense.* Minneola, NY: Foundation Press.

Lykken, D. T. (1959). The GSR in the detection of guilt. *Journal of Applied Psychology, 43,* 385–388.

Lykken, D. T. (1960). The validity of the Guilty Knowledge Technique: The effects of faking. *Journal of Applied Psychology, 44,* 258–262.

Lykken, D, T. (1974). Psychology and the lied detector industry. *American Psychologist, 29,* 725–739.

Lykken, D. T. (1981). *A tremor in the blood: Uses and abuses of the lie detector.* New York: McGraw-Hill.

Lykken, D. T. (1988). The case against polygraph testing. In A. Gale (Ed.), *The polygraph test: Lies, truth and science* (111–125). London: sage.

Lynn, S. J., Myers, B., & Malinoski, P. (1997). Hypnosis, pseudomemories, and clinical guidelines: A socio-cognitive perspective. In D. Read & S. Lindsay (Eds.), *Recollections of trauma: Scientific research and clinical practice*. New York: Plenum Press.

Maccoby, E. E., & Mnookin, R. H. (1988). Custody of children following divorce. In E. M. Hetherington & J. D. Aresteh (Eds.), *Impact of divorce, single parenting, and stepparenting on children* (pp. 110–149). Hillsdale, NJ: Erlbaum.

Maccoby, E. E., & Mnookin, R. H. (1992). *Dividing the child: Social and legal dimensions of child custody.* Cambridge, MA: Harvard University Press.

Maccoby, E. E., Mnookin, R. H., Depner, C. E., & Peters, E. H. (1992). *Dividing the child: Social and legal dimensions of child custody.* Cambridge, MA: Harvard University Press.

MacCoun, R. J., Lind, E. A., & Tyler, T. R. (1992). Alternative dispute resolution in trial and appellate courts. In D. K. Kagehiro & W. S. Laufer (Eds.), *Handbook of psychology and law* (pp. 95–118). New York: Springer-Verlag.

MacKain, S. J., Tedeschi, R. G., Durham, T. W., & Goldman, V. J. (2002). So what are the master's-level psychology practitioners doing? Surveys of employers and recent graduates in North Carolina. *Professional Psychology: Research and Practice, 33*(4), 408–412.

Magaletta, P. R., Patry, M. W., Dietz, E. F., & Ax, R. K. (2007). What is correctional about clinical practice in corrections? *Criminal Justice and Behavior, 34*, 7–21.

Magaletta, P. R., & Verdeyen, V. (2005). Clinical practice in corrections: A conceptual framework. *Professional Psychology: Research and Practice, 36*(1), 37–43.

Magdol, L., Moffit, T. E., Caspi, A., & Silva, P. A. (1998). Developmental antecedents of partner abuse: A prospective-longitudinal study. *Journal of Abnormal Psychology, 107*, 373–389.

Magley, V. J., Waldo, C. R., Drasgow, F., & Fitzgerald, L. F. (1999). The impact of sexual harassment on military personnel: Is it the same for men and women? *Military Psychology, 11*, 283–302.

Mahalik, J. R., Good, G. E., & Englar-Carlson, M. (2003). Masculinity scripts, presenting concerns, and help seeking: Implications for practice and training. *Professional Psychology: Research and Practice, 34*(3), 123–131.

Malpass, R. S., & Devine, P. G. (1981). Eyewitness identification: Lineup instructions and the absence of the offender. *Journal of Applied Psychology, 66*, 482–489.

Mannheim, C. I., Sancilio, M., Phipps-Yonas, S., Brunnquell, D., Somers, P., Farseth, G., & Ninonuevo, F. (2002). Ethical ambiguities in the practice of child clinical psychology. *Professional Psychology: Research and Practice, 33*(1), 24–29.

Marston, W. M. (1917) Systolic blood pressure changes in deception. *Journal of Experimental Psychology, 2*, 143–163.

Mason, M. A., & Quirk, A. (1997). Are mothers losing custody?: Read my lips: Trends in judicial decision-making in custody disputes—1920, 1960, 1990, and 1995. *Family Law Quarterly, 31*, 215–236.

Masten, A. S. (2001). Ordinary magic: Resilience processes in development. *American Psychologist, 56*, 227–238.

Matarazzo, J. D. (1990). Psychological assessment versus psychological testing. *American Psychologist, 45*, 999–1017.

Maudsley, H. (1898). *Responsibility in Mental Disease.* New York: D. Appleton & Co.

Mauer, M. (1999). *Race to incarcerate.* New York: The New Press.

Mauet, T. A. (1992). *Fundamentals of trial techniques* (3rd ed.). Boston: Little, Brown.

Mcelvain, J. P., & Kposowa, A. J. (2008). Police officer characteristics and the likelihood of using deadly force. *Criminal Justice and Behavior, 35,* 505–521.

*McCabe v. Hoberman,* 33 A. D.2d 547 (1st Dept. 1969).

McCann, J. T. (1990). A multitrait-multimethod analysis of the MCMI-II clinical syndrome scales. *Journal of Personality Assessment, 55,* 465–476.

McCann, J. T., & Dyer, F. J. (1996). *Forensic assessment with the Million Inventories* New York: Guilford Press.

McCarter, W. D. (1999). Juror nondisclosure. *Journal of the Missouri Bar, 55,* 214–220.

McCloskey, K., & Grigsby, N. (2005). The ubiquitous clinical problem of adult intimate partner violence: The need for routine assessment. *Professional Psychology: Research and Practice, 36,* 264–275.

*McDonald v. United States,* 312 F.2nd 844 (D.C. Cir. 1962).

McEvoy, M. (2005). Psychological first aid: replacement for critical incident stress debriefing? *Fire Engineering* (pp. 63–67).

McEvoy, M. (2006). Psychological first aid: replacement for critical incident stress debriefing? *Fire Engineering,* 63–66.

McGrath, M. G. (2000). Criminal Profiling: Is there a role for the forensic psychiatrist? *Journal of the American Academy of Psychiatry and Law, 28*(3), 314–324.

McGrath, M., & Turvey, B. E. (2002). Sexual asphyxia. B. Turvey (Ed.), *Criminal profiling: An introduction to behavioral evidence analysis* (2nd ed., pp. 479–496). New York: Academic Press.

McGrath, R. E., Wiggins, J. G., Sammons, M. T., Levant, R. F., Brown, A., & Srock, W. (2004). Professional issues in psychopharmacotherapy for psychologists. *Professional Psychology: Research and Practice, 35*(2), 158–163.

McGrath, R. J., Hoke, S. E., & Vojtisek, J. E. (1998). Cognitive-behavioral treatment of sex offenders. *Criminal Justice and Behavior, 25,* 203–225.

McGuire, J. (2001). Treatment approaches for offenders with mental disorder. In L. Motiuk & R. Serin (Eds.), *Compendium 2000 on effective correctional programming* (pp. 122–134).

McIntosh, J. A., & Prinz, J. A. (1993). The incidence of alleged sexual abuse in 603 family court cases. *Law and Human Behavior, 17,* 95–101.

*McKune v. Lile,* U.S. (2002).

McMains, M. (1988). Psychologists' roles in hostage negotiations. In J. Reese & J. Horn (Eds.), *Police psychology: Operational assistance* (pp. 281–317). Washington, DC: U.S. Government Printing Office, Federal Bureau of Investigation.

McNulty, M. J. (2000). Practical tips for effective voir dire. *Louisiana Bar Journal, 48,* 110–114.

*McWilliams v. Fairfax County Bd. Of Supervisors,* 72 F.3d 1191, 69 FEP 1082 (4th Cir. 1996).

Medoff, D. (1999). MMPI-2 validity scales in child custody evaluations: Clinical vs. statistical significance. *Behavioral Sciences and the Law, 17,* 409–411.

Meehl, P. (1954). *Clinical versus statistical predictions: A theoretical analysis and a review of the evidence.* Minneapolis: University of Minnesota.

Meichenbaum, D., & Turk, D. C. (1987). *Facilitating treatment adherence: A practitioner's guidebook.* New York: Plenum Press.

Melton, G. B. (1987). Training in psychology and law. In I. B. Weiner & A. K. Hess (Eds.), *Handbook of forensic psychology* (pp. 681–697). New York: Wiley.

Melton, G. B., Petrila, J., Poythress, N., & Slobogin, C. (1997). *Psychological evaluations for the courts: A handbook for mental health professionals and lawyers* (Rev. ed.) New York: Guilford Press.

Melton, G. B., Petrila, J., Poythress, N. G., & Solbogin, C. (2007). *Psychological evaluations for the courts: A handbook for mental health professionals and lawyers* (3rd ed.) New York: Guilford Press.

Melton, G. B., Weithorn, L. A., & Slobogin, C. (1985). *Community mental health centers and the courts: An evaluation of community-based forensic services.* Lincoln: University of Nebraska Press.

*Meritor Savings Bank v. Vinson*, 106 S. Ct. 2399, 40 EPD 36, 159 (1986).

Merry, S., & Harsent, L. (2000). Intruders, pilferers, raiders, and invaders: the interpersonal dimension of burglary. In D. Canter & L. Alison (Eds.), *Profiling property crimes* (pp. 31–56). Dartmouth, UK: Ashgate.

Meyerhoff, J. L., Saviolakis, G. A., Koenig, M. L., & Yourick, D. L. (2000). *Physiological and biochemical measures of stress compared to voice stress analysis using the computer voice stress analyzer (CVSA)* (Report No. DoDPI98-P-0004). Ft. Jackson, SC: U.S. Department of Defense Polygraph Institute.

Meyers, J. R., Schmidt, F. (2008). Predictive validity of the structured assessment for violence risk in youth (SAVRY) with juvenile offenders. *Criminal Justice and Behavior*, 344–355.

Michel, W., & Michel, H. N. (1977). *Essentials of psychology.* New York: Random House.

Milan, M. A., Chin, C. E., & Nguyen, Z. X. (1999). Practicing psychology in correctional settings: Assessment, treatment, and substance abuse programs. In A. K. Hess & I. B. Weiner (Eds.), *The handbook of forensic psychology* (2nd ed., pp. 580–602). New York: Wiley.

Miller, D. (2002). Advancing mental health in political places. *Professional psychology: Research and Practice*, 33(3), 277–280.

Miller, H. A. (2001). *M-Fast: Miller Forensic Assessment of Symptoms Test.* Sarasota, FL: Psychological Assessment Resources, Inc.

Miller, J. (2001). The use of debriefing in schools. *Smith College in Social Work*, 71, 259–272.

Miller, R. D. (2003). Hospitalization of criminal defendants for evaluation of competence to stand trial or for restoration of competence: Clinical and legal Issues. *Behavioral Sciences and the Law*, 21, 369–391.

Millon, C., & Davis, R. (1994). MCMI-III Manual: Millon Clinical Multiaxial Inventory–III. Minneapolis, MN: National Computer Systems.

Moleski, S. M., & Kiselica, M. S. (2005). Dual relationships: A continuum ranging from the destructive to the therapeutic. *Journal of Counseling and Development*, 83(1), 3–11.

Monahan, J. (Ed.). (1980). *Who is the client?: The ethics of psychological intervention in the criminal justice system.* Washington, DC: American Psychological Association.

Monahan, J. (1993). Limiting therapist exposure to *Tarasoff* liability: Guidelines for risk containment. *American Psychologist. 48*, 242–250.

Monohan, J. (2003). Violence risk assessment. In I. B. Weiner (Series Ed.) & A. M. Goldstein (Vol. Ed.), *Handbook of Psychology: Vol. 11. Forensic psychology* (pp. 527–540). New York: Wiley.

Monahan, J., Steadman, H. J., Silver, E., Appelbaum, P. S., Robbins, P. C., Mulvey, E. P., et al. (2001). *Rethinking risk assessment: The MacArthur Study of Mental Disorder and Violence.* New York: Oxford University Press.

Monahan, J., & Walker, L. (1988). Social science research in law: A new paradigm. *American Psychologist*, 43, 465–472.

Montgomery, L. M., Cupit, B. E., & Wimberly, T. K. (1999). Complaints, malpractice, and management: Professional Issues and personal experiences. *Professional Psychology: Research and Practice*, 30, 402–410.

Moran, G., & Comfort, J. C. (1986). Neither "tentative" nor "fragmentary": Verdict preference of impaneled felony jurors as a function of attitude toward capital punishment. *Journal of Applied Psychology, 71,* 146–155.

Moran, G., Cutler, B. L., & De Lisa, A. (1994). Attitudes toward tort reform, scientific jury selection and juror bias: Verdict inclinations in criminal and civil trials. *Law and Psychology Review, 18,* 309–328.

Moran, G., Cutler, B. L., & Loftus, E. F. (1990). Jury selection in major controlled substance trials: The need for extended voir dire. *Forensic Reports, 3,* 331–348.

Moran, R. (1981). *Knowing right from wrong: The insanity defense of Daniel McNaughten.* New York: The Free Press.

Morey, L. C. (1991). *The Personality Assessment Inventory: Professional manual.* Odessa, FL: Psychological Assessment Resources.

Morgan, R. (2003). Basic mental health service: Services and issues. In T. Fagan & B. Ax (Eds.), *Correctional mental health handbook* (pp. 59–72). Thousand Oaks, CA: Sage.

Morgan, R. D., Beer, A. M., Fitzgerald, K. L., & Mandracchia, J. T. (2007). Graduate students' experiences, interests, and attitudes toward correctional/forensic psychology. *Criminal Justice and Behavior, 34,* 96–107.

Morgan, R. D., Rozycki, A. T., & Wilson, S. (2004). Inmate perceptions of mental health services. *Professional Psychology: Research and Practice, 35*(4), 389–395.

Morgan, R. D., Winterowd, C. L., & Ferrell, S. W. (1999). A national survey of group psychotherapy services in correctional facilities. *Professional Psychology: Research and Practice, 30,* 600–606.

Moriarty, A. R., & Field, M. W. (1994). *Police officer selection: A handbook for law enforcement administrators.* Springfield, IL: Thomas.

Morris, G. H., & Meloy, J. R. (1993). Out of mind? Out of sight: The uncivil commitment of permanently incompetent criminal defendants. *U.C.-Davis Law Review, 27,* 1–96.

Morris, J. S., Friston, K. J., Buchel, C., Frith, C. D., Young, A. W., Calder, A. J., et al. (1998). A neuromodulatory role for the human amygdale in processing emotional facial expressions. *Brain, 121,* 47–57.

Morse, S. J. (1978). Law and mental health professionals: The limits of expertise. *Professional Psychology, 9,* 389–399.

Morse, S. J. (2003). Involuntary competence. *Behavioral Sciences and the Law, 21,* 311–328.

Moser, C. (1994). The unthinkable happens. *OH&S Canada, 10,* 38–48.

Mossman, D. (1994). Assessing predictions of violence: Being accurate about accuracy. *Journal of Consulting and Clinical Psychology, 62,* 783–792.

Mufson, D., & Mufson, M. A. (1998). Predicting police officer performance using the Inwald Personality Inventory: An illustration from Appalachia. *Professional Psychology: Research and Practice, 29*(1), 59–62.

Mumford, G. (2004). A rallying cry for psychological science. *Monitor on Psychology, 35*(6), 78–79.

Murphy, W. D., & Peters, J. M. (1992). Profiling child sexual abusers: Psychological considerations. *Criminal Justice and Behavior, 19*(1), 24–37.

Murray, H. (1943). *Analysis of the personality of Adolph Hitler with predictions of his future behavior and suggestions for dealing with him now and after Germany's surrender.* Office of Strategic Services Archive DD247 HS MH7. Retrieved April 5 2005, from http://www.lawschool.cornell.edu/library/donovan/hitler/

Myers, B., & Arena, M. (2001). Trial consultation: A new direction in applied psychology. *Professional Psychology: Research and Practice, 32*(4), 386–391.

Myers, B., & Lecci, L. (1998). Revising the factor structure of the juror bias scale: A method for the empirical validation of theoretical constructs. *Law and Human Behavior, 22,* 239–256.

Myers, D., & Wee, D. (2005). Critical incident stress management in large-scale disasters: effectiveness of CISD and CISM: research issues and findings. In *Disasters in mental health: A primer for practitioners* (pp. 188–200).

Myers, J. E. B. (1998). *Legal issues in child abuse and neglect* (2nd ed.). Newbury Park, CA: Sage.

Myers, J. B., & Erickson, R. (1999). *Legal and ethical issues in child custody litigation.* In R. M. Galatzer-Levy & L. Kraus (Eds.), *The scientific basis of child custody decisions* (pp. 12–32).

Myers, J. R., & Schmidt, F. (2008). Predictive validity of the structured assessment for violence risk in youth (SAVRY) with juvenile offenders. *Criminal Justice and Behavior, 35,* 344–355.

Myers, L. (2005). 1943 psychological profile of Hitler accessible on CU Law Library site. *Cornel Chronicle.* Retrieved April 5, 2005, from http://www.news.cornell.edu/Chronicle/05/3.17.05/Hitler_papers.html

Myers, R. G. (1983). *The clinician's handbook: The psychopathology of adulthood and late adolescence.* Boston: Allyn & Bacon.

Myron, N., & Goldstein, A. (1979). *Hostage.* New York: Pergamon Press.

Narby, D. J., & Cutler, B. L. (1994). Effectiveness of voir dire as a safeguard in eyewitness cases. *Journal of Applied Psychology, 79,* 724–729.

*National Advisory Commission on Criminal Justice Standards and Goals: Police.* (1967). Washington, DC: U.S. Government Printing Office.

National Center for Educational Statistics. (1997). *The impact of the baby boom echo on U.S. school enrollments* (NCES 98039). Washington, DC: U.S. Government Printing Office.

National Center for Health Statistics of the United States. (2001). Table 1. Provisional number of marriages and divorces, 1997–1999. *Monthly Vital Statistics Report, 48,* 1–2.

National Conference of Bar Examiners. (2000). Index: to cases reported in the *Bar Examiner* 1989–1999. *The Bar Examiner, 69,* 35–51.

National Institute of Justice. (1999). At a glance: Recent research findings. *National Institute of Justice Journal, 27.*

National Institute on Alcohol Abuse and Alcoholism. (1995). *A guide to substance abuse services for primary care physicians* (DHHS Pub. No. SMA 97-3139). Washington, DC: U.S. Government Printing Office.

National Interdisciplinary Colloquium on Child Custody. (1998). *Legal and mental health perspectives on child custody law: A deskbook for judges.* Danvers, MA: West Group.

*Neil v. Biggers,* 409 U.S. 188 (1972).

Neubauer, D. (1992). *America's courts and the criminal justice system.* Pacific Grove, CA: Brooks/Cole.

Newman, R. (2004). Leading psychology forward: Staying the course in uncertain times. *Professional Psychology: Research and Practice, 35,* 36–41.

Newman, R. (2005) APA's Resilience Initiative. *Professional Psychology: Research and Practice, 36,* 227–229.

Nicholson, R. A., & Kugler, K. E. (1991). Competent and incompetent criminal defendants: A quantitative review of comparative research. *Psychological Bulletin, 109,* 355–370.

Nicholson, R. A., & McNulty, J. (1992). Outcome of hospitalization for defendants found incompetent to stand trial. *Behavioral Sciences and the Law, 10,* 371–383.

Nicholson, R. A., Norwood, S., & Enyart, C. (1991). Characteristics and outcomes of insanity acquittees in Oklahoma. *Behavioral Sciences and the Law, 9,* 487–500.

Nicholson, R. A., Robertson, H., Johnson, W., & Jensen, G. (1988). A comparison of instruments for assessing competency to stand trial. *Law and Human Behavior, 2,* 313–321.

Niederhoffer, A. (1967). *Behind the blue shield: The police in urban society.* Garden City, NY: Doubleday.

Nielsen, E. (1990). Traumatic Incident Corps: Lessons learned. In J. T. Reese, J. M. Horn, & C. Dunning (Eds.), *Critical incidents in policing* (pp. 315–323). Washington, DC: Federal Bureau of Investigation.

Nietzel, M. T., & Dillehay, R. C. (1986). *Psychological consultation in the courtroom.* New York: Pergamon Press.

Nietzel, M. T., McCarthy, D. M., & Kerr, N. L. (1999). Juries: The current state of the empirical literature. In R. Roesch, S. D. Hart, & J. R. P. Ogloff (Eds.), *Psychology and law: The state of the discipline.* New York: Kluwer Academic/Plenum Press.

Nixon, M. (1990). Professional training in psychology: Quest for international standards. *American Psychologist, 45*(11), 1257–1262.

Norcross, J. C., Castle, P. H., Sayette, M., & Mayne, T. J. (2004). The Psy.D: Heterogeneity in practitioner training. *Professional Psychology: Research and Practice, 35*(4), 412–419.

Norvell, N., Hills, H., & Murrin, M. (1993). Understanding female and male law enforcement officers. *Psychology of Women Quarterly, 17,* 289–301.

Oberlander, L. B. (1998, April). *Evaluating parenting capacity and allegations of child maltreatment.* Paper presented to the American Academy of Forensic Psychology, San Juan, Puerto Rico.

Oddenino, M. (1994). Helping your client navigate past the shoals of a child custody evaluation. *American Journal of Family Law, 8,* 81–95.

O'Donohue, W., & Fisher, J. (Eds.). (1999). *Management and administration skills for the mental health professional.* New York Academic Press.

Office of the Inspector General. (2004, March). *The Federal Bureau of Prisons Inmate release preparation and transitional reentry programs.* Report No. 04-16. Retrieved March 15, 2005, from http://www.usdoj.gov/oig/audit/BOP/0416/intro.htm

Office of Technology Assessment. (1983). *Scientific validity of polygraph testing: A research review and evaluation* (OTA-TM-H-15). Washington, DC: Government Printing Office.

Olgoff, J. R. (2000). Two steps forward and one step backward: The law and psychology movement(s) in the 20th century. *Law and Human Behavior, 24*(4), 457–483.

Ogloff, J. R., & Otto, R. K. (1993). Psychological autopsy: Clinical and legal perspectives. *Saint Louis University Law Journal, 37,* 607–646.

O'Hair, D., & Cody, M. J. (1987). Gender and vocal stress differences during truthful and deceptive information sequences. *Human Relations, 40,* 1–13.

Olczak, P. V., Kaplan, M. F., & Penrod, S. (1991). Attorney's lay psychology and its effectiveness in selecting jurors: Three empirical studies. *Journal of Social Behavior and Personality, 6,* 431–452.

On-the-Job Stress in Policing: Reducing it, preventing it. (2000). *National Institute of Justice Journal* (pp. 18–24).

*Oncale v. Sundowner Offshore Oil,* 83 Fed. 118, 70 FEP. 1303 (5th Cir. 1996).

*Oncale v. Sundowner Offshore Oil,* 118 S. Ct. 998, 76 FEP 221 (1998).

Ones, D. S., Viswesvaran, C., & Schmidt, F. L. (1993) Comprehensive meta-analysis of integrity test validities: Findings and implications for personnel selection and theories of job performance. *Journal of Applied Psychology, 78*, 679–703.

Orne, M. T., Axelrad, A. D., Diamond, B. L., Gravitz, M. A., Heller, A., Mutter, C. B., et al. (1985). Scientific status of refreshing recollection by the use of hypnosis. *Journal of American Medical Association, 253*, 1918–1923.

Oswald, J. D., & Johnson, R. G. (1994). A law school's duty to report student bar application misconduct. *The Bar Examiner, 63*, 7–14.

Otto, R. K. (1998). The rain of managed care and the perceived oasis of forensic psychology. *Bulletin of the American Academy of Forensic Psychology, 19*(1), 1–3, 9.

Otto, R. K. (2003). *Teaching psychology and law in the 21st century.* Poster session presented at the annual meeting of the Teaching of Psychology Symposium. Saint Petersburg, FL.

Otto, R. K. (2005). *Current challenges to forensic psychology.* Paper presented at the annual meeting of the Southeastern Psychological Association, Nashville, TN.

Otto, R. K., Buffington-Vollum, J. K., & Edens, J. F. (2003). Child custody evaluation. In I. B. Weiner (Series Ed.) & A. M. Goldstein (Vol. Ed.), *Handbook of psychology: Vol. 11. forensic psychology* (pp. 179–208). New York: Wiley.

Otto, R. K., & Collins, R. P. (1995). Use of the MMPI-2/MMPI-A in child custody evaluations. In Y. S. Ben-Porath, J. R. Graham, G. C. N. Hall, R. D. Hirshman, & M. S. Zaragoza (Eds.), *Forensic applications of the MMPI-2* (pp. 222–252). Thousand Oaks, CA: Sage.

Otto, R. K., Edens, J. F., & Barcus, E. (2000). The use of psychological testing in child custody evaluations. *Family and Conciliation Courts Review, 38*, 312–340.

Otto, R. K., & Heilbrun, K. (2002). The practice of forensic psychology. *American Psychologist, 57*(1), 5–18.

Otto, R. K., Poythress, N. G., Nicholson, R. A., Edens, J. F., Monahan, J., Bonnie, R. J., et al. (1998). Psychometric properties of the MacArthur Competence Assessment tool-criminal adjudication. *Psychological Assessment, 10*, 435–443.

Packer, I. K., & Borum R. (2003). Forensic training and practice. In A. K. Hess & Wiener (Eds.), *The handbook of forensic psychology* (2nd ed., pp. 21–32) New York: Wiley.

Palm, K. M., & Gibson, P. (1998). Recovered memories of childhood sexual abuse: Clinicians' practices and beliefs. *Professional Psychology: Research and Practice, 29*(3), 257–261.

Palmatier, J. J. (1996). *The Validity and comparative accuracy of voice stress analysis as measured by the CVSA: A field study conducted in a psychophysiological context.* Appeared as incomplete Report No. DoDPI97-P-0003 (published in 1996), under the same title. Note: Also unfinished draft title assigned Report No. DoDPI97-P-0002. U.S. Department of Defense Polygraph Institute, Ft. Jackson, SC.

Paoline, III, E. A., & Terrill, W. (2007). Police education, experience, and the use of force. *Criminal Justice and Behavior, 34*, 179–196.

Parhar, K. K., Wormith, J. S., Derkzen, D. M., & Beauregard, A. M. (2008). Offender coercion in treatment. *Criminal Justice and Behavior, 35*, 1109–1135.

Parry, J. (1994). Involuntary civil commitment in the 90s: A constitutional perspective. *Mental and Physical Disability Law Reporter, 18*, 320–333.

Pasewark, R. A., & Pantle, M. L. (1981). Opinions about the insanity plea. *Journal of Forensic Psychology, 8*, 63.

*Pate v. Robinson*, 383 U.S. 375 (1966).

Patrick, C. J. (Ed.). (2005). *Handboodk of psychopathy.* New York: Guilford Press.

Patterson, C. (1995). Lesbian and gay parenthood. In M. Bornstein (Ed.), *Handbook of parenting* (Vol. 3, pp. 255–276). Mahwah, NJ: Erlbaum.

Patterson, D. R., Goldberg, M. L., & Heed, D. M. (1996). Hypnosis in the treatment of patients with severe burns. *American Journal of Clinical Hypnosis, 38*, 200–212.

Pavlidis, I., Eberhardt, N. L, & Levine, J. A. (2002). Seeing through the face of deception. *Nature, 415*, 35.

Pendergrass, M. (1999). Smearing in the name of scholarship. *Professional Psychology: Research and Practice, 30*(6), 623–625.

Pendergrast, M. L., Farabee, D., Cartier, J. M., Henkin, S. (2002). Involuntary treatment within a prison setting. *Criminal Justice and Behavior, 29*, 5–26.

Pennebaker, J. W., Francis, M. E., & Booth, R. J. (2001). Linguistic inquiry and word count: LIWC 2001. Mahwah, NJ: Erlbaum.

Penrod, S. D., Fulero, S. M., & Cutler, B. L. (1995). Expert psychological testimony on eyewitness reliability before and after *Daubert*: The state of law and the state of science. *Behavioral Sciences and the Law, 13*, 229–259.

*Penry v. Limbaugh*, 492 U.S. 302 (1989).

Petrila, J. & Otto, R. K. (1996). *Law and mental health professionals, Florida.* Washington, DC: American Psychological Association.

Piotrowski, S. D. (1996). Use of the Rorschach in forensic practice. *Perceptual and Motor Skills, 82*, 254.

Plichta, S. B. (1996). Violence and abuse: Implications for women's health. In M. M. Falk & K. S. Collins (Eds.), *Women's health: The Commonwealth survey* (pp. 237–270). Baltimore: John Hopkins University Press.

Police Executive Research Forum (1997). *The police response to people with mental illness: Including information on the Americans with Disabilities Act requirements and community policing approaches. Trainers Guide and Model Policy.* Washington, DC: Police Executive Research Forum.

Polich, J. (2007). Updating P300: An integrative theory of P3a & P3b. *Clinical Neurophysiology, 118*(10), 2128–2148.

Polich, J., & Kok, A. (1995). Cognitive and biological determinants of P300: an integrative review. *Biological Psychology, 41*(2), 103–146.

Pollina, D. A., & Ryan, A. (2002). *The relationship between facial skin surface temperature reactivity and traditional polygraph measures used in the psychophysiological detection of deception: A preliminary investigation.* Ft. Jackson, SC: U.S. Department of Defense Polygraph Institute.

Pomerantz, A. M. & Handelsman, M. M. (2004). Informed consent revisited: An updated written question format. *Professional Psychology: Research and Practice, 35*(2), 201–205.

Poole, D. A., & Lindsay, D. S. (1995). Interviewing preschoolers: Effects of nonsuggestive techniques, parental coaching, and leading questions on reports of nonexperienced events. *Journal of Experimental Child Psychology, 60*, 129–154.

Pope, H. G. (1997). *Psychology astray: Fallacies in studies of "repressed memory" and childhood trauma.* Boca Raton, FL: Upton Books.

Pope, K. S. (1990). Therapist-patient sex as sex abuse: Six scientific, professional, and practical dilemmas in addressing victimization and rehabilitation. *Professional Psychology: Research and Practice, 21*, 227–239.

Pope, K. S. (1996). Scientific research, recovered memory, and context: Seven surprising findings. *Women and Therapy, 19*, 123–140.

Pope, K. S. (n.d.) M*alingering research update.* Retrieved March 14, 2005, from http://kspope.com/assess/malinger.php

Pope, K. S., Butcher, J. N., & Seelen, J. (2000). *The MMPI, MMPI-2, MMPI-A in court: A practical guide for expert witnesses and attorneys* (2nd ed.). Washington, DC: American Psychological Association.

Pope, K. S., & Tabachnick, B. G. (1995). Recovered memories of abuse among therapy patients: A national survey. *Ethics and Behavior, 5,* 237–248.

Porter, S., Yuille, J. C., & Lehman, D. R. (1999). The nature of real, implanted, and fabricated memories for emotional childhood events. *Law and Human Behavior, 23,* 517–538.

Posey, A. J., & Wrightsman, L. S. (2005). *Trial consulting.* New York: Oxford University Press.

Powell, B., & Downey, D. B. (1997). Living in single-parent households: An investigation of the same-sex hypothesis. *American Sociological Review, 62,* 521–539.

Powers-Stafford, K. (2003). Assessment of competence to stand trial. In I. B. Weiner (Series Ed.) & A. M. Goldstein (Vol. Ed.), *Handbook of psychology: Vol. 11. Forensic psychology* (pp. 360–380). New York: Wiley.

Poythress, N., Nicholson, R., Otto, R., Edens, J., Bonnie, R., Monahan, J., et al. (1999). *Professional manual for the MacArthur Competence Assessment Tool—Criminal Adjudication.* Odessa, FL: Psychological Assessment Resources.

Poythress, N., Otto, R. K., Darkes, J., & Starr, L. (1993). APA's expert panel in the congressional review of the USS Iowa incident. *American Psychologist, 48,* 8–15.

Prentky, R. A., & Burgess, A. W. (2000). *Forensic management of sexual offenders.* New York: Kluwer Academic/Plenum Press.

Presser, L., & Van Voorhis, P. (2002). Values and evaluation: Assessing processes and outcomes of restorative justice programs. *Crime and Delinquency, 48,* 162–188.

Pruitt, D. G., Pierce, R. S., McGillicuddy, N. B., Welton, G. L., & Castrianno, L. M. (1993). Long-term success in mediation. *Law and Human Behavior, 17,* 313–330.

Pryor, J. B. (1987). Sexual harassment proclivities in men. *Sex Roles, 17,* 269–290.

Pryor, J. B., Giedd, J. L., & Williams, K. B. (1995). A social psychological model for predicting sexual harassment. *Journal of Social Issues, 51,* 69–84.

Rabin, A.I. (1981). *Assessment with projective techniques: A concise introduction.* New York: Springer.

Rafilson, F., & Sison, R. (1996). Seven criterion related validity studies conducted with the national police officer selection test. *Psychological Reports, 78*(1), 163–176.

Ratner, M. (2001). In the aftermath of *Troxel v. Granville:* Is mediation the answer? *Family Court Review, 39,* 454–468.

Reaves, B. (1996). *Local police departments, 1995.* Washington, DC: Bureau of Justice Statistics, U.S. Department of Justice.

Redding, R. E., Floyd, M. Y., & Hawk, G. L. (2001). What judges and lawyers think about the testimony of mental health experts: A survey of the courts and bar. *Behavioral Sciences and the Law, 19,* 583–594.

Reese, J. T., Horn, J. M., & Dunning, C. (1990). *Critical incidents in policing.* Washington, DC: Federal Bureau of Investigation.

Reiser, M. (1972). *The police department psychologist.* Springfield, IL: Thomas.

Reiser, M. (1980). *Handbook of investigative hypnosis.* Los Angeles: LEHI.

Reiser, M. (1982). Selection and promotion of policemen. In M. Reiser (Ed.), *Police psychology: Collected papers* (pp. 84–92). Los Angeles: LEHI.

Reitzel, L. R. (2006). Sexual offender update: Incarcerated offense behavior and community risk. *The Correctional Psychologist, 38,* 1–4.

Renninger, S. M., McCarthy-Veach, P., & Bagdade, P. (2002). Psychologists' knowledge, opinions, and decision-making processes regarding child abuse and neglect reporting laws. *Professional Psychology: Research and Practice*, 33(1), 19–23.

Resnick, P. J. (1997). Malingering of post traumatic stress disorders. In R. Rogers (Ed.), *Clinical assessment of malingering and deception* (2nd ed., pp 130–152). New York: Guilford Press.

Rey, A. (1964). *L'examen clinique en psychologie* [ The clinical examination in psychology]. Paris: Presses Universitaires de France.

Rice, M. E. (1997). Violent offender research and implications for the criminal justice system. *American Psychologist*, 52, 414–423.

Rieber, R. W., & Green, M. (1981). *Milestones in the history of forensic psychology and psychiatry*. New York: Da Capo Press.

Rigaud, M., & Flynn, C. (1995). Fitness for duty (FFD) evaluation in industrial and military workers. *Psychiatric Annals*, 25, 246–250.

*Riggins v. Nevada*, 112 S. Ct. 1810 (1992).

Ritchie, E. C., & Gelles, M. G. (2002). Psychological autopsies: The current Department of defense effort to standardize training and quality assurance. *Journal of Forensic Science*, 47, 1370–1372.

Robbennolt, J. K., Groscup, J. L., & Penrod, S. (2006). Evaluating and assisting jury competence in civil cases. In I. B. Weiner & A. K. Hess (Eds.), *The handbook of forensic psychology* (3rd ed., pp. 392–425). Hoboken, NJ: Wiley.

Robins, L. N., Tipp, J., & Przybeck, T. (1991). Antisocial personality. In L. N. Robins & D. Regier (Eds.), *Psychiatric disorders in America: The Epidemiologic Catchment Area study* (pp. 258–290). New York: Free Press.

Robinson, R. C., & Mitchell, J. T. (1995). Getting some balance back into the debriefing debate. *Bulletin of the Australian Psychological Society*, 17, 5–10.

Rodgers, D. (1992). The MMPI-2: Improvement or marketing ploy? *The National Psychologist*, 1(3), 14–15.

Rodriguez, M. A., Bauer, H. M., McLoughlin, E., & Grumbach, K. (1999). Screening and intervention for intimate partner abuse: Practices and attitudes of primary care physicians. *Journal of the American medical Association*, 282, 468–474.

Roesch, R., Goulding, S. L., Hans, V. P., & Reppucci, N. D. (1991). Social science and the courts: The role of amicus curiae briefs. *Law and Human Behavior*, 15, 1–11.

Roesch, R., Grisso, T., & Poythress, N. G. (1986). Training programs, courses, and workshops in psychology and law. In M. F. Kaplan (Ed.), *The impact of social psychology on procedural justice* (pp. 83–108). Springfield, IL: Thomas.

Roesch. R., Zapf, P. A., Golding, S. L., & Skeem, J. L. (1999). Defining and assessing competency to stand trial. In A. K. Hess & I. B Weiner (Eds.), *The handbook of forensic psychology* (2nd ed.). New York: Wiley.

Rogers, R. (1984). *Rogers Criminal Responsibility Assessment Scales (R-CRAS) and test manual*. Odessa, FL: Psychological Assessment Resources.

Rogers, R. (1988). *Clinical assessment of malingering and deception*. New York: Guilford Press.

Rogers, R. (Ed.). (1997). *Clinical assessment of malingering and deception* (2nd ed.). New York: Guilford Press.

Rogers, R. (1998). *Malingering and deception: Clinical and legal issues*. Paper presented at the 8th Annual Symposium: Mental Health and the Law, Miami, FL.

Rogers, R., Bagby, R. M., & Dickens, S. E. (1992). *Structured Interview of Reported Symptoms (SIRS) and professional manual*. Odessa, FL: Psychological Assessment Resources.

Rogers, R., & Bender, S. D. (2003). Evaluation of malingering and deception. In I. B. Weiner (Series Ed.) & A. M. Goldstein (Vol. Ed.), *Handbook of psychology: Vol. 11. Forensic psychology* (pp. 109–129). New York: Wiley.

Rogers, R., & Ewing, C. P. (1989). Ultimate issue prescriptions: A cosmetic fix and plea for empiricism. *Law and Human Behavior, 13,* 357–374.

Rogers, R., Fitch, W. L., Frumkin, I. B., Slobogin, C., Fredrick, R., Myers, J. E. B., et al. (1998, March). *Malingering and deception: Clinical and legal issues.* Symposium conducted at the meeting of the 8th Annual National Symposium: Mental Health and the Law, Miami, Florida.

Rogers, R., Gillis, J. R., Dickens, S. E., & Bagby, R. M. (1991). Standardized assessment of malingering: Validation of the Structured Interview of Reported Symptoms. *Psychological Assessment, 3,* 89–96.

Rogers, R., & Sewell, K. W. (1999). The R-CRAS and insanity evaluations: A re-examination of construct validity. *Behavioral sciences and the Law, 17,* 181–194.

Rogers, R., & Shuman, D. W. (2000). *Conducting insanity evaluations.* New York: Guilford Press.

Rogers, R., Wasyliw, O. E., & Cavanaugh, J. L. (1984). Evaluating insanity: A study of construct validity. *Law and Human Behavior, 8,* 293–303.

Rohman, L., Sales, B., & Lou, M. (1987). The best interests of the child in custody disputes. In L. Weithorn (Ed.). *Psychology and child custody determinations* (pp. 59–105). Lincoln; University of Nebraska Press.

*Roper v. Simmons,* 543 U. S. (Supreme Court 2005). Retrieved March 21, 2007, from http://www.supremecourtus.gov/opinions/04pdf/03-633.pdf

Rose, M. R. (1999). The peremptory challenge accused of race or gender discrimination? Some data from one county. *Law and Human Behavior, 23,* 695–702.

Rosenfeld, J. P. (2005). "Brain fingerprinting": A critical analysis. *Scientific Review of Mental Health Practice, 4*(1), 20–33.

Rosenthal, R., & Jacobson, L. (1968). *Pygmalion in the classroom: Teacher expectation and pupils' intellectual development.* New York: Rinehart and Winston.

Rotter, J. B., Lah, M., & Rafferty, J. (1992).*Rotter incomplete sentences blank manual* (2nd ed.). New York: Psychological Corporation.

Rottman, D. (2000). Does effective therapeutic jurisprudence required specialized courts (and do specialized courts imply specialist judges)? *Court Review, 37,* 22–27.

*Roulette v. Department of Central Management Services,* 490 N.E.2d 60, (Ill. App. 1 Dist. 1987).

Rowan, J. R., & Hayes, L. M. (1995). *Training curriculum on suicide detection and prevention in jails and lockups* (2nd ed.). Mansfield, MA: National Center on Institutions and Alternatives.

Rowley, W. J., & MacDonald, D. (2001). Counseling and the law: A cross-cultural perspective. *Journal of Counseling and Development, 79,* 423–429.

Ruis, M. A., Drake, E. B., Glass, A., Marcotte, D., & van Gorp, W. G. (2002). Trying to beat the system: Misuse of the internet to assist in avoiding the detection of psychological symptom dissimulation. *Professional Psychology: Research and Practice, 33*(3), 294–299.

Saks, M. J. (1987). Social scientists can't rig juries. In L. S. Wrightsman, S. M. Kassin, & C. E. Willis (Eds.)., *In the jury box: Controversies in the courtroom* (pp. 185–203). New York: Springer-Verlag.

Saks, M. J. (1990). Expert witnesses, nonexpert witnesses and nonwitness experts. *Law and Human Behavior, 14,* 291–313.

Saks, M. J. (1993). Improving APA science translation amicus briefs. *Law and Human Behavior, 17,* 235–247.

Sales, B. D., Manber, R., & Rohman, L. (1992). Social science research and child-custody decision making. *Applied and Preventive Psychology, 1*, 23–40.

Sales, B. D., Miller, M. O., & Hall, S. R. (2005). *Laws affecting clinical practice.* Washington, DC: American Psychological Association.

Sales, B. D., & Shuman, D. W. (1993). Reclaiming the integrity of science in expert witnessing. *Ethics and Behavior, 3*, 223–229.

Sales, B. D., & Shuman, D. (2005). *Experts in court: Reconciling law, science, and professional knowledge.* Washington, D.C: American Psychological Association.

Samuelson, S. L., & Campbell, C. D. (2005). Screening for domestic violence: Recommendations based on a practice survey. *Professional Psychology: Research and Practice, 36*, 276–282.

Sanchez, H. G. (2001). Risk factor model for suicide assessment and intervention. *Professional Psychology: Research and Practice, 32*(4), 351–358.

Santrock, J., & Warshak, R. (1979). Father custody and social development in boys and girls. *Journal of Social Issues, 35*, 112–125.

Sarason, I. G., & Sarason, B. R. (2005). *Abnormal psychology: The problem of maladaptive behavior* (11th ed.). Upper Saddle River, NJ: Pearson Education.

*Schall v. Martin*, 467 U.S. 253 (1984).

Scheck, B., Neufeld, P., & Dwyer, J. (2000). *Actual innocence.* New York: Random House.

Scheflin, A. W., Spiegel, H., & Spiegel, D. (1999). Forensic uses of hypnosis. In A. K. Hess & I. B. Weiner (Eds.), *The handbook of forensic psychology* (2nd ed., pp. 474–498). New York: Wiley.

Schlenger, W. E., & Kukla, R. A. (1987, August). *Performance of the Keane-Fairbank MMPI Scale and other self-report measures in identifying post traumatic stress disorder.* Paper presented at the 95th annual meeting of the American Psychological Association, New York.

Schmolck, H., Buffalo, E. A., & Squire, L. R. (2000). Memory distortions over time: Recollections of the O. J. Simpson trial verdict after 15 and 32 months. *Psychological Science, 11*, 39–47.

Schneider, B. E. (1987). Graduate women, sexual harassment, and university policy. *Journal of Higher Education, 58*, 46–65.

Schoenfeld, L. S., Hatch, J. P., & Gonzalez, J. M. (2001). Responses of psychologists to complaints filed against them with a state licensing board. *Professional Psychology: Research and Practice, 32*(5), 491–495.

Schultz, B., Dixon, E., Lindenberger, J., & Ruther, N. (1989). *Solomon's sword: A practical guide to conducting child custody evaluations.* San Francisco: Jossey-Bass.

Scogin, F., Schumacher, J., Gardner, J., & Chaplin, W. (1995). Predictive validity of psychological testing in law enforcement settings. *Professional Psychology: Research and Practice, 26*, 68–71.

Scrignar, C. B. (1996). *Post-traumatic stress disorder: Diagnosis, treatment, and legal issues* (3rd ed.). New Orleans, LA: Bruno Press.

Settle, S. A., & Lowery, C. R. (1982). Child custody decisions: Content analysis of a judicial survey. *Journal of Divorce, 6*, 125–138.

Seppa, N. (1997, May). Sexual harassment in the military lingers on. *APA Monitor* (pp. 40–41).

Settle, S. A., & Lowery, C. R. (1982). Child custody decisions: Content analysis of a judicial survey. *Journal of Divorce, 6*, 125–138.

Shapiro, D. L. (1984). *Psychological evaluation and expert testimony: A practical guide to forensic work.* New York: Van Nostrand Reinhold.

Shapiro, D. L. (1999). *Criminal responsibility evaluations: A manual for practice.* Sarasota, FL: Professional resource Press.

Shaw, J. (1986). MMPI selection procedures. In J. Reese & H. Goldstein (Eds.), *Psychological services for law enforcement*. Washington, DC: U.S. Government Printing Office.

Sheehan, D. C. (Ed.). (2000). *Domestic violence by police officers*. Washington, DC: Federal Bureau of Investigation.

Sheehan, D. C., Everly Jr., G. S., Langlieb, A. (2004). Coping with major critical incidents. *FBI Law Enforcement Bulletin, 73*, p1–13, 13p, 5c.

Sheehan, D. C., Everly, Jr., G. S., & Langlieb, A. (2004). Current best practices: Coping with critical incidents. *FBI Law Enforcement Bulletin, 73*, 1–13.

Sheehan, P., & Tilden, J. (1983). The effects of suggestibility in hypnosis on accurate and distorted retrieval from memory. *Journal of Experimental Psychology: Learning, Memory, Cognition, 9*, 283–293.

Sherrod, T. J., Anderson, H. J., & Tyron, E. (1991). Neuropsychologists and neurolawyers. *Neuropsychology, 5*, 293–305.

Shneidman, E. S. (1981). The psychological autopsy. *Suicide and Life-Threatening Behaviors, 11*(4), 325–340.

Shuman, D. W. (1994). *Psychiatric and psychological evidence* (2nd ed.). Deerfield, IL: Clark Broadman Callaghan.

Shuman, D. W., & Foote, W. (1999). *Jaffee v. Redmond's* impact: Life after the Supreme Court's recognition of a psychotherapist–patient privilege. *Professional Psychology: Research and Practice, 30*, 479–487.

Shuman, D. W., Cunningham, M. D., Connell, M. A., & Reid, W. H. (2003). Interstate forensic psychology consultations: A call for reform and proposal of a model rule. *Professional Psychology: Research and Practice, 34*(3), 233–239.

Shuman, D. W., & Greenberg, S. A. (2003). The expert witness, the adversary system, and the voice of reason: Reconciling impartiality and advocacy. *Professional Psychology: Research and Practice, 34*(3), 219–224.

Shusman, E., & Inwald, R. (1991). A longitudinal validation study of correctional officer job performance as predicted by the IPI and the MMPI. *Journal of Criminal Justice, 19*(4), 173–180.

Silver, E. (1995). Punishment or treatment?: Comparing the lengths of confinement of successful and unsuccessful insanity defendants. *Law and Human Behavior, 19*, 375–388.

Silver, E., Cirincione, C., & Steadman, H. J. (1994). Demythologizing inaccurate perception of the insanity defense: legal standards and clinical assessment. *Applied and Preventive Psychology, 2*, 163–178.

Skolnick, J. H. (1966). *Justice without trial: Law enforcement in a democratic society*. New York: Wiley.

Slind-flor, V. (1994). Helping judges to judge science. *National Law Journal*, A5, A12.

Slobogin, C. (1989). The "ultimate issue" issue. *Behavioral Sciences and the Law, 7*, 259–266.

Small, M. A., Lyons, P. M., & Guy, L. S. (2002). Liability issues in child abuse and neglect reporting statues. *Professional Psychology: Research and Practice, 33*(1), 13–18.

Smith, D. H., & Scotland, E. (1973). A new look at police officer selection. In J. R. Snibble & H. M. Snibble (Eds.). *The urban policeman in transition* (pp. 5–24). Springfield, IL: Thomas.

Smith, V. L. (1991). Prototypes in the courtroom: lay representation of legal concepts. *Journal of Personality and Social Psychology, 61*, 857–872.

Smith-Bailey, D. (2003). Alternatives to incarceration. *APA Monitor, 34*(7), 54–56.

Solomon, M. F., & Wrightsman, L. S. (2009). *Forensic psychology* (3rd ed.). Belmont, CA: Wadsworth, Cengage Learning.

Sorenson, E. D., & Goldman, J. (1990). Custody determination and child development: A review of the current literature. *Journal of Divorce, 13*, 53–67.

Southworth, R. N. (1999). *Taking the job home.* In L. Territo & J. D. Sewell (Eds.), *Stress management in law enforcement* (pp. 141–147). Durham, NC: Carolina Academic Press.

Spiegel, D., & Spiegel, H. (1987). Forensic uses of hypnosis. In J. Weiner & A. Hess (Eds.), *Handbook of forensic psychology.* New York: Wiley.

Spielberger, C. D., Ward, J. C., & Spaulding, H. C. (1979). A model for the selection of law enforcement officers. In C. D. Spielberger (Ed.), *Police selection and evaluation: Issues and techniques.* Washington, DC: Hemisphere.

Spitzer, R. L., Williams, J. B. W., Gibbon, M., & First, M. B. (1992). The structured clinical interview for DSM-III-R (SCID). I: History, rationale, and description. *Archives of General Psychiatry, 49*, 624–629.

Sporer, S. L., & Schwandt, B. (2007). Moderators of nonverbal indicators of deception: A meta-analytic synthesis. *Psychology, Public Policy, and Law, 13*(1), 1–34.

Stafford, K. P. (2003). Assessment of competence to stand trial. In I. B. Weiner (Series Ed.) & A. M. Goldstein (Vol. Ed.), *Handbook of psychology: Vol. 11. Forensic psychology* (pp. 359–380). New York: Wiley.

Stahl, P. (1994). *Conducting child custody evaluations: A comprehensive guide.* Thousand Oaks, CA: Sage.

Standards Committee, American Association for Correctional Psychology. (2000).

Standards for psychology services in jails, prisons, correctional facilities, and agencies. *Criminal Justice and Behavior, 27*, 433–494.

Stapp, J. (1996, January). An interesting career in psychology: Trial consultant. *Psychological Agenda.* Retrieved August 1, 2005, from http://www.apa.org/science/ic-stapp.html

*State of Connecticut v. Laquan Ledbetter* (2005). 275 Conn. 534,881 A.2d 290.

*State v. Hurd*, 86 N.J. 525, 432 A.2d 86 (1981).

*State v. Lozano*, 616 So.2d 73 (Fla. App, 1993).

Steadman, H. J., & Hartshorne, E. (1983). Defendants incompetent to stand trial. In J. Monahan & H. J. Steadman (Eds.), *Mentally disordered offenders: Perspectives from law and social science* (pp. 39–64). New York: Plenum Press.

Steadman, H. J., McGreevy, M. A., Morrissey, J. P., Callahan, L. A., Robbins, P. C., & Cirincione, C. (1993). *Before and after Hinkley: Evaluating insanity defense reform.* New York: Guilford Press.

Steadman, H. J., Monahan, J., Hartstone, E., Davis, S. K., & Robbins, P. C. (1982). Mentally disordered offenders: A national survey of patients and facilities. *Law and Human Behavior, 6*, 31–38.

Steadman, H. J., & Veysey, B. M. (1997). *Providing services for jail inmates with mental disorders.* Washington, DC: U.S. Department of Justice, National Institute of Justice.

Steblay, N. M. (1997). Social influence in eyewitness recall: A meta-analytic review of lineup instruction effects. *Law and Human Behavior, 21*, 283–297.

Steblay, N. M., Besirevic, J., Fulero, S. M., & Jimenez-Lorente, B. (1999). The effects of pretrial publicity on juror verdicts: A meta-analytic review. *Law and Human Behavior, 23*, 219–235.

Steblay, N. M., & Bothwell, R. K. (1994). Evidence for hypnotically refreshed testimony: The view from the laboratory. *Law and human behavior, 18*, 635–651.

Stolle, D. P., Robbennolt, J. K., & Weiner, R. L. (1996). The perceived fairness of the psychologist consultant: An empirical investigation. *Law and Psychology Review, 20*, 139–173.

Stone, A. (1984). *Law, psychiatry, and morality.* Washington, DC: American Psychiatric Press.

Stone, A. (1990). Psychological fitness for duty evaluations. *Police Chief, 52,* 39–53.

Stone, A. (2002).*Fitness for duty: Principles, methods, and legal issues.* Boca Raton, FL: CRC Press.

*Stovall v. Denno,* 388 U. S. 293 (1967).

Strausburger, L. H., Gutheil, T. G., & Brodsky, A. (1997). On wearing two hats: Role conflict in serving as both psychotherapist and expert witness. *American Journal of Psychiatry, 154,* 448–456.

Strawbridge, P., & Strawbridge, D. (1990). *A networking guide to recruitment, selection, and probationary training of police officers in major police departments in the United States of America.* New York: John J. College of Criminal Justice.

Streier, F. (1999). Whither trial consulting? Issues and projections. *Law and Human Behavior, 23,* 93–115.

Streier, F., & Shestowsky D. (1999). Profiling the profilers: A study of the trial consulting profession, its impact on trial justice and what, if anything, to do about it. *Wisconsin Law Review, 3,* 441–499.

Stricker, G., & Cummings, N. A. (1992). The professional school movement. In D. K. Freedman (Ed.), *History of psychotherapy: A century of change* (pp. 801–828). Washington, DC: American Psychological Association.

Studebaker, C. A., & Penrod, S. D. (1997). Pretrial publicity: The media, the law, and common sense. *Psychology, Public Policy, and Law, 3,* 93–115.

Sullivan, M. J. (1999). Psychologists as legislators: results of the 1998 elections. *Professional Psychology: Research and Practice, 30*(3), 250–252.

Super, J. (1997). Legal and ethical aspects of pre-employment psychological evaluations. *Journal of Police and Criminal Psychology, 12,* 1–6.

Super, J. (1999). Forensic psychology and law enforcement. In A. K. Hess & I. B. Weiner (Eds.), *The handbook of forensic psychology* (2nd ed.). New York: Wiley.

Swets, J., Dawes, R., & Monahan, J. (2000). Psychological science can improve diagnostic decisions. *Psychological Science in the Public Interest, 1,* 1–26.

Swenson, L. C. (1997). *Psychology and law for the helping professions* (2nd ed.). Pacific Grove, CA: Brooks/Cole.

Swenson, W. M., & Grimes, P. B. (1969). Characteristics of sex offenders admitted to a Minnesota state hospital for pre-sentence psychiatric investigation. *Psychiatric Quarterly Supplement, 34,* 110–123.

Swisher, K. (1994, February). Corporations are seeing the light on harassment. *Washington Post National Weekly Edition* (p. 21).

Swogger, M. T., & Kosson, D. S. (2007). Indentifying subtypes of criminal psychopaths. *Criminal Justice and Behavior, 34,* 953–970.

Szaj, C. M. (2002). The fine art of listening: Children's voices in custody proceedings. *Journal of Law and Family Studies, 4,* 131–150.

Technical Working Group for Crime Scene Investigation. (1999a). *Crime scene investigations: A guide for law enforcement.* Washington, DC: United States Department of Justice, Office of Justice Programs.

Technical Working Group for Eyewitness Evidence. (1999b). *Eyewitness evidence: A guide for law enforcement.* Rockville, MD: National Criminal Justice Reference Service.

Terr, E. (1994). *Unchained memories.* New York: Basic Books.

Territo, L., Halsted, J. B., & Bromley, M. L. (2004). *Crime and justice in America: A human perspective.* Upper Saddle River, NJ: Prentice Hall.

Tesler, P. H. (1999). Collaborative law: A new paradigm for divorce lawyers. *Psychology, Public Policy, and Law, 5,* 967–1000.

The Correctional Psychologist. (2008). Newly-ratified version of the international association for correctional and forensic psychology bylaws. *The Correctional Psychologist, 40,* 10–15.

The Innocence Project. (2007). Eyewitness identification resource guide: a primer for reform. *The Innocence Project*, New York: NY.

The Psychological Corporation. (1997). *Wechsler Adult Intelligence Scale—Third Edition, Wechsler Memory Scale Technical Manual* (3rd ed.). San Antonio, TX: The Psychological Corporation.

Thomas, J. (2005, July 15). Is jury pool of 104 big enough? Nope. *St. Petersburg Times*, p. 1A.

Ticillo, J. A., DeFilippis, N. A., Denney, R. L., & Dsureny, J. (2002). Licensure requirements for interjurisdictional forensic evaluations. *Professional Psychology: Research and Practice*, 33(4), 377–383.

Travis, J., & Lawrence, S. (2002). *Beyond the prison gates: The state of parole in America*. Washington, DC: Urban Institute.

Tjaden, P., & Thoennes, N. (2000a). *Extent, nature, and consequences of intimate partner violence: Findings from the National Violence Against Women Survey* (No. NCJ-181867). Washington, DC: U.S. Department of Justice.

Tjaden, P., & Thoennes, N. (2000b). Prevalence and consequences of male-to-female and female-to-male intimate partner violence as measured by the National Violence Against Women Survey. *Violence Against Women, 6*, 142–161.

Toch, H. (2002). *Stress in policing*. Washington, DC: American Psychological Association.

Tondo, C., Coronel, R., & Drucker, B. (2001). Mediation trends: A survey of states. *Family Court Review, 39*, 431–453.

Turvey, B. (2000). Modus operandi. In *Encyclopedia of forensic science*. London: Academic Press.

Turvey, B. (Ed.). (2000). *Criminal profiling: An introduction to behavioral evidence analysis* (2nd ed.). New York: Academic Press.

Tversky, B., & Tuchin, M. (1989). A reconciliation of the evidence on eyewitness testimony: Comments on McCloskey and Zaragoza. *Journal of Experimental Psychology: General, 118*, 86–91.

Uniform Marriage and Divorce Act, 9 A.U.L.A. 197, 402 (West, 1979).

United States General Accounting Office. (2001). Investigative techniques: *Federal agency views on the potential application of "Brain Fingerprinting."* GAO-02-2.

*United States v. Ash*, 413 U.S. 300 (1973).

*United States v. Brawner*, 471 F.2d.969 (D.C. Cir. 1972).

*United States v. Duhon*, 104 F. Supp. 2d 663 (W.D. La. 2000).

*United States v. Hinkley*, 525 F. Supp. 1342 (D.D.C., 1982).

*United States v. Robinson*, 94 F. Supp. 2nd 751 (2000).

U.S. Bureau of the Census. (1989). *Statistical abstract of the United States*. Washington, DC: U.S. Bureau of the Census.

U.S. Bureau of the Census. (1998). *Household and family characteristics: March 1998 (update)*. Current Population Reports, P20-515. Washington, DC: U.S. Bureau of the Census.

U.S. Department of Justice. (2002). *Recidivism of prisoners released in 1994*. Washington, DC: U.S. Department of Justice, Bureau of Justice Statistics.

Van Emmerik, A. A., Kamphuis, J. H., Hulsbosch, A. M., & Emmelkamp, P. M. (2002). Single session debriefing after psychological trauma: a meta-analysis. *Lancet, 360*, 766–772.

Van Harreveld, F., Claassen, L., & Van Dijk, W. W. (2007). Inmate emotion coping and psychological and physical well-being. *Criminal Justice and Behavior, 34*, 697–708.

Van Horne, B. A. (2004). Psychology licensing board disciplinary actions: The realities. *Professional Psychology: Research and Practice, 35*, 170–179.

Van Sickel, A. D. (1992). Clinical hypnosis in the practice of anesthesia. *Nurse Anesthesiologist, 3*, 67–74.

Varela, J. G., Boccaccini, M. T., Scogin, F., Stump, J., & Caputo, A. (2004). Personality testing in law employment settings: A meta-analytic review. *Criminal Justice and Behavior, 31*(6), 649–675.

Vasquez, M. J. T., Baker, N. L., & Shullman, S. L. (2003). Assessing employment discrimination and harassment. In I. B. Weiner (Series Ed.) & A. M. Goldstein (Vol. Ed.), *Handbook of psychology: Vol. 11. Forensic psychology* (pp. 259–278). New York: Wiley.

Vernon, A. (2006). Response to critical incidents. *Fire Engineering*, pp. 5–10.

Victor, T. L., & Abeles, N. (2004). Coaching clients to take psychological and neuropsychological tests: A clash of ethical obligations. *Professional Psychology: Research and Practice, 35*(4), 373–379.

Viljoen, J. L., Scalora, M., Cuadra, L., Bader, S., Chavez, V., Ullman, D., & Lawrence, L. (2008). Assessing risk for violence in adolescents who have sexually offended. *Criminal Justice and Behavior, 35*, 5–23.

*Vinson v. The Superior Court of Alameda County*, 740 P.2d 404 (Cal. 1987).

Visher, G. (1987). Juror decision making: The importance of evidence. *Law and Human Behavior, 11*, 1–14.

Walker, L. E. (1979). *The battered woman.* New York: Harper & Row.

Walker, L. E. (1984). *The battered woman syndrome.* New York: Springer.

Walker, L. E. (1992). Battered woman syndrome and self-defense. *Notre Dame Journal of Law, Ethics, and Public Policy, 6*, 321–334.

Wallerstein, J. S., & Lewis, J. (1998). The long-term impact of divorce on children: A first report from a 25-year study. *Family Conciliation Courts Review, 36*, 368–383.

Waln, R. F., & Downey, R. G. (1987 ). Voice stress analysis: Use of telephone recordings. *Journal of Business and Psychology 1*, 379–389.

Ward, T., & Stewart, C. (2003). Criminogenic needs and human needs: A theoretical model. *Psychology, Crime and Law, 9*(2), 124–143.

Wareham, J., & Dembo, R. (2007), A longitudinal study of psychological functioning among juvenile offenders. *Criminal Justice and Behavior, 34*, 259–273.

*Washington v. United States*, 129 U.S. App. D.C. 29 (1967).

Washington State Department of Health. (2000, July 7). Prevalence of intimate partner violence and injuries. *Morbidity and Mortality Weekly Report, 49*, 313–316.

Weathers, F. W., Keane, T. M., & Davidson, J. R. T. (2008). Clinician-administered PTSD scale: A review of the first ten years of research. *Depression and Anxiety*, 132–156.

Wechsler, D. (1944). *The measurement of adult intelligence.* Baltimore: Williams & Wilkins.

Weinberger, L. E., & Screenivasan, S. (1994). Ethical and professional conflicts in correctional psychology. *Professional Psychology: Research and Practice, 25*(2), 161–167.

Weiner, I. B. (1996). Is the Rorschach welcome in the courtroom? *Journal of Personality Assessment, 67*, 422–425.

Weissman, H. N., & DeBow, D. M. (2003). Ethical principles and professional competencies. In I. B. Weiner (Series Ed.) & A. M. Goldstein (Vol. Ed.), *Handbook of psychology: Vol. 11. Forensic psychology* (pp. 33–53). New York: Wiley.

Weithorn, L. A. (1987). *Psychology and child custody determinations: Knowledge, roles, and expertise.* Lincoln: University of Nebraska Press.

Weitzman, L. J. (1985). *The divorce revolution: the unexpected social and economic consequences for women and children in America.* New York: Macmillan.

Welch, B. L. (1998a). Reducing liability in a litigious era. *Insight, 1*, 1–4.

Welch, B. L. (1998b). Walking the documentation tightrope. *Insight, 2*, 1–6.

Welch, W. N., McGrain, P., Salamatin, N., & Zajac, G. (2007). Effects of prison drug Treatment on inmate misconduct: A repeated measures analysis. *Criminal Justice and Behavior, 34*, 600–615.

*Wellman v. Faulker.* 715 F.2d 269 (1983).

Wells, C. Getman, R., & Blau, T. (1988). Critical incident procedures: The crisis management of traumatic incidents. *The Police Chief, 55*(1), 70–74.

Wells, G. L. (1978). Applied eyewitness testimony research: System variables and estimator variables. *Journal of Personality and Social Psychology, 36*, 1546–1557.

Wells, G. L. (1984). The psychology of lineup identification. *Journal of Applied Social Psychology, 14*, 89–103.

Wells, G. L. (1993). What do we know about eyewitness identification? *American Psychologist, 48*, 553–571.

Wells, G. L. (1995). Scientific study of eyewitness testimony: Implications for public and legal policy. *Psychology, Public Policy, and Law, 1*, 726–731.

Wells, G. L. (1998). *Eyewitness identification: A system handbook.* Toronto: Carswell.

Wells, G. L. (2001). Police lineups: Data, theory, and policy. *Psychology, Public Policy, and Law, 1*, 791–801.

Wells, G. L., & Bradfield, A. L. (1998). "Good, you identified the suspect": Feedback to eyewitnesses distorts their reports of the witnessing experience. *Journal of Applied Psychology, 83*, 360–376.

Wells, G. L., Leippe, M. R., & Ostrom, T. M. (1979). Guidelines for empirically assessing the fairness of a lineup. *Law and Human Behavior, 3*, 285–29.

Wells, G. L., & Loftus, E. F. (2003). Eyewitness memory for people and events. In I. B. Weiner (Series Ed.) & A. M. Goldstein (Vol. Ed.), *Handbook of psychology: Vol. 11. Forensic psychology* (pp. 149–160). New York: Wiley.

Wells, G. L., Small, M., Penrod, S., Malpass, R. S., Fulero, S. M., & Brimacombe, C. A. E. (1998). Eyewitness identification procedures: Recommendations for lineups and photospreads. *Law and Human Behavior, 22*, 603–647.

*Westbrook v. Arizona,* 384 U.S. 150 (1966).

Westen, D., & Weinberger, J. (2004). When clinical description becomes statistical prediction. *American Psychologist, 59*(7), 595–613.

Westendorf, M. J. (1999). Essentials of competency to stand trial assessment. In A. S. Kaufman & N. L. Kaufman (Series Eds.) & M. J. Ackerman (Vol. Ed.), *Essentials of psychological assessment: Essentials of forensic psychological assessment* (pp. 100–135). New York: Wiley.

Wester, S. R., & Lyubelsky, J. (2005). Supporting the thin blue line: Gender-sensitive therapy with male police officers. *Professional Psychology: Research and Practice, 36*(1), 51–58.

Weston, P., & Wells, K. (1974). *Criminal investigation: Basic perspectives* (2nd ed.). Englewood Cliffs, NJ: Prentice Hall.

Wetterm, M. W., & Corrigan, S. K. (1995). Providing information to clients about psychological tests: A survey of attorneys' and law students' attitudes. *Professional Psychology: research and Practice, 26*, 1–4.

Wexler, D. B. (1990). *Therapeutic jurisprudence: The law as a therapeutic agent.* Durham, NC: Carolina Academic Press.

Wexler, D. B. (1996). Therapeutic jurisprudence and the criminal courts. In D. B. Wexler & B. J. Winick (Eds.), *Law in a therapeutic key* (pp. 157–170). Durham, NC: Carolina Academic Press.

Wexler, D. (n.d.). *Therapeutic jurisprudence: An overview*. Retrieved March 28, 2005, from http://www.law.arizona.edu/depts/upr-intj/

Wexler, D. B., & Winick, B. J. (1991). *Essays in therapeutic jurisprudence*. Durham, NC: Carolina Academic Press.

Wexler, D. B., & Winick, B. J. (Eds.). (1996). *Law in a therapeutic key*. Durham, NC: Carolina Academic Press.

Whisenand, P. (1989). Personnel selection. In W. G. Bailey (Ed.), *The encyclopedia of police science*. New York: Garland Publishing.

White, T. W. (2008). The psychological autopsy: Is it a research, clinical, forensic, or risk management tool? *The Correctional Psychologist, 40*, 4–6.

Wiener, R. L., Watts, B. A., & Stolle, D. P. (1993). Psychological jurisprudence and the information processing paradigm. *Behavioral Sciences and the Law, 11*, 79–96.

Williams, C. (2002). *Outcome of the Commission on Education and Training Leading to Licensure in Psychology: Impact and implications for students and new psychologists*. Washington, DC: American Psychological Association. Available: www.apa/apags/comontrain.html

Williams, D. J. (2008). Offender gambling in prisons and jails: Is it hidden leisure experience? *The Correctional Psychologist, 40*, 7–10.

Williams, G. (1963). *The proof of guilt* (3rd ed.). London: Steven & Sons.

Winerman, L. (2004). Criminal profiling: the reality behind the myth. *Monitor on Psychology 35*(7), 66–69.

Winick, B. J. (n.d.). *Therapeutic jurisprudence defined*. Retrieved March 28, 2005, from http://www.brucewinick.com/Therapeutic%20Jurisprudence.htm

Wolber, G. J., & Carne, W. F. (2002). *Writing psychological reports: A guide for clinicians* (2nd ed.). Sarasota, FL: Professional Resource Press.

Woocher, F. D. (1986). Legal principles governing expert testimony by experimental psychologists. *Law and Human Behavior, 10*, 47–61.

Woody, R. H. (1988). *Fifty ways to avoid malpractice*. Sarasota, FL: Professional Resource Exchange.

Wormith, J. S., Althouse, R., Simpson, M., Reitzel, L. R., Fagan, T. J., & Morgan, R. D. (2007). The rehabilitation and reintegration of offenders: The current landscape and some future directions for correctional psychology. *Criminal Justice and Behavior, 34*, 879–892.

Wortz, C. (1999, Winter). 1998 membership survey report. *Court Call*, p. 15.

Wrightsman, L. S. (2001). *Forensic psychology*. Belmont, CA: Wadsworth/Thomson Learning.

Wrightsman, L. S., Batson, A. L., & Edkins, V. A. (2004). *Measures of legal attitudes*. Belmont, CA: Thomson.

Wrightsman, L. S., Greene, E., Nietzel, M. T., & Fortune, W. H. (2002). *Psychology and the legal system* (5th ed.) Belmont, CA: Wadsworth/Thomson Learning.

Wulsch, J. S. (1980). The incompetency plea: Abuses and reforms. *Journal of Psychiatry and Law, 8*, 317–328.

Yarney, A. D. (1979). *The psychology of eyewitness testimony*. New York: Free Press.Yarney, A. D., Yarney, M. J., & Yarney, A. L. (1996). Accuracy of eyewitness identification in showups and lineups. *Law and Human Behavior, 20*, 459–477.

Youngjohn, J. (1995). Confirmed attorney coaching prior to neuropsychological evaluation. *Assessment, 2*, 279–283.

Yuille, J. C. (1993). We must study forensic eyewitnesses to know about them. *American Psychologist, 48*, 572–573.

Zeisel, H., & Diamond, S. S. (1978). The effect of peremptory challenges on jury and verdict: An experiment in a federal district court. *Stanford Law Review, 30,* 491–531.

Ziskin, J. (1995). *Coping with psychiatric and psychological testimony* (Vols.1–3, 5th ed.) Los Angeles: Law and Psychology Press.

Ziskin, J., & Faust, D. (1994) *Coping with psychiatric and psychological testimony* (5th ed.). Marian Del Rey, CA: Law and Psychology Press.

Zlotnick, C., Kohn, R., Peterson, J., & Pearlstein, T. (1998). Partner physical victimization in a national sample of American families. *Journal of Interpersonal Violence, 13,* 156–166.

Zvolensky, M. J., Herschell, A. D., McNeil, D. W. (2000). Learning to administrate, administrating to learn. *Professional Psychology: Research and Practice, 31*(5), 553–558.

# Glossary

*Actus rea*: The criminal act, including omissions of behavior that result in a criminal act.

**Adjudication:** The judgment rendered in a civil or criminal case.

**Advocacy brief:** Letter to the court advocating for a specific outcome of the case.

**Advocate:** One who pleads on behalf of another individual; an advocate will promote the interests of their client. An attorney typically serves as a legal advocate for their client.

**Affirmative defense:** Defendant admits guilt, but claims he did not possess *"mens rea"* at the time of the offense. Examples include self-defense, insanity, and committing a crime under duress.

**American Psychological Association:** Based in Washington, D.C., the American Psychological Association (APA) is a scientific and professional body that represents psychology in the United States (*www.apa.org*).

*Amicus curiae* **brief:** Letter to the court from a "friend of the court," typically a person or organization that provides information to the court relevant to a case before the court.

**Antisocial personality disorder (APD):** A personality disorder listed in the *Diagnostic and Statistical Manual of Mental Disorders* characterized by infringing on the rights of others; includes behaviors such as aggressiveness, deceitfulness, impulsivity, recklessness, lack of remorse, and failure to conform to social norms.

**Arbitrator:** Someone who helps opposing sides in a dispute come to an agreement and has the authority to make the decision. See Mediator.

**Attitudinal predictors:** Attitudes relevant to a particular case that are related to verdict inclinations among jurors.

**Authoritarianism:** A personality trait characterized by endorsement of conventional values, respect for authority, and acting punitively toward people who defy authority or conventional norms; individuals high in authoritarianism are generally more willing to convict defendants in criminal trials.

**Batson challenge:** A claim that opposing counsel's use of a peremptory strike during voir dire is based solely on race or gender.

**Battered woman syndrome:** Collection of symptoms and behaviors that are believed to occur in women who are the victims of repeated physical and psychological abuse.

**Belief in a just world hypothesis:** A belief that bad things happen to bad people and good things happen to good people; attitude sometimes used in jury selection.

**Best interest of the child standard:** The standard used in child custody disputes that suggests custody decisions should be made with regards to the best interests of the child, as opposed to parental rights.

**Beyond a reasonable doubt:** A standard of proof of such convincing nature that one would be willing to rely upon it in his or her own personal affairs; typically defined as a belief to a moral certainty.

**Big Five personality factors:** Personality trait theory suggesting individuals can be described using five personality factors: openness, conscientiousness, extraversion, agreeableness, and neuroticism (OCEAN).

**Brain fingerprinting:** A technique using EEG patterns to detect if an individual has specific knowledge, used in investigative psychology. The technique uses an event related-potential, termed the P300, to determine if an individual has knowledge of a crime-related fact. The presence of the P300 after the fact displayed to the individual indicates that the individual possessed knowledge of the fact.

**Brandeis brief:** *Amicus curiae* to the court (a letter to the court) using social science research to support arguments.

**Burden of proof:** The necessity of proving facts in dispute, the burden of proof typically rests with the prosecution in criminal trials (beyond a reasonable doubt) and the plaintiff in civil trials (preponderance of the evidence).

**Capital charge:** A felony for which the defendant can face the death penalty.

**Challenge for cause:** Removal of a prospective juror during voir dire because of a prejudice the juror holds that would interfere with rendering a fair verdict.

**Change of venue request:** The process in which an attorney requests that a trial be moved to a different jurisdiction, usually based on concerns that the defendant could not get a fair trial in the presiding jurisdiction.

**Circumstantial evidence:** Evidence that links someone to the crime scene but does not place them directly at the scene at the time of the crime.

**Civil law:** The area of law that deals with the infringement upon the civil rights of an individual or organization; noncriminal law.

**Clear and convincing proof:** A level of proof or persuasion that produces a firm belief as to the facts; greater than *a preponderance of the evidence* but not as strict as *beyond a reasonable doubt*.

**Clinical evaluation:** The use of psychological assessment and treatment with the goal of helping the client.

**Clinical prediction:** Using clinical observation and prior clinical experience to predict future behavior, as compared to statistical prediction.

**Clinical psychologist:** A doctoral-level psychologist (PhD or PsyD) trained to work with individuals with mental illness. Clinical psychologists are regulated by state law and must be licensed to practice.

**Coercion:** In correctional psychology, the process of requiring offenders to participate in treatment programs.

**Cognitive psychology:** A subfield of psychology concerned with the study of cognition and mental processes including memory and eyewitness testimony.

**Community survey:** A randomly administered survey of jury-eligible individuals that collects information on demographics, case-relevant attitudes, and potential verdict decisions. A community survey is commonly used in change of venue requests and jury selection by trial consultants.

**Competency:** The ability or capacity to perform a specific task or function with rationality. The Dusky standard is used to determine competency to stand trial.

**Competency Screening Test (CST):** A brief screening instrument consisting of 22 sentence stems related to legal scenarios used to help determine competency to stand trial.

**Concurrent validity:** Two measures of a construct are assessed at the same time and should correlate with one another; one measure is compared with an already established measure.

**Confidentiality:** The mental health professional's obligation to the client to keep communications between the client and therapist private.

**Confirmation bias:** The deliberate or inadvertent use of subtle cues to bias an eyewitness's identification.

**Control-question technique:** A technique used in polygraph examinations in which the comparison of physiological responses is between relevant questions and control questions. Control questions are questions about possible past infractions that should elicit anxiety in all examinees.

**Core competencies:** Skills and knowledge that enable a professional to engage in a scientifically minded practice. Suggested core competencies in the practice of psychology include competence in psychological assessment, interventions, consultation and interprofessional collaboration, supervision, and professional development.

**Correctional psychologist:** A psychologist working in a correctional facility who may or may not have specialized training in correctional psychology.

**Correlation coefficient:** A mathematical expression indicating how two or more variables vary together; both the direction and strength of the relationship are expressed by a numerical value ranging from $-1.0$ to $1.0$.

**Counseling psychologist:** A doctoral-level psychologist (PhD or EdD) trained to work with individuals with adjustment problems, such as a relationship or occupational problem.

**Court-appointed evaluator:** Mental health professional who is appointed by the court to gather information for the court.

**Crime scene analysis:** The process of examining evidence from a crime scene to help develop the offender description.

**Criminal law:** The area of law that deals with offenses committed against the safety of society or acts against the state.

**Criminal profile:** A written report that describes an offender's characteristics when the offender is not known.

**Criminal profiling:** Any process used to infer distinctive personality traits, behavioral tendencies, physical and demographic characteristics, or even geographic locations of individuals responsible for committing criminal acts from physical and/or behavioral evidence.

**Criminal responsibility:** Culpability for a crime; accountability for criminal behavior; often discussed with the insanity defense.

**Criminogenic needs:** Dynamic risk factors related to criminal behavior, such as attitudes and cognitions.

**Criminology:** The study of crime from a sociological perspective.

**Criterion keying:** Identifying a criterion group and a control group, and using their responses to identify which questions reliably distinguish between the two groups; the method used to develop the MMPI scales.

**Critical incident:** Situations that threaten the life or bodily harm of an individual or others near the individual; police officers may encounter critical incidents and suffer psychological consequences as a result of the trauma.

**Database analysis:** Using an existing database to explore the attitudes and opinions of laypersons, typically used in jury selection.

**Daubert standard:** Case law establishing how judges can determine if expert testimony meets criteria for reliability and relevancy.

**Death-qualified jurors:** Jurors who are not opposed to deliberating the death penalty, in capital cases jurors must all be death-qualified jurors.

**Decisional competence:** The ability to make necessary decisions before, during, and after a trial.

**Defendant:** In both civil and criminal court the defendant is the individual against whom legal action is brought.

**Deinstitutionalization:** The process of releasing mental health patients in the 1970s from large mental health hospitals after the discovery of antipsychotic medications and reform that sought to place individuals in the least-restrictive environment.

**Delayed reporting statues:** A law that allows a victim of alleged abuse to file a claim within a set time period after the abuse is remembered. The statute of limitations is not linked to when the crime occurred but is linked to when it is recalled.

**Delusions:** Irrational beliefs, such as believing that one is being controlled by powerful transmissions from another planet; often associated with severe mental illness.

**Demand characteristics:** The aspects of a situation may influence a participant to respond in a particular manner. For example, the demand characteristics of a courtroom may convince a potential juror to affirm that they can offer an impartial verdict in a case even when the juror may hold a bias.

**Deterrence:** The notion that the threat of punishment will deter individuals from committing a crime.

**Developmental psychology:** A subfield of psychology that focuses on the study of the changes in behavior and mental processes over time due to aging and maturation.

**Diplomate:** Recognition by a professional association that a member has advanced training, skills, and competence; commonly referred to as board certified.

**Direct evidence:** Evidence that directly places the suspect at the crime scene around the time of the offense. Contrast with circumstantial evidence.

**Direct examination:** The questioning of a witness during the trial by the attorney who called the witness. The direct examination occurs before cross-examination.

**Directed verdict:** A judge rules that there is insufficient evidence to support a tort claim.

**Discovery:** The process of both parties obtaining all information that will be submitted as evidence before a trial.

**Discrimination:** Acting with bias because of a person's race, color, religion, national origin, age, or sex.

**Discriminatory effects:** Discrimination against a protected group, as in employment law, where the entire group suffers.

**Discriminatory treatment:** Discrimination against an individual in a protected group.

**Dismissed with prejudice:** Refers to a judge's decision to dismiss a case and the case cannot be brought before the court again.

**Dismissed without prejudice:** Refers to a judge's decision to dismiss a civil case but allows for the possibility of refiling the case at a later date; associated with tort law.

**Disparate impact:** Occurs when an entire protected group (sex, race, or age) is adversely affected by discrimination.

**Dissociative amnesia:** Inability to recall a traumatic event that is not attributable to head injury or drug use.

**Duress:** Unlawful threat or coercion used to cause another to act in a manner that they otherwise would not.

**Dusky standard:** The standard used to determine competency to stand trial. A defendant must understand the nature of the proceedings against him or her and must be able to rationally assist his or her attorney.

**Dynamic risk factors:** Factors that are likely to be malleable over time that can pose a risk for criminal behaviors, such as attitudes and opinions.

**Episodic memories:** Memories of events such as a wedding or graduation, as compared to memories of facts (semantic memory).

**Estimator variables:** Factors out of police control that typically occur before the police arrive on the scene and can affect eyewitness accuracy.

**Evaluation anxiety:** Anxiety caused by the desire to be judged positively by others.

**Experimenter bias:** Research indicating that the expectations of the experimenter can influence the behavior of research participants in a study.

**Expert witness:** Any individual who has been qualified as an "expert" by the trial judge due to specialized knowledge or skill. A fact witness is generally not allowed to offer an opinion, whereas an expert witness may.

**External locus of control:** Personality style characterized by the belief that you can do very little to affect outcomes in your life; compared to an internal locus of control.

**Face validity:** Refers to whether a test *appears* to measure what it purports to measure.

**Facial thermography:** A procedure that measures radiant energy emitted from a subject's face; used to detect deception with the assumption that when an individual is lying they emit higher amounts of radiant energy.

**Fact witness:** A person who testifies about things they know or have personally perceived.

**False memory syndrome:** False memories that have been implanted inadvertently through suggestive therapy techniques but the individual believes the memories to be real.

**Felony:** A criminal offense punishable by incarceration in prison or the death penalty.

**Fitness-for-duty evaluations:** Psychological evaluations conducted to determine if individuals in high-risk occupations (e.g., law enforcement) are psychologically capable of performing their jobs.

**Forensic pathology:** Applying medical knowledge and procedures to solving problems in the legal arena.

**Forensic psychology:** The application of clinical specialties to legal institutions and people who come into contact with the law.

**Frye test:** Case law regarding admissibility of scientific evidence; the evidence must be based on scientific work that is *generally accepted* by the appropriate scientific community.

**Functional size:** Used in research on the validity of a lineup; it is the number of members in a lineup who physically match the suspect, plus the suspect.

**Gender role conflict (GRC):** Traditional gender role socialization resulting in behaviors that are inappropriate for the current situation, such as a man's inability to express a weakness.

**General acceptance rule:** For scientific expert testimony to be admissible, it must be based on *generally accepted* scientific methods.

**Georgia Court Competency Test (GCCT):** A screening instrument that uses a drawing of the courtroom to prompt defendants on courtroom protocol and personnel.

**Guidelines:** Statements regarding recommended professional behavior or conduct; used to establish a standard of care.

**Hallucinations:** Hearing, seeing, or feeling things that are not actually present, typically associated with severe mental illness.

**Hostage negotiation:** Mediation between hostage-taker and law enforcement personnel.

**Hostile work environment:** An intimidating, hostile, or offensive working environment due to sexual harassment.

**Hypnosis:** An altered state of consciousness characterized by varying degrees of willingness to engage in changes in behavior or conscious experience.

**Hypnotically refreshed memories:** Memories that have been enhanced under hypnosis; used to help victims or witnesses recall details of a crime; not admissible as evidence in many jurisdictions.

**Imagination inflation:** The process whereby a person comes to believe that a fictitious event actually occurred as a result of imagining the event.

**Impeachment:** Calling into question the credibility of a witness's testimony.

**Incapacitation:** One of the goals of incarceration based on the premise that the offender is unable to reoffend as long as they are incarcerated.

**Industrial/organizational psychology:** Specialty in psychology that works with industry on assessment and classification of workers, organizational morale and culture, and workers' performance.

**Insanity:** A legal term addressing a defendant's culpability for a crime. Different standards are used in different jurisdictions, such as the McNaghten standard and the Durham standard.

**Integrity tests:** Standardized tests that are used to assess personality traits such as conscientiousness, dependability, and honesty.

**Interdisciplinary Fitness Interview (IFI):** A joint interview by a psychologist and a lawyer to assess clinical psychopathology and understanding of legal concepts for a competency to stand trial evaluation.

**Internal locus of control:** The belief that your actions affect the outcomes in your life, in contrast to an external locus of control, which is characterized by the belief that regardless of what you do, you cannot control situations. This is a personality trait sometimes considered in jury selection.

**Investigative hypnosis:** A tool used to help enhance a victim's recollection of a crime.

**Investigative phase:** Analysis of behavioral evidence in order to develop an offender description; used during the process of criminal profiling.

**Investigative psychology:** The application of behavioral science methods to criminal investigative work.

**Irrelevant question:** Control questions that have nothing to do with the topic of investigation, used with polygraph testing.

**Irresistible impulse:** Understanding the difference between right and wrong, but being unable to control one's behavior.

**Jail:** Detention centers for criminal suspects and inmates; typically run by the local government and used to temporarily hold defendants. Jails generally do not offer a wide variety of mental health services.

**Joint custody:** In child custody cases the parents share legal authority but the children reside predominantly with one parent.

**Jurisdiction:** Synonymous with the word "power" and is the authority to preside over a given case.

**Jury consultant:** A trial consultant who assists an attorney during voir dire and the selection of jurors, as well as other activities such as witness preparation and a change of venue request.

**Jury nullification:** Occurs when a jury ignores the evidence and acquits the defendant. The jury essentially finds a guilty defendant innocent. This may occur if the jury does not agree with the law or the enforcement of a particular law in a specific situation.

**Least detrimental standard:** A standard used in child custody evaluations that attempts to identify the custody resolution that does the least amount of harm to the children.

**Legal parental authority:** The decision-making role regarding the child's long-term welfare; used in child custody decisions.

**Legal psychology:** The scientific study of the effect of the law on people, and the effect people have on the law. Areas of legal psychology discussed in the text include eyewitness identification and investigative psychology.

**Legal sufficiency:** A criterion used in determining the admissibility of expert testimony. Legal sufficiency relates to whether the testimony is likely to assist the jury. Expert testimony on the fallibility of eyewitness identification has sometimes been refused on the premise that it is unlikely to assist the jury.

**Liable:** In civil court the judge or jury states that the plaintiff has proven his or her claim against the defendant and the defendant is responsible for damages to the plaintiff.

**Limited joint custody:** A child custody arrangement in which both parents share legal authority, but one parent has exclusive physical authority.

**Litigation:** The conduct of a lawsuit in civil court.

**Magnetic resonance imaging (MRI):** Exposes the brain to a magnetic field and measures the radio frequency waves, providing an image of the anatomical structures of the brain.

**Malingering:** An individual attempts to feign symptoms or exaggerate symptoms during assessment, usually for secondary gain. For example, a defendant may fake a mental illness with the intention of being found incompetent to stand trial.

**Manslaughter:** The killing of someone without malice. Involuntary manslaughter is unintentional but through actions that place others at risk. Voluntary manslaughter is reckless or impulsive behavior but nonetheless intentional homicide.

**Match-to-description strategy:** The known innocents in a lineup should match the witness's prelineup description of the suspect.

**Mediator:** Someone who helps opposing sides in a dispute come to an agreement; does not have the authority to make decisions. See Arbitrator.

**Misdemeanor:** A criminal offense punishable by a fine or incarceration in jail for a year or less. Contrast with a felony.

**Mitigating circumstance:** Factors in a defendant's life or related to the crime that can reduce the culpability or punishment of a defendant. Psychologists may testify regarding a defendant's mitigating circumstances, such as an impoverished and abusive childhood in capital cases and determinate sentencing to reduce the punishment.

**Memory:** What the witness recalls about the event.

**Memory testimony:** A witness's statement of what he or she recalls about a prior event.

**Mens rea:** A "guilty mind" or free will with the intention of doing harm; required for conviction in criminal court.

*Modus operandi*: Latin for "method of operating" or the choices and behaviors by the criminal in order to commit the crime; a term used in criminal profiling.

**Negligence:** The failure to act or an action that a "reasonable person" would not have committed or failed to commit that results in injury to another.

**Nominal size:** The number of persons in a lineup, used in eyewitness identification.

**Noncriminogenic:** The dynamic factors that need to be addressed with regards to a offender but are not seen as playing a role in criminal behavior.

**Normal distribution:** The scores of a sample of a population that, when graphed, fall on or close to a normal curve, where the highest frequency is in the middle, and this frequency diminishes the farther you get away from the center on either end.

**Offender description:** A general description that can include personality traits, psychopathologies, behavior patterns, and demographic variables of the offender, which is arrived at through the process of criminal profiling.

**Opinion testimony:** Testimony based on what the witness infers about the facts. Generally only expert witnesses may offer opinion testimony.

**Optimality hypothesis:** A concept related to eyewitness testimony that posits that the more optimal the conditions in which the offender was viewed, the stronger the relationship between confidence of eyewitness identification and level of accuracy of the identification by the witness.

**Own-race bias:** Research suggests people can better discriminate among members of the race to which they belong than among members of a different race.

**Penultimate issue:** Elements that define the ultimate issue and do not appear to unduly influence the jury.

**Per se exclusionary role:** The prohibition of all testimony based on hypnotically refreshed memories.

**Peremptory challenge:** Removal of a prospective juror for no stated reason during voir dire. This is distinguished from *for-cause* challenges, which requires a reason to remove a potential juror.

**Personal injury lawsuit:** A lawsuit seeking compensation for damages to the person, their mental health, or reputation.

**Photo lineup:** The use of photos instead of live people in a lineup. This technique is used in eyewitness identification.

**Physical authority:** The decision-making role affecting daily activities and with whom the child lives; used in child custody evaluations.

**Poison pill strategy:** Attempting to retain jurors during voir dire whose personalities would clash during deliberations in the hopes of a mistrial.

**Police psychology:** Area of forensic psychology that focuses on law enforcement personnel; includes the assessment and treatment of law enforcement personnel.

**Position emission tomography (PET):** Localize brain cell activity by identifying specific brain regions that are active during certain psychological tasks.

**Postidentifications feedback effect:** Giving positive feedback after making an eyewitness identification increases the witness's level of certainty.

**Posttraumatic stress disorder (PTSD):** A severe anxiety disorder resulting from exposure to a traumatic event outside the range of usual human experience.

**Predictive validity:** How well test scores predict future behavior.

**Preponderance of the evidence:** The evidence for one side is more convincing than the evidence for the other side; the lowest burden of proof. Used in competency evaluations as well as civil court.

**Prison:** Operated by state or federal government for individuals serving sentences of more than 1 year for a felony conviction.

**Privilege:** The law's recognition of confidentiality in legal proceedings and therapeutic settings in which the individual can prevent disclosure of information during legal consultation or treatment, respectively.

**Profiling:** A technique used in investigative psychology to identify the characteristics of unknown criminal suspects related to a specific crime. It is the process of inferring distinctive personality characteristics of individuals using physical and/or behavioral characteristics of a crime scene.

**Projective hypothesis:** Assumes that people project their unconscious into their responses to ambiguous stimuli and is associated with the use of projective assessment techniques.

**Proximate cause:** Refers to the event closest to the injury, which had it not occurred the injury would not have occurred; also consider legal cause.

**Psychodynamic viewpoints of personality:** Assumes that a great deal of the causes of behavior derive from unconscious motives.

**Psycholegal soft spots:** Areas involving legal issues or procedures that may harm or help the psychological well-being of the parties involved.

**Psychological assessment:** The entire evaluative process used to measure a person's psychological status.

**Psychological autopsy:** A retrospective examination of social and psychological events prior to an individual's death; used to determine if the death was accidental or a suicide.

**Psychology:** The study of behavior and mental processes.

**Psychopathology:** Any form of a mental illness.

**Psychopathy:** Personality pattern consisting of characteristics of antisocial personality disorder along with superficial charm, egocentricity, insincerity, shallowness, and grandiosity.

**Punitive damages:** Financial awards to the plaintiff paid by the defendant in a lawsuit; serves as punishment for the defendant.

**Questionable validity generalization:** The possibility that the actuarial model was developed on a population very different from the individual being evaluated.

**Quid pro quo:** Tit for tat; used to describe sexual harassment when job retention, promotion, or raises are contingent on sexual relations.

**Race-norming:** An individual's scores are compared to norms for their ethnic group.

**Racial profiling:** Suspecting an individual of illegal activity because of ethnic background, such as pulling over an African American male driver simply because of his race. Racial profiling has been ruled illegal in many states.

**Rare risk or protective factors:** Identification of factors not considered in the development of the actuarial model.

**Recidivism rates:** The rate at which individuals convicted of a crime reoffend.

**Rehabilitation:** Changing behavior patterns so the individual can return to society.

**Relative judgment:** Selecting the individual in a lineup that most closely resembles the witness's recollection.

**Relevance:** Expert testimony must be directly related to the issues of the case; one criterion used to determine admissibility of expert testimony.

**Relevant question:** Used in polygraph testing in which the question deals directly with facts related to the offense.

**Repressed memory:** The unconscious psychological process of keeping the memory of an event out of awareness for an extended period of time.

**Restorative justice (reintegration):** Addressing both the individual and certain aspects of the individual's environment to make a successful transition to life outside of prison.

**Retribution:** Punishing people for violating the rights of others.

**Role theory:** Suggests that hypnosis is a social role being played by the "hypnotized" subject.

**Same-sex parenting:** The belief that a boy living with his father and a girl living with her mother was necessary for the adjustment of the child; was an early consideration regarding child custody decisions.

**Schema:** Mental representations for people, objects, places, and events.

**Science-translation brief:** Provides the court with an objective, neutral summary of social science research relevant to the case.

**Scientific jury selection:** Attempting to identify characteristics that will be associated with a favorable verdict using scientific methods such as community surveys, questionnaires, etc.

**Selective incapacitation:** The confinement of an individual based on presumed dangerousness.

**Semantic memories:** Memories of facts.

**Sequential lineup:** The suspect and known innocents appear one at a time.

**Sexual harassment:** Unwelcome, sex-based advances; requests for sexual favors or verbal or physical conduct of a sexual nature that renders harm to an individual.

**Shadow jury:** Group of individuals similar in demographics to the seated jury who watch the trial as it progresses and provide feedback to the attorney.

**Showup:** A lineup with only one suspect presented to the eyewitness(es).

**Signature behavior:** Personal aspects of criminal behavior carried out to satisfy emotional and psychological needs.

**Simultaneous lineup:** Suspect and known innocents appear together.

**Social framework testimony:** Expert testimony that presents conclusions based on social science research to assist the court in making a decision.

**Social psychology:** The study of how people influence others' behavior and attitudes; the study of the individual within a group.

**Sociology:** The study of social institutions and groups in society.

**Sole custody:** One parent has both physical and legal authority over the child; used in child custody decisions.

**Specialty competencies:** Skills distinctive to a particular specialty; for example, legal knowledge is a specialty competency for forensic psychologists. See Core competencies.

**Specific deterrence:** The assumption that the experience of being punished prevents an individual from reoffending.

**Split custody:** In cases with more than one child, legal and physical authority of one or more children is awarded to one parent, and the other parent has legal and physical authority of the remaining children.

**Standard deviation:** The amount of variability among scores on a test around the mean score.

**Standard error of measurement:** The amount of variation in a score each time it is assessed, which is considered the result of measurement error.

**Standard of care:** The appropriate practice for the delivery of mental health or medical services; a standard of care should be based on scientific evidence and is the expected minimum care within the profession.

**Standard of practice:** The usual or typical level of care provided by the majority of practitioners; the *standard of practice* may be lower than the *standard of care*, particularly if a standard of care has not been established.

***Stare decisis:*** Latin meaning *let the decision stand*; used in case law as the standard that states that legal rules decided in cases govern subsequent cases; contributes to the consistency of laws.

**State theory:** Hypnosis is an altered state of consciousness that has specific changes in behavior.

**Statistical prediction:** Using an actuarial formula to make predictions.

**Stealth jurors:** Individuals who misrepresent themselves to get on a jury in order to further their own goals.

**Stockholm syndrome:** Hostage identifying with the hostage-takers; named after a hostage situation in Stockholm in which the hostages agreed with their takers after the incident.

**System variables:** Preventable variables introduced by police procedure.

**Tender-years doctrine:** Assumes the mother is the most appropriate parent for young children.

**Test battery:** A group of assessment instruments and techniques selected to answer a specific referral question.

**Therapeutic jurisprudence:** Using social science to guide legal decisions so that all involved benefit psychologically or therapeutically.

**Time-sharing:** Term used to describe visitation rights in child custody cases.

**Tort:** A lawsuit.

**Totality of circumstances test:** Used by courts to determine if a hypnotically refreshed memory can be admitted into testimony; usually depends on whether a variety of guidelines were followed before, during, and after the hypnosis.

**Traditional jury selection:** Any traditional strategy used by attorneys to identify jurors who are favorable, or unfavorable, to their case.

**Transsituational consistency:** The proposition that behavior is consistent across situations.

**Transtemporal consistency:** The proposition that behavior is consistent over time.

**Treatment:** Providing psychological services to an individual for the purpose of helping the individual improve functioning.

**Trial phase:** Analysis of forensic evidence and the offender to assist in various aspects of a trial, part of criminal profiling.

**Ultimate issue:** The final question that must be decided by the court; usually left to the trier of fact to decide (i.e., guilt or innocence).

**Unconscious transference:** The process of confusing a person seen in one situation as having been seen in another situation.

**Validity:** The extent to which an instrument is an accurate measure of what it claims to measure.

**Vanity boards:** Certification boards that have minimal or nonexistent requirements for board certification.

**Victimology:** The thorough study of all available information regarding the victim of a crime.

**Voir dire:** An examination of prospective jurors to determine if the individual should serve on the jury; during the process of voir dire, attorneys may use trial consultants to assist with jury selection.

**Witness:** An individual called to testify as to what he or she has seen or heard.

**Witness immunity:** When an expert witness is exempt from criminal or civil liability for actions or testimony as an expert witness.

**Work product doctrine:** Maintains the privacy of a trial consultant's meetings with witnesses.

# Index